KNOWLEDGE ARCHITECTURES

Knowledge Architectures reviews traditional approaches to managing information and explains why they need to adapt to support 21st-century information management and discovery.

Exploring the rapidly changing environment in which information is being managed and accessed, the book considers how to use knowledge architectures, the basic structures and designs that underlie all of the parts of an effective information system, to best advantage. Drawing on 40 years of work with a variety of organizations, Bedford explains that failure to understand the structure behind any given system can be the difference between an effective solution and a significant and costly failure. Demonstrating that the information user environment has shifted significantly in the past 20 years, the book explains that end users now expect designs and behaviors that are much closer to the way they think, work, and act. Acknowledging how important it is that those responsible for developing an information or knowledge management system understand knowledge structures, the book goes beyond a traditional library science perspective and uses case studies to help translate the abstract and theoretical to the practical and concrete.

Explaining the structures in a simple and intuitive way and providing examples that clearly illustrate the challenges faced by a range of different organizations, *Knowledge Architectures* is essential reading for those studying and working in library and information science, data science, systems development, database design, and search system architecture and engineering.

Denise Bedford is currently an adjunct professor, Georgetown University's Communication Culture and Technology program, USA; Visiting Scholar at the University of Coventry, UK, and Distinguished Practitioner/Virtual Fellow with the U.S. Department of State. She currently serves as Associate Editor of the *Journal of Knowledge Management*. Her educational background includes a B.A. triple major in intellectual history, Russian language, and German language; an M.A. in Russian and East European history; an M.S. in information science; and a Ph.D. in Information Science with focus on systems analysis and design, and economics of information.

KNOWLEDGE ARCHITECTURES

Structures and Semantics

Denise Bedford

Routledge
Taylor & Francis Group

LONDON AND NEW YORK

First published 2021
by Routledge
2 Park Square, Milton Park, Abingdon, Oxon OX14 4RN

and by Routledge
52 Vanderbilt Avenue, New York, NY 10017

Routledge is an imprint of the Taylor & Francis Group, an informa business

British Library Cataloguing-in-Publication Data
A catalogue record for this book is available from the British Library

Library of Congress Cataloging-in-Publication Data
A catalog record for this book has been requested

ISBN: 978-0-367-21943-7 (hbk)
ISBN: 978-0-367-21944-4 (pbk)
ISBN: 978-0-429-26891-5 (ebk)

Typeset in Bembo
by Apex CoVantage, LLC

CONTENTS

SECTION 5
Pulling it all together – the big picture knowledge architecture

FIGURES

TABLES

PREFACE

Overview of the subject matter

The economy is continually evolving. Over the past 70 years, the U.S. economy has been shifting from an advanced industrial to a knowledge-based economy. Machlup first observed this shift in the 1950s (1962). His work has been chronicled and expanded by other leading economists and researchers (Antonelli & David, 2015; Baumol et al., 1981; Bell, 1976; Drucker, 2013; Porat & Rubin, 1977; Wolff & Baumol, 1989). Since the 1950s, economists have attributed the change to the rise in importance of services, information, an increasingly educated and trained workforce, technology, an increasingly virtual work environment, and increases in artificial intelligence and automation. The common element to all of these perspectives is the increased value of knowledge. In the 21st century, knowledge is now a primary factor of production (Garcia-Perez et al., 2019). It is equivalent to financial and physical capital in the industrial economy and to land and physical labor in the agricultural economy.

Transitioning from an industrial economy to a knowledge economy is the primary business challenge of the 21st century (Allee, 2000, 2009, 2012; Bedford, 2012a, 2012b; Bontis, 2003; Ceruti et al., 2019; Handa et al., 2019; Snowden, 2003). In a knowledge economy, the fundamental assumptions and behaviors are changing. The balance of capital is shifting. The knowledge economy increases the role and value of knowledge capital, whereas earlier economies place higher values on financial and physical capital. Knowledge capital has a different set of economic properties and behaviors from that of physical and financial capital (LaFayette et al., 2019). The new properties and behaviors change how markets and economic transactions behave. In this new economic environment, the future is more effectively defined by what we want it to be. Organizations with visions and strategies grounded on knowledge capital and knowledge capacity will thrive in the new economy (Ceruti et al., 2019). Those organizations guided by industrial era visions and strategy may not fare as well. Leaders, executives, and managers need to ensure that their vision and strategy align with economic changes. Leaders, executives, and managers need to expand their vision and strategy to build knowledge capacity for the future.

To survive in the knowledge economy, organizations must adjust their mental models and business strategies to invest in, leverage, and safeguard this important new type of capital. The first challenge for managers and staff alike is understanding what we mean by knowledge and learning to see it in our business and working environments. Our treatment of knowledge over the centuries has been both general and specific. It has been characterized as an amorphous thing we all strive to gain, and as something distinct and discrete like a book or a data set. Extensive work in the field of intellectual capital and knowledge economies offers working characterizations of knowledge. We have learned from this field that knowledge is an asset with very different economic behaviors and properties than other types of capital assets. Our management strategies and methods, and our 'internal built environments,' are not sufficient to manage knowledge capital.

These new and different economic properties are driving the rapid rate of economic change. Our production operations, our markets, and consumption patterns are changing. Sources, channels, and consumers are changing. To survive in this new environment means learning how to see change and adapt to it. The new environment is anathema to all of the massive investments we have made in standardized and 'built solutions.' Not only is the business environment changing rapidly, but so is the rate of change of technologies. Succeeding in the knowledge economy means being able to design solutions to suit a business context at a given point in time.

What does this all mean? It means that we need a better understanding of knowledge assets and more suitable functional architectures to help us grow, leverage, and persistently manage those assets (Handa et al., 2019). For these reasons, we need a knowledge architecture. The topic of knowledge architecture is not well-defined or supported today. We lack the broad foundation for understanding what we mean by knowledge assets, because we do not yet have a place in the world of enterprise architecture that focuses on knowledge. This book aims to fill these needs and gaps.

Knowledge architecture is a form of architecture. It leverages and spans all of the layers of enterprise architecture, but it has no clear and distinct home in that context. This text aims to make a case for formally integrating knowledge architecture into the profession and practice of enterprise architecture (Zachman, 1997). This new subject requires engagement in stakeholders in the fields of management, economics, intellectual capital management, knowledge management, library and information science, enterprise architecture, computer sciences, and software development. These are relevant stakeholders because they represent the 'built environments' we have in place today. Traditional information or knowledge architecture approach has focused on construction and build rather than design – this text aims to shift the focus back to design. The stakeholders we must engage in to achieve our goal will come from the field of design thinking.

Where the topic fits in the world today

Knowledge architecture is a multifaceted topic. While anchored in the field of architecture – specifically enterprise architecture – it draws models, practices, and processes from knowledge management, economics, information and library science, information engineering, computer science, and management science. It is not just a matter of finding common ground across these fields, but instead developing new strategies and approaches to bring all these fields into the modern business environment. In essence, the answer to where this topic fits in the world today – the issue is the concern, responsibility, and purview of business managers. It fills a gap that has only recently been exposed.

Knowledge architecture is fundamentally a variety of architecture. We draw from and adapt the principles, reference models, methods, and tools of architecture to fill this new gap. We anchor knowledge architecture in the principal activity of design. We might associate architecture with buildings or artifacts. We interpret architecture in the classic sense – the practice of designing form to suit the function and designing to a purpose. Design methods are well suited to supporting the fluid and dynamic nature of the knowledge economy. We need to plan for environments where different functions will develop and change at different rates, where the roles of stakeholders are evolving rapidly.

Knowledge architecture must go beyond traditional design to suit this new economic environment. The topic of knowledge architecture gives us reason to question our existing professional perspectives, assumptions, and processes. Can we adapt the standards and procedures we developed for explicit information to suit relational capital? Can we expand the methods developed by network architects to support reputational capital? Or do we need a radical new design approach? We need to be open to new design methods and new functional architecture designs.

Where the book fits in the literature today

In designing this book's structure and content, the author hoped to fill an existing gap and engage professionals and practitioners from several disciplines in a dialog to fill that gap. This text is not a replacement for any current book. This book provides an umbrella treatment and interpretation of all the books on the market today. The most definite affinity, though, is with the fields of enterprise architecture and knowledge management. It is a supplement to the enterprise architecture literature. It is a fundamentally new foundation for knowledge management. We hope the book will contribute to the fields of information management and library science by describing a future focus that holds both challenges and opportunities.

Intended audience of the book

The intended audience is broad. It includes business managers, knowledge management professionals and practitioners, library and information scientists, information engineers, systems developers, and information architects. We hope that the book will serve as a blueprint for information and knowledge architects as they face new challenges. We expect the book will paint a realistic picture of the future environment that business managers will develop and manage. The challenge of writing the book is to achieve a narrative that will stimulate discussion within and across disciplines, serve as an instructional tool for practitioners, and be a source of practical guidance for business managers.

More particularly, though, the audience includes academics – teachers, students, researchers, and active learners – in the fields of information and library science, knowledge sciences, enterprise architecture, and business administration. The book is written in a way that allows professors and instructors to develop course syllabi, and to design exercises. Each chapter has an extensive bibliography from which targeted readings may be drawn.

Structure of the book

The book is organized into five sections and 23 chapters. The first section focuses on the purpose and context of knowledge architecture and consists of five chapters. Sections 2 through 4 focus on knowledge architecture segments in which knowledge is made available, accessed, and consumed. Section 2 focuses on designing architectures that support knowledge availability and consists of five chapters. Section 3 focuses on designing functional architectures that support knowledge accessibility and consists of six chapters. Section 4 focuses on designing functional architectures that promote the consumption of knowledge and consists of five chapters. Finally, the two chapters in Section 5 focus on blueprinting the whole knowledge architecture and integrating it into the enterprise architecture practice.

Section 1. Context and Purpose of Knowledge Architecture

- Chapter 1. Making the case for knowledge architecture
- Chapter 2. The landscape of knowledge assets
- Chapter 3. Knowledge architecture and design
- Chapter 4. Knowledge architecture reference model
- Chapter 5. Knowledge architecture segments

Section 2. Designing for availability

- Chapter 6. Knowledge object modeling
- Chapter 7. Knowledge structures for encoding, formatting, and packaging
- Chapter 8. Functional architecture for identification and distinction
- Chapter 9. Functional architecture for knowledge asset disposition and destruction
- Chapter 10. Functional architecture designs for knowledge preservation and conservation

Section 3. Designing to accessibility

- Chapter 11. Functional architectures for knowledge seeking and discovery
- Chapter 12. Functional architecture for knowledge search
- Chapter 13. Functional architecture for knowledge categorization
- Chapter 14. Functional architectures for indexing and keywording
- Chapter 15. Functional architecture for knowledge semantics
- Chapter 16. Functional architecture for knowledge abstraction and surrogation

Section 4. Functional architectures to support knowledge consumption

- Chapter 17. Functional architecture for knowledge augmentation, derivation, and synthesis
- Chapter 18. Functional architecture to manage risk and harm
- Chapter 19. Functional architecture for knowledge authentication and provenance
- Chapter 20. Functional architectures for securing knowledge assets
- Chapter 21. Functional architectures for authorization and access management

Section 5. Putting it all together – the big picture knowledge architecture

- Chapter 22. Functional architecture for knowledge metadata and metainformation
- Chapter 23. The whole knowledge architecture – pulling it all together

Chapter summaries

The focus of each chapter is described briefly in this section.

Chapter 1 explains the role that knowledge plays in the knowledge economy and why it is important to see knowledge as part of an organization's stock of capital assets. The chapter discusses the different perspectives of knowledge and highlights the work of intellectual capital researchers in identifying working categories of knowledge assets. The chapter also describes how knowledge assets are different from other forms of capital and how we identify and characterize these different economic properties and behaviors.

Chapter 2 describes the literature and research on knowledge typologies and identifies a common framework for designing a functional knowledge architecture. The chapter takes Bontis's work in modeling intellectual capital as a foundation and designs a set of five types of knowledge capital assets to use for architectural design. The five types include (1) human knowledge assets, (2) explicit knowledge assets, (3) procedural knowledge assets, (4) cultural knowledge assets, and (5) relational knowledge assets. We define each type, provide examples, and discuss their essential behaviors and properties.

Chapter 3 introduces the concept of architecture and explains the importance of design to good architecture practice. The difference between design and construction is described. The chapter considers current and relevant architecture practices in organizations today, including enterprise, business, and information architecture. We make a case for a more inclusive and comprehensive knowledge architecture practice. Here we lay out the elements and methods of good architecture design, including future state visions, design principles, reference models, architecture segments, blueprints, and governance models. The chapter interprets these common architecture elements for knowledge architecture.

Chapter 4 presents a working knowledge architecture reference model. Architectures are labor- and time-intensive to develop and are difficult to design in a densely built environment, particularly when grounded in well-established and heavily entrenched practices and activities. The chapter suggests that developing a new knowledge architecture in established business practices, development, and technology practices can be challenging. The chapter lays out the role and elements of architecture reference models in harmonizing and synthesizing existing perspectives and developing a shared vision for the future. This chapter introduces a reference model intended to help the reader learn to see this new architecture and to guide others in the process of understanding that vision.

Chapter 5 describes architecture segments and explains their role in designing how all the layers of architecture fit together. The chapter identifies three primary segments for knowledge architectures, including knowledge availability, knowledge accessibility, and knowledge consumability. We consider how these architecture segments relate to the functions we need to manage our knowledge assets. We elaborate on the functional architectures required to support each segment. This chapter provides the structure for more detailed discussions of each architecture in Chapters 6 through 22.

Chapter 6 discusses the development of object models for knowledge assets and the five activities that support the creation of these models. The chapter explains why it is essential to have a good understanding of object models and their components; the difference between object models and functional, process, and information models, object modeling methods, languages, and object mapping methods. This chapter also explains what we have to work with, where we lack good precedents, and where we can adapt and expand existing practices. The chapter offers sample structures that organizations can leverage to develop their object models.

Chapter 7 discusses what we mean by encoding structures, formats, and packages and explains why they are essential and how to discover them across your organization. The chapter lays out six activities that support the management of encoding, formats, and packaging of functional architectures. This chapter explains why it is essential to have a good understanding of encoding and decoding methods, historical and current formatting structures, and methods. The chapter explains why we should be aware of common forms of packaging for knowledge assets, future trends for formatting, and common kinds of vulnerabilities and risks associated with each type of packaging. The chapter explains why it is essential to focus on knowledge assets and to be prepared to do object model mapping in times of rapid technological change.

Chapter 8 discusses what it means to identify and distinguish knowledge assets. It explains why these factors are essential and how to determine them across all assets. Here we will cover seven activities that support the discovery of identification and distinction. This chapter explains why it is essential to understand common practices for identifying an asset's identity, attribution, dates, versions, and copies, and it describes the advantages and limitations of unique reference identifiers. Three methods of determining identity are laid out, including through direct examination of an asset, inference, and inheritance of context, and through demonstration, testimonials, or analytic methods. The chapter also explains how semantic or other scientific methods can be leveraged to discover highly similar knowledge assets.

Chapter 9 explains what it means to disposition and destroy knowledge assets and why it is crucial to have an active asset disposition capability. The chapter describes the five activities that support asset disposition and destruction. The chapter also considers why it is vital to have a good understanding of general asset management practices, the criteria for assessing the business value of and for auditing knowledge assets, common disposition practices, and tools, and of managing destruction activities. Here we consider the design challenges we must address in the wide variation in accepted practice for managing these different kinds of assets and the absence of accepted methods for some of these assets.

Chapter 10 explains what we mean by preservation and conservation of knowledge assets, and how these traditional functions relate to the dynamic technology context. The chapter outlines six activities that support knowledge asset preservation and conservation and that are essential to designing a supporting functional architecture. The chapter considers why it is vital to have a good understanding of preservation, conservation, content migration, preservation, or conservation practices for different types of assets. Here I explain that the primary challenge in designing this functional architecture is maintaining the focus on the knowledge assets rather than the package and in thinking long term rather than short term.

Chapter 11 discusses what is meant by knowledge seeking and discovery and why it is essential to be able to see the broader knowledge landscape. This chapter also distinguishes between seeking and discovery and searching. The chapter describes the five activities vital to designing an effective seeking architecture. The chapter explains why it is crucial to have a good understanding of common knowledge-seeking practices and patterns, discovery methods such as berrypicking, browsing, grazing, and satisficing. The chapter describes the difference between seeking and findability and explains how to use scenarios to understand your stakeholders' behaviors. It will demonstrate that the primary challenge is to expand the productive base of knowledge and practice to include all types of knowledge assets.

Chapter 12 explains what it means to search for knowledge assets and why it is essential to design a knowledge search architecture intentionally. The chapter lays out the six activities that support knowledge search architecture designs, and it considers why it is crucial to have a good understanding of search as a system – the inputs, processes, and outputs – that determine performance and effectiveness. We will examine the components of a search system and learn how these parts have evolved to support today's search methods. We will consider the primary challenge in designing this functional architecture for search – the high level of marketing and costs of search systems and the absence of active management of search system designs.

Chapter 13 explains the role that categorization plays in supporting access to knowledge assets. The chapter describes the seven activities that support the design of categorization architectures. The chapter also considers why it is essential to have a good understanding of categories, categorization schemes and their principles, categorization processes and methods, and both human and machine techniques. The chapter explains the differences between categorization, indexing and keywording, and other semantic structures. Here we consider the primary challenge in designing this functional architecture for categorization: adapting common and traditional perceptions, practices in and procedures, and the existing 'built' environment.

Chapter 14 explains the role that concept indexing and keywording plays in supporting access to knowledge assets. The chapter outlines the six activities that support the design of an indexing and keywording architecture for knowledge assets. The chapter also considers why it is vital to understand the use of language to describe concepts and ideas, domain vocabularies, focal vocabularies, listening vocabularies, speaking vocabularies, reading vocabularies, and writing vocabularies. The chapter also explains the difference between unmanaged and managed vocabularies and explains how structured vocabularies are different from managed vocabularies. We will consider the primary challenge in designing this functional architecture for designing effective conceptual indexing and keywording. It is the integration and harmonization of terms used to index from different sources and over time.

Chapter 15 explains the role that semantic structures play in knowledge access. The chapter lays out the seven essential activities that support designing a semantic architecture. The chapter also considers why it is crucial to have a good understanding of thesauri, semantic networks, concept and topic maps, semantic relationships, semantic relatedness, and meaning in different contexts. The chapter lays out the similarities and differences in human and machine approaches to defining meaning and relatedness. We consider the primary challenge in designing this functional architecture is developing a harmonized, common design strategy for designing semantic structures that suit different communities.

Chapter 16 explains the role that abstracting and surrogation plays in making knowledge accessible. Here we will look at the five activities essential to developing abstracts and surrogates of knowledge assets. The chapter also considers why it is crucial to have a good understanding of forms abstracts can take, the different ways we structure abstracts, and the design of abstracts for various formats such as images, audio and visual formats, and text. This chapter shows why we still develop abstracts, including supporting access to knowledge in other languages, access to any asset we can experience directly, for marketing and promotion, and overcoming impediments to full asset access. We will consider the primary challenge in designing this functional architecture for abstracting. It is raising awareness of the growing importance of abstracts to access in the age of full text, and of learning to see abstracts and summaries in non-traditional information professions.

Chapter 17 considers a range of ways we can consume knowledge assets. We abstract these different practical actions into three general types – asset translations, asset interpretations, and asset augmentations. The chapter outlines the four essential activities we need to consider when designing an architecture to support this rich set of practices. The chapter also discusses why it is crucial to have a good understanding of the way the knowledge management field describes knowledge use, exchange, transfer, uptake, and sharing. It also describes the limitations inherent to historical definitions of knowledge assets and explains the activities included in translating, interpreting, and augmenting knowledge assets. We will consider the primary challenge in designing this functional architecture. It is learning to see and understand how we are consuming our knowledge assets and keeping pace with the rapid evolution of different patterns of consumption.

Chapter 18 considers the types of harm and risk an organization can incur from making available, accessible, and consumable knowledge assets. We consider the types of harm that might naturally result from the use of knowledge. The chapter explains the importance of working with business managers to determine the degree of risk any business might encounter. The chapter reminds us that every organization has a unique business context. This chapter walks through several design activities and tasks, including identifying risk factors; identifying the business custodians and stewards who can advise on the degree of risks, determining the cost-benefit model for safeguarding assets; and designing a risk management portfolio. This chapter also considers why it is essential to understand the spectrum of harm, including knowledge loss, knowledge theft, knowledge damage or misuse, asset tampering, and the creation of fake knowledge. We suggest the primary challenge in designing this functional architecture is exposing the harm that has occurred in the past and shaping systems and human behaviors to protect against harm.

Chapter 19 explains the role that authentication plays in making knowledge assets consumable. The chapter lays out the six activities that support the design of functional architectures that enable authentication of knowledge assets. The chapter considers why it is essential to have a good understanding of authenticity, authentication methods, package-based authentication, product-based authentication, and inferred authentication. The chapter also identifies and describes the range of authentication concepts, challenges, and practices. Here we consider the primary problem in designing this functional architecture for authentication. It is raising awareness of the need to authenticate all types of knowledge assets and the importance of adopting technologies for different assets.

Chapter 20 explains the role that knowledge asset security plays in making knowledge assets consumable. The chapter lays out the five activities that support designing appropriate security methods for knowledge assets. The chapter also considers why it is essential to understand the harm, forms, and degrees of harm, types of risk, harm, and risk mitigation. It is also essential to understand how different approaches to security may or may not reduce harm and risk. The primary challenge we face in designing this functional architecture is developing security measures and methods that are suited to types and levels of harm and avoiding the temptation to adopt security classifications structures and practices from other organizations without full consideration.

Chapter 21 explains how authorizing knowledge assets and designing privileges enables us to consume these assets. The chapter looks at the five activities that support authorization and access privileges. The chapter also considers why it is crucial to have a good understanding of access, access controls, access rights, access control mechanisms, user identity management, and all of the different approaches to privilege access management: authorization and authorization methods. A primary challenge to designing this functional architecture is understanding who is requesting access, why, and what harm or risk they present, and overcoming the tendency to revert to the principle of least privilege – which results in lower knowledge flows and constrains the business value of knowledge assets.

Chapter 22 explains the role that metadata and metainformation play in making knowledge assets accessible. The chapter lays out the six activities that support designing metadata and metainformation architecture to support knowledge assets. The chapter also considers why it is vital to have a good understanding of the designing to essential access points, why we need to understand metadata specifications and business rules, the semantics of each attribute, and how we instantiate or manage metadata structures. The chapter makes a case for designing metadata to suit your organization rather than merely adopting a standard framework. Here we consider the primary challenge in designing this functional architecture for metadata. It integrates and harmonizes deeply entrenched metadata practices across domains and rethinks these practices to support knowledge asset mobility and extensibility.

Chapter 23 assesses the current state of knowledge architecture, working across architecture segments and across types of knowledge assets. We consider what we need to do to bring the current state up to an acceptable level – that is, an equilibrium state across all assets. Drawing from the factors identified in the evolution of the 17 functional architectures, we observe that knowledge architecture has followed the path of economic systems. We align the knowledge architecture segments with the basic elements of an economic system. We explore what economists, media, and broadcasting experts tell us about the economic trends that will shape the future. And, we translate these trends to understand the future knowledge architecture.

How the book impacts the field

This book presents a framework for understanding where we've been, where we are, and where we might be going in designing functional architectures to support organizations in the knowledge economy. The book is designed to synthesize and anchor the literature of knowledge management to address the full spectrum of knowledge capital. The book is intended as a new instructional tool for young professionals in the fields of information engineering, library and information science, knowledge management, and systems development. The book is also written to help the reader analyze their current 'built environment' and to reverse engineer and redesign it to suit the new environment.

How to read this book

Knowledge management is not a new discipline, but knowledge architecture is a relatively new interdisciplinary practice. There are no experts in the field today, including the author. The author is an avid learner who has had the benefit of many wonderful mentors and coaches over many decades. Each chapter represents what the author has learned over 40 years of working in several related disciplines, explained from an interdisciplinary and blended view. The explanations do not represent the views or practices of any single discipline. They are presented so that a reader or practitioner from any of those disciplines can see the bigger picture.

The book is designed to help you assess and build your organization's knowledge architecture. The book is written to be read one chapter at a time, with pauses for thinking and discussion before tackling the next. Each reader will develop a different and unique architecture solution. We hope readers will bring their thoughts and work back to the community to share what they have learned.

References

Allee, V. (2000). The value evolution: Addressing larger implications of an intellectual capital and intangibles perspective. *Journal of Intellectual Capital*, 1(1), 17–32.

Allee, V. (2009). *The future of knowledge*. Routledge.

Allee, V. (2012). *The knowledge evolution*. Routledge.

Antonelli, C., & David, P. (2015). *The economics of knowledge and the knowledge driven economy*. Routledge.

Baumol, W. J., Branunstein, Y., Fisher, D. M., & Ordover, J. A. (1981). *Manual of pricing and cost determination of organizations engaged in dissemination of knowledge*. New York University.

Bedford, D. A. (2012a). Expanding the definition and measurement of knowledge economy-integrating triple bottom line factors into knowledge economy index models and methodologies. In *Proceedings of the European conference on intellectual capital* (pp. 67–74). Academic Conferences and Publishing International (ACPI).

Bedford, D. A. (2012b). The role of knowledge management in creating transformational organizations and transformational leaders. *Journal of Knowledge Management Practice*, 13(4), 32–44.

Bell, D. (1976, May). The coming of the post-industrial society. In *The Educational Forum* (Vol. 40, No. 4, pp. 574–579). Taylor & Francis Group.

Bontis, N. (2003). Intellectual capital disclosure in Canadian corporations. *Journal of Human Resource Costing and Accounting*, 7(1), 9–20.

Ceruti, M., Williams, A., & Bedford, D. (2019). Translating the vision into strategies. In *Translating knowledge management visions into strategies*. Emerald Publishing Limited.

Drucker, P. (2013). *Managing for the future*. Routledge.

Garcia-Perez, A., Cegarra-Navarro, J. G., Bedford, D., Thomas, M., & Wakabayashi, S. (2019). *Critical capabilities and competencies for knowledge organizations*. Emerald Group Publishing.

Handa, P., Pagani, J., & Bedford, D. (2019). *Audit methodology for knowledge assets*. Knowledge Assets and Knowledge Audits (Working Methods for Knowledge Management). Emerald Group Publishing.

LaFayette, B., Curtis, W., Bedford, D., & Iyer, S. (2019). *How work changes in the knowledge economy*. Knowledge Economies and Knowledge Work (Working Methods for Knowledge Management). Emerald Group Publishing.

Machlup, F. (1962). *The production and distribution of knowledge in the United States* (Vol. 278). Princeton University Press.

Porat, M. U., & Rubin, M. R. (1977). *The information economy: Definition and measurement* (Vol. 77, No. 12). The Office.

Snowden, D. (2003). Innovation as an objective of knowledge management. Part I: The landscape of management. *Knowledge Management Research and Practice, 1*(2), 113–119.

Wolff, E., & Baumol, W. J. (1989). Sources of postwar growth of information activity in the United States. In *The information economy: The implications of unbalanced growth* (pp. 17–46). New York, NY: C.V. Starr Center for Applied Economics, New York University

Zachman, J. A. (1997). Enterprise architecture: The issue of the century. *Database Programming and Design, 10*(3), 44–53.

ACKNOWLEDGMENTS

Over 40 years I have had a wealth of opportunities to learn from and work with some remarkable individuals. Some taught me directly, and others indirectly through their behaviors, values, and simple ways of working. I owe what I know and how I learned to 'see things' to these individuals. Each of these individuals played a role in building my professional knowledge, developing my professional practice, and in shaping my ethics, norms, attitudes, and behaviors. Starting from the earliest years of my career, I am grateful to David Weber, Sally Buchanan, Carol Fleischauer, and Carolyn Henderson (Stanford University); Yale Braunstein and Mike Cooper (University of California, Berkeley); Sally Hambridge (Intel Corporation); Bonnie Carroll (Information International Associates); Janet Ormes, Jim Erwin, and Adelaide del Fratte (NASA); Elizabeth Aversa (Catholic University); Anna Flavia Fonseca, Klaus Tilmes, and Hinda Kada (World Bank); John Zachman (Zachman International); Robert Walker (Kent State University); Pawan Handa and Dean Testa (Goodyear); Elias Carayannis (George Washington University); Alexeis Garcia-Perez (Coventry University); and Linda Garcia and David Lightfoot (Georgetown University).

That I was able to learn from these amazing individuals is due to the encouragement of my parents, Dorothy and Tasman Dowding, and the unwavering support of my husband, Cliff Bedford, and son, Chris Bedford.

SECTION 1

Context and purpose of knowledge architecture

This section makes a case for knowledge architecture. It explains the landscape of knowledge architecture in the knowledge economy. The building blocks of knowledge architecture are laid out, including the essential elements of design, architecture methods, and tools. The second describes a working reference model for knowledge architecture and details three upper knowledge architecture domains. Each upper knowledge architecture domain is broken down into its functional architecture components.

1

MAKING THE CASE FOR KNOWLEDGE ARCHITECTURE

Chapter summary

This chapter explains the role that knowledge plays in the knowledge economy and why it is essential to see knowledge as part of an organization's stock of capital assets. The chapter discusses the different perspectives of knowledge and highlights the work of intellectual capital researchers in identifying working categories of knowledge assets. The chapter also describes how knowledge assets are different from other forms of capital and how we identify and characterize these different economic properties and behaviors.

Why we care about knowledge

Knowledge is an essential commodity in the knowledge economy. It is a new form of capital. It is the most critical business tool and competitive advantage of any organization. While there has been much talk about managing knowledge over the past 25 years, our treatment and support of knowledge warrants more serious consideration, we must also see and understand knowledge from a design perspective. Because knowledge is complex and dynamic, this means understanding its essential properties and behaviors. Our current architectures are designed to support tangible information objects rather than all types of knowledge.

When we think of knowledge in the broadest and holistic sense, even processes and methods must expand. Most of what we currently define as knowledge or knowledge engineering and management is in factor information engineering and management. It is predicated on the assumptions that knowledge can be better managed when it is tangible and when a decision has been made about the legal or security value of the information. This assumption negates many of the basic properties and behaviors of knowledge and limits the amount we can draw from it.

These assumptions restrict our understanding of knowledge – and are the source of many of our fundamental challenges. Our challenge is that we are not working in a vacuum. All of the existing architectures and solutions we have to work with today lock us into working with static and tangible objects. Designing new knowledge architectures provides an opportunity to translate and adapt these solutions to suit the full suite of knowledge. As a foundation for making this mental shift, we need a good grounding in knowledge – all types, and their properties and behaviors.

Knowledge – perspectives and definitions

The challenge we face in talking about and working with knowledge is not the lack of a good working definition. Instead, the problem is that there are many definitions of knowledge, and each of these definitions makes good sense in its original context. There is value in each of these definitions for knowledge architecture (Bontis, 1996, 1998, 2003; Bontis et al., 2000; Bornemann et al., 1999; Brainerd, 1978; Edvinsson & Malone, 1997; Gourlay, 2006; Gruber & Voneche, 1977; Nazari & Herremans, 2007; Nonaka & Takeuchi, 1995; Roos et al., 1997; Saettler, 1990; Zins, 2006). Our challenge in this text is to identify a working definition of knowledge that allows us to design practical and sustainable architectures. Conversely, our working definition must make sense to many different perspectives and work in all these different disciplines. What are some of the disciplines we draw from and must consider in developing our working definition? At a minimum, we must consider philosophy, communications, learning and education, human resource management, business, economics, technology, and information management.

Philosophy addresses knowledge through the study of epistemology. The definition of knowledge in philosophy dates back to Plato. Plato famously defined knowledge as justified true belief (Cornford, 2003) – a core element of the definition adopted by the field of knowledge management. Over the centuries, philosophers have focused on what knowledge is, how it is acquired, and the extent to which individuals can acquire knowledge. In the context of philosophy, knowledge is closely related to truth, belief, justification, intelligence, and wisdom.

Communications treat knowledge as the message or content exchanged between two or more agents to convey or receive meaning. Knowledge is understood to include intent and message, and the processes around knowledge include composition, message encoding and decoding, and message interpretation. In communications, knowledge is defined as a shared system of signs and semiotic rules. Knowledge is the symbolic representation of the sender's intended meaning. Knowledge is also conveyed or received through observation, imitation, verbal exchange, audio, and video channels.

Learning and education treat knowledge as both a resource and an end state. As a resource, it includes the stock of facts, information, descriptions, or skills associated with an individual. As a process, knowledge is acquired through experience, perception, discovery or learning, storytelling, discovery, teaching, training, or research. In this context, knowledge refers to a theoretical or practical understanding of a subject, area of practice, or discipline. Education is a formal process whose end game is to build knowledge in the individual. Education is achieved through formal institutions and methods, whereas learning and knowledge acquisition take place through real-life experiences. In education, Piaget proposes three types of knowledge: physical, logical-mathematical, and social knowledge. Physical knowledge is knowledge about objects in the world, which can be gained through their perceptual properties. Logical-mathematical knowledge is abstract knowledge that must be invented. Social-arbitrary knowledge is culture-specific knowledge learned from people within one's culture-group (Driscoll, 1994). We can find all three of these characterizations in common definitions of knowledge from the field of knowledge management. Piaget's three principles of knowledge development (Piaget, 1976) are represented in Nonaka's Spiral Model (Nonaka & Takeuchi, 1995; Baumol, 1968), including assimilation, accommodation, and equilibrium. These principles help us to understand the continuous development and essential transitory nature of knowledge.

Business managers and accountants treat knowledge capital as an intangible asset (Carayannis, 2009; Carayannis & Formica, 2008; Carayannis & Sipp, 2005). This perspective compares the tangible and quantifiable attributes of physical and financial capital to the intangible and hidden value of knowledge capital. Business managers and accountants have long recognized the value of human capital – the way they refer to knowledge capital. From this perspective, knowledge capital includes reputation, know-how, and process knowledge – no business process or operation can function without some working knowledge. Business managers also understand the value of knowledge to an organization's competitive status in a market, to the role it plays in redefining or remaking those markets, and to the composition of those markets. We can already see the impact of businesses that have realized the value and leverage that knowledge capital offers.

Human resource professionals frame knowledge capital as human capital, social capital, or emotional intelligence. Knowledge capital is still an emerging concept in this field – human resource management training has traditionally focused on the management of people as a supporting resource for the business. We manage people through their salaries, their job classifications, skills, and competencies. This perspective is expanding to strategic workforce management and planning.

Economists frame knowledge capital as intellectual capital (Bassi & van Buren, 1999; Baumol & Braunstein, 1977; Bornemann et al., 1999; Edvinsson & Malone, 1997; Goldkuhl & Rostlinger, 2000; Kanchana & Mohan, 2017; Kianto et al., 2017; Prochazkova & Jelinkova, 2014; Roos et al., 1997; Silva et al., 2017; Sveiby, 1997a, 1997b, 2001). There is a high-profile journal focused entirely on intellectual capital – the *Journal of Intellectual Capital*. Economists treat knowledge as an asset that produces wealth, multiplies the output of physical assets, gains competitive advantage, and enhances the value of other types of capital. Recently, economists have described intellectual capital as a real capital cost because (1) investment in (and replacement of) people is equivalent to or greater than the investment in machines and plants, and (2) expenses incurred in education and training (to maintain the shelf life of intellectual assets) are equivalent to depreciation costs of physical assets.

Technologists and futurists often focus on the role that technology plays in advancing the industrial economy to leverage artificial intelligence, robotics, and the embodiment and use of business rules repositories. While this perspective is essential, it places technology in the dominant role and considers how it impacts human workers.

Information professionals treat knowledge as a form of information. There are many, and many different, characterizations of knowledge in information science. The most significant challenge we face in this context is the interchangeability of two terms – knowledge and information. In this context, information is described as both a thing and a process. Knowledge is assumed to be part of the broader context of information. For some, knowledge is derived from information. For others, knowledge is interchangeable with the term – document – in its broadest characterization. For some, a document is any representation of or encoding of meaning. There is a close alignment of the idea of a generic document and a knowledge object. Here, a document is a fundamental, abstract idea – anything and everything that may be represented or memorialized to serve as evidence. A document can include anything that can be an object of study or understanding. It has some tangible representation that allows us to derive meaning and understanding. However, this characterization is far from commonly accepted in the field of information science. While the fields of information science and knowledge science are closely related, they do not offer a well-developed characterization of knowledge. What we can derive from this field, though, are some basic methods for supporting knowledge availability, accessibility, and consumability. These methods provide a starting point – though not an endpoint – for understanding architecture design.

Our working definition must make sense and be a practical tool we can use to design our knowledge architectures. What can we leverage from across these perspectives? What are the core elements? What is common to all of these perspectives? And, what makes knowledge different from other commodities and resources? From all of these perspectives, we observe that knowledge:

- is both a thing and a process;
- is inherently human;
- is dependent upon context;
- has both intrinsic and conditional value;
- has behaviors and properties that are different from commodities and resources.

Based on what is common to all of these perspectives, the scope and coverage of knowledge for knowledge architecture include any object – regardless of encoding, packaging, or format – that contains knowledge. This means knowledge extends far beyond simple textual representations such as books, documents, or social media. It means that knowledge can be embedded in and take many forms, including art objects, an artifact, a person, a group or community, an antique Persian rug, an antique American sampler or quilt, or a movie performance. Each of these representations encodes, packages, and formats knowledge differently. Each of these representations requires different methods and processes to make the embedded knowledge accessible, available, and consumable.

There is a characterization of knowledge that is sufficiently rigorous and inclusive to help us design a supportive knowledge architecture. The field of knowledge sciences provides this characterization. In Chapter 2, we offer a deep dive into the scope and coverage of a subfield of knowledge sciences – knowledge and intellectual capital. Each of these dimensions and characterization can accommodate the work of researchers in that field.

Shifting knowledge environment

In 2020, each of these representations is governed and managed by a channel – meaning the mechanism we use to make it available, to access it, or to consume it – that is best suited to that representation. Over the millennia, channels have changed – they have evolved. But, they have not developed with the level of speed we have experienced since the second half of the 20th century – the scale of change has been challenging to accommodate. The rate of change will not slow in the 21st century – it will only accelerate. Managers, designers, and knowledge producers need better strategies for managing the scale of this change.

We are accustomed to finding and using particular types of knowledge through specific channels and in particular packages. For example, we report research in print or digital journals or books. We are accustomed to finding people in directories and learning about their knowledge through CVs, resumes, and professional networks. We expect to see process know-how in manuals, procedures, instructional materials, or patents. Music, stories, and documentaries may be packaged in film, recorded on vinyl or magnetic tape, or burned on CDs. Each of these packages presumes a channel and has a 'built architecture,' which makes it challenging to find, access easily, and use embedded knowledge. Knowledge architecture is about designing a functional environment that recognizes the challenges of the built environment but looks beyond the package and the channel to leverage the object's embedded knowledge.

While the scale of change is noteworthy, the scope of change will be greater. Technology will continue to produce new packages and new channels for distribution. The old packages and channels will persist, though, increasing the scope of the design challenge. We can no longer rely on a single type of packaging as a target for persistent access and preservation. It will be necessary to assess the business value of knowledge assets continually. It will no longer be cost-effective or efficient to stockpile all of these assets, just in case the knowledge might have a future value. We can no longer presume that the package and channel in which a knowledge asset was created will be its only package and channel. Once available, any representation will mutate to accommodate access and consumption in other new and different channels.

Distinctive economic properties and behaviors of knowledge

Designing solutions in the future will not be as simple as choosing an archival format, establishing standards for packaging, or selecting a suite of products for procurement. Designing a solution will not be as simple and manageable as simply transforming from one medium to another. Knowledge assets have different economic properties and behaviors from those of other physical and financial capital assets. Understanding these properties and behaviors is essential to understanding why we need a new kind of knowledge architecture.

Let's begin with a review of the properties and behaviors of knowledge (Amidon et al., 2005). The properties of knowledge capital are different from those of the economic properties of physical and financial capital. The economics literature identifies 15 properties that affect the behaviors of knowledge capital, including:

- scarcity;
- experience goods;
- extensibility;
- public goods;
- non-competitive markets;
- opportunity costs;
- cost of time;
- openness;
- collaborative;
- transparency;
- interactiveness;
- perishability;
- embeddedness;
- infinite useful life;
- dynamic.

Each of these economic properties will influence how we think about and design knowledge architectures – how we design to make knowledge available, access knowledge, and consume knowledge. What is the significance of each of these properties? How does it affect the behavior of knowledge and how we design environments to support that behavior?

Property 1. Abundance versus scarcity

Properties of knowledge vary from other kinds of capital because the concept of scarcity does not apply; they grow rather than diminish through use and expenditure. Knowledge is a non-depleting resource. Knowledge itself doesn't go away when it is used or consumed in a production process. This is one reason we characterize it as a capital asset. Rather than diminishing through use and expenditure, knowledge generally increases in value, and rather than diminishing through use, knowledge increases in value.

Our knowledge architecture must be capable of making knowledge available and accessible in a way that allows the knowledge owner or custodian to define degrees of control. Degrees of control will vary in different contexts and business practices. The greater the exposure, consumption, and use of knowledge, the more likely its value is to increase. Stockpiling or hoarding knowledge will diminish its value.

Property 2. Knowledge is an experience good

An experience good is a product or service where features or characteristics such as quality or price are difficult to observe in advance of a purchase. You may not be able to judge its value in advance of purchase, but once you've read it, watched it, or used it, you no longer need to purchase it. Defining value is challenging. We meet this challenge by building an understanding of the production and consumption behaviors of knowledge assets. Individuals, collective groups, communities, organizations, and even cities leverage knowledge to create wealth. It is their collective brainpower or packaged useful knowledge.

This means that we cannot judge the value of knowledge until we have experienced it. The knowledge that is not experienced by others cannot be valued or validated. So, what does this mean? It means that we need an architecture that focuses on access and availability. A knowledge architecture must ensure that knowledge architecture must align with and support all business practices that leverage knowledge.

Property 3. Knowledge is extensible

Knowledge rarely remains in its original form. To consume knowledge, an individual must interpret it and integrate it into their stock of knowledge capital. There is a kernel of the initial knowledge, but it is no longer in its original form. An individual may understand part of the kernel or may embed it into existing knowledge. It is no longer the pristine entity it was before consumption.

This means that it is difficult to say that any two individuals have the same form of knowledge. When we consume knowledge from another, it is inherently unique. So, what does this mean? It means that our knowledge architecture must support dynamic objects, objects that continuously change. It means the architecture must be able to capture the value-added in all business contexts. It means that the architecture must be integrated into and support the tracking and discovery of knowledge in all business practices.

Property 4. Knowledge is a public good

A public good is one that is non-rivalrous and non-excludable. Non-rivalrous means it can be consumed by a collective of consumers (radio broadcasting, national defense, air, etc.). Non-excludable means if one individual consumes the good, the amount of the good does not diminish – the good is still available for consumption by others (creative works, information, patents, etc.). Exclusionary goods are goods that individuals cannot use unless they pay for their use. Exclusionary products reflect clearly defined property rights. Non-exclusionary goods are goods that some people can use without paying for them. Those who consume knowledge without paying for them are called free riders. Public goods require unique mechanisms to ensure that an efficient solution is achieved for both the producer and the consumer.

No one individual or organization can claim exclusive ownership of knowledge. The knowledge architecture must be able to account for and recognize source ownership and other value-added contributions. The architecture must account for multiple creator roles. The knowledge architecture must support interaction and have a process component to support access and use. We must design the knowledge architecture for those who have and those who want it.

Property 5. Knowledge is non-competitive

Knowledge is a non-competitive good, which means its availability does not change regardless of how many times we consume it. Acquisition and consumption of knowledge do not guarantee sole ownership. It means that the foundational assumptions of economic goods cannot be applied to knowledge. There is a need to adapt and adjust the foundation.

Knowledge architectures need to be able to track and race knowledge throughout its full business life. Today we have internal and external markets for knowledge. The demand for knowledge is great within an organization as well as outside the organization. Every business process is grounded in and leverages knowledge. It should be easier to find and to consume in that business context. Consider how knowledge is created and leveraged by organizations and their partners – suppliers, producers, and clients. Once accessed, further use and modification are challenging to control because of its non-competitive properties. The number of people who have access grows as knowledge is exposed in these internal and external environments.

Property 6. Opportunity costs of knowledge

Knowledge has opportunity costs. An opportunity cost is a cost of making a decision or consumption choice over an alternative one. Opportunity costs go beyond pure financial losses – in the case of information, it includes any other investment that might have been made instead of managing knowledge capital. We meet this challenge by ensuring that liabilities and potential failures are identified before making any investment decisions. Opportunity costs are significant considerations in the development of knowledge assets. Without access to sources, means, and opportunities, individuals and groups will not develop knowledge. A lack of knowledge puts an individual and a group at a disadvantage in the knowledge economy.

Every action to make knowledge available requires effort. Every step to discover and consume knowledge requires effort. Accessibility, availability, and consumption all have significant opportunity costs. Knowledge architecture needs to be able to optimize indirect and automatic methods to manage the amount of human effort required.

Property 7. Cost of time

Individuals need time to grow knowledge capital. Individuals must have the time to develop their tacit knowledge, to engage with others in the production and consumption of structural knowledge, and to engage in broader networks to expose themselves to other sources of knowledge and relationships. Individuals who work three part-time jobs and have no time to grow their knowledge capital find it challenging to advance in the knowledge economy. Communities and organizations suffer when individuals lack or have diminished knowledge capital.

The knowledge architecture designs must fit invisibly into the working environment. They cannot be obtrusive, and additional functional components add to the effort required for doing the organization's business.

Property 8. Knowledge is open

Knowledge permeates physical barriers. Barriers that do exist are not material. 'Knowledge is open' means that it is the natural behavior of knowledge to move. It is difficult, if not impossible, to contain or constrain the flow of knowledge in any context. It means that individuals and groups will gain more from encouraging production, use, sharing, and consumption of knowledge than from trying to control it.

Any solution we design must be dynamic. It must accommodate versions and editions. It must be embedded in a way that allows it to see and distinguish knowledge objects.

Property 9. Knowledge is collaborative

Knowledge is the property of communities and groups. Collaborative knowledge also means that through curation, review, evaluation, and feedback, the quality of knowledge assets will grow. The value of knowledge increases in its aggregate or shared form. Knowledge thrives in an environment of exchange and aggregation.

The knowledge architecture must have interactive and collaborative processes at its core. It is more than a simple business or workflow design. It must be adaptable to any business context in which people interact.

Property 10. Knowledge is transparent

We can identify the methods, sources, assumptions, outcomes, and other properties that allow a potential consumer to understand how the asset was designed or produced (e.g., its provenance). There is traceability and attribution of sources. It means that knowledge is more complex to value and trust than are other forms of capital and commodities.

The knowledge architecture must accommodate complex objects. It must be extensible beyond traditional information models. The knowledge architecture must be capable of embodying all those properties that help us to support transparency.

Property 11. Knowledge is interactive

Interactivity is inherent to the nature and flow of knowledge. Knowledge flows are inherently interactive – through face-to-face exchanges, internalization (e.g., reading and absorbing, listening and absorbing, etc.), externalization (e.g., communicating, documenting, recording, etc.), or a combination of any of these processes. Individuals and groups should expect to engage with other sources and actors in their questions to grow their human and structural capital. This property speaks directly to the importance of relational or network capital.

The knowledge architecture must support and have interaction at its core – any form of interaction related to the business's tasks.

Property 12. Knowledge is perishable and transitory

Knowledge is elusive, but once it is discovered and exploited, it may provide an organization with a new resource base from which to compete and win (Bontis, 1996). Cohen (2011) warn that just like the human body's muscles, knowledge suffers from lack of use – 'if you do not use it, you lose it.' It matters because if knowledge is not shared, recorded, or kept alive through some form of use, it will perish. While it is always possible to recreate knowledge, the recreation will come at great cost and with significant consequences. It is easy to dismiss or disregard the perishable nature of knowledge because it is intangible. There is no predictable fixed form. Because it is often intangible, it is also often invisible. Like information, knowledge has a structure. It is often difficult to see these structures, though, when they are invisible. Our knowledge architecture needs to be able to represent knowledge models embedded in the minds of its holders and custodians.

The knowledge architecture must be able to capture some form of knowledge in its various stages. It means it must have the ability to track the types of changes that are inherent to that type of knowledge. It is not sufficient to be able to represent different physical versions or editions.

Property 13. Knowledge is embedded

Knowledge is not a stand-alone asset – there are always antecedents. Knowledge is embedded in a process or activity, an inherent element of a culture or behavior. Knowledge is innate to every environment. This property is related to the extensible nature of knowledge. Knowledge always has a context. It is essential to understand the context in order to assign a value or before deciding to consume it.

The knowledge architecture must be able to represent the context of the knowledge. We must know the context in which knowledge was created to understand its purpose and intention.

Property 14. Knowledge is a dynamic and continuously changing asset

Two great thinkers have distinguished between knowledge and knowledge in books. Albert Einstein famously said that the knowledge recorded in books is dead because it is no longer alive, learning, and changing. Peter Senge, the author of Fifth Discipline and other knowledge management texts, has famously said that there is no knowledge in books, suggesting that knowledge is dynamic, changing, and perishable, and encoded and physically represented knowledge of books is unchanging. These distinctions are important because they caution us against assuming that prices for encoded information can be translated to valuations of knowledge capital. They also remind us that we need new and different strategies for managing knowledge capital.

The knowledge architecture must be designed around principles of change. It means that knowledge curation expands beyond reformatting and making decisions about which version is the final authoritative version. Knowledge curation must now pay attention to business value, and the architecture must support this type of activity.

Property 15. Knowledge has an infinite useful life

We do not associate the normal life cycle of birth, growth, maturity, and death with knowledge. Knowledge has an intrinsic useful life and value – just by its existence. That same knowledge, though, also has a useful business life – meaning that its value will be determined by the context in which it is consumed. There is no single value assigned to knowledge. The cost of production or the willingness of a consumer to pay is an estimate of value. Still, estimates of value will always vary with the context and the individual judgments of the producer and the consumer. It means that economy transactions for knowledge are perhaps the purest form of capital valuation.

The context of the use of knowledge has expanded well beyond our assumption of the useful life of information. It also means that we cannot assume that there is one useful or universal rationale for managing knowledge. It means that each organization must define business value for itself. It means the architecture must be able to support the assignment and management of value to knowledge.

These properties and behaviors constitute a compelling argument for a distinctive knowledge architecture. We cannot assume we are managing an easily defined, persistent, easily controlled commodity. There is no clear and evident knowledge architecture for us to draw from – we must identify the elements of a knowledge architecture. Like all forms of architecture, defining knowledge architecture begins with establishing a set of design principles.

Design principles for knowledge architecture

Each property and behavior discussed earlier gives rise to a knowledge architecture design principle. Here are the 16 principles that were identified in our descriptions.

- Principle 1. Knowledge architecture must make knowledge available and accessible in a way that allows the knowledge owner or custodian to define degrees of control. Degrees of control will vary in different contexts and business practices.
- Principle 2. Knowledge architecture must ensure that knowledge architecture must align with and support all business practices that leverage knowledge.
- Principle 3. Knowledge architecture must support dynamic objects, objects that continuously change. It must be able to capture the value-added in all business contexts. The knowledge architecture must be integrated into and support the tracking and discovery of knowledge in all business practices.
- Principle 4. Knowledge architecture must be able to account for and recognize source ownership and other value-added contributions, to account for multiple creator roles.
- Principle 5. Knowledge architecture must support interaction and have a process component to support access and use.
- Principle 6. Knowledge architecture needs to be able to track and race knowledge throughout its full business life.
- Principle 7. Knowledge architecture needs to be able to optimize indirect and automatic methods to manage the amount of human effort required.
- Principle 8. Knowledge architecture designs must fit invisibly into the working environment and not require distinct or different efforts of knowledge producers and consumers.
- Principle 9. Knowledge architecture must be embedded and dynamic and capable of accommodating versions and editions.
- Principle 10. Knowledge architecture must have interactive and collaborative processes at its core, and these processes must be adaptable to any business context in which people interact.
- Principle 11. Knowledge architecture must accommodate complex objects and be capable of embodying all those properties that help us to support transparency.
- Principle 12. Knowledge architecture must support and have interaction at its core, both synchronous and asynchronous.
- Principle 13. Knowledge architecture must be able to represent knowledge models that are embedded in the minds of its holders, and custodians and must be able to track and trace changes that are inherent to that type of knowledge.
- Principle 14. Knowledge architecture must be able to represent the context in which knowledge was created.
- Principle 15. Knowledge architecture assumes that there is no single authoritative final version of knowledge. The architecture must support active knowledge curation to ensure any version of value is available, accessible, and consumable.

- Principle 16. Knowledge architecture must be capable of recording and updating the business value of any knowledge object.

These principles should guide all of our work to define a knowledge architecture framework. There is no one knowledge architecture that will work in every business context. They can be used to determine a framework from which any organization can design a knowledge architecture that will meet their needs.

Practical working definition of knowledge

We have a good understanding of the nature, properties, and behavior of knowledge. We have identified important new design principles to guide our development of knowledge architecture. Is there a working definition of knowledge we can use to ground our architecture design? Is there a characterization of knowledge that aligns with these properties, behaviors, and principles? The answer is yes. The definition comes from researchers in the field of intellectual capital. The definition takes the form of working descriptions of intellectual capital which are the equivalent of categories of knowledge. Let's review that characterization in Chapter 2.

Chapter review

After reading this chapter, you should be able to:

- explain the role of knowledge in the knowledge economy;
- discuss and contextualize the many definitions of knowledge;
- describe the increased scale of change of access to knowledge;
- describe the expanded scope of change of availability of knowledge assets;
- explain the distinct economic properties and behaviors of knowledge.

References and recommended future readings

Amidon, D., Formica, P., & Mercier-Laurent, E. (2005). *Knowledge economics: Emerging principles, practices and policies.* Tartu University Press.

Bassi, L. J., & Van Buren, M. E. (1999). Valuing investments in intellectual capital. *International Journal of Technology Management, 18*(5–8), 414–432.

Baumol, W. J. (1968). Entrepreneurship in economic theory. *The American Economic Review, 58*(2), 64–71.

Baumol, W. J. (1993). *Entrepreneurship, management, and the structure of payoffs.* Cambridge, MA: MIT Press.

Baumol, W. J., & Braunstein, Y. M. (1977). Empirical study of scale economies and production complementarity: The case of journal publication. *Journal of Political Economy, 85*(5), 1037–1048.

Bontis, N. (1996). *Intellectual capital: An exploratory study that develops measures and models.* Paper prepared for the Seventeenth McMaster Business Conference, London, Ontario, Canada: Richard Ivey School of Business, University of Western Ontario, January 24–26.

Bontis, N. (1998). Intellectual capital: An exploratory study that develops measures and models. *Management Decision*. ISSN: 0025-1747.

Bontis, N. (2003). Intellectual capital disclosure in Canadian corporations. *Journal of Human Resource Costing and Accounting*, 7(1/2), 9–20.

Bontis, N., Keow, W. C. C., & Richardson, S. (2000). Intellectual capital and business performance in Malaysian industries. *Journal of Intellectual Capital*, 1(1).

Bornemann, M., Knapp, A., Schneider, U., & Sixl, K. I. (1999, June). Holistic measurement of intellectual capital. In *International Symposium Measuring and Reporting Intellectual Capital: Experiences, Issues, and Prospects*. OECD.

Brainerd, C. J. (1978). *Piaget's theory of intelligence*. Prentice-Hall.

Carayannis, E. G. (2009). Firm evolution dynamics: Towards sustainable entrepreneurship and robust competitiveness in the knowledge economy and society. *International Journal of Innovation and Regional Development*, 1(3), 235–254.

Carayannis, E. G., & Formica, P. (2008). *Knowledge matters: Technology, innovation and entrepreneurship in innovation networks and knowledge clusters*. Springer.

Carayannis, E. G., & Sipp, C. (2005). *E-development toward the knowledge economy: Leveraging technology, innovation and entrepreneurship for "smart" development*. Springer.

Cohen, J. A. (2011). *Intangible assets: Valuation and economic benefit* (Vol. 273). John Wiley & Sons.

Cornford, F. M. (2003). *Plato's theory of knowledge: The theaetetus and the sophist*. Courier Corporation.

Driscoll, M. P. (1994). *Psychology of learning for instruction*. Allyn and Bacon.

Edvinsson, L., & Malone, M. S. (1997). *Intellectual capital: The proven way to establish your company's real value by finding its hidden brainpower*. Piatkus.

Goldkuhl, G., & Röstlinger, A. (2000). *Beyond goods and services: An elaborate product classification on pragmatic grounds*. Universitet, Centrum för studier av människa, teknik och organisation.

Gourlay, S. (2006). Conceptualizing knowledge creation: A critique of Nonaka's theory. *Journal of Management Studies*, 43(7), 1415–1436.

Gruber, H. E., & Voneche, J. J. (1977). *The essential Piaget*. Basic Books.

Kanchana, N., & Mohan, R. R. (2017). A review of empirical studies in intellectual capital and firm performance. *Indian Journal of Commerce and Management Studies*, 8(1), 52.

Kianto, A., Inkinen, H., Ritala, P., & Vanhala, M. (2017, July). A temporal perspective to intellectual capital dynamics: How has IC changed in Finnish firms from 2013 to 2017? In *Proceedings of the 14th international conference on intellectual capital* (pp. 134–138). Knowledge Management & Organizational Learning.

Nazari, J. A., & Herremans, I. M. (2007). Extended VAIC model: Measuring intellectual capital components. *Journal of Intellectual Capital*, 8(4), 595–609.

Nonaka, I., & Takeuchi, H. (1995). *The knowledge-creating company: How Japanese companies create the dynamics of innovation*. Oxford University Press.

Piaget, J. (1976). Piaget's theory. In *Piaget and his school* (pp. 11–23). Springer.

Prochazkova, P. T., & Jelinkova, E. (2014, October). The importance of intellectual capital in entrepreneurial companies. In *ECIC2014-proceedings of the 6th European conference on intellectual capital: ECIC 2014*. Academic Conferences Limited.

Roos, J., Edvinsson, L., & Dragonetti, N. C. (1997). *Intellectual capital: Navigating the new business landscape*. Springer.

Saettler, P. (1990). *The evolution of American educational technology*. Libraries Unlimited, Inc.

Silva, R., Leal, C., Marques, C. S., & Ferreira, J. (2017, March). The strategic knowledge management, innovation and competitiveness: A bibliometric analysis. In *European Conference on Intellectual Capital* (p. 303). Academic Conferences International Limited.

Sveiby, K. E. (1997a). The intangible assets monitor. *Journal of Human Resource Costing & Accounting*, *2*(1), 73–97.

Sveiby, K. E. (1997b). *The new organizational wealth: Managing & measuring knowledge-based assets*. Berrett-Koehler Publishers.

Sveiby, K. E. (2001). A knowledge-based theory of the firm to guide in strategy formulation. *Journal of Intellectual Capital*, *2*(4), 344–358.

Zins, C. (2006). Redefining information science: From "information science" to "knowledge science." *Journal of Documentation*, *62*(4), 447–461.

2

THE LANDSCAPE OF KNOWLEDGE ASSETS

Chapter summary

This chapter describes the literature and research on knowledge typologies and identifies a common framework for designing a functional knowledge architecture. The chapter takes Bontis's work in modeling intellectual capital as a foundation and designs a set of five types of knowledge capital assets to use for architectural design. The five types include (1) human knowledge assets; (2) explicit knowledge assets; (3) procedural knowledge assets; (4) cultural knowledge assets; and (5) relational knowledge assets. We define each type, provide examples, and discuss their essential behaviors and properties.

Why we care about knowledge

The value of knowledge to organizations in the knowledge economy is substantial. As a starting point for knowledge architecture, we need to have a working definition of knowledge. Understanding the full scope and coverage of knowledge assets is essential to ensuring that the architecture we design to support knowledge availability, accessibility, and consumability. We need to select a framework that incorporates all of these definitions. We must understand knowledge in a systematic, comprehensive, and practical way. We need to translate what we learned in Chapter 1 to a working framework we can use to design a knowledge architecture. This framework needs to be usable by any organization.

Knowledge typologies from the literature

In this chapter, we look at the excellent work of researchers in knowledge and intellectual capital for guidance (Carr et al., 2001; Diniz, 2015; Kianto et al., 2017; Leal et al., 2016, 2019; Nafukho et al., 2004; Navarro, 2015; Ng & Chatzkel, 2015;

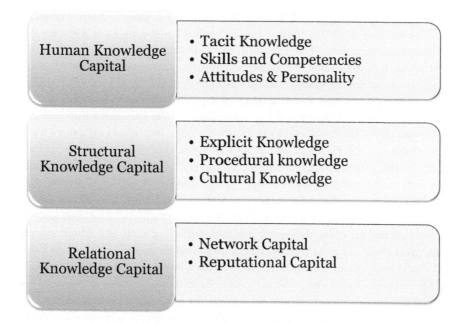

| Human Knowledge Capital | • Tacit Knowledge
• Skills and Competencies
• Attitudes & Personality |

| Structural Knowledge Capital | • Explicit Knowledge
• Procedural knowledge
• Cultural Knowledge |

| Relational Knowledge Capital | • Network Capital
• Reputational Capital |

FIGURE 2.1 Types of Intellectual Capital

Sweetland, 1996). Intellectual capital researchers offer several different typologies of knowledge capital. The works of Bontis (1996), Andriessen (2004), and Amidon (2005) are the most widely referenced and cited. These researchers define three broad categories (Figure 2.1), including: (1) human capital – tacit knowledge and skills, and attitudes; (2) structural capital – culture, procedural knowledge, and explicit knowledge; and (3) relational capital – communication, knowledge and social networks, as well as overall reputation and brand. We take three categories of knowledge capital as a starting point, to which we've mapped existing frameworks and treatments. These categories include human capital, structural capital, and relational capital.

We describe each type, break each type down into its practical components, and provide examples to help the reader develop a broad understanding of the landscape of knowledge assets. A full view of this landscape is essential to ensuring that our knowledge architecture supports any context and function and supports all assets.

Human capital – definitions and examples

Human capital represents a foundational shift in our conceptualization and characterization of capital because (1) everyone has it; (2) everyone has the opportunity to develop it; and (3) everyone owns their knowledge capital. Unless an individual is living in a society or economy that tolerates slavery, no other individual can own or claim title to an individual's knowledge capital. This form of capital – and its value to the new knowledge economy – is now a point of leverage (Bontis et al.,

2007; Chatzkel, 2003; Choo & Bontis, 2002; Curado & Bontis, 2007; Malhotra, 2002; Serenko et al., 2010). And, every individual has this point of leverage. An individual can accumulate human capital, but unless they share it, use it, or ensure it circulates, it loses its value. No single individual can amass such a level of human capital as to 'corner the market,' as you could if you could gain ownership over a commodity or if you were to hoard financial capital. Every individual must understand this fundamental change and the implications of the change for their actions.

Human capital has the most evident focus on a single individual of the three types of intellectual capital. Human capital flows to an individual. While the focus is clear, there is nothing simple about an individual's human capital. Every person has multiple forms and types of tacit knowledge – professional or occupational knowledge, tacit knowledge of the legal and political worlds in which they exist, knowledge of medical conditions that may govern their health, and financial and economic knowledge. A person has many different kinds and degrees of skills and competencies. Some individuals can grow their food, others can repair their cars, some can bake, and others have various talents they've developed as hobbies. Every person has multiple personality characteristics. Sociologists refer to these variations as 'registers' – a variety of behavior or language used for a particular purpose or specific situation. To fully leverage knowledge capital in the knowledge economy, it is essential to understand the richness and complexity of an individual's knowledge registers.

Human capital focuses on an individual – it represents a person's knowledge, including their tacit knowledge, skills and competencies, and attitudes and behaviors. There is a strong consensus among intellectual capital researchers around the definition and characterization of human capital. Tacit knowledge includes everything an individual knows and has learned throughout a lifetime. Tacit knowledge is gained through formal and informal learning experiences – the total of what they know. Skills and competencies include all of those things an individual 'can do' – what they can demonstrate. These may be skills and competencies defined by professional associations, industry standards, training professionals, or things a person learns to do in living each day. Attitudes and behaviors describe an individual's characteristics and traits, including their ability to engage socially, their emotional intelligence, their ability to work with others, their values, perspectives, personal morals, ethics, and beliefs. Skills and competencies may also include all of the knowledge that an individual gains through experience. Attitudes and behaviors are necessary because they may determine how an individual consumes, produces, and values knowledge capital.

So, what are some examples of human capital? Examples of *tacit knowledge* might include an individual's ability to diagnose an electrical system problem, an individual's ability to predict a computer system failure, an architect's understanding of how to design a building to fit a slope near a river, or a chemist's ability to predict the rate of production of a new chemical compound. Examples of *skills and competencies* might include enterprise architecture certification, enterprise content management certificates, teaching credentials, automotive mechanics' brand certification, a license to practice law, or a license to practice medicine. Examples of an individual's *attitude and behavior* include a chief economist's ability to work with

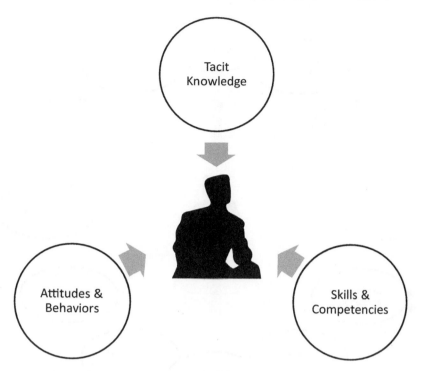

FIGURE 2.2 Individual as the Focus of Human Capital

junior economists, a tenured faculty member's ability to mentor junior faculty or to teach an undergraduate course in their field, a customer service representative's emotional intelligence quotient, the combined ratings of individual team members, or a CEO's ability to abide by and promote ethical and moral codes of conduct.

Tacit knowledge

Tacit knowledge is the total of everything a person knows – all of the knowledge in their head. Tacit knowledge is complex and multidimensional. It represents what an individual has learned formally and informally, through self-study, through experience, by working with others, learning by doing, from insights gained through critical thinking or creative activities, from extracurricular activities, by talking with others, and through mentoring and coaching (Bontis & Fitz-enz, 2002; Collins & Hitt, 2006; Fitzsimons, 1999; Nerdrum & Erikson, 2001; Olaniyan & Okemakinde, 2008). In short, any activity that generates new knowledge creates knowledge gaps or corrects existing knowledge. Tacit knowledge is aimed at and acquired by an individual. Others leverage it, but it is the property of a single individual. In the knowledge economy, a person's tacit knowledge is their prime source of capital – what they know, what they have learned, their understanding – and is an essential source of wealth and comparative advantage in the knowledge economy.

FIGURE 2.3 Graphic Representation of Tacit Knowledge

How do we design knowledge architecture to support the availability of, access to, and consumption of tacit knowledge? What does this mean when the source of tacit knowledge is an individual? We begin by understanding the facets and structures of tacit knowledge (Figure 2.3), including:

- continuous education;
- conversations;
- critical thinking;
- experience;
- extracurricular activities;
- formal courses;
- informal learning;
- learning by doing;
- mentoring and coaching;
- problem-solving;
- self-study;
- teamwork.

Tacit knowledge enables individuals to apply their understanding and experience to everyday business problems. It also means understanding the behavior of tacit knowledge – how it grows, how it diminishes, and the factors that affect growth or depletion. Tacit knowledge grows through formal and informal learning processes. Tacit knowledge grows through exposure to problem situations, opportunity to detect and diagnose problems, posing questions, developing the capacity to explain what you know and how you think about something to others, through exposure to failures, and by learning from mistakes. Contrary to popular thinking, tacit knowledge is not built from resource-based learning alone. Rather, experience and working with others is essential. Despite the common perception that tacit knowledge grows from and is demonstrated through formal education and advanced degrees, tacit knowledge would appear to grow over time through exposure to different contexts, to working with others in teams, and in project environments. An individual's tacit knowledge may gain a foothold in formal education and training, but it grows through experience. The more dynamic the knowledge domain, the more important it is after formal education and training.

Skills and competencies

Skills and competencies can include everything from formal certificates and credentials to general life skills such as communication and learning skills. Skills and competencies are acquired through formal training programs, formal degree programs, credentialing courses, and through self-study and testing. Skills and competencies may be defined by external or authorizing bodies such as the American Bar Association, the American Medical Association, American Library Association, National Court Reporters Association, carpentry certification and licensure programs, teacher certification programs, and so on. Every profession, every trade has some way to gauge and assess the proficiency of its practitioners. Skills and competencies have an inherent tacit knowledge element. What distinguishes tacit knowledge from skills and competencies is the act of 'doing' – the translation of that tacit knowledge into action.

How do we design knowledge architecture to support the availability of, access to, and consumption of skills and competencies? What are the sources of skills and competencies, and how are they represented as an individual's human knowledge? We begin by understanding the facets and structures of skills and competencies (Figure 2.4), including:

- certification;
- credentialing and licensing;
- demonstrations;
- formal coursework;
- formal training;
- learning capacity;
- life skills;
- practical experience;
- technical competencies;
- testing and examinations.

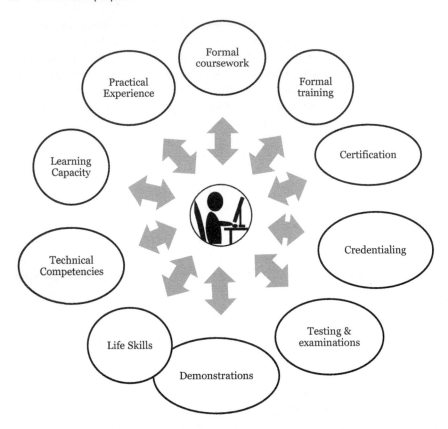

FIGURE 2.4 Graphic Representation of Skills and Competencies

The knowledge architecture must be designed to identify formal learning courses and degree programs, as well as official training sources; these are essential to growing formally recognized skills and competencies. Such structured training and education require preparation for examinations and tests, access to adequate coaching and mentoring, recognition of credentialing sources, professional associations, and vendor supporting credentials. Just as growing tacit knowledge extends beyond formally structured learning activities, so does building our skills and competencies. One of the most often-cited sources of skills development is on-the-job experience or self-directed informal learning, and as the work environment shifts from process-related competencies to context-sensitive capabilities, informal and self-directed learning will be the primary source of learning essential skills. Research suggests that skills and competencies will see the most significant shift and change as we advance further into the 21st century.

Attitudes and behaviors

Attitudes and behaviors are the most natural forms of human capital to develop – they are inherent to every individual's growth and development. They are the most challenging to assess. Human resource professionals have traditionally referred to this type of human capital as 'soft skills' or behavioral competencies. This category of human capital includes but is not limited to moral and ethical behaviors, norms, values, emotional intelligence, social intelligence, general personality types and behaviors, a capacity for learning, a capacity for teamwork, cultural intelligence, and propensity for reciprocity (Nahapiet & Ghoshal, 1998).

How do we design knowledge architecture to support the availability of, access to, and consumption of attitudes and behaviors? What does this mean when the source of attitudes and behaviors is an individual? We begin by understanding the facets and structures of tacit knowledge (Figure 2.5), including:

- behavior;
- capacity for learning;
- capacity for teamwork;
- cultural intelligence;
- emotional intelligence;
- ethics;
- morals;
- norms;
- reciprocity;
- social intelligence;
- values.

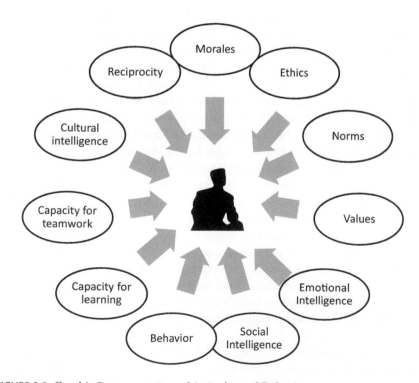

FIGURE 2.5 Graphic Representation of Attitudes and Behaviors

What does it mean to grow our attitudes and behaviors? It is a complex design challenge. Attitudes and behaviors receive only passing attention in command-and-control cultures of the industrial economy. Attitudes and behaviors come into focus when they are negative. Yet, attitudes and behaviors will be critical to the knowledge economy. Consider the role that an individual's attitude might play in effectively collaborating with a team, or whether their behavior encourages trust sufficient to share a new idea. Attitudes and behaviors determine how effectively we can learn by example, to demonstrate strong ethical and moral behaviors, the form with which one can receive or offer constructive feedback, or receive and confer rewards and acknowledgments. Growing this kind of capital requires having exposure to good role models, mentors, and teachers. Research highlights how often this kind of knowledge capital is learned through engagement in extracurricular activities, cultural and spiritual upbringing, sports clubs, sports teams, and social clubs. We gain this kind of capital by mentoring others, by supporting and sponsoring others, by learning how to listen and to be empathetic. Individuals are recognized to have these attributes through their informal reputations, in ratings and feedback, and by general referrals from others. We demonstrate our capacity by making ethical choices and explaining our options.

Structural capital – definitions and examples

Whereas human capital focuses on the knowledge of individuals, structural capital focuses on the knowledge of groups, communities, and organizations. In the knowledge economy, a group's or an organization's structural knowledge is their prime source of capital – what they know, how they do things, the norms and values they value collectively (De Pablos, 2004; Morrison & Siegel, 1998). Structural knowledge is more than the simple sum of all of its human capital. Individuals pool their knowledge to create something exponentially more significant. Individuals in the group refresh and grow their human capital drawing from the knowledge of the collective. In this chapter, we consider what it means for groups, communities, and organizations to produce and consume structural knowledge.

Structural capital is critical to developing organization-wide knowledge capabilities. While structural capital is associated with groups, communities, and the organization, it also has implications for individuals. Through their individual and collective activities, individuals contribute to the creation of structural capital. Chapter 12 provides an extended discussion of how individuals and organizations can grow their explicit knowledge, procedural knowledge, and organizational culture attributes and examines these issues in the context of learning cultures and learning spheres. These issues include determining sources, opportunities and challenges, risks, and the inherent interrelatedness of human capital, structural capital, and relational capital assets.

There is no restriction on the nature of the type of the 'group.' The vital point to understand about structural capital is that it represents an aggregate of the human capital of the individuals who make up the group. Structural capital represents an aggregation of knowledge that is generated by a group of individuals. Structural capital may also represent a level of agreement, consensus, or justification. All of the members of a group – whether it is a workgroup, a neighborhood, a social group, a corporation, or a professional association – participate in creating structural capital. They pool their knowledge capital to create something new – something that is greater than the simple sum of their knowledge. All members of the group have access to the knowledge, and each member of the group incorporates the structural knowledge into their human capital. The flows are bidirectional.

The growth of human capital is exponential given the interactions and exposure within groups, units, communities, and organizations. Our perspective is also more focused because structural capital describes the behavior of knowledge in a given context. The context represents the group's common interests – whether that is a neighborhood, a social club, a business unit in an organization, or an entire organization.

The first category of structural capital is *explicit knowledge or information*, which is codified knowledge in any format (Figure 2.6). This may include books, journals, conference papers, magazine articles, formal communications, intranets, newspapers, websites, documentaries, recorded music or videos, and so forth. Some researchers characterize these as 'what is left behind after the people leave' because there is no

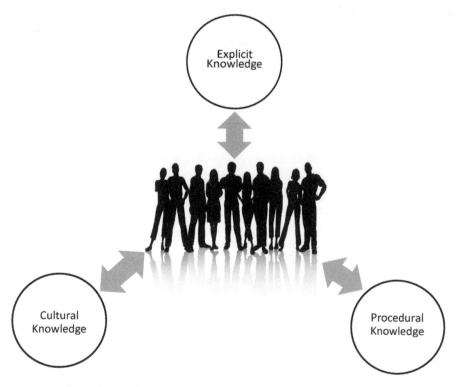

FIGURE 2.6 The Focus of Structural Capital Is Group, Community, and Organization

apparent interaction or contact with the source. The knowledge represented in this type of explicit information is static and, according to Albert Einstein, 'dead knowledge.' This definition reduces the economic properties of this kind of knowledge capital.

The second category of structural knowledge is referred to as *procedural capital*. Structural knowledge represents the group's process knowledge, their knowledge of how to do something – whether it is to produce a product or advocate on behalf of a neighborhood. It represents the collective knowledge of individuals – tested, validated, activated, and continually evolving and improving. This type of structural knowledge is dynamic and continually changing through input and learning of the individuals and agents who support the process. When this procedural knowledge is recorded in a design manual or a repair manual, the codified form becomes explicit information. The underlying knowledge, though, retains the characterization of procedural knowledge.

The third category of structural capital is *organizational capital*. Organizations with substantial structural capital will have a supportive culture that allows individuals to try new things, to learn, and to fail. Organizational culture is complex. Organizational cultures encourage individuals to grow their human capital, contribute to procedural capital, encourage individuals to try new things, learn, and fail safely to succeed and excel in the knowledge economy. Every group – whether a business unit, a club, a professional association, or a corporation – has multiple levels of culture and numerous cultural registers. Every individual comes to work with numerous cultural registers, meaning they operate within multiple cultures every day – family cultures, national cultures, social cultures, political cultures. One of the most substantial types of culture is the culture inherent to a function or subject area. The accounting profession, the marketing profession, and the information management professions each have their assumptions and beliefs, values and behaviors, and artifacts. These cultures are often invisible, but their impact is significant. Crafting a knowledge culture is essential to leveraging any knowledge capital available to the group. Harmful or destructive cultures can negate the inherent value of knowledge capital and influence the growth not only of groups but of individuals. It is easy to feel trapped in these negative cultures, without a better option. While cultures change slowly, they can change.

What is consistent across the existing research is a common assumption of collective and aggregated knowledge capital. Collective knowledge may represent the aggregated knowledge of as few as two or three individuals, or it may be as many as or more than 10,000. Additionally, aggregation may include human and non-human sources. In this section, we look more closely at the breakdown of structural capital and consider its specific properties, behaviors, production and consumption opportunities and challenges, and useful life.

Explicit information

Explicit information includes any knowledge that is important for a group, a community, or an organization to make explicit for management, access, availability, use, and preservation. Explicit means making it tangible in some way so that it is available to, accessible to, used by, and preserved for entities other than its source.

Explicit knowledge may be available as documented text, in audio form, in video form, as a transcript, a captured dialog or discussion thread – any format. This means defining some tangible and persistent form of representation. Examples of explicit knowledge might include an engineering design manual, a corporation's quarterly financial reports, a peer-review journal article, a conference presentation, a community newsletter, a national newspaper, a record of a conversation, a website, a chemistry textbook, a documentary, or a best-selling decorating book.

How do we design knowledge architecture to support the availability of, access to, and consumption of explicit knowledge? The good news is that there are many methods and practices in place now. The bad news is that these methods derive from many different professions and areas of practice, each specific and suited to the physical representation of the type of object. Explicit knowledge often draws from the principles and practice of information management. The extensive practice of information management is an essential foundation for this type of knowledge capital. While this category can draw from those practices, there is one crucial distinction – context. Information management may treat all explicit knowledge equally. While all explicit knowledge has intrinsic value, it does not have equal extrinsic value. Experience suggests that organizations – businesses in particular – may focus on what is most natural to 'capture' rather than what is most important to make available. A common mistake is to capture and preserve everything the organization generates, which has a tangible form, rather than identifying business-critical knowledge and ensuring it has a tangible form. Capturing and storing everything that has tangible form is information management – we can draw from the principles and practices of information management to support this category of knowledge capital. However, information management should not be confused with the management of knowledge capital.

What does this mean for designing a knowledge architecture? It means that we need to identify the common elements across all these areas of practice and be prepared to expand, extend, and adapt them to the new environment. We begin by understanding the facets and structures of explicit knowledge (Figure 2.7), including:

- audio recordings of conversations;
- engineering design specifications;
- meeting photographs;
- meeting transcripts;
- performance feedback;
- personal profiles;
- policy documents;
- procedural manuals;
- project reports;
- quality control reports;
- regulatory guidelines;
- text capture of conversations;
- video recordings of processes;
- websites.

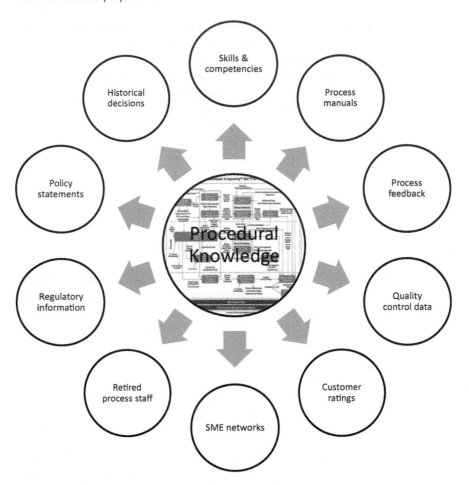

FIGURE 2.7 Graphic Representation of Explicit Knowledge

Procedural knowledge

The knowledge management literature is rich with references to process knowledge and business 'know-how.' The research is sparse, though, on specific examples. Procedural capital includes the way an organization markets to its customers, an assembly line process for building a car, the method a baker follows to bake a tiramisu cake, the procedures a carpenter follows for framing a house, or how a legislator works with others to pass a law (Banks & Millward, 2007; Capello & Faggian, 2005; Carr et al., 2001; Fayol, 1994; Glisky, 1992; Lynn & Akgun, 2000; Martínez-Torres, 2006; Matsuo & Kusumi, 2002; Surif et al., 2012; Yitmen, 2011; Yli-Renko et al., 2001). Examples of organizational culture might include how the organization treats its employees and the value it assigns to those people as individuals, the unit level knowledge-sharing behaviors, managerial cultures for rewarding and recognizing the contributions of employees, the organizational policy that allows or restricts employees from bringing personal decorations into their offices, or leaders' support for and encouragement for staff participation in clubs and associations

Like other forms of structural knowledge, procedural knowledge is relevant to a context. Unlike explicit knowledge, procedural knowledge draws from all sources and may take any form. The critical factor is whether the knowledge is related to a given process. The process may be relevant to any group or organization – it may be a core business process, or it may be a support process. Is it related to a process? Is it needed to perform that process? Does it mean the difference between acceptable and high-quality products or outcomes?

Procedural knowledge draws from all other types of knowledge capital, including the tacit knowledge of those involved in or related to the business process, the skills and competencies required to carry out any step or make any decision in that process, attitudes and behaviors that make it possible for all sources to contribute their knowledge, process manuals, process feedback, quality control data, customer ratings, and networks of subject matter experts and retired process staff. The deciding factor is whether it pertains to a step in the process. Knowledge pertinent to a process is one degree more focused than knowledge related to business. Procedural knowledge may take an explicit or a tacit form – it must simply be known, accessible, and available. It must be usable by the business process – at that point in the process where it is needed.

What does this mean for designing a knowledge architecture? It means we need to understand the facets and structures of procedural knowledge (Figure 2.8), including:

- customer ratings;
- historical decisions;
- policy statements;
- process documents;
- process feedback;
- quality control data;
- regulatory information;
- retired process staff;
- skills and competencies;
- subject matter expert groups.

Where do we begin to identify process knowledge? We start by focusing on the process. Some organizations start with detailed workflow diagrams or process manuals. Procedural knowledge is often embedded in other knowledge forms. Procedural knowledge includes any knowledge assets that pertain to each step in the process. Assets are leveraged by individuals or agents performing steps in the process, but they are organized at the whole process level.

What are the design factors for procedural knowledge? In the early 21st century, we see a trend across organizations to extract this procedural knowledge and represent it in business rules repositories or explicit business decision systems. This trend towards formalizing business knowledge is also pertinent to the automation of business processes, the increased use of intelligent agents, robotics, and automated

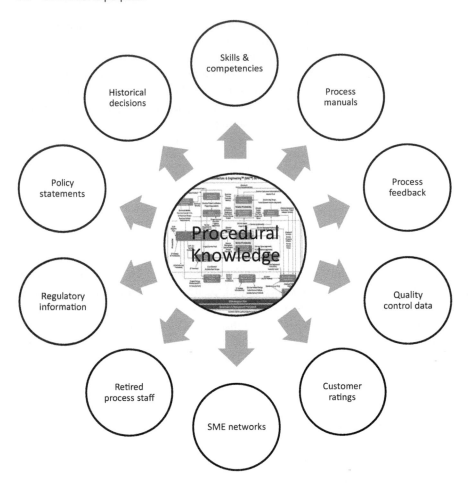

FIGURE 2.8 Graphic Representation of Procedural Knowledge

decisions. A related trend is the development of business language and business organization tools. Historically, access has been dominated by general or specialized subject matter vocabularies. Business-related vocabularies may be defined for an economic sector or for an area of business practice, but it must always be adapted to the business context of an organization.

Organizational culture knowledge

Cultural capital is collective, and it is also context-relevant. Cultural capital includes all of those assumptions and beliefs, behaviors, values, and artifacts that are pertinent to the way a group or an organization functions. Those aspects of culture that pertain to the collective consensus or assumptions related to knowledge capital are of the highest interest. Does the collective culture value knowledge capital? Does the culture indicate that the knowledge of all staff has value? Is there an expectation that quality control of knowledge, that knowledge validation and reliability are essential behaviors? Does the behavior of leaders and managers reify the espoused knowledge culture, or do they contradict it?

Culture is difficult to recognize – it is difficult to see and expose, but every member of an organization lives it every day. Culture is complex – as a collective asset, it is an aggregation of the cultures of individuals, business units, and the entire membership of the group or organization. Culture is refined and expanded at each level. Culture is dynamic and continuously evolving. Culture is multidirectional. Individuals share their cultural behaviors and values with others – they influence everyone they come in contact with. The collective supporting a business unit defines its culture then – a change in membership or a change in leadership can significantly change the culture. The organizational or whole culture will be substantially influenced by the inherent cultures of leaders, but leaders will also be affected by the cultures of the collective. While culture is manifested in the collective, it is lived by each individual. Individuals absorb elements of every culture they are exposed to – it becomes part of their fundamental attitudes and behaviors.

What does this mean for designing a knowledge architecture? It means that we need to identify the three levels of cultural representation and to understand how these are manifested in any business context. We begin by understanding the facets and structures of explicit knowledge (Figure 2.9), including:

- business cultures;
- functional cultures;
- informal group cultures;
- individual cultures.

While many factors influence an organization's culture, five core elements (Figure 2.10) are essential, including (1) assumptions, (2) beliefs, (3) values, (4) behaviors,

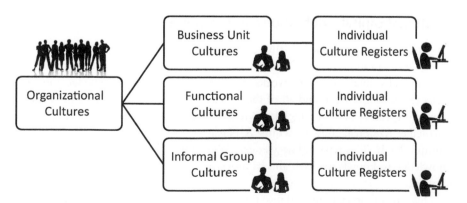

FIGURE 2.9 Graphic Representation of Cultural Knowledge Capital

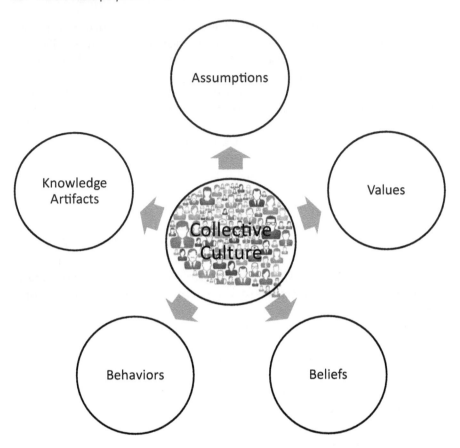

FIGURE 2.10 Essential Elements of Collective Culture

and (5) artifacts. Representing culture at all three levels means defining and making these five elements accessible at each of these levels.

Relational capital – definitions and examples

The more common name for this category of knowledge is relational capital, though it might more accurately be described as network capital. The main themes of relational capital are the networks, the knowledge flows, knowledge sources, social relationships, trust, and all of those factors that speak directly to the movement, flow, and velocity at which knowledge moves and transforms (Capello, 2002; Carmeli & Azeroual, 2009; Dewhurst & Navarro, 2004; Liu et al., 2010; Tymon & Stumpf, 2003). This type of knowledge capital shifts the focus from the source of knowledge to knowledge itself and its movement across and transformation across networks.

This type of capital is divided into two forms – *relational or network knowledge*, and *reputational knowledge*. Relational capital focuses on individuals, their connections,

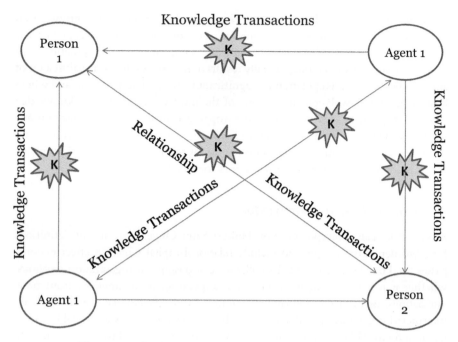

FIGURE 2.11 The Focus of Relational Capital – Knowledge, Relationships, and Flows

and the flows of knowledge across networks. This type of knowledge capital is one step greater in intensity and volume than either human or structural capital. This form leverages the knowledge capital of many individuals and is unconstrained by any given context. Relational knowledge includes all of the human capital of the individual nodes and the aggregated structural capital of groups of nodes. It is a level of richness and complexity beyond structural knowledge. For this text, relational capital can include networks of humans, non-human actors such as machines and intelligent agents, or pure knowledge networks. Common examples of networks include communities of practice, neighborhood networks, community groups, informal clubs, online social networks, professional communities, invisible colleges, and others. Non-human or hybrid networks might include robotics, automated personal assistants, networks of processes and business rules repositories, etc.

Relational or network knowledge is critical to knowledge flows and transfers, and, as it turns out, also to the growth of all other forms of knowledge capital. Any attempt to grow human or structural knowledge without leveraging networks and network relationships will, by definition, be insufficient. And we know that network engagement is dependent upon reputation. For an extended discussion of how individuals and organizations can grow their networks, network relationships, and reputation, see Chapter 12. That chapter also examines issues such as determining sources, opportunities and challenges, risks, and the inherent interrelatedness of human capital, structural capital, and relational capital assets.

Reputational knowledge focuses on the reputation or image of a group or an individual within a group. Reputation is an aspect of relational knowledge because it is a value that is formed and held by multiple agents or sources. Reputation is an opinion about that source and generally results from some evaluation against a set of agreed-upon criteria. Reputation is a significant factor in whether, how, and where knowledge will flow. Reputation is one of the most valuable forms of knowledge capital – it speaks to identity, trust, and comparative advantage. Examples of reputational knowledge might include an individual's curriculum vitae, a corporation's social responsibility rating, a community's social following, and friend's links, or publication citation rates and impact factors for an academic department.

Networks and network knowledge

Although initially conceptualized by Hubert Saint-Onge, more recent definitions have broadened the category to include relational capital which in effect encompasses the knowledge embedded in all the relationships an organization develops, whether it is from customers, from the competition, from suppliers, from trade associations, or from the government (Bontis, 2001). Relational capital has been interpreted differently by different researchers. The variation is attributable to the research focus. Where the research is relevant to commercial businesses or private sector organizations, networks will, by definition, include the knowledge of customers, suppliers, producers, shareholders – within and beyond the company's formal boundaries. Where the research focuses on the community, the network will include any individual or group functioning within the community's geographical boundaries. The research focus is a subject discipline; the network will consist of any member of the invisible college, human, and non-human sources of knowledge.

Examples of networks and relationships might include an individual staff's contacts lists and virtual Rolodex, a business unit's network of social contacts, a network analysis of who people go to for advice and answers, or past employment professional networks.

Networks and network relationships can be found in any network where humans or knowledge-rich agents engage in knowledge transactions (Figure 2.12). Networks might include neighborhoods, community groups, informal clubs, online social networks, professional communities, invisible colleges, business groups, business units, and so on. Because relational capital focuses on connections, flows, and the knowledge itself, we assume that all forms of knowledge are of interest.

Network and network relationships include four essential components – the sources and targets of a transaction (e.g., network nodes), the relationships and connections between sources and destinations (e.g., network links), and the knowledge content or messages that flow across those links, and the knowledge transactions that occur across those links. Network sources and targets can include human and non-human actors or agents. The nature of the relationships between nodes will vary depending on whether the source and destination are human or non-human. How humans interact with other humans is different from how they

FIGURE 2.12 Graphic Representation of Relational Capital

interact with non-human actors, i.e., robotics, machines, intelligent agents. We are just beginning to understand the relationships and transactions between machines and non-human actors. How do machines talk to and share knowledge? Do they share knowledge, or do they share only data or explicitly captured information? Is knowledge exchanged only between human actors? If this is true today, will this be true in the future?

What happens to the knowledge that is transacted is a network? We know that knowledge is extensible, mutable, and dynamic. We know that this transaction will change, as will the human capital of the source and the target involved in the transaction. What factors affect whether a transaction takes place, and what kind of a relationship must be established for a social knowledge transaction to occur? For a political knowledge transaction? Or a business knowledge transaction? These questions relate to an individual or a group's human capital, structural capital, and reputational capital. As in other categories, relational capital is highly dependent on other forms of human and structural capital.

Networks and network relationships are not an asset that most organizations formally acknowledge. Instead, they are treated as a personal preference or activity. Developing network capital involves creating contacts from professional events and conferences, identifying people through reading, reaching out to communities, participating in professional associations, engaging in virtual or physical communities of practice, and developing social relationships. In some cases, networks exist, and we simply need to join them. In other cases, we may grow our networks – our virtual Rolodex. Typically it takes years for a network to develop, or it may take years to connect to the right people when the network exists but is invisible. Organizations can conduct network analyses to discover hidden networks and to ensure that new individuals are quickly connected and to make missing connections. Organizations can also encourage individuals to share their networks, to acknowledge their participation, and allocate time for participation. Lack of organizational support or approval translates to the organizations not having the rights to leverage those networks. They are then personal knowledge capital.

Reputational knowledge

Reputational capital includes the beliefs or opinions held about someone or an entity such as a group or an organization. Reputations are owned by and associated with an entity, but others define them. A company's reputation is determined by its customers, suppliers, and producers. A club's reputation is determined by its members and those who interact with the members. Their actions influence an individual's reputation, but it is created and defined by peers and associates. Reputation may include the individual or the organization's level of trust, their integrity and honor, their honesty, their stature in a field or area of practice or a community, their numerical evaluations and ratings, their capacity for innovation and flexibility, their social responsibility, their level of transparency, and their capacity for leadership.

What does this mean for designing a knowledge architecture? It means that we need to identify the facets of reputational knowledge and how these are manifested in any business context. We begin by understanding the facets and structures of explicit knowledge (Figure 2.13), including:

- flexibility;
- honesty;
- honor;
- innovation;
- integrity;
- leadership;
- ratings;
- social responsibility;
- stature;
- transparency;
- trust.

What are the architectural design factors related to reputational knowledge? We know that to develop reputational capital, we need to consider two aspects – the production of the reputation, and how it is represented and communicated. In the traditional environment, a reputation is based on a CV or a resume. In this case, an individual needs to know how to create and present a CV or resume effectively – to have good writing, publishing, and coaching skills. Individuals need the social skills

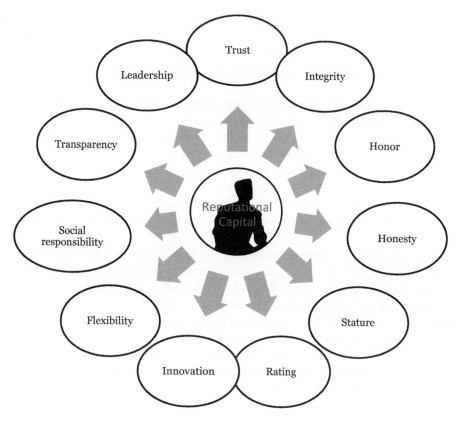

FIGURE 2.13 Graphic Representation of Reputational Capital

to cultivate relationships in order to crate perceptions, recommendations, references, and reviews that form the foundation of reputation. There are many ways to grow a reputation. Every other form of knowledge capital is an element of an individual's reputation – their tacit knowledge, skills and competencies, attitudes and behaviors, and publications and reports. The challenge individuals encounter is that organizations typically leave the development of this asset to the individual. Individuals learn it through trial and error. A simple remedy to this gap is to expect every individual to create and maintain a personal profile, which is the equivalent of an extended CV or resume. Ironically, many organizations make personal profiling applications available through institutional directories and contact systems. The connection between reputation and profile, though, is not always clear.

Designing architectures to support knowledge

How do we design an architecture to support this broad and diverse landscape of knowledge assets? First, we look at the future state and determine the functional architectures we will need to have in place. Second, we assess the current state – what we have to work with today. Finally, we develop a roadmap from where we are today to where we need to go. Organizations should begin by focusing on the highest level of commonality across assets. Essentially, looking at the highest level, we see five high-level categories of knowledge assets, including:

1   human capital – the knowledge of individuals, including tacit knowledge, skills and competencies, and attitudes and behaviors;
2   explicit knowledge – tangible forms of knowledge, including everything from text to oral-audio, visual, art and artifacts, and any combinations of these;
3   procedural knowledge – the collective knowledge of groups, units, and communities that has business value;
4   culture knowledge – the living knowledge of groups – and its levels and elements;
5   relational knowledge – the paths and flows of knowledge through networks.

These five high-level categories remind us that knowledge is inherent to, embedded in, and grown by people. The common element to all of these categories is the essential nature of people. Consider the focal point of all of the graphic models we presented earlier in this chapter – people. The five high-level categories are more practical to work with than abstract research concepts to design a knowledge architecture. These categories provide a practical and easy way to understand focus for sketching out the landscape. Working within these five categories, organizations can identify more targeted types of knowledge assets, specifically those called out by knowledge capital researchers.

Envisioning the knowledge landscape of the future

The knowledge landscape of the future means that we need to design for:

*   knowledge mobility;
*   knowledge mutability and transformation;
*   chunked, recombinant, translated and interpreted knowledge;
*   many different strategies for managing knowledge rather than a single established process;
*   informal and less structured forms of assets – different formats and packages;
*   the core elements of knowledge kernels of objects;
*   the first stages of knowledge creation rather than the last stages;
*   managing the relationships among knowledge assets as well as other assets;
*   teaching non-professionals and less experienced practitioners to recognize and manage their knowledge assets;
*   multiple segments and working in teams that represent numerous skill sets and competencies.

Once we have a sense of the current and future knowledge landscape, we can focus on designing to function and domains.

Chapter review

After reading this chapter, you should be able to:

* explain the working definition of knowledge in the intellectual capital research domain;
* explain what is included in the definition of human capital;
* explain what is included in the definition of structural capital;
* explain what is included in the definition of relational capital;
* describe where these types are found and how they are managed across the organization.

References and recommended future readings

Amidon, D. M. (2005). Knowledge zones fueling innovation worldwide. *Research Technology Management, 48*(1), 6–8.

Andriessen, D. (2004). *Making sense of intellectual capital: Designing a method for the valuation of intangibles*. Routledge.

Banks, A. P., & Millward, L. J. (2007). Differentiating knowledge in teams: The effect of shared declarative and procedural knowledge on team performance. *Group Dynamics: Theory, Research, and Practice, 11*(2), 95.

Bontis, N. (1996, January 24–26). *Intellectual Capital: An Exploratory Study That Develops Measures and Models*. Paper prepared for the Seventeenth McMaster Business Conference Richard Ivey School of Business, University of Western Ontario, London, Ontario, Canada.

Bontis, N. (2001). Managing organizational knowledge by diagnosing intellectual capital: Framing and advancing the state of the field. In *Knowledge management and business model innovation* (pp. 267–297). IGI Global.

Bontis, N., Bart, C. K., & Kong, E. (2007). The strategic importance of intellectual capital in the non-profit sector. *Journal of Intellectual Capital*, 8(4), 721-731.

Bontis, N., & Fitz-enz, J. (2002). Intellectual capital ROI: A causal map of human capital antecedents and consequents. *Journal of Knowledge Management, 14*(1), 3–23.

Capello, R. (2002). Spatial and sectoral characteristics of relational capital in innovation activity. *European Planning Studies, 10*(2), 177–200.

Capello, R., & Faggian, A. (2005). Collective learning and relational capital in local innovation processes. *Regional Studies, 39*(1), 75–87.

Carmeli, A., & Azeroual, B. (2009). How relational capital and knowledge combination capability enhance the performance of work units in a high technology industry. *Strategic Entrepreneurship Journal, 3*(1), 85–103.

Carr, D. L., Markusen, J. R., & Maskus, K. E. (2001). Estimating the knowledge-capital model of the multinational enterprise. *American Economic Review, 91*(3), 693–708.

Chatzkel, J. L. (2003). *Knowledge capital: How knowledge-based enterprises really get built*. Oxford University Press.

Choo, C. W., & Bontis, N. (Eds.). (2002). *The strategic management of intellectual capital and organizational knowledge*. Oxford University Press on Demand.

Collins, J. D., & Hitt, M. A. (2006). Leveraging tacit knowledge in alliances: The importance of using relational capabilities to build and leverage relational capital. *Journal of Engineering and Technology Management, 23*(3), 147–167.

Curado, C., & Bontis, N. (2007). Managing intellectual capital: The MIC matrix. *International Journal of Knowledge and Learning, 3*(2/3), 316–328.

De Pablos, P. O. (2004). Measuring and reporting structural capital. *Journal of Intellectual Capital, 5*(4), 629–647.

Dewhurst, F. W., & Navarro, J. G. C. (2004). External communities of practice and relational capital. *The Learning Organization, 11*(4/5), 322–331.

Diniz, L. M. (2015). Impact of investments in human capital on corporate market value. In *European Conference on Intellectual Capital* (p. 369). Academic Conferences International Limited.

Fayol, M. (1994). From declarative and procedural knowledge to the management of declarative and procedural knowledge. *European Journal of Psychology of Education, 9*(3), 179–190.

Fitzsimons, P. (1999). Human capital theory and education. *Encyclopedia of Philosophy of Education, 1*–5.

Garicano, L., & Rayo, L. (2017). Relational knowledge transfers. *American Economic Review, 107*(9), 2695–2730.

Glisky, E. L. (1992). Acquisition and transfer of declarative and procedural knowledge by memory-impaired patients: A computer data-entry task. *Neuropsychologia, 30*(10), 899–910.

Kianto, A., Inkinen, H., Ritala, P., & Vanhala, M. (2017). A temporal perspective to intellectual capital dynamics: How has IC changed in Finnish firms from 2013 to 2017? In *Proceedings of the 14th international conference on intellectual capital* (pp. 134–138). Knowledge Management & Organizational Learning.

Leal, C., Bessa, R., Loureiro, M., Nunes, R., & Marques, C. (2019). Intellectual Capital in healthcare, a social exchange approach. In *European Conference on Intangibles and Intellectual Capital* (pp. 163-XII). Academic Conferences International Limited.

Leal, C., Marques, C., & Marques, C. (2016). Mediating effects of intellectual capital and corporate strategy on firms' sustainable value creation. In *European conference on knowledge management* (p. 520). Academic Conferences International Limited.

Liu, C. L. E., Ghauri, P. N., & Sinkovics, R. R. (2010). Understanding the impact of relational capital and organizational learning on alliance outcomes. *Journal of World Business, 45*(3), 237–249.

Lynn, G. S., & Akgun, A. E. (2000). A new product development learning model: Antecedents and consequences of declarative and procedural knowledge. *International Journal of Technology Management, 20*(5–8), 490–510.

Malhotra, Y. (2002). Knowledge assets in the global economy: Assessment of national intellectual capital. In *Intelligent support systems: Knowledge management* (pp. 22–42). IGI Global.

Martínez-Torres, M. R. (2006). A procedure to design a structural and measurement model of intellectual capital: An exploratory study. *Information & Management, 43*(5), 617–626.

Matsuo, M., & Kusumi, T. (2002). Salesperson's procedural knowledge, experience and performance. *European Journal of Marketing, 36*(7/8), 840–854.

Morrison, C. J., & Siegel, D. (1998). Knowledge capital and cost structure in the US food and fiber industries. *American Journal of Agricultural Economics, 80*(1), 30–45.

Nafukho, F. M., Hairston, N., & Brooks, K. (2004). Human capital theory: Implications for human resource development. *Human Resource Development International, 7*(4), 545–551.

Nahapiet, J., & Ghoshal, S. (1998). Social capital, intellectual capital, and the organizational advantage. *Academy of Management Review, 23*(2), 242–266.

Navarro, J. G. C. (Ed.). (2015). *ECIC2015–7th European conference on intellectual capital: ECIC 2015.* Academic Conferences and Publishing Limited.

Nerdrum, L., & Erikson, T. (2001). Intellectual capital: A human capital perspective. *Journal of Intellectual Capital, 2*(2), 127–135.

Ng, A., & Chatzkel, J. (2015). Knowledge management for CSR and sustainability performance: Renewing the business model through systematic innovation for value creation.

In *International conference on intellectual capital and knowledge management and organisational learning* (p. 176). Academic Conferences International Limited.

Olaniyan, D. A., & Okemakinde, T. (2008). Human capital theory: Implications for educational development. *Pakistan Journal of Social Sciences, 5*(5), 479–483.

Serenko, A., Bontis, N., Booker, L., Sadeddin, K., & Hardie, T. (2010). A scientometric analysis of knowledge management and intellectual capital academic literature (1994–2008). *Journal of Knowledge Management, 14*(1), 3–23.

Strassmann, P. A. (1999). *Measuring and managing knowledge capital.* The Executive Report on Knowledge, Technology & Performance, Knowledge Inc. http://www.providersedge.com/docs/km_articles/Measuring_and_Managing_Knowledge_Capital.pdf

Surif, J., Ibrahim, N. H., & Mokhtar, M. (2012). Conceptual and procedural knowledge in problem solving. *Procedia-Social and Behavioral Sciences, 56*, 416–425.

Sweetland, S. R. (1996). Human capital theory: Foundations of a field of inquiry. *Review of Educational Research, 66*(3), 341–359.

Tymon, W. G., & Stumpf, S. A. (2003). Social capital in the success of knowledge workers. *Career Development International, 8*(1), 12–20.

Wiig, K. M. (1997). Integrating intellectual capital and knowledge management. *Long-Range Planning, 30*(3), 399–405.

Yitmen, I. (2011). Intellectual capital: A competitive asset for driving innovation in engineering design firms. *Engineering Management Journal, 23*(2), 3–19.

Yli-Renko, H., Autio, E., & Sapienza, H. J. (2001). Social capital, knowledge acquisition, and knowledge exploitation in young technology-based firms. *Strategic Management Journal, 22*(6–7), 587–613.

3

KNOWLEDGE ARCHITECTURE AND DESIGN

Chapter summary

This chapter introduces the concept of architecture and explains the importance of design to good architecture practice. We describe the difference between design and construction. The chapter considers architecture practices, including enterprise, business, and information architecture. The chapter makes a case for a more inclusive and comprehensive knowledge architecture practice. Here we lay out the elements and methods of good architecture design, including future state visions, design principles, reference models, architecture segments, blueprints, and governance models. The chapter interprets these common architecture elements for knowledge architecture.

Why we care about architecture

We care about architecture because most of the solutions we have to work with today are engineered and constructed applications. Given the range of properties and behaviors of knowledge discussed in Chapter 1 and the typologies we described in Chapter 2, we need to design a new solution. Architecture is the most compelling design method. Our knowledge architecture needs to support a much broader set of capabilities. We can learn much from our current information management solutions, but they do not speak to the essential and guiding principles of knowledge architecture.

This chapter focuses on what we mean by architecture and its relationship to design. In this chapter, we clearly distinguish between design that supports form and function and the translation of that design into physical systems and applications. The former is called architecture; the latter is called development or construction. For too many decades, we have focused on a small scale or isolated solutions that were constructed from collected requirements. Today's knowledge architecture landscape is a hodge-podge of solutions that do not work together.

They are built from haphazard requirements, present redundancies, duplication across the organization, or large-scale solutions that become functions in their own right. Given the rapid rate of change in channels and the increasing scale and scope of knowledge assets, it is essential to step back and refocus our attention on the design. Technologies will change, applications will come and go, but design basics and conceptual models will persist.

Architecture – definitions and characterizations

What is architecture? Architecture can describe buildings and other physical structures (Gutheim, 1941; Harris, 1975; Holl, 2012; Lewis, 1985; Wright, 1953). It can represent the and science of designing buildings and nonbuilding structures. It can also refer to the style of design and method of construction. Architecture is both an art and a science, a process and a result, an idea and a reality. People often use the words 'architecture' and 'design' interchangeably. If you can 'design' your own career goals, aren't you the architect of your own life?

What is design? Design is a plan or specification for the construction of an object or system (Brooks, 2010; Corbusier, 2007; Craven, 2008; Dorst & Nigel, 2001). Design is the implementation of an activity or process, leading to a prototype of a product. What purpose does it serve? When considering the design of something, you must think about how everything fits together in harmony.

While we ground architecture design in structural and traditional product architectures and draw from many of the other kinds of architectures in use today, there is another consideration which is essential to knowledge architecture. In the end, our organizations must adopt and leverage the knowledge architecture we develop. How does this happen? What is the context in which our knowledge architecture would be adopted? There are two critical points of integration and adoption. The first point of integration is the organization's enterprise architecture practice. Regardless of who is involved in developing the components of knowledge architecture, adoption, and implementation are dependent upon the enterprise architecture team. We must have a good understanding of that enterprise architecture framework and must be able to propose reasonable and practical ways to adopt knowledge architecture. The second point of integration is the organization's relevant business segments, i.e., all of those business units that have responsibility for the business capabilities and operations that produce or consume the knowledge assets we discussed in Chapters 1 and 2.

How does enterprise architecture relate to knowledge architecture? Enterprise architecture (EA) is a well-defined practice for conducting enterprise analysis, design, planning, and implementation, using a holistic approach at all times, for the successful development and execution of strategy (Bouwman et al., 2011; Chief Information Officer Council, 2001; Clemente, 2016; Harrison, 2018; Len, 2012; McDermott et al., 1996; Pereira & Sousa, 2004; Richards, 2020; Ross et al., 2006; Spewak & Hill, 1992; Urbaczewski & Mrdalj, 2006; Whittle & Myrick, 2004). Enterprise architecture applies architecture principles and practices to guide organizations through the business, information, process, and technology changes necessary to execute their strategy. These practices utilize the various aspects of an enterprise to identify, motivate, and achieve these changes. Enterprise architects are responsible for performing the analysis of business structure and processes. They are often called upon to conclude from the information collected to address the goals of enterprise architecture: effectiveness, efficiency, agility, and durability. Why is this important? What can we leverage from this architecture?

Integrating knowledge architecture into the enterprise architecture framework

What is the enterprise architecture framework? How might our work on a knowledge architecture fit into this framework? The traditional enterprise architecture 'stack' or model (Figure 3.1) identifies between four and six layers of architecture.

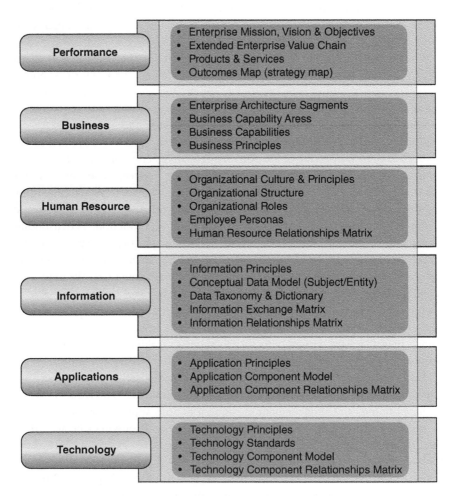

FIGURE 3.1 Traditional Enterprise Architecture Reference Model

In all of the models, the top layer focuses on performance or strategy. This layer represents the organization's business goals, strategies, and performance expectations. This layer may have different labels, but the focus is consistent. In some models, particularly the earliest models, this layer also combines the business architecture layer. In the past ten years, though, the business architecture layer has been called out because it supports the need to describe the full set of business operations and capabilities. In a few models, you may find a people or human resources architecture called out. This is a recent addition and is still exceptional in most architecture models. The business architecture layer is essential because it represents real-world aspects of a business, along with how they interact. It focuses on defining and positioning all of the other layers to support what business does, how it does it, how it is organized, and how it realizes value. It is the most critical layer for any organization – it ensures that the architecture is aligned with and not impeding the organization's work. Architectures that do not begin with a focus on this layer will always – by definition – be suboptimal, rigid, and constructed rather than designed.

The next layer, which is consistent and has been included since the earliest days of enterprise architecture practice, is the data–information architecture layer. In the earliest models, it was referred to generically as the data architecture layer (Martin et al., 2010; Otto, 2012; Otto & Schmidt, 2010; Toms, 2002; van den Hoven, 2004). More recently, though, it has been expanded to include information architecture. It is rarely the case that you will find these two views split into two layers. Another standard layer is the application layer, which focuses on all of those applications that are used anywhere in the organization to support business operations. Finally, the technology layer always has been the foundation of the enterprise architecture stack. This layer focuses on hardware, communications, and networking technologies, excluding those functional applications that are used directly in business operations.

Where would we place knowledge architecture in this framework? Do we call out a new layer? Do we integrate it into existing layers? Do we redefine or combine existing layers? The placement or designation of knowledge architecture is less critical than ensuring that all of the architecture segments and functional elements are completely and inclusively covered in the framework. If we were to make the argument for a new layer, it would most likely be inserted between human resources/people and information, combined with the human resource/people and information layer and renamed knowledge. Or, we could simply rename the human resource/people layer as knowledge given the hefty focus on people as a knowledge asset.

Any of these options works well because it places the knowledge layer close to the business layer but positions it more prominently than the application layer. What is perhaps more important, though, is to ensure that all of the functional architecture segments required to support knowledge asset management are clearly and distinctly called out across the architecture layers. To ensure this, we need to walk layer by layer to consider the best alignment and position.

How does *business architecture* relate to knowledge architecture? Business architecture is a blueprint of the enterprise that provides a common understanding of the organization and is used to align strategic objectives and tactical demands (Clemente, 2016; Elliott et al., 2015; Ghahramany et al., 2015; Hadaya & Gagnon, 2017; Poulin, 2013; Ulrich & McWhorter, 2010; Versteeg & Bouwman, 2006; Whelan & Meaden, 2012). Business architecture is the bridge between the enterprise business model and enterprise strategy on one side, and the business functionality of the enterprise on the other. Typically, a business architecture models the organizational business capabilities and functionalities. Why is this important? What can we leverage from this architecture?

How does *information architecture* relate to knowledge architecture? There are many different forms of information architecture. Essentially, information architectures are the underlying designs of system applications that support all of our areas of practice. Information architectures can broadly include data architecture, usability and user interface architectures, digital asset management architectures, publishing architectures, document and information architecture models, web content management architectures, search architectures, and information security architectures. Each of these architectures has value for knowledge architectures, but no one of them satisfies the design principles or aligns with all the types of knowledge. Perhaps our most effective approach is to look at the capabilities these architectures offer and consider how we can adapt them to support knowledge architecture.

How does knowledge architecture relate to applications and technology architecture? These layers are often referred to by other terms in the trade literature, peer-reviewed, and trade publications. For example:

- computer architectures map to the technology layer;
- network architectures map to the technology layer;
- system architectures may map to both the applications layer and the technology layer;
- software architectures map to the applications layer.

Software architecture refers to the fundamental structures of a software system, the discipline of creating such structures, and the documentation of these structures. These structures are needed to reason about the software system. The *architecture* of a software system is a metaphor, analogous to the architecture of a building. Software architecture is about making fundamental structural choices that are costly to change once implemented. Software architecture choices, also called architectural decisions, include specific structural options from possibilities in the design of the software. For example, the systems that controlled the space shuttle launch vehicle had the requirement of being very fast and very reliable. Therefore, an appropriate real-time computing language would need to be chosen. Additionally, to satisfy the need for reliability, the choice could be made to have multiple redundant and independently produced copies of the program, and to run these copies on independent hardware while cross-checking results.

Computer architecture is a set of rules and methods that describe the functionality, organization, and implementation of computer systems. Some definitions of architecture define it as describing the capabilities and programming model of a computer but not a particular implementation. Why is this important? What can we leverage from this architecture?

Network architecture is the design of a communication network. It is a framework for the specification of a network's physical components and their functional organization and configuration, operational principles and procedures, and data formats. In telecommunication, the specification of a network architecture may include a detailed description of products and services delivered via a communications network. Why is this important? What can we leverage from this architecture?

The system architecture is a conceptual model that defines the structure, behavior, and more views of a system. An architecture description is a formal description and representation of a system, organized in a way that supports reasoning about the structures and behaviors of the system. A system architecture can comprise system components that will work together to implement the overall system. Why is this important? What can we leverage from this architecture?

In addition to the architecture layers listed in the framework, and those other references from the literature, we should consider three additional architectures, including:

- cognitive or mental architectures;
- interior or spatial architectures;
- urban or neighborhood architectures.

These three architectures are relevant because they tell us about the mental processes supporting the development of human capital (e.g., tacit knowledge, skills, and competencies, attitudes, and behaviors), as well as the environments that influence our cultures and networks (e.g., collective knowledge, relational knowledge).

Cognitive architecture can refer to a theory about the structure of the human mind. The formalized models can be used to refine a comprehensive theory of cognition further. Why is this important? What can we leverage from this architecture?

Interior architecture is the design of a space that has been created by structural boundaries and the human interaction within these boundaries. It can also be the initial design and plan for use. Later, it can be redesign to accommodate a changed purpose or a significantly revised design for adaptive reuse of the building shell. The latter is often part of sustainable architecture practices, conserving resources through 'recycling' a structure by adaptive redesign. Generally referred to as the spatial art of environmental design, form, and practice, interior architecture is the process through which the interiors of buildings are designed, concerned with all aspects of the human uses of structural spaces. Put simply, interior architecture is the design of an interior in architectural terms.

Urban design is the process of designing and shaping cities, towns, and villages, in contrast to architecture, which focuses on the design of all the urban landscape components. It is an interdisciplinary field that utilizes elements of many built environment professions, including landscape architecture, urban planning, architecture, civil engineering, and municipal engineering. Why is this important? What can we leverage from this architecture?

Integrating and adapting knowledge architecture across business segments

The other challenge we face in moving knowledge architecture forward is to ensure that all of the different areas of practice, and existing architectures, are aligned with and are supported by knowledge architecture. How do we approach this? Does the enterprise architecture framework help us to achieve that? The answer is 'Yes!' As Figure 3.1 suggests, with knowledge architecture as a new layer in the framework, we are well-positioned to align all of those variant areas of practice – all those stakeholders. They have a role to play in creating or using those different kinds of knowledge.

The designed versus the built environment

In the industrial economy, tangible information and tangible data were treated as commodities – as additional inputs to decision and business processes. In that environment and starting from that perspective, we 'constructed and built' solutions that enabled us to manage information and data in the business context directly. The design resembled engineering, and engineering was to requirements and specifications. Design – from an architecture perspective, and with a view to knowledge – was not common practice. The legacy of this era is a landscape and landfill of systems, applications, and solutions that serve an isolated purpose or process. Applications are solutions configured to support work in a specific context. Unfortunately, in too many cases, the work has been re-engineered to support the solution.

Beginning in the early 1990s, a few insightful individuals understood that as the value of information and data grew, information and data would need to be accessible through and processable by many different applications. In the past, each functional or administrative area of an organization had its applications and technologies. For 50 years, the solution developed focused on the 'process.' In this context, information and data were embedded in the applications. It took several decades for developers to realize that it was essential to separate applications from source information. This breakthrough came from the pioneering work of information engineers in the 1980s and 1990s. It took another ten years for developers to realize that computer architectures were distributed and that functions could be more reliably supported in a federated environment. The increased capacity in computing and the explosion of applications forced us to consider that development without a view to enterprise integration was unwise, unsustainable, and unaffordable. The science of enterprise architecture developed from these early insights. It took another 20 years for us to understand that we must go deeper than data and information – to access the underlying knowledge – and to design for availability, access, and consumption. And, that we need to think of context beyond the enterprise.

When we study all of these parts and processes independently – in different contexts, and in various professions – we create isolated architectures. While this makes sense from an industrial economy perspective and supports research and scientific inquiry, it creates an artificial environment that does not meet business needs. This has significant consequences for how we represent, access, and consume knowledge. It is critical to developing a holistic architecture designed to support the whole knowledge landscape.

Knowledge architecture tools and products

The design process relies upon and is supported by several tools and including (1) vision of the future state; (2) architecture design principles; (3) knowledge architecture reference models; (4) architecture segments; (5) blueprints; and (6) governance models and methods (Figure 3.2). In this section, we explain each of these tools and methods.

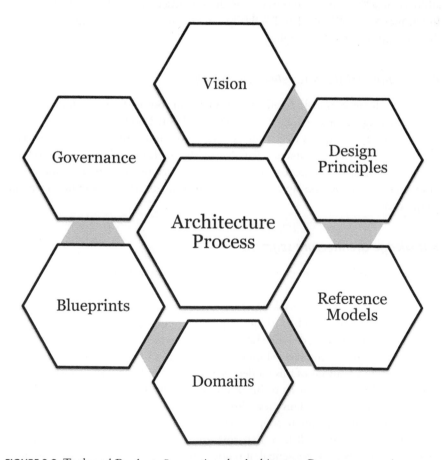

FIGURE 3.2 Tools and Products Supporting the Architecture Process

Knowledge architecture visions

The purpose of this phase in establishing an architecture practice is to define or review the vision, stakeholders, and principles of the architecture practice. The focus in this phase would be on the architecture practice as a whole and not on a particular architecture project.

Knowledge architecture design principles

A good set of principles will be founded in the beliefs and values of the organization and expressed in language that the business understands and uses. Principles should be few in number, future-oriented, and endorsed and championed by senior management. They provide a firm foundation for making architecture and planning decisions, framing policies, procedures, and standards, and supporting the resolution of contradictory situations. A poor set of principles will quickly become disused, and the resultant architectures, policies, and standards will appear arbitrary or self-serving, and thus lack credibility. Essentially, beliefs drive behavior. In Chapter 1, we identified 16 knowledge architecture design principles that meet the standards of sound principles.

Knowledge architecture reference models

What is a reference model? A reference model is an abstract framework or description consisting of an interlinked set of clearly defined concepts produced by an expert or body of experts to encourage clear communication. A single view lays out the organization's architecture framework, the methods and processes it follows to maintain the architecture, the blueprints and descriptions of architectural specifications for segments and layers, and the supporting governance and management components.

Knowledge architecture segments

The most essential element of a reference model is a description of the architecture segments.

There are two ways of looking at an architecture domain (Figure 3.3). Both are essential to understand. Both are required to build out a practical enterprise architecture reference model. The first view of an architecture domain is that of the architecture layers themselves – business, data/information, applications, technology. There are variations of this model – some include a layer for people or human resources. This view helps us to break out and work through all of the different elements of architecture. This view also ensures that we will construct that model and design the architecture to support our unique business environment and goals. No two organizations will have the same enterprise architecture for that simple reason. While this view is essential, it is not sufficient. The second view helps us to

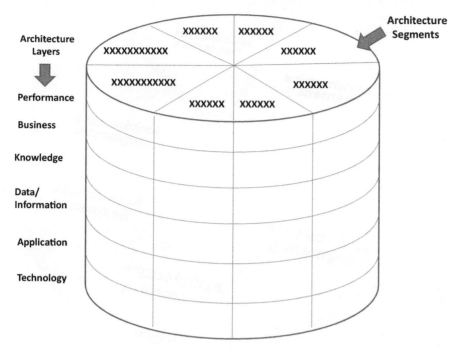

FIGURE 3.3 Enterprise Architecture Layers and Segments

see what some models refer to as 'architectural segments' or 'business capabilities.' Whereas the first view helps us to understand how to design all the layers to work together, the second view allows us to take a vertical slice of the cake and more closely examine how those layers are designed to support a specific and unique set of business capabilities. The reason why no two organizations have the same enterprise architecture is that the 'slices' of the cake are different.

The process of defining enterprise architecture is an iterative one. We begin by identifying the layers at a very general level. Then we step back and look at the business capabilities – all the slices we need to create to make up the whole, layer by layer (Figure 3.4). We build out the architecture for each slice and consider how the slices fit back together. When we put the slices back into the cake and look across all the layers, we see what elements of each layer are (1) core to all of the organization's work; (2) are common to some areas of work; and (3) are unique to one area. In this way, we support all of the organization's work, but we do so in a way that is adaptable, agile, and flexible.

We already know from practical experience in enterprise and knowledge architecture that knowledge assets – specifically the five categories we defined in Chapter 2 – are universal to all 'slices' of the layer cake. The challenge today is that they are scattered across different layers of the cake and receive different levels of focus and treatment. The goal of knowledge architecture is to make that design

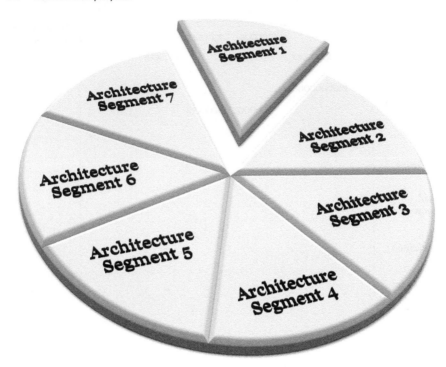

FIGURE 3.4 Conceptual Model of Architecture Segments

process both more consistent and even, and to strengthen its presence in the architecture framework.

We define three segments, including (1) knowledge availability, (2) knowledge accessibility, and (3) knowledge consumption (Flannagan et al., 2018), displayed in Figure 3.5. Where our knowledge architecture supports these three segments, we have a strong foundation for designing an effective working environment. Knowledge availability focuses on those aspects of design that ensure the persistence or long-term representation and availability of the knowledge. Knowledge accessibility focuses on those aspects of design that support accessibility of and to the knowledge asset. Finally, knowledge consumability focuses on those aspects of design aimed to enable actors and agents to use, work with, repurpose – and consume in any other way. These segments and the functions they support are described in greater detail in Chapter 5.

No knowledge architecture is designed from or in a vacuum. Availability, accessibility, and consumability exist to some extent, for some kinds of knowledge in every organization. There are existing methods and work practices to create, leverage, and safeguard different types of knowledge. The challenge is that most of these are disjointed. The challenge is that most of these focus on one particular kind of knowledge – explicit information. We can build upon what exists, but we must carefully examine and expand each of these segments. How do we approach this task?

FIGURE 3.5 Knowledge Architecture Segments

Knowledge architecture blueprints

One of the outputs of a knowledge architecture process is a blueprint. A blueprint is a diagram, schema, or visualization that gives an architect or engineer an overview of all essential concepts, the logical elements, physical components, attributes, and interrelationships throughout the organization. Blueprints also reference standards and regulations. Each set of knowledge architecture blueprints will describe the technology foundation, the applications leveraged, the knowledge models, all the functionality that support capture, organization, discovery, and use, and how the components integrate with other systems and applications.

Knowledge architecture governance models and methods

Architecture is dynamic – it adapts, extends, and expands to support form and function. Given the properties and behaviors of knowledge, it is clear that architecture is a continuous and universal business process. Knowledge architecture governance is not limited to a small group of design specialists, technologists, or managers. Knowledge architecture governance should involve business managers and any staff who have or leverage knowledge.

To ensure a knowledge architecture supports form and function in the future, there must be an active and representative governance model. Conventional governance models consist of four components (Figure 3.6), including (1) incoming proposals to adapt, adjust, or change the knowledge architecture; (2) governance

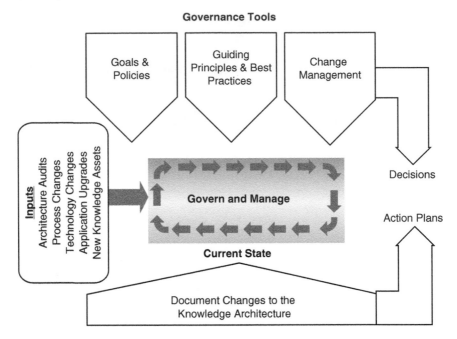

FIGURE 3.6 Architecture Governance Model

tools and processes, including strategic plans, guiding principles, standards, and rules, and change management processes; (3) architecture board reviews and decisions; and (4) action plans and updated architecture blueprints.

Knowledge architecture process

The knowledge architecture design process follows an established set of six steps, including:

    Step 1. Identify stakeholders and establish a vision

    Step 2. Define strategic and business architecture capabilities

    Step 3. Define knowledge architecture segments

    Step 4. Design future state knowledge architecture vision

    Step 5. Define current state knowledge architecture

    Step 6. Design roadmap to achieve the future state knowledge architecture vision

Step 1. Identify stakeholders and concerns, business requirements, and architecture vision

This step provides the first effort to scope the architecture. It provides the early, very high-level definitions of the baseline and target environments, from a business and knowledge perspective. We look first to stakeholders to help us understand business requirements, a future vision, current challenges, and opportunities. We launch this step by asking some key questions. What are your business goals? Who are your stakeholders and clients? What are your current challenges? What do you see as opportunities?

Step 2. Define the strategic and business architecture capabilities

Standard enterprise architecture processes focus on business capabilities to complete this step. You may already have identified these high-level capabilities. If you have not, though, this does not impede building out the knowledge architecture. Knowledge architecture segments cross all business capabilities. It may be easier to identify patterns for knowledge architecture segments if you can work within business capabilities, but it is not a requirement. What is critical is a good working knowledge of the kinds of knowledge assets, and what it means to make those assets available across the organization, to access those assets, and to consume those assets in the course of doing business. We are interested in 'knowledge-related' capabilities rather than business capabilities.

Step 3. Define knowledge architecture segments

This text proposes three high-level knowledge architecture segments that any organization can use as a framework to define their segments. The segments are determined first by their top-level scope and coverage, and second by the functional architectures needed to support that scope and coverage. In this case, we expect organizations to adapt or adjust the framework to serve as a foundation for their knowledge architecture blueprint.

Step 4. Determine desirable future state knowledge architecture

This is a crucial step in the process. It is always critical to focus on the future state, not the current state, of your architecture. Try to project out five to ten years in defining that future state. Lead the stakeholders in a visioning exercise that paints a picture of what availability, accessibility, and consumability looks like in five to ten years. Once you have that future vision, you can do what is referred to as backcasting to determine what needs to be in place to achieve that future vision. The future vision also helps you to manage the tendency to exclude options because they are not 'doable now.' Focusing on the current state, and trying to project forward, is always dominated by existing constraints and concerns. It is, by definition, problem-focused rather than opportunity-focused.

Step 5. Define current state knowledge segments

Once you have the future vision sketched out, the next step is to audit or take inventory of the current situation. At this stage, it is essential to look beyond the 'built environment.' The tendency will be to look at the applications and technology we have in place – but this gives us only a limited perspective of the current knowledge architecture. It is challenging to 'see' the full current knowledge architecture landscape. The most effective approach will be to use the framework outlined in this text as a guideline. First, look at each functional architecture in isolation to ensure you are comprehensively inventorying the current state. Look across the functional architectures within the segment to make sure that all critical connections are in place. At the end of this step, you should have put together a current state picture for the whole knowledge architecture.

Step 6. Develop a roadmap from where you are today and where you want to be in the future

This is the final step in the process. You begin with the future state vision, compare it to the current state, and develop a practical roadmap. The best approach is to build the roadmap in increments of two years, five years, and ten years. Keep in mind that the roadmap is a living resource. As the context changes, the roadmap should be updated as you make progress, as there are new developments, innovations, or lessons learned.

Chapter review

After reading this chapter, you should be able to:

- define knowledge architecture and explain how it relates to building architecture;
- define design and the role it plays in knowledge architecture;
- explain how knowledge architecture aligns with enterprise architecture practice;
- distinguish between designing architecture and building a solution;
- describe common knowledge architecture tools and products;
- describe the six steps in the knowledge architecture process.

Reference and recommendations for future readings

Bouwman, H., van Houtum, H., Janssen, M., & Versteeg, G. (2011). Business architectures in the public sector: Experiences from practice. *Communications of the Association for Information Systems, 29*(1), 23.

Brooks, F. P. (2010). *The design of design: Essays from a computer scientist.* Addison-Wesley Professional. ISBN: 0-201-36298-8.

Chief Information Officer Council. (2001, February). *A practical guide to federal enterprise architecture.* Version 1.0 (Extended by GAO-03-584G).

Clemente Minonne. (2016). *Business Analyse – Konzepte, Methoden und Instrumente zur Optimierung der Business-Architektur* (in German) (1. (deutsche) ed.). Schäffer-Poeschel. ISBN: 978-3-7910-3308-2.

Corbusier, L. (2007). *Toward an architecture.* Getty Publications.

Craven, J. (2008). *What is "adaptive reuse"?* http://architecture.about.com/od/preservation/g/reuse.htm.

Dorst, K., & Cross, N. (2001). Creativity in the design process: Co-evolution of problem – solution. *Design Studies, 22*(5), 425–437.

Elliott, E. S., Fons, F., & Randell, A. (2015). *Business architecture and agile methodologies.* Copyright © 2015 Business Architecture Guild.

Flannagan, C. A., Lyle, J., Carlson, J., & Bedford, D. A. (2018). A guide to ensure access to the results of federally funded transportation research. *NCHRP Research Report* (936).

Ghahramany Dehbokry, S., & Chew, E. (2015). *Toward a multi-disciplinary business architecture reference model for SMEs.* https://aisel.aisnet.org/ecis2015_cr/56.

Gutheim, F. (Ed.). (1941). *Frank Lloyd Wright on architecture: Selected writings (1894–1940).* Grosset's Universal Library.

Hadaya, P., & Gagnon, B. (2017). *Business architecture – the missing link in strategy formulation, implementation and execution.* ASATE Publishing.

Harris, C. M. (Ed.). (1975). *Dictionary of architecture and construction.* McGraw-Hill.

Harrison, R. (2018). *Togaf (r) 9 foundation study guide.* Van Haren.

Holl, S. (2012, May 18). *Five minute manifesto.* AIA Gold Medal Ceremony.

Len, B. (2012). *Software architecture in practice* (3rd ed.). Addison-Wesley Professional.

Lewis, R. K. (1985). Introduction. In M. Builders & D. Maddex (Eds.), *National Trust for Historic Preservation* (p. 8). Wiley Preservation Press.

Martin, A., Dmitriev, D., & Akeroyd, J. (2010). A resurgence of interest in information architecture. *International Journal of Information Management, 30*(1), 6–12.

McDermott, R., Mikulak, R. J., & Beauregard, M. (1996). *The basics of FMEA.* SteinerBooks.

McIntire, M. (2005, March 5). Enough about 'gates' as art: Let's talk about that price tag. *The New York Times.*

Otto, B. (2012). How to design the master data architecture: Findings from a case study at Bosch. *International Journal of Information Management, 32*(4), 337–346.

Otto, B., & Schmidt, A. (2010). *Enterprise master data architecture: Design decisions and options.* ICIQ.

Pereira, C. M., & Sousa, P. (2004). A method to define an enterprise architecture using the Zachman framework. In *Proceedings of the 2004 ACM symposium on applied computing* (pp. 1366–1371). ACM Press.

Poulin, M. (2013). *Architects know what managers don't: Business architecture for dynamic market.* BuTechCon.

Richards, M. (2020). *Fundamentals of software architecture: An engineering approach.* O'Reilly Media.

Ross, J., Weill, P., & Robertson, D. C. (2006). *Enterprise architecture as strategy: Creating a foundation for business execution.* Harvard Business Review Press.

Spewak, S., & Hill, S. C. (1992). *Enterprise architecture planning: Developing a blueprint for data, applications, and technology.* QED Publishing Group.

Toms, E. G. (2002). Information interaction: Providing a framework for information architecture. *Journal of the American Society for Information Science and Technology, 53*(10), 855–862.

Ulrich, W., & McWhorter, N. (2010). *Business architecture: The art and practice of business transformation.* Megan-Kiffer Press.

Urbaczewski, L., & Mrdalj, S. (2006). A comparison of enterprise architecture frameworks. *Issues in Information Systems, 7*(2), 18–23.

van den Hoven, J. (2004). Data architecture: Standards for the effective enterprise. *Information Systems Management, 21*(3), 61.

Versteeg, G., & Bouwman, H. (2006). Business architecture: A new paradigm to relate business strategy to ICT. *Information Systems Frontiers, 8*, 91–102.

Whelan, J., & Meaden, G. (2012). *Business architecture: A practical guide.* Ashgate. ISBN: 978-1-4094-3859-5.

Whittle, R., & Myrick, C. (2004). *Enterprise business architecture: The formal link between strategy and results.* CRC Press. ISBN: 978-0849327889.

Wright, F. L. (1953). *The future of architecture.* New American Library, Horizon Press.

4

KNOWLEDGE ARCHITECTURE REFERENCE MODEL

Chapter summary

Architectures are labor- and time-intensive to develop and are challenging to design in a densely built environment, particularly when grounded in well-established and heavily entrenched practices and activities. Creating a new knowledge architecture amid established business practices, development, and technology practices can be challenging. Architecture reference models are essential to harmonizing and synthesizing existing perspectives and developing a shared vision for the future. This chapter introduces a reference model intended to help the reader learn to see this new architecture and to guide others in the process of seeing that vision. The reference model builds on the MASK models developed by Dr. Jean-Louis Ermine.

Reference models

The core element of any knowledge architecture or architecture is a reference model.

A reference model is an abstract framework or domain description consisting of an interlinked set of clearly defined concepts produced by an expert or body of experts to encourage clear communication (Espinosa et al., 2011; Fischer et al., 2007; Greefhorst & Proper, 2011; Gregor et al., 2007; Iacob et al., 2014; Ross et al., 2006; Schekkerman, 2004; Sessions, 2007; Urbaczewski & Mrdalj, 2006; Winter & Fischer, 2006). In the case of architecture, a reference model, these concepts typically represent domains. A reference model is essential for design because it provides a framework that guides our work. Chapter 3 offered a reference model that needs to support a wide range of functions. These functions need to align with and support the three architecture segments we identified in Chapters 1 and 3. Our reference model identified 11 essential functions that are needed to support these domains. How do these functions align with the three knowledge domains? The challenge is that there is not a one-to-one alignment. Every functional component supports all three of the segments – directly or indirectly. With these caveats in mind, this chapter offers an alignment that reflects dependencies and relationships among functional architectures. On this basis, we can conceptually place these functions within the knowledge segment model.

Working knowledge architecture reference model

In Chapter 3 we explained that segments are essential components of every architecture reference model. Consider the design domain in physical building architectures – business environments, residential environments, recreational environments, infrastructure environments. Segments in enterprise architecture tend to focus on and be defined by collections of business capabilities – what an organization does to deliver value to its stakeholders. Segments in communication architecture are determined by the flows and the types of messages that flow between nodes. In these segments, nodes are not sources of knowledge but distribution and direction points. Segments in community and social networks are defined by a purpose, shared goals, and the community's environment.

In Chapter 3, we identified three essential segments of knowledge architecture, including knowledge availability, knowledge accessibility, and knowledge consumability. We also identified some critical components that support these segments (see Figure 3.5). We define a working knowledge architecture reference model by aligning these functions with the three domains, and by explaining the role each plays in supporting the segment. We represent knowledge segments based on those activities that support the full set of knowledge types and transactions. It is essential to avoid using an existing life cycle model that represents a current characterization of knowledge. We define the knowledge domain as groups of activities that support our design principles. In Chapter 3, we identified three segments (shown in Figure 4.1), including (1) knowledge availability, (2) knowledge accessibility, and (3) knowledge consumability.

Knowledge availability means there is an awareness of the knowledge – we can determine it exists. We know what knowledge assets exist, how they are structured and packaged, and their characteristics. Availability also speaks to the knowledge assets persistence – will it be retained or preserved in its context? Or, will it be disposed of and destroyed? It means that the source from which the asset is made available is future-proof and sustainable through changing technology environments. All of these availability considerations are essential for accessibility.

Knowledge accessibility means the knowledge asset is accessible to its intended consumers. Knowledge is accessible where they meet the following criteria:

- the creator or custodian of the asset assumes that others will seek or look for it;
- it is accessible in a context that supports access by others – whether through search, browse, promotion, automated discovery, or recommendation;
- applications needed to discover and find the asset are known and accessible;
- we have meta-information about the object, its creation, quality, and intended uses.

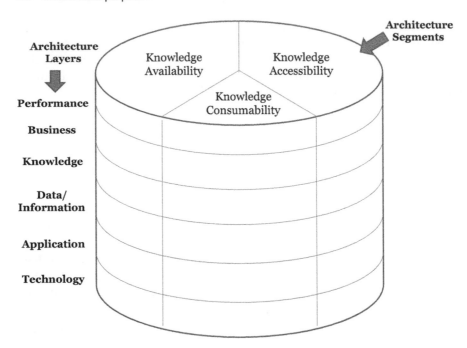

FIGURE 4.1 Core Knowledge Architecture Domains

Consumability speaks to the actual use of a knowledge asset, and what use can be made of that asset.

Because of the range of knowledge types, it helps to understand what the potential uses might be for each kind of asset. There is a spectrum of use – from being able to view the asset at one end, to being able to add to, revise, or change the asset, to being able to redesign, reformat, or restructure the asset. This spectrum resembles the conceptual models that network directory architects and security experts use. These architects focus on four critical elements, including authenticating and provenance tracking, asset management and security, asset privileging and permissions, and support for annotation, changes, revisions, and so on.

Each of the three segments consists of several functional architectures (Figure 4.2). The functional architecture is the essence of our knowledge architecture reference model. The challenge we face – and the opportunity this text presents – is understanding how the various current practices, solutions, and architectures align with these functional architectures. Additionally, there are many dependencies within and across each domain. No one of these functions stands alone – no single functional architecture is a solution in itself. They are part of the larger picture. When we design for future knowledge functional architectures, we must design to the whole picture. Those functional architectures in Figure 4.2 that have no shading are central to the knowledge architecture practice. Where a knowledge architecture practice does not yet exist, these would tend to align with the information

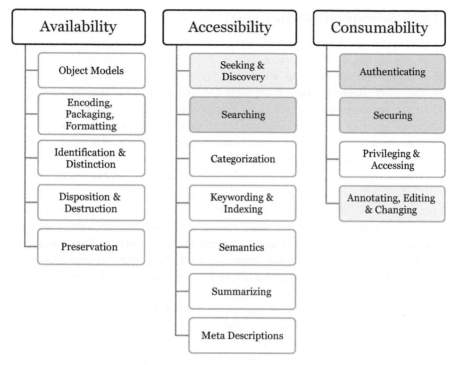

FIGURE 4.2 Working Knowledge Architecture Reference Model

architecture practice. Those functional architectures shaded in light gray would more closely align with the business architecture practice. Finally, those functional architectures shaded in dark gray have a stronger affinity with the application architecture practice.

Chapter 5 provides a high-level overview of the 17 functional architectures. We provide in-depth walk-throughs of these architectures in Chapters 6 through 22. Their functions and activities best define knowledge architecture segments. Knowledge is not an isolated business capability that we can identify and manage separately. Instead, it is a universal business process that touches every other business activity across the organization. As such, the activities that make up a knowledge segment are those we would expect every individual, unit, or team to support.

This knowledge architecture reference model serves as general guidance and a learning source for those involved in any level or aspect of knowledge architecture work. The framework is generic. Like any architecture design tool, it supports the architect as they work through all of the essential views and issues. It is not a rigid standard. It should be treated as a design book from which every organization or community derives ideas, translates those ideas to their context, and adapts and develops those ideas into formal working knowledge architectures. Remember, context is the critical architecture design principle!

The knowledge architecture design process

Operationalizing a knowledge architecture design process means having a future vision, taking stock of the current state, and developing a roadmap that gets you from where you are today to where you want to be (McGovern et al., 2004; Minoli, 2008; Riege & Aier, 2008; Simon et al., 2014; Wegmann et al., 2007). The three segments and the functional component alignment gives us an idea of where we want to go. Each organization, though, must develop its vision of its architecture. It means defining priorities and determining how to design the architectural elements into the existing environment. Given the broad range of support functions, we need a systematic approach to describing the current environment.

It is not sufficient to simply describe the current application and technology environment. We know that knowledge is a complex asset that carries with it assumptions and values. In every organization, we know that there are established and approved ways of support availability, access, and consumption. Every organization has multiple behaviors around these segments. And, every organization has a sense of why knowledge is essential. Every organization has its knowledge flows, sources, influencing factors, and consequences. Because knowledge architectures must support the environment in which it exists, and the business of the organization, a level of awareness and understanding is an essential part of the design process.

Is there a systematic way of working through these issues? We approach this challenge through a series of views common to enterprise architecture design, knowledge engineering, and modeling. As we noted earlier, we approach the design process by first focusing on the architecture segments. Then we work through the business architecture, data/information architecture, application architecture, and technology architecture layers for that segment. This can be a challenging task, but we can manage the process by leveraging Ermine's MASK methodology (Barthelmé et al., 1998; De Vries & Van Rensburg, 2008; Ermine, 2007, 2013; Ermine et al., 2006). Ermine defines four views that provide a full understanding of any architecture segment.

Additionally, they help us to bridge the future and current state, to understand how we got to where we are today with our build environment. Developing these four views provides an understanding of (1) the design environment; (2) the historical, current, and evolving design work supporting this function; (3) the essential design concepts; and (4) the activity and task designs (Figure 4.3). The Design Environment view helps us to build the strategic architecture layer: the Activity and Task Design view map to the business architecture view. The Design Concepts view maps to the data/information architecture layer. Finally, the Historical and Evolutionary Design perspective helps us to understand the current situation and how we got there. We do not expect to address the application and technology layers in this text because our focus is on designing a knowledge architecture.

What is the focus and purpose of each of the four views? The design view is crucial if we want to see the function as an inclusive environment to ensure we identify all of our existing processes and critically assess whether they can be adaptable and extensible to knowledge and understand the inputs, outputs, and influence factors. We need to understand the fundamental design concepts and

FIGURE 4.3 Four Views of a Knowledge Domain

components – many would suggest this is the essence of any architecture. We need to know how we got to where we are and where we're going in the future – because we are too often rooted in our current practices and solutions, and the channels and assets are changing rapidly. We need to understand the activities and processes that define each functional knowledge architecture – to help us understand how the architecture design will be 'used' or 'lived-in.'

The two most important views are (1) the design environment – equivalent to where the building exists and those essential external and internal factors that affect how it works; and (2) the activity and task views which tell us how the building will be used and lived in every day. The challenge for knowledge architecture is that we are never beginning with a blank sheet of paper – our task more closely resembles the reclamation and redesign of an essential historical building than it does the design of a new building. We have many different 'businesses' living in this historically significant building – and they must all be willing and eager to move back into the building following the redesign. Working through the four views allows us to consider all of our 'current tenants' – and to factor their design requirements into the new architecture blueprint. The remainder of this chapter explains how each of these views helps us to understand the environment we're designing for and ensures that we design to a dynamic and evolving environment. Architectures and knowledge architectures, in particular functional designs, help us understand how to leverage and adapt to whatever engineering solutions exist. They are not constructed or engineered elements.

The design environment

To see and understand the big picture, we need to understand six factors. We need to understand the events or rationale that trigger events, sources, targets, consequences, activity flows and tasks, and influence factors (Figure 4.4).

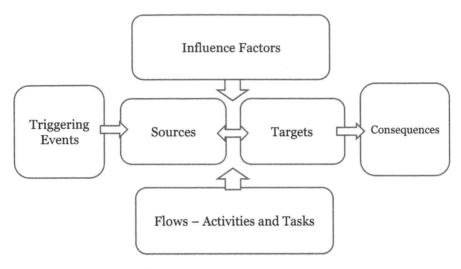

FIGURE 4.4 Big Picture of Knowledge Architecture

Triggering event

A triggering event is anything that sets the activity into motion. In this case, the activity is anything that causes us to create, access, use, or consume and make knowledge available. Triggering events will be both common and distinct in each of the segments we defined in Chapter 2. Also, the triggering event may be influenced by the business context, the type of knowledge, and the specific knowledge transaction instance. How do understanding triggering events contribute to the architecture design process? Triggering events help us to surface and discuss where we start any knowledge creation, use, or management activity. Because we have expanded the scope and coverage of knowledge assets, we take the opportunity to think about the best point to leverage. We need to think through these issues for the other seven kinds of knowledge we've defined. We cannot merely assume that what works for explicit information works for procedural knowledge, for network relationships, or tacit knowledge. Asking 'What are the triggering events for tacit knowledge?' allows working through these issues.

Sources

Sources are inputs to the activity or the general process. In this case, we're talking about sources and types of knowledge. In addition to the knowledge resource itself, though, architecture inputs also include the people or agents involved, the support applications and technologies, any tools or other supports that make it possible for us to use the source. Sources will vary with each triggering event, the type of knowledge, and the knowledge domain. How does understanding sources contribute to the architecture design process? We must design sources into the solution.

Again, we cannot assume that sources of tacit knowledge or network relationships will be the same as those for explicit information.

Consequences

The outcomes of the process are the results we expected to achieve and those we did achieve. These are the goals we expect to accomplish with a well-developed and executed operation. Consequences are specific to the business environment and an incident. How does understanding consequences contribute to the architecture design process? Consequences are essential because they keep the purpose and outcome front and center to the design process. We may capture explicit information as a legal or financial record of a business transaction. We obtain tacit knowledge, skills, and competencies, and procedural knowledge for a different reason – to sustain and support our business operations.

Targets

Targets are those products, services, and outputs generated by an event, designed to achieve a result. Targets will vary with the business context, the sources including the type of knowledge, and the expected consequences. How does understanding targets contribute to the architecture design process? Targets are an essential consideration because they tell us about the intended recipient or receptor of the knowledge asset. We cannot merely design around triggering events and sources – we must understand how those targets can best receive or manage the assets.

Flows

Flows are those activities and tasks that we choose and follow to 'do' the process. In this case, activities and tasks describe the actual knowledge transaction. Depending on the type of knowledge, these flows may be simple or complex. How does understanding activity flows contribute to the architecture design process? It is critical to understand flows and tasks, particularly when there are established solutions in place. Understanding how we do it now – step by step – is essential to determine if that process will work for other kinds of knowledge. It also is a starting point for designing new or expanded processes where they do not currently exist.

Influence factors

Influence factors are those considerations which affect the way we do a knowledge transaction. These factors may set the goals, objectives, and performance we strive to achieve, determine the resources and assets we have to work with, provide the tools to evaluate our results, or help to guide the way we think about and approach the process. How does understanding influence factors contribute to the architecture design process? Influence factors are what distinguish one environment from another. Engineered solutions – particularly commercially available solutions – presume a standardized workflow and a standardized set of influence factors. We know that influence factors will vary by organization and even by unit or team because goals, objectives, and performance expectations vary. If we ignore these in the design process, they will harm any solution we put in place.

Design concepts

As noted in Chapter 2, knowledge architecture does not exist in a vacuum. There is a significant history; there are meaningful connections to other architectures and established behaviors and assumptions. Exposing and defining key concepts are essential to developing a shared vision of the architecture. Key concepts are represented in well-entrenched definitions, procedures, and tools. We must surface and discuss these concepts to ensure they are adapted and translated to the vision of a knowledge architecture.

How does an understanding of factors contribute to the architecture design process? Key concepts are essential to design for two reasons. First, they help us to bridge different levels of architecture and different domains. If our collaboration solutions use a particular software vocabulary, it is essential to ensure the design factors are understood at a functional level by anyone in the organization. Second, a simple term can be interpreted in many different ways. We may each make assumptions about what that term means and what it does. But, these assumptions may not hold in the current or proposed solutions. It is essential to break down the key concepts to expose these assumptions and to arrive at a common level of understanding.

Activity and task designs

The flow view describes those activities and tasks that comprise and support the transaction. In this case, we're talking about any kind of knowledge transaction. This is an essential view to understand because it speaks to the reason we're designing a solution. The challenge we face in knowledge transactions is how we have historically defined and scoped these kinds of transactions. Most of the flow models related to knowledge architecture are information management flow models. Or, they speak only to the last stage of tasks and processes in the activity.

A flow view is defined around five essential components, including the tasks that comprise the activity, the inputs, outputs, roles and actors, and resources and tools (Figure 4.5). An activity view describes how we do things today. It also provides a picture of how we might do something in the future or different contexts.

Inputs to the activity

Inputs include the knowledge object itself, all those applications that might support it, the technologies we might leverage, any tools or resources we need to complete

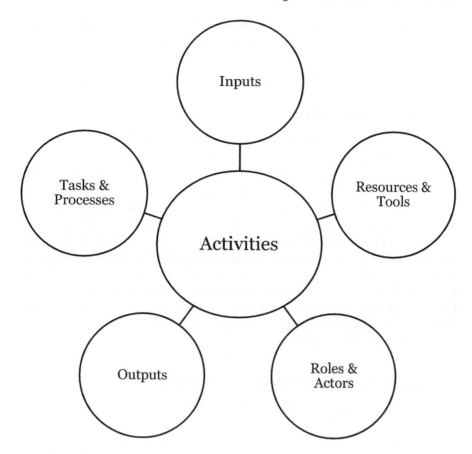

FIGURE 4.5 Designing Architectures That Support Activities and Tasks

the process, and any actors or agents who are essential to the successful completion of the process. This is an essential part of the model because often, the way they support the process may tend to limit our view of how that process might be designed to suit the future. We should describe the current state of inputs because they must, by definition, change with our redesign. But, like in other architecture contexts, we should not be bound by these inputs. Consider, for example, the importance of designing around different types of knowledge as inputs.

Outputs to the activity

As noted earlier, most of the outputs we expect from our current architectures support current business capabilities and activities. When we shift our focus to knowledge architectures, we hope to expand these outputs. We should also expect that the outputs will change with the nature of the channel. As channels continue to develop and evolve, we will need new kinds of knowledge outputs to make available, accessible, and consumable knowledge. An output from a task or process is defined as whatever that process generates. Outputs might be physical or digital, may be simple or complex. And, depending on the task, outputs from one process may be inputs to another process.

Roles, actors, and agents

Roles, actors, and agents include those individuals who 'do' the process and those who support it. Primary actors are those who play a primary, leading, or responsible role in the process. For human knowledge, this is the individual who holds the knowledge and those who draw from it and leverage it. Secondary actors are those who play supporting or enabling roles in the process – the architects, the support teams, the professionals, trainers, and coaches. Given the rapid evolution of technology and artificial intelligence, we must remember to include both human and non-human actors. We tend to think of these agents and roles as sources of technology or technology tools. In many cases, however, an automated analyst or a robot is the actor responsible for performing the process. In this case, it is vital to identify and distinguish those tools which support the process from those who perform the operation. Consider how roles and actors will expand when we design for different types of knowledge.

Resources supporting or leveraged in the activity

Resources are all of those tools that will contribute to the implementation of a thorough, relevant, and pertinent process. Resources will vary with every activity model. Perhaps more importantly, resources will vary significantly with the type of knowledge they are designed to support. There may be some persistent categories of resources we can identify to ensure that our analysis of resources is complete. We must also expose all those resources we use or may need to leverage to support our knowledge architecture design. It is crucial to keep in mind that most of the resources in place today were designed to support a particular kind of knowledge – explicit knowledge – moving through defined channels. Our challenge in designing for the future is to understand what resources we might need and how to design them for functionality. The critical question is whether these resources can be adapted and redesigned to support new channels, or whether a new resource will be needed.

Tasks

Tasks are what results when we break down activities. Tasks describe 'how' we do something – they represent a step-by-step process. What are the processes we follow to create, capture, and represent knowledge? What are the processes we put in place to support organizing knowledge? Or to find and use knowledge? In most cases, the processes we have in place are specific to specific kinds of knowledge assets. While it is essential to continue to respect these tasks, we need to understand them from a more generic perspective.

Tasks describe the actual processes we follow today to support an activity, including all of the critical decision points. Task views inherit and leverage all of the components of an activity model – such as actors, inputs, outputs, and resources – and details how they are leveraged today. Attempting to design a new solution for a knowledge transaction is a high risk unless we understand how it works today. Change and disruption should be well planned and executed if they are to be effective. To realize a functional design, we must always interpret it in the context of how it will work. Consider designing a house without views of the rooms and elements. We would never create or sign off on an architectural design if we cannot see how we will walk from room to room, where the windows and doors are, and the layout of each room.

Most organizations have reliable processes in place to leverage explicit information in a process context, but few to address the other seven types of capital. Can we leverage what we know from explicit information management processes and apply them to other kinds of knowledge? Or, do we need to adapt them or replace them with new processes? These questions are essential to the architecture design process. We may find that there are some processes in place, but they are embedded in applications or solutions that are not in the knowledge architecture landscape.

There may be processes that individuals follow to leverage human capital. But, tacit knowledge is managed by individuals as they best understand. Skills and competencies are managed jointly by the individuals who hold them, those who teach and coach them, and those who define the skills and competencies needed to support the business. Norms, rewards, and punishments govern attitudes and behaviors. While there are tools and training sources, individuals are left to manage this type of knowledge independently and as they choose. This is not an efficient or effective way for an organization to manage its human capital. We need to design and implement new processes to support the management of human capital.

Procedural knowledge has gained greater recognition in the last decade, but it is still undervalued. Most organizations 'manage' procedural knowledge in terms of procedural manuals or instructional materials. This is a small portion of the iceberg that represents all of the process knowledge an organization creates and leverages to do what it does. Organizational culture is a particularly challenging form of knowledge to manage. While culture is recognized in business management as a potential impediment or support for strategy, it is only rarely recognized as a form of knowledge that should be managed. The challenge with structural capital is the gaps that exist for procedural and cultural knowledge. These require more complex processes than human capital because they involve multiple players – they are collective activities.

There are few processes for leveraging relational capital. We acknowledge this type of capital to some degree, yet few processes are in place to support and encourage representation. More recently, knowledge management has developed activities to support communities and social networks actively, but professional networks and business networks are often the choice of individuals. Reputation is managed in terms of CVs and resumes, and individuals may use some support processes to manage their reputations. By and large, though, these are very undervalued and under-supported activities.

It is crucial to keep in mind that it is the responsibility of an organization or a group to translate the knowledge architecture framework and design principles to the process level. Architecture designs provide guidance, but they do not produce the results – they may produce a blueprint that the engineers or developers use, but architects do not construct solutions. Moving from the activity to the task or the process level represents this critical transition point – from design to build. Organizations must be particularly mindful of 'off-the-shelf' solutions designed for generic processes. It is critical to ask whether the solution can be designed or configured to support the way your architecture blueprint defines functionality. If the answer is no, consider the implications it will have to represent your business operations and goals.

Evolution of design and build architectures

The historical and evolutionary view helps us to see where we have come from, why we do things the way we do today, and where we might go in the future (Figure 4.6). Knowledge transactions are timeless. Humans have created knowledge back to ancient times, and they continue to create, use, and manage knowledge today. Little has changed in terms of basic types and properties of knowledge. What has changed, though, are the channels through which knowledge is transacted. The historical model will vary by

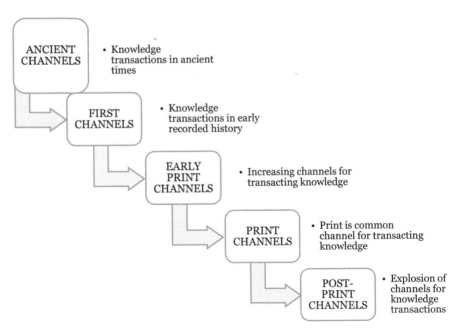

FIGURE 4.6 The Historical and Evolutionary View

domain and by context, but each of these segments has a broad historical context. The evolutionary view is particularly crucial to knowledge architecture because we know the number and complexity of channels continue to grow and change. We can predict within some degree of the reason the form some of these channels may take, but there is a risk in not being able to see and design for future channels. In the mid-20th century, we assumed the channels would focus on electronic broadcast and print. We prepared to manage knowledge that was captured in print, but we did not prepare to manage knowledge transmitted through electronic broadcast channels. As a result, much of this knowledge has been lost to future generations.

The historical view is essential for understanding how we got to where we are today and how we came to do things as we do today. It helps us to put 'the way we do things' in context and allow us to revisit and redesign new solutions. Architecture is not just about designing something new or designing in a vacuum. The historical view helps us to see the constraints we may have imposed upon our designs. The evolutionary perspective is an essential management tool for the future. It reminds us to continue to update our historical view – and to track how the environment is changing. This helps us to transition to new or revised solutions more effectively and efficiently.

There is not one evolutionary model for all knowledge architecture segments. Looking across the phases of evolution for each segment helps us to understand what factors trigger a massive change or shift in that segment. The segments are persistent, but the functional architectures must be able to adapt. Understanding the evolution of each knowledge segment increases our sensitivities to shift and changes that will impact us. Being forewarned is being forearmed – increased awareness leads to more effective change management strategies.

Iterating and synthesizing views

The knowledge architecture design process is both challenging and exciting. It is exciting to expose all four views for all 17 of our functional architectures – and to see that broader picture emerge for each functional area. It is also challenging because while we're concentrating on these functional architectures, we must also remember to pull it all back to the high level 'whole picture.' Remember that there are significant dependencies across the knowledge domains. A functional design for availability will have considerable consequences for accessibility and consumption. New expectations and norms for consumption and knowledge re-engineering will have significant implications for knowledge accessibility – some encouraging and some cautionary.

Chapter review

After reading this chapter, you should be able to:

- explain the elements of the knowledge architecture reference model;
- describe the knowledge architecture design process;

- describe how we identify design concepts for a knowledge architecture;
- explain why it is important to know the design environment;
- describe the design activities we follow for each functional architecture;
- explain why it is important to understand the evolution of design and build in each functional architecture.

References and recommended readings for the future

Barthelmé, F., Ermine, J. L., & Rosenthal-Sabroux, C. (1998). An architecture for knowledge evolution in organisations. *European Journal of Operational Research, 109*(2), 414–427.

De Vries, M., & Van Rensburg, A. C. (2008). Enterprise architecture-new business value perspectives. *South African Journal of Industrial Engineering, 19*(1), 1–16.

Ermine, J. L. (2007). Introduction au knowledge management. *Management des connaissances en entreprise. Lavoisier. Paris, Hermes Science, 23.*

Ermine, J. L. (2013). *Knowledge management with the MASK method.* Edition Hermès.

Ermine, J. L., Boughzala, I., & Tounkara, T. (2006). Critical knowledge map as a decision tool for knowledge transfer actions. *Electronic Journal of Knowledge Management, 4*(2), 129–140.

Espinosa, J. A., Boh, W. F., & DeLone, W. (2011). The organizational impact of enterprise architecture: A research framework. In *2011 44th Hawaii international conference on system sciences* (pp. 1–10). IEEE.

Fischer, R., Aier, S., & Winter, R. (2007). A federated approach to enterprise architecture model maintenance. *Enterprise Modelling and Information Systems Architectures (EMISAJ), 2*(2), 14–22.

Greefhorst, D., & Proper, E. (2011). *Architecture principles: The cornerstones of enterprise architecture.* Springer Science & Business Media.

Gregor, S., Hart, D., & Martin, N. (2007). Enterprise architectures: Enablers of business strategy and IS/IT alignment in government. *Information Technology & People, 20*(2), 96–120.

Iacob, M. E., Meertens, L. O., Jonkers, H., Quartel, D. A., Nieuwenhuis, L. J., & Van Sinderen, M. J. (2014). From enterprise architecture to business models and back. *Software & Systems Modeling, 13*(3), 1059–1083.

McGovern, J., Ambler, S. W., Stevens, M. E., Linn, J., Jo, E. K., & Sharan, V. (2004). *A practical guide to enterprise architecture.* Prentice Hall Professional.

Minoli, D. (2008). *Enterprise architecture A to Z: Frameworks, business process modeling, SOA, and infrastructure technology.* CRC Press.

Riege, C., & Aier, S. (2008). A contingency approach to enterprise architecture method engineering. In *International conference on service-oriented computing* (pp. 388–399). Springer.

Ross, J. W., Weill, P., & Robertson, D. (2006). *Enterprise architecture as strategy: Creating a foundation for business execution.* Harvard Business Press.

Schekkerman, J. (2004). *How to survive in the jungle of enterprise architecture frameworks: Creating or choosing an enterprise architecture framework.* Trafford Publishing.

Sessions, R. (2007). A comparison of the top four enterprise-architecture methodologies. *Microsoft Developer Network Architecture Center,* 1–31.

Simon, D., Fischbach, K., & Schoder, D. (2014). Enterprise architecture management and its role in corporate strategic management. *Information Systems and e-Business Management, 12*(1), 5–42.

Urbaczewski, L., & Mrdalj, S. (2006). A comparison of enterprise architecture frameworks. *Issues in Information Systems, 7*(2), 18–23.

Wegmann, A., Regev, G., Rychkova, I., Le, L. S., De La Cruz, J. D., & Julia, P. (2007). Business and IT alignment with SEAM for enterprise architecture. In *11th IEEE international enterprise distributed object computing conference (EDOC 2007)* (p. 111). IEEE.

Winter, R., & Fischer, R. (2006). Essential layers, artifacts, and dependencies of enterprise architecture. In *2006 10th IEEE international enterprise distributed object computing conference workshops (EDOCW'06)* (p. 30). IEEE.

5

KNOWLEDGE ARCHITECTURE SEGMENTS

Chapter summary

This chapter describes architecture segments and explains their role in designing how all the layers of architecture fit together. The chapter identifies three primary segments for knowledge architectures, including knowledge availability, knowledge accessibility, and knowledge consumability. We consider how these architecture segments relate to the functions we need to manage our knowledge assets. The functional architectures needed are elaborated for each knowledge architecture segment. This chapter provides the structure for more detailed discussions of each architecture in Chapters 6 through 22.

Architecture segments – definition and characterization

What is an architecture segment? What are some common architecture segments? Consider the design domain in physical building architectures – business environments, residential environments, recreational environments, infrastructure environments. Segments in enterprise architecture tend to focus on and are defined by collections of business capabilities – what an organization does to deliver value to its stakeholders. What do we need to know about segments to design a suitable architecture? And what do the four critical design points we described in Chapter 4 look like for each segment?

In Chapter 3, we described the role of segments in the broader architecture context, and in Chapter 4, we identified three high-level knowledge architecture segments. This chapter's focus is scoping out those three knowledge architecture segments, providing a foundation for more detailed descriptions in Chapters 6 through 22.

As a starting point, we should keep in mind that a knowledge architecture segment should be:

- designed to support the organization's business functions and operations;
- designed to be process-agnostic and focused on capabilities for greater stability;
- organization- and administrative-agnostic as well as time- and location-neutral;
- technology-agnostic to enable us to acquire, design, and swap out as the market changes;
- designed to identify and reduce unnecessary redundancies or unintended variations;
- aware of all of the current investments into the 'built environment,' including all forms of 'stakes' and 'established investments' in the current landscape, including current standards, certifications, credentials, or curricula;
- focused on identifying, acknowledging, leveraging, integrating, and harmonizing existing architecture good practices regardless of which domains have developed them;
- designed to support the way the organization works, as well as what it does, to ensure the result is practical;
- designed to suit knowledge assets and their different properties and behaviors;
- designed by teams of individuals who see the challenges and opportunities from multiple perspectives;
- understandable to and useful to end users as well as architects, managers, professionals, and developers;
- supported by a robust but flexible governance structure that allows the segment to continue to adapt and adjust based on input from stakeholders.

Business segments are organized around business capabilities (Bernard, 2012; Jonkers et al., 2006; Lankhorst, 2009; Ross et al., 2006; Schekkerman, 2004; Sessions, 2007; Tamm et al., 2011; Urbaczewski & Mrdalj, 2006; Wagter et al., 2005; Winter & Fischer, 2006). There are internal segments and external segments. Internal segments are defined to support groups of functional capabilities the organization performs to support its business goals. Every organization also exists in a broader business context – generally defined as an economic sector or an economic industry. For example, a financial services organization will determine its architectures to support similar kinds of financial functions. A university organizes its internal activities around capabilities such as teaching, research, advocacy, and advising. A legal firm will define its architecture segments around its areas of legal expertise and the services it offers. Within an economic sector, we will find general architecture design patterns – taking the form of off-the-shelf applications, procedures, and practices that are common to the profession or area of practice.

Each example describes architecture designed to support optimal performance. Ideally, the domain architectures are designed to support the particular context in which these capabilities exist. Similarly, the architectures of community and social networks are designed around the segments of interest of those communities. The primary activity in these environments is conversation and exchange, so the architecture is designed to support interactions.

Information segments are relevant to our discussion of knowledge architecture. It is relevant because it pertains to one type of knowledge assets, but it is not clear that the existing architectures will be sufficient to support the other types of knowledge. Because there is a long history of support for the information domain, it can be challenging to take a new perspective. The traditional information domain architecture is defined around stages in an information life cycle. As the life cycle model does not apply as well to other types of knowledge, we propose to define domains by the high-level activities we might leverage to make knowledge available to make it accessible and consumable. Within these broad domains, we can align the traditional information domains and expand them to address all of the challenges associated with knowledge.

Knowledge architecture segments

What do we know about knowledge architecture domains? We know they exist in every organization. We know they are pervasive in all business processes – no business process can exist without a knowledge foundation. We know they must be able to support the very nature of knowledge and the full range of kinds of knowledge (Figure 5.1). Given these fundamental assumptions, knowledge domains:

- are best defined by their *activities and functions* – of the five high-level views we reviewed in Chapter 4, the activity and task flow view is perhaps the most instructive for us as we build out our knowledge domains;
- represent *universal business processes* that touch every business activity across the organization – these segments are not isolated business capabilities but must be designed into the underlying architecture of every business activity;
- relevant to every individual, unit, or team, and should be designed to support the way *people work* every day;
- support the *full set of knowledge types* and transactions and extends beyond the current information life cycle model;
- must support *all forms of availability and access*, including collaboration and community formation, networking, and interactions;
- must be *unobtrusive* in how they integrate with and support business processes;
- support *all uses* including all actions that support revising, restructuring, partitioning, editing, review, supplementing, evaluating, and reconstruction;
- support the representation of *context and provenance*;
- provide for appropriate *levels of control* by knowledge creators and custodians;
- enable *discovery and promotion* within the business context.

We define knowledge segments as groups of functional activities that support availability, accessibility, and consumability (Flannagan et al., 2018). Availability and

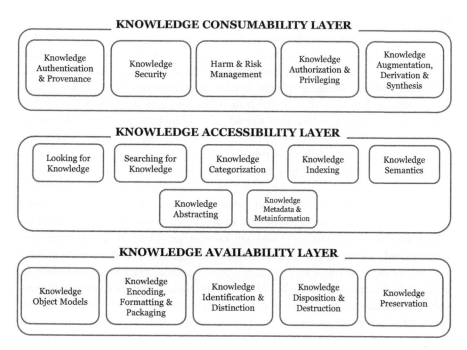

FIGURE 5.1 Aligning Functional Architectures With Segments

accessibility refer to how the organization and its policies ensure or strive to ensure that stakeholders have the means to find, read, understand, trust, and otherwise use knowledge assets. Availability helps us to define the scope and coverage of knowledge of interest to the business. We're focused on ensuring that the knowledge of interest to us for business within the larger university of knowledge is available. Availability ensures that the assets are known and can be discovered. Accessibility pertains to an individual's ability to access the knowledge asset in some way and some form. The owner or custodian may control access, and the access mechanisms designed and supported by the owner and custodian. Consumability refers to the actual use, trust, and understanding of the knowledge asset. Consumability is heavily dependent upon editing, review, editing, evaluation, and general curation activities. Consumability also relies on extensive information about the context in which the knowledge was created, the methods used to create it, and any underlying assumptions. In the statistical and data management field, this is referred to as metainformation. The creator or the expert curator generates metainformation. The individual generating the metainformation must understand and be able to describe the context and methods followed to create it.

Why is availability essential, and why should we not take it for granted? Because a knowledge asset exists does not mean it is available to create value wherever value is needed. For example, tacit knowledge is available to the individual who holds it, but it may not be readily available to others within the organization who would benefit from the exposure. How do we make tacit knowledge more widely available? It is not as simple as creating a physical representation of tacit knowledge. Tacit knowledge changes continuously – it increases in value through exposure, review, and critique. The tacit knowledge of an individual differs from similar records of that knowledge in papers, books, or memoranda. The challenge is to design mechanisms that allow individuals to explain and share their knowledge. The other challenges architecture should address include whether and how to make such availability persistent, to protect the source, and to ensure appropriate controls when the knowledge is exposed.

Why is accessibility important? Because knowledge assets are available does not mean it is accessible. How do we find and discover existing knowledge? Accessibility requires specialized functions and deliberate actions. Accessibility is a critical domain for businesses because it speaks to the entry point for every team, individual, unit, and organization to leverage knowledge. There are many established methods and tools to support access to explicit and tangible information assets. Can we use the same methods to make these other kinds of knowledge accessible, or are new designs needed? How should we expand these functions to ensure all these stakeholders have access to human capital, structural capital, and relational capital? Are there other functions we need to consider in this domain to ensure this access?

Why is consumability essential, and why should we not take it for granted? In Chapter 1, we made the case that knowledge is dynamic – it generates value through use and consumption. To derive value from the knowledge, it must be used. The value of knowledge diminishes when it is simply stockpiled. The challenge with consumability is that by coming in contact with others in the work environment, we naturally exchange and consume human capital. But, our consumption will always be limited by the natural boundaries of availability and accessibility. An individual in Team A would benefit from learning what a member of Team X knows, but they are separated by countries and organizational structures. How do we make Team X's human capital available to Team A? It is more than simply packaging it and posting it. Human capital is best exchanged directly and interactively. In this case, it is knowing that Team X has relevant knowledge and having the support and capability to interact with them in an essential aspect of availability. The same might be said of skills and competencies. While Team C members can attend the same training as Team Z, Team C works in an environment where they can put that training to work and adapt the new competencies to support the organization. In contrast, Team Z has the resource-based knowledge they gained in the training course, but no context in which to test or develop that knowledge and transform it into competencies. Nor do they have contact with Team C, which would allow them to continue their development through the new experiences of others.

As we see, the three segments of availability, accessibility, and consumability are highly interdependent. We consider this when defining our working reference model. We will cover how the 13 functions support these three domains, but with the caveat that the boundaries between these three segments are very porous. The interdependence of these functions and segments is a primary consideration when we translate our working reference model into actual designs and blueprints.

We organize sets of activities into these three broad segments. Perhaps the most critical alignment factor is how the 13 functions interact with one another. How do these functions work together to form a whole knowledge architecture? The alignment of functions into segments is guided by logical connections and flows. Our working reference model addresses each function in terms of its purpose and consequences, its fundamental activities and tasks including resources, standards, and business rules, its historical grounding, and its key concepts and assumptions. The reference model expands these functions to apply to all types of knowledge. The functions built into the reference model also allows us to track a knowledge asset as it moves throughout its business life. The functions generate new value from and for each knowledge asset. There are inherent challenges and impediments to supporting the flow of knowledge assets and their value-added properties across domains. One challenge is the disruption of flows due to system and technical solutions. The reference model introduces elements of availability that allow knowledge assets and their value to transcend the three domains more easily.

Functional architectures that support availability

Which of the functional architectures are most relevant to knowledge availability? What are the underlying processes we need to pay attention to and expand to cover all types of knowledge assets? They are:

- knowledge object modeling and representation;
- knowledge asset encoding, formatting, and packaging;
- knowledge asset identification and distinction;
- knowledge asset disposition and destruction;
- knowledge asset preservation.

Knowledge object modeling and representation

This functional architecture must support several activities and tasks, including (1) the grouping and reverse engineering of all five categories of knowledge assets to identify the core knowledge; (2) creating new object models for the group and all of its instances, and desk checking the models against the organization's knowledge assets to ensure the models work for mapping; (3) assigning models to instances and ensuring that the models are accessible to asset owners and custodians; and (4) identifying those assets at most significant risk of loss or harm and developing a plan for transforming the knowledge content. To develop this functional architecture, we must have a good understanding of object models and their components, the difference between object models and functional, process, and information models, object modeling methods and languages, and object mapping methods. The major challenge we face in designing this functional architecture is the absence of good precedents for modeling knowledge assets.

Knowledge asset encoding, packaging and formatting

This functional architecture must support several activities and tasks, including (1) conducting an audit of the encoding structures, formats, and packages in which the organization's assets are represented; (2) aligning formats with asset types and classes; (3) identifying the formats at most significant risk of loss or harm and develop a strategy for transforming those assets; (4) conducting a desk check transformation of selected assets to test availability; (5) documenting the transformations in the metadata records for individual assets; and (6) working with asset owners and custodians to develop strategies for future transformations. To develop this functional architecture, we must have a good understanding of encoding structures and methods including encoding and decoding methods, historical and current formatting structures and methods, awareness of future trends and projects of formatting, common forms of packaging for knowledge assets, and common forms of vulnerabilities and risks associated with each type of packaging. The major challenge we face in designing this functional architecture is the pace of change and development of these methods, the cost of keeping up with the change, and the risk of loss and harm due to not being able to provide continued availability.

Knowledge asset identification and distinction

This functional architecture must support several activities and tasks, including (1) defining and identifying the attributes that identify and distinguish the high-level classes of knowledge assets; (2) developing a strategy for determining whether these attributes are embedded, inferred or inherited, or discovered; (3) defining the current state and capture methods for these attributes; (3) identifying gaps for these attributes; (4) developing strategies to backfill these gaps for business-critical knowledge assets; (5) developing methods for identifying versions of assets, are redundant or duplicate of other assets; (6) developing strategies for tracking and linking versions and copies; and (6) developing new training and processes to create these attributes in the future. To develop this functional architecture, we must have a good understanding of common practices for attribution or identifying the creator of the asset; naming and titling practices for all kinds of assets; establishing and representing the dates associated with the creation or the acquisition of an asset; unique reference identifiers; common practices for managing versions, editions, and copies; and knowledge of semantic or other scientific methods for discovering highly similar knowledge assets.

Knowledge asset disposition and destruction

This functional architecture must support several activities and tasks, including (1) identifying current practices for disposing of and destroying knowledge assets, (2) conducting a review of knowledge assets and their business value, (3) developing and assigning practical retention and disposition rules and schedules to all five classes of knowledge assets, (4) developing methods for making and communicating disposition decisions, and (5) destroying knowledge assets at the end of their useful business life. To develop this functional architecture, we must have a good understanding of general asset management practices; the criteria for assessing the business value of kinds of knowledge assets; common disposition practices and tools; asset audit and inventory methods; metadata retention practices; and acceptable destruction practices for different kinds of knowledge assets and their packaging. The major challenge we face in designing this functional architecture is the wide variation in accepted practice for managing these different kinds of assets, and the absence of accepted practices for some of these assets.

Knowledge asset preservation and conservation

This functional architecture must support several activities and tasks, including (1) defining strategies for preserving and conserving (e.g., transforming) the organization's knowledge assets to ensure continued availability; (2) conducting desk checks of the transformation strategies; (3) defining preservation and conversation infrastructures, internal capabilities, and competencies; (4) developing decision criteria for preservation and conservation actions; (5) scheduling the transformation of knowledge assets dispositioned for conservation; and (6) ensuring the asset metadata is updated to document the transformation. To develop this functional architecture, we must have a good understanding of preservation, conservation, content migration, preservation, or conservation practices for different types of media, including their inherent encoding and formatting; emulation strategies; reinterpretation strategies; as well as traditional preservation and conservation cultures. The primary challenge we face in designing this functional architecture is maintaining the focus on the knowledge assets rather than the package, and in acting for the long term, and in ensuring that preservation and conservation are undertaken for availability and access rather than lockdown and storage.

Functional architectures that support accessibility

We align seven functions with knowledge accessibility, including:

- seeking and discovering knowledge assets;
- searching for knowledge assets;
- categorizing knowledge assets;
- knowledge asset indexing and Keywording;
- semantics for knowledge assets;
- knowledge abstraction and surrogation;
- metadata for knowledge assets.

Seeking and discovering knowledge assets

This functional architecture must support several activities and tasks, including (1) identifying the knowledge-seeking and discovery needs of people in the business environment; (2) developing profiles of knowledge seeking for business-critical environments; (3) defining the knowledge discovery landscape including current sources and gaps; (4) designing a discovery environment start at the business level and progress to the whole environment; (5) developing a discovery monitoring and feedback capability to ensure the landscape supports current business needs. To develop this functional architecture we must have a good understanding of common knowledge-seeking practices and patterns: discovery methods such as berrypicking, browsing, grazing, and satisficing; the difference between seeking and findability; use of case modeling methods; and the rich base of research focused on information and knowledge seeking. The primary challenge we face in designing this functional architecture is expanding the rich base of knowledge and practice to include all of the types of knowledge assets. Additionally, a critical challenge is distinguishing seeking and discovery from searching architectures designed for particular sources.

Searching for knowledge assets

This functional architecture must support several activities and tasks, including (1) defining the sources that must be searchable; (2) identify and defining appropriate search capabilities; (3) assessing current search capabilities against need; (4) designing appropriate index structures and architectures; (5) designing indexing updating and rebuilding practices; and (6) designing search logging and feedback capabilities. To develop this functional architecture, we must have a good understanding of those concepts that pertain to search inputs, search processes, and search outputs. More specifically, search input concepts include query formulation, searching methods for personal collections, web content, databases, catalogs, directories, and business applications. Search process concepts include index structures such as query processing and transformation, query expansion, query profiling, common index designs, full-text indexes, parameterized indexes, hybrid indexes, federated search architectures, enterprise index structures, index build methods, index monitoring, indexing balancing, and rebuilt methods. Search output concepts include results display and sorting, citation display and downloading, results linking, deduplication of results, results page design, and other user services such as current awareness, search recommendations, social tagging, syndication services, and search profile development. The primary challenge in designing this functional architecture is translating the rich body of knowledge and extensive research into all five classes of knowledge assets.

Categorizing knowledge assets

This functional architecture must support several activities and tasks, including: (1) identifying those access points to knowledge access that require some level of language control to be effective; (2) defining the categories of control for those access points; (3) developing a whole organization category structure to manage these categories; (4) mapping existing categories and labels to this new structure; (5) conducting a desk check of categories with seekers and stakeholders; (6) developing a method for categorizing assets; and (7) developing a capability for assessing categorization actions. To develop this functional architecture, we must have a good understanding of categories, their structures and behaviors, and categorization schemes and their principles; categorization processes and methods; and common types of categorization methods such as human, machine-assisted, and automated. The primary challenges we face in designing this functional architecture are adjusting prevalent perceptions, practices in, and procedures in specific domains, and seeing other design options that transcend current 'build solutions.'

Knowledge asset indexing and keywording

This functional architecture must support several activities and tasks, including (1) defining acceptable types of indexing values and their specifications; (2) identifying indexing principles, policies, and performance thresholds; (3) inventorying the current state of indexing and keywording; (4) developing a strategy for harmonizing and integrating existing index terms; (5) defining acceptable indexing methods; and (6) defining monitoring and assessment methods for indexing. To develop this functional architecture, we must have a good understanding of the use of language to describe concepts and ideas, domain vocabularies, focal vocabularies, listening vocabularies, speaking vocabularies, reading vocabularies, writing vocabularies, subject indexing schemes, subject headings, controlled versus uncontrolled vocabularies, professional indexing practices, generalized keywording practices, indexing exhaustivity, pre- and post-coordinated index terms, and indexing for precision and recall. The primary challenge we face in designing this functional architecture is integrating and harmonizing terms used to index from different sources and over time.

Semantics for knowledge assets

This functional architecture must support several activities and tasks, including (1) developing an understanding of the structure of the language of the domain or the context; (2) increasing awareness of the linguistic registers in place for stakeholders of the domain; (3) developing an understanding of the semantic structures and relationships common to the domain; (4) assessing current semantic structures in the domain for suitability to the business context; (5) defining scope and coverage of the domain suited to business purposes; (6) working with stakeholders to develop and test the semantic structures; and (7) designing a process for deploying the structures in existing applications and tools such as metadata templates, search interfaces, automated indexing tools, and so on. To develop this functional architecture, we must have a good understanding of thesauri; semantic networks, concept and topic maps; semantic relationships such as synonym rings, hierarchical and associative relationships; semantic relatedness, distance, and centrality; vocabularies designed for administrative functions and business functions; and semantic principles, policies, and governance processes. The primary challenge in designing this functional architecture is developing a harmonized, common design strategy for designing semantic structures that suit different communities.

Knowledge abstracting and surrogation

This functional architecture must support several activities and tasks, including (1) defining the purpose and goal of the abstract or summary; (2) identifying the environment that will host or manage the abstract; (3) defining the type and structure of the abstract; (4) defining the abstracting process and rules; and (5) producing the abstract or summary. To develop this functional architecture, we must have a good understanding of the types of abstracts including extracted highlights, summaries, explanations, lists, descriptive abstracts, informative and indicative abstracts; structured and unstructured abstracts; summarization methods for different formats such as images, audio and visual formats, and text; embedded versus linked abstracts; author-generated summaries; professional abstracting methods; and the full range of goals for abstracting and summarizing, including surrogate access for other language assets, marketing and promotion, and overcoming impediments to full asset access. The primary challenges we face in designing this functional architecture are recognizing the importance and growing need for abstracts in the age of full text, and of learning to see abstracts and summaries in non-traditional information professions.

Metadata for knowledge assets

This functional architecture must support several activities and tasks, including (1) defining the access points needed to support knowledge asset seeking, searching and management; (2) inventorying and profiling current metadata structures and methods; (3) identifying new structures and access points for knowledge assets; (4) harmonizing and integrating existing structures and methods; (5) developing embedding mechanisms for metadata properties and assets; and (6) developing new practices, policies, and assessments methods to support the new structures. To develop this functional architecture, we must have a good understanding of the principle of access points; metadata attributes, specifications, and business rules; metadata semantics; metadata profiles and records; metadata architectures; catalog and inventory applications; and metadata practices, policies, and standards. The primary challenges we face in designing this functional architecture are learning to see metadata as a kind of abstract description of the asset, integrating and harmonizing well-established and well-entrenched metadata practices and policies across domains, and making a case for redesigning metadata structures and referencing practices for knowledge asset mobility and extensibility.

Functional architectures that support consumability

We align five functions with knowledge consumability, including:

- knowledge augmentation, derivation, and synthesis;
- knowledge harm and risk management;
- knowledge authentication and provenance tracking;

- knowledge security management;
- knowledge asset control and privileging.

Knowledge asset authentication and provenance tracking

This functional architecture must support several activities and tasks, including (1) identifying the authentication factors and methods that are suited to the organization's knowledge assets; (2) conducting a desk check of knowledge assets to determine the extent of the authentication challenge; (3) developing authentication and provenance tracking practices for classes of knowledge assets; (4) developing a strategy for routinely identifying and marking knowledge assets for authentication; (5) developing a strategy for tracking provenance for critical business assets; and (6) retrospectively identifying and remedying assets that require authentication. To develop this functional architecture, we must have a good understanding of authenticity; authentication methods; package-based authentication; product-based authentication; inferred authentication; plagiarism; digital signatures; watermarking; archival stamps; seals; plagiarism; provenance; custodial history; provenance tracking and recording; the chain of custody; proof markup language; and scientific workflow systems. The primary challenge we face in designing this functional architecture is to raise awareness and to keep up with the technologies and practices that make it easier to create copies and new versions, to falsify and misrepresent, and to appropriate or engage in knowledge theft.

Knowledge asset harm and risk management

This functional architecture must support several activities and tasks, including (1) identifying risk factors; (2) identifying business custodians; (3) determining the degree of risk; (4) considering the cost-benefit model for safeguarding; and (5) designing a risk management portfolio. To develop this functional architecture, we must have a good understanding of the full spectrum of harm, including (1) asset loss; (2) asset theft; (3) physical harm; (4) tampering and misuse of assets; and (5) the creation of false and fake assets. We also need to understand business risk, risk mitigation, and risk portfolio development. The primary challenge we face in designing this functional architecture is recognizing the harm that can occur, raising awareness among staff, and providing the support structures for recording harm and alerting users to risk.

Knowledge asset security management

This functional architecture must support several activities and tasks, including (1) defining the types of harm and the levels of risk for knowledge assets; (2) developing security criteria based on harm and risk levels; (3) inventorying and assessing the current security infrastructure for knowledge assets; (4) designing activities to assign security to knowledge assets; and (5) designing security monitoring and management methods. To develop this functional architecture, we must have a good understanding of harm, including legal harm, economic harm, willful harm, and negligent harm; reputational damage; physical hurt or damage; levels and degrees of harm; risk reduction; risk of faults; risk from errors; uncertainty; unauthorized use; insurance against harm; security classes; security classification; overclassification; and underclassification. The primary challenge we face in designing this functional architecture is developing security measures and methods that are suited to types and levels of harm, and avoiding the temptation to adopt security classifications structures and methods from other organizations without full consideration.

Knowledge asset privileging and authorization

This functional architecture must support several activities and tasks, including (1) defining common access behaviors and control risks; (2) assessing current directory and access structures in place across the organization; (3) designing privilege levels appropriate to each class of knowledge asset; (4) designing new strategies for supporting access based on privilege levels; and (5) designing methods for assigning or inferring privileges based on user information and credentials. To develop this functional architecture, we must have a good understanding of access; access control; access rights; access control mechanisms; user identify management; privilege access management; discretionary access control; mandatory access control; attribute-based access control; personally identifiable information; user accounts; risk privileged accounts; the principle of least privilege; authorization; and authorization methods. The primary challenge we face in designing this functional architecture is understanding who is requesting access, why, and what harm or risk they present. Another challenge is the tendency to revert to the principle of least privilege – which results in lower knowledge flows and constraints the business value of knowledge assets.

Knowledge augmentation, interpretation, and translation

This functional architecture must support several activities and tasks, including (1) developing an understanding and awareness of the knowledge consumption patterns across the organization; (2) identifying those patterns that align with business-critical capabilities; (3) assessing the existing architectures to support knowledge consumption; (4) designing solutions to support knowledge consumption; and (5) designing solutions to represent the augmented, translated, and interpreted knowledge back into the business. To develop this functional architecture, we must have a good understanding of the full spectrum of use, including knowledge translation, interpretation, and augmentation. To understand knowledge translation, we need to have a good grasp of knowledge exchange, transfer, uptake, and sharing. Translated knowledge makes the source knowledge actionable, including translations of research into practice, clinical procedures, explanations, testing procedures and results, representations of knowledge in other languages, or any other activity that transforms the knowledge asset to generate business value. Knowledge interpretation is the representation of knowledge in other forms, such as performance or rendering in other channels, creating knockoffs and copies, plagiarism, adaptations, parodies or satires, critical reviews, peer reviews – in essence, any type of use that is best understood in the context of the original asset. Interpretive knowledge cannot be fully understood or its meaning realized without knowledge of the source. Knowledge augmentation changes the original knowledge asset, including annotations in all media forms (e.g., text, film, image, audio, dramatic, story), errata and corrections, versions and revisions, renditions, redactions, or partially censored versions, annotations, markups, comments, and note bene. The primary challenge we face in designing this functional architecture is learning to see and understand how we are consuming our knowledge assets, and keeping pace with the rapid evolution of different patterns of consumption, changing roles in consumption, and the rapidly expanding and evolving knowledge use landscape. This functional architecture not only supports knowledge consumption but also increases our awareness of common forms of consumption.

Chapter review

After reading this chapter, you should be able to:

- explain the purpose and role of an architecture segment;
- describe the three knowledge architecture segments;
- describe the functional architectures that make up the knowledge availability segment;
- describe the functional architectures that make up the knowledge accessibility segment;
- describe the functional architectures that make up the knowledge consumability segment.

References and recommended future readings

Bernard, S. A. (2012). *An introduction to enterprise architecture.* AuthorHouse.

Jonkers, H., Lankhorst, M. M., ter Doest, H. W., Arbab, F., Bosma, H., & Wieringa, R. J. (2006). Enterprise architecture: Management tool and blueprint for the organisation. *Information systems frontiers, 8*(2), 63.

Lankhorst, M. (2009). *Enterprise architecture at work* (Vol. 352). Springer.

Ross, J. W., Weill, P., & Robertson, D. (2006). *Enterprise architecture as strategy: Creating a foundation for business execution.* Harvard Business Press.

Schekkerman, J. (2004). *How to survive in the jungle of enterprise architecture frameworks: Creating or choosing an enterprise architecture framework.* Trafford Publishing.

Sessions, R. (2007). A comparison of the top four enterprise-architecture methodologies. *Microsoft Developer Network Architecture Center,* 1–31.

Tamm, T., Seddon, P. B., Shanks, G., & Reynolds, P. (2011). How does enterprise architecture add value to organisations? *Communications of the Association for Information Systems, 28*(1), 10.

Urbaczewski, L., & Mrdalj, S. (2006). A comparison of enterprise architecture frameworks. *Issues in Information Systems*, 7(2), 18–23.

Wagter, R., Van Den Berg, M., Luijpers, J., & Van Steenbergen, M. (2005). *Dynamic enterprise architecture: How to make it work*. John Wiley & Sons.

Winter, R., & Fischer, R. (2006). Essential layers, artifacts, and dependencies of enterprise architecture. In *2006 10th IEEE international enterprise distributed object computing conference workshops (EDOCW'06)* (p. 30). IEEE.

SECTION 2

Designing for availability

The chapters in Section 2 focus on those functions that help us establish a robust architecture for ensuring that knowledge is available to those who need it, when needed, where it is needed, and how it is needed. We must understand but move beyond traditional practices and constraints. We must see knowledge assets from a business asset management perspective, not as a secondary information object. It means being able to look beyond the package and the distribution channel to see the embedded knowledge, and to learn to manage the embedded knowledge rather than just the package or the distribution channel.

6

KNOWLEDGE OBJECT MODELING

Chapter summary

This chapter discusses the development of object models for knowledge assets and the five activities that support the creation of these models. The chapter explains why it is vital to have a good understanding of object models and their components: the difference between object models and functional, process, and information models, object modeling methods, languages, and object mapping methods. This chapter also explains what we have to work with, where we lack good precedents, and where we can adapt and expand existing practices. The chapter offers sample structures organizations can leverage to develop their object models.

Why we care about knowledge object models

We care about knowledge object models because representation is the foundation of all three of our knowledge domains. Every activity and process designed to support these segments begins with the underlying assumption that we have something that can be 'made available,' something that can be 'accessed' and something that can be consumed and leveraged (Bachman, 1969; Becker et al., 2000; Berner, 2019; Broch et al., 1991; Chen, 1976; Date, 2003; ISO, 1994; Lee, 1999; Loomis et al., 1987; Moss, 2012; Quatrani, 1996; Rumbaugh et al., 1991, 1994; Roberts, 2018; Terje Totland, 1997). A knowledge object model is a unifying representation because knowledge objects run the range of abstract ideas and attitudes to physical documents and data sets to virtual and physical networks.

We care about having a reliable and valid object model of a knowledge asset because the credibility of any business transformation depends on the object itself. We must have access to the object model of the asset to ensure that:

- there is a working object model associated with every knowledge asset regardless of when, where, or how the organization created them;

- we can associate a knowledge asset with a working object model irrespective of where it comes from or where it travels to;
- what we are encoding is either an accurate or close representation of the asset;
- there is direct access to the asset to ensure that any new formatting design or packing does not alter the asset – we need design control of the object;
- we are not relying on metadata descriptions alone because these are abstractions of the object and are often inferred or interpreted rather than extractions;
- we can authenticate and validate the knowledge asset and protect it from theft, misuse, and misappropriation;
- we can track and account for changes to the original knowledge asset and describe its provenance;
- we can ensure that we have a full understanding of the asset to assign appropriate levels of privileges and authorizations;
- we can assign and embed security properties in the asset itself rather than to simply infer it from its application or metadata;
- we can establish a persistent anchor for extensions, abstractions, and surrogates and explain the relationships;
- assets are defined distinctly from processes and applications and can be consumed by any other application.

Object models, if well-articulated, can help ensure that the object remains understandable and interpretable with whatever applications or technologies that come along. Without object models, asset availability depends on the changing abilities of application or humans. Absent object models, knowledge assets may be at risk of unintentional loss.

Object models and knowledge object models – design concepts

To develop this functional architecture, we must have a good understanding of object models and their components, the difference between object models and functional, process, and information models, object modeling methods and languages, and object mapping methods. The major challenge we face in designing this functional architecture is the absence of good precedents for modeling knowledge assets.

Object models can take many forms. They may include conceptual models, logical models, physical system models, physical scale models, and blueprints. Models may be dynamic or functional, data models, information models, web templates, business information models, entity-relationship models, and UML models. How do these models relate to the object models we need to design for knowledge assets?

> *Data models* are an abstract model that organizes elements of data and standardizes how they relate to one another and the properties of real-world

entities. A data model may specify that the data element representing a car be composed of several other factors, which, in turn, represent the color and size of the vehicle and define its owner. A data model can refer to an abstract formalization of the objects and relationships found in a particular application domain: the customers, products, and orders found in a manufacturing organization. A data model can refer to the set of concepts used in defining such formalizations: for example, concepts such as entities, attributes, relations, or tables. So the 'data model' of a banking application may be defined using the entity-relationship 'data model.'

Conceptual models are structured business views of the data required to support business processes, record business events, and track related performance measures. This model focuses on identifying the data used in the business but not its processing flow or physical characteristics.

Logical models describe the data in as much detail as possible, without regard to how they will be physically implemented in the database. A logical data model includes all entities and their relationships, all of the attributes, the primary key for each asset, the foreign keys that identify relationships with other entities.

Physical models explain how the model will be built in a database. It describes table structures, column names, column data types, column constraints, primary keys, foreign keys, and relationships between tables.

Functional models are a kind of semantic model that uses functional representations to create associations between objects. The purpose of a functional model is to support an understanding of the formalisms of the relationships.

Information models are representations of concepts and the relationships, constraints, rules, and operations to specify data semantics for a chosen domain of discourse. Typically it defines relations between kinds of things, but it may also include relationships with specific items.

Business information models specify meta-information used to achieve a common understanding of business objects, their definition, structure, and contents as well as all relationships to other business objects. A description of information that is important to the business independent of any underlying information technology.

Entity-relationship models describe interrelated things of interest in a specific domain of knowledge. A basic ER model is composed of entity types and specifies relationships that can exist between entities. An entity set is a group of similar objects, and these entities can have attributes. An entity-relationship model shows the complete logical structure of an entity by showing relationships, entities, and attributes. These are typically used to describe databases and tables.

Unified Modeling Language (UML) models are visual representations of software programs using a collection of diagrams. The notation has evolved from the work of Grady Booch, James Rumbaugh, Ivar Jacobson, and the Rational Software Corporation to be used for object-oriented design. It has since been extended to cover a wider variety of software engineering projects. Today, UML is accepted by the Object Management Group (OMG) as the standard for modeling software development.

In developing a knowledge architecture practice, you will likely find all of these object models in use across your organization. Each type of model can provide some understanding for you as you design and develop knowledge object models. Understanding the purpose and nature of each of these models will help you understand how to relate these models to knowledge object models.

Knowledge object models are essential to all three types of knowledge – to human knowledge, structural knowledge, and relational knowledge. The existing models are not sufficient to serve as a foundation for the vision of a knowledge architecture. Current models often reflect the needs of the distribution channels for which they were packaged or the applications in which the asset was created. Knowledge object models must describe the encoding, format, and package, but they must be agnostic. Existing models are not sufficient for a well-defined, extensible, and comprehensive knowledge architecture because they focus on the external rather than essential elements of the knowledge asset. These models are scattered across areas of practice and subject domains and are not readily available outside of those contexts.

Knowledge objects must be atomic, extensible, flexible, and descriptive. What does this mean? And, how is it different from what we have today?

- *Atomic*: Historically, we have associated knowledge with explicit information objects. We have assumed that knowledge came to us encoded, formatted, and packaged to suit the distribution channel. In future knowledge architecture, we need to be able to get to the core knowledge object while still having access to the information that tells us about the encoding, formatting, and packaging. An atomic object model focuses on the elements and design of the knowledge itself. An atomic object model treats encoding, formatting, and packaging as attributes of the object rather than elements.
- *Extensible and additive*: In Chapter 1, we explained that knowledge is dynamic and continually changing. With change comes new value in the business context. It is crucial to be able to track those changes and new values and link them to the source asset. Historically, we have managed extensibility sporadically through version control. And, we have applied version control to official information documents or new editions. In the future, we will manage extensibility by linking and establishing relationships among knowledge object models.
- *Flexible*: Object models cannot be developed with a 'one and done' intent. Objects will change, and the change will not always warrant the creation of a new object model. They may simply involve a change to

the existing model. We must have conceptual, logical, and physical models to ensure continued access and ongoing management. We must be able to manage object models at the element level – not just the model level.

- *Descriptive*: Object models must have sufficient detail to contain and embody all of the descriptive attributes needed to continue to make them available, accessible, and consumable. The descriptive attributes will vary with each organization and each business context. It is essential, though, that they be a core element of the model.

The human capital object model

A human capital object model takes as a focus a person. Our human capital model intends to make it easier for individuals to promote and for others to discover their human capital assets. The more individuals tell us about their human capital, the easier it is for others to discover that capital and to increase the circulation of knowledge. We are not modeling the physical characteristics of an individual – as we would in a medical profile – or the financial characteristics of an individual – as in a banking or credit profile. These do not tell us about the individual's human capital.

Human capital object classes

Our human capital object model will include elements that represent the dimensions of an individual's tacit knowledge, their skills and competencies, their behavior and attitudes, their work histories, and their reputations. There are two object classes for this type of knowledge asset – a People Object Class and an Agent Object Class (Table 6.1). The People Object Class represents living individuals who have tacit knowledge, skills, competences, attitudes and behaviors, work history, and reputation. In a world where decisions and actions and knowledge are increasingly made by robotics and automated agents, it is important to begin to think of an object class that defines the kinds of human capital assets embedded in these agents.

Object Class Secondary and Tertiary Object Classes for Human Capital would be those subclasses that represent the individual's (1) tacit knowledge; (2) skills and competencies; (3) attitudes and behaviors; (4) cultural profiles; and (5) relational knowledge. Each of these assets has unique behavior and is best modeled as a subobject.

Object Class Attributes, Specifications, and Behaviors for People and Agents would include any attributes needed to identify and distinguish the object (e.g., name, dates, physical characteristics or packages, encoding such as language, estimated business life span and value, authenticity and provenance, security credentials, and access privileges). The subobject classes would have additional attributes about the type and nature of tacit knowledge, the identification and characterization of skills and competencies, characterizations of attitudes and behaviors, cultural

TABLE 6.1 Human Capital Object Classes

Class	Description	Examples
People Object Class	Describes the individual whose tacit knowledge, skills and competencies, attitudes and behaviors, cultural knowledge, and relational knowledge have potential business value.	• A mechanical engineer who is a lead on a tire engineering team • An electrician involved in designing solar energy panels for a business • A mason who works with industry and construction crews to design and product large building materials • An elementary school organization with experience working with children from challenging homes
Agent Object Class	Any agent, whether physical, programmatic or hybrid, has the organization's embedded knowledge and is designed to provide operational support. The agent qualifies as human capital when it has embedded tacit knowledge, skills, and competencies, and is connected to other agents or people (e.g., relational knowledge).	• The automated agent an organization uses to provide physical labor for a production process • An AI application that makes management decisions to solve complex problems • An engineered machine that provides support for instrument production

attributes, and membership and roles in networks). These attributes apply equally to People and Agents and would provide for significantly improved management of Agent assets if applied.

Object Class Link Categories for People would include links to explicit knowledge assets, to procedural knowledge assets, and to the community, group, or social groups with which the individual is affiliated.

The explicit knowledge object model

Explicit knowledge assets will represent the most common stocks of existing knowledge assets (Austerberry, 2004; Appleton Company, 1985; Briet, 1951; Buckland, 1991; Frohmann, 2009; Hjerppe, 1994; Houser, 1986; Larsen, 1999; Levy, 1994; Lund, 2008; Ørom, 2007; Repa, 2012; Veryard, 1992; Riles, 2006; Schamber, 1996; Schenck & Wilson, 1994; Signer, 2010; Smith, 2012, 2013; Swift, 1997; Wood et al., 1998). The breadth and range of assets are significant. Rather than begin with detailed typologies, though, we begin by defining four high-level object classes whose architectures will differ significantly from one another but are relatively consistent when broken down into their secondary and tertiary subclasses.

These object classes include (1) documents or text-based assets, (2) visual assets, (3) audio assets; and (4) artifacts (Table 6.2). The differentiating factors across these four classes will derive from their encoding, formatting, and packaging attributes. Their commonalities will derive from the remaining attributes.

Object Class Secondary and Tertiary Object Classes for Explicit Knowledge would include those subclasses representing the assets semantic or structural elements. Secondary and tertiary subclasses will depend on the nature of the primary object class – consider that we might break books down into chapters and sections. For project documents, internal reports might have abstracts, sections, glossaries,

TABLE 6.2 Explicit Knowledge Object Classes

Class	Description	Examples
Documents	Describes any type of text-based asset, whether formally published or internally generated, authorized by an organization or generated by an individual, regardless of its structure, enumeration, or chronology, that has business value to the organization.	• Internal project plans and formal business strategies • Performance evaluation documents • Published scientific books • Published fiction books • Social science journals • Organic chemistry bi-annual compilations (series)
Visual Assets	Describes any type of visual or image-based asset that has business value to the organization, regardless of whether they are in physical or digital forms.	• Photographs, logos, illustrations, animations, audiovisual media, presentations, business images, films, streamed visual assets
Audio Assets	Describes any asset of business value that has audible content, including audio recordings, performed music, telephone conversations, audio meeting transcripts, narrated experiments, narrated processes, narrated after-action reviews, performed stories, and so on.	• Founders' speeches on tape • Recorded transcripts of conferences • Recorded business conversations • Oral history interviews • Business manager's experiential stories • Recordings of holiday celebrations • Brand jingles and marketing music
Artifacts	Any object that has a three-dimensional shape, whether physical or digital, that has business value or purpose.	• Scale model of a new building • Print or digital model of a new product or product line • Brand artifacts that represent the organization's identity or are used to promote its image • Sculptural representations of founders or critical experts

and appendices. Visual objects may be broken down into different visual elements, depending on the format and package. Films would have various subclasses than would illustrations or logos. Audio would ultimately break down into sounds, but those sounds might be organized into variant secondary classes.

Object Class Attributes, Specifications, and Behaviors for Explicit Knowledge would include any attributes needed to identify and distinguish the document, visual asset, audio asset, or artifact (e.g., name, dates, physical characteristics or packages, encoding such as language, medium), the estimated business life span and value, attributes that enable access (e.g., authenticity and provenance, security credentials, and access privileges). Additionally, any descriptive attributes describe the knowledge kernel (e.g., its topical focus, its business focus, its geographical focus). The subobject classes would have additional attributes about the type and nature of the audio asset, the visual asset, or the artifact.

There are two essential categories of Explicit Knowledge Object Class Links. The first category includes links to containers or other parts of an explicit compound object, including links from parent to child or siblings such as books in series, issues in journal runs, episodes in installments, or artifacts in a defined set. The second category of links includes chunked object links – extracted smaller pieces not originally intended to be a separate and distinct object. Examples might consist of shots from a movie, quoted passages from a report, or extracted conversations from a more extended meeting.

The procedural knowledge object model

The challenge with procedural knowledge is to describe those assets that are not otherwise covered as explicit knowledge assets. The differentiating factor is its relationship to business processes and operations (Camarinha-Matos & Afsarmanesh, 2006; Curtis et al., 1992; Mendling et al., 2010). The primary differentiating factor for procedural knowledge object classes is the type of business process or operation (Table 6.3). The secondary and tertiary subclasses describe the type of task.

TABLE 6.3 Procedural Knowledge Object Classes

Class	Description	Examples
Process	A defined business operation that generates products and services and represents a business capability. The process will represent a spectrum from heavily scripted, routinized, and controlled to creative, unpredictable, and variant. Any process that is assigned to a Person or an Agent should be included in this object class.	• Assembly line production process for generating plastic bottles • Software engineering process that supports construction project management • An agricultural process that involves the planting, harvesting, and packaging of soybeans • The chemical discovery process for developing a new agent to address the dangerous class of pollutants

If we accept this explanation, there is only one primary object class for procedural knowledge – the process. And there is only a single second object class – the task. Depending on the complexity of the task or its variability, there may be a tertiary subclass – step. The challenge of determining whether procedures manuals, audio recordings of process team after-action review meetings, or an oral history interview with a process expert are explicit or procedural knowledge is easier to resolve when we define the object class in this way. These examples would be mapped to explicit knowledge object models but linked to the Process Object Models as Object Class links. Additionally, we would expect to have a more extensive list of link categories to ensure that all of the Human Capital, Explicit Capital, and Cultural Capital assets could be easily discovered from the process, task, and step object models.

Procedural Knowledge Secondary and Tertiary Object Classes for procedural knowledge would focus progressively on the tasks that comprise a process, and the steps that comprise a task. We have types of tasks, and not all tasks will have intentional or defined actions. The value of identifying and modeling tasks and steps is that tasks are often replicated or reused across administrative units and processes. There may be little opportunity to access these knowledge assets outside of the process, which can lead to an unnecessary hoarding or hiding of task-level knowledge. Calling out subclass models for tasks and steps provides a significant step forward for procedural knowledge discovery, access, and consumption across an organization. It may also provide an opportunity for those who perform the tasks to see their work beyond the organization's boundaries.

Procedural Knowledge Object Class Attributes, Specifications, and Behaviors include any attributes needed to identify and distinguish the process (e.g., name, dates, physical characteristics or packages, encoding such as language), attributes that are essential to access (e.g., authentication and provenance descriptors, security credentials, and access privileges). Additionally, the attribute would include any essential categorizations that help us to understand the criticality of the process to the business (e.g., its associated business capability or function), the nature of the process (e.g., type of process, type or level of effort, business criticality), or description of the process that is important to discovery. The subobject classes would have additional attributes that pertain to the type and nature of the task and the step. The challenge in developing these subclass models is to ensure that the attributes have been normalized, e.g., they are not repeated or redundant across classes. For example, a process may be comprised of several task subclasses which are different in their nature and results. The characterization of the process, the task, and the step should be logical and consistent across the instantiations of the model.

Of all the knowledge object classes, procedural knowledge models may have the most productive set of links. From process models we expect to link to other knowledge assets including (1) Products and Services generated; (2) Process Designs and Specifications; (3) Process Demonstrations; (4) Process Explanations; (5) Process Errors, Faults, and Mistakes; (6) Process Applications, Tools, and Ingredients; (7) process training resources; (8) patents; (9) associated job classifications; and (10) associated automated Agents.

The cultural knowledge object model

We encounter many of the same challenges for cultural knowledge object models as for procedural knowledge object models. When is a cultural performance an explicit knowledge asset, and when is it a cultural knowledge asset? Our challenge is made more complicated by the general use of the word, culture, to represent any kind of social or celebratory event (Orellana et al., 2010). The solution to this challenge is to refer back to the basic definitions of cultural elements – those assumptions and beliefs, values and behaviors, and artifacts that represent what the organization, units, and individuals hold to be most important. Working from this definition, we have three object classes for culture – the culture of the organization, the culture of the group or unit, and the culture of the individual. These object models have comparable secondary subclasses that deconstruct these cultural assets into their essential assumptions and beliefs, values and behaviors, and artifacts (Table 6.4).

TABLE 6.4 Cultural Knowledge Object Classes

Class	Description	Examples
Organizational Culture Profile	This profile describes the espoused culture of the organization and the actual or practiced cultures of leaders. This profile changes with changes in people, particularly leadership.	• Culture profile of GM in the 1950s • Cultural profile of GM in the 1970s • Cultural profile of Harvard in 1932 • Cultural profile of Harvard in 2020 • Cultural profile of World Bank in the 1970s under McNamara • Cultural profile of World Bank in the 2000s under Wolfensohn
Group Culture Profile	The Group Culture describes the group's actual culture and all the factors that shape it, as well as the practiced culture of the group members. This cultural profile is more complicated than the Organizational Culture because it blends elements from an organization and its interpretation by groups and individuals.	• Cultural profile of the human resources unit • Cultural profile of the sales and marketing group • Cultural profile of the budget and financial management group • Cultural profile of a production unit in field operation • Cultural profile of the engineering group • Cultural profile of the external communications team
Individual Culture Profile	The Individual Culture Profile describes the cultures of individuals and the factors that shape them. As individuals move around or out of the organization, this profile helps us to understand how they shape the group culture.	• Cultural profile of the group manager • Cultural profile of a subject matter expert • Cultural profile of the unit secretary or executive assistant • Cultural profile of a corporate trainer • Cultural profile of a financial analyst

Cultural Knowledge Secondary and Tertiary Object Classes represent the elements of culture as defined by professionals and practitioners, including (1) assumptions and beliefs; (2) values and behaviors; and (3) artifacts. Academicians have explored the characterization of these elements of culture, but they continue to evolve on a practical level. Tertiary object classes may emerge with the modeling of cultural profiles. They may take the form of assumptions and beliefs, types of values and behaviors, and artifacts. At this point, though, we recommend focusing on the primary and secondary object class models.

As for other types of knowledge assets, Cultural Object Class Attributes, Specifications, and Behaviors focus on those needed to support identity and distinction of the profile (e.g., who it is a profile of, the date range of the profile, the form the profile takes – a model or a text description), the business value and useful life of the profile, the attributes that testify to its authenticity and provenance, its security and access parameters, and the factors described in the profile.

Several categories of links and relationships are essential to Cultural Object Classes, including (1) links to the people the profiles describe; (2) links to the groups the profiles describe; and (3) links to any audio, visual, and artifacts – any explicit assets – that illustrate or represent that culture.

The relational knowledge object model

There is one primary object class for relational capital – the network or community. This object class describes the community as a whole and defines nodes, links, and messages as secondary object classes (Table 6.5). The advantage of defining object class models for communities and networks is that there is a rich literature on network models and network metrics. This means that stakeholders will more readily adopt our proposed network object classes. One secondary class that is not typically modeled in network research is the message content and the knowledge characterization of the network nodes. We add these to our knowledge architecture framework.

TABLE 6.5 Relational Knowledge Object Classes

Object Class	Description	Examples
Network	Describes the network, community, group, unit, as a whole entity, and the knowledge generated that has business value for the organization	• A community of practicing technicians who meet monthly to share experiences • Ski club of members across the organization • Cross-functional communities of interest focused on community outreach • Cross-organization networks of trainers • Project team assembled to carry out a defined mission • Hastily formed disaster management teams

Relational Capital Secondary Object Classes include (1) network nodes; (2) network links; and (3) network messages and communications. Network nodes are any source or target from which a message originates or to which it is received. Nodes can refer to People, Agents, or any form of explicit knowledge object. Network links are the connections or relationships established between two nodes, usually through some form of communication or connection. Messages are the essential knowledge that is packaged and exchanged between the source and the target. All three of these secondary object classes describe vital knowledge assets. Consider the extent of the literature on knowledge sharing, transference, exchange, hoarding, and translation. This literature pertains directly to this set of knowledge object classes. The challenge is that the literature is rarely tied to networks or community models.

Relational Capital Object Class Attributes, Specifications, and Behaviors are not unlike those described for the other types of object models and classes. These attributes are essential to identifying and distinguishing networks as knowledge assets, defining their business value and tracking their useful business life span, determining the access and security restrictions that need to be observed for a network, and any descriptors that help us to discover and access the inherent knowledge assets in the network.

The most common relationships and links to other knowledge assets for Relational Capital Object Classes include links to the People and Agents who take the role of a node, or any explicit knowledge object that serves as a node. Messages will be modeled as subclasses in a network but may also relate to any other kind of knowledge asset through direct or indirect references. The relationships modeled between nodes are essential reference points for the relational capital subclass of individuals.

What does an object modeler need to know when building out an object model? You need to be able to define (1) the object classes – categories of objects – that make up the model; (2) the attributes that define each object class; (3) the specifications and behaviors of those attributes; (4) the kinds of relationships that object might have to other objects (Figure 6.1).

Elements of a knowledge object model

Each knowledge object model will have multiple *object classes*. Object classes are the essential design of the object model. Object classes of knowledge objects represent the categories of knowledge. We define categories because they allow us to find common elements across knowledge assets and have the flexibility to reuse object elements and attributes across categories. For knowledge objects, we envision three classes: a primary knowledge class, a secondary knowledge class, and a tertiary class (Table 6.6). Our experience suggests a three-tier object class structure is sufficient to cover all kinds of knowledge assets.

It is common practice for an object class to be defined by a few essential *variables* to ensure they can be used by other human and machine applications. These

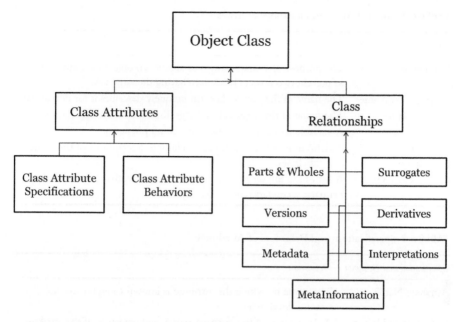

FIGURE 6.1 Elements of a Formal Object Model

TABLE 6.6 Knowledge Object Model Classes

Object class	Definition
Primary Knowledge Object Class	The object model that describes the whole object.
Secondary Knowledge Object Class	The object models that describe the highest level 'parts' of the object. Secondary object classes represent sub-assets that can stand on their own.
Tertiary Knowledge Object Class	The object models that describe the lowest level of deconstruction of the object. Tertiary object classes are parts of secondary object classes.

variables include a unique key, a display name, a short name, an object class name, an object class description, and a reference to the object class set. Table 6.7 provides a brief description of what we mean by each variable.

Additionally, each object class will have a set of *inherent attributes*. These attributes define the knowledge asset. We need to know what the attributes are, their specifications, and their behaviors (Table 6.8). Attributes will be appropriate and unique for each object class. These attributes are described later in this chapter. The object modeler needs to know how these attributes are likely to be defined and how they are to behave in their organization. This is a design effort in each

TABLE 6.7 Essential Attributes for Object Classes

Variable	Description
Unique Key	The purpose of a unique key is to identify an object class uniquely and to prevent two object classes from having the same key.
Object Class Name	The name of the object class that uniquely describes it for developers.
Display Name	The name of the object class that is displayed in the application.
Short Name	A variable name may be used for coding purposes.
Object Class Description	A definition of the object class including descriptions of the classes and subclasses.
Object Class Set	A list of the full set of object types assigned to that class, including primary, secondary, and tertiary classes.

TABLE 6.8 Specifications and Behaviors of Attributes

Specification and Behavior	Definition
Attribute Name	The name by which the attribute is known to architects and systems developers.
Definition and Purpose	A description of the purpose, scope, and coverage of the attribute.
Management Obligation	Whether the attribute is required in an application, and what exceptions are possible.
Recordkeeping Obligation	Whether the attribute is required from a recordkeeping perspective (e.g., officially required by records managers)
Repeatable	Determines whether there can be more than one instance of the attribute for any object model, or if only one is permitted.
Attribute Length	The maximum number of characters allowed in the attribute.
Variable Type	The type of values the attribute can accept, i.e., text, date, numbers, etc.
Entry Value	Defines how data can be added to the attribute, i.e., from a controlled drop-down list, a controlled scrolled or popup list, free text, authorized terms, etc.
Entry State	Defines whether the field is empty upon access or has a linked source.
Attribute Syntax	Defines the representation of the attribute's values, i.e., string, date, unique ID format, ISBN format, Social Security number format, etc.
Status	Defines whether the attribute is in active use, is inactive, or historical.
Indexed	Defines whether the attribute values are added to an index, and which index.
Default Value	Defines a default value that must be overridden or changed.
Conversion and Capture	The source of the value, i.e., new creation, copy from a source system, machine-generated, etc.
Authoritative Reference Source	The controlling reference source that defines the allowable values for the attribute.
Alternative Reference Source	The secondary controlling reference source if the first is not available to the asset creator.
Subattribute Maps	Links to any related subfields.
Business Stewards	The business steward responsible for governance and management decisions about the attribute.

organization because it means synthesizing and harmonizing across sources currently constructed and those not yet managed.

The final element of the object model is *essential relationships and links* for the knowledge asset. This is an element of the object model commonly found in metadata records, in metainformation records, or by dynamic links. The challenge with this approach is that while these objects may be persistent, they are vulnerable to disconnection from the source assets. If we define classes of links into the object model, it gives us the capability to record them in the object model for the knowledge asset. A baseline categorization of essential links might include links to (1) versions and editions; (2) abstracts and surrogates; (3) derivative assets; (4) interpreted assets; and (5) translated assets.

Knowledge object models – the design environment

In Chapter 4, we laid out the dimensions of the design environment. We walk through design factors by walking through those dimensions in the form of questions and answers.

What triggers the need for this functional architecture? We need knowledge object models: (1) to cover any new kind of knowledge asset or any variations that have business value; (2) to map older formats and packages to ensure they are accessible and consumable through new applications and channels; (3) whenever machines or business operations need to consume knowledge assets directly and yet their physical format or package makes this difficult; (4) when we have a risk of loss of knowledge and must take action to migrate or conserve knowledge objects from earlier formats or packages; (5) when we have conflicting knowledge assets, and we need to compare the two at an atomic level; and (6) when we have redundant knowledge, and it is necessary to combine assets.

What do we need to think about when we're designing? What are the factors that will influence how we develop knowledge object models? From practical experience, we know that it is easier to model a knowledge asset that has a tangible rather than an intangible or tacit form. We understand that the sources we need to draw from may be varied and diverse. We know that sources may be difficult or cumbersome to find and access, depending on their format, packaging, and rarity. We want to give priority to developing models of business-critical knowledge assets and focus secondarily on those with lesser or diminishing value. Those business assets whose formats are at risk of deterioration or degradation should have practical models. We also need to consider the language and form of the models to ensure they are manageable and widely accessible.

What is the impact or outcome of having this functional architecture in place? If we have a knowledge object model in place for our knowledge assets, we have the capability – regardless of the original format, structure, or packaging – to make that asset available, accessible, and consumable in the future. It means that we can access the kernel of that knowledge without repeatedly transforming it into every new format or channel. It means that we can manage our knowledge assets without creating large landfills of copies and without destroying or damaging the original asset. It means a more cost-efficient and cost-effective knowledge management environment. It means a lower risk that knowledge with business value will unintentionally be lost or destroyed.

What sources do we have to leverage? The sources depend on the type of knowledge asset we're modeling. The primary source for developing human capital object models are people, directories, social profiles, financial profiles, CVs and resumes, references and recommendations, personnel, and human resource records. The primary source for explicit knowledge is the rich world of formal and packaged information; any existing models developed over time in an operational context, and data models. The primary sources for structural knowledge are groups, teams, operational staff, managers, any representations of how things are done regardless of format, discoveries of errors, mistakes or faults, quality control reports, process evaluations, customer or consumer feedback, and so on. The primary sources of cultural knowledge include formal and informal cultural profiles of individuals, business units, and organizations. These formal and organizational self-assessments describe the factors that influence cultures at all levels. The primary sources for network knowledge include professional networks, business groups, internal communication patterns, external and internal social networking platforms, email systems, telephone logs, organizational clubs, and staff activities.

What are the outputs and products of this architecture? Knowledge object models intend to apply them to all of the organization's knowledge assets as needed to ensure continued availability, accessibility, and consumability. The intent is to ensure that these representations are application, technology, and distribution-channel agnostic. Knowledge object models must be sufficiently flexible to be managed by practitioners and non-professionals. They must be extensible to allow us to see the full spectrum of value, assessment, and use of the knowledge assets.

Designing knowledge object modeling activities and tasks

What activities and tasks does this functional architecture need to support? As a baseline, we identified five high-level activities that should be supported. These may serve as a framework for further design work. Each activity is briefly described in terms of essential inputs, outputs, roles and responsibilities, resources including applications and technologies, and tasks. The five activities for knowledge object modeling include:

- Activity 1. Deconstruct or reverse engineer the knowledge asset
- Activity 2. Construct the object model
- Activity 3. Desk check the object model against instances
- Activity 4. Associate existing knowledge assets to object models
- Activity 5. Begin the object model transformation process

Activity 1. Deconstruct or reverse engineer the knowledge asset

How do we do this? The first step in developing an object model is understanding the nature of the thing we're trying to model. In this case, we're focusing on different types of knowledge assets. The most effective way to approach this is to deconstruct the asset. Deconstruction is a way of understanding how something was created – to break it down into smaller parts, to look at the initial design of the asset, and to understand how it was built out (Figure 6.2). We can also understand this activity as reverse engineering – a simulated reproduction or reconstruction of another designer or engineer's product following a detailed examination of its construction or composition. This activity involves discovery across the organization, communication with various units and practitioners, and a search for good practice examples across professional domains. Deconstruction involves mentally taking the object apart piece by piece. We have to learn to see the asset from a new perspective.

What are the inputs? Deconstruction and reverse engineering are effective where we have good practice products or examples of leveraging. As we look across our five kinds of knowledge assets, we understand that we have models for some assets but not for others. So our first task in deconstructing is to look for as good an example as you can find. Remember, the model has to work for your organization, and your context – today and going forward.

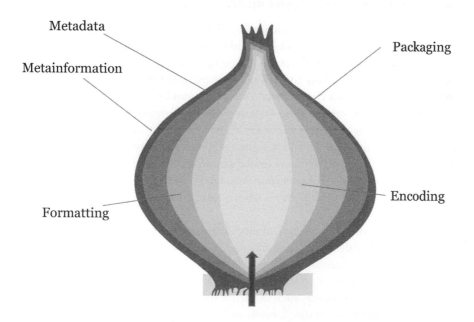

Knowledge Kernel

FIGURE 6.2 Learning to See Layers of the Knowledge Asset

In most cases, you'll want to find a good example that will serve as a baseline. You'll need to look across the business to discover how other practices and applications are characterizing and managing this kind of asset. You'll need to be sure to consider those practices because you want your model to be widely accepted and used widely across the organization. In other cases, you may have to come up with a baseline model and integrate all the practices and applications you find – simply because there isn't a common baseline to work from. One way to be sure your design will serve as a baseline is to make sure you focus on the essential nature of the asset – not the package, its metadata, or its spin-offs. While all of those factors will be recorded in the model as attributes or related objects, they will distract you from seeing the asset's core or the kernel.

What does this activity produce? This activity should produce the general conceptual outline of a model. You should have a good sense of whether you know enough to define object classes, their attributes, and the kinds of relationships you will need to support. At this point, you should have a good sense of who is going to be using these models and how they will be used. Who will be the primary user of the model? Who are the secondary users?

What resources does it use? This activity relies heavily on the architect's abilities to investigate, to communicate, and to analyze. These abilities will provide access to the sources you need to work with for deconstruction and reverse engineering.

Activity 2. Construct the object model

How do we do this? This is a design activity. We use what we have gathered in the construction exercise to design object models of our knowledge assets. We should not attempt this activity without having completed the deconstruction exercise. We first look at what we have to work with. Begin by defining the object classes for the model. Look at your best practice examples, consider the other examples from other business areas, other industries, and professional domains. If these examples do not have clearly defined categories of assets or object classes, develop object classes by working with a basic definition. Remember that an object class is a grouping or set of objects that have similar characteristics and behaviors. We expect to have multiple instances of assets in a class. Do not define an object class based on a single instance. You'll refine these classes as you work through all of the elements of the model.

Once you have a set of draft object classes, begin to add the attributes. In defining attributes, their specifications, and behaviors, you must look across all of the instances in the category. They may have multiple labels, different values, and sources. This is normal. For some attributes, you'll have to select one specification as the primary attribute, such as the creation date and format. You'll have to accommodate all the other date formats and ensure you either map them or have a method for conversion. For others – for example, creator name – you may need to exercise what librarians call authority control. There are many variations of every name, and there will be a need to select a single authoritative value. This requires

the power of names in a separate source. For other attributes – for example, country – there can be only one source and one format. However, there may be variants allowed for seeking and discovery, such as the ISO country code or a UN code. And for other attributes – such as subject or theme – you may define a single specification and behavior but allow values from an unlimited number of sources, all of which are mapped to a common source. Finally, we need to consider any inherent or embedded relationships. Most of the instances you'll be working with represent a particular business context. It is crucial to identify the context and make sure it is core to the asset rather than a kind of relationship. Is the asset part of a larger asset? Is it routinely broken into parts, or does it have multiple pieces?

What are the inputs? The inputs to this activity are what you collected in the first activity, and the working conceptual model you produced in the first step.

What outputs does it produce? This step should produce your first pass at a fully elaborated conceptual model. It will take several iterative steps to arrive at this model. The model should be good enough for the knowledge architecture to use in a rigorous desk check exercise against existing instances.

What resources does it use? This activity relies heavily on the knowledge architect's design abilities. The architect must be familiar with object modeling techniques, but designing a model that will be easily understood by all the intended consumers is paramount. This means understanding the format of the model that is most easily understood by the range of consumers. The resource that is essential to producing the model is some form of modeling software. While the architect may create hand-sketched concept models as he or she works through the process, a formal and cleaner example is needed to share with others. Try to leverage the organization's preferred or most commonly used modeling method, i.e., UML models, Entity-Relationship models, formal Data Object models, natural language models, and so on.

Activity 3. Desk check the object model against instances

How do we do this? This activity is a rigorous internal check of the draft object model we developed against all of the instances we collected, as well as verification against other examples that may not have been used to design the model. The knowledge architect should develop a set of critical questions to use to ensure objectivity and rigor. These questions might include:

- Does the instance fit well into the data class? Does it fit into only one data class, and is that class quickly and easily determined?
- Are all of the attributes in the example accommodated in some way in the model? If so, what kind of alignment do they require? Will you have to adjust the specifications or behaviors? What kind of treatment do we need to support to accommodate values?
- Are there other new support capabilities we need to have in place to support the mapping? How will we control all of the variant sources? Or will we

simply decide to acknowledge them and let the business practice adapt them as needed?

- Have we defined the kinds (i.e., classes) of relationships sufficiently to support what we see in the instances? Is the type of relationship clear and distinct, or is there more than one that might apply? If there is more than one, be sure to adjust the definition and class to ensure it is orthogonal (e.g., distinct) from other classes.

An essential task in this activity is to share your model with potential stakeholders to hear their feedback. Keep in mind that some of the examples you may have worked with may not reflect current practice. Realistically, we make changes to our working environment continuously, but we do not always take the time to document those changes. Encourage stakeholders to tell you what works, what doesn't work, or what will result in more work or a more complicated capture, preservation, or transformation process. Don't share the model only for the propose of gaining approval.

Finally, remember that these are working models – they will change in the future, and those changes need to be reviewed, approved, and published. This means that you need to ensure these models become part of your governance processes and are treated as critical business resources across the organization.

What are the inputs? The inputs for this activity are all of the instances collected for Activity 1, and any others we may discover through communications or extended discovery. As you work through the desk check and make adjustments, you may have other ideas of what to look for and where to look for instances. You need to make sure that you have a representative population to work from when developing your model.

What outputs does it produce? The product from this activity is a working model that you can hand to stakeholders. It is also a model that is formally published for anyone to work with across the organization.

What resources does it use? The resources that support this activity are the feedback and evaluation tools and governance tools. If these are not in common use, the knowledge architect should create some processes to use to support the process.

Activity 4. Associate existing knowledge assets to object models

How do we do this? The knowledge architect should make the first pass at determining which assets align with which models and object classes. This provides a systematic roadmap for working with business unit managers. In this activity, the knowledge architect needs to work with business units to ensure that the knowledge object models are associated with the unit's knowledge assets. This means ensuring that business unit managers are aware of the models and how to use them for mapping assets. Additionally, the unit managers need to be alerted to the need to inform the knowledge architect whenever changes are made to those assets that would affect the model.

What are the inputs? The primary input to this activity is the knowledge architect's knowledge of the types and uses of assets that align with each model and each object class. The mapping is the basis for communicating with the business unit managers. Another primary input is the knowledge architect's desk check of the model to the unit's knowledge assets. This is the basis of the conversation between the architect and the manager.

What outputs does it produce? The result of this activity is a well-prepared and well-informed business unit. Units will more cost-effectively and cost-efficiently manage transitions to the applications and technologies.

What resources does it use? This activity leverages the accumulated products, knowledge, and learning of all the stakeholders across all five activities.

Activity 5. Begin the object model transformation process

How do we do this? Since this task is a 'built' or an 'engineering' kind of activity, the knowledge architect's role is to work with the asset owners and developers to ensure that the mapping is used properly for distribution, transformation, or conservation. Ideally, the knowledge architect maintains a design focus rather than a 'build' focus. This does not mean that the architect should not engage in the mapping process, provide guidance or advice to the developers, or follow up and review the results. These are essential design tasks because they provide input to the next stage or iteration of design work.

What are the inputs? The primary input here is the knowledge assets at risk, the relevant knowledge object model, and the instructions or procedures developers would follow to undertake the mapping of assets to the models. The knowledge architect should expect to guide the mapping, particularly of attributes and relationships, to ensure an effective transformation.

What outputs does it produce? This activity generates a representation of the asset for use in a possible future and different environment, a preserved representation of the asset for potential, or a conserved and transformed asset depending on the fragility and risk of the original format and package.

What resources does it use? The primary resources are the knowledge architect, developers, the assets and models, and any applications and technologies that will support the mapping and transformation work.

Evolution of knowledge object model designs

To understand where we are today, we must understand how we got here. The challenge of architectural design is that we are rarely working with a blank canvas – there are almost always existing structures and practices in place. To design a way forward, we need to understand where we are today, what is disposable, what is adaptable, and what must be continued. Experience and a review of the literature suggest knowledge objects have evolved over five phases (Figure 6.3).

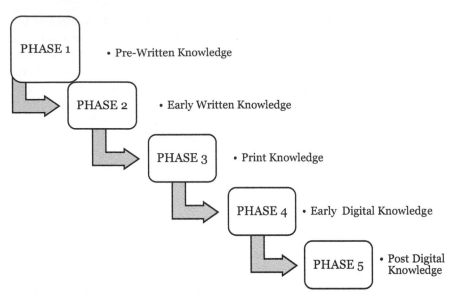

FIGURE 6.3 Evolution of Knowledge Object Modeling

While we have always had knowledge assets, we have not always had explicit object models. Though they were only recently explicit and object-oriented, we have always had mental and conceptual models of knowledge assets. How would we describe a model of knowledge in ancient times – before we had commonly accessible writing systems (Phase 1: pre-written knowledge)? What form did our earliest models of written knowledge assets take – of early manuscripts, letters, or early handwritten journals, diaries, and books (Phase 2: early written knowledge)? How did those models change when we had new distribution channels that reached a broader audience (Phase 3: print knowledge)? How did new technologies further change these models – early audio or video recordings, digitization of content (Phase 4: early technologies)? Finally, what will the next generation of representation mean for knowledge models (Phase 5: post-digital knowledge)? When is knowledge integrated into and embedded in other objects?

Over these five phases, several factors appear to have influenced how we model knowledge. As the intended consumer or audience has expanded, we have moved from informal and conceptual models to formal and physical models. When we expected to share a carpentry skill with our apprentices, the model may have taken the form of a demonstration, explanation, or correction. We imparted the model directly to the mentee. As we began to record knowledge to share it with others in the monastery, in our guild, or our scientific circles, we developed structures that served as models for others to follow. These models were suited to how we expected others to work with those assets. As the learned portion of the population began to grow, distribution channels grew, and there was a demand to produce greater quantities of knowledge. We standardized and routinized the models for publishing and communication. The richness of structures and forms grew exponentially with the introduction of new mass-market production and distribution capabilities. We moved rapidly from conceptual models and structures to build and customize models. This trend continued with advances in digitization and expanded to support greater creativity with increased producer competencies. With the proliferation of structures and forms, we moved away from models and design to construction and manufacturing. In the future, it will be impossible to stop the spread of designs and customizations. We must develop the capability to reverse engineer knowledge assets to knowledge models to maintain and to ensure the availability of assets in the future.

The earliest models focused on the modeling of systems such as databases. These early models focused on semantic or linguistic factors rather than entities (Chen, 1976). The development of object models and object modeling is relatively recent. The first entity-relationship model was developed in 1976 (P. Chen). These models were designed to overcome manual normalization challenges. Over the years, we have developed modeling methods for information objects (Integrated Definition Language 1 Extended (IDEF1X), the EXPRESS language, and the Unified Modeling Language (UML). Chen's entity-relationship modeling methods were extended in the 1980s (C. Rolland) and formed an essential element of the information engineering movement of the 1990s (Lee, 1999; Martin et al., 1991). The shift to client-server architecture and the uncoupling of data and information from applications helped us to see the need to apply modeling to the objects themselves. Today, the modeling of information and data objects is a common practice. There is greater availability of and access to modeling methods and languages. Object models are no longer the purview of systems or information engineers but are generated by a wide range of practitioners and professionals.

The average business or organization has, in its knowledge stocks today, assets that represent all five of the phases in our timeline. It is helpful to understand the different types of models in place to ensure we take an inclusive approach.

Knowledge object models in the knowledge architecture blueprint

This functional architecture is core to the knowledge architecture practice. As we will see in subsequent chapters, knowledge object models are the foundation on which all other functional architectures depend. We begin to see why it has been challenging to design and develop other sustainable, functional knowledge architectures when we become aware of this gap.

The knowledge architect must be integrated into the business operations and the enterprise architecture practices of the organization. We've talked about how we put the models into the hands of business managers. The last step is to determine where this work fits into the enterprise architecture framework. This will depend on the nature of the knowledge architecture practice and approach. If the practice sees a combined data and information layer and has data and information architects, it should be added to that practice area. This makes sense because this is the traditional place where object models live. The knowledge object models should also be made available to that practice if there is a people or a human resource architecture practice. If there is a knowledge architecture practice, the models form the core of this layer. Most architecture practices have an application architecture practice. Because applications leverage object models, they should be available to application architects. This alignment also helps us to understand who is involved in governance reviews and decisions.

Chapter review

After reading this chapter, you should be able to:

- describe the purpose and role of object models;
- understand where we might find object models across the organization;
- explain the elements of a knowledge object model;
- explain what we mean by knowledge object model classes;
- explain what we mean by knowledge object model attributes;
- describe the specification and behaviors of attributes;
- provide examples of knowledge object models for each type of knowledge capital.

References and recommended future readings

Austerberry, D. (2004). *Digital asset management.* Taylor & Francis.

Bachman, C. W. (1969). Data structure diagrams. *ACM SIGMIS Database: The DATABASE for Advances in Information Systems, 1*(2), 4–10.

Becker, J., Rosemann, M., & von Uthmann, C. (2000). Guidelines of business process modeling. In *Business process management* (pp. 30–49). Springer.

Berner, S. (2019). *Information modelling, A method for improving understanding and accuracy in your collaboration.* Vdf Zurich. ISBN: 978-3-7281-3943-6.

Briet, S. (1951). *Qu'est-ce que la documentation?* Documentaires Industrielles et Techniques.

Broch, G., Rambaugh, J., & Jacobs, I. (1991). The unified modeling language (UML): User guide. Addison-Wesley.

Buckland, M. K. (1991). Information as thing. *Journal of the American Society for Information Science, 42*(5), 351-360.

Buckland, M. (1998). What is a digital document? *Document Numérique, 2*(2). [1] Archived 2011–10–02 at the Wayback Machine, Paris.

Camarinha-Matos, L. M., & Afsarmanesh, H. (2006, September). A modeling framework for collaborative networked organizations. In *Working conference on virtual enterprises* (pp. 3–14). Springer.

Chen, P. (1976, March). The entity-relationship model – towards a unified view of data. *ACM Transactions on Database Systems, 1*(1), 9–36.

Curtis, B., Kellner, M. I., & Over, J. (1992). Process modeling. *Communications of the ACM, 35*(9), 75–90.

D. Appleton Company, Inc. (1985, December). *Integrated information support system: Information modeling manual, IDEF1 – Extended (IDEF1X).* ICAM Project Priority 6201,

Subcontract #013-078846, USAF Prime Contract #F33615-80-C-5155, Wright-Patterson Air Force Base.

Date, C. J. (2003). Edgar F. Codd: A tribute and personal memoir. *ACM SIGMOD Record, 32*(4), 4–13.

Flannagan, C. A., Lyle, J., Carlson, J., & Bedford, D. (2018). *Developing a guide to ensuring access to the publications and data of federally funded transportation research* (No. NCHRP Project 20-110). Transportation Research Board.

Frohmann, B. (2009). Revisiting "what is a document?" *Journal of Documentation, 65*(2), 291–303.

The history of conceptual modeling at uni-klu.ac.at.

Hjerppe, R. (1994). A framework for the description of generalized documents. *Advances in Knowledge Organization, 4*, 173–180.

Houser, L. (1986). Documents: The domain of library and information science. *Library and Information Science Research, 8*, 163–188.

ISO 10303–11:1994(E), *Industrial automation systems and integration*. Product Data Representation and Exchange – Part 11: The EXPRESS Language Reference Manual.

Larsen, P. S. (1999). Books and bytes: Preserving documents for posterity. *Journal of the American Society for Information Science, 50*(11), 1020–1027.

Lee, T. Y. (1999). *Information modeling from design to implementation*. National Institute of Standards and Technology.

Levy, D. M. (1994). Fixed or fluid? Document stability and new media. In *European conference on hypertext technology 1994 proceedings* (pp. 24–31). Association for Computing Machinery. Retrieved October 18, 2011, from http://citeseerx.ist.psu.edu/viewdoc/download?doi=10.1.1.119.8813&rep=rep1&type=pdf Archived 2013-06-06 at the Wayback Machine

Loomis, M. E., Shah, A. V., & Rumbaugh, J. E. (1987, June). An object modeling technique for conceptual design. In *European conference on object-oriented programming* (pp. 192–202). Springer.

Lund, N. W. (2008). Document theory. *Annual Review of Information Science and Technology, 43*, 399–432.

Martin, B. E., Pedersen, C. H., & Bedford-Roberts, J. (1991). An object-based taxonomy for distributed computing systems. *Computer, 24*(8), 17–27.

Mendling, J., Reijers, H. A., & van der Aalst, W. M. (2010). Seven process modeling guidelines (7PMG). *Information and Software Technology, 52*(2), 127–136.

Moss, K. (2012, April). The entity-relationship model. In *Proceedings of the 2012 IEEE global engineering education conference (EDUCON)* (pp. 1–6). IEEE.

Orellana, M. F., Reynolds, J., & Martínez, D. C. (2010). Cultural modeling: Building on cultural strengths as an alternative to remedial reading approaches. In *Handbook of reading disability research* (pp. 285–290). Routledge.

Ørom, A. (2007). The concept of information versus the concept of document. I: Document (re)turn. In R. Skare, N. W. Lund, & A. Vårheim (Eds.), *Contributions from a research field in transition* (pp. 53–72). Peter Lang.

Quatrani, T., & Chonoles, M. J. (1996). *Succeeding with the Booch and OMT methods: A practical approach*. Addison Wesley. ISBN: 978-0-8053-2279-8.

Repa, V. (2012). *Information modeling of organizations*. Bruckner Publishing. ISBN: 978-80-904661-3-5.

Riles, A. (Ed.). (2006). *Documents: Artifacts of modern knowledge*. University of Michigan Press.

Roberts, S. (2018). Introduction to information engineering (PDF). *Oxford Information Engineering*. Retrieved October 4, 2018, from http://www.robots.ox.ac.uk/~sjrob/Teaching/b4_intro_all.pdf.

Rumbaugh, J., Blaha, M., Premerlani, W., Eddy, F., & Lorensen, W. E. (1991). *Object-oriented modeling and design* (Vol. 199, No. 1). Prentice-Hall.

Rumbaugh, J., Blaha, M., Premerlani, W., Eddy, F., & Lorensen, W. (1994). *Object-oriented modeling and design*. Prentice Hall. ISBN: 0-13-629841-9.

Schamber, L. (1996). What is a document? Rethinking the concept in uneasy times. *Journal of the American Society for Information Science, 47,* 669–671.

Schenck, D., & Wilson, P. (1994). *Information modeling the express way.* Oxford University Press.

Signer, B. (2010, November). What is wrong with digital documents? A conceptual model for structural cross-media content composition and reuse. In *Proceedings of the 29th international conference on conceptual modeling (ER 2010).* http://www.beatsigner

Smith, B. (2012). How to do things with documents. *Rivista di Estetica, 50,* 179–198.

Smith, B. (2013). Document acts. In A. Konzelmann-Ziv & H. Bernhard Schmid (Eds.), *Institutions, emotions, and group agents. Contributions to social ontology* (Philosophical Studies Series). Springer.

Swift, A. (1997). A brief introduction to midi. www.doc.Ic.ac.uk/~nd/surprise_97/journal/vol1/aps2, 6

Totland, T. (1997). *5.2.7 Object modeling technique (OMT) Thesis,* Norwegian University of Science and Technology (NTNU), Trondheim.

Veryard, R. (1992). *Information modelling: Practical guidance.* Prentice Hall.

Wood, L., Le Hors, A., Apparao, V., Byrne, S., Champion, M., Isaacs, S., . . . Wilson, C. (1998). Document object model (dom) level 1 specification. *W3C Recommendation, 1.*

7

KNOWLEDGE STRUCTURES FOR ENCODING, FORMATTING, AND PACKAGING

Chapter summary

This chapter discusses what we mean by encoding structures, formats, and packages and explains why they are essential and how to discover them across your organization. The chapter lays out six activities that support the management of encoding, formatting, and packaging functional architectures. This chapter explains why it is essential to have a good understanding of encoding and decoding methods, historical and current formatting structures, and methods. The chapter explains why we should be aware of common forms of packaging for knowledge assets, future trends for formatting, and common forms of vulnerabilities and risks associated with each type of packaging. The chapter explains why it is essential to focus on knowledge assets and to be prepared to do object model mapping in times of rapid technological change.

Why we care about encoding, formatting, and packaging

In Chapter 6, we emphasized the importance of learning to see the knowledge asset – looking beyond its package and format. Having accomplished this conceptually to develop the models, we now take on the task of building the encoding, formatting, and packaging layers back into the models. We care about how an asset is encoded, formatted, and packaged because our knowledge stocks are complex. They include all encoding schemes, all formats, and all kinds of packages. We need to understand what these are and how they work through those knowledge stocks to prepare transformation strategies for all of our business-critical assets. What is packaging, and why is it important? How will packaging continue to change? How will evolving channels affect packaging? What kinds of tools do we need to have to open or unlock a package to get to the knowledge asset? How has the package affected or been affected by the format and the encoding scheme?

Knowledge architects should care about encoding, formatting, and packaging because they represent the 'built' environment. These are processes that are commonly left to engineers and system designers. They follow industry standards or common practices to ensure the package is suitable for delivery and distribution. But these practices may not always be the best choice for persistently accessing the knowledge asset. Knowledge architects can bring a design perspective to these processes.

Knowledge encoding, formatting, and packaging – design concepts

To develop this functional architecture, we must have a good understanding of encoding structures and methods, including historical and current formatting structures and methods, an awareness of future trends in formatting, common forms of packaging for knowledge assets, and common packaging vulnerabilities and risks.

In Chapter 6, we described a knowledge asset as a multilayered object. In this chapter, we begin to peel back those layers (Figure 7.1). If we look at these layers from the construction perspective, the first layer is the encoding layer – how we represent the essential knowledge. Encoding is not just for digital assets. Encoding for tacit knowledge means encoding knowledge in a person's brain, converting it into a language to share with another person, using a writing scheme to record it on paper, or using voice or visual tools to encode it as music, or portray it in a painting. The next layer we encounter is formatting – the appearance, layout or structure, or presentation. The format is essential to access and consumption. If we do not have the tools to read or decipher the format, we cannot access the knowledge. The outer layer is the packaging. The packaging is developed to support distribution and

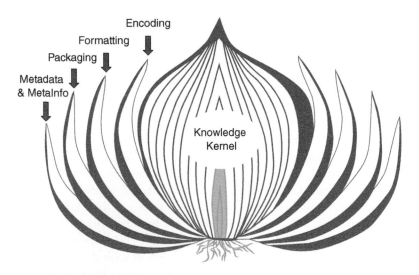

FIGURE 7.1 Peeling Back Layers of a Knowledge Asset

access – but over time, packaging and formatting have blended in some products. We need to understand each of these layers to ensure we can reverse engineer them in the future to ensure continued availability, accessibility, and consumability. And, we need to translate these three layers to all five of our high-level knowledge asset types. It is also important to remember that each of these three layers becomes an important attribute of each object class in our knowledge object model.

These three layers have blended and integrated over the centuries. There are strong dependencies among encoding types, the formats that embed those encoding schemes, and the packaging we choose to distribute those formats. Additionally, we'll also discover that the distribution channel, while not a part of the knowledge asset itself, will dictate encoding, formatting, and packaging. Although it seems logical to begin with the outer layers we can see – the package – it is more effective to start with encoding because it allows us to make some assumptions about historical choices. Let's begin with the design concepts for encoding and work our way through formatting and packaging.

What is encoding?

Encoding is the representation of content in a structure or scheme to make it accessible and readable, generally by people, machines, and applications (Alvestrand, 1998; Bradshaw & Anderson, 1982; Brandenburg, 1987; Bub et al., 1988; Elias & Perfetti, 1973; Ide, 1994; Jot et al., 1999; Li & Momoi, 2001; Llewellyn, 2013; Merrill et al., 1981; Mozaffari et al., 2005; Whistler et al., 2008; Wren-Lewis, 1983; Wu et al., 2014; Zölzer, 2008). Encoding tells us what we need to open the package. Encoding is defined as representing ideas or expressions in a scheme that can be presented to a consumer or stored for later consumption. In essence, any knowledge we sense and attempt to share, process, store, or later retrieve must be represented in a way that people – through the use of their senses – can transform into a way that our minds and bodies can understand. The process of breaking the information down into a form we can understand is the process of encoding. Encoding is essential for getting the knowledge into the memory system – human or machine – for preservation and later use. Decoding is the process of recalling this knowledge later. The encoding process begins with perception, which is the identification, organization, and interpretation of any sensory information to understand it within the context of a particular environment. (Figure 7.2).

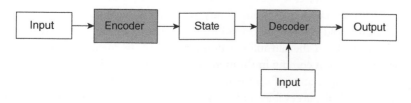

FIGURE 7.2 Encoding–Decoding Process

Encoding is generally a representation of a standard or set of expected–agreed upon fields for communicating or sharing knowledge. Knowledge architects understand that (1) they will need to translate their information into one or more schemes to share it with internal and external consumers, and (2) encoding schemes in and of themselves are not standard protocols. An encoding scheme should be adopted only to support information exchange. Encoding should not be confused with encryption, a process in which data is deliberately altered to conceal its content. Encryption can be done without changing the particular code that the content is in, and encoding can be done without deliberately concealing the content.

The terms encoding and decoding are often used about the processes of analog-to-digital conversion and digital-to-analog conversion. However, encoding is much broader than this. Considering the breadth of knowledge assets, we need to remember that encoding can apply to any form of knowledge, including ideas, conversations, actions and demonstrations, text, images, audio, video, multimedia, computer programs, or signals in sensors, telemetry, and control systems. There are four primary categories of encoding, including visual, acoustic, elaborative, and semantic. All four types are essential to knowledge assets.

Semantic encoding is the processing and encoding of sensory input that has a particular meaning or that can be applied to a context. We encode tacit knowledge to support our access and consumability, represent it so we can share with others, and preserve it in our memories. Encoding of memories in the brain can be optimized in a variety of ways, including mnemonics, chunking, and state-dependent learning. Memory encoding allows information to be converted into a construct that is stored in the brain indefinitely; once it is encoded, it can be recalled from either short- or long-term memory. Semantic encoding reflects the intended structure and meaning of knowledge. Echoic encoding – another form of semantic encoding – imitates a sound – is onomatopoeic. Mnemonic encoding is anything we create – often verbal forms – to help us remember knowledge. Semantic encoding applies to all types of human capital – tacit, skills and competencies, behaviors, and attitudes – as well as to cultural knowledge.

Elaborative encoding is the process of actively relating new information to knowledge that is already in memory. The elaborative encoding uses information that is previously known and compares it to the new information being experienced. The nature of a new memory becomes dependent as much on previous information as it does on the new information. Elaborative encoding makes new knowledge easier to retain – it makes it 'stick' to our tacit knowledge more effectively. It speaks directly to understanding and our ability to translate meaning. Memories are a combination of old and new information, so the nature of any particular memory depends as much on the old information already in our memories as it does on the new information coming in through our senses. Knowledge architects need to recognize the importance of elaborative encoding in making human and cultural knowledge available, accessible, and consumable. Treatment of both semantic and elaborative encoding is absent from the knowledge management literature.

Character encoding pertains to representing knowledge in written language and text. Character encoding is not new, though it is largely unrecognized and unacknowledged by both academics and businesses today. Texts are written by creating marks on some kind of medium. Written marks are a part of our writing systems they are used in and are bundled into written language. Our awareness of character encoding increased when the physical text became digital, and it became necessary for machines to read and understand the digitally encoded language. At that time, many organizations realized that their documents, websites, accounting system text, presentations, and social media texts were nothing more than images. They could be interpreted and understood only by humans who knew the language. Ideally, today text is created in UNICODE, which is the universal encoding system for characters across languages. The challenge for knowledge architects, though, is that the majority of the historical digital texts must be converted to continue to be 'available' to more than direct human consumption in the future. Conversion may be achieved by scanning an image with OCR software or creating a new digitally encoded version of the asset. Machines need semantic applications to understand and add structure to the encoded text. The consuming application needs to be able to decode and understand characters. And, it also needs to understand that character in the semantic or grammatical context of the language. This is another attribute we need to consider in our data class. If the asset travels, we need to tell the application that captures it what the encoding scheme is or whether it is merely an image.

Visual encoding is the process of encoding images and visual sensory information. The creation of mental pictures is one way that people use a visual encoding. Again, we need to consider how both humans and machines encode and decode visually represented knowledge assets. Visual encoding is the process of encoding images and visual sensory information. This means that people can convert the new information that they stored into mental pictures (Harrison and Semin 2009)

Acoustic encoding is the use of auditory stimuli or hearing to implant memories. Acoustic encoding is essential to knowledge architecture today when so many of our knowledge practices are shifting from text and physical communications to audio, speech, and digital communications. Consider all of the new ways we are recording procedural knowledge exchanges and experiments, how we're exchanging ideas over social media, and how we're using voice technologies to record our thoughts and ideas. Also, consider the audio recordings that are on fragile media and at risk of being lost forever. Consider the historical recordings of sermons by famous clergy or the historical audio recordings of famous orators. Consider audio recordings of interviews with your organization's founders or past executive officers. It is true people can transcribe them, but this is time-consuming and costly. Can your organization afford to take the time to transcribe these? Will they be used if they are available only on the current media? Also, consider how important it is to convert text to audio for those who cannot consume the text. In our digital worlds, we're also accustomed to consuming knowledge while we're doing something else – driving, exercising, shopping. We need to be able to take the text and encode it in audio form. How will these assets be decoded for access and consumption? Can we decode with a sufficient level of accuracy and quality to use the text for other purposes? For translation? For use by those who cannot read the text? Or those who cannot hear the audio? The machine process of the audio encoding and decoding process is as complex as the human encoding and decoding process.

What is the formatting?

The format of something is the way or order in which it is arranged and presented – the shape, size, and general makeup of a knowledge asset (Besser, 2001; Bhabatosh, 2011; Eden & Eshet-Alkalai, 2013; Enticknap, 2005; Faller, 2004; Fridrich et al., 2002; Larobina & Murino, 2014; Library of Congress, 2020; Miano, 1999; Solomon & Breckon, 2011; Wiggins et al., 2001). It is the general plan of organization, arrangement, or choice of material or a method of organizing knowledge. When we refer to formats, people most often think of digital formats represented as MIME extensions. While MIME extensions are essential, they are not the only types of formats we must consider when looking at the full range of our knowledge stocks. We must also consider other text, audio, and visual formats

In its simplest form, *text formatting* refers to the organization, plan, style, or structure of the text asset. Why is it essential for us to understand format? While people can read and interpret the meaning of these structures, machines cannot derive this same meaning unless we can characterize these structural elements and encode the meaning of these structures. This means identifying the structural elements and developing rules for machine interpretation. What are these elements? There are many types of textually rendered assets. In Chapter 6, we identified several object classes, but within each of these classes, there are several different formats. There may be some core formatting elements across the variations. For example, we might find title statements, sections, paragraphs, and footnotes in fiction and non-fiction books, serials, and series, technical memoranda, email messages, speeches, and social media posts. But, we do not find tables of contents, references, footnotes, or formulae in works of fiction, whereas we would find them in non-fiction books, or in messages, speeches, or social media.

The knowledge architect must also understand *audio formatting* because knowledge can be represented as an audio asset. Audio assets include any form of audio recording – sounds and music. Whenever we hear something, we are engaging around an audio asset. The challenge for discovering formatting is that it is often deeply embedded with the package. The knowledge architect needs to understand the audio file format and the audio coding format at the format level. The audio file format is a file format for storing digital audio data on a digital application. The audio data can be a raw bitstream, or embedded in the format of the package, or in a format defined by the application. The bit layout of the audio data is called the audio coding format. The format is directly related to the type of equipment or application on which it is used or played. It is essential to distinguish between the audio coding format, the package that holds the raw audio data, and an audio codec. A codec performs the encoding and decoding of the raw audio data while the encoded data is stored in a package file. Most audio file formats support only one type of audio coding data – the data created with an audio coder.

We must also understand format compression because we are concerned about being able to access the knowledge kernel – whether it is a recorded interview, speech or memorandum, or a cultural performance funded by a community organization. Compression is essential to all kinds of formats, but mainly to audio file formats because it is a way to manage file size. Compression choices are typically made by network and technology architects to conserve storage space. Their decisions, though, can impact the knowledge architect's ability to provide continuous availability to digital assets well into the future. Knowledge architects should understand the three types of compression, including (1) uncompressed audio (WAV, AIFF, AU or raw header-less PCM); (2) lossless compression files (FLAC, WavPack, TTA, ATRAC, ALAC, PGEG-4, MPEG-4ALS, MPEG-4DST, Windows Media Audio Lossless) and (3) lossy compression (i.e., Opus, MP3, Vorbis, Musepack, AAC, ATRAC, Windows Media Audio Lossy). Uncompressed audio is an audio file with no compression applied to it – the sound remains the same as when it was recorded. Lossless formats use compression algorithms that preserve audio data, so the audio is the same as the source. The lossy audio produces a lower-quality sound and has a smaller file size. Lossy compression produces a smaller file size and has a lower quality sound. It is called lossy because this approach to compression is not reversible – it is impossible to rebuild any elements that were stripped away. The encoding standards you choose will impact what is and is not available in the knowledge asset as you transform or map it for use in new applications.

Visual formatting

Visual formatting is how any visual form is arranged to appear, whether this is printed or displayed on a screen. The format depends heavily on the type and nature of the visual asset. Visually represented assets can include still images, moving images, paintings, textiles with text, photographs, visual representation of statistics, graphics, and so on. This type of formatting is less settled and standardized than either text or audio format. Practices and standards are still evolving. There are two dimensions of common practices for the visual representation of any digital images, including (1) vector vs. raster; and (2) high resolution vs. low resolution. Additionally, we need to be concerned about file size, since image files can have a wide range and some can be very large. The knowledge architect needs to understand the formats in which the organization's visual assets have or will be represented. First, let's talk about raster or vector images. Then we'll address the issue of resolution.

Raster images are created from a series of pixels, or individual blocks, to form an image. Raster files include JPEG, GIF, and PNG. Every photo you find online or in print is a raster image. Pixels have a defined proportion based on their resolution (high or low). When the pixels are stretched to fill space they were not originally intended to fit, they become distorted, resulting in blurry or unclear images. The pixel quality is affected by any resizing of a raster image. It changes the resolution. Raster files must be saved in the exact dimensions called for by the interpreting equipment or application. Vector images are constructed using proportional formulas rather than pixels. *They* are more flexible and include EPS, AI, and PDF. These are ideal for creating graphics that require frequent resizing. These might consist of logos and brand graphics. Typically, organizations would create and retain a master version of the essential knowledge asset. The change in size or dimensions will not degrade the resolution or quality of a vector image.

High or low resolution pertains to the number of dots per inch in the representation. Your choice of resolution will affect how well the image conveys the visual knowledge as your transform or map it to new applications in the future. The density of the pixels determines which application is appropriate for the image. DPI translates to dots per inch, and PPI translates to pixels per inch. DPI refers to the output resolution of a printer or an imagesetter – when an image is reproduced as a real physical object. PPI refers to the input resolution of a photograph or an image. In printing, DPI (dots per inch) refers to the output resolution of a printer or imagesetter, and PPI (pixels per inch) refers to the input resolution of a photograph or image.

File sizes can have a significant impact on accessibility and consumability, particularly for consumers in environments with low or unstable internet connections. The file size is dependent upon the number of pixels. Uploading and downloading of dense images can have significant performance consequences. Also, consider that images can be captured and stolen. Many organizations have multiple resolutions of an image, one for presentation to a consuming external audience and one for the internal audience. The external resolution may be a smaller file size and lower resolution to discourage theft and encourage permission acquisitions. Knowledge architects need to understand what compression and file size are optimal for your knowledge designs. If left to developers, they may make a choice that will have consequences for your architecture. It is also essential to set guidelines for how physical images will be converted to digital images, as you may be creating a new working master version of the image.

Moving images

Moving images have many of the same parameters, but moving image sequences are additional considerations as a visual presentation. These additional parameters include (1) image change rate; (2) moving image capture methods; and (3) aspect ratio.

There are several *image changes or frame rates* in common use today. The change rate affects how easily the motion plays on the screen. Moving images may be (1) film-based material, where the images have been captured by the camera 24 times per second, and (2) video-based material, where the image is captured 50 to 60 times a second. The video-based capture captures motion very well and looks fluid on the screen. The film–based capture is sufficient but does not represent fluid motion. There are capture rates in the middle as well.

There are two types of *capture methods* for moving images – mechanical and electronic shutters. These capture methods define the frame rate of the image sequence. Early television cameras did not have shutters. Shutters allow the image for a single frame to be integrated over a shorter period than the image change period.

Aspect ratio is the ratio of the width of a television or motion-picture image to its height. An aspect ratio of 4:3 can refer to an image (or screen) that is 4 feet wide and 3 feet tall, or one that is 12 feet wide and 9 feet tall. An easy way to think of this is the number of perforations on the earliest cellulose film strip. Each image was four perforations high. As the channels expanded to talking films and television broadcasts, aspect ratios increased to accommodate sound. A wide range of aspect ratio standards is in practice today. The variation is often aligned with industry and the common forms of capture and presentation at play in those industries. Knowledge architects should be aware of the full range of standards used to represent their moving images, particularly when a need arises to translate the images, preserve the moving image, or capture images from the whole set of frames. Knowledge architects must understand the current practices and be able to explain why those current practices are the best choices for the organization.

Physical images

Every organization has a stock of historical images. Some images of these may require preservation and conservation, depending on their business or cultural value. Physical images have significant accessibility and consumability limitations. They can be accessed and consumed only where they exist and by those who are permitted to view them. There may be constraints applied to how they can be handled. One strategy for increasing availability, accessibility, and consumability is to create a digital surrogate of the image. The knowledge architect must leverage the knowledge of image representation practices to ensure an effective choice is made for each image. For example, a photograph of an oil painting of the ten presidents of the organization may be sufficient for an organizational history website. It may not, though, be sufficient for insurance valuation purposes. A physical sculpture created by a prominent artist for display in the foyer may best be captured in a moving image for off-site access and use to ensure that all aspects of the sculpture are available. Sketches or print drawings may be amendable to scanning, and depending on the size of the original image may require one or more representations.

This type of design activity may be considered outside of a knowledge architect's roles and responsibilities. That kind of thinking may be acceptable if we only think of explicit knowledge represented as text. When we think of the full range of knowledge assets, these design activities fall in the knowledge architect's work. While these design activities are within the knowledge architect's work, the knowledge architect will not be a methodological expert. For this type of expertise, the knowledge architect should turn to the museum – particularly virtual museum – curators.

What is packaging?

Finally, we consider the outer layer – the package. The package is the container in which the asset is delivered to the consumer (Becker et al., 2011; Chen et al., 1994; Fang et al., 1993; Frear & Thomas, 2003; Hernandez & Rue, 2015; Sonsino, 1990; Twede, 2016). The package is the presentation of a person, product, or action in a particular way. The package is how we recognize something. The packaging is the activity of designing and producing the container or wrapper for the product. The wrapping material around a consumer item serves to contain, identify, describe, protect, display, promote, and otherwise make the product marketable and keep it clean. Packages also protect goods and assets. Food, electronics, clothes, furniture, and other consumer goods all come in packaging meant to protect them during transportation and storage. Different types of packaging solutions and materials suit the form, function, and marketing of each product. Packages are designed to support physical mobility and use – the mobility of the asset. Packaging has been designed to support distribution and controlled accessibility and indirect consumption. The packaging is what we need to make something available – to deliver it, to acquire it. The broader and less controlled the distribution, the greater the need to integrate metadata and metainformation into the package. Packaging also involves describing the product, including what it looks like, how to use it, what it contains, any cautions, who produced it, and so on.

The package is what we see, and in many cases, it tells us what the asset is, how to access it, and how to consume it. For some professionals and practitioners, – the knowledge asset is equivalent to the package or container. For example, a book is a physical package that contains some aspects of the author's knowledge, but we cannot say that it 'is' the author's knowledge. It is a small portion, a version, or an interpretation of the author's knowledge. Most books tell us enough about who the author is to begin to make a connection to the author. The physical paperback book is one package for distributing knowledge. The same knowledge may be distributed through a kindle digital version of the text, an audio recording, or full dramatic performance. In these cases, the source knowledge is consistent, but the packaging is significantly different. With each different package come different formats and encoding schemes. Similarly, an interview with a senior corporate executive may be captured on film, as an audio recording, and as a transcribed text translated to the other corporate languages. Every organization – and every knowledge architect – must be aware of the full range of packages applied to its knowledge stocks.

Encoding, packaging, and formatting human capital

What does it mean to encode, format, and package human capital? Given the nature of human capital, perhaps the questions we must ask are 'Who encodes, formats, and packages human capital?' and 'How can we best distribute the package?' Human capital is inherent to an individual. It is part of the basic and essential coding of that individual. Consider our earlier discussions of semantic, elaborative, audio, and visual encoding. Humans create and store their human capital using all of these methods. Extracting or learning from an individual is the same task as trying to open the package that is a text or an audio file, except that we don't have ready access to information about the format and the encoding scheme the individual uses. We need to understand how the individual has mentally encoded their tacit knowledge, experience, skills, and competencies so that we can 'decode it' for others to access. We need to understand how others learn, think, and encode knowledge to understand what the best encoding scheme is for their consumption. How do we discern these human encoding and decoding schemes (Figure 7.3)?

The first step is to understand how the individual learns. We rarely ask or document what a person's preferred learning style is. This is an essential 'people metadata attribute' for ensuring knowledge availability. Another encoding consideration is the individual's native language. Consider how crucial those guiding questions are when the individuals involved in the exchange do not share a common native language. We have another level of encoding and decoding to consider. Is there a language interpreter or translator also involved in the exercise? How does formatting relate to human capital? Does it describe how an individual mentally structures and organizes information? This is difficult to describe, so the way we discover an individual's preferred 'formatting scheme' is by asking questions to help them translate those formats into a structure that other humans understand. This means that any tacit knowledge transfer exercise should begin with a standard set of questions. Individuals should know what these questions are, how to use them, and how their responses will work for others. In other words, the questions may serve as a common formatting scheme that both the knowledge producer and consumer can work with to understand the embedded meaning.

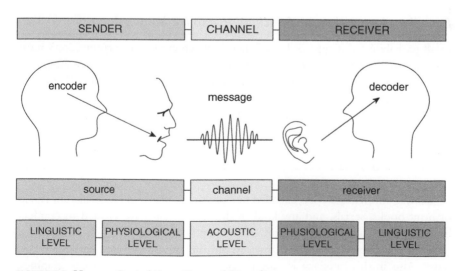

FIGURE 7.3 Human Capital Encoding and Decoding

Today, most of our profiling of people tends to focus on the physical package. Consider how we are using biometrics or DNA modeling. Knowledge architects are interested in this type of packaging only when we need to authenticate the individual. Authenticating the person as the package does not identify, distinguish, or authenticate their human capital. We need only to have enough understanding of an individual to ensure that we're working with the intended source. We need to be clear that we are not interested in all of an individual's knowledge – only that knowledge that has business value, and business value then and in that place in time. Knowledge architects are interested in unlocking and accessing what an individual knows (e.g., tacit knowledge) that has business value, what an individual can do (e.g., skills and competencies) that the business can leverage, and the attitudes and behaviors of that individual that contribute to the business value of the organization.

Our methods today are fragmented and scattered across disciplines. We create people profiles in organizational directories that provide some metadata about the individual. We have CVs and resumes that provide more extensive metadata and metainformation. We have learning profiles and development strategies that tell us about an individual's aspirations. We may be able to find all of the publications, documents, and communications an individual has authored if those other assets have trusted and consistent identification metadata. There is no intentional people or human capital reference model in organizations today that pulls all of this together and provides a holistic view of an individual. This is a starting point for knowledge architects – to create this core knowledge asset. It is in a people reference model that we can most effectively enable an individual to tell us about their preferred learning styles, the way they see things, and how they most effectively share what they know with others.

Encoding, formatting, and packaging explicit knowledge

In all probability, this type of knowledge asset represents the organization's most extensive stock of existing knowledge stocks. The stock consists of three categories of assets from encoding, formatting, and packaging practices, including (1) knowledge that is already physically encoded, formatted, and packaged according to some past practice; (2) knowledge that is already digitally encoded, formatted, and packaged according to some past practice; and (3) knowledge that is created according to intentionally defined practices that align with good knowledge architecture practices. Each of these stocks presents a unique set of challenges for knowledge architecture.

Existing knowledge assets encoded in a physical package include all your stocks of print books, serials, and any kind of document you have created to conduct business. This stock consists of all of your audio tapes and cassettes, any vinyl recordings, videotapes or video cassettes, old film stocks, or even early slide cassettes. Also in this category are any physical artifacts such as paintings, graphics, master trademarks and logos, physical models, sculptures, and so on. Each of these instances represents an earlier encoding practice, earlier formatting conventions, and packaging standards. The knowledge architect must understand enough about these original practices to ensure that there are strategies to reach back from the current and future application and technology environment to access the knowledge kernel. For this stock, the knowledge architect needs to have a working strategy for assessing and transforming these assets. Standard practice for unpackaging, unformatting, and decoding all of these physical assets will need to be standard practice to ensure that future transformations do not create new problems that cannot be reverse engineered. Which assets are destroyed or preserved is a discussion covered in Chapters 9 and 10.

We have been living and working in a digital environment for several decades now. Just because they are in a digital form does not mean access is safeguarded or ensured in the future. These assets are more complex to manage in a future environment because unless they are stored in an open or standards-based encoding scheme or format, we need the application to open them. These assets are already encoded. An additional challenge to be aware of is that you may be working with a knowledge asset that has already been re-encoded, re-formatted, and re-packaged. Consider all of the PDF documents that your organization has created to support records management requirements. Were these scanned to PDF using OCR (optical character recognition) software to give you a machine-readable document? Or, do you simply have a scanned image? If you simply have a scanned image and need to create a machine-readable version, you may not have the original print copy to work from. You may have to create a new print copy, and that print copy may not be of sufficiently good quality to generate a good OCR version. These were good practices in many organizations before they understood that the digital environment would continue to evolve. While these early practices may have supported a degree of availability, they do not support accessibility or consumability.

For this stock, the knowledge architect needs to understand all of the historical practices and applications used to create knowledge assets over the past 40 years. The challenge is that this information may be discovered only by looking at the file itself or its metadata. In addition to opening and decoding the asset, we need to add some form of markup coding or some rules for discovering the asset's embedded format. In some cases, the encoding and format will be deeply embedded in the package. The package may need to be re-engineered so that it is machine consumable and machine-readable. We need the application to translate and understand the format. And we need the application to decode the knowledge kernel. A knowledge architect needs a two-pronged strategy for these assets – one to open and decode the asset, and another to transform it into a future environment.

The third stock of knowledge assets is those assets that are digitally encoded to good practices defined by the knowledge architect. These assets will have the most effective transition to a future environment. To accomplish this, though, the knowledge architect needs to establish those good practice guidelines for all business units to follow. Consider how people are managing their digital assets every day. Consider how developers and engineers are making decisions that have organization-wide implications. All of these practices need to be aligned with good practices.

Encoding, formatting, and packaging procedural knowledge

We have the same three stocks of procedural knowledge assets as we did explicit knowledge assets. The challenge with past explicit knowledge practices is that the encoding, formatting, and packaging conform to the practices in place at a time in the past. The practice does not acknowledge the type of asset that is encoded, formatted, or packaged. Existing stocks of procedural knowledge will be found in existing repositories, network drives, dedicated servers, or in digital asset management systems. The challenge the knowledge architect faces with this stock is recognizing the type of embedded asset and ensuring that any transformation or future mapping accounts for or can expose the procedural knowledge elements. The encoding–decoding and packaging issues will be similar to those for other classes of assets (Figure 7.4). What is different, though, is the way the asset is formatted. The format of procedural knowledge should be capable of reflecting the structure, organization, and attributes of procedural knowledge object classes. This is a challenge because the activity requires some understanding of the organization's operations and processes over time.

Every organization has a wealth of digitally packaged procedural knowledge. Consider the design manuals that were designed as navigable websites to facilitate their use. Consider procedural details that were stored in Lotus Notes databases

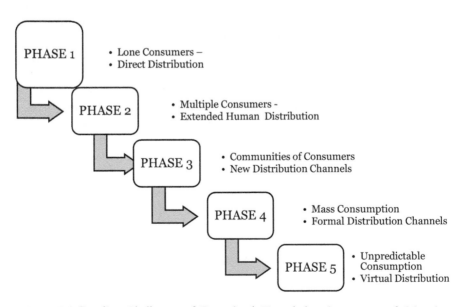

FIGURE 7.4 Peculiar Challenge of Procedural Knowledge Structure and Meaning Translation

or formatted as SGML files. And, consider the extensive use of links and references that have been contributed by process team members. Procedural capital focuses on the joint, contributed, and agreed-upon knowledge that has business value to the organization. Consider all of the procedural knowledge encoded into workflow applications, CAD applications and drawings, taped oral histories, video recordings of back-to-office experiences, best practices or lessons learned for a specific task, transcripts of critical incident analysis review meetings, processes, and formulas recorded in digital laboratory notebooks, expert narrations of process videos, e-science or e-engineering collaboratories, or knowledge books of expert knowledge. These are explicit, digitally packaged procedural assets that have all of the challenges of other kinds of assets. The challenge with this stock of assets is that it is easy to overlook. They are likely to be stored on dedicated servers, on department or unit drives, or even in personal collections. Knowledge architects must expand their knowledge of these operations-specific formats and conventions to ensure there is a strategy for managing them.

Perhaps the most extensive stock of procedural knowledge, though, are those assets that are neither physically nor digitally represented. For this stock, the knowledge architect should develop good practice guidelines for both print and digital encoding, formatting, and packaging. We should start with a template or a working strategy before we attempt to represent procedural knowledge. Encoding should follow the organization's standards for the type of asset – character, audio, visual, moving image, or physical. There should be a working template that architects can use to design the organization, structure, and meaning of the asset. Templates should support and align with procedural object classes and should reflect the attributes identified for those classes.

An additional complication is that procedural knowledge is highly dynamic. Teams continuously improve the way they do things; products have new features, make corrections, and change ingredients. This means that whatever package and format we choose should be easy to modify and update. The practices we adopt cannot be so rigid as to require a new representation each time an aspect of the process or the product changes.

Encoding, formatting, and packaging cultural knowledge

While cultural capital is challenging to represent, the opportunity is that we do not have large existing stocks of encoded, formatted, or packaged cultural knowledge assets. Where these do exist in the form of print reports or digital profiles, they should follow the organization's good practices for encoding, formatting, and packaging. It may be the case that the organization has physical and digital stocks of cultural artifacts that have or might be represented as knowledge assets. For these instances, the knowledge architect should consider those factors that are important to encoding, formatting, and packaging other types of physical assets. Formatting, in particular, should reflect the object classes and attributes for cultural knowledge.

Encoding, formatting, and packaging relational knowledge

What does it mean to encode, format, and package relational and network capital? From Chapter 6, we have a working model of the components of a network that are important to encode, format, and package. We're encoding two elements for this model – what we need to know about the business value of the network and the business value of the individual who engages with the network. Again, we're not interested in all networks, just those that have business value. We need to pay attention to and encode networks that connect people within the organization and help to build cross-team or cross-unit relationships. We need to know about networks that help individuals to construct human or structural capital. Does working in a maker space with other people to invent new ideas and methods have value to the team? It might. Does participating in a community network add to the organization's business reputation in the community? It might. We also need to encode how the individual engages with the network to ensure there is business value.

What does it mean to format network capital? Formatting network capital is an essential consideration. In addition to serving as a representation of the knowledge, it is also a connection point for individuals who may wish to join the network. The format should consider openness and availability – and should align with and be integrated with whatever general communication channels the organization uses.

What does it mean to package network capital? As in other cases, here we're talking about filling in the product – building out the profile. Individuals with business knowledge and roles should be responsible for packaging the network profiles with individual input. Individuals should be responsible for packaging their roles in the networks. We also note that these roles should be linked to the human capital 'packages.'

Encoding, formatting, and packaging design environments

What do we need to think about when designing the functional architecture? The major challenge we face in designing this functional architecture is the pace of change and development of these methods, the cost of keeping up with the change, and the risk of loss and harm due to not being able to provide continued availability. While it is critical for us to focus on the knowledge kernel – the essence of the knowledge asset – we must also understand other layers and learn how to interpret and work with them. Consider the result if we threw away the package that contained instructions (e.g., metainformation), or lost the container label that told us what it was (e.g., metadata), or what tool or application to use to read, play, or consume it (e.g., format)? All of these layers are essential to the continued availability of the asset. Several factors influence how we design this functional architecture. We need to consider the level of awareness of the importance of these layers to the long-term availability, accessibility, and consumption of business-critical knowledge assets. In most organizations, these decisions are given only passing consideration – the knowledge architect should consider preparing guidance and training materials to improve the organization's choices.

What triggers a need to encode, format, or package? We need to make encoding, formatting, and packaging choices when:

- *a new knowledge asset with business value* is created;
- existing objects that have business value are at risk of being lost or cannot be accessed by those who need them;
- there is a need to project forward to protect knowledge assets at risk;
- to bring some older objects into the current knowledge architecture;
- there is a need to create new knowledge objects from existing objects – as recombinations, in other versions, or for different audiences;
- when consumption is labor-intensive, and there is a need for a more efficient representation for business purposes;
- the tools and applications used to consume the original asset are obsolete, and there is a need to preserve to a new platform;
- the skills and competencies needed to support the tools and technologies have disappeared, and the people who can operate the machinery are no longer available;
- when the knowledge to decode the original asset is no longer available because instructions were not written, procedural knowledge was never passed on, or the supplies needed to operate the machines or keep them running (e.g., ink, chemicals, film, or microfilm) are no longer produced.

What is the impact of encoding, formatting, and packaging? Having a supporting functional architecture ensures that the organization can:

- formulate actionable policies to safeguard these types of knowledge;
- actively manage the full suite of their knowledge capital;
- access and consume a broader range of knowledge to self-invest and to grow;
- leverage reliable and accessible knowledge because there are fewer and better-quality reproductions, surrogates, and preserved representations;
- new objects make more consistent, effective, and sustainable choices during the development process;
- access historical physical assets whose consumption was severely restricted;
- support more effective mobility of knowledge assets and more informed consumption;
- continue to make knowledge assets available regardless of the changes in distribution channels.

What are the sources we need for encoding, formatting, and packaging? We need a basic knowledge of encoding and decoding practices, formats and their factors, and awareness of packages and the additional metadata and metainformation they may contain. Essentially, the knowledge architect should have a basic familiarity with standard practices, and with the organization's historical choices for different kinds of assets. The architect also should understand how these practices pertain to different types of knowledge assets, including all of the instances we used to test our object classes for object models. These practices will likely vary within and across object classes. However, understanding how they align will help to develop guidelines for good design practices for object classes.

What is the intended use of encoding, formatting, and packaging? By designing a functional architecture, we increase the probability that our physical and digital representations of knowledge assets will be accurate, accessible, and consumable by a variety of consumers. We also increase the likelihood that the design choices we make will be suitable for the asset and to its intended consumption.

Design activities and tasks for encoding, formatting, and packaging

Five essential activities support this aspect of the architecture design process:

1. define current state formatting practices for knowledge assets – organize by types of knowledge capital and then create an inventory of practices;
2. define preferred future encoding, formatting, and packaging practices;
3. identify knowledge stocks at risk for availability, accessibility, and consumability;
4. ensure there is a business contingency plan in place for supporting any at-risk knowledge assets;
5. ensure there are good training and guidance for future encoding, formatting, and packaging of knowledge assets.

Activity 1. Define current state encoding, formatting and packaging practices for knowledge assets – organize by types of knowledge capital and then create an inventory of practices

How do we do this? A two-front strategy will help you define the organization's current and historical practices. First, focus on the largest body of assets – those that have been explicitly encoded, formatted, and packaged. To find these, begin with a review of those repositories and sources that hold the most significant number of assets. Include in this inventory your enterprise applications, web content management systems, document and archives management systems, and library catalogs and collections. Developers and administrators should be able to give you a list of all of the MIME types that are used in the source system. These repositories will not be comprehensive, though, so you'll need to look at other common sources for storing assets such as network drives, unit servers, and personal collections. The goal of this exercise is to compile a working list of formats. Once you have this list, consult with application and technology architects to ensure you haven't missed any formats. Also, learn from them how these packages have handled both formatting and encoding over the years. With a working knowledge of these stocks, you have a foundation for identifying practical strategies for advising custodians and developers on how to map these resources in the future.

What are the inputs? Three necessary inputs are: (1) the working inventory; (2) the knowledge object models, developed in Chapter 6; and (3) the knowledge architect's knowledge of encoding, formatting, and packaging practices – and his or her knowledge of good practices. The knowledge architect must maintain awareness of encoding, formatting, and packaging practices sufficient to support design. That knowledge need not be as in-depth, though, like that of engineers and developers.

What outputs does it produce? This activity generates summaries of current and past practices, lists of challenges the organization may face when trying to access or use assets in these packages, and a set of guidelines for anyone who is tasked to transition or transform these assets.

What resources does it use? This activity relies on access to sources and knowledge of sources. To develop a good enough understanding of past practices, the knowledge architect may need to examine specific examples.

Activity 2. Define preferred future encoding, formatting, and packaging practices

How do we do this? This activity is challenging because we don't know what future practices might come. The most effective approach may be to begin by developing a set of best practice guidelines for choosing an encoding scheme, a format, and a package. As practice emerges, the guidelines should be supplemented with what is learned. The best practice guidelines should be designed to align with the knowledge object classes.

What are the inputs? The inputs for this task are the working knowledge object models, knowledge of current applications, and good practices such as those published by the Library of Congress and other recognized authorities. Another critical input is any existing guidelines or instructions or policies that may reflect past practices. These guidelines and policies should be updated to reflect preferred practices.

What outputs does it produce? This activity produces two outputs – a set of preferred practice guidelines for others to use in managing their assets, and increased awareness of practitioners and managers on preferred practices.

What resources does it use? Resources include the same as those used in the first two activities.

Activity 3. Identify knowledge stocks at risk for availability, accessibility, and consumability

How do we do this? Working with the inventory of past and current practices, the knowledge architect should consult with business managers to identify business-critical knowledge assets in packages, formats, or encoding schemes that present a risk to future availability, access, and consumption. The list should be prioritized by the value of assets to the organization.

What are the inputs? In addition to the working inventory, an essential input to this activity is the guidance of business managers.

What outputs does it produce? This activity generates a prioritized list of assets at risk by the business area.

What resources does it use? The primary resources for this activity are the knowledge of the business managers of the value of assets and the knowledge architect's knowledge of types and degrees of risk.

Activity 4. Ensure there is a business contingency plan in place for supporting any at-risk knowledge assets

How do we do this? The knowledge architect should prepare a long- and short-term plan to ensure these assets are safeguarded from risk. The plan should define timelines, levels of effort, budgets, and applications needed to support the plan. The plan should be consistent with good practice guidelines but should be designed for business managers to take responsibility for implementation.

What are the inputs? This activity continues to leverage the good practice guidelines developed earlier, the working inventory, and the business managers' input as to the business value of individual assets.

What outputs does it produce? This activity generates practical business contingency plans for business-critical knowledge assets that are at risk from availability, accessibility, and consumption.

What resources does it use? In addition to the resources used for the previous three activities, the knowledge architect should leverage the organization's strategy for business contingency planning.

Activity 5. Ensure there are good training and guidance for future encoding, formatting, and packaging of knowledge assets

How do we do this? Finally, it is essential to turn the best practice guidelines, the working inventory, contingency plans, and the knowledge developed into training and learning materials. It is essential to ensure that the organization's preferred practices are widely adopted to ensure that day-to-day operations do not revert to past practices.

What are the inputs? All of the guidelines, inventories, plans, and knowledge developed throughout the process.

What outputs does it produce? The primary output is a set of training materials that can be used to promote learning across the organization. The primary outcome, though, is a change in behavior and an increased awareness of the importance of making smart choices for encoding, formatting, and packaging.

What resources does it use? The knowledge architect will leverage training strategies and templates to ensure effective learning in addition to all of the new resources generated in activities 1 through 4.

Evolution of encoding, formatting, and packaging designs

Of the three layers we addressed in this chapter, packaging has the longest history. Packaging has been around since the beginning of humankind. To develop a historical perspective, we must understand the factors that have signaled major shifts and architectural design changes. Taking packaging as the baseline allows us to see how formats and encoding are developed to address the challenges of the kinds of products in the packages. Our review of the historical literature suggests five general phases (Figure 7.5):

- Phase 1. Lone consumers and direct distribution;
- Phase 2. Multiple consumers and extended human distribution;
- Phase 3. Communities of consumers and new intentional distribution channels;
- Phase 4. Mass consumption and formal distribution channels;
- Phase 5. Unpredictable consumption and virtual distribution.

These five phases are defined by who the consumers are, how many there are, whether we know who will be consuming the product and how, and how distribution is controlled and managed. The fewer the number of consumers, the simpler the access and consumption, and the greater control over distribution, the simpler the design and the lower the need for complex encoding and formatting. As the number of consumers increases, and our degree of familiarity decreases, the need for encoding and formatting increases. As encoding and formatting increase, so does the sophistication of the package design. As distribution distances increases, durability

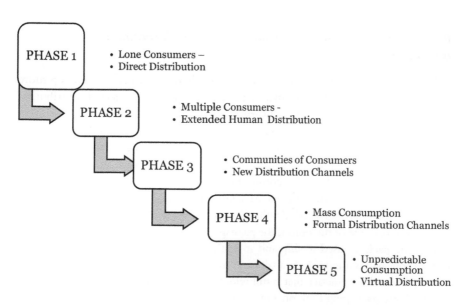

FIGURE 7.5 Evolution of Encoding Formatting and Packaging Design

becomes a package design concern. As the asset itself changes from single to multiple consumptions, we must be concerned about durability and preservation in packaging.

Phase 1. Lone consumers and direct distribution

This early phase is characterized by direct exchange of knowledge assets between a few known producers and consumers, through direct contact, and of a known asset. The encoding was embedded in the product itself. It was formatted as a natural product. The package was designed by the producer using natural materials that worked for that transaction. There was no need to design a more complex package, or to add formatting to the product – its meaning, structure, and presentation were self-evident. The producer directly explains to the consumer through the use of a common encoding scheme – language – what the product is. Historically, packages included leaves, wooden barrels, crates, and fabric containers. The role of protecting the asset was shifted from the producer to the consumer during the transaction.

Phase 2. Multiple consumers and extended human distribution

As transactions and distribution expanded from a controlled and limited environment to multiple consumers and distribution to more than one consumer, packaging and formatting evolved. The packaging needed to be efficient and easy to produce to accommodate multiple consumers. Packaging advanced to pots and mugs, woven materials, tree bark as earliest forms of paper, glass, more extensive wood packages, and the earliest metal containers. Packages also needed to be more durable, and reuse became an issue as more people were involved in producing goods.

Phase 3. Communities of consumers and new intentional distribution channels

With the advances of the industrial revolution, there was a need to develop more durable and robust packaging materials. We had new 'engineered' distribution systems in the form of postal delivery services and even rudimentary forms of shipping. Serial production generated the scale and scope of products, and the rate of consumption grew. There was a need to explain the meaning, organization, and structure of products to consumers we did not know. We had to format and encode those products for consumption by a broader consumer base. Paper and cardboard became the primary packaging materials, through all of the earlier packaging materials persisted. At this time packaging also evolved into multiple layers – the package of the object, the package used to deliver the object to the consumer, the package used to ship and store the object in transit. During the Great Depression, packaging took on a sales and marketing aspect. The package became a 'silent salesman' – a practice that is still widely used today for marketing knowledge assets. Plastic packaging took on a more prominent role after World War II when a disposable shopping culture developed.

The broader scale of distribution and the introduction of increased risks added another dimension to packaging – protecting and safeguarding the product.

Phase 4. Mass consumption and formal distribution channels

The rise of the digital economy has expanded the importance of encoding, formatting, and packaging. It is with the growth of the digital economy that a need for universal encoding schemes emerges. The rise of the digital economy that increases our need to add semantics to our products ensures that any consumer can access and interpret their meaning, organization, and structures. The digital economy allows us now to acquire products over time and space. Consumers need formatting to interpret and translate meaning regardless of where they are and what they know.

Phase 5. Unpredictable consumption and virtual distribution

Today, production and consumption transactions occur in any environment. Knowledge assets are mobile – they can travel anywhere, can be consumed by anyone, and modified and repurposed by anyone. This new environment exponentially increases the need for knowledge assets in particular to have embedded information about their encoding, formatting, and packaging conventions. The risk of not having this available is the creation of unusable or fugitive knowledge assets.

Encoding, formatting, and packaging in the knowledge architecture

This functional architecture is an essential component in the knowledge architecture practice. When this functional architecture is missing, we tend to focus on the package rather than the knowledge kernel. This leads to suboptimal transformation and migration choices, particularly in highly volatile technology environments. In the end, the absence of this functional architecture is a trigger for a loss of availability and access to essential business knowledge.

As a general practice, encoding, formatting, and packing should live in the information or the knowledge layer of the enterprise architecture stack. Because the primary consideration for most organizations is storage and cost of maintaining the package, these functional architectures live in the application and technology layer. We need to work towards shifting these back to the knowledge architecture layer, or at a minimum to ensure that the knowledge asset design aspects of these architectures are part of the application and technology architecture practice.

Chapter review

After reading this chapter, you should be able to:

- define encoding and explain how it applies to knowledge assets;
- define formatting and explain how it applies to knowledge assets;

- define packaging and explain how it applies to knowledge assets;
- explain the layers of encoding, formatting, and packaging in knowledge architecture;
- discuss why these layers are essential to knowledge architecture designs.

References and recommended future readings

Alvestrand, H. (1998, January). *IETF policy on character sets and languages*. BCP 18, RFC 2277.

Becker, L., van Rompay, T. J., Schifferstein, H. N., & Galetzka, M. (2011). Tough package, strong taste: The influence of packaging design on taste impressions and product evaluations. *Food Quality and Preference, 22*(1), 17–23.

Besser, H. (2001). Digital preservation of moving image material. *The Moving Image, 1*(2), 39–55.

Bhabatosh, C. (2011). *Digital image processing and analysis*. PHI Learning Pvt. Ltd.

Bradshaw, G. L., & Anderson, J. R. (1982). Elaborative encoding as an explanation of levels of processing. *Journal of Verbal Learning and Verbal Behavior, 21*(2), 165–174.

Brandenburg, K. (1987). Evaluation of quality for audio encoding at low bit rates. In *Audio Engineering Society Convention* (Vol. 82). Audio Engineering Society.

Bub, D. N., Black, S., Hampson, E., & Kertesz, A. (1988). Semantic encoding of pictures and words: Some neuropsychological observations. *Cognitive Neuropsychology, 5*(1), 27–66.

Chen, Y., Wu, Z., Agrawal, A., Liu, Y., & Fang, J. (1994). Modeling of Delta-I noise in digital electronics packaging. In *Proceedings of IEEE multi-chip module conference (MCMC-94)* (pp. 126–131). IEEE.

Eden, S., & Eshet-Alkalai, Y. (2013). The effect of format on performance: Editing text in print versus digital formats. *British Journal of Educational Technology, 44*(5), 846–856.

Elias, C. S., & Perfetti, C. A. (1973). Encoding task and recognition memory: The importance of semantic encoding. *Journal of Experimental Psychology, 99*(2), 151.

Enticknap, L. D. G. (2005). *Moving image technology: From zoetrope to digital*. Wallflower Press.

Faller, C. (2004). *Coding of spatial audio compatible with different playback formats* (No. CONF).

Fang, J., Liu, Y., Chen, Y., Wu, Z., & Agrawal, A. (1993). Modeling of power/ground plane noise in high speed digital electronics packaging. In *Proceedings of IEEE electrical performance of electronic packaging* (pp. 206–208). IEEE.

Frear, D. R., & Thomas, S. (2003). Emerging materials challenges in microelectronics packaging. *MRS Bulletin, 28*(1), 68–74.

Fridrich, J., Goljan, M., & Du, R. (2002). Lossless data embedding for all image formats. In *Security and watermarking of multimedia contents IV* (Vol. 4675, pp. 572–583). International Society for Optics and Photonics.

Harrison, C., & Semin, A. (2009). *Psychology*. New York: New York Press, p. 222

Hernandez, R. K., & Rue, J. (2015). *The principles of multimedia journalism: Packaging digital news*. Routledge.

Ide, N. (1994, August). Encoding standards for large text resources: The text encoding initiative. In *Proceedings of the 15th conference on Computational linguistics-Volume 1* (pp. 574–578). Association for Computational Linguistics.

Jot, J. M., Larcher, V., & Pernaux, J. M. (1999). A comparative study of 3-D audio encoding and rendering techniques. In *Audio engineering society conference: 16th international conference: Spatial sound reproduction*. Audio Engineering Society.

Larobina, M., & Murino, L. (2014). Medical image file formats. *Journal of Digital Imaging, 27*(2), 200–206.

Li, S., & Momoi, K. (2001). A composite approach to language/encoding detection. In *Proceedings 19th International Unicode Conference* (pp. 1–14). Google Scholar.

Library of Congress. (2020). *Format descriptions for moving images. Sustainability of digital formats: Planning for library of congress collections*. Retrieved January 31, 2020, from www.loc.gov/preservation/digital/formats/fdd/video_fdd.shtml.

Llewellyn, S. (2013). Such stuff as dreams are made on? Elaborative encoding, the ancient art of memory, and the hippocampus. *Behavioral and Brain Sciences, 36*(6), 589–607.

Merrill, E. C., Sperber, R. D., & McCauley, C. (1981). Differences in semantic encoding as a function of reading comprehension skill. *Memory & Cognition, 9*(6), 618–624.

Miano, J. (1999). *Compressed image file formats: Jpeg, png, gif, xbm, bmp*. Addison-Wesley Professional.

Mozaffari, S., Faez, K., & Ziaratban, M. (2005). Character representation and recognition using quad tree-based fractal encoding scheme. In *Eighth international conference on document analysis and recognition (ICDAR'05)* (pp. 819–823). IEEE.

Solomon, C., & Breckon, T. (2011). *Fundamentals of digital image processing: A practical approach with examples in Matlab*. John Wiley & Sons.

Sonsino, S. (1990). *Packaging design*. Van Nostrand Reinhold.

Twede, D. (2016). History of packaging. In *The Routledge companion to marketing history* (pp. 139–154). Routledge.

Whistler, K., Davis, M., & Freytag, A. (2008). The XXXrganiz character encoding model. *The Unicode Consortium, Technical Report, 17*.

Wiggins, R. H., Davidson, H. C., Harnsberger, H. R., Lauman, J. R., & Goede, P. A. (2001). Image file formats: Past, present, and future. *Radiographics, 21*(3), 789–798.

Wren-Lewis, J. (1983). The encoding/decoding model: Criticisms and redevelopments for research on decoding. *Media, Culture & Society, 5*(2), 179–197.

Wu, J., Zhang, Y., & Lin, W. (2014). Towards good practices for action video encoding. In *Proceedings of the IEEE conference on computer vision and pattern recognition* (pp. 2577–2584). IEEE.

Zölzer, U. (2008). *Digital audio signal processing* (Vol. 9). Wiley.

8

FUNCTIONAL ARCHITECTURE FOR IDENTIFICATION AND DISTINCTION

Chapter summary

This chapter discusses what it means to identify and distinguish knowledge assets. It explains why these factors are essential and how to determine them across all assets. The chapter lays out seven activities that support the discovery of identification and distinction. This chapter explains why it is vital to have a good understanding of common practices for identifying an asset's identity, attribution, dates, versions, and copies. The chapter also describes the advantages and limitations of unique reference identifiers. The chapter also lays out the three methods of determining identity, including through direct examination of an asset, inference, and inheritance of context, and through demonstration, testimonials, or analytic methods. The chapter also explains how semantic or other scientific methods can be leveraged to discover highly similar knowledge assets.

Why we care about identifying and distinguishing knowledge assets

Today, our stocks of knowledge include assets from the past century and the present day. There is business value in all of these assets. Managing the continued availability of these assets in the future depends on our ability to identify these assets, determine what they are, and distinguish them from other assets. Also, there is a greater need to authenticate assets, to secure them from loss and misappropriation, and to ensure they are authorized for use by individuals we can identify. We have always had instances of fakes, forgeries, versions, and copies. With widespread access to digital tools, it is now possible to create, promote, distribute, and market things – including knowledge – that is not what it says it is. In the past, it took effort and time to identify what was real and distinguish what was real from not real – and it involved experts or expert tools. Today it is easier to do both, and awareness is just increasing. Identification is the starting point for authentication, security, and access to functional architectures. If we do a better job at the initial stage of identification and providing sufficient information to allow the user or consumer to identify and distinguish knowledge assets, our work in the forensic stage will decrease.

Identification and distinction – design concepts

To develop this functional architecture, we must have a good understanding of common practices for identifying and distinguishing knowledge assets. Much of what we know today and the source of current practice derives from information and archival sciences, specifically bibliographic design (Bothmann, 2004; Burress et al., 1982; Daily, 1967; Demner et al., 2005; Fellows, 1922; Gladd, 1980; Levy, 1995; Lubetzky, 1953) and descriptive cataloging (Blake, 2002; Bull, 1963; Fox, 1990; Gorman, 1989; Gregor & Mandel, 1991; Henderson, 1976; Hill, 1977; Jeng, 1986; Keisch et al., 1967; Krogh, 2009; Levy, 1995; Lubetzky, 1969; Lundy, 2008; Moriarty, 2004; Papakhian, 2000; Pass and ARL, 2003; Rockwell, 1999; Stalker & Dooley, 1992; Tillett, 1991; Truelson, 1969). It is important to leverage this historically significant foundation, as we also consider new approaches for identifying the creator of the asset; naming and titling practices for all kinds of assets; establishing and representing the dates associated with the creation or the acquisition of an asset; unique reference identifiers; common practices for managing versions, editions, and copies; and knowledge of semantic or other scientific methods for discovering highly similar knowledge assets.

A starting point for availability is knowing what an object is and how it is distinct from other assets. Identity is defined generally as the condition of being the same as something described or distinguished from others in some way. Identification is the action or process of identifying someone or something. Identifying something means that we can prove through some means that a thing is what it claims to be. Traditionally, we have identified a person through their official documents – birth certificates, marriage certificates, passports, driver's licenses, Social Security numbers, or another identifying document or badge issued by the organization that is vouching for the identity. The means of identification may include a name, a number, date of birth, biometric information, fingerprints, of any combination of these attributes.

What are the essential identifying attributes or factors for knowledge assets? It depends on the object class. In Chapter 6, we defined a set of crucial attributes of knowledge assets. We leverage a combination of these to determine the identity of an asset. Regardless of the object class identity, there are a set of essential attributes that help us to establish identity with reasonable certainty. Let's translate how we identify a person to how we might identify knowledge assets. We need to know the name of an asset (e.g., official name on a birth certificate, marriage certificate), who created it (e.g., name of parents or ancestors), the date it was created (e.g., birth date), physical characteristics (e.g., height, weight, eye color), and any official authoritative, unique identification number.

A distinction is a difference or contrast between similar things or people. Distinguishing is the process of defining the differences among things, in this case, knowledge assets. We might have two people who look the same, two people with the same name, the same birth date, or the same parents. It is the combination of attributes that allow us to distinguish one asset from another. Or, perhaps we want to see all of the knowledge assets associated with a person. Still, we want to be able to distinguish which are his or her tacit knowledge assets, project roles, network memberships, and scholarly articles he or she has published. In this case, we need to be able to reliably identify the individual but distinguish assets based on their association with the individual. Identification is also the foundation for authentication (we are authenticating an instance against a known identity), for assigning security classifications, and for determining surrogates, derivatives, interpretations, and translations of knowledge assets. Without a reliable form of identity, these architectures and functions are less reliable. All of these are dependent upon our ability to determine that an asset is what it purports to be.

We are inclined to believe that identification and distinction are well-managed processes for some assets and in some contexts. For example, an organization may have strong controls over personnel records and secure personal identification documents. However, these systems may still allow names to vary considerably – in personnel records, in the enterprise directory, in the people profile pages, and in document metadata. The corporate or agency library may have good authority control routines in place for author information. But, authors are not limited to agency personnel, and agency personnel may have different authoritative published names. Knowledge assets in published collections may have well-established identities because publishers, music producers, and media publishers have major processes to manage it. For organizations and their internal explicit information products, their documents, videos, audio recordings, and graphics offer the same challenges as other types of knowledge. The challenge is to discover what the established processes are and to determine whether they can be adopted or adapted to support the knowledge architecture.

Attributes that identify and distinguish

We know from our design of knowledge objects that we need multiple attributes to establish identity reliably, and to provide sufficient definition of those identities to distinguish one knowledge asset from another. The challenge is multidimensional because we are working with such a rich stock of knowledge. There is no single element of a knowledge asset that will allow us to determine that it is different from another. Rather than rely on a single attribute, it is a combination of elements that will enable us to both identify and distinguish. What are the essential attributes that must be available for all knowledge assets to create this foundation? We suggest six attributes. These apply to every knowledge object class described in Chapter 6.

- creator or agent: the entity that is responsible for the knowledge;
- name of the entity: what it calls itself and how others refer to it;
- date of creation: when it was created;

- medium or format: the medium on which it is stored;
- issuing or authorizing source: the source that vouches for or acknowledges responsibility for the asset;
- encoding language: the language in which it is represented.

How would we define each of these attributes? What are the specifications for each attribute? And how do they behave or 'work'? Let's walk through each attribute.

Creator or agent attribute

What is it? Person(s), unit(s), or organization(s) primarily responsible for the intellectual content of the resource. The agent's purpose is to define the authenticity of the material. There are variations of agents, some personal agents, and corporate agents. Personal agents are named people. Corporate agents can be organizational units, institutions, government agencies, etc. The values for individual agent names also vary. For example, J. Thomas Smith, John Thomas Smith, and J. T. Smith are all the same agent, but there are variations in the way the agent name is presented. We use authority control to manage and harmonize named agents.

What is its status and obligation in an object model? This attribute is essential and mandatory.

Can there be more than one value? For some assets, there can only be one creator, e.g., when an asset is a person or a node in a network or a business role. For other kinds of assets, there can be more than one creator, e.g., the creator of a book, a report, a communication, or an artifact.

Is there a fixed length for the attribute? Yes, one should be established.

Is it a structured attribute? Are there syntax considerations? Yes, and the attribute should be character-based. There are syntax issues for personal agents and corporate agents. For example, a name in the directory might consist of three subfields – first name, middle name, last name, or the name may be a single text string.

Can the attribute be edited? Yes, by authorized personnel and manually.

Is there a default value? No.

Should the attribute be indexed for accessibility? Yes.

How do we find values for the attribute? By capture from the asset itself, by inheritance from source systems or inference from an authoritative source, or through other forms of proof and demonstration.

Should there be an authoritative reference source? Organizations may or may not use authority control. The decision will be made based on the size and complexity of their knowledge stocks and the effort and cost to create and maintain an authority control solution.

Title or name attribute

What is it? The name given to the object by the creator or publisher. It provides a textual description of the intellectual content of the object. Its purpose is to provide some minimal descriptive access and disambiguation of the intellectual content for IW users.

What is its status and obligation in an object model? This attribute is essential and mandatory.

Can there be more than one value? Yes, but only one current value. There can be superseded values.

Is there a fixed length for the attribute? Yes; one should be established. Length should be set to accommodate the longest values across attributes.

Is it a structured attribute? Are there syntax considerations? Yes, and the attribute should be character-based. Syntax and structure should accommodate complex titles such as those with subtitles or title qualifiers.

Can the attribute be edited? Yes, by authorized personnel and manually.

Is there a default value? No.

Should the attribute be indexed for accessibility? Yes.

How do we find values for the attribute? By capture from the asset itself, by inheritance from source systems or inference from an authoritative source, or through other forms of proof and demonstration.

Should there be an authoritative reference source? Establishing a title is a creative exercise by the creator. It is not possible to identify a single authoritative value across assets. There may be a need to establish rules for titles of authoritative assets, but these are not controlled through authority control systems.

Date created attribute

What is it? Two attributes are related – an actual date value and a date qualifier. The date may take one of several meanings or types. The default, most common meaning is the date the resource was made available in its current form, date created. The actual date value, though, adheres to ISO 2014 format.

What is its status and obligation in an object model? This attribute is essential and mandatory.

Can there be more than one value? No. If there are multiple kinds of dates, other attributes should be used to represent those values.

Is there a fixed length for the attribute? Yes, and this should conform to the organization's guidelines for 'Date' values.

Is it a structured attribute? Are there syntax considerations? Yes, there should be one accepted syntax. Dates are and have been represented by many formats and languages over time. For this attribute to support accessibility, a single acceptable syntax should be established.

Can the attribute be edited? Yes, by authorized personnel and manually.

Is there a default value? No.

Should the attribute be indexed for accessibility? Yes.

How do we find values for the attribute? By capture from the asset itself, by inheritance from source systems or inference from an authoritative source, or through other forms of proof and demonstration.

Should there be an authoritative reference source? There cannot be a single trustworthy date value, but dates should follow international standards for syntax and form, e.g., ISO 2014.

Format attribute

What is it? Data representation of the resource, e.g., text/HTML, ASCII, Notes, PDF, etc. It defines the format or media in which the information was issued. Its purpose is to provide the necessary information to allow people or machines to determine what is required to use the information object. The same intellectual content may be available in more than one format.

What is its status and obligation in an object model? This attribute is essential and mandatory.

Architecture/structure: hierarchical classification.

Can there be more than one value? Generally, no. However, in the case of a compound asset, e.g., a multimedia format, it may be necessary to describe more than one format. Ideally, though, each part of the asset is described separately.

Is there a fixed length for the attribute? Yes; one should be established. Length should be defined to conform to the longest MIME extension name.

Is it a structured attribute? Are there syntax considerations? No; it is a single value attribute.

Can the attribute be edited? Yes, by authorized personnel and manually.

Is there a default value? While an organization may find circumstances where a business unit defaults to a single format for all its assets, it is essential to create this attribute intentionally. Errors in assignments can have an impact.

Should the attribute be indexed for accessibility? Yes, if there is a demand to discover or sort by formats and packaging.

How do we find values for the attribute? By capture from the asset itself, by inheritance from source systems or inference from an authoritative source, or through other forms of proof and demonstration.

Should there be an authoritative reference source? An authority-controlled list of MIME types and formats should be established to reduce the uncertainty and manage choices.

Issuing or authorizing source

What is this? It is the entity responsible for making the resource available. It is the source we look to when we are authenticating a knowledge asset at other functional architecture points.

What is its status and obligation in an object model? This attribute is essential and mandatory.

Can there be more than one value? No. Values may be edited or superseded, but there can be only one value at a time. Multiple issuing agencies suggest multiple assets.

Is there a fixed length for the attribute? Yes, the organization should determine the length based on the maximum likelihood value.

Is it a structured attribute? Are there syntax considerations? It is a simple single attribute without further qualification or subdivision.

Can the attribute be edited? Yes, by authorized personnel and manually.

Is there a default value? No.

Should the attribute be indexed for accessibility? Generally, no. This attribute is not widely used for discovery or search.

How do we find values for the attribute? By capture from the asset itself, by inheritance from source systems or inference from an authoritative source, or through other forms of proof and demonstration.

Should there be an authoritative reference source? There cannot be a single authoritative date value as the possibilities and variations are too numerous to manage efficiently.

Language attribute

What is it? Language of the intellectual content of the knowledge asset. Use CDS codes as available or map to ISO codes in the absence of CDS-approved language codes. In the case of human capital assets, language is the primary or native language of the human whose knowledge assets we are referencing.

What is its status and obligation in an object model? This attribute is essential and mandatory.

Can there be more than one value? Yes, because some assets can be represented in multiple languages. However, multiple languages should not be used to describe multiple language surrogates that are not an integral part of the asset.

Is there a fixed length for the attribute? Yes. The organization should determine the length based on the maximum likelihood value – this length can also be determined by consulting the ISI list of official language names.

Is it a structured attribute? Are there syntax considerations? It is a simple single attribute without further qualification or subdivision.

Can the attribute be edited? Yes, by authorized personnel and manually.

Is there a default value? No, unless the organization never uses or access assets in other than a single language.

Should the attribute be indexed for accessibility? Yes, if the knowledge assets represent multiple languages, and there is a choice that is important for discovery and search.

How do we find values for the attribute? By capture from the asset itself, by inheritance from source systems or inference from an authoritative source, or through other forms of proof and demonstration.

Should there be an authoritative reference source? The organization may maintain an authoritative list of language names. If so, this should be used as an authoritative source. Otherwise, the ISO 639–2 Codes language names or codes should serve as a reference. This source provides normative text names for languages, bibliographic codes, and terminology codes.

Identifiers and descriptors

All of these attributes serve as critical identifiers for knowledge assets. However, it is important to distinguish our characterization of an identifying attribute from an 'identifier.' An identifier has a special meaning in data science and information science. In data science, an identifier refers to a data type with a one-to-one correspondence between the entity and the data type. In other words, it is possible to have a correct or authoritative value that defines the entity. In many cases, an identifying attribute will also serve as a primary key for an object class or an instance. In information science, this translates to a single approved name of something, i.e., names of people, places, and things. These identifiers have been authorized or established in a particular form. Because they have a single approved form, they are used consistently throughout an architecture. An authorized ID is trusted as a real value. Identifiers are different from descriptors. A descriptor, on the other hand, can use any of several values to describe the entity. Several names over their career may have known a person, or they may use familiar rather than formal names. When that name is a crucial attribute for identifying human capital, an author of a book, a process team lead, or a node is a network, we need to have established a single authoritative form. Several names over its history may have known an organization or a group. These may include full names as well as acronyms. Pulling all of these variations together adds coherence to our knowledge architecture. Identifiers are different from descriptors. A descriptor may use any of several values to describe the entity. Descriptors support accessibility and take many forms. But, identifiers play a different and vital role in establishing the identity and authenticity of an entity.

Identifiers are what are called essential attributes – they must be present. Identifiers commonly derive from a set of rules and guidelines that help us to understand how to establish the original form. They may also be supported by an authoritative source, a data structure that identifies the authorized form and provides references to other conventional forms and variations. In this way, an identifier is a controlled value in terms of its scope and usage. We can use authority control to manage descriptors. In that case, though, there is no single correct and authorized value that defines the attribute or the object.

Identification methods

Identification has always depended on some form of direct contact with the asset. Not all identifying attributes are fully visible through simple contact with the asset itself. For some assets, we need to be able to do more than just 'see' the asset – we need to look inside the asset or query the asset to learn enough to identify it with certainty. Based on experience and a review of the literature for all types of assets, we suggest three methods for identifying and distinguishing assets (Figure 8.1):

- identification through direct examination of the asset;
- identification through inference and inheritance of context;
- identification through demonstration, testimonials, or analytic methods.

Different types of knowledge assets require different identification methods. Some assets are simple and defined based on their inherent and intrinsic attributes. In most cases, the elements that identify and distinguish one asset from another are embodied

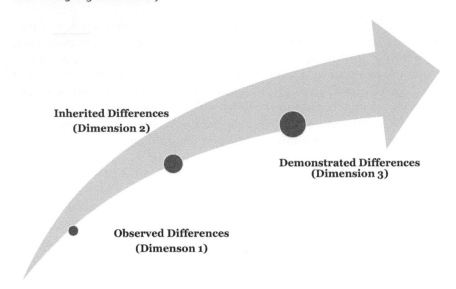

Inherited Differences
(Dimension 2)

Demonstrated Differences
(Dimension 3)

Observed Differences
(Dimenson 1)

FIGURE 8.1 Three Methods of Identification

in the asset itself. We can open a book and find the author, title, and creation date. We can watch a video and the title, writer, and product names, and the release date will be displayed. Other objects are complex and are identified and distinguished through a combination of inherent and contextual attributes. For example, we may recognize people by sight, but if we don't know them, we may have to infer they are who they are from photos, their identification documents, or through an introduction by a colleague. A document may have a title, but that title was derived from the type of report's official name. It is not unique to the document. That same document may have the issuing or authorizing department, but it is only through examination or by interference to the project team that we can determine who created it. The bottom line is that there is more than one way to establish identity, and more than one way to find the values for these identifying attributes.

Identification through direct examination of the asset

This method works when the attributes we need are authoritatively present in the asset and directly observable through direct access. This includes explicit knowledge objects we can examine directly. These assets have embedded in their inherent structure and organization the identifiers we would use to determine identity. In other words, we can view the image, open the book, examine the journal article, or watch the video to find the creator, the asset's name, its creation date, and its language. We can also verify the issuing or authorizing agency or organization; we have a reasonable certainty that the asset is what it purports to be. We need to look to other dimensions to verify the asset identity, where we cannot verify the issuing and authorizing agency or organization.

Identification through inference and inheritance of context

When assets are created distinctly, and without regard to a context, we can examine them directly and discover what we need to know to identify them. As our work environments became more complex and more supportive, these assets were created in systems and applications, workflow processes, workshops, or places that held essential clues to their identity. We were not concerned about embedding these clues into the asset because we did not assume the asset would leave the context. Today, though, assets are mobile. They leave the context intentionally and unintentionally, deliberately and inadvertently. For these assets, we need to understand the context to infer or inherit those identifying attributes. One of the most common examples of this method is metadata records that contain live metadata registries or catalogs. Metadata or properties that are embedded in the asset are examples of the first method. But, metadata records that are not attached to the asset are inherited or inferred. We infer this is the metadata record for this asset because they have the same inventory number or are connected through a web link.

What are some less recognized examples, and what practical methods can we adopt to provide full identification? We may be less familiar with these examples, but they are quite common across organizations today. And, how do we extract identifying attributes from these contexts?

- email messages;
- documents filed in document management systems;
- web communications;
- organizational unique reference identifiers;
- files on network drives;
- reports created from portal templates;
- reports generated from rules in ERP systems.

Email messages infer the author as the sender and the title as the subject line. Most email messages are automatically dated and time-stamped. While we have a sender's email account name, we do not have the authoritative version of their name. We have to infer this or interpret it from another source system. We can assume that the message text is the object, but what if there are attachments? Attachments may have different identities, and it may not be reliable to assume attribution to the email author.

Documents filed in document management systems may have authors and titles, but it is unlikely that they have a clearly stated identifier for the authorizing or issuing agency. And, consider that some organizations have hundreds of kinds of documents – each with a different format and structure. Some may not have any indication of the creator, and the general practice may be to infer the title from the type of document in combination with the creation date. In some cases, the context of the document – a country or an industry – may be defined as a folder label and not inherited to the project. This is a common practice in document and records management systems.

Web content management systems make it easy for us to create communications, press releases, and other forms of organizational assets. These may be generated from templates and do not exist as complete assets except as displayed. The identifying attributes may be embedded in templates or web workflows. Taking a snapshot of the display is equivalent to interpreting the asset.

An organization may create and issue a unique identifier for people, for documents, for equipment, etc. Those identifiers are essential internal management controls, but they must be interpreted to access the identifying value. Once an asset leaves the organization, that unique identifier loses its value.

Files on network drives may be valuable knowledge assets. Still, unless the identifying attributes are embedded in the asset or embedded in the file as properties, we must infer the identifying attributes. Some organizations develop elaborate file naming conventions that include identifying values such as title and date. The creator, though, is often inherited from the file structure of the drive.

Many organizations are using reporting portals that use templates with predefined fields to generate routine reports. This situation is similar to web communications, where the report information lives in the template and is assembled in the background for submission to an internal transaction system. These portal templates may or may not create all of the identifying attributes we need to identify and distinguish one report from another. It may be necessary to look at system-level metadata to identify some of the values we need.

Larger organizations with more automated business operations may generate reports and explicit knowledge assets based on internal rules and trigger dates. These may produce a virtual asset that does not have a persistent form. Additionally, these rules may generate dynamic data graphics and statistical comparisons. These examples require that we infer or inherit attribute values if no persistent form is created.

Identification through demonstration, testimonials, or analytic methods

When assets have neither embedded nor inherited identifying attributes, we need to demonstrate or prove what they are. This method has its roots in the world of art and antiques, but it is increasingly important to other types of knowledge assets. In these instances, we need to analyze the asset to determine what it is. Chemical analysis may be used to verify the age or composition of an asset. Semantic analysis or image analysis may be used to determine whether an asset is an exact copy of another asset, a version, an extraction or derivative, a convenience copy, a stolen or misappropriated copy, or even a misrepresentation of the asset. There are assets whose identifying attributes are embedded in the package, but the packaging is distinct from the asset, and the package has been lost. The asset itself has no identifying attributes. Consider a CD that contains all of an individual's email messages for the past six months. The CD comes in a sleeve with a label, but the jacket is lost. There is no label on the CD, and we can open the CD only if we have the email application to do so. To get to the identifying attributes, we need to open the package, interpret the format, and decode the asset. Ideally, this method is rarely used. But it is a method the knowledge architect should be prepared to promote to ensure we can identify all of our knowledge assets.

Identifying attributes for human capital

Human capital identifiers define who owns the tacit knowledge, skills and competencies, attitudes and behaviors, work history, and reputation. The identifier for all of the human capital knowledge classes is the person. How do we interpret each of these identifying attributes for a person (Table 8.1)?

For both the Person and the Agent object class, we use the credentials of the individual as the identifying attributes. For the Person object class, we design tacit knowledge, skills and competencies, attitudes and behaviors, work experience, and reputation as subobject classes. For the Agent object class, we use these subclasses to explain what knowledge stores and rules we have embedded in the agent, the tasks the agent performs, the processes to which it has been applied, and any quality control or feedback about its performance. We will infer most of the values for the Person attributes. The developer and the asset manager will create through direct examination and inference.

What are the concerns we should be aware of when establishing and maintaining identifying attributes? First and foremost, we need to consider privacy and security boundaries. If a people object class was created, there must be adequate protections to ensure that the individual has full control over the profile. Second, it is crucial to understand what the primary source for people object models will be – at a minimum, we should consider a context with multiple levels of access privileges and security and do not routinely involve data or information exchanges with the external environment. The source application or repository must have

TABLE 8.1 Identifying Attributes for Human Capital

Identifying Attribute	Person Object Class	Agent Object Class
Creator or Agent	The person who is creating the profile – in this case, it should be the individual	Agent developer or designer
Name of the Entity	Person's official name	Agent control number
Date of Creation	Person's date of birth	Date first launched
Medium or Format	Person	Physical (robot); software (automated analyst or expert system)
Issuing or Authorizing Source	Individual and/or organization	Owning unit
Encoding Language	The native language of the individual	Programming or machine language

refined levels of access controls and rigorous security infrastructures. A good practice example would be archival vital records systems. Finally, we must also consider that while the organization's perspective of the individual is the most relevant in the business context, this definition needs to make sense and be interpreted if the profile is used outside the organization.

Identifying attributes for explicit knowledge

We need to define identifying attributes for the three knowledge object classes we described in Chapter 6, including documents, visual assets, audio assets, and artifacts.

Identification practices for this knowledge asset class reflect well-established practices from the publishing industry, the broadcast and film industries, and the art world. The challenge is that these practices have long histories and need to be adapted to support a more generic knowledge architecture. This may shift our perspectives slightly in adapting these practices. Where the document object class

TABLE 8.2 Identifying Attributes for Explicit Knowledge

Identifying Attribute	Document Class	Audio Class
Creator or Agent	Person(s) or application responsible for content	Individuals whose knowledge is recorded in the audio
Name of the Entity	Title of document	Title assigned to the audio
Date of Creation	Date published or issued	Date issued or the date the event occurred
Medium or Format	May be any physical or digital	One of the audio formats
Issuing or Authorizing Source	Publisher, owning organization, or unit	Publisher, owning organization, or unit
Encoding Language	Language of the document	The language spoken in the audio

TABLE 8.3 Identifying Attributes for Explicit Knowledge (cont.)

Identifying Attribute	Image Class	Artifact Class
Creator or Agent	Artist, filmmaker, producer	Artifact creator or producer
Name of the Entity	Name assigned by the creator	Name assigned by the creator
Date of Creation	Date published or offered	Date completed
Medium or Format	Any print or digital format	Physical medium
Issuing or Authorizing Source	Owning agency or source	Owning agency or source
Encoding Language	Language expressed in an asset, if applicable	Language expressed in an asset, if applicable.

refers to internal organizational documents, though, practices are less well established. They will vary with the context and with the management philosophy of the unit. Methods for visual and audio assets may be well developed within the general industry but will vary with the market. Identification practices in commercial markets may differ from academic or internal corporate environments. Of the three identification methods, direct observation, inheritance, and inference will be most common for document classes. For audio and image classes, all three ways will be necessary.

Identifying attributes for procedural knowledge

We need to define identifying attributes for the nine knowledge object classes we described in Chapter 6, including procedural documentation, process demonstrations, process explanations, process and workflow diagrams, and process patents. We walk through three of the object classes to illustrate sources and methods (Table 8.4).

The key identifying attribute for these object classes is the name or title of the process. The challenge is that only the largest and most sophisticated organizations track processes with any degree of consistency and control over their operations. For most organizations, procedures will be referenced in job descriptions or as activities in strategies and plans. Being able to distinguish one process from another may require an additional authoritative source. This situation makes the argument for the process being treated either as the creating agent or the name of the entity. We may be inclined to define the creating agent as the business unit – but business units change as well – as multiple units may use a process or process object. In this case, you would expect to have multiple creators. While we may be able to examine procedural documentation directly, most of the other classes will require inference and inheritance, and demonstration.

TABLE 8.4 Identifying Attributes for Procedural Knowledge

Identifying Attribute	Procedural Documentation	Process Demonstrations
Creator or Agent	The unit that owns the process	Individuals performing the demo
Name of the Entity	Name of the activity or process	Name of the activity or the process
Date of Creation	The date this process was first implemented	The date the demo was created
Medium or Format	May be any format including applications or drawings	Likely moving image with sound; may also be a simulation in specialized software
Issuing or Authorizing Source	The organization that owns the process	Business unit supporting the demo
Encoding Language	Language of the support team	The language spoken in the demo

Identifying attributes for cultural knowledge

We need to define identifying attributes for the five knowledge object classes we described in Chapter 6, including organizational culture profiles, unit culture profiles, team culture profiles, community culture profiles, and individual culture profiles. We take two of these object classes as examples (Table 8.5).

Few organizations have conducted cultural assessments or developed cultural profiles. Where they exist, they may or may not be treated as internal documents. It is crucial to identify the name of the entity assessment or profiled so the assessment can be associated with the other types of knowledge related to the unit or the person. We would expect to find cultural profiles generated for organizations, business units, communities, teams, and individuals. The challenge for knowledge architects is that the communities and teams profiled will not be well controlled. It is possible to identify the business unit if the organization manages its administrative unit names over time. Typically, these names and codes are managed by a central authority as master data. Where they are not controlled, though, it may be challenging to achieve consistent identification. For teams, it may be possible only to identify the team lead as the 'owner' or 'custodian' of the profile. Identifying individuals is dependent upon having authoritative people's names and sources. Of the three methods, direct observation, inference, and inheritance, will be most common.

Identifying attributes for network capital

We need to define identifying attributes for the three knowledge object classes we defined in Chapter 6, including network nodes, network links, and network messages (Table 8.6).

TABLE 8.5 Identifying Attributes for Cultural Knowledge

Identifying Attribute	Organizational Cultural Profile	Individual Cultural Profile
Creator or Agent	The individual who conducted the assessment	The individual who conducted the assessment
Name of the Entity	Name of organization profiled	Name of the Individual assessed
Date of Creation	The date the assessment was completed	The date the assessment was completed
Medium or Format	Likely print or digital but may also be application-specific	Likely print or digital but may also be application-specific
Issuing or Authorizing Source	The organization that accepted and approved the assessment	Name of the organization that accepted and approved the assessment
Encoding Language	Language of the assessment	Language of the assessment

TABLE 8.6 Identifying Attributes for Network Knowledge

Identifying Attribute	Network Nodes	Network Messages
Creator or Agent	Network administrator	Name of originating person
Name of the Entity	Name of individual in the network	Message subject or title
Date of Creation	The date the individual entered the network	Date message was posted
Medium or Format	Network profile or application	Network application
Issuing or Authorizing Source	Agency or organization supporting the network	Agency or organization supporting the network
Encoding Language	Language of the network	Language of the message

The focus of these object classes is on the components of the network. The primary challenge is the fluidity and dynamic nature of networks. Networks exist, but they are rarely managed or controlled by the organization. The closest we may come to a controlling source would be the network administrator or facilitator. Nodes will also be fluid, but we should be able to identify when an individual joins the network. We create or define the names of networks, but unless they are an official or formally supported organizational network, there is little probability of verifying the network name. Of the three identification methods, direct observation, inference, and inheritance are most common.

The design environment for identification and distinction of knowledge assets

What factors do we have to consider in designing the functional architecture? Historically, identification focused on the asset, but over time, the focus has shifted to the package and away from the asset itself. There are different sets of rules for identifying and distinguishing different kinds of knowledge assets. There are different models and structures, properties, metadata, and metainformation. The challenge for knowledge architects has been that with the focus on explicit knowledge – we have become accustomed to a 'one and done' kind of activity – we don't expect to have to change the identification or distinction attributes once it has been created. The knowledge architect needs to be aware of the organization's inclination and culture to leverage existing knowledge. The architect also needs to take into consideration the organization's propensity and culture to invest in existing knowledge and to build new knowledge. No one size architecture suits all organizations. We need to know how to identify and distinguish those knowledge assets with the highest business value in terms of identification and distinction. It is also essential to understand the organization's reward and recognition systems because the architect needs to build incentives for individuals to identify the knowledge assets they create.

What triggers the need to identify or distinguish knowledge assets? We need to make decisions about identification and distinction when:

- the business has developed a new service and needs to find staff with the human capital to support it;
- a business team has invented a new way of manufacturing a product and will update all of its procedural knowledge;
- a business is scaling up production and needs to expand its operations to three new countries and six new plants – the procedural knowledge needs to be readily available to the new managers;
- a business needs to scale up its training in one area, and it needs access to staff who have the skills and competence to bring them into the training program;
- an organization wants to enter a new market, and it will leverage networks to identify and build networks of suppliers and to target new audiences.

What are the impacts and consequences of this functional architecture? The effect is a higher level of knowledge and awareness of knowledge assets, and understanding of what these assets are and how unique or redundant they are. It is a starting point for assessing the long-term value of those assets. The impact of a well-designed environment is that outdated, 'spoiled,' or superseded knowledge can be identified to reduce business risk. Knowledge assets that are redundant or duplicative can be reduced to manage knowledge and information landfills better.

What sources do we need to design this functional architecture? The design environment includes the full range of knowledge assets and all of the sources and places where they might live.

What are the outputs and outcomes? This architecture provides the capability to track and account for all of our knowledge assets and to identify those with business value. This architecture is the foundation of every other functional architecture in practice. We need to have a good handle on what assets we have before we can manage them for future availability, accessibility, and consumability. The product of this architecture is a working, practical architecture that identifies and distinguishes knowledge assets across the organization.

Design activities and tasks for identification and distinction

Five essential activities are required to support this functional architecture:

- Activity 1. Define and describe the specifications and behaviors of attributes that identify knowledge assets by object class
- Activity 2. Identify the authoritative and controlled reference sources needed for the functional knowledge architecture
- Activity 3. Develop a working inventory of current practices for these attributes
- Activity 4. Design a functional architecture to support these attributes

- Activity 5. Develop good practice guidelines for contributing to and leveraging the institutional architecture

Activity 1. Define and describe the specifications and behaviors of attributes that identify knowledge assets by object class

How do we do this? This is a challenging design task – you're looking to the future and for a synthesized design definition, but you have to accommodate current and past practices. You need to have a design that leverages current practices, or you will not get buy-in for your knowledge architecture. This process is iterative – first, you need to look across the knowledge object models, then you need to look within each asset class. We should remember that a 'class' of assets contains not just one type of asset but many similar characteristics. Similar characteristics will include the identifying attributes, but there will be variations you'll have to accommodate. Brainstorm a set of identifying attributes that will work across all your asset types – you should be able to look at your object models to create your working list. Looking across all asset types, brainstorm the best representation of that attribute for the object class – take those identifying attributes and do a more in-depth analysis of the assets assigned to each object class. Here you're identifying the type of value you'll use to represent each attribute. You will need to accommodate all assets in the final design. Still, it is essential to ensure that your design works for (1) the business-critical assets, and (2) the most significant number of assets. For example, you may be tempted to take published books and journals as your good practice model for the Document Object Class – and while this is a natural starting point, it will not be a useful starting point if your internal documents have greater business value and if there are 10 million documents and only 100,000 books and journal titles. Next, look at those behaviors. Does there need to be more than one value for a kind of asset? (More than one creator? Different creator roles?) Do some need support from an authoritative reference source? Brainstorm the specifications for these attributes.

What are the inputs? There are four essential inputs, including: the knowledge object models; inventories of the knowledge assets we created when establishing a functional architecture to address encoding, formatting, and packaging; system and repository administrative documents and data dictionaries that describe field specifications; and any relevant external standards for metadata practices for different kinds of assets.

What does this activity produce? This activity generates a working list of identifying attributes that work across all kinds of assets, a preliminary working list of source definitions for attributes by asset class, and an initial description of the attribute specifications and behaviors.

What resources does it use? Several resources are essential to this activity, including the knowledge architect's knowledge, data dictionaries or other system and repository administrative manuals, external metadata standards and procedures, the working asset inventory from format and package discovery exercise, and the knowledge object models.

Activity 2. Identify the authoritative and controlled reference sources needed for the functional knowledge architecture

How do we do this? There are several parts to this activity. First, we need to review the attribute list and specs you produced in Activity 1, and to identify those attributes that need support from a reference source. We need to examine each source by walking through a set of critical questions. The key questions might include:

- Is there an existing source?
- Is the source intentionally controlled, or merely an aggregation?
- Is there just one source?
- Is there a unit that is responsible for managing this source?
- Will that source work for all assets?
- Does the source need to be expanded?
- Is there a governance model? And, will governance work for all assets? Does it have policies and guidelines?
- Can people access the source easily?

What are the inputs? To accomplish this activity, the knowledge architect needs a working list of attributes with sources, examples of assets, the data dictionaries and administrative documents describing the attributes, access to source systems to review the sources, and policies and guiding principles for each existing sources.

What does this activity produce? This activity generates a set of draft specifications for harmonized and consolidated sources for identifying attributes.

What resources does it use? Several resources are essential to this activity. We need all of the inputs noted earlier in addition to the knowledge architect's knowledge. We need the tacit knowledge of different repository and systems developers to understand how sources are supported and used. We need the tacit knowledge of individuals who manage or use the existing sources. And, we need the tacit knowledge of individuals responsible for governing the sources.

Activity 3. Develop a working inventory of current practices for these attributes

How do we do this? This activity focuses on developing the documentation for the identifying attributes – we're pulling together everything we've learned and designed in the first two tasks. First, we need to create descriptions of each identifying attribute across asset classes, including their specifications and behaviors. Next, we need to describe the specifications and behaviors of these attributes by the knowledge asset object class. These two perspectives give us the full view we need to design the architecture.

What are the inputs? For this activity, we need everything we learned, and all of the information we collected in Activities 1 and 2. We also need good practice models of how the organization documents and describes attributes – also called fields in some contexts.

What does this activity produce? This activity generates the first draft of specifications and behaviors for identifying attributes across all kinds of knowledge assets. This activity also produces a description of how these work and behave that are understandable by all current stakeholders, and an explanation that even makes sense to developers and engineers.

What resources does it use? This activity leverages all of the inputs from Activities 1 and 2, the knowledge architect's knowledge, and those organizational conventions for documenting field and attribute specifications.

Activity 4. Design a functional architecture to support these attributes

How do we do this? This activity involves developing a high-level conceptual model – a conceptual blueprint on a single page – a blueprint that describes the identifying attributes. This activity also consists of developing blueprints that describe each attribute in greater detail and that explain the full architecture, including (1) design principles, (2) attributes, (3) attribute specifications and behaviors, (4) attribute sources, and (5) stakeholders for each attribute.

What are the inputs? This activity is grounded in a list of the architectural elements outlined in Chapter 4 to ensure that the blueprints and the supporting documentation cover all of the key elements of functional architecture. It is also essential to encourage input from other enterprise, information, and data architects to prepare your blueprints and documentation in a way that supports current methods and tools. Finally, we need to make sure that the blueprints and documentation make sense to stakeholders, e.g., assets custodians, stewards, and owners, since their day-to-day behaviors will determine success or failure.

What does this activity produce? This activity creates blueprints that can be shared with stakeholders to collect feedback. It also produces a working functional architecture that supports identification and distinction of the full range of knowledge assets

What resources does it use? This activity leverages everything you produced in the earlier activities, examples of current architecture blueprints and supporting documentation, and feedback from other architects and stakeholders.

Activity 5. Develop good practice guidelines for contributing to and leveraging the institutional architecture

How do we do this? After we've received feedback on blueprints and made adjustments, the next step is to develop a working set of guidelines and good practices for moving this functional architecture forward. It involves working with the existing enterprise architects and information/data architectures to ensure the guidelines and blueprints are integrated into existing architecture practice. This activity also consists of integrating asset identity management into the architecture governance model. If an architecture governance model is not in place, you need to set up at least one such model to manage knowledge assets. Eventually, this governance model should cover all of the functional architectures discussed in this text.

What are the inputs? Essential inputs for this activity include the blueprints and supporting documentation, good practice governance models, and the policies, tools, and methods that support other architecture practices.

What does this activity produce? This activity produces a practical working knowledge architecture for identification and distinction.

What resources does it use? In addition to the inputs described earlier, this activity leverages governance models, as well as any applications or traditions for making, recording, and promoting decisions.

Historical, current, and future design for identification and distinction

Identification becomes increasingly complex with more assets and more complex assets. A distinction was not significant when the community of producers and consumers and the range of assets were small. As the communities grew, as the range of assets grew, and as the complexity of assets increased, the need for distinction grew. As the need to distinguish increased, identification methods evolved. We identified five phases of evolution (Figure 8.2) of knowledge identification and distinction, including:

- Phase 1. Unique assets and limited production (direct observation)
- Phase 2. Multiple instances and increased production (need to identify and distinguish)
- Phase 3. High rates of reproduction and duplication – multiple producers
- Phase 4. High rates of rendering, chunking, and repurposing
- Phase 5. Unlimited producers and lack of systematic attribution

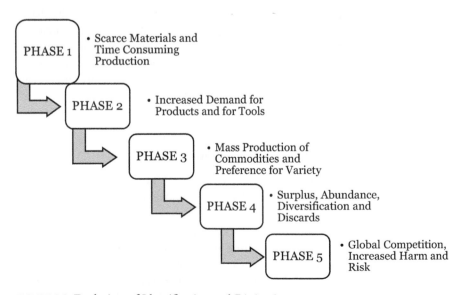

FIGURE 8.2 Evolution of Identification and Distinction

Phase 1: unique assets and limited production
(direct observation)

This phase describes the earliest centuries of civilization. Identification was self-evident and self-explanatory, and access to the product was sufficient identification for the consumer to acquire it and consume it. Both the producer and the consumer knew the product, and there was only one form. The bottom line is that there was no need to distinguish one person or product from another.

Phase 2: multiple instances and increased production
(need to identify and distinguish)

Looking forward to centuries with population growth, increased communications and travel, and growth in products, the need to identify and distinguish people and things increases. As the number of product variations or the number of sources increased, there was a need to determine what the producer was offering and what the consumer was acquiring. The idea of choice came into the decision – by definition, choice means we have to distinguish one asset from another. We need to be able to both identify and distinguish. Which asset should we use, and how do we know what it is? But the number of choices is still limited. Consider how we evolved the identification of people when we expanded beyond our initial family groups into tribes – when there was a need to distinguish and recognize differences. Consider that the evolution of naming people by surnames came when the distribution or mobility of those tribal members went beyond their immediate location – when people traveled outside of their village, they needed to be able to explain who they were in a way that was beyond their original context or familiarity

Phase 3: high rates of reproduction and
duplication – multiple producers

Fast forward to the industrial revolution. During this time, people came into contact with people and products from places they did not know first-hand. There was a need to identify people and assets in this new world by more than one attribute or characteristic. Essentially, this was the emergence of people and product 'metadata' – multiple ways of defining a person or a product. At that point, we started to identify people by: (1) their dates – when they were born or when they died; (2) their physical attributes – height, color of hair, skin color, weight, etc.; (3) their location – where they were born and where they lived; (4) what they do – their work; and (5) the language they spoke. As commerce increased and capital became an attribute, we began to describe people in terms of their social and financial status, and ultimately their politics. The more complex the set of characteristics, the more complicated the processes used to define these attributes. Some identification and distinction attributes must be interpreted, intuited, or inferred. Other attributes are embedded in the asset, but the practice is uneven. For some products and assets, we must understand the context to distinguish which is the original asset, and which is the authentic asset.

Phase 4: high rates of rendering, chunking, and repurposing

Fast forward to today, and we find the proliferation of technologies and an increased level of skills and competencies across the population. These include the capabilities of individuals to reverse engineer, repurpose, render, chunk, or repurpose any product or asset available. Identification and distinction serve a new purpose – we use these methods to determine whether the object is what it purports to be or whether we are acquiring a copy, a knockoff, a changed version, or a compromised product or asset. Because this has economic implications, the need for security arises, and with the increased demand for security, we need to apportion privileges to users based on their identity and attributes. Identification is now vital for both the producer and the consumer. Economic and social transactions may be conditioned on identity rather than identity playing a secondary consideration.

Phase 5: unlimited producers and lack of systematic attribution

In the future, we need to look to the models and methods of bioinformatics and air travel to understand how we will track identity by the information the asset carries with it. This shift began in Phase 3, but it has now escalated. Future consumers expect that they will be able to query the asset, and it will disclose and explain its properties. The shift here is that the burden for determining identity is now on the producer – the burden is to ensure that all of the identifying attributes must be embedded in the object. We cannot assume it will be discoverable by the context. Consumers will have little patience to demonstrate or analyze the item. In addition to embedding 'metadata' properties, we also need to embed metainformation – those extended attributes that explain why the consumer can trust the asset. Trust must be supported by highly reliable identification and authentication methods. Authentication must be supported when the object is created, not just at a later point in the consumption stage. We can look to traditional methods such as watermarking – but these must be available to anyone who can create an asset, affordable, and easy to use. Some form of registration must be incorporated for watermarks, trademarks, and copyrights. Metadata must be embedded and be able to travel with the object. There is also a need for an extensible metadata model to allow supplemental contextual information as use expands.

Identification and distinction in the knowledge architecture blueprint

This functional architecture is a critical dependency for many other functional architectures. When we do not have rigorous methods of identifying and distinguishing knowledge assets, we set the stage for unauthorized access, misuse, misrepresentation, misappropriation, and the simple inability to establish trust, authenticity, and provenance. Research suggests that trust and provenance are essential to knowledge consumption – if we cannot determine the source, the asset's validity is in question. Rather than reducing uncertainty and risk, this increases it. It means that we are less likely to leverage and derive value from our stocks of knowledge assets. Lack of ability to identify knowledge assets is a trigger for knowledge loss – if we cannot identify an asset, if we do not track its business value or life span, what prevents us from discarding it or disposing of it unwisely?

This functional architecture aligns with the information architecture layer and in the knowledge architecture layer if one exists. It terms of positioning it in that practice, we should place it closer to the business architecture practice because we're focused on attribution and comparison to other business assets.

Chapter review

After reading this chapter, you should be able to:

- explain how identification and distinction is important for knowledge assets;
- describe those attributes that help us to identify knowledge assets;
- describe those attributes that help us to distinguish knowledge assets;
- explain what we mean by identification through direct examination;
- explain what we mean by identification through inference and inheritance;
- explain what we mean by identification through demonstrations, testimonials, and analysis.

References and recommended future readings

Blake, V. L. (2002). Forging the anglo-american cataloging alliance: Descriptive cataloging, 1830–1908. *Cataloging & Classification Quarterly, 35*(1–2), 3–22.

Bothmann, R. L. (2004). Cataloging electronic books. *Library Resources & Technical Services, 48*(1), 12.

Bull, C. (1963). Sample catalog cards illustrating solutions to problems in descriptive cataloging. *Bulletin of the Medical Library Association, 51*(1), 143.

Burress, E., Mikel, S., Pringle, B., Kane, A., & Black, B. (1982). *Comparison of DTIC COSATI cataloging and AACR-II cataloging in the MARC communications format* (No. RSAG/CRC-82/01). Resource Sharing Advisory Group Alexandria Va Committee on Cataloging Rules.

Daily, J. E. (1967). *The selection, processing, and storage of non-print materials: A critique of the Anglo-American cataloging rules as they relate to newer media.* http://hdl.handle.net/2142/6383.

Demner-Fushman, D., Hauser, S., & Thoma, G. (2005). The role of title, metadata and abstract in identifying clinically relevant journal articles. In *AMIA Annual Symposium Proceedings* (Vol. 2005, p. 191). American Medical Informatics Association.

Fellows, J. D. (1922). *Cataloging rules: With explanations and illustrations.* HW Wilson Company.

Fox, M. J. (1990). Descriptive cataloging for archival materials. *Cataloging & Classification Quarterly, 11*(3–4), 17–34.

Gladd, B. (1980). *DTIC cataloging guidelines.* http://www.dtic.mil/gils/documents/naradoc/.

Gorman, M. (1989). Yesterday's heresy-today's orthodoxy: An essay on the changing face of descriptive cataloging. *College & Research Libraries, 50*(6), 626–634.

Gregor, D., & Mandel, C. (1991). Cataloging must change! *Library Journal, 116*(6), 42–47.

Henderson, K. L. (1976). *Treated with a degree of uniformity and common sense, 1876–1975.* Descriptive Cataloging in the United States.

Hill, J. S. (1977). *Developments in map cataloging at the library of congress.* Library of Congress, Geography and Map Division.

Jeng, L. H. (1986). An expert system for determining title proper in descriptive cataloging: A conceptual model. *Cataloging & Classification Quarterly, 7*(2), 55–70.

Keisch, B., Feller, R. L., Levine, A. S., & Edwards, R. R. (1967). Dating and authenticating works of art by measurement of natural alpha emitters. *Science, 155*(3767), 1238–1242.

Krogh, P. (2009). *The DAM book: Digital asset management for photographers.* O'Reilly Media, Inc.

Levy, D. (1995). *Cataloging in the digital order.* Presented at The Second Annual Conference on the Theory and Practice of Digital Libraries.

Lubetzky, S. (1953). *Cataloging rules and principles: A critique of the ALA rules for entry and a proposed design for their revision.* Prepared for the Board on Cataloging Policy and Research of the ALA Division of Cataloging and Classification. Processing Department, Library of Congress.

Lubetzky, S. (1969). *Principles of cataloging.* Final Report. Phase I: Descriptive Cataloging.

Lundy, M. W. (2008). Provenance evidence in bibliographic records: Demonstrating the value of best practices in special collections cataloging. *Library Resources & Technical Services, 52*(3), 164.

Moriarty, K. S. (2004). *Descriptive cataloging of rare materials (books) and its predecessors: A history of rare book cataloging practice in the United States.* Chicago, CA: Rare Books and Manuscripts Section of the   Association of College and Research Libraries.

Papakhian, A. R. (2000). Cataloging. *Notes, 56*(3), 581–590.

Pass, G. A., & Association of College and Research Libraries. Bibliographic Standards Committee. (2003). *Descriptive cataloging of ancient, medieval, renaissance, and early modern manuscripts.* Association of College and Research Libraries.

Rockwell, K. (1999). Problem areas in the descriptive cataloging of sheet maps. *Cataloging & Classification Quarterly, 27*(1–2), 39–63.

Stalker, L., & Dooley, J. M. (1992). Descriptive cataloging and rare books. *Rare Books and Manuscripts Librarianship, 7*(1), 7–22.

Tillett, B. B. (1991). A summary of the treatment of bibliographic relationships in cataloging rules. *Library Resources & Technical Services, 35*(4), 393.

Truelson Jr, S. D. (1969). The need to standardize descriptive cataloging. *Bulletin of the Medical Library Association, 57*(1), 21.

9

FUNCTIONAL ARCHITECTURES FOR KNOWLEDGE ASSET DISPOSITION AND DESTRUCTION

Chapter summary

This chapter explains what it means to disposition and destroy knowledge assets and why it is essential to have an active asset disposition capability. The chapter lays out the five activities that support asset disposition and destruction. The chapter also considers why it is crucial to have a good understanding of general asset management practices, the criteria for assessing the business value of and for auditing knowledge assets, common disposition practices, and managing destruction activities. Here we consider the design challenges we must address in the wide variation in accepted practice for managing these different kinds of assets and the absence of accepted practices for some of these assets.

Why we care about knowledge asset disposition and destruction

We've made the case that knowledge is a capital asset, so it needs to be managed over its useful business life like a capital asset. Organizations do asset management for all of their capital assets and have done so for decades or centuries. We haven't always referred to it as asset management, but the essential asset management practices and models have remained relatively constant. We need to take our cues from the asset management world. Given the different economic properties and behaviors of knowledge assets, we'll need to translate traditional asset management practices to suit knowledge assets.

Knowledge management practices have provided some useful guidance, but they do not rise to how we manage other kinds of capital assets. In the past, we have viewed knowledge as an explicit resource whose 'management' involves making it accessible through descriptive cataloging, indexing, and security classification. This view is insufficient for the knowledge economy. As a capital asset, we need to look at dispositioning as an asset management decision and action.

Drawing from the asset management world, why do we care about disposition-ing knowledge assets? How do these reasons translate to knowledge assets? In our review of the asset management and knowledge management literature, we find four reasons that capital assets may be disposed of:

- dispositioning to reduce costs of surplus knowledge assets;
- dispositioning to avoid diminished business value;
- dispositioning to avoid business risk or loss;
- dispositioning to avoid business harm.

Reducing costs of surplus knowledge assets

What is the common business rationale and practice? We dispose of knowledge assets because they are a surplus or because it no longer has business value. The asset is costing us more to maintain than it generates business value. In this scenario, we have too many capital assets, and they carry the organization's cost to manage and maintain (Arnold, 2002; Ayres Ferrer & Van Leynseele, 1997; Corrigan, 2010; Franks, 2017; Jonassen & Colaric, 2001). These assets confuse and lead to poor business decisions because it leads to fragmentation and scattering of assets. The assets also detract from the organization's overall architecture because it becomes unnecessarily complex. In this scenario, assets are dispositioned to streamline and achieve increased efficiency. From a procurement perspective, we stop purchasing these and limit our new acquisitions to a particular asset product line, set timelines for de-accessioning or disposing of other assets as they age out, or release a new ver-sion. Another reason we surplus computer assets is because there is a new version, and the vendor no longer supports the older version. In this case, dispositioning just means setting a timeline for replacement, setting expectations, and disposing of the application or the hardware. Theoretically, the knowledge assets are not deeply coupled with the applications. Too many organizations have realized too late that the major ERP systems may not transition data and explicit information assets well. In these cases, you'll need to make sure you have that encoding/decoding, format transitioning, or repackaging strategy. We offer caution for this scenario.

Avoiding diminished business value

What are the common business rationale and decision for this scenario? In this scenario, the asset no longer generates business value or does so at a higher cost (old equipment, old processes, 'old people') (Black et al., 1998; Handa et al., 2019; Harrison, 2007; Hastings, 2010; Hsiang & Jina, 2019; Jolicoeur & Barrett, 2005; Nomura & Momose, 2008; Posey et al., 2015; Tungare et al., 2010). In the physi-cal asset world, this scenario is equivalent to using an outdated piece of equipment whose performance has decreased due to simple wear and tear. The equipment that a carpenter uses wears down over time and has to be replaced. A shipping company has to replace its loading equipment every five or ten years because the engines wear down. Think about how long you keep your automobiles and how often you have to buy a new one, just because it has worn down. Or, perhaps the equipment simply becomes outdated and there is no one available to maintain it. Perhaps the business supplies required to support it are no longer available. The person who knows how to fix the mimeograph machine is no longer available. The supplies we need to continue to use this printer are no longer produced. We can no longer extract business value from the asset, so we choose to dispose of it.

What is an equivalent in the financial environment? Currencies may become obsolete, or they are reduced in value. In this case, we might exchange the currency for another or change it to another kind of asset. We dispose of the financial asset in favor of another asset with higher business value. The same is true of knowledge assets – some knowledge becomes out of date because we've learned something new; there is a better way to do it. So, this new knowledge supersedes earlier knowledge. Unfortunately, when we don't actively manage our knowledge assets, we might continue to keep outdated knowledge in circulation. Outdated knowledge isn't always 'bad knowledge,' but it can result in diminished business value. Unfortunately, we have also looked at people as 'resources to be retired.' We haven't assigned a disposition schedule to individuals – we haven't planned for transition periods when we would ensure that everything they knew how to do was transitioned off to another source. We simply looked at them as expenses to be retired and to de-accessioned. Or when the knowledge asset or custodian simply has reduced capacity or limited capacity to interact with and leverage the knowledge asset to best advantage.

Avoiding business risk and loss

What are the rationale and the decision for this scenario? The asset is prone to error and failure; it creates faulty products and results and presents a risk. Trucking companies and health care providers disposed of equipment because keeping defective or degraded assets in use can generate substantial business risks and losses for the organization. Consider what happens when a dump truck driver is required to transport a load of construction debris on a public highway with faulty brakes. Or, when a hospital is required to reuse personal protective equipment that increases the spread of diseases. Consider a financial analyst who advises you not to dispel your financial resources but to maintain them in an investment that demonstrates an increased level of risk. When it comes to knowledge assets, there are several ways we can experience risk and loss. For example, knowledge assets can be unintentionally but recklessly lost through poor planning of migration of applications and technologies. They can be lost through poor or inappropriate levels of security protection, or by poor design of access privileges. Business harm in these scenarios may be equivalent to theft or the cost of replacement. The business's impact is a temporary loss or a low level of business risk that can be rectified. The knowledge can be replaced, the individual or the expert has a backup. Knowledge assets can pose a risk when they are misappropriated or stolen, released to a competitor.

Avoiding business harm

What are the rationale and the decision for this scenario? It generates harm if knowledge is misused, stolen, or destroyed unintentionally. It has business value, but it needs to be protected. A doctor fails to update her knowledge about treatment and continues to use a procedure that has been demonstrated to have significant consequences. She fails to read the medical literature or follow her specialized advice, and her patients experience the harmful effects. As a result, she is hit with lawsuits and is forced to retire from practice. A staff member believes that his manager is doing something unethical. The manager refuses to acknowledge this. To alert others, the staff member releases internal emails to the local news media. The organization's reputation is significantly damaged. Both the manager and, ultimately, the CEO who authorized the behavior lose their positions. The organization's reputation is one of its primary assets – this has significantly degraded as a result. An individual is hired as CIO because of his political network rather than his competencies. His background is in accounting, and he does not know rapidly changing security threats and protections. He disregards his CTO's advice and does not invest in new security systems because of the expense. There is a major data breach of the organization's financial operations, and coveted financial investment strategies are stolen in the process. The core competency of the organization is now exposed to others. An entirely new approach must be designed because those who created the strategies have long since retired and are not available to explain the strategy. A manufacturing company does not save the chemical formula used to produce an ingredient that is the crucial ingredient of their core product. The expert who developed the formula has retired and is no longer in the company's network. The company is hit by a tornado (force majeure), and all records of the formula are lost when paper files, servers, and repositories are destroyed. It takes the company years to recover because they have to reinvent the formula.

Knowledge asset disposition and destruction – design concepts

To develop this functional architecture, we must have a good understanding of general asset management practices, the criteria for assessing the business value of kinds of knowledge assets, common disposition practices and tools, asset audit and inventory methods, metadata retention practices, and acceptable destruction practices of different types of knowledge assets and their packaging. The major challenge we face in designing this functional architecture is the wide variation in accepted practice for managing these different kinds of assets, and the absence of customary practices for some of these assets.

What is disposition?

Disposition is a concept with origins in several fields, including legal, criminal justice, and records management, Disposition in a legal or law enforcement context is the final settlement of a matter and concerning decisions announced by a court; a judge's ruling is commonly referred to as disposition, regardless of the level of resolution. In criminal procedure, it is the sentencing or other final settlement of a criminal case. Disposition also has a meaning in real estate or real property; it describes property acquisition and disposition. It also has a meaning in the financial investment and capital context; the most common form of disposition would be selling a stock investment on the open market, such as a stock exchange. Other types of dispositions could involve donations to charities or trusts. We dispose of real estate, facilities, land, and other asset types.

Disposal is an umbrella term for the ultimate fate of an asset, which could be that it is kept, recycled, discarded, or destroyed. In the context of knowledge management, though, the treatment of asset disposition is scattered and fragmented. In some cases, there are strict, almost rigid practices in place (e.g., records management, archival science) (Bradsher, 1985; Brynjolfsson, 1994; Carlucci, 1986; Dollar, 1993; Drewry, 1955; Franks, 2013; Matthews & Gibson, 2009; Park, 2004; Penn & Pennix, 2017; Sabourin, 2001; Schiller & Merhout, 2011; Summers, 1991; Zhenquan, 2001). In other instances, dispositioning is unrecognized for what it is (e.g., retirement, outsourcing, artificial intelligence replacement, transfers, reductions in force). In yet other cases, it is addressed only from a legal rather than a business value perspective (e.g., copyright, trademarks, patents). In yet others, it is recognized only after the value of the asset has expired (e.g., when the physical object has deteriorated or degraded). The most significant challenge for this functional architecture is to establish a comprehensive and consistent framework applicable to all knowledge asset classes.

Disposition decisions and decision criteria

Disposition decisions are serious management actions that have cost and business value implications. A poor decision can significantly affect a company or organization's business health. Every business decision must be made through careful deliberation and in a defensible way. Disposition decisions are carried out one asset at a time, even when we have guidelines and criteria that pertain to classes of assets. Disposition decisions should involve the knowledge architect, the asset custodian, and the cognizant business manager.

The traditional industry and service sector practices guide the disposal of assets, and for the criteria for making disposition decisions. Experience and an extensive review of the applied research tell us that there are four types of disposition decisions and actions (Figure 9.1). The four choices are a decision to:

- preserve an asset;
- dispose of through repurposing and recycling;
- dispose of through discard without reuse;
- dispose of through destruction.

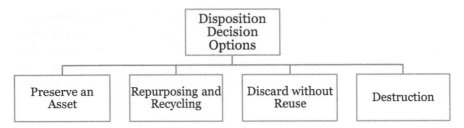

FIGURE 9.1 Disposition Decisions and Actions

Decisions to preserve

We decide to preserve a knowledge asset because it (1) has business value for the foreseeable future; (2) would present a risk if it were damaged, lost, or misused; (3) is deteriorating, is becoming obsolete, or is at risk of not being accessible in the future because of its package or format; (4) it represents a trade secret or core capability of the organization which must be safeguarded.

Decisions to dispose of through repurposing or recycling

We decide to repurpose or recycle knowledge assets because we no longer need them, but someone else might derive value from them. By recycling or repurposing these assets, our business value does not diminish, and the value of the knowledge asset can continue. If the knowledge asset is scarce and would be difficult to reproduce – for example, an expert's tacit knowledge – the organization needs to repurpose and recycle it by teaching it to others. For example, libraries or departments may have physical copies of publications or physical media assets. They decide to dispose of these collections and copies by donating them to a non-governmental organization with limited resources. Another example is an individual who has expertise in a particular process has trained and coached others to operate just as well as possible. She has now announced that she is leaving the organization to take on a leadership role in another organization. Her tacit knowledge assets, skills, and competencies are being recycled to another organization where she will teach and train others. A network that was developed in house in a collaboratory fashion has value outside of the organization. The organization transfers ownership and administration of the network to a professional association. The network is still available to all of the staff, but it is no longer an internal asset the organization must retain.

Decisions to discard without reuse

We may decide to discard knowledge assets because they have spoiled, they no longer have business value to any other business, they may present a business risk if not discarded, they are no longer needed – they are redundant or duplicative, or cost the business more to maintain and manage than they generate business value. An example is an individual whose skills and competencies have been replaced by offshoring the work to another country, or by a robot that can now perform the work. The business can 'discard' the individual without considering what happens to their knowledge in the future, as that knowledge is now redundant. For example, the work process is no longer part of the company's operations, so all of the knowledge that supports that process that was unique is no longer important. Unless these people have other competencies, they will be discarded. A second example might focus on a knowledge asset's business value that has expired; say it is out of date, or the equivalent of spoiled. In this case, we do not want to repurpose it because repurposing can cause damage to anyone continuing to use it. Also, we might encounter a situation where a business unit has a counterproductive work culture that harms the unit's productivity. The source of the negative culture is the manager and her management style. The manager has some expertise that has value but should not be in a management role. The organization decides to 'discard' this person's management role and not repurpose it in any other management capacity. Through this action, the organization prevents further damage but without additional loss.

Decisions to destroy

We decide to destroy knowledge assets intentionally and unintentionally. Intentional destruction decisions may be taken because there is no further business value; there is no need to keep the asset for learning or cautionary purposes. There are multiple copies of the asset, and convenience copies are costly to manage. Unintentional destruction decisions are made through a failure to prepare or take precautions, individual mistakes, negligence, or force majeure.

Decision criteria

Disposition decisions are made based on a set of factors, including (1) the projected useful business life of the knowledge asset; (2) the business value of the knowledge asset; (3) the scarcity of the asset; (4) the cost to recreate or reproduce it; and (5) the cost of retention of the asset versus the value of the asset. These are the traditional decision criteria for asset disposition across all industries. Developing these criteria for each asset category is what businesses do for their physical and financial assets. It is the first thing we need to address in designing a functional architecture for disposition and destruction.

Destruction

Asset destruction is a set of processes and methods that may be applied to all types of capital assets that fall into two of our disposition categories, specifically where we decide (1) to discard the asset without reuse, or (2) to deliberately and intentionally destroy the asset (Bradshaw & Linneker, 2015; Coates, 2014; Cox et al., 2002; Curiac & Pachia, 2015; Geambasu et al., 2009; Goza, 2013; Harris, 2000; Oesterle, 1982; Perlman, 2005; Plastoi & Curiac, 2009; Plastoi et al., 2009). Unintentional destruction actions are not considered a managed disposition. Processes for the destruction of assets are unique to the type of asset. Destruction is not a simple single action. Just as for other kinds of capital assets, we need to account for the destruction. We may need to keep and update its metadata and metainformation to show its earlier existence, physical destruction, or erasure from digital sources or directories. It may also involve the removal of its metadata and metainformation. Destruction of explicit knowledge assets or procedural knowledge assets will involve consultation with the business owner. Destruction pertains both to any authoritative sources and any copies or reproductions of those assets.

Ideally, destruction occurs within a well-defined set of disposition rules and decision criteria. Preferably, there are specific guidelines for appropriate destruction methods (i.e., shredding, pulping, burning, electronic wiping, reprimanding, firing, instituting robust practices for cleaning electronic trash bins, etc.). Destruction practices should always be distinguished from recycling, reuse, repurposing, or recovery actions. Destruction is designed to prevent theft, recomposition, or reverse engineering.

Disposition of human capital assets

What does it mean to the disposition of human capital assets? Dispositioning means deciding what to do with these assets long term. There are several levels of human capital disposition decisions. Does the first decision pertain to who decides to dispose of tacit knowledge? Of skills and competencies? Of behaviors and attitudes? Of relationships? The first decision is made by the individual who is the owner and custodian of these assets. Theoretically, an individual does not 'lose' or destroy their human capital. Rather, they may let it degrade, or put it aside in favor of other types of capital, depending on the rewards and incentives of the business environment. An individual can replace their skills and competencies with others if the need arises. If those skills and competencies are no longer of value, they will be discarded or updated to those with value. Human capital disposition can be incentivized or disincentivized by organizations. For example, an organization that encourages individuals to take early retirement is making a human capital disposition decision. The disposition action is not destruction but rather one of discard. An organization should not be able to destroy human capital, but it can decide it no longer has business value and is expendable. If an individual leaves an organization for another position, they take their human capital out of the organization, but it is neither discarded nor destroyed. The knowledge asset is simply no longer accessible to the organization.

Disposition of explicit knowledge assets

Dispositioning of explicit knowledge assets is more straightforward. Most of our disposition and destruction methods are drawn from the work of information professionals, records managers, and archivists to establish standard protocols and tools to manage explicit assets. The chances are good that your organization already has disposition and destruction policies and procedures for these types of assets. The challenge is to ensure they are expanded to apply to all four types of explicit knowledge object classes.

Disposition of cultural knowledge assets

What does it mean to dispose of knowledge of cultural assets? What are the natural processes that trigger the disposition of these assets? When cultures change, the profiles change – because of the nature of cultural profiles, though, it is not accurate to say that a culture changes, rather than adapts. Cultures are slow to change because many different factors mold them. Some changes are intentional, and others are unintentional. If an organizational leader retires and is replaced by another, that new leader's culture influences the organization-level profile. However, organizational culture is deeply embedded in all of the other units and people; the change will take time – maybe as long as ten years – to take shape. Where the new leader is brought in to change the culture deliberately, there may be a backlash and fragmentation. All of these are forms of dispositioning of the culture. Consider how the cultural profile of a unit or team changes as team members are added or removed, and how the project team leads or managers influence the culture. If a new manager arrives, the cultural change may be more dramatic and immediate.

The main point to consider here is that disposition of culture is not likely to be explicitly managed but is expected to occur as an ordinary course of staffing actions. Perhaps the most important trigger point for dispositioning cultural assets is significant staffing changes. Significant changes might trigger a 'cultural audit' or an 'after-action cultural assessment' to determine whether – and if so, how – the culture has changed. These suggestions pertain to the organization- and group-level profiles. We must acknowledge that an individual's culture is changing continuously. It makes more sense to look at cultural dispositioning at this level as simple periodic profile updates to check for changes.

Disposition of procedural knowledge assets

What does it mean to disposition procedural knowledge? It could mean to update or change the process – when we update or improve the process or alter the materials or applications we use. A process may be discarded when an organization outsources it, stops investing in a business line, or sells it to another company. The human form of a process may be archived if the process is fully automated with robotics. A process may be destroyed if it is found to produce harmful results. Disposition decisions and actions can be applied to all levels of procedural knowledge – the process, the task, or the step. It is more likely that steps and tasks will be changed than whole processes.

The danger or risk here is threefold: (1) the unintentional dispositioning or destruction of a process, task, or step and the loss of knowledge that results; (2) the intentional changing of processes without recording the disposition action; or (3) intentional destruction of the process through malicious activities. In any of these scenarios, having a record of disposition actions is an effective way to safeguard procedural knowledge.

Disposition of network knowledge assets

Dispositioning of network and relational knowledge assets resembles dispositioning of cultural knowledge assets. The essential challenge is that we do not have management- or business-level awareness of network knowledge, and so we pay little attention to it when it is lost, destroyed, or walks out the door. We can reverse this only by raising our awareness of our existing networks and communities, and identifying who contributes to them. The primary trigger for a loss of networks and communities is the loss of individuals or agents who comprise them. As with cultural assets, the most effective strategy may be to periodically audit for networks and communities. Such an audit or review might be triggered by conducting annual performance assessments and asking individuals to explain how they contribute to or derive knowledge from these sources. Knowledge communities and networks are destroyed only when all of their members withdraw their participation. At this point, it is too late to capture the knowledge that was generated in the network. Dispositioning in the form of archiving must begin early on in the life of the network. We can lose access to a network if the network is external, and our connection to that network leaves the organization withdrawing participation due to job change or transfer. Loss of access can be equivalent to the destruction of the network for the organization. Like cultural knowledge disposition, network knowledge disposition should be proactively managed periodically, unlike the design of record retention schedules defined for explicit knowledge assets.

The design environment for knowledge asset disposition and destruction

What factors do we need to consider when designing this architecture? There are many factors to take into account when designing this functional architecture. Business custodians and stewards need to be aware of the value of knowledge assets. They need a new awareness of risks and harm that 'spoiled' or bad knowledge assets can have on the business. We need the buy-in and participation of business actors to help us identify these business assets, to establish suitable disposition decision structures, to carry out good disposition actions, and to record those actions.

What triggers the need to identify or distinguish knowledge assets? We realize the importance of dispositioning and the need to plan to dispose of assets when our awareness of the business value of those assets increases, and we understand that we need to safeguard these assets. We understand the need to plan for different disposition actions as we better understand the risks to those assets. New versions of applications and technologies emerge to raise our awareness of the risk of loss of access if we do not have a disposition plan in place. Accidental and unintentional discard reminds us that we need to have policies and practices in place for individuals. Mistakes, faults, and errors remind us of the need to have backups as part of a dispositioning plan. All of these conditions remind us of the need for good working inventories of our knowledge assets.

What are the impacts and consequences of this functional architecture? The consequence of this functional architecture in place is that the organization manages its knowledge assets effectively and consistently. Indirectly, this increases organizational awareness of the business value of these assets, and the need to treat them as capital assets. We can better see and understand risks and act proactively to safeguard assets. When this architecture is not in place, the consequences are the unintentional and intentional loss of valuable assets, the retention of low-value assets at a cost to the organization, and a comparative disadvantage to those seeking assets for business purposes.

What sources do we need to design this functional architecture? The critical inputs are the knowledge asset object classes and models, well-articulated disposition classes and schedules, characterization of assets by their business value, and knowledge of current practices across the organization.

What are the outputs and outcomes? This functional architecture generates new values for our knowledge asset object models – we can now describe the retention class and schedule that pertains to each kind of knowledge asset. This architecture also generates a practical working method for routinely reviewing and identifying assets that should be dispositioned, along with recommended actions for each asset. This architecture also produces a new capability for joint decision-making between business custodians and stewards, and the knowledge architect.

Design activities and tasks for knowledge asset disposition and disposal of knowledge assets

Five high-level activities define this functional architecture, including:

- Activity 1. Define and develop the knowledge asset disposition schedules and criteria
- Activity 2. Conduct a review of knowledge assets and their business value – remember that disposition is always contextual
- Activity 3. Ensure that all knowledge assets with business value have an obvious and assigned retention and disposition class
- Activity 4. Make disposition recommendations for knowledge assets
- Activity 5. Dispose of knowledge assets – destruction or moving on to preservation

Activity 1. Define and develop the knowledge asset disposition schedules and criteria

How do we do this? This activity requires two tasks, which may be simply described but are labor-intensive and iterative. The first task is the development of a working framework for what it means for these assets to (1) create surplus stocks or inventories; (2) lose business value or outlive their useful business life; (3) create risk or introduce an opportunity for loss; and (4) create a threat of harm for the organization. The second task is the development of a working framework of explanations of the disposition actions that can be taken to mitigate the adverse effects. There should be an identification of actions for each knowledge asset class, and an explanation of acceptable procedures for each action.

What are the inputs? The knowledge architect should begin with a template drawn from industry good practices and translate the template to make sense for each knowledge asset class. Another critical input is knowledge of how these assets are managed today. Is there a conscious disposition capability? Or, do we treat knowledge assets like interchangeable resources rather than capital assets? What is possible, and what is necessary to protect the organization and the knowledge asset? This knowledge can be informally collected by reviewing current management decisions or procedural documentation. We can also learn this through conversations with asset custodians and stewards who make this decision.

What does this activity produce? In a nutshell, this activity provides a set of draft disposition schedules and guidelines for knowledge object classes. This is a crucial starting point for effectively managing knowledge assets, and it is absent in most organizations.

What resources support this activity? In addition to knowledge of current practices, this activity depends on the knowledge of knowledge architects, asset disposition experts from other industries, and knowledge custodians and stewards. Knowledge is the key resource.

Activity 2. Conduct a review of knowledge assets and their business value – remember that disposition is always contextual

How do we do this? Business value and useful business life spans are essential business concepts, but they are rarely applied to knowledge assets. They are important decision criteria for dispositioning. This a challenging task because it requires the engagement of business managers who may not yet think in these terms. The knowledge architecture needs to have a strategy in mind for estimating the business value of assets. The most effective approach to use at the outset is one that provides some form of a rating or assessment scale rather than a financial valuation approach. Is the asset business-critical? Is it important, but substitutes are available? Is it disposable, or does it have a limited business life because it is superseded so often? Is it a common asset that can be easily replaced? Managers can provide a more accurate response when allowed to respond in this way.

What are the inputs? The three critical inputs to this activity are the working inventory of knowledge asset classes, the knowledge architect's development of a valuation strategy, and the business manager's characterization of the relative value of the assets pertinent to their operations.

What does this activity produce? This activity provides a disposition schedule for a unit. This unit-level schedule is an essential input to developing the whole organization disposition schedule for a class of knowledge assets. It is not an idea for individual units to have individual and distinct schedules, as this can lead to variations in decisions and actions. But it is an essential input that allows us to identify decisions and practices across units.

What resources support this activity? In addition to the inputs noted earlier, the business manager's knowledge of their knowledge assets and their ability to assign a relative value to those assets.

Activity 3. Ensure that all knowledge assets with business value have an obvious and assigned retention and disposition class

How do we do this? Two tasks support this activity. The first task is to look across all of the disposition schedules developed for units to design a whole organization disposition schedule for each asset class. The knowledge architect will initiate this task. The synthesis of schedules, though, produces a new proposed class for each asset class. It is up to the knowledge architect to fully elaborate on the knowledge asset disposition classes. While the schedules provide a broader view of all the asset classes and the actions, disposition classes provide the details of disposition timelines, disposition decision criteria, and disposition methods for that particular class. They are the detailed set of instructions. The whole new synthesized set of schedules for all knowledge asset classes will need to be reviewed by business managers. Once the knowledge architect has the last round of feedback from business managers, he or she will update the knowledge object class models with reference to the disposition class for that asset. Assigning it to the knowledge asset model ensures it will be persistently available to any consumer or in any transformation. Assigning it to a metadata record in a database introduces vulnerabilities.

What are the inputs? The unit schedules, the feedback from business managers, and the original knowledge asset object models are the most important inputs.

What does this activity produce? This activity produces outputs, including (1) a unified set of disposition schedules for all knowledge assets; and (2) updated knowledge asset object models, with the notation of the appropriate disposition class.

What resources support this activity? All of the activities generated in the two earlier activities, the knowledge asset object models, and the feedback of business managers.

Activity 4. Make disposition recommendations for knowledge assets

How do we do this? This activity represents the implementation of the classes for individual assets. Implementing disposition classes means creating an asset auditing and review process. The problem with the current approach is that it is reactive rather than proactive. To shift to a proactive approach, we need to have a sense of what the near and short-term future looks like for these assets. What is happening in the next year that might generate a surplus? Or reduce business value? Or shorten the useful business life of an asset? Are there any risks or opportunities for harm on the horizon? Are there assets that need to be or may be dispositioned? What kind of action is required in each case? Can we protect these assets from risk or harm by acting now? The more managed and orderly this process, the more effective overall management of knowledge assets.

What are the inputs? The most crucial input for this activity, besides the disposition schedules and classes, is the business manager's knowledge of the business environment. The knowledge architect can develop an application to support inventory, audit, and review of knowledge assets. The business manager, though, will make the disposition decision and take the disposition action.

What does this activity produce? This activity creates a working knowledge asset disposition capability.

What resources support this activity? The most critical resource for this activity is an application that allows the business manager to track their knowledge assets and conduct periodic audits and reviews to make disposition recommendations. It is also essential to provide the business manager with the capability to record the decision and to describe the disposition actions.

Activity 5. Dispose of knowledge assets – destruction or moving on to preservation

How do we do this? This activity represents the actual disposition action. Disposition may take any of four actions. The manager can recommend the knowledge asset for preservation and conservation, in which case it is moved to experts' control. More detailed discussions of preservation and conservation actions are provided in Chapter 10. This activity also includes the repurposing or recycling of knowledge assets, the discarding of those assets without reuse, and the deliberate destruction of assets. For each action, the business manager is expected to follow the guidelines outlined in the disposition class, and to record the details of the action.

What are the inputs? The inputs required for this activity are the knowledge assets themselves, and the prescribed disposition action in the disposition class.

What does this activity produce? This activity either moves assets to the preservation, or it results in de-accessioned and destroyed knowledge assets.

What resources support this activity? In addition to the inputs described earlier, this activity requires the means and applications used to perform discards, de-accessioning, and destruction.

Evolution of disposition and destruction designs

Experience and a review of the literature suggest there are five phases of evolution of disposition and destruction design factors (Figure 9.2), including:

- Phase 1. Scarce materials and time-consuming production
- Phase 2. Increased demand for products and tools
- Phase 3. Mass production of commodities and preference for variety
- Phase 4. Surplus, abundance, diversification, and discards
- Phase 5. Global competition, increased harm and risk

Experience and a review of the asset management literature suggest four factors have contributed to the evolution of our disposition and destruction practices over the centuries. The first is the scarcity of materials and the assets. A second is how those assets are produced – manually, machine, or mass-produced. The third factor is who has the knowledge to produce these assets and how widespread that knowledge is. The final factor is the ease of access to and the abundance of those assets. The greater the scarcity, the greater the knowledge and effort it takes to create the assets, the less likely we are to discard them readily. The easier and cheaper the products, the easier the access, and the greater the knowledge of how to produce,

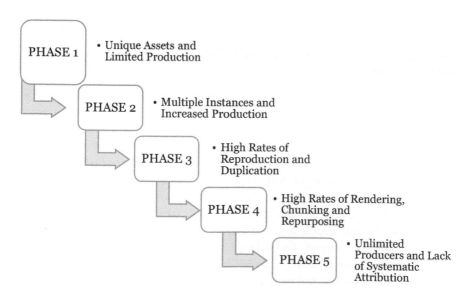

FIGURE 9.2 Evolution of Asset Disposition and Destruction

the more likely we are to discard because replacement is more cost-effective than production.

Phase 1. Scarce materials and time-consuming production

In the earliest phase, we created things ourselves, and we replaced them when they wore out. Materials were scarce, and we had to manage our commodities and tools to ensure we had either a sufficient stock or a replacement to carry us into the future. We had to plan. Few people knew how to produce commodities and tools, and fewer knew how to fix them. During this phase, tools and products were the primary sources of capital and our livelihoods. The demand for tools and products was manageable because the population was smaller, and life spans were shorter. We fixed, repaired, and patched them to extend their useful business lives. We discarded commodities and tools only when they spoiled or no longer served a useful purpose.

Phase 2. Increased demand for products and tools

Over the centuries, populations and their life spans grew. There was an increasing demand for commodities and tools. And with increased availability, there was increased knowledge of how to use and make them. The growing demand meant that more people had to learn how to fix them. Scarcity became a widespread concern because we needed to make more of everything. The scarcity of materials and tools increased the risk of theft, misappropriation, misrepresentation, fault, or error. New economic consequences and remedies emerged to address demand and scarcity.

Phase 3. Mass production of commodities and preference for variety

Fast forward to the industrial age, where materials for producing commodities are more widely available now due to market expansions. There is a continued increase in demand, but there is increased demand for variations and versions. The choice becomes an option for those populations with expendable resources. Advances in transportation increase options for delivery and access to commodities. The time to delivery for ready-made goods decreases, which means that demand is satisfied more quickly. Widespread access to commodities and materials means that more people can learn how to produce goods and tools themselves. 'Homemade' versions increase because people have the knowledge and means to create. A surplus is a new economic concept. Discarding becomes routine for some populations, and this new economic behavior creates secondary markets for 'used materials.' The concept of recycling and reuse becomes the norm in populations with fewer resources.

Phase 4. Surplus, abundance, diversification, and discards

All of the factors that we have called out for disposition of knowledge assets are now firmly in place in our basic economic behaviors. It set the stage for mass production of commodities and mass consumption. The cost of commodities and tools is now affordable to the majority of the population. Everyone wants new because it conveys a level of economic status. No one has to know how to fix it because replacement is more cost-effective. Discarding is now considered part of social standing – if you can discard, you must be well-positioned. Discarding produces landfills of discarded assets around the country and the globe. Versions and variation are the new normal – people want what is different. Design shifts to style over function. Balancing supply and demand is now a major consideration. Because we have increased production capacity, quality has decreased. We now have increased product deterioration – life spans shorten. Pulp paper deteriorates. We throw away low-quality products at an increasingly frequent rate because they are not worth fixing. People forget how to fix, and knowledge about tools and assets begins to disappear.

Phase 5. Global competition, increased harm and risk

The future holds more global competition for resources, increased costs and prices, and greater scarcity. Asset landfills inside organizations grow, and new methods of acquisition develop to reduce disposition activities. Organizations lease versus buy because it routinizes disposition. Secondary markets for recycling and reuse grow for some kinds of assets. Repurposing and reuse increases across the population, as awareness of pollution grows. There is a resurgence of interest in 'how to make' and 'how to fix,' and a need for knowledge of assets increases. Knowledge of how to produce variations and how to create from existing (upcycling) expands rapidly across the population, and with the aid of technology advances. Everyone is now a producer. Given the decentralization of production, there is an increased risk of faults, errors, risks, and harm because of controls over production decrease. There is an increased risk of theft, and misrepresentation also increases. Market sources are not always known or trusted. The emerging challenges of discovering information and knowledge in organizational landfills raises concerns about convenience copies and redundancies.

Knowledge asset disposition and destruction in the knowledge architecture blueprint

This functional architecture most closely aligns with the data and information architecture practice. It has a close affinity with business capabilities and business architecture practice. It is business managers and stakeholders who determine whether an asset still has business value. Within the knowledge architecture segment, it has extensive dependencies for all of the earlier functional architectures.

Chapter review

After reading this chapter, you should be able to:

- define disposition and destruction for knowledge assets;
- discuss the four reasons organizations should have architectural support for dispositioning and destruction;
- describe dispositioning through preservation;
- describe dispositioning through repurposing and recycling;
- describe dispositioning through discard without reuse;
- describe dispositioning through destruction.

References and recommended future readings

Arnold, S. E. (2002). *Content management: Role and reality.* Pre-publication draft. http://www.arnoldit.com/articles/cmkoenigJuly2002.pdf.

Ayres, R., Ferrer, G., & Van Leynseele, T. (1997). Eco-efficiency, asset recovery and remanufacturing. *European Management Journal, 15*(5), 557–574.

Black, E. L., Sellers, K. F., & Manly, T. S. (1998). Earnings management using asset sales: An international study of countries allowing noncurrent asset revaluation. *Journal of Business Finance & Accounting, 25*(9–10), 1287–1317.

Bradshaw, S., & Linneker, B. (2015). The gendered destruction and reconstruction of assets and the transformative potential of "disasters." In *Gender, asset accumulation and just cities* (pp. 176–192). Routledge.

Bradsher, J. G. (1985). An administrative history of the disposal of federal records, 1789–1949. *Provenance, Journal of the Society of Georgia Archivists, 3*(2), 2.

Brynjolfsson, E. (1994). Information assets, technology and organization. *Management Science, 40*(12), 1645–1662.

Carlucci, T. N. (1986). The asset, transfer dilemma: Disposal of resources and qualification for Medicaid assistance. *Drake Law Review, 36*, 369.

Coates, S. (2014). BYOD business issues: Auditors need to ensure their organization has a map in place for connecting personal devices to corporate networks and data. *Internal Auditor, 71*(1), 21–23.

Corrigan, M. (2010). Cleaning up your information wasteland. *Information Management, 44*(3), 26.

Cox, R. J., Wallace, D. A., & Wallace, D. (Eds.). (2002). *Archives and the public good: Accountability and records in modern society.* Greenwood Publishing Group.

Curiac, D. I., & Pachia, M. (2015). Controlled information destruction: The final frontier in preserving information security for every organisation. *Enterprise Information Systems, 9*(4), 384–400.

Dollar, C. M. (1993). Archivists and records managers in the information age. *Archivaria, 36*.

Drewry, E. B. (1955). Records disposition in the federal government. *Public Administration Review, 15*(3), 218–221.

Franks, P. C. (2017). Even in a "never delete anything" world, compliant information disposition has its place. *Information Management, 51*(6), 45–46.

Franks, P. C. (2013). *Records and information management.* American Library Association.

Geambasu, R., Kohno, T., Levy, A. A., & Levy, H. M. (2009, August–October 4–6). Vanish: Increasing data privacy with self-destructing data. In *USENIX security symposium. (OSDI)*, (Vol. 316, pp. 299–315). USENIX Association.

Goza, R. (2013). The ethics of record destruction. *Journal of Management Policy and Practice*, *14*(6), 107–115.

Handa, P., Pagani, J., & Bedford, D. (2019). *Identifying and categorizing organization's knowledge assets*. Knowledge Assets and Knowledge Audits (Working Methods for Knowledge Management), 79–104.

Harris, V. (2000). *"They should have destroyed more": The destruction of public records by the South African state in the final years of apartheid, 1990–1994*. ISSN 0258-7696.

Harrison, R. J. (2007). Creating value in a medical device company through intellectual assets. In *2007 29th annual international conference of the IEEE engineering in medicine and biology society* (pp. 4381–4385). IEEE.

Hastings, N. A. (2010). *Physical asset management* (Vol. 2). Springer.

Hsiang, S. M., & Jina, A. S. (2019). *Replication data for: Geography, depreciation, and growth*. American Economic Association.

Jolicoeur, P. W., & Barrett, J. T. (2005). Coming of age: Strategic asset management in the municipal sector. *Journal of Facilities Management*, *3*(1), 41–52.

Jonassen, D. H., & Colaric, S. (2001). Information landfills contain knowledge: Searching equals learning; hyperlinking is good instruction; and other myths about learning from the internet. *Computers in Schools*, *17*(3), 159–170.

Matthews, D., & Gibson, E. (2009). Fixed asset disposal: Methods and strategies for disposing of personal property in the public sector. *International Handbook of Public Procurement*, 591.

Nomura, K., & Momose, F. (2008). *Measurement of depreciation rates based on disposal asset data in Japan*. Paper presented, Economic and Social Research Institute (ESRI).

Oesterle, D. A. (1982). Private litigant's remedies for an opponent's inappropriate destruction of relevant documents. *Texas Law Review*, *61*, 1185.

Park, Y. J. (2004). A study on the operation and special quality of the records disposition schedule. *Journal of Information Management*, *35*(1), 71–91.

Penn, I. A., & Pennix, G. B. (2017). *Records management handbook*. Routledge.

Perlman, R. (2005). The ephemerizer: Making data disappear. *Information System Security*, *1*(1), 51–68. [Crossref], [Web of Science ®].

Plastoi, M., & Curiac, D. L. (2009, May 28–29). Energy-driven methodology for node self-destruction in wireless sensor networks. In *Proceedings of the 5th international symposium on applied computational intelligence and informatics (SACI'09)* (pp. 319–322). IEEE.

Plastoi, M., Curiac, D. L., Banias, O., Volosencu, C., Pescaru, D., & Doboli, A. (2009, July 7–10). Self-destruction procedure for cluster-tree wireless sensor networks. In *Proceedings of the international conference on wireless information networks and systems (WINSYS 2009)*, (pp. 63–67). INSTICC Press.

Posey, C., Roberts, T. L., & Lowry, P. B. (2015). The impact of organizational commitment on insiders' motivation to protect organizational information assets. *Journal of Management Information Systems*, *32*(4), 179–214.

Sabourin, P. (2001). Constructing a function-based records classification system: Business activity structure classification system. *Archivaria*, *51*, 137–154.

Schiller, S., & Merhout, J. W. (2011). *IT asset disposition services: A green solution for the enterprise*. AMCIS.

Summers, J. (1991). Asset disposal: Follow company policies or follow the law? *Journal of Healthcare Materiel Management*, *9*(4), 54–56.

Tungare, M., Pérez-Quiñones, M., Pyla, P. S., Hanrahan, B., Murthy, U., & Quintana-Castillo, R. (2010). *Sustainability of Bits, not just Atoms*. Manuel Pérez-Quiñones.

Zhenquan, L. H. H. G. D. (2001). Study of semi-structurd information disposition pattern based on EC-MAS. *Computer Engineering* (12), 6.

10

FUNCTIONAL ARCHITECTURE DESIGNS FOR KNOWLEDGE PRESERVATION AND CONSERVATION

Chapter summary

This chapter explains what we mean by preservation and conservation of knowledge assets, and how these traditional functions relate to the dynamic technology context. The chapter outlines six activities that support knowledge asset preservation and conservation and are essential to designing a supporting functional architecture. The chapter considers why it is essential to have a good understanding of preservation, conservation, content migration, preservation, or conservation practices for different types of assets. Here we explain that the primary challenge in designing this functional architecture is maintaining the focus on the knowledge assets rather than the package and in thinking long term rather than short term.

Why we care about knowledge asset preservation

Preservation of knowledge assets is one of the four disposition decision outcomes we discussed in Chapter 9. We preserve knowledge assets because they have a continuing useful business life for the organization. The goal is to maintain that kernel of knowledge that has enduring or at least situational business value. The challenge for preservation is to determine when this means preserving the encoding, formatting, and packaging, and when it is acceptable simply to maintain the embedded knowledge. Business experts and the knowledge architects make these decisions on a case-by-case basis.

Is it essential to preserve and retain the original version of the movie *Metropolis*? Or the recording of Enrico Caruso's performance of an opera? Or is it good enough to have an authenticated reproduction, particularly where the reproduction will serve the purpose of knowledge access and consumption more efficiently and effectively than the original? Here is where the decision about long-term availability – which is at the heart of preservation – depends on the expected accessibility and consumability.

Preservation is essential to the 21st-century knowledge economy because channels are changing so rapidly that even well-intended preservation efforts are at risk of being out of date. Preservation is critical to all three knowledge domains – to availability, accessibility, and consumption. If we focus on the package, we run the risk of having to redefine the package to suit the channel continually. Consider all the knowledge that we have already lost because of shifting media and sources. Locking down assets supports the preservation, but it does not support availability, access, or use – it is critical to expanding how we think about 'change' – not just the asset but in terms of the channel. We cannot presume that direct human consumption will be the rule going forward. We want to avoid spending money and devoting resources to knowledge assets that do not have business value and not artificially constraining access to or using knowledge assets based on some artificial principles of originality.

There is a balance to be achieved – and the discussion of this balance has not yet received the attention it should have received. It is essential to define 'business value' based on context and situations. What business value means in a public education situation is different from what it means in a Fortune 100 company. We also must learn to differentiate between preservation and conservation and to make decisions pertinent to the asset and its business value. We focus on preserving the context to ensure legal and regulatory trustworthiness is respected.

At this point, we have already decided to preserve the asset. Now we must decide on what aspects of the object to preserve and how to preserve them. How we preserve the asset depends on the nature of the risk. Is the object deteriorating? Is the medium itself no longer available to read it? Does it have historical value? You need to have a set of conservation guidelines for when you simply preserve it and when that preservation becomes conservation. Conservation may be required – and we may need to do a full restoration of the knowledge asset as a whole or the layers of the knowledge asset.

Knowledge asset preservation and conservation – design concepts

To develop this functional architecture, we must have a good understanding of preservation, conservation, content migration, preservation, or conservation practices for different types of media, including their inherent encoding and formatting, emulation strategies and reinterpretation strategies, as well as traditional preservation and conservation cultures. The primary challenges we face in designing this functional architecture are maintaining the focus on the knowledge assets rather than the package, in acting for the long term, and in ensuring that preservation and conservation are undertaken for availability and access rather than lockdown and storage.

Preservation

Preservation is defined as the protection of something – especially from loss, injury, or danger. Preservation is an umbrella term for activities that reduce or prevent damage to extend the life expectancy of a knowledge asset (DAITSS, 2004; Heslop et al., 2002; Lindlar et al., 2013; Lorie, 2004; Lundy, 2008; Maniatis et al., 2003; North East Document Conservation Center, 2019; Rothenberg, 1995; Van Wijngaarden & Oltmans, 2004). It is a process that helps to keep knowledge assets alive or in existence, to extend their useful business life, to keep something safe from harm, to protect it, or to retain it. Preservation intends to prevent deterioration or loss of the essential asset. We focus on preserving the original state, but not the formatting and the packaging – it will always depend on the asset. This means that it is not sufficient just to define asset preservation schedules based on asset type. Preservation requires additional decision criteria that allow the decision-maker and expert to make a preservation decision based on the business value of the asset itself and its state. This means we also likely need additional metainformation to document how we have preserved any specific knowledge asset following preservation.

Preserving knowledge presumes that we can identify the asset and have a sense of its business value to the organization. Organizations preserve knowledge to maintain access to their business value. The business value may be defined in many ways, including legal requirements or financial requirements. Organizations may focus on digital preservation, which may mean the transformation or migration of formats to ensure continued access and availability.

New media preservationists work to integrate new preservation strategies with existing documentation techniques and metadata standards. This effort is made to remain compatible with previous frameworks and models for archiving, storing, and maintaining variable media objects in a standardized repository utilizing a systematized vocabulary. We can draw guidelines from the practices of digital preservation, web archiving, and digital resource curation. This is true for explicit knowledge assets and any structured knowledge assets. They may not apply equally well, though, to other types of assets represented in non-text or non-data formats. Scientific data and legal records may be easily migrated from one platform to another without losing their essential knowledge. Still, images, audio, and works of art are often sensitive to the look and feel of the media in which they are embedded.

Conservation

Preservation may also involve retaining and protecting physical materials by minimizing physical deterioration and damage to reduce loss and extend the life of an asset. This aspect of a preservation decision is better described as conservation. Preservation is distinguished from conservation, which addresses treatment to repair the damage. Records are those materials that warrant preservation due to their business value. Archives management also contributes significantly to this stage as it is concerned with the maintenance of archival collections and materials. Archival materials may be either digital or physical. Archives management focuses on the acquisition, care, arrangement, description, and retrieval of records once they have been tagged for either preservation or disposition.

Conservation speaks to the preservation of our experience of the asset (American Institute for Conservation, 2019; Dow, 2009; Frey & Heller, 2008; Liang & Wan, 2017; Ockerbloom, 1998; Remondino, 2011; Shi et al., 2009; Sitts, 2000; van der Wal & Arts, 2015; Walker & Thoma, 2004). The way we consume the asset determines access. Conservation also refers more specifically to the physical treatment of individual damaged items. Preventive conservation describes those activities that address the longevity of knowledge assets. Restoration refers to returning an object to its original state, or what is thought to have been its original state. In other words, we might try to restore those old rolls of B-film rather than transfer the audio and moving images to a DVD.

While the most apparent vulnerability or new media art is rapid technological obsolescence, conservation addresses other challenges, including hybrid, contextual, or 'live' qualities. We need new strategies for preserving conceptual art, performance, installation art, video art, and even to a limited extent, painting and sculpture. For conservation guidance, we look to the field of art conservation and restoration, which has expertise in addressing conditions of neglect, willful damage, or routine decay caused by the effects of time and human use. Conservation addresses protection from future damage and deterioration. Art conservation has become an essential tool of research; it is a standard practice among professional conservators to document treatments with photographs and written reports.

Knowledge asset preservation is the term we use to refer to what the knowledge management literature defines as knowledge retention. It is a critical knowledge management process linked to knowledge loss. As outlined earlier, knowledge loss refers to knowledge attrition when part of the created knowledge base is not retained by the organization (DeLong & Storey, 2004). Unfortunately, there is no systematic approach to preservation or conservation across the full range of knowledge asset types. Practices are scattered and fragmented, and there is little grounding theory. We need to redefine what we mean by 'preservation' when it comes to human capital, collective knowledge capital, cultural capital, and network knowledge capital. We have a good sense of preservation for explicit knowledge assets, but we may need to redefine what we mean by preservation – preservation may not be infinite.

Preservation and conservation decisions

Once the decision to preserve has been made, the knowledge architect and the business manager need to determine the best preservation strategy. Ideally, there are guidelines in place that help them to make the decision. These guidelines should be referenced in the disposition schedules, and for each asset class. The disposition classes may describe the preferred strategies, but they cannot tell us about the asset's

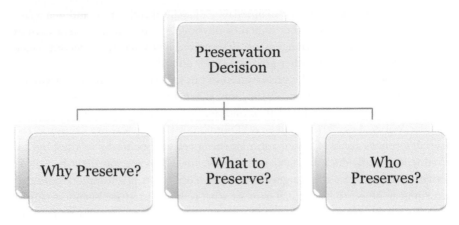

FIGURE 10.1 Preservation–Conservation Decision Process

business value. For each asset, we need to walk through a series of questions to arrive at the best preservation strategy (Figure 10.1).

The first question we need to answer is, 'What is the business value of this particular asset?' Is this a good business choice? Will this strategy ensure continued availability, accessibility, and consumability in our day-to-day business operations? Will it meet these criteria ten years from now, or will we need to preserve it again? What is the expected life span of the new preservation strategy? If there are ten possible preservation strategies, the business manager should choose the one that serves the business purpose. In this case, the business purpose also includes considering any legal or financial regulatory requirements.

The second critical question is, 'What elements of the asset will we preserve?' This question speaks to whether we will preserve only the knowledge asset without regard to the package or format, or whether we need to preserve the encoding, formatting, and packaging. In this step, we must consider those elements of the asset that may serve as evidence. Is it necessary to preserve the full email for e-discovery and legal documentation? Or, do we need to keep a snapshot of the financial system to validate the data asset? If there are legal or financial considerations, or if the asset has historical value in its original state, the business decision should be able to preserve the asset. Where the original asset needs to be preserved in its original state, we need to look at conservation options.

For any class of assets, there are many possible preservation strategies available. We can create an archival print copy of a digital email. We can create digital copies of print records. We can migrate a structured data set from an application-specific format to a generic spreadsheet or database format. We can copy a B-film role to a digital multimedia asset by playing it on an old projector and recording it. We can make a digital copy of an old vinyl audio recording. The possibilities of what we can do are unlimited. Preservation should apply all of those critical questions we posed for choosing standards in Chapter 7 to each preservation decision. Is the format choice open-source or proprietary? Does it lock down the asset without regard to access or use? Does it have documented standards to support it? Is it lossless or lossy? Is there a single version in use across the organization? Does it have an earlier version viewer?

An important architectural aspect of this decision point is, 'Do we have the applications and tools we need to preserve the asset?' Can our functional architecture support this process? Or, do we need to have outside services or support? These questions are essential where legal or financial rules apply, and where the asset must be conserved.

We expect the preservation of functional architecture to make extensive use of the knowledge asset object models, any applications needed to complete transformations or conservation, and the capture of preservation metadata. Preservation metadata encompasses all information necessary to manage and preserve digital assets over time. Preservation metadata captures technical information supporting preservation decisions and actions, documents preservation actions taken, records the effects of preservation strategies, ensures the authenticity of digital resources over time, and contains essential information about rights management.

We need to be cautious about simple solutions to preservation questions – one common approach today is for organizations to simply 'store things in the cloud.' Keep in mind that while this may be a cost-effective storage option, it is not necessarily a cost-effective preservation option. If storing it in the cloud does not address the encoding, formatting, and packaging issues, you do not focus on preservation.

Finally, the last question is, 'Who can best do the preservation?' Does the strategy require engineering expertise? Archival or media expertise? Or, given the appropriate instructions and guidelines, can the business unit complete it? Can the preservation action be automated and simply set up as a periodic process?

An example might be the scheduled and automatic copying of six months of email communications to a backup server or a physical storage medium. Is the business custodian or steward aware of how to document the preservation action? Do they have access to the applications they need?

Preservation methods

What are some of the methods our functional architecture may need to support? And how does it provide support? The most common form of preservation is asset migration. We tend to talk about migration only in terms of format migration, but knowledge asset preservation needs to look at all layers of that asset model. It is not limited to formats. Migration can include copying data from one type of storage material to another to ensure continued access to the information as the data structure becomes obsolete. It can consist of converting data from an obsolete structure to a new structure to prevent risk, harm, or loss. It may involve changes in the internal structure of a data file as needed to keep pace with changing software versions, or a radical change in structure, such as changes from one application to another. Making changes in the essential knowledge assets encoding and format structures place the original at risk. The new structure may not accurately capture the form and function of the original.

Some preservation strategies may focus on the environment in which the assets are stored. In this case, the functional architecture may include environmentally controlled storage. Here the functional architecture is both physical and digital – ensuing physical conditions are appropriate to protect materials from adverse effects of temperature, humidity, air quality, light, and biological infestation, as well as human risks associated with housekeeping procedures, security, and fire and water damage.

Preservation and conservation of human capital assets

What does it mean to 'preserve' an individual's tacit knowledge? Their skills and competencies? Their attitudes and behaviors? On a practical level, only the individual can preserve their knowledge. We cannot 'retain' the individual indefinitely. We can ensure that the individual's knowledge is actively transferred to others while he or she is with the organization. We can ensure the individual passes on their skills and competencies and learn from their constructive attitudes and behaviors. Any tangible representation we create takes the form of explicit knowledge representation. From a knowledge architecture design perspective, the question is, how do we preserve the representation we created? We begin by focusing on the personal reference model of the individual. These are often embedded within the supporting applications. Preserving profiles means exporting them from the application and transforming them into a format that can be read by other applications. We don't need to preserve all elements of the profile, but we do need to be able to decide which are the elements that have principal business value.

The probability is high that what we want to preserve are those representations of how they did what they did, the kinds of decisions they made, and what they knew that was relevant to the business. What knowledge is retained is part of the review and decision process of the business. The challenge is that human capital assets are dynamic. Preservation is not a one-time task – we have to essentially identify snapshots of an individual's human capital for preservation. In essence, this is curation practices applied to preservation. The final preservation action occurs only when the individual retires or leaves the organization.

Preservation and conservation of explicit knowledge assets

An organization needs to develop preservation strategies for explicit knowledge asset classes. The challenge is that your starting point may be either physical or digital. Just because the source is print does not mean that the preferred preservation form is digital. Just because the source differentiator will be whether those assets in the asset class are in physical or digital form, the digital form may not transform into other digital forms. There may be a need to create a long-term print version.

Those decision points identified earlier, and the criteria for making preservation decisions outlined earlier, are well suited to explicit knowledge. While the preservation options may be well articulated in practice and the literature, the challenge is to choose an 'end state' goal that will serve your business goals. In most organizations, these decisions are left to the archivists, the records managers, and the data management teams. While they are experts in preserving assets for protection purposes, they may not have the same insights as business managers, stewards, and custodians on the nature of the future use of these assets. Additionally, it is always important to seek your legal and internal regulatory advice to ensure that any strategy you choose will meet requirements.

As with the other functional architectures, we always start with the knowledge asset classes we defined in Chapter 6. This provides some guidance, but there are so many options that it may be difficult to determine one preservation strategy for a class. One way to break the decision down to a manageable level is to consider a short- and long-term strategy. This framework would be similar to how records managers think of 'semi-active' and 'inactive' business assets. Business managers would not consider keeping inactive equipment or financial capital because they cost more to maintain than they add value. But, they might sideline an asset with the intent to use it in contingency or backup situations, or for future reference. This may be helpful if your legal and regulatory environment is unsettled or if you know the asset has business value for the next ten years. Still, it is difficult to project beyond that timeline. It is this type of knowledge asset that adds the most volume to our digital landfills. It is essential not just to preserve forever and forget.

Preservation and conservation of procedural knowledge assets

What is the best format and package for preserving procedural knowledge, so it is accessible and usable in the future? This is perhaps the most important type of knowledge asset to preserve because it represents your organization's 'treasured recipes' for doing what you do. In the disposition stage, we determined which procedural knowledge assets had persistent value. At this stage, we need to think about why we're preserving those assets. Most likely, we're preserving this knowledge because we need (1) to use if for teaching those who need to learn how to do it well; (2) to analyze processes for critical incident analyses and after-action reviews; (3) to identify problems and demonstrate how not to do it; (4) to preserve the ways or methods of particular experts; or (5) to serve as documentary evidence of the organization business operation's overtime. In four of the five scenarios, we're preserving for active use.

What does this mean in terms of a preservation strategy? Is a migration or transformation sufficient? Or, do we need to think about a better way to represent or document procedural knowledge for the future? Ideally, we would begin with the object classes we identified for procedural knowledge and establish a set of strategies based on expected future use. This is quite a different approach from what we currently take, so it will involve some creative thinking and brainstorming with business custodians and stewards. Additionally, procedural knowledge assets are not well managed or controlled by the average organization. You should assume source assets will come in a variety of states. For example, what do you have to work within terms of procedures? What do we have to work within terms of process demonstrations and explanations? What is the nature of assets representing errors, faults, and mistakes?

Or, process 'recipes' or resource lists? Workflow or process engineering documents may be created for robotics or managers. Do we want to preserve them in their original state, or is there a better target form that works better for long-term preservation? What about process training materials? Or patents?

Preservation of procedural knowledge assets goes beyond locking down and storing the evidence forever. It means being able to envision how to make these assets accessible and consumable for active learning. This is a significant change to preservation. From a functional architecture perspective, it means planning for transformations that not only access and deconstruct the original knowledge asset, but to re-represent it in a forward-looking form. We should expect the preservation process for procedural knowledge assets to be iterative because we are preserving for active learning and continuous business investment. As the environment – business and technology – changes, we will need to reassess our preservation strategies. Our functional preservation architecture should include monitoring, auditing, and reporting capabilities.

Preservation and conservation of cultural knowledge assets

Cultural assets have been defined as profiles. There are documentary and report versions – preservation strategies would follow guidelines for explicit assets. Preservation might seem straightforward – simply create a persistent form of the assessment or the profile. But, we're preserving cultural knowledge to help reinforce or shift our cultures – we want to remember where we came from, our organizational heritage, where we are now, and to shape our organizational culture for the future. This is more than a 'profile' or a 'report.' There are audio or visual representations of our culture from the past that we need to 'experience' – performances, events, artifacts that represent our culture. What will be more effective for helping a recruit understand our ethics and values than an interview with the company founder? Or, a noteworthy speech by a critical expert. How we behave, how we treat each other can best be taught through good practice examples we can see and feel. Records of a significant event, meetings, celebrations – all are now possible to capture and record.

The challenge is that many will be in physical form and like procedural knowledge. Or they may be in digital form or on a media that requires conservation as well as preservation. Here you will need specialized expertise to guide the decision-making process. Starting with your knowledge asset classes, develop a series of questions that will help you assess the source object scheduled for preservation. Consult with business managers about the potential future use of these assets. Be sure to consider the future value of these assets to develop organizational narratives and storytelling. Ideally, the knowledge architect will have a cultural expert to work with to understand future uses.

Preservation and conservation of network capital assets

Network assets present a different kind of preservation challenge. We have a good idea of the knowledge asset classes of a network: nodes, links, and messages. But the network is the most dynamic of all of our knowledge asset types. Depending on the level of activity of a network, this may mean the network changes hourly, or daily. Ideally, the knowledge architect has defined a schedule for capturing representations of these asset classes. This is where our preservation strategy begins. The organization has decided which elements have business value, and which elements should be preserved. The essential decision points for preservation are how to preserve these assets for access and use in the future. Because these assets can represent such a high volume of data, future use of the preserved asset is essential. Are we preserving network representations for persistent knowledge of who has tacit or procedural knowledge to contribute to a topic? If so, we need to preserve the network in a way that makes it easy for us to access the nodes or those who represent those nodes. Are we preserving the network assets so we can trace an idea's evolution or how a team assessed and resolved a problem? We need to focus on preserving the messages and discourse.

We may not need to preserve the whole network. Like procedural knowledge, the knowledge architect's work will be simplified if there is a set of critical questions for business managers that helps them zero in on the business value of any given network. This allows the knowledge architect to focus on the structure of the network, and to consider how to ensure preservation strategies are application-agnostic. Network applications are emerging, and they represent many structures.

The design environment for knowledge asset preservation

What triggers the need to identify or distinguish knowledge assets? There are several reasons to preserve knowledge assets. First, the cost of maintaining and managing explicit knowledge becomes overwhelming, and not all of these assets have current business value. We need to balance business value with the costs of preservation. Second, everyday organizations lose knowledge assets because there is no preservation strategy in place. Loss of human capital adversely affects the organization's business. Organizations fail to make their existing human capital available, and it spends additional resources to recreate or reinvent that knowledge. Third, procedural knowledge can leak outside the organization when adequate preservation strategies are not in place, resulting in comparative business harm to the organization. Finally, organizations can lose vital network connections or knowledge generated through professional networks when those network connections are lost.

What sources do we need to design this functional architecture? This functional architecture pulls together the knowledge object models we developed early on, the disposition process that generates the preservation action, the knowledge assets, defined preservation strategies, and an affordable and effective preservation architecture and infrastructure.

What are the outputs and outcomes? The specific outputs and outcomes from this functional architecture are updated knowledge object models, practical and pertinent preservation strategies, and affordable and sustainable preservation infrastructure.

What are the impacts and consequences of this functional architecture? This functional architecture provides support for the preservation of all knowledge assets that have business value regardless of their form or representation. This functional architecture also supports the decision-making process for choosing a preservation strategy for classes of knowledge assets, and to apply those strategies to specific assets. It also ensures that the assets are accessible and consumable for business use in the future. In the longer term, consequences are that knowledge assets with long-term business value are safeguarded. Historical knowledge that has business value has been transformed to work with current channels, tools, and methods. Historical knowledge that has business value can continue to be used. Finally, this functional architecture makes the task of preservation practical and affordable for business managers.

How do we do this? This functional architecture supports five essential activities, including: (1) defining organization's preservation strategies; (2) defining the organization's preservation infrastructures; (3) developing preservation decision criteria – supplemental to retention schedules; (4) identifying knowledge assets scheduled for preservation disposition; and (5) supplementing the metadata and metainformation for any preserved assets.

What factors do we need to consider when designing this architecture? This functional architecture represents a new and expanded capability for the organization. Historically, preservation has been limited to enterprise resource systems and structured data or internal documentation representing official business transactions. This functional architecture represents a shift from the 'preserve to store and protect' mindset to 'preserve for use.' In designing this architecture, the knowledge architecture ensures that preservation storage is easily accessible to anyone in the business context who may need it. We include preserving 'bad' knowledge to ensure that it is not repeated and that we are preserving the knowledge asset, not just the package. Additionally, the knowledge architecture should ensure that the organization's understanding of conservation expands to include the restoration of the original asset in a way that supports knowledge availability, knowledge accessibility, and knowledge consumability.

Design activities and tasks for knowledge asset preservation

Five high-level activities support this functional architecture, including:

- Activity 1. Define the organization's preservation strategies
- Activity 2. Define the organization's preservation infrastructures and sources

- Activity 3. Update the Object Model Preservation Attributes
- Activity 4. Identify knowledge assets scheduled for preservation disposition
- Activity 5. Supplement the metadata and metainformation for any preserved assets

Activity 1. Define the organization's preservation strategies

How do we do this? This activity provides a foundation from which we can draw strategies for classes of knowledge assets and business contexts. We can design a more effective functional architecture if we focus on and develop the competencies to support those preservation actions that are effective for our organization. Having a single functional architecture does not mean there is just one strategy; i.e., everything is transformed to PDF and stored in a designated archival system. It means that we have an identified set of strategies that we know we can sustain that will work across all of our knowledge assets. Essentially, we look across our asset classes, consult with business managers and engineers, and develop a decision framework that supports a range of scenarios. This activity should also include a 'desk check' to ensure that any scenarios recommended will produce assets that remain available, accessible, and consumable – not simply stored and locked down.

What inputs does this activity need? The activity produces a decision framework, the asset's long-term business value and use, the current source encoding, format, and package, the preferred final form, and the transformation process. Traditional preservation strategies and sources must be adapted because they have been designed to preserve the package primarily. Traditional approaches often presume the asset is being stored 'just in case' there is a need rather than an expectation that the asset will be put into service in some way in the future.

What products does this activity generate? This activity produces a decision framework that business managers and the knowledge architect can use to narrow down options for specific knowledge asset classes.

What resources does this activity require? This activity requires the knowledge object models, the details on the range of encoding, formatting and packaging practices for those classes, and the knowledge of business managers, preservation experts, and the knowledge architect.

Activity 2. Define the organization's preservation infrastructures and sources

How do we do this? Preservation requires specialized applications and technologies. An important checkpoint for our preservation decision framework is an understanding of what applications and technologies are needed, their cost, what competencies they require to support them, and what new roles and responsibilities might be required. As noted earlier, preservation is often a back-room operation that archivists and data managers perform at the end of an asset's useful business life or periodically to manage storage capacity. Preservation typically targets explicit knowledge assets and structured explicit knowledge assets. Even with this limited focus, preservation can have high costs to an organization – costs of personnel, applications, and technologies. A preservation strategy for all kinds of knowledge assets dramatically expands the possibilities. A preservation decision framework is an essential tool for identifying this infrastructure. It is also essential that we have an efficiently designed infrastructure. Allowing each business unit to define its infrastructure will carry a huge direct cost (e.g., redundant and diverse applications and technologies) and indirect costs (e.g., redundant and variant competencies across processes). The knowledge architect should work closely with preservation experts and developers to identify the optimal applications and technologies to support each scenario in the decision framework. Additionally, the knowledge architect should work closely with business managers and preservation experts to identify the competencies, roles, and responsibilities, and to design a whole organization support strategy.

What inputs does this activity need? The preservation decision framework and the knowledge asset object classes are the essential inputs for this activity.

What products does it generate? This activity should produce a draft whole organization preservation infrastructure blueprint, supported by estimated costs and necessary skills and competencies to support it. The architecture blueprint should also be integrated into the application and technology architecture practice of the organization.

What resources does this activity require? This activity is heavily dependent upon the preservation experts, developers and engineers, business managers, and the knowledge architect.

Activity 3. Update the Object Model Preservation Attributes

How do we do this? This activity involves backfilling the knowledge object models with options and values for preservation attributes. These attributes should describe the preservation action is taken, the changes to the asset, the date of the transformation, and any documentation required for legal, evidentiary, or regulatory purposes.

What inputs does this activity need? This activity is heavily dependent upon the preservation decision framework and the scenarios pertinent to each class of knowledge assets.

What products does it generate? The product of this activity is updated object model preservation attributes for each class of assets.

What resources does this activity require? The most important resource is the knowledge object models. We use the decision framework and the advice of preservation experts and business managers to assign strategies to each knowledge asset class.

Activity 4. Identify knowledge assets scheduled for preservation disposition

How do we do this? This activity involves applying the preservation actions to knowledge assets that require preservation. At any point in time, on any given day, every organization has knowledge assets with a business value at risk of deterioration, damage, loss, or loss of access. The knowledge object models will guide timelines for preservation review. Initially, though, a process will need to be established to act on disposition decisions that recommend preservation assets.

What inputs does this activity need? The knowledge object models provide a set of scenarios for transformation. The business manager and preservation experts will have to select one of these options and prepare a plan for that asset.

What products does it generate? This activity creates a list of assets to be preserved and the recommended preservation actions. It should also produce preservation actions and preserved assets.

What resources does this activity require? This activity requires access to the assets, the preservation recommendations, and any applications and technologies needed to complete the transformation.

Activity 5. Supplement the metadata and metainformation for any preserved assets

How do we do this? Once the asset has been preserved, the metadata for the specific asset should be updated. This activity differs from the object model update in that it changes the asset's metadata and goes beyond merely describing the possible scenarios for attributes.

What inputs does this activity need? This activity requires access to the asset's metadata or properties.

What products does it generate? This activity updates the metadata about the knowledge asset to provide a tracing of the changes made to the asset.

What resources does this activity require? It requires some form of metadata description, whether as an extended set of properties or a standardized metadata record structure. It also requires knowledge of the preservation attributes. This activity should be completed by a preservation expert, working with the business managers.

Evolution of knowledge asset preservation designs

The evolution of preservation has been influenced by several factors, including (1) what we're preserving and its value; (2) why we're preserving it; (3) to whom it has value; and (4) the preservation techniques that are available for us to leverage. As these factors change, we see shifts across five phases (Figure 10.2):

- Phase 1. Cultural and art collection preservation
- Phase 2. Cultural and art conservation
- Phase 3. Archival collection preservation
- Phase 4. Object level preservation
- Phase 5. Print and digital media preservation

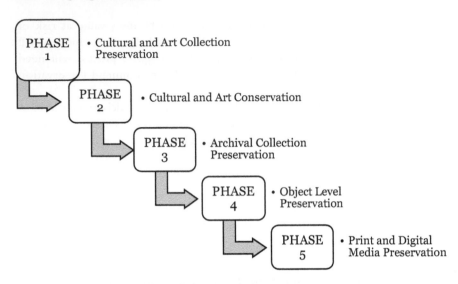

FIGURE 10.2 Evolution of Knowledge Asset Preservation

Phase 1. Cultural and art collection preservation

The earliest preservation was applied to cultural artifacts and art, and to manuscripts that had value to the wealthiest individuals. In this earliest phase, these assets were preserved because they had status value to their owners. They were preserved as representations of the culture and history of the region or nation. The earliest preservation strategies were primitive and rudimentary and often involved focusing on the environment in which the resources were stored. Preservation also included keeping these resources from heavy use by storing them in private collections or monastery collections with limited users. Because preservation techniques were primitive, many resources were lost, damaged, or deteriorated beyond repair. In the earliest centuries, conservation was also primitive and rudimentary.

In some cases, these techniques added to the risk, loss, and damage of the assets. In most cases, the preservation of manuscripts and documents involved making new copies. The one advantage we had in the earliest centuries was that the materials on which these manuscripts and documents were created were of higher quality than in later centuries. The use of manuscripts and documents was also limited by definition because literacy rates were low. Fewer people could read, and the demand for access to written knowledge was lower.

Phase 2. Cultural and art conservation

The second phase of the evolution of preservation sees some advances in art and cultural artifact conservation techniques. These advances were not yet applied to manuscripts and documents. These materials were not as highly valued as were works of art or cultural artifacts. As we moved into the Enlightenment and there was a renewed interest in historical knowledge, our awareness of manuscripts and early books increased. We became aware of their condition and the need to preserve them, and we made them more widely available to scholars.

Phase 3. Archival collection preservation

The widespread availability of written text, in the form of printed books, increases literacy rates and the demand for access to knowledge. Education and literacy are still not widespread, but the awareness of the value of printed knowledge is growing. Scholarship increases among the wealthy and scholarly communities arise. There is a growing interest in creating collections of print materials among scholarly communities. With this increased interest, written knowledge grows in scale and scope. We now have scholarly letters, the earliest examples of scholarly journals, and scientific disciplines. Journals and diaries of scientific work and knowledge are created. Scholars create collections of scholarly knowledge and the first rudimentary elements of collecting emerge. In this phase, the focus is on assembling collections of domain knowledge. This sets the stage for collection management and preservation.

Phase 4. Object level preservation

At this point in history, we have significant private collections and emerging public collections. The first libraries appear, and the proliferation of books grows. The increased demand for access to written knowledge results in lower-quality materials and lower prices. This introduces new risks of potential damage and deterioration to print materials. This phase also sees the earliest forms of other physical media develop – photographs, prints, more accessible forms of art. The scale and the scope of assets we're collecting, accessing, and using is growing. And, the quality of the media on which they're being recorded is decreasing. The available stock is increasing, and the economic environment is one of increased discard and unrestrained consumption. A significant development during this phase, though, is the increased focus on public and private museums – a significant shift from private collections. The increased interest in museums raises our awareness of the need to preserve art and artifacts for long-term public access and consumption.

Additionally, the rapid move to mechanized production of physical products increases awareness of hand-made artifacts and craftsmanship's artistic value. This leads to a new preservation strategy – art and antique conservation. Our industrialized environments create new hazards for collections, and increasingly frequent natural disasters and force majeure events increase these assets' potential loss. During the 19th century, there was a great impetus, partly due to the loss of some prominent collections to fire, to disseminate the information found in records by publishing them. The discipline of archival science emerges to meet the demand for preserving and conserving written assets.

Phase 5. Digital media conservation

Fast forward to the information age where we have a proliferation of knowledge assets, increased literacy levels, increased resources to acquire, and consume information and knowledge. The rapid advance of technology further accelerates these trends and turns everyone into a knowledge producer and a knowledge consumer. Collections of knowledge assets are commonplace, and the value of knowledge assets increases. By the mid-20th century, however, archivists increasingly focused on preserving original documents that were deteriorating. Archivists adopted many of the techniques for the conservation of individual documents set forth by organizations, among them deacidification and lamination, a process later found to be damaging. In the mid-1960s, the acid-free box was developed, with partial support from the Council on Library Resources (CLR).

Our awareness of the poor-quality production of many historical materials, the rapid deterioration, and the vulnerability to these assets increases. New conservation and preservation strategies emerge, with increased scientific knowledge. Our ability to apply conservation techniques to resources increases the need to make decisions on the value of these assets. Archivists began to see how severe the problem of physical deterioration was – and how little time and money was available to address it. As a result, they began to consider how to choose those records that deserved preservation in their original form, and those that should be dealt with in other ways, such as reformatting.

Like librarians, archivists have increasingly focused on improving environmental control and storage facilities to ensure that their collections of enduring value have as long a life as possible. The techniques and methods of art conservation and restoration go hand in hand and became the province of trained professionals in the 20th century. They have become an increasingly important aspect of the work not only of museums but also of civic authorities and all those concerned with works of art, whether artists, collectors, or galleries. Advances in science and technology and the development of conservation as a profession in the 20th century have led to safer and more effective approaches to studying, preserving, and repairing objects. Modern conservation practice adheres to the principle of reversibility, which dictates that treatments should not cause permanent alteration to the object. Just as we are developing preservation and conservation strategies to manage print and physical assets, the rise of digital assets exponentially increases conservation and conservation challenges. In this phase, we see conservation strategies take on the additional challenge of transformation to preserve access given dynamic applications and technologies.

Knowledge asset preservation and conservation in the knowledge architecture blueprint

Knowledge asset preservation and conservation functional architectures are centered in the knowledge architecture layer. Absent a knowledge architecture practice, this functional architecture must live in the information/data layer.

Within those practices, it must maintain ties to the business architecture practice and the application practice. Business managers, custodians, and stewards are essential decision-makers and advisers to the knowledge architect. All preservation and conservation infrastructure – supporting applications and technologies – are firmly grounded in the application architecture practice.

Chapter review

After reading this chapter, you should be able to:

* define and explain the difference between preservation and conservation of assets;
* explain why we preserve assets;
* explain how we decide what to preserve;
* explain who should preserve;
* describe preservation methods, and explain how they apply to knowledge assets.

References and recommended future readings

American Institute for Conservation of Historic and Artistic Works. (2019). *Definitions of conservation terminology*. Retrieved February 2, 2020, from www.conservation-us.org/docs/default-source/governance/definitions-of-conservation-terminology.pdf.

DAITSS Overview. (2004). www.fcla.edu/digitalArchive/pdfs/DAITSS.pdf.

DeLong, D. W., & Storey, J. (2004). *Lost knowledge: Confronting the threat of an aging workforce*. Oxford University Press.

Dow, E. H. (2009). *Electronic records in the manuscript repository*. Scarecrow Press.

Frey, F., & Heller, D. (2008). *The AIC guide to digital photography and conservation documentation*. American Institute for Conservation.

Heslop, H., Davis, S., & Wilson, A. (2002). *National archives green paper: An approach to the preservation of digital records*. Retrieved February 2, 2020, from www.naa.gov.au/recordkeeping/er/digital_preservation/Green_Paper.pdf.

Liang, J., & Wan, X. (2017). Prototype of a pigments color chart for the digital conservation of ancient murals. *Journal of Electronic Imaging, 26*(2), 023013.

Lindlar, M., Friese, Y., Müller, E., Bähr, T., & von Trosdorf, A. (2013). Benefits of geographical, organizational and collection factors in digital preservation cooperations: The experience of the Goportis consortium. In *Proceedings of the 10th international conference on preservation of digital objects, Lisboa* (pp. 110–117). Digital Preservation of a Process.

Lorie, R. (2004). Preserving digital documents for the long-term. In *IS&T archiving conference* (pp. 88–92). Vimeo.

Lundy, M. W. (2008). Provenance evidence in bibliographic records: Demonstrating the value of best practices in special collections cataloging. *Library Resources & Technical Services, 52*(3), 164.

Maniatis, P., Roussopoulos, M., Giuli, T., Rosenthal, D. S. H., Baker, M., & Muliadi, Y. (2003, October). Preserving peer replicas by rate-limited sampled voting. In *Proceedings of the nineteenth ACM symposium on operating systems principles* (pp. 44–59). Rate-Limited Sampled Voting.

North East Document Conservation Center. (2019). What is preservation? Session 1: Introduction to preservation. Retrieved February 2, 2020, from www.nedcc.org/preservation101/session-1/1what-is-preservation.

Ockerbloom, J. (1998). *Mediating among diverse data formats.* Tech. Rep. CMU-CS-98-102, Carnegie-Mellon University.

Remondino, F. (2011). Advanced 3D recording techniques for the digital documentation and conservation of heritage sites and objects. *Change Over Time, 1*(2), 198–214.

Rothenberg, J. (1995). Ensuring the longevity of digital documents. *Scientific American, 272,* 1.

Shi, G. W., Wang, Y. T., Liu, Y., & Zheng, W. (2009). Digital conservation of cultural heritage using augmented reality. *Journal of System Simulation, 7,* 2090–2097.

Sitts, M. K. (2000). *Handbook for digital projects.* Northeast Document Conservation Center.

Van der Wal, R., & Arts, K. (2015). Digital conservation: An introduction. *Ambio, 44*(4), 517–521.

Van Wijngaarden, H., & Oltmans, E. (2004). Digital preservation and permanent access: The UVC for images. In *IS&T archiving conference* (pp. 254–258). ISSN: 1082-9873.

Walker, F., & Thoma, G. (2004). A web-based paradigm for file migration. In *IS&T archiving conference* (pp. 93–97). http://docmorph.nlm.nih.gov/docmorph/IST2004.pdf.

SECTION 3

Designing for accessibility

Accessibility is critical to realizing the business value of knowledge assets. For accessibility, we shift our focus from the architectures, whose goal is to ensure the availability of knowledge assets, to how people and agents access them. Accessibility architectures continue to consider the full range of knowledge assets. The 'functions' and 'actions' are controlled by how people and agents seek, search for, categorize, describe, and summarize assets. Access is grounded in what social, and knowledge scientists refer to as our knowledge registers – how we mentally make sense of the world of knowledge. This knowledge architecture segment is supported by a rich body of knowledge on searching for information discovery, search, and information retrieval. However, the literature does not cover the full range of knowledge assets. Access to knowledge assets is time-consuming and cumbersome because the lack of design places the burden for discovery and searching on the person. This section addresses those concerns and expands our perspective to include how functional architectures can improve and simplify access.

SECTION 3

Designing for accessibility

11

FUNCTIONAL ARCHITECTURES FOR KNOWLEDGE SEEKING AND DISCOVERY

Chapter summary

This chapter discusses what we mean by knowledge seeking and discovery, and why it is essential to be able to see the broader knowledge landscape. This chapter also distinguishes between seeking and discovery and searching. The chapter describes the five activities vital to designing an effective seeking architecture. The chapter explains why it is essential to have a good understanding of common knowledge-seeking practices and patterns, discovery methods such as berrypicking, browsing, grazing, and satisficing. The chapter describes the difference between seeking and findability and explains how to use scenarios to understand your stakeholders' behaviors. Here, the primary challenge is to expand the rich base of knowledge and practice to include all types of knowledge assets.

Why we care about knowledge seeking and discovery

Over the past century, the literate and educated population has increased dramatically. Businesses thrive when their critical knowledge assets are effective, efficient, and easily accessed when needed. Managers and staff are increasingly challenged to navigate the knowledge landscape when they need the knowledge to make a decision, to do their job, to develop a new product or service, and to troubleshoot a problem simply. This is because the knowledge landscape has exponentially increased due to the widespread availability of technologies, the dramatic increase in knowledge producers, and the increased awareness of the business value of knowledge. We care about the functional architecture of knowledge seeking because it is designed to map and help navigate this new landscape.

Mapping and navigating the landscape of knowledge assets is an effective mental model for understanding the challenge and how we design it. There are many different source destinations, and there are multiple paths to each destination. People and agents have preferences for how they find those destinations and which destinations they choose to access. Think about the landscape of sources as a map – we all need a map to learn what sources are available. We need a map to help us figure out how to get to those sources and how to access them once we arrive. Maps present the entire landscape – they tell us what exists and the possible routes. There has been little effort to lay out the landscape of knowledge assets with business value within organizations or the landscape of knowledge assets that have business relevance outside the organization. Where an effort has been made to sketch out this landscape and provide even rudimentary tools of navigating it, the results have been noteworthy. An enterprise search engine is not the same as a landscape or a navigation tool because it treats each destination as equivalent and essentially hides the landscape. This increases the challenge of discovering relevant assets rather than reduce it.

Why do we care about how well we can 'see' the landscape and how well we can navigate it? We care because:

- every individual navigates the landscape differently;
- every source's destination has multiple paths and offers different business value – to obscure the paths and neutralize the values is detrimental to discovering the most relevant assets from among many;
- until today, most sources have been designed in isolation and in a haphazard way – there are few good practice conventions for designing and constructing a source, and as a result, the designs vary widely; these variations add to the seeker's burden by first having to 'learn' the source before deciding whether it will be a good source for their task at hand;
- source destinations that have a lower volume or different kinds of assets will have a lower priority and treatment in a federated search environment – seekers need to be able to assess the full range of sources, and maps that highlight only the most popular restaurants may prevent us from finding a highly desirable family-owned restaurant;
- seekers need to be able to define how they navigate the landscape today, and to vary that route tomorrow depending on the reason they're looking for assets – different people look for different things in different contexts;
- seeking is a discovery process in itself – research has shown that people learn more about what they are looking for as they look – having a full landscape of source destinations is an essential element of learning;
- seekers have different capacities for seeing and absorbing what is on the landscape – if we design for one kind of seeker, other seekers will be disadvantaged;
- there is a business risk to satisficing in the discovery and seeking task – individuals with a lower capacity for navigation or absorption will take the first asset they find, whereas others may be more deliberate and intentional in their navigation – laying out the landscape levels the task by giving seekers a choice of where to start and where to end up.

Where the landscape of knowledge assets is not designed to address these effects, its impact will be significant. Internal use cases have demonstrated that, on average, every individual in an organization wastes up to 30 minutes a day looking for information. Internal use cases have shown that individuals never give up finding knowledge to reduce uncertainty and risk – but the cost of finding that information may have a prohibitive cost in terms of time and opportunity costs. Consider how many individuals there are in your organization. Then consider the average hourly wage. Keep in mind that the individuals who spend more time looking for knowledge may also be the most highly paid in your organization. For a single year, ineffective and labor-intensive knowledge seeking can cost an organization many millions of dollars. Consider how this time could have otherwise been spent on productive work and innovation. This factor alone provides the rationale we need to develop a functional architecture for knowledge seeking and discovery.

Knowledge seeking and discovery – design concepts

To develop this functional architecture, we must have a good understanding of common knowledge-seeking practices and patterns, discovery methods such as berrypicking, browsing, grazing, and satisficing; the difference between seeking and findability; use case modeling methods; and the rich base of research focused on information and knowledge seeking. The primary challenge we face in designing this functional architecture is expanding the rich base of knowledge and practice to include all of the types of knowledge assets. Additionally, a critical challenge is distinguishing seeking and discovery from searching architectures designed for particular sources.

For this purpose of this text and from an architecture perspective, 'seeking' and 'searching' are two different functions. Our distinction is simple. Seeking is something we do when we're looking across sources when we're navigating the broader landscape of options. Searching is something we do in a defined system or context. People seek regardless of whether there has been any deliberate attempt to structure the environment for them. People search in a setting that has been designed and deliberately built to support access to a predefined collection of knowledge assets.

Every search system or engine has a predefined target because every search system leverages an index that serves as the primary access point to the collection. Seeking is across any and every source, regardless of whether it has an intentionally designed search system or index (Figure 11.1). From a research and peer-reviewed literature perspective, these two approaches may blend under the general term of information retrieval. From an architecture perspective, though, these are two entirely different design challenges.

Seeking and discovery include two essential categories of tasks, specifically those that include 'looking for' information in the broader business environment, and those activities that pertain to searching within systems. How individuals look for information depends upon their experiences, their knowledge, their sources, and the type of information they seek. To support all the ways that people might look

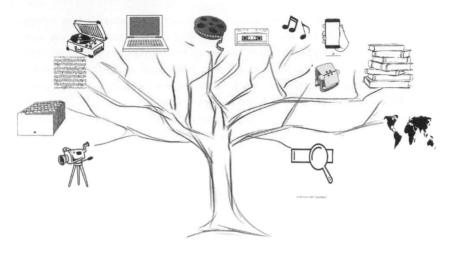

FIGURE 11.1 The Richness of Internal Sources of Knowledge Assets

FIGURE 11.2 How Individual Seekers Navigate the Knowledge Landscape

Source: Lifewire (www.lifewire.com/)

for information, an organization should ensure there are multiple points of access and discovery, including directories, navigation and browse structures, and easy access to individuals, reference services, and search support (Figure 11.2).

Designing a functional architecture to support knowledge seeking focuses on defining and describing the landscape and designing paths that allow seekers or 'travelers' to navigate that landscape to arrive at any destination successfully. In a nutshell, our functional architecture provides a way to identify, inventory, and describe each destination, and to map out all of the possible paths to that source. The functional architecture should not prescribe how any traveler might arrive at the destination just as Google Maps describes routes and gives us information about those routes so each traveler can make their own choices. If one source has no search but only browsing, we need to know before we spend time going there. If another source does not have references to people, we need to know that. If another source is only updated every three months, we need to know that. Despite these limitations, though, any one of these sources may be the best destination – hold the most relevant asset – for the task at hand. These are decisions the seeker needs to be able to make for themselves. Merely using an enterprise search option removes these choices and that essential information from your control.

The functional architecture for knowledge seeking speaks to our view of the world of knowledge that has business value. Internal organization landscapes should lay out the landscape of internal sources. External landscapes should be two-tiered. The first external tier should be the landscape of essential business sources (e.g., destinations) that we know are relevant to what we do. The second tier is the landscape of the whole knowledge landscape. The first tier is often what our internal library websites provide – they represent the sources most commonly accessed and used to answer business questions by the information professionals. Directories of sources for business sectors typically represent the second tier and web search systems.

What are the essential concepts we need to understand to design this functional architecture? We need to understand (1) social and linguistic registers of seekers; (2) sources of knowledge assets and their essential characteristics and features; (3) the seeking process, i.e., information grazing and berrypicking; (4) typical seeking models and use case scenarios; (5) architectures that support browsing; and (6) architectures that support search. This chapter touches upon search system functional architectures only lightly because Chapter 12 is devoted to these functional architectures.

Social and linguistic registers and the knowledge landscape

Each of us has a set of mental models and registers we use to navigate the world. Mental models are how we visually organize the world to handle complexity. Registers are the different ways we learn to communicate with others. Registers are designed to suit the environment. While mental modes are our own and we develop them independently and over time, registers are negotiated vocabularies developed by a community. Consider how you talk to your manager or to your coworkers each day. Consider how you shift that language when you talk to your family, or your banker, or your doctor. There are fundamental concepts that define each domain and conventions for interacting in each domain. Our mental models, our linguistic and social registers, determine how we think about and describe what we seek, and how we design the task change with the environment. Sociologists talk about registers as orienting strategies (Berger & Zelditch, 1993; Wagner, 1984; Wagner & Berger, 1985). They treat mental models and registers as metatheories – what concepts are included, how those concepts are related, and how they represent what we know and how we make sense of things (Kuhn's paradigms; Wagner & Berger, 1985).

Similarly, any environment or source we encounter while we're looking for something has its domain language and an underlying knowledge structure. We begin with a mental model of what we're looking for, and some language that describes what we're looking for. The challenge of successful seeking is to adapt that mental model and language to work with any source. This is no small task. It is a mental negotiation we each undertake several times a day. Sometimes we're successful, and sometimes we're not. But, it is always the case that we learn something new with each attempt. In designing a functional architecture to support knowledge seeking, we need to design like a map. We need to identify all the possible sources, explain what they are, and show multiple paths and ways to get to those sources. We design the architecture not to prescribe which destinations people will choose or how they get to them, but to explain the options. This is very different from the way we design search systems.

Knowledge sources and designing a flexible knowledge landscape

The starting point for our functional architecture is identifying all the sources and destinations that need to be on the map for anyone in our business environment. This sounds like a daunting task, but in fact, it is not unlike what reference and collection development librarians do every day. They consider the domain, look at the most authoritative sources, and assess authoritativeness, costs, ease of use, and goodness of fit to the kinds of seeking their stakeholders do. These sources often include formal published information and data. They can consist of any source – a database, a website, a directory, a collection of FAQs, a departmental collection, and so on. Information professionals lean towards promoting sources that are curated, collected, and managed to quality and reliability. While this is important, it tends to include the informal sources that often contain applied knowledge, discussions, and knowledge about specific tasks and practices.

Additionally, the sources are often presented as an alphabetical listing with metadata records that provide some high-level descriptions. In other words, they catalog these sources and publish them in a way that will make sense to the simplest mental model – alphabetic by name. The challenge is often that few of the stakeholders use these sites. They are most effectively used by people who know the source they're looking for and need to find. Navigating the long list is too time-consuming. And, you need to navigate the whole list if you don't know the landscape.

Each stakeholder has preferred sources, and these sources often reflect the professional networks and business groups they rely on for advice and guidance. These may be internal networks, external networks, or a hybrid. These networks and how we navigate them provide the best explanations of our landscapes and how we use them. The professional sources and activities of information professionals are a good starting point. But, we need to design the landscape to resemble the map more closely – almost a concept or a topic map that links to sources. And there should be multiple ways to access and navigate the map; in other words, the seeker should be able to scope and manipulate the map.

Additionally, the seeker should be able to add sources to the map – with their descriptions and recommendations. What do seekers want to know about a source they might find on a source map? What seekers want to know might include:

- who put it together, and who is responsible for maintaining it;
- why they put it together;
- what it covers in terms of subjects, periods, and how sources are selected for inclusion;
- what it does not include – what is excluded;
- how we navigate the source;
- how often it is updated;
- whether it is reliable, or whether there is a bias;
- whether there is a direct cost;
- whether there are restrictions on what I can see and what I can do with what I find;
- what tools are available for me to work with for this source;
- who recommended it for the map.

What we can learn from the information retrieval and information science research

There is a rich body of knowledge around the topics of information behaviors and information retrieval. This research is grounded in rigorous cognitive models, user information interface design, general information behaviors, and information retrieval. Cognitive models describe the relationship between a person's cognitive mental model of the knowledge sought and how the landscape and its sources are laid out. These models attempt to understand how a person is searching for information so that the database and the search of this database can be designed in such a way as to serve the user best. Information retrieval may incorporate multiple tasks and cognitive problems. This is particularly so because different people may have different methods for attempting to find this information and expect the information to be in various forms. Cognitive models of information retrieval may be attempts at something as prosaic as improving search results or may be something more complex, such as attempting to create a database that can be queried with natural language search (Baeza-Yates & Ribeiro-Neto, 1999; Garfield, 1984; Gupta & Jain, 1997; Ingwersen, 1992; Manning et al., 2008; Meadow et al., 1999; Salton, 1968).

The challenge is that the research is used to design specific systems and sources, rather than to design the broader knowledge landscape. While this research is rigorous, reliable, and groundbreaking, it tends to focus on the use and seeking of formal information sources, and to draw from academic or high-end information seekers. The literature provides an excellent description of the challenges we often find in a single knowledge domain and context. While most of the literature is robust and reliable, it will not always be reliable for business managers. The literature does not translate easily to seeking in a business context. The richness of this literature paints an artificial view of the seeking environment rather than one that more closely represents a test and laboratory environment than a business context (Case, 2007; Chang & Rice, 1993; Chatman, 1999; Dervin et al., 2003; Foster, 2005; Johnson Andrews & Allard, 2001; Kuhlthau, 2006; Leckie, 2006; Leckie et al., 1996; Miller & Jablin, 1991; Pomerantz, 1988; Qu & Furnas, 2008; Strickland, 2009; Talja & Mckenzie, 2007; Wagner, 1984; Wagner & Berger, 1985; Waterworth, 1991; Wilkinson, 2001; Wilson, 1999; Zipf, 1949).

The information science literature provides strong guidance in the research on information grazing, berrypicking, and browsing. These more closely resemble how we conceptualize and manage the knowledge landscape. They also provide more significant insights into the seeker's experiences, mental models, and registers.

What we can learn from information grazing and berrypicking

Information grazing refers to the ability to quickly obtain knowledge and facts in time to solve new problems or answer questions. It includes 'information jumping' – moving quickly from source to source and cherry-picking information and knowledge along the way. Information grazing changes our mental models and refines our registers as we go along to the extent that we focus on something long enough to understand its relevance fully. The research on information grazing realizes that some landscapes are so large, so dynamic, so interdependent and focused, that traditional methods of sense-making will not be effective or efficient (Dearle et al., 1990). We tend to leverage information-grazing methods when we are presented with an overwhelming number of search results. Information grazing is more common in landscapes like science and engineering, or commercial markets where the newest knowledge is dynamic.

Each time we look for knowledge, we need to reset our understanding of the landscape – because the landscape has changed. Information grazing is particularly relevant to the business environment, where the landscape and sources change daily.

The need to support information grazing in a knowledge landscape raises risks. Explicitly, sources may not be consistent or objectively verifiable, may continuously change, offer cutting-edge but untested advice from practitioners, and may be unverified or incorrect. Information grazing is what knowledge seekers do today – every day, in every business context. A well-designed knowledge-seeking functional architecture will not change this behavior, but it might mitigate the risks. A well-designed functional architecture that manages the landscape can at least identify and describe sources and offer cautions. This is a new reality of the knowledge economy. We have argued that knowledge is dynamic and continuously evolving. Our knowledge landscape cannot ignore these sources. We can, though, mitigate their risks and gain a better understanding of our stakeholders' sources.

Perhaps the most important research, though, to understand the function of seeking is Marcia Bates's breakthrough work on information grazing and berrypicking (Bates, 1989a). Her findings and guidance apply to the design of landscapes as well as to individual sources and systems. Bates argues that 'berrypicking' better reflects how users seek knowledge and information. Her work builds upon and incorporates cognitive issues. Most information behavior and retrieval research present the task as a simple linear match between a query and an asset. Rather, Bates suggests every discovery action evolves and develops bit by bit (Figure 11.3). She argues that a person continuously learns and adapts his mental model and register in response to what they find. If the landscape is limited, and the sources they encounter do not advance their understanding of the problem or the landscape, it is suboptimal. A simple linear model that describes a single, one-time event with a positive or negative result is not a realistic representation of knowledge seeking. Every response, every new step generates feedback that causes the seeker to modify the cognitive model.

How do knowledge architects gain an understanding of the knowledge-seeking behaviors of their stakeholders? It is the starting point for designing our knowledge

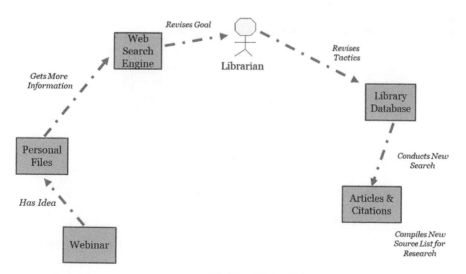

FIGURE 11.3 Bates Characterization of a Typical Knowledge Seeking Event

landscape. One of the most effective methods has been to develop use case scenarios from real-world practical examples. We should select a representative set of stakeholders, identify a range of typical knowledge-seeking activities, and work through a use case model with each stakeholder. Use case scenarios to help us to understand the stakeholder's experiences and to identify the essential sources to include in the landscape (Figure 11.4). These scenarios help us see where success and failure points represent gaps or suspect sources. They also provide an easy-to-understand graphic representation of a wide range of stakeholder experiences. Use case scenarios can provide a critical starting point for defining destinations on the knowledge landscape.

These use cases help us to understand what stakeholders mean when they tell us that search doesn't work, and what a discovery failure looks like (Figure 11.5).

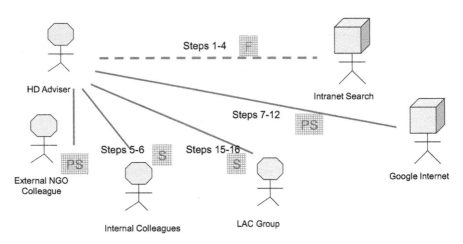

FIGURE 11.4 Representation of a Seeking Use Case Scenario

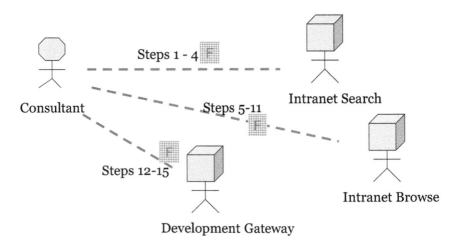

FIGURE 11.5 Representation of a Seeking Use Case Scenario

We also learn a critical lesson. Stakeholders do not give up looking for knowledge even if the sources we design for them do not satisfy the need. They will continue to seek out sources until they get an answer. Use case scenarios also help us to understand their seeking strategies – where they begin, what causes them to change paths, how they adapt their mental models and registers, and what failure looks like. They also tell us what success looks like, so we have a better sense of the goodness of the knowledge they're using.

When use cases are developed, we typically learn that absolute success rates are high because stakeholders do not give up. We also learn that most seeking activities look precisely like Bates's berrypicking models – they involve multiple steps and multiple sources. The success rates for individual sources, though, vary widely. This is often due to design and a mismatch between the seeker's mental models, registers, and the source architecture. We realize how vital human knowledge and networks are to successful seeking, and how often formal sources and databases are the least effective. Because most seekers are confronted with rigidly defined landscapes, they often choose the least effective source as a starting point.

Two other research bodies are relevant to designing the functional architecture, but they are insufficient and more limited in their scope. The limitation is because, for the most part, they focus on a single source rather than on the larger landscape of sources. These research domains include both browsing and search.

What we can learn from the browsing research

Browsing is relevant, but like search, it presumes that we are navigating through predefined collections of documents. Browse structures may be constructed for any classification schemes defined for a system, where the values have been associated with metadata records for documents (Bates, 1989b, 2007; Berger & Zelditch, 1993; Cove & Walsh, 1988; Hildreth, 1982; Hjørland, 2011; Kurth & Peters, 1995; Marchionini, 1997; Morse, 1973; Rice et al., 2001; Schmeltz Pedersen, 1993). This function also includes the ability to generate and browse search transaction logs. Search and Browse also includes maintaining the search indexes and classification schemes to ensure the efficient performance of these tools for users. Chapter 11 presents critical decision points related to finding and discovery of information assets, including considerations for different business and working environments. This function is discussed in detail in Chapter 12.

Browsing is a kind of orienting strategy. It is designed to identify relevant assets. For example, people browse search results; they browse shelves in stores, shelves of books and artifacts in libraries, or by topics through databases. The most prominent research in this literature is Gary Marchionini (1997). Marchionini suggests that browsing represents a distinct behavior from the analysis. For Marchionini, analysis requires planning, the intentional selection of search terms, and iterative searching. In contrast, browsing is heuristic and opportunistic and relies heavily on mental models and registers. The analysis represents a discourse between a source and a person – question and answer. If an individual does not ask the right question, the source does not give a relevant answer. If the individual asks the question in the wrong way, the source will not understand what they are looking for. Browsing is more interactive and represents a real-time exchange and collaboration between the seeker and the source. Browsing requires a lower cognitive load upfront and leaves room for learning and adapting.

What we can learn from the research on search

Search system creation and maintenance include the configuration of the search system architecture, definition of searchable fields and search index parameters, search system interface and search results display and presentation, search results sorting and manipulation options, and the configuration of query processing algorithms (e.g., exact and fuzzy pattern matching, Boolean operators, query expansion, etc.). It is relevant to using individual sources, but it does not help us to understand or design the larger functional architecture that supports the knowledge landscape.

Seeking and discovery – the design environment

What triggers the need to develop a functional architecture for knowledge seeking? Several events can trigger knowledge seeking. An individual realizes they have a question that needs to be resolved. A problem develops for which there is no proven solution, and we need to identify and contact several experts to help us resolve the issue. We hear that there is a new substitute resource that can be used in the manufacturing process, and it is more cost-effective than what we are using now. A process consistently generates products that have quality control problems. We need to learn everything we can about what factors might generate these kinds of failures. We simply want to verify something, and we have to look at the trade literature to find an answer.

What sources do we need to consider when designing the architecture? The sources that help us to design the functional architecture include business stakeholders' understanding of their job-related asset business needs, knowledge of the most commonly and frequently used sources by capability, and an understanding of how and when a business unit uses these sources. We also leverage any information we have about success and failure rates, and the time spent looking for information. The knowledge architect's understanding of dynamic mapping applications and designs is also essential to this task.

What outputs and outcomes result from having this architecture in place? This functional architecture produces a product and a capability that are critical today and in the knowledge economy. In essence, this functional architecture allows us to manage the landscape of knowledge sources and present it to the business in a flexible, adaptable, and navigable way. The knowledge landscape includes all five kinds of knowledge assets and internal and external sources, and it allows stakeholders to adapt and maintain it directly. Ideally, having these knowledge landscapes makes it cost-effective and cost-efficient to look for knowledge, rather than to recreate it. Ideally, it reduces business risks and uncertainties by providing higher quality and relevant knowledge for decision-making and problem-solving. A navigable, adaptable knowledge landscape should reduce the time we spent looking for knowledge, reduce the lost time and opportunity costs of failed seeking, and reduce the risk of finding and using bad or suboptimal knowledge.

What are the consequences we expect from having this architecture in place? If the navigable knowledge map is effectively designed, it should change our knowledge-seeking behaviors – from informal, fragmented, and based on individual preferences, to more reliable, predictable, and systematic. Ideally, it will increase our capacity to learn while seeking, to share information about new sources, to identify gaps, and to make greater business use of knowledge.

What activities does this architecture support? A well-designed knowledge landscape lets us better discover what knowledge we need, to find relevant sources better, and to understand better how the business looks for and uses knowledge. From a management perspective, this functional architecture enables us to better leverage those knowledge assets we have internally, and to ensure that they are exposed for everyone to access. This functional architecture supports knowledge discovery – central adaptable and flexible access point, behind-the-scenes discovery architectures, targeted discovery 'push' agents, and presentation of results to support learning. This functional architecture also enables us to capture quantitative and qualitative information about our knowledge-seeking behaviors to use to improve behaviors continuously.

What factors do we need to consider when designing this architecture? We need to consider how much we know about knowledge seeking and how much we have yet to learn at the outset. We need to develop a better understanding of why business stakeholders need knowledge, and to design an architecture that supports 'just in time' seeking, not only 'just in case' seeking. We need to know whether our current behaviors are effective or creating business risk – is there a need to change behaviors? Of all the functional architectures, this is likely the one we know the least about – simply because we tend to focus on 'searching within sources' rather than on 'seeking across sources.'

Design activities and tasks for seeking and discovery

Five activities support the design of this functional architecture, including:

- Activity 1. Identify the knowledge discovery needs
- Activity 2. Develop profiles of knowledge seeking for business-critical capabilities
- Activity 3. Inventory sources and design a discovery environment
- Activity 4. Design an environment for discovery
- Activity 5. Design logging capabilities to understand discovery patterns

Activity 1. Identify the knowledge discovery needs

How do we do this? This activity begins with the identification of a representative set of seekers from across the organization. We need to ensure that the sample includes multiple people from business-critical capabilities. The knowledge architect should work with information professionals to develop a use case methodology, instructions, and materials for interviewers to use. Interviewers can be anyone from the organization – they do not have to be information professionals or knowledge managers. We should conduct a pilot test and incorporate feedback before we apply the methodology across the organization.

What inputs does this activity need? The methodology and instructions should include all five categories of knowledge assets and include lists of all the object models to ensure the use cases are focused not just on explicit knowledge but on all types of knowledge.

What products does it generate? With the feedback, we make adjustments to the methodology and move forward to the development of use case scenarios. Working with all of the scenarios, the knowledge architect and information professionals should prepare a report and presentation for review across the organization. This activity provides a baseline understanding of what your stakeholders are looking for, where, how, and how successful they are. From this baseline, you can identify the primary sources, understand the order in which they are used and the sequence of steps, and the types of assets they're looking for.

What resources does this activity require? This activity will leverage use case scenario tools, survey tools, and any other methods routinely used to assess the effectiveness of access to knowledge assets.

Activity 2. Develop profiles of knowledge-seeking for business-critical environments

How do we do this? With a first-pass understanding of the knowledge landscape, we can focus on knowledge-seeking landscapes and strategies that will have value for individual business capabilities and units. Our goal is not to design a rigid structure or directory, but to provide a flexible and adaptable map to the sources we know are most valuable to the business unit. We leverage the results of the first activity and formulate new use case scenarios to distribute to individuals in business-critical units to 'self-complete.' This activity attempts to reach everyone in the unit, rather than to sample across the organization.

What inputs does this activity need? We need to ensure there is a representative set of seeking tasks in the next round of use cases. This activity enables individuals to complete the use case scenarios. From the broader set of scenarios, we can develop a comprehensive list of knowledge sources and begin to characterize these sources to support navigation. We want to analyze the use case results for success, failures, and gaps and consult with information professionals to fill gaps.

What products does it generate? We have an opportunity in this step to identify issues with individual sources and design solutions. We can also make a first pass at prioritizing the sources by their quality, trustworthiness, ease of use, and value to the capability. Over time the stakeholders can update these descriptions. The final step in this activity involves validating sources with managers and staff involved in that operation.

What resources does this activity require? This activity requires knowledge of and access to business units and their knowledge needs. It includes the kinds of knowledge they use in business processes and the types of knowledge they generated throughout the process.

Activity 3. Inventory sources and design a discovery environment

How do we do this? Working with the list of sources for each business capability, we identify those sources that have the greatest value to a particular business operation. We share the list with the business unit and solicit feedback on coverage and gaps. Once you have a working list, develop a description of each source, including its location, scope and coverage, sources and update rates, access methods, and any cautions about risks.

What inputs does this activity need? Input from information professionals is also crucial at this point – there may be relevant sources the unit is unaware of.

What products does it generate? This activity generates a comprehensive list of knowledge sources essential to the business unit's work and goals.

What resources does this activity require? The primary resource is the input from individuals in the business unit. The input should also include information about the source applications, their advantages, and disadvantages.

Activity 4. Design an environment for discovery

Designing an environment for discovery includes a central access point, behind-the-scenes discovery architectures, targeted discovery 'push' agents, and presentation of results to support learning

How do we do this? At this point, we also design an interface that allows stakeholders to display sources and to manipulate the display to align with what we are looking for then. The display should be 'navigable' – it allows stakeholders to display the sources and change their position and links to better align with the task. Ideally, the knowledge architect designs an interface that works like an interactive topic list – that allows the user to organize sources by any of the attributes in the description. The architect also works with developers to design a function in the architecture that allows individuals to add sources to the landscape and to provide descriptions of those sources. Together they also design a reporting and monitoring function that allows knowledge architects, business managers, and information professionals to increase their awareness of the unit, the organization's knowledge-seeking patterns.

What inputs does this activity need? The primary input is the inventory of sources, what works well, and what needs improvement. Another input is the knowledge of interface designs and source use from information professionals and systems developers.

What products does it generate? This activity produces a working design and specifications for a comprehensive knowledge landscape. Ideally, the landscape is defined for each business unit distinctly and then synthesized into a navigable resource for the organization as a whole.

What resources does this activity require? This activity leverages any existing publishing or design interfaces the organization has at its disposal.

Activity 5. Design logging capabilities to understand discovery patterns

How do we do this? The knowledge architect working with information professionals and business stakeholders should be prepared to update the sources on the landscape continuously. Information professionals should also continuously monitor the suggestions and additions of business stewards to ensure the descriptions are accurate and complete, and any risks or deficiencies are known. In a nutshell, this activity involves monitoring the knowledge landscape, learning how it is used, and ensuring it works to support the business. This activity also provides critical insights that can be used to improve general and individual training in particular. This task also puts us in a position to develop and track metrics to better manage knowledge seeking.

What inputs does this activity need? For this activity, we leverage the reports that are routinely generated by the functional landscape architecture to understand how the unit satisfies its needs for knowledge. The knowledge landscape is dynamic – it reflects the current state of the business. As business changes, we may need new sources.

What products does it generate? This activity provides the management and monitoring capabilities required to sustain the knowledge landscape. It also produces a set of metrics and assessment methods that are the focus of routine reporting.

What resources does this activity require? This activity leverages any inherent logging capabilities in source applications and definitions of metrics for knowledge discovery and navigation.

Evolution of knowledge seeking and discovery designs

Humans have sought out knowledge as long as they have existed. What has changed over time is the nature of the knowledge landscape and the methods we use to discover and use sources on the landscape. Our experience and review of the literature suggest five general phases that describe the evolution of the factors that contribute to seeking and discovery (Figure 11.6):

*   Phase 1. Local and known source destinations
*   Phase 2. Expanded landscape and lesser-known sources
*   Phase 3. Seekers develop new skills and competencies
*   Phase 4. Seeking agents emerge and seek for us
*   Phase 5. The shift from generic to personalized landscapes

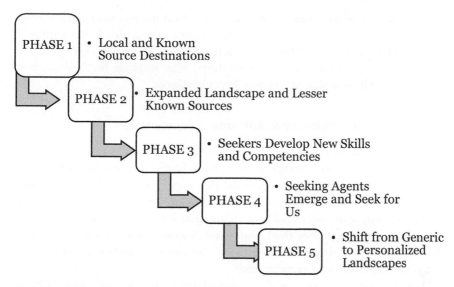

FIGURE 11.6 Evolution of Knowledge Seeking

Phase 1. Local and known source destinations

Seeking in the earliest times focused on sources that were close by, known, familiar, and part of our immediate world. Finding and accessing these sources did not require complex tools or descriptions. People are the primary knowledge source in the landscape. Seeking was grounded on our ability to ask questions, listen, and absorb the knowledge shared with us. The smaller the local community or social group, the fewer choices for sources. We have little control over sources – the choice is limited. The quality of the source determines the quality of the knowledge we discover. Knowledge seeking is simple and straightforward. The challenge is that social and economic status may restrict access to sources – in this phase, the source controls access. Additionally, the limited choice means that the source controls the cost of access as well. All of the factors that later contribute to a complex seeking environment are present – but the options and choices are significantly restricted.

Phase 2. Expanded landscape and lesser-known sources

As the community expands, as our ability to travel grows, the landscape of knowledge sources expands. Choice increases, and we now must be able to discern one source from another. Rudimentary choices are still sufficient, but we may not know all of the available sources. As our proximity to sources increases, our range of knowledge also expands. Some sources are familiar, others are not. The process of learning how to access and use a source increases – the first sign of learning while seeking. Costs increase – the idea of the 'cost' of accessing each source arises.

Cost does not necessarily mean a financial cost – what the producer and the consumer decide is a fair exchange; there is an incentive to negotiate because there is some competition. A broader landscape means the complexity of access to sources increases – where are they, can we get to them, what language do they use, is it validated, etc. All those descriptors now become relevant.

Phase 3. Seekers develop new skills and competencies

Over centuries, access and choice have increased. While there is a more abundant knowledge landscape, navigating this landscape is more complex. We have always had mental models to help us navigate the landscape, but now these models and registers need to work in a more complex space. How we each see the world now becomes important to understand how we navigate the landscape. What is important to each of us, how they think about and describe what we are looking for, who we turn to now shapes what we know. Our mental models and registries are the foundation of our new competencies.

These patterns begin to take shape as patterns in an emerging profession of library and information science. Understanding seeking becomes an area of study, and we begin to do both applied and theoretical research. Due to the broad nature of the task, though, this research spans multiple fields. The more professional competencies are increasingly important to a smaller and smaller set of professional analysis, intelligence officers, and forensic experts. The fragmentation of these different discovery environments is the primary consideration for design – it is no longer sufficient to develop the technologies to support searching for something simply – rather, a holistic discovery environment is essential.

Different working and social environments give rise to different discovery needs – so the everyday competencies of discovery are increasingly crucial to everyone. It is essential to distinguish between what we know from formal and informal theories of seeking and discovery behavior. The early theories focus on explicit information, final products, and finished and published information. (e.g., Zipf's Principle of Least Effort, Brenda Dervin's Sense-Making, and Elfreda Chatman's Life in the Round) investigate the processes that surround information seeking). A review of the literature on information-seeking behavior shows that information seeking has generally been accepted as dynamic and non-linear (Foster, 2005; Kuhlthau, 2006; Ross, 1983). People experience the information search process as an interplay of thoughts, feelings, and actions (Case, 2007; Kuhlthau, 2006; Robinson, 2010; Wilson 1999); therefore, they developed a nested model of conceptual areas, which visualizes the interrelation of the here-mentioned central concepts. Wilson defines models of information behavior to be 'statements, often in the form of diagrams, that attempt to describe an information-seeking activity, the causes and consequences of that activity, or the relationships among stages in information-seeking behavior' (1999, p. 250). These representations are not unlike the use case scenarios described earlier. These theories are groundbreaking, though they do not address the challenge of different levels of quality of information and the means of distinguishing between what to trust and what not to trust. Instead, they focus on the goodness of search and its results. This early research dates back to the early 1950s and 1960s and comes from the early documentalists and engineers. This early research evolved into a focus on library collections and databases of information. From this foundation, our focus on search evolved. This area of practice establishes a good understanding of how people seek and discover explicit information.

Phase 4. Seeking agents emerge and seek for us

In recent years, information seeking has expanded to include automated agents programmed to look for information and knowledge on our behalf. An increasingly automated and industrialized environment and the exponential expansion of the landscape creates a need for designing and developing agents or tools to help us effectively and efficiently navigate the landscape. Search systems emerge as a vital tool – because they can leverage existing and common practices of collecting, inventorying, and searching through inventories. We lose sight of the larger landscape, though, as our focus shifts to search applications and tools. While search applications provide access to a broader set of sources, the nature of those sources and our ability to assess them decreases. As technology is also applied to these new sources and volumes, we have needed new competencies – but the new competencies are increasingly differentiated into professional and non-professional competencies.

Phase 5. The shift from generic to personalized landscapes

Looking to the future, we can no longer expect people to adapt to the system or the technology. Expectations are increasing to adapt the technology and the sources to suit the individual and the task. The available sources have grown exponentially, and the landscape is now crowded and complex to navigate. Our mental models no longer suffice to help us navigate the environment. We need first to redefine the landscape before we apply those mental models and registers. We make sense of the landscape by redefining the landscape. It will be essential to give each individual the capability to design their discovery environments and adapt them to suit the task at hand. This calls for the development of new architectures and methods, particularly tools that help us manage the landscape and hide the complexity.

The future will be radically different from the present. Individuals will design the knowledge landscape and personalize the tools that help them to navigate the landscape. The landscape is no longer limited to text but includes all types of knowledge and all forms of encoding and packaging. It means that there will be an increasing fragmentation and distinction between professional and formal seeking and discovery (for analytical and intelligence work). There will be everyday seeking and discovery, which will include everything. Seeking capabilities will need to include not just search which is controlled and managed by seekers, but also 'push agents,' user profiles, and automated discovery agents. These agents will be more sophisticated and tailored versions of today's current awareness and recommender engines.

Knowledge seeking and discovery in the knowledge architecture blueprint

Knowledge seeking and discovery should live squarely in the knowledge architecture practice, where that practice exists. Where it does not exist, though, it should live in the information architecture practice. This practice requires close collaboration with the business side of the organization, waiting for business architects, and with the application architects.

Chapter review

After reading this chapter, you should be able to:

*   define information seeking and discovery and explain how they relate to information retrieval and information science research;
*   explain how information seeking and discovery relate to and differ from knowledge seeking and discovery;
*   describe your organization's knowledge landscape;
*   explain social and linguistic registers and how they relate to seeking and discovery;
*   discuss berrypicking, information grazing, and browsing;
*   explain how seeking and discovery relate to but are different from searching.

References and recommended future readings

Baeza-Yates, R., & Ribeiro-Neto, B. (1999). *Modern information retrieval* (Vol. 463). ACM Press.

Bates, M. J. (1989a). *The design of browsing and berrypicking techniques for the online search interface*. Retrieved February 2, 2020, from https://pages.gseis.ucla.edu/faculty/bates/berrypicking.html.

Bates, M. J. (1989b). The design of browsing and berrypicking techniques for the online search interface. *Online Review* (5), 407–424. https://pages.gseis.ucla.edu/faculty/bates/berrypicking.html.

Bates, M. J. (2007). What is browsing-really? A model drawing from behavioral science research. *Information Research, 12*(4), paper 330. Retrieved February 2, 2020, from http://InformationR.net/ir/12-4/paper330.html.

Berger, J., & Zelditch, M. (1993). Orienting strategies and theory growth. In J. Berger & M. Zelditch (Eds.), *Theoretical research programs: Studies in the growth of theory* (pp. 3–22). Stanford University Press.

Case, D. O. (2007). *Looking for information: A survey of research on information seeking, needs, and behavior*. Elsevier/Academic Press.

Chang, S-J., & Rice, R. E. (1993). Browsing: A multidimensional framework. *Annual Review of Information Science and Technology, 28*, 231–276.

Chatman, E. A. (1999). A theory of life in the round. *Journal of the American Society for Information Science, 50*(3), 207–217.

Cove, J. F., & Walsh, B. C. (1988). Online text retrieval via browsing. *Information Processing & Management, 24*(1), 31–37.

Dearle, A., Cutts, Q. I., & Kirby, G. N. C. (1990). Browsing, grazing and nibbling persistent data structures. In J. Rosenberg & D. M. Koch (Eds.), *Persistent object systems* (pp. 56–69). Springer-Verlag.

Dervin, B., Foreman-Wernet, L., & Lauterbach, E. (Eds.). (2003). *Sense-making methodology reader: Selected writings of Brenda Dervin.* Hampton Press.

Foster, A. E. (2005). A non-linear model of information seeking behaviour. *Information Research, 10*(2), 222.

Garfield, E. (1984, October 29). Scanners of the world unite: You have nothing to lose but information overload. *Current Contents.* Reprinted in his *Essays of an information scientist.* ISI Press, 1985, 346. Retrieved February 2, 2020, from www.garfield.library.upenn.edu/essays/v7p346y1984.pdf.

Gupta, A., & Jain, R. (1997). Visual information retrieval. *Communications of the ACM, 40*(5), 70–79.

Hildreth, C. R. (1982). Online browsing support capabilities. *ASIS Proceedings, 19,* 127–132.

Hjørland, B. (2011). The importance of theories of knowledge: Browsing as an example. *Journal of the American Society for Information Science and Technology, 62*(3), 594–603.

Ingwersen, P. (1992). *Information retrieval interaction* (Vol. 246). Taylor Graham.

Johnson, J. D., Andrews, J. E., & Allard, S. (2001). A model for understanding and affecting cancer genetics information seeking. *Library & Information Science Research, 23*(4), 335–349.

Kuhlthau, C. C. (2006). Kuhlthau's information search process. In K. E. Fisher, S. Erdelez, & L. McKechnie (Eds.), *Theories of information behavior* (pp. 230–234). Information Today.

Kurth, M., & Peters, T. A. (Eds.). (1995). Browsing in information systems. An extensive annotated bibliography of the literature. *Library Hi Tech.* (Special Theme), *10*(x), 275.

Leckie, G. J. (2006). *General model of the information seeking of professionals.* In K. E. Fisher, S. Erdelez, & L. McKechnie (Eds.), *Theories of information behavior* (pp. 158–163). Information Today.

Leckie, G. J., Pettigrew, K. E., & Sylvain, C. (1996). Modeling the information seeking of professionals: A general model derived from research on engineers, health care professionals, and lawyers. *Library Quarterly, 66*(2), 161–193.

Manning, C. D., Raghavan, P., & Schütze, H. (2008). *Introduction to information retrieval.* Cambridge University Press.

Marchionini, G. (1997). Information seeking in electronic environments. Chapter 6. *Browsing Strategies.* Cambridge University Press.

Meadow, C. T., Kraft, D. H., & Boyce, B. R. (1999). *Text information retrieval systems.* Academic Press, Inc.

Miller, V. D., & Jablin, F. M. (1991). Information seeking during organizational entry: Influences, tactics, and a model of the process. *The Academy of Management Review, 16*(1), 92–120.

Morse, P. M. (1973). Browsing and search theory. In C. H. Rawski (Ed.), *Toward a theory of librarianship. Papers in honor of Jesse Hauk Shera* (pp. 246–261). The Scarecrow Press.

Pomerantz, A. (1988). Offering a candidate answer: An information seeking strategy. *Communication Monographs, 55*(4), 360–373.

Qu, Y., & Furnas, G. W. (2008). Model-driven formative evaluation of exploratory search: A study under a sensemaking framework. *Information Processing & Management, 44*(2), 534–555.

Rice, R. E., McCreadie, M., & Chang, S. L. (2001). *Accessing and browsing information and communication.* MIT Press.

Robinson, M. A. (2010). An empirical analysis of engineers' information behaviors. *Journal of the American Society for Information Science and Technology, 61*(4), 640–658.

Ross, J. (1983). Observations of browsing behaviour in an academic library. *College and Research Libraries, 44*(4), 269–276.

Salton, G. (1968). *Automatic information and retrieval* (Computer Science). McGraw-Hill Inc.

Schmeltz Pedersen, G. (1993, June 27–30). A browser for bibliographic information retrieval, based on an application of lattice theory. In *SIGIR'93 conference* (pp. 270–279). ACM Press.

Strickland, J. (2009). HowStuffWorks "How web 3.0 will work". *HowStuffWorks "Computer".* Retrieved February 2, 2020, from http://computer.howstuffworks.com/web-30.htm.

Talja, S., & Mckenzie, P. J. (2007). *Editor's introduction: Special issue on discursive approaches to information seeking in context.* The University of Chicago Press.

Wagner, D. G. (1984). *The growth of sociological theories.* Sage.

Wagner, D. G., & Berger, J. (1985). Do sociological theories grow? *American Journal of Sociology, 90*(4), 697–728.

Waterworth, J. A. (1991). A model for information exploration. *Hypermedia, 3*(1), 35–58.

Wilkinson, M. A. (2001). Information sources used by lawyers in problem-solving: An empirical exploration. *Library & Information Science Research, 23*(3), 257–276.

Wilson, T. D. (1999). Models in information behaviour research. *Journal of Documentation, 55*(3), 249–270. doi:10.1108/eum0000000007145. Archived from the original on 21 October 2014. Retrieved 28 October 2017.

Zipf, G. K. (1949). *Human behavior and the principle of least effort: An introduction to human ecology.* Addison-Wesley.

12

FUNCTIONAL ARCHITECTURE FOR KNOWLEDGE SEARCH

Chapter summary

This chapter explains what it means to search for knowledge assets and why it is important to intentionally design a knowledge search architecture. The chapter lays out the six activities that support knowledge search architecture designs. The chapter also considers why it is important to have a good understanding of search as a system – the inputs, processes, and outputs – that determine performance and effectiveness. The chapter walks through the components of every search system and explains how these parts have evolved to support what we are searching for and how. Here we consider the primary challenge in designing this functional architecture for search – the high level of marketing and costs of search systems and the absence of active management of search system designs.

Why we care about searching for knowledge

Some readers may wonder why we differentiate between 'looking for' and 'searching'. One explanation we offer is that looking for is an activity that is undertaken across many different kinds of functional architectures, whereas search has a specific context and meaning. Looking for, as Bates and Marchionini suggest, can be serendipitous, can span time and space. In contrast, a search is a deliberate and intentional action working with a specific application or source. The semantics can be somewhat confusing since looking for, seeking, search, and discovery may be used as synonyms in a single research paper. They are used as synonyms in the field of information sciences and information retrieval. From a design perspective, though, these concepts represent two different functional architectures. What is particularly distinctive about search is that (1) there is a deliberate action undertaken, and (2) this action is executed against a defined source.

When we talk about finding knowledge, most people think of a search engine and search system. It is true that today, a search is an important tool for finding information. Within the broader knowledge landscape, search plays an important role. It is the tool that provides the easiest and fastest way to discover the knowledge and information that has been intentionally collected by a source. Most sources have a search capability of some kind. From our institutional repositories to our commercial databases, and even web search engines – search is an application that helps us to navigate the content of that source.

We often refer to search as an engine because today's search can be added to any source as a distinct capability. Search is a system – with three essential parts. The first component is the input side – what it is we're going to be searching for. The second component is the process – the index structure, query processing rules, query matching rules. Finally, outputs include all those rules that determine how the results are displayed and what we can do with those results.

What we can find with search depends entirely on the scope and coverage of the source. Some engines search a single database, whereas others may search across many sources. We care about the functional architecture of search because it determines what is and is not possible, what we will find, and what we will not find. When we don't find what we're looking for, when the results are not what we expected, we often decide that the knowledge doesn't exist. In fact, in most cases, it is the source and the search architecture that may be the problem. We must understand the coverage and scope, and the capabilities of the search, before we use any source.

We care about search architecture because it is often the most significant direct expenditure any organization makes in knowledge management. The promotion of search engines often leads us to believe that they are turnkey. A turnkey system requires no configuration – it can be installed and simply turned on. Every search engine requires careful and thoughtful design work. In our experience, organizations often acquire search products that cannot be configured because the architectural components are designed around predefined settings and defaults. The more we understand about search functional architecture, the better choices we can make, and the more appropriate our configuration.

The architectural design of search systems is not well understood. They are not complex to understand. Search system designs have remained fairly constant over the decades. Advances have been made to individual components. The primary advancement has been the increased computer capacity that makes it possible to develop more sophisticated and comprehensive index architectures. The promotion of search engine optimization we have seen in the past decade pertains to the output side of the search process – how the results are presented to the searcher. It is the input and the process components where the additional design would have the greatest impact on performance.

Searching for knowledge – design concepts

To develop this functional architecture, we must have a good understanding of those concepts that pertain to search inputs, search processes, and search outputs.

More specifically, search input concepts include query formulation, searching methods for personal collections, web content, databases, catalogs, directories, and business applications. Search process concepts include index structures such as query processing and transformation, query expansion, query profiling, common index designs, full-text indexes, parameterized indexes, hybrid indexes, federated search architectures, enterprise index structures, index build methods, index monitoring, indexing balancing, and rebuilt methods. Search output concepts include results display and sorting, results citation display and downloading, results linking, results deduplication, results page design, and other user services such as current awareness, search recommendations, social tagging, syndication services, and search profile development. The primary challenge we face in designing this functional architecture is translating the rich body of knowledge and extensive research to apply to all five classes of knowledge assets.

Search system architectures have steadily developed over the past 70 years. Designs have evolved from library catalogs (Adkins & Bossaller, 2007; Buijs, 2017; Colglazier, 1996; Cooper, 1973, 1983a, 1983b, 2001; Cooper & Chen, 2001; Hancock, 1987; Kilgour, 1981; Tribbett, 2019) to commercial databases (Feinglos, 1983; Tenopir, 1983; Trzebiatowski, 1984; Younger & Boddy, 2009), to web search systems (Bollegala et al., 2007; Broder, 2002; Chen et al., 2006; Costa et al., 2013; Henzinger et al., 2002; Penniman, 1975; Trotman & Zhang, 2013), and to today's intelligence-embedded search tools (Amberg et al., 1996; Blanken et al., 2003; Guha et al., 2003; Karakostas, 1992; Lei et al., 2006; Madhu et al., 2011; Ohta et al., 2006; Zhong et al., 2002). This provides a good foundation from which to design a solution for any business source and context. The challenge is to determine how to adapt the existing architectures to support searching for knowledge assets.

We begin with the design principles. For this text, we begin with these two key design principles: search is intentional, and search is executed against a defined source. Looking for may be both unintentional and serendipitous, and sometimes intentional. But looking for will include many different sources. Search architectures focus on the design of the source, whereas looking for and discovery architectures focus on the design of human behavior. There is a hint of this variation in the information science literature – in the terms information seeking, information behaviors, and information retrieval. In each case, we are searching for a source that has been deliberately created based on an intentional collection of knowledge or information. That collection may be private, small, and time-limited, or it may be public, large, and time-independent. The parameters of any search are entirely constrained by the definition of the collection and the nature of the items in the collection. Even web search engines are not all-encompassing. They are grounded on rules defined for web crawlers to include or exclude source materials. Another distinction is that in searching, the source is 'hardwired' or its design and behavior are predefined. In contrast, looking for and discovery takes place in a much broader knowledge landscape.

We need to expand our definition of search to include not just looking for formal, packaged, and finalized knowledge products and services – but all forms and stages of knowledge (Cooper, 1998; Girod et al., 2011; Walker et al., 2002; Zhou et al., 2006). What does it mean to search for an idea? For an event? A process, an object, or a person? While there are search systems that support searching for all these forms of knowledge, they do so in different ways, and they interpret what we are looking for in different ways.

Architectural components of a search system

We know a lot about the functional architecture of search because of the research undertaken in the fields of library science, information sciences, information retrieval, and computer science (Fenichel, 1981; Fidel, 1984; Jansen et al., 2009; Meadow & Cochrane, 1981; Sewell & Teitelbaum, 1986; Siegfried et al., 1993; Tremain & Cooper, 1983). What we do not know is how to make all kinds of knowledge searchable in a way that supports looking for, seeking, and discovery. The challenge for designing a functional architecture for knowledge searching is adapting the architecture to support this expanded landscape. Search architectures today are designed to search for explicit information, and people as entities. Searching for the tacit knowledge, skills, and competencies of individuals, the procedural knowledge of businesses and organizations, and networks is an indirect and multistep search challenge. We discover an individual's tacit knowledge by searching their names, hoping to find a social media or professional profile, or discovering their citation rate. Once we have retrieved their CV or resume, we can scan that and make assumptions about what the person might know. We can access their books and publications (assuming they have published), read them, and learn more about their tacit knowledge. Consider that most internal organization people profiles and directories do not link to an individual's work or papers, and do not trace back to any of the projects or operations they have supported.

With tacit knowledge, skills, and competencies a valuable business asset today, this cumbersome approach to search is not acceptable. We face a similar challenge when we need to find procedural knowledge across the organization or even in the larger business community. This is typically informal or internal knowledge that is stored in applications that do not have rigorous search capabilities (i.e. Lotus Notes, Facebook, Slack). This information is typically not published or described on external organization websites, so it is not indexed by the index crawlers of major web search engines. And, the assets themselves are often short postings, dialogs, or conversations which are difficult to discover when they are indexed for internal enterprise search engines – simply because their low density does not promote them to the top 30 search results.

The challenge of designing a functional architecture for knowledge search is that we must adapt and extend all three of the components of the traditional design. The opportunity is that we have a foundational architecture and a body of knowledge about search functionality from which to draw. Search systems can be complex applications. But, these applications are 'systems,' and every system has three essential components, including (1) search inputs, (2) search processes, and (3) search outputs (Figure 12.1).

Elements of Search System

**Contextualization, Personalization, Recommender,
Content Syndication, Q&A Systems, Intelligent Search**

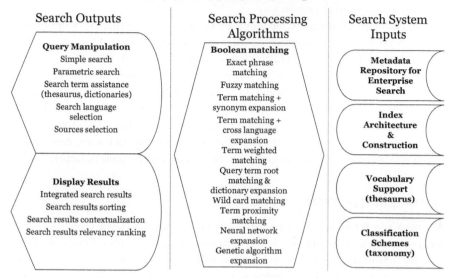

Search Outputs	Search Processing Algorithms	Search System Inputs
Query Manipulation Simple search Parametric search Search term assistance (thesaurus, dictionaries) Search language selection Sources selection	**Boolean matching** Exact phrase matching Fuzzy matching Term matching + synonym expansion Term matching + cross language expansion Term weighted matching	**Metadata Repository for Enterprise Search**
		Index Architecture & Construction
Display Results Integrated search results Search results sorting Search results contextualization Search results relevancy ranking	Query term root matching & dictionary expansion Wild card matching Term proximity matching Neural network expansion Genetic algorithm expansion	**Vocabulary Support (thesaurus)**
		Classification Schemes (taxonomy)

FIGURE 12.1 Three Components of a Search System

Search system inputs

A search system interface is our point of interaction with the search system's inputs. We can tell a lot about a search system's functionality by discovering what we can and cannot do from the interface. Can we create our search terms, or do we have to select a term from a predefined list? Can we search by fields, or only by a string of keywords? Do we have to tell it all the different forms a term might take (e.g., synonyms, acronyms, initialism, misspellings), or does it have an embedded dictionary to include them? If we can search by fields, what fields can we search? Can we tell the search engine how to treat our terms or how to prioritize the fields? Can we tell it to search for a name as a person or as an author? Can we tell what kind of knowledge we are searching for? Does the source include people, websites, journal articles, books, networks? Who selected what is included in the search system? Can we target our search for one kind of asset? Or to one collection or site?

These design issues are particularly important for knowledge search because the assets we're looking for have a context – and the search system may not understand the context. Most search systems are word- and text-based. Knowledge assets will be increasingly represented in audio or visual form. Does the search system include images? Or, do we need to have a different search architecture to find those assets? Consider how we access different kinds of assets through the Google search interface – we have distinct tabs for distinct formats. Most of the search systems we use each day, though, can identify and process only the words we give it to work with.

Knowledge search needs to go beyond this. Your initial functional design may need to focus on ensuring that these other formats are readily discovered in the knowledge landscape. It may take additional effort and resources to prepare them for inclusion in a search architecture.

The challenge of designing the inputs to a search system is that every option has a corresponding process component. We cannot search by fields if the index is not designed for identifying the field context of a term in an asset. We cannot expand the query to include acronyms or misspellings or synonyms if there is not an embedded thesaurus. We cannot tell the system how to prioritize our terms unless we give the searcher control over search operators. We cannot tell it to search for a person as staff versus a person as an author unless we have distinct metadata fields to use in indexing. While the interface is what we see and interact with, designing a search functional architecture begins with the process components (Cooper, 1971).

Search system processes

An index is a list of words or phrases ('headings') and associated pointers ('locators') to where useful material relating to that heading can be found in a document or collection of documents. Search system indexes are extensions of the everyday index we find in a book. An index is essentially a roadmap to the book, listing names, places, and things in alphabetical order and giving the page numbers associated with each topic. For nonfiction books, packed with valuable information, a well-made index can help quickly direct the reader to the information they're trying to find.

There are many different forms and types of indexes, but they all serve a common purpose. Every index is designed as a roadmap to 'something.' The 'something' is a source – a database, a website, a book, the full run of a journal and all its issues, the World Wide Web, or even a simple document. Indexes tell us exactly how to find the idea or thing we're looking for. The index gives us the shortest path from what we know or where we're starting to where we want to go in the source. The purpose of the index is to make this journey as short and effective as possible. Using an index is much more efficient than reading through the whole landscape, and far more effective than guessing at coverage from a table of contents. Indexes are efficient and effective because they focus on concepts and ideas that are discussed – not categories, topics, high-level functions, or subjects.

Search system processes revolve around one component – an index. An index helps us to locate important information in an asset. Indexes are used to quickly locate data without having to search every row in a database table every time a database table is accessed. Derived from Latin, an index means one who points out, an indication or a forefinger. Examples are a back-of-the-book (BOTB) index or a library catalog. In a traditional BOTB index, the headings will include names of people, places, events, and concepts selected by the indexer as being relevant and of interest to a possible reader of the book. The indexer may be the author, the editor, or a professional indexer working as a third party. The pointers are typically page numbers, paragraph numbers, or section numbers. A library catalog is another form of index. A catalog record contains authors, titles, subject headings, and pointers to where the item is found in the collection, either in the form of a call number or a weblink. Internet search engines (such as Google) and full-text searching help provide access to information but are not as selective as an index, as they provide non-relevant links and may miss relevant information if it is not phrased in exactly the way they expect.

Designing any kind of index involves deciding:

- what we will index – every word in an asset (e.g. a full-text index), the asset metadata, the first 4,000 characters of a source, only the asset abstract;
- whether we have more than one index – an index for each metadata field (e.g. parameterized index), an index for titles, an index for dates;
- whether we create a dedicated central index or use the indexes of other systems (e.g., federated index);
- whether we will create the index by crawling sources and sites, or whether we will leverage human processes to index;
- what each index entry looks like – whether it is just a word, a word with a pointer to the asset, or a word with a location in the asset;
- how we will treat each index entry – e.g., whether words are all treated equally, whether words in the title have greater weight, whether we record the position of the word in the asset or simply reference the whole asset;
- whether we make any changes to what we index before we add it to the index – e.g., whether we stem it, expand it, or tag it with a meaning;
- how we manage the index performance – whether we monitor its growth to ensure balanced performance;
- how often we update the index – whether it is overnight, every 15 minutes – and how long it takes to refresh the whole index – one week, or six weeks;
- whether we ever rebuild the index.

What do we index? Any information landscape can be indexed. Index architectures focus on the design of the index. Indexes are designed to support ways we expect to navigate the landscape and the nature of the destination. What are some of the design dimensions we need to consider? We need to consider what the destination is – is it a word, a concept or phrase, a paragraph, a general treatment, references to people, places, or names of things? A BOTB index may be a combination of these types of entries, or there may be multiple indexes – one dedicated to people and places, one dedicated to concepts or topics. Consider a Google search result. Google's core design function is a full-text index – this means that every word in every source Google indexes is an entry or destination in the index. That is why we're able to see the word in its context in the results.

Two other important process components of a search system include (1) search query processing, and (2) search matching and relevance. What we can do with these components and how they work is heavily impacted by the design of the search index.

Search query processing

Search query processing is simply defined as what the search system does with the search terms you tell it to look for. What might a search engine do with your search terms? If you entered more than one word, the system might search each term separately and return a combined set of results (e.g., word X AND word Y but in any order – Polish car and Car polish). It might assume you meant either term (e.g., word X OR word Y – Polish or Car). The search engine might decide you meant these as a phrase and look for a match to the exact phrase (e.g.: word X word Y word Z – 'Polish car'). The search system might decide that your term is not in its list of controlled terms, and so it will not match any results; no other words or terms are indexed. It might also decide you wanted only to see results when they appeared in the title (e.g., fielded search) or anywhere in the text (e.g., full-text search). The search engine might also expand your term to include singular and plural forms (e.g., dictionary lookup), or it might look up the word 'car' in an embedded thesaurus and also search for autos, automobiles, and vehicles. If you have designed a multilingual search architecture, query processing might translate your terms into German, French, or Polish to find additional matches. In designing your knowledge search architecture, you should think about what the search system needs to know about your search terms and what you expect it to do with them. This component in itself demonstrates that no search system should be viewed as a 'plug and play' application.

Search matching and relevance

Let's assume we've told the search system what to do with your terms, or given the searcher the option to specify what to do with it (e.g., by designing an interface that lays out the choices). Now we need to think about how the system will decide what is and is not a match. Depending on the source you're searching for, there may be many instances of a word or phrase in the index. Some results may be more relevant, popular, or authoritative than others. How does the system rank results before it displays them? Ranking and relevance methods vary widely. And, how does it decide which is the best match, and what is a less important match? If the index tracks the number of times the terms occur in a single asset, some search systems may decide that this higher incidence is an indication of greater relevance. If the index includes words from the title, the abstract, and the metadata fields, these results will not 'appear' to be as important to the same search system. They will be assigned a lower relevance. This means they will appear lower in the results list. Some search systems, though, can be configured to assign a greater weight to words that appear in a title or an abstract than anywhere in the text. If the system is not configured, the defaults will remain in place.

If the search terms appear anywhere in the indexing architecture, though, you should be able to define how to match results. This may take the form of filtering the results, where we can override the relevance ranking and see results by field.

For example, in Google, we can *filter* by date by using the search tools. Results matching and ranking might also depend on the proximity of your search terms in the asset. For example, it might match on a title – 'Car manufacturing and labor unions in Polish factories' – if you set the proximity factor anywhere in the same sentence. If you limit a match to adjacent terms, it will not consider this title a match.

Search system outputs

Just as the process component of the architecture determines inputs, the process components determine what we can do with the results. What we can display is determined by what has been stored in the index – is it just a pointer to a call number and enough information to identify the item on the shelf? Is it a link to the asset? Is it just a citation? The type of index determines whether you can sort the results – you need to have fields or parameters to sort on. Indexes that have meta-data can provide more descriptive information about the asset. Who is responsible for it? Does it have a name or title? What is the format? Full-text indexes do not allow you to sort results. Do the results highlight your search terms in the results? If they do, this means the index has some way of locating where those terms exist in the asset. Can you find other versions of the result? If the index leverages metadata, results may also include recommendations or pointers to other assets with similar characteristics, e.g., recommendations and 'others like this.' If you have designed a federated index – in which you search the indexes of other sources – you will need to have results deduplication processes. Results duplication eliminates redundant results pulled from multiple sources.

Additionally, search systems offer services at the output stage. These may include storing results in a cache and selecting citations to download. A system may allow you to create personal search profiles that can be run periodically – to alert you to the appearance of new and relevant assets. Some search systems allow us to set up syndication or current awareness services also based on predefined search profiles.

Searching for human capital

Consider the variety of results and intentions we encounter when we search for a person or an organization. How many different sources do we have to search for? There are people searches, web searches, directories, publication databases. What does Google assume we mean? What does a commercial database such as Lexis Nexis assume we mean? Or LinkedIn, or a library catalog? To search for information about a person, you need to select the most pertinent source and then understand 'how' to search in that source. This is a significant challenge for knowledge search – it is a result of designing search architectures to support explicit information and knowledge products. This functional architecture must be expanded and rethought in the 21st century.

Consider the results when we search for an idea. The results we generate are just the starting point to uncovering that idea – what the different sources think about it, disambiguating what we intended and what the source thought, and assessing the trustworthiness of the sources. The small task that constitutes a search of a source is one small action in the larger 'looking for' and 'discovery' context. For example, searching for an idea in a library catalog search is challenging unless that catalog includes a full-text search of books and journal articles – because ideas are not represented in subject headings.

Searching for explicit knowledge

Most search engines today are targeted at explicit information sources. A search system that provides access to knowledge assets, though, must go beyond explicit knowledge. It is important to continue to provide access points for books, journal articles, presentations, technical reports, and patents, regardless of whether they are in a digital or a physical format. But, explicit knowledge comes in the form of audio recordings of books, of speeches, of testimony, of events and performances, of YouTube videos, art, and images of artifacts. Today we search for these other forms in distinct systems. Google is perhaps the closest we have to a cross-asset search by offering a federated search that displays different formats in different tabs. This is a significant design and engineering challenge because searching different types of assets means building multiple indexes, and defining different sets of indexing rules and methods.

While search systems are effective at providing access to some important fields – i.e., author, title, date, format – these access points reflect the design of the original catalogs and card catalogs. A knowledge search system should be able to understand the context and meaning of references in knowledge assets – i.e., determine when a person is being referred to as an author, being able to recognize a place name as a geographic location, etc. Search systems for explicit knowledge should be able to index a document for more than a simple occurrence of words. As a BOTB index, they should be able to identify and distinguish different access points. This means we need to begin adding semantic analysis tools to our indexing methods.

Searching for procedural knowledge

How do we design a system to search for procedural knowledge? The challenge begins with identifying sources to include in the index. Unlike explicit knowledge, procedural knowledge is unlikely to be stored in well-developed or well-managed collections or repositories. Where an organization has created procedural manuals, they are likely to be treated simply as 'manuals' or 'documents' and included in other storage systems. They may also be created as a dynamic website that may be captured in an enterprise search crawl. It may be a structured object in a Lotus Notes database that has its dedicated search system. Or, it may be a single document stored in a folder on a unit's network drive. To meet the first challenge of search, we need to have a 'collection policy' that intentionally identifies and tracks these assets and ensures they are indexed – whether manually or programmatically. This holds for all other types of procedural knowledge, including audio or video recordings of process performance, after-action review conversations about a critical incident, an interview with an expert explaining how to perform a specific step, engineering specifications or blueprints for a process layout, or a knowledge book that captures essential steps.

To enable effective searching, we need new indexing rules and new access points. We search for procedural knowledge by the name of the process, the products they generate, or the materials and ingredients they consume. These are not common access points in most catalog indexes and have not been designed into most search engines. Inventory systems and supply catalogs have access points for product and part names, but not for processes. This is a critical new access point that must be developed. Given that we are starting from scratch for this type of search, the most effective approach may be to address building semantic analysis tools into our indexing methods.

Searching for cultural knowledge

We have a similar challenge to designing a search system to find cultural knowledge. It is unlikely that these assets are managed distinctly. We start our search design process by developing methods to identify and collect these materials. They will likely be scattered across repositories and storage locations. Some may be stored in document management systems. Examples of cultural events or performances may be recorded as moving images, as photographs, as audio recordings. These may be stored in physical archives, in digital asset management systems, in boxes on shelves in communications offices, or in special collections. Index design may rely on metadata to provide effective access across formats and sources. Because cultural events and activities have dates, performances, and participants, we will need new access points.

Searching for network knowledge

How do we design a search for network knowledge? A network knowledge search should help us to find a network by the focus or purpose of the network, to find the people who are members of the network or community, and to find the knowledge that is created or exchanged in the network. While this sounds straightforward, consider where most networks exist – in closed social media platforms, or community-specific applications. Most networks and online communities are not curated or deliberately collected. Most applications that support networks do not have robust search systems. To design a search system for network knowledge, we have to first identify and intentionally curate the networks that have value to our business. Assuming these networks have a structure we can navigate with an indexing routine, we might be able to create an internal index for each network.

This approach, though, will not be effective for supporting the important access points. This type of search should have an indexing method that identifies people as entities.

Searching for knowledge – the design environment

What factors do we need to consider in designing a search functional architecture? There are several factors we need to consider in designing this functional architecture. We need to consider the complexity of the environment in terms of sources. We need to consider the complexity of the business environment and the focus of the work. We need to be aware of the volatility of knowledge in this business context, and the rate of change of the external business environment. We need to understand the level of competitiveness of the external business environment – how critical is it for our business stakeholders to access cutting-edge knowledge to retain a market position? What is the level and nature of the knowledge assets the organization has to work with? Are they all well managed and intentionally collected? Perhaps most critically, what search architecture competencies does the organization have to design and develop a knowledge search architecture?

What events trigger the need to search for knowledge? We become aware of the need to support a knowledge search when we realize how much time is lost in failed searches, or the opportunity costs of time spent in learning and relearning how to search and navigate individual sources. Wherever we have high rates of knowledge recreation or the use of suboptimal knowledge assets, we realize the importance of improving knowledge search. The challenge, though, is to ensure that knowledge architects and business stakeholders are aware of these situations, and how unacceptable they are from a business perspective. Essentially, this is any time we know we have internal knowledge assets that are relevant to the task at hand, but we cannot locate those assets.

What are the impacts of having a knowledge search function in place? The impacts go well beyond the outputs. When knowledge search works well, we reduce lost time to failed or unproductive searches. We reduce the opportunity costs of spending time on a search that could be spent on other business tasks. Knowledge assets are reused and improved. Knowledge gaps are filled. We have a choice between multiple assets across the organization, rather than just what is easily accessible to us in our unit or community.

What sources do we leverage to search for knowledge? We have several sources to leverage, including centralized index structures, database and application indexes, existing search tools and architectures, and library catalogs with embedded architectures and engines. The challenge is what is missing – the experience with new access points and the need to better manage some categories of knowledge assets.

What are the outputs and outcomes of searching for knowledge? This functional architecture generates higher levels of knowledge asset discoveries, better access to people and their inherent knowledge, procedural and cultural knowledge, and networks.

Designing knowledge search activities and tasks

This functional architecture must support several activities and tasks, including:

- Activity 1. Define the source(s) to be searched
- Activity 2. Define search capabilities
- Activity 3. Design to support search capabilities
- Activity 4. Design search architecture
- Activity 5. Design index update capabilities
- Activity 6. Define logging and feedback capabilities

Activity 1. Define the source(s) to be searched

How do we do this? This activity leverages the information you collected to define your knowledge landscape. If a source is important enough to be included in your landscape, it should have some form of searchable access. Each organization must ask and answer a key set of questions to define the landscape their search system will support. These questions focus initially on each source:

- Does the source have its search application, and is it good enough?
- Does it need to be enhanced to support searching for knowledge assets by knowledge access points?
- If there is no searchable access, what kind of search capability can you provide for it?
- Can you access the source content to crawl it or expose the assets to search?
- How well will this sourcing fare in an enterprise search?
- Is the content sufficiently dense to be able to compete with other sources included in your enterprise search?
- Do you need to add semantic technologies to your indexing methods to ensure you can surface the other important access points?

What inputs does this activity need? The most important source is an understanding of the knowledge landscape. While it is important to enhance the knowledge source capabilities of existing sources, it is important to start with a sense of whether the important knowledge sources are or are not searchable. This means we need to have a high-level description of the sources on the landscape. Also useful to this activity is feedback from business stakeholders whether current forms and levels of access to these sources are sufficient.

What products does it generate? This activity should produce a sense of answers to the essential design questions. It provides us with a sense of where we need to start our design.

What resources does this activity require? The inventory of the knowledge landscape, feedback from business stakeholders, and answers to the key design questions. The knowledge architect should synthesize all of these inputs into a rough sketch of what the high-level knowledge search design.

Activity 2. Define search capabilities

How do we do this? This activity requires a deeper dive into the functionality of the knowledge search. Working with the rough architecture design from Activity 1, and the feedback from the business stakeholders, the architect should focus on (1) identifying the access points that should be searchable, (2) map them to potential index structures, and (3) design a simple and detailed results display. The architect should walk through this process for each index identified in Activity 1. Looking across all indexes, the architect should then

What inputs does this activity need? To complete this activity, we need to leverage our knowledge object models, and we need to know the access points and variables for each object model. We also need to leverage the understanding we have developed about how our business stakeholders look for knowledge. It is also important to understand the current search and indexing architectures to understand what we can leverage, what is working, and what needs to be improved.

What products does it generate? This activity generates a working framework of important search access points, a search interface design that supports these access points and makes sense to business stakeholders, the index architectures that align with each access point, and the rules for constructing those indexes.

What resources does this activity require? This activity requires synthesizing and designing the connections between the inputs to the search system and its underlying architecture. In addition to the inputs noted, the knowledge architect's ability to work with business stakeholders, business architects, application architects, and information architects is important.

Activity 3. Design to support search capabilities

How do we do this? For each search field on the interface, we need to define the query processing rules. For each query, we need to define the matching and relevance rules. To complete this activity effectively, we need to understand how each access point works. Each access point should have a purposeful and intentional design for query processing and query matching. One size does not fit all types of searches. What works for matching descriptors does not work for matching names of people. People indexes perform best when we can apply Soundex matching methods. But, Soundex algorithms are designed to work with Western European languages, not with Asian or African languages. Using an embedded dictionary from the *Financial Times* might work well in a financial services context, but it is not likely to be an effective choice for query expansion in a transportation agency. And, it is important to leverage what is already in place and working. This means we have to look across the organization and not limit our reference points to those that apply to explicit knowledge assets.

What inputs does this activity need? For this activity, we need to know the specifications and behaviors for each attribute we're adding to the index, if any, from our object models. We need to understand how business stakeholders are likely to speak about or form a search query. We need to understand how to manage that query to better prepare the query for matching with the source assets. Query processing may mean that we have to semantically analyze the query terms entered into a general keyword search box, and tag them to a specific index, before we attempt to find a match. We need to be able to extract meaning from the query to understand whether the searcher is asking a question, looking for a specific item, or in search of a high-level description of a topic. We need to know whether we should expand the query terms, stem them and match them, or simply take them as entered. Expanding the search term China to include Asia may degrade the relevance of results, and it may hide important results in too large a results set. We also need to know how we will match the search terms – exact matching, fuzzy matching, single term matching? And, we need to decide how we will calculate relevance. Is it simply incidence? That may be effective for a descriptor, but it will not be effective for people's names or organization names.

What products does it generate? This activity produces a set of design guidelines for query processing and query matching for knowledge search.

What resources does this activity require? The primary resource is our knowledge of the behavior of the access points, and how business stakeholders search for different kinds of knowledge assets.

Activity 4. Design search architecture

How do we do this? Looking across all the sources in your landscape, the knowledge architect should work with the developers and business stakeholders to design an architecture for knowledge search. These are questions we highlighted earlier in the chapter, including:

- Do you have a centralized, federated, or a hybrid architecture?
- What limitations does a federated search introduce?
- Do these limitations constrain searching for knowledge assets?
- What resources are needed to support a centralized or hybrid architecture?
- Does the organization have the competencies and knowledge to support either a centralized or hybrid architecture?
- Is it parameterized and fielded, or simple keyword searching supported?
- How do parameterized search leverage the knowledge object models, variables, and reference sources?

With the answers to these questions, you should be able to determine the design for the overall knowledge search architecture. Having defined the high-level architecture, the next step is to define the indexes you will need, and the structure of each of those indexes. An index that supports searching for identifiers, e.g., formally named things, will have a different set of fields and indexing rules than an index that searching for topics or dates. You will need to define the indexing methods and the indexing rules for each index. Will you extract and map metadata from sources, will you include end user-generated keywords, and will you include web crawled valued? How will you map these different inputs to the structures, and how will you weight them? Will you control the syntax for some fields but not others?

What inputs does this activity need? The primary input for this activity is what you learned about your knowledge landscape, the knowledge your business stakeholders need to support the organization's work, and the behavior of the sources on that landscape. All of this is input for the knowledge architect who must have sufficient knowledge of search to design a suitable architecture.

What products does it generate? This activity should produce a working blueprint for knowledge search which can be handed to the developers for review and feedback.

What resources does this activity require? The primary resource is the knowledge architect, and the knowledge architect's ability to work with the business architect and the application architect to communicate and operationalize the design.

Activity 5. Design index update capabilities

How do we do this? This activity addresses the management of indexes. Indexes are living structures. The knowledge architect and the application architect need to determine the rate at which entries are added to the index, how often people expect to find new search results, and common practices for the major source systems. These questions are particularly important if you're working with federated architecture design because varying update rates will become obvious in the search results. If you're working with a centralized architecture, you can better manage the updates to the indexes from individual sources. Index rebuilds are resource and time intensive. We only want to rebuild an index when the performance of the indexing is declining because it is unbalanced. Of course, this assumes we're working with an inverted index rather than a table structure. Table structures require less maintenance. Unfortunately, relational indexes that resemble database structures are performance-inefficient and performance-poor. Tall table structures have better performance, but they are not as effective as inverted index structures. Depending on the rate of the update, indexes may be rebalanced monthly. Indexes like those that support web search engines are continuously rebuilt and rebalanced. They leverage rolling rebuilds in the background. These update routines can take up to six weeks to complete a complete index refresh.

What inputs does this activity need? This activity is heavily dependent upon knowledge of the index designs, and the search system. This means the knowledge architect must work closely with the application architect to achieve an efficient design.

What products does it generate? This activity generates specifications for index management.

What resources does this activity require? As noted earlier, this is a knowledge-intensive activity. Its success is heavily reliant on having an experienced knowledge architect and application architect on the team.

Activity 6. Define logging and feedback capabilities

How do we do this? The first step is to define the kind of information we need to make decisions about how to manage knowledge search. What does performance look like? What is acceptable performance and what is not? What are effective search results? Do we have high rates of failure in some sources? Do we have high failure rates for different kinds of searches? Is search aligning with and supporting our knowledge landscape, or do we have gaps? We need to decide who should receive the reports. We need to determine when and how we need to search for scenarios. Just as we built use case scenarios to understand the knowledge landscape, we need a periodic sampling of performance from a business perspective, not just an application perspective. What do we need to capture in the log? Are the logs continuous, or do we sample different sources? We need to determine how long we will maintain our search logs. Will we offload them to a storage source? Who will analyze them? What are the rates of the collection?

What inputs does this activity need? We need to make sure that our search systems have logging capabilities. Where these are missing, we have to rely on periodic sampling and scenario building. The application architects should construct the search logs, but the knowledge architect and the business architect should manage and interpret the output.

What products does it generate? This activity generates reports on search performance and effectiveness.

What resources does this activity require? Search logs are resource-intensive to generate and to interpret. Not every organization will have the resources to set up and support this activity. Business managers must also have the capacity to learn from and provide feedback from these reports. Search systems require continuous management just like any other organization application.

Evolution of knowledge search designs

Searching and search systems have a different history and evolution from those of seeking and discovery. This is because the focus point is different. Search systems focus on a defined context, whereas seeking and discovery include the entire landscape. Experience and a review of the literature suggest five general phases have brought us to where we are today with a search (Figure 12.2):

- Phase 1. Single source searching
- Phase 2. Catalog-based searching
- Phase 3. Multidimensional catalog searching
- Phase 4. Online catalog searching
- Phase 5. Distinct search applications and tools

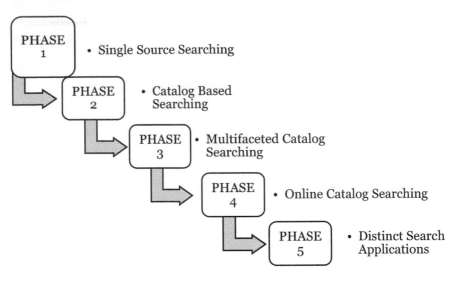

FIGURE 12.2 Evolution of Search System Architectures

Phase 1. Single source searching

In the earliest times, a search was defined by and predicated on a specific source. Sources were limited because our contact was limited. Knowledge had not yet been formally represented or codified – we did not yet have large collections of information or knowledge. Sources were close to the searcher. From a formal search perspective, the most sophisticated sources may take the form of lists or inventories of personal or private resources. For example, a monastery or a local lord may have had small collections of handwritten or manuscript collections. To manage the collections, they may have created handwritten lists of private or monastery collections. These early lists would have been linear in simple chronological order.

Phase 2. Catalog-based searching

Over time, as the stocks of knowledge and codified knowledge increase, those with resources began to assemble collections. They were collecting not for preservation but as status symbols or personal use. We see the emergence of scientific collections, scholarly collections, religious collections, and literary collections. As collections increased and proliferated, we see the emergency of catalogs. Catalogs provide an expansion over inventory lists – they include more extensive descriptions of the items in the collection. Print catalogs were intended to be used on-site or in proximity to the location of the collection. These early catalogs were difficult and cumbersome to update. Any changes require a new version or a supplement. As national libraries emerged, print catalogs were produced and distributed as reference materials to support the location and borrowing of materials from remote collections. An example of this is the British Museum Library

Blue Book Catalogs —an initial edition covered a collection to a certain date, and supplementary volumes were produced to represent new acquisitions.

Catalogs also represented inventories of producers. The catalog has been a vital part of the shopping experience and has a very rich and interesting history. The first catalog was published by Aldus Pius Manutius in Venice in 1498. The invention of the printing press earlier that century made it possible for Manutius to efficiently produce the first printed editions of many Greek and Latin classics. When he wanted to introduce his books to Venice, he *printed a catalog of all the books he was printing* – the first-ever published catalog.

Fast forward 200 years. Seed companies take the next step in catalog evolution. The roots of these seed catalogs lie in 1667, when William Lucas, an English gardener, published a catalog with seed products and prices for his customers. The practice was continued in colonial America in 1771 when William Prince published a catalog of fruit trees. These were not only sales and marketing tools but also horticultural literature. The use of catalogs for product offerings and prices accelerated in the late 1700s. Consider Benjamin Franklin's invention and promotion of the mail order business. One of Franklin's earliest catalogs was *A Catalogue of Choice and Valuable Books, Consisting of Near 600 Volumes, in Most Faculties and Sciences*. Franklin's business and his catalog were precursors of the retail mail-order businesses and catalogs of the 1800s and 1900s. The rise of manufacturing and production centers and a dispersed population made mail order shopping the norm. Catalogs described and promoted the inventories of all of the major retail companies. Consider Tiffany & Company's *Blue Book*, first published in 1845. Pryce-Jones was one of the first to sell by mail order on a large scale in 1861. The first Montgomery Ward catalog was produced in 1872, the first catalog intended for the general public. In 1894, Sears published one of their earliest catalogs. The larger these catalogs became, the more important it was to include an index to help the shopper find products. The rise of shopping malls reduced the demand for mail order shopping, but the rise of online shopping transformed the traditional catalogs into online search and navigation. The essential designs and structures of these earlier catalogs served as the prototype for today's online shopping. Despite the demise of mail order shopping, catalogs remain a tool of direct marketing and advertising even today.

The purpose of our discussion of these early catalogs serves to remind us that searching catalogs are a natural process for the larger population. The general public is not unfamiliar with indexes, catalog descriptions, and the mental processes of navigating catalogs. We need to understand how catalogs are designed and used because they are the prototype for today's search systems.

Phase 3. Multidimensional catalog searching

A simple architectural advancement was designed and promoted by libraries. With the advent of the French Revolution and the opening of the collections of the aristocracy to public use, there was a need to provide broader and more flexible access to collection inventories. Print catalogs transformed into physical card catalogs. Card catalogs provided a single physical record for each item in the collection. We describe this phase of catalog design as flexible because for the first time they provided multiple access points. These are still representative of a single collection and typically were limited to books and journal titles. They were intended to be used on-site and close to the collection. Similar structures were created by businesses to track their products and parts inventories. We now had multiple parameters from which we can access the collection – the first fielded or parameterized catalog. But the size and space requirements of these physical catalogs were expensive to maintain. While they provided access from multiple perspectives, the space limitations introduced restrictions and impediments to how many parameters could be supported. Every parameter required another separate physical instance of the catalog. At a point in time, filing rules were designed to enable us to integrate all access points into a single physical catalog – integrated author and subject catalogs. As interests in parameters expanded, we found a need to combine access points into subject headings. This lead to the practice of pre- or post-coordinated indexing terms. These early parametric card catalogs and the practices that grew up around them introduced design architectures that are with us today. Unfortunately, we have done little to critically evaluate these early designs.

Phase 4. Online catalog searching

With the advancement of technology and the increased computing capacity, these early library catalogs were transformed into online instances. The earliest online catalogs combined a database of metadata and a search architecture. They were tightly integrated designs. As functional applications such as cataloging and acquisitions were automated, we redesigned the architecture to include separate databases, distinct index structures, and distinct search engines. These early integrated library systems provided the first models for our early search systems.

These early designs allowed us to expanded the search to include multiple parameters. These early catalogs also took guidance from commercial databases and search designed to support journal titles and articles. The print indexes of long runs of journal publications were simply too extensive to navigate. And, demand was rapidly increasing for access to the scientific and engineering literature.

The earliest examples include the DIALAOG system, the BRS service, ERIC, and the earliest University Microfilms service. These search systems provided direct access to the resources in addition to metadata descriptions. The earliest online library catalogs were available internally – to people who could access the terminals on-site. The earliest commercial databases, though, were open to broader communities – for a price. These developments give us our first opportunity to think about the design and functionality of a search architecture. This phase forced us to begin to design search applications, as well as to consider how we might re-engineer the traditional 'index' as a core component of search.

The increased availability of online catalogs and the ability to search catalogs remotely created a demand for direct access to the source materials. While it was a great benefit to know what was in a collection, now the challenge was how to get the source materials. When catalogs and collections were 'adjacent,' this was not a challenge, but this new advance created a demand for digital versions of source materials. Online catalogs spurred developments in three new directions: (1) retrospective conversions of existing print and card sources; (2) focus on creating and acquiring digital versions of resources in commercial databases; and (3) conversion of print resources to digital resources. Additionally, the idea of online catalogs spurred the development of search capabilities for specialized formats and types of collections including. Consider the development of specialized search engines for music collections, for art collections, and people or business searching.

Phase 5. Distinct search applications and tools

As publishers moved to increase the scale and scope of digital offerings online, the universe of information available to search online expanded exponentially. Shifting from the original focus on bibliographic databases (e.g., the online equivalent of abstracting and indexing services), databases have now expanded to include full-text versions of journal articles, books, technical reports, conference presentations, and so on. Consider the Google Books search, which provides full-text level access to books of scholarly significance.

As more types of resources are brought online, however, the searcher has a more complex search environment to navigate. The complexity increases the types of sources to search and the search techniques designed into different sources. The development of distinct applications as products also increases the challenge for organizations. Many designs are now possible, and the need to understand architectures and performance increases. This phase aligns with two major developments – the appearance of client-server architectures and the first forms of the Web. Stand-alone search applications can now be applied to any source. As the scale of sources increases, the earliest database structure indexing methods fall short of our expectations. New index designs are needed. But, this means that organizations must take responsibility for designing and maintaining those indexes – they cannot assume they are part of the whole application architecture. We now have the opportunity to build enterprise search, collection-specific search, site-specific search, and even search for network drives and personal collections. This new capability increases the complexity and variation of the searcher's experience.

Going forward, we expect two new developments. First, we expect a search to be designed to meet personal needs. As our understanding of search architectures increases, and as the availability of tools grows, individuals will be able to design their search environment. This new architecture might reflect those personal social and linguistic registers described earlier. Rather than the individual having to adapt to every search system they encounter, they should be able to navigate sources using their search systems. Second, we expect a search to be less intrusive and to become a back-end operation. This does not mean it is embedded into other applications; rather, it is an invisible service that supports our dialogs with and queries of different sources. This will result from the integration of ratification intelligence and semantic technologies as an intermediate application. We also expect search engines to become smarter in terms of how they construct indexes. Rather than focus on those traditional access points supported in early library catalogs, the rapid expansion of the knowledge economy will highlight the importance of new and user-defined access points. Again, this will be a result of the development and application of semantic technologies and artificial intelligence capabilities.

Knowledge search in the enterprise architecture blueprint

Knowledge search is likely to live in the application layer of most current architecture practices. This is challenging because it means that search tends to be treated like a plug-and-play application, rather than a resource that needs to be managed and monitored. Ideally, knowledge search lives in the knowledge architecture, but with strong ties to the business architecture practice. The management and design of knowledge search functional architectures should reside with the business and the knowledge architect, in support of the application architects.

Chapter review

After reading this chapter, you should be able to:

* define searching, and explain what it means to search for knowledge;
* describe the architecture of a search system;
* explain what it means to search for explicit knowledge;
* describe searching for other types of knowledge capital.

References and recommended future readings

Adkins, D., & Bossaller, J. E. (2007). Fiction access points across computer-mediated book information sources: A comparison of online bookstores, reader advisory databases, and public library catalogs. *Library & Information Science Research, 29*(3), 354–368.

Amberg, A., Domschke, W., & Voß, S. (1996). *Capacitated minimum spanning trees: Algorithms using intelligent search.* Darmstadt Technical University, Department of Business Administration, Economics and Law, Institute for Business Studies (BWL).

Blanken, H., Grabs, T., Schek, H. J., Schenkel, R., & Weikum, G. (Eds.). (2003). *Intelligent search on XML data: Applications, languages, models, implementations, and benchmarks* (Vol. 2818). Springer Science & Business Media.

Bollegala, D., Matsuo, Y., & Ishizuka, M. (2007). Measuring semantic similarity between words using web search engines. *www, 7*(757–766), 10–1145.

Broder, A. (2002, September). A taxonomy of web search. In *ACM Sigir forum* (Vol. 36, No. 2, pp. 3–10). ACM Press.

Buijs, J. (2017). *A visual history of the catalog.* Retrieved February 2, 2020, from www.publitas.com/blog/a-visual-history-of-the-catalog/.

Chen, Y. Y., Suel, T., & Markowetz, A. (2006, June). Efficient query processing in geographic web search engines. In *Proceedings of the 2006 ACM SIGMOD international conference on Management of data* (pp. 277–288). https://doi.org/10.1145/1142473.1142505.

Colglazier Jr, M. L. (1996). Prologue for a synoptic catalog: Combining a hospital library catalog and a bookseller's catalog. *Bulletin of the Medical Library Association, 84*(1), 41.

Cooper, M. D. (1971). *Evaluation of information retrieval systems: A simulation and cost approach.* Berkeley, CA: School of Librarianship, University of California.

Cooper, M. D. (1973). A simulation model of an information retrieval system. *Information Storage and Retrieval, 9*(1), 13–32.

Cooper, M. D. (1983a). Response time variations in an online search system. *Journal of the American Society for Information Science, 34*(6), 374–380.

Cooper, M. D. (1983b). Usage patterns of an online search system. *Journal of the American Society for information Science, 34*(5), 343–349.

Cooper, M. D. (1998). Design considerations in instrumenting and monitoring web-based information retrieval systems. *Journal of the American Society for Information Science, 49*(10), 903–919.

Cooper, M. D. (2001). Usage patterns of a web-based library catalog. *Journal of the American Society for Information Science and Technology, 52*(2), 137–148.

Cooper, M. D., & Chen, H. M. (2001). Predicting the relevance of a library catalog search. *Journal of the American Society for Information Science and Technology, 52*(10), 813–827.

Costa, M., Gomes, D., Couto, F., & Silva, M. (2013, May). A survey of web archive search architectures. In *Proceedings of the 22nd international conference on world wide web* (pp. 1045–1050). ACM Press.

Feinglos, S. J. (1983). MEDLINE at BRS, DIALOG, and NLM: Is there a choice? *Bulletin of the Medical Library Association, 71*(1), 6.

Fenichel, C. H. (1981). Online searching: Measures that discriminate among users with different types of experiences. *Journal of the American Society for Information Science, 32*(1), 23–32.

Fidel, R. (1984). Online searching styles: A case-study-based model of searching behavior. *Journal of the American Society for information Science, 35*(4), 211–221.

Girod, B., Chandrasekhar, V., Grzeszczuk, R., & Reznik, Y. A. (2011). Mobile visual search: Architectures, technologies, and the emerging MPEG standard. *IEEE MultiMedia, 18*(3), 86–94.

Guha, R., McCool, R., & Miller, E. (2003, May). Semantic search. In *Proceedings of the 12th international conference on world wide web* (pp. 700–709). Google Scholar.

Hancock, M. (1987). Subject searching behaviour at the library catalogue and at the shelves: Implications for online interactive catalogues. *Journal of documentation, 43*(4), 303–321.

Henzinger, M. R., Motwani, R., & Silverstein, C. (2002, September). Challenges in web search engines. In *ACM SIGIR forum* (Vol. 36, No. 2, pp. 11–22). ACM Press.

Jansen, B. J., Booth, D., & Smith, B. (2009). Using the taxonomy of cognitive learning to model online searching. *Information Processing & Management, 45*(6), 643–663.

Karakostas, V. (1992). Intelligent search and acquisition of business knowledge from programs. *Journal of Software Maintenance: Research and Practice, 4*(1), 1–17.

Kilgour, F. G. (1981). *Library catalog design* (pp. 169–173). International Online Information Meeting, London. Retrieved from May 1, 2020, from http://pascal-francis.inist.fr/vibad/index.php?action=getRecordDetail&idt=PASCAL82X0330207.

Lei, Y., Uren, V., & Motta, E. (2006, October). Semsearch: A search engine for the semantic web. In *International conference on knowledge engineering and knowledge management* (pp. 238–245). Springer.

Madhu, G., Govardhan, D. A., & Rajinikanth, D. T. (2011). Intelligent semantic web search engines: A brief survey. arXiv preprint arXiv:1102.0831.

Meadow, C. T., & Cochrane, P. A. (1981). *Basics of Online Searching*. Wiley-InterScience, 605 Third Ave.

Ohta, T., Miyao, Y., Ninomiya, T., Tsuruoka, Y., Yakushiji, A., Masuda, K., . . . Tateisi, Y. (2006, July). An intelligent search engine and GUI-based efficient MEDLINE search tool based on deep syntactic parsing. In *Proceedings of the COLING/ACL 2006 interactive presentation sessions* (pp. 17–20). Association of Computational Linguistics. ACLWeb. https://www.aclweb.org/anthology/P06-1000.pdf.

Penniman, W. D. (1975). *Rhythms of dialogue in human-computer conversation* (Doctoral dissertation), The Ohio State University, Ohio.

Sewell, W., & Teitelbaum, S. (1986). Observations of end-user online searching behavior over eleven years. *Journal of the American Society for Information Science, 37*(4), 234–245.

Siegfried, S., Bates, M. J., & Wilde, D. N. (1993). A profile of end-user searching behavior by humanities scholars: The getty online searching project report no. 2. *Journal of the American Society for Information Science, 44*(5), 273–291.

Tenopir, C. (1983). Dialog's knowledge index and BRS/after dark: Database searching on personal computers. *Library Journal, 108*(5), 471–474.

Tremain, R., & Cooper, M. D. (1983). A parser for on-line search system evaluation. *Information Processing & Management, 19*(2), 65–75.

Tribbett, T. S. D. (2019). *Next generation catalog design for an international law firm*. Advised Key Safety Systems Inc.

Trotman, A., & Zhang, J. (2013). Future web growth and its consequences for web search architectures. arXiv preprint arXiv:1307.1179.

Trzebiatowski, E. (1984). End user study on BRS/after dark. *RQ*, 446–450.

Walker, M. J., Hull, R. D., & Singh, S. B. (2002). CKB− the compound knowledge base: A text based chemical search system. *Journal of Chemical Information and Computer Sciences, 42*(6), 1293–1295.

Younger, P., & Boddy, K. (2009). When is a search not a search? A comparison of searching the AMED complementary health database via EBSCOhost, OVID and DIALOG. *Health Information & Libraries Journal, 26*(2), 126–135.

Zhong, J., Zhu, H., Li, J., & Yu, Y. (2002, July). Conceptual graph matching for semantic search. In *International conference on conceptual structures* (pp. 92–106). Springer.

Zhou, Z. Y., Yu, P., Chelba, C., & Seide, F. (2006). Towards spoken-document retrieval for the internet: Lattice indexing for large-scale web-search architectures. In *Proceedings of the main conference on human language technology conference of the North American chapter of the association of computational linguistics* (pp. 415–422). Association for Computational Linguistics.

13

FUNCTIONAL ARCHITECTURE FOR KNOWLEDGE CATEGORIZATION

Chapter summary

This chapter explains the role that categorization plays in supporting access to knowledge assets and details the seven activities that support the design of categorization architectures. It explains why it is essential to have a good understanding of categories, categorization principles, schemes, processes, and methods, including both human and machine techniques. The chapter lays out the differences between categorization, indexing and keywording, and other semantic structures. Here we consider the primary challenge in designing this functional architecture for categorization: adapting common and traditional perceptions, practices in and procedures, and the existing 'built' environment.

Why we care about categorizing

Categorization serves a very human need to impose order on nature and make sense of a complex environment. It helps us to more effectively and efficiently store and retrieve knowledge by grouping organisms and species together. Additionally, categorizing gives us a way to describe an item to others. It provides connections between ideas for similarities/differences. It provides us with a way to group our thoughts. As the scale and scope of information and knowledge have grown over the centuries, people have found it helpful to organize things into categories. Organizing things into a structure is a way for people to manage their world. Consider the categorization schemes you use without thinking every day – the layout of grocery stores, store and mall directories, website browsing structures, yellow pages, or online store categories for grouping similar things.

Categorization also helps us to understand the scope and coverage of a collection, a domain, an industry, or even a grocery store. It is essential to understand the scope and coverage of a field before we search for information in that domain. Domains can be described from many different perspectives, using different language and terminologies. A categorization scheme can help us to see what terms and concepts are within or out of scope for a domain. Fields can be defined by an organization – the topics they work in, the kinds of work they do, the types of knowledge created, the countries or regions where they work.

Despite this widespread use, there is only one published standard. This standard, *ISO 11179-2 Information Technology – Metadata Registries (MDR). Part 2: Classification (2005)*, guides the data structures and relationships that should be used to represent a classification scheme. It does not, though, guide how to create or maintain the values in a classification scheme. While organizing is a critical design factor for knowledge architecture, there is considerable misunderstanding about categorizing knowledge, categorizing knowledge objects, and judging the goodness of categorization actions. The misunderstanding and confusion is a consequence of the impediments and constraints imposed by a built environment, and by a historical lack of capacity to design categorization to suit the definition and need. This confusion and confounding is a serious impediment to good functional architecture designs – because there are a variety of design principles, design environments, and design concepts at play. There is a need to clarify what a category is and how it fits into a categorization scheme – and to different categories and schemes for controlled vocabularies, topic or concept maps, and concept clusters. These topics are discussed in greater detail in Chapter 15; this chapter focuses on categorization.

The biggest challenge we face in achieving this clarity is the extent of the 'built environment' for this functional area, the level of investment made in these applications, and their embeddedness in other applications and professional practice. An additional impediment is the tendency to teach method rather than design principles and concepts. So most professionals and experts charged with developing or applying a categorization scheme have little foundation from which to work. In many cases, the action of categorizing is a subjective decision that may or may not have a good result.

Categorizing knowledge – design concepts

We must have a good understanding of categories, their structures and behaviors, categorization schemes and their principles; categorization processes and methods; and common types of categorization methods such as human, machine-assisted, and fully automated. The primary challenges we face in designing this functional architecture are adjusting prevalent perceptions, practices in and procedures in specific domains, and seeing other design options that transcend current 'built solutions.'

What is the category?

A category is a group to which entities or concepts belong based on the definition of the group and the characteristics of the objects. We can define categories in different ways. In mathematics, a category is a set of entities defined by a common set of attributes or characteristics. In biology, a class or category is defined by the differentiation of characteristics – in other words, we create a group based on a single attribute rather than on multiple attributes. What are some examples of categories? A geographic region is a category of countries defined based on their geographical location. A subject or topic category is defined by all of those dimensions that make up the category. A subject or topic category may be defined in the scope of issues and concepts defined in an area of study or research. A topic may also be described by how an organization defines its interests in a topic. A business category might be defined by the processes or products produced by the businesses in an industry. A business category might also represent a single organization's business operation based on the way it does what it does. Grocery stores may define a set of categories that define standard product offerings. But, a vegetarian grocery story may define categories for its products and services in a slightly different way. We all develop personal categories. Consider how we each organize our kitchen shelves, our closets, and our drawers. Consider how we each organize the assets in our office. These personal organization schemes are the personal categories we define to help us make sense of our environments.

What is the categorization scheme?

A categorization scheme is the whole set of categories we define to describe the context or the environment. A categorization scheme helps us to make sense of a bounded space. Categorization schemes represent our way of seeing and making sense of any defined context (Borko, 1962; Devlin, 1993; Rafferty, 2001; Ranganathan, 1957; Van der Walt, 1998; Zins and Santos, 2011). They can tell us about the scope and definition of physics, mathematics, or medieval history. They can tell us about the different sets of skills that automotive engineers might develop. What are some of the common categorization schemes we encounter every day? Think about how your organization structures work into job categories, or the Standard Industrial Accounting Codes, Amazon or eBay's product listings, restaurant's wine categories, motion picture categories and ratings, chemical categories, medical specialization categories, your grocery store's physical layout and the signs above the aisles (Figure 13.1), the way stores organize camping and hiding gear (Figure 13.2), or the security categories your organization uses to classify sensitive information.

There are many different perceptions of how we structure and design the whole set of categories. The expanse of the categorization scheme reflects our need to organize assets of interest. A grocery store's categorization scheme does not include categories for products they do not offer. A topic scheme does not cover topics that are not of interest to an organization. A categorization scheme is structured in a way that reflects how we expect to use the scheme. For the most part, humans expect a scheme of categories to be organized into a hierarchy. It is an intuitive design – we assume that more attributes or broader scope definitions define higher-level categories.

FIGURE 13.1 Common Categorization Schemes for Grocery Shopping

Camping & Hiking Gear

Backpacks
Backpacking Packs
Day Packs
Hydration Packs
Baby Carrier Packs
Waist Packs
Accessories

Tents
Backpacking Tents
Camping Tents
Roof-top Tents
Shelters
Bivy Sacks
Accessories

Sleeping Bags
Men's
Women's
Double
Kids'
Bag Liners
Blankets

Pads & Hammocks
Sleeping Pads
Hammocks
Cots
Air Mattresses
Pillows

Camp Kitchen
Stoves
Coolware
Dinnerware
Coffee & Tea
Utensils
Cooers

Camp Furniture
Chairs
Hammocks
Tables
Camp Kitchens

FIGURE 13.2 Common Categorization Scheme for Outdoor Gear Shopping

In contrast, lower- or narrower-level categories are defined by fewer attributes. We expect to be able to navigate a categorization scheme. If we start with a category that describes 'women's clothing,' we expect the next set of categories to define 'clothing' – dresses, jackets, blouses, pants, pajamas. A categorization scheme can also help us to partition a collection into subdomains that help to improve the relevance of searching. It is much more efficient and effective to look for a blue jacket in the 'collection of women's jackets' than to look for jackets as soon as we walk into the store. We first navigate to the women's section, then to the jacket section, and finally, look for blue products.

A categorization scheme also defines how we manage and govern the organization of entities and the representation of the context. Contexts are dynamic – no closet, no grocery store, no topic remains static. We are always expanding and contracting the context. We demote a topic because it is no longer of interest. A business decides to carry children's clothing no longer. A library expands its collections to make way for a significant acquisition of old films, or an art museum expands its collections from textiles to pottery. Every one of these actions prompts a redesign of the categorization scheme.

Categorization schemes are developed by defining the scope of the context and partitioning that scope into sets or groups that make sense to us. We may define the common attributes upfront and explicitly, or we come to them intuitively. Our categorization schemes can be defined as intuitively and based on how we see things. But, categorization schemes that will be used by others should have clearly defined design principles and assumptions. This is a critical decision point in navigating the layers of categorization schemes we encounter each day. It is a negotiation we perform every day when we encounter a different environment. We negotiate our definitions of the categories with the categories we're offered. It is a process of interpretation. It may seem to be a simplistic explanation of how we make sense of the world. But, it is a critical design factor for anyone designing a categorization scheme for others to understand.

A critical initial design question for developing any categorization scheme is, do we expect the scheme to be applied to a defined collection whose parameters we can observe and define? Or do we expect this to be a scheme applied to many different unknown collections or environments? If it is the former, we can define the scope of the scheme based on what is. If it is the latter, we begin the design with a set of high-level categories of what might be and provide flexibility to define how others might interpret that scheme depending on their collections or environments. Both of these approaches can be effective. But, applying these approaches to the wrong context can have quite adverse effects. Consider the design origins of some of our historical generic and universal categorization schemes. The American Mathematical Society's categorization scheme was designed to organize reviews of mathematical research published in a journal. This scheme provides a different representation of the field of mathematics from that of the Library of Congress Classification Scheme or the Dewey Decimal System. The AMS scheme was developed in collaboration with the mathematical community and represents how mathematicians make sense of the field. In contrast, the Dewey Decimal System's original structure was designed around the St. Louis Public Library's collection and a general public library community and was applied to the library collection of the Amherst Collect Library and its academic community. The mathematical collections of these two sources and the perspectives of the two communities varied. Both are well suited to their function and purpose, but neither would work well in the other context.

The development of categorization schemes became a popular activity in the early 2000s with the advent of websites. The limited entry point to a collection of digital resources increased the need to help the visitor anticipate and make sense of what they could expect to find within site. A variety of guidelines and methods for developing and applying categorization schemes have emerged over the past 20 years. The challenge is that these methods and guidelines have been developed for a point in time and not well supported by governance structures. As a result, the natural tendency is to allow categorization schemes to evolve outside of a logical framework. It typically results in a structure that is unbalanced, unpredictable, and unusable for its intended purpose. While there is value in each of these, Ranganathan remains the supreme authority on design principles for a well-architected categorization scheme.

S.R. Ranganathan's *Prolegomena to Library Classification* (1957) has provided strong design principles for information scientists to draw from in developing a categorization scheme for half a century (Baker & Shepherd, 1987; Beghtol, 2008; Berlin, 2014; Bliss, 1929; Broughton & Slavic, 2007; Chan, 1995; Dahlberg, 1976; Dobrowolski, 1964; Hjørland, 2008; International Standards Organization, 2006; Losee, 1993; Ma, 1954; Painter, 1974; Ranganathan, 1937, 1945, 1965, 1989; Satija, 2000). For a discussion of the full set of principles, we refer the reader to Ranganathan's text. We select seven of Ranganathan's principles to explain the essential design principles in this text. These principles are: exclusiveness, uniqueness, and relevance; ascertainability; consistency; affinity; currency; differentiation; and exhaustiveness.

> *Exclusiveness, Uniqueness, Relevance.* No two categories should overlap or should have the same scope and boundaries. Each category should have a set of concepts, derivation rules, and content that define its focus, which should be relevant to the scheme's goal.
> *Ascertainability.* Each category should be definitively and immediately understandable from its name.
> *Consistency.* The rules for creating, managing, and retiring categories should be consistently adhered to across application systems, across types of information, and in different contexts.
> *Affinity.* This is characterized by decreasing extension and context. Each category in a scheme should be defined in the light of its parent category. The intention of the categories should increase while moving down a hierarchy from top to bottom, and the extension of the categories should decrease.

Currency. Names of categories in a classification scheme should reflect the
language of the knowledge domain.

Differentiation. When differentiating a category, it should give rise to at least two
subcategories. However, not all levels in the scheme must be differentiated.

Exhaustiveness. The categories in the scheme should be exhaustive of their
common immediate universe; in other words, they should provide comprehensive coverage of the knowledge domain of interest.

These are excellent starting points for designing any categorization scheme. The
design process, though, should facilitate the human navigation and translation process. We need to consider all of the categorization schemes that our community
might be accustomed to working with every day. We should consider the underlying design principles of these other schemes and how those communities use them.

A significant design challenge for categorization schemes is that we often fail
to teach individuals how to design them. We teach them how to interpret and
apply them but not how to discover their underlying principles. If we encounter
problems in applying a categorization scheme, it is often because the scheme's fundamental design principles were not well articulated or followed over time.

Navigation in categorization schemes

Categorization schemes provide a structure for mentally and physically organizing
ideas and things. In addition to organizing things into similar groups, categorization schemes also offer a controlled and flexible architecture for us to navigate. The
design challenge is to understand how stakeholders will most naturally navigate the
structure. We might leverage a categorization scheme to organize things that have
some similar features but are of different formats and packages. Building on one of
the essential design principles of search, a categorization scheme must 'make sense'
to stakeholders. We should design the structure that is intuitive for users and does
not require extensive explanation to use.

Most of the categorization structures and principles in use today apply to tangible
'things.' Will they translate to other types of knowledge assets? If not, how do we
expand or enhance them? That is our design challenge. How do we categorize human
capital – tacit knowledge, skills and competences, cultural knowledge, and network
capital? How do we organize and structure these kinds of knowledge? Is there one
universal scheme, or do we have layers of schemes – that begin with the individual's
way of seeing and making sense of these assets, to the unit, to the organization, the
domain, and a generic scheme? How do these vary with the nature of the asset?

What is the categorization process?

We should not overlook the dependencies between a well-formed categorization
scheme and a well-executed categorization decision while considering the evaluation of the scheme and the decision separately. Making an optimal classification

choice depends on a good representation of the class, a well-formed class, and a well-formed classification scheme. The context in which taxonomies are used has expanded significantly in the past 20 years; the evaluation criteria have not changed. The expansion in affordable computing power and the availability of semantic technologies provide the capacity to make and evaluate classification decisions in low-risk and objective ways.

Categorizing is a distinct process from the development of a categorization scheme (Borko, 1964; Boros et al., 1998; Ciesiak & Chowla, 2009; Hammer et al., 2004; Hanson & Brennan, 1990; Lee & Brennan, 2009; Lee et al., 2002; Sayers, 1918). These two processes are often conflated into a single action. When conflated, the result is both a suboptimized schema and suboptimized categorization of entities into groups. Categorization is the act of distributing or assigning objects into classes or groups based on common attributes or relationships. Categorization is a decision-making process that involves making choices. Decisions are frequently made in the context of an existing categorization scheme by a human or machine categorizer and for a given object (Figure 13.3). In theory, this choice seems like a straightforward decision process. The categorizer knows the categorization scheme, considers the object and what they know about the possible categories, and chooses the categories that are the best for the object.

Knowledge economists tell us that optimal decisions result from reducing uncertainty. One way to improve a categorization decision is to reduce the uncertainty in the process. Several kinds of uncertainty characterize categorization. The categorizer may have an incomplete understanding of the object. Uncertainty may

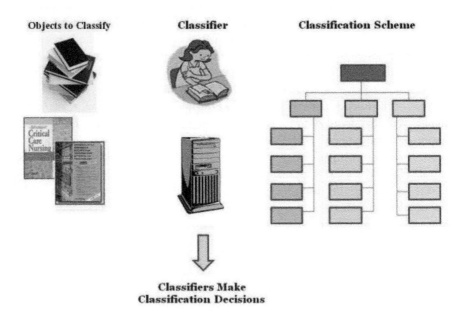

FIGURE 13.3 Overview of the Categorization Process

be high, where the categorizer has access only to an abstract or summary of the object. The categorizer may be uncertain as to what properties or attributes define the class. Uncertainty about the category may result from an incomplete understanding of the scheme or an incomplete specification of the domain – perhaps not all relevant categories have been defined in the schema. Perhaps the categorizer has imperfect knowledge of all the topics covered in the scheme. The scope and coverage of the classes may not be explicitly available, requiring subjective interpretation by the classifier.

Any of these uncertainties may lead to a suboptimal categorization decision. In some cases, making a less-than-perfect categorization decision may be acceptable – perhaps the risk resulting from a categorization decision is not significant. If a young reader overlooks a book about snakes in a desert ecosystem for a school project because it was miscategorized, the risk is low. In other cases, though, the risk of miscategorization may be significant. Where an energy-materials scientist overlooks a critical report of a chemical experiment, national security risks may arise. We should strive to reduce these uncertainties both when making a categorization decision, and evaluating a categorization decision.

How can we reduce the uncertainty we find in the categorization decision? How can we improve the information we need to evaluate categorization decisions? The answer is simple – by expanding what we know about the object, individual classes, and the overall makeup and purpose of the categorization scheme. Uncertainty is highest when we rely on subjective interpretation of objects, where there is no direct access to objects and no formal and extensive representation of a class. High levels of uncertainty may result in higher probabilities of misclassification.

Today, we are not likely to encounter uncertainty about an object because the categorizer – human or machine – will have the object in hand or will be able to access it in its entirety in digital form. It is more probable that we will encounter uncertainty about a class. While humans have constructed hierarchical categorization schemes for centuries, often they have not provided rigorous characterizations of those classes sufficient to reduce uncertainty in the decision process. For example, categorization schemes are often represented (1) through narrative scope notes, (2) by de facto practice as defined in collections, and (3) through associated subject headings and descriptors. In each of these cases, the categorizer has little explicit knowledge with which to work. As a result, the choice is made based on a subjective interpretation of the class. A human categorizer relies on personal subject knowledge and experience. The decision made by the machine categorizer will be simple word matching and relevancy ranking.

The human categorizer can look for more information to help interpret and understand the intent of a category and its relationship to other categories. A human can examine the other items in the category and deduce what the common characteristics are. If there is no scope description, they can look at all of the other items in the category to understand the scope. If we were to observe a good human categorizer, we would find they do exactly this. Expert categorizers will talk about the art and the science of what they do. The science involves following the explicitly stated rules. The art lies in understanding what is not expressly stated. It is essential to understand both of these aspects of categorization when we consider how machines categorize (Bedford, 2013).

Human and machine categorization methods

Categorization is essentially the process of interpreting the scheme and the object and deciding which category is the best fit between the two. We do not have an infinite universe of categories, so we're making the best decisions. A person has an understanding of the scheme, of the object, of what constitutes a good fit, and the risks of a wrong decision. Humans often seek additional information to reduce uncertainty and to increase the goodness of this decision. Categorization is labor-intensive and time-consuming. It is simply not possible to expect that humans will be able to categorize all of the knowledge assets we are creating today, those historical assets we have not yet categorized, or assets that we want to recategorize or categorize differently. We need to look for automated methods to support this process. Like many other processes, though, we cannot merely apply automation to what we see. We have to create all of the human elements of the process and make them understandable to the machine (Borko & Bernick, 1963, 1964; Chen et al., 2004; Garland, 1983; Larson, 1992; Wang, 2009).

Consider what machines need to know to categorize well. Under the best circumstances, a machine must have access to the categorization scheme, a scope and attribute-level understanding of each category, category definitions that distinguish one category from another, and a detailed-level understanding of the object we're categorizing. The machine needs to understand not just the instance or occurrence of words but their relationship and the density of treatment of topics or concepts in an object. A human indexer makes these judgment calls by looking at the title, the abstract, the table of contents, or the section headings. A machine simply sees these as a series of words unless we're working with semantic technologies.

Semantic technologies understand words, word forms, grammatical structures, and languages. They can understand a text object, but they cannot understand a categorization scheme at the same level unless they have equivalent semantic elaborations of each category. Machines need fully elaborated conceptual or attribute definitions to make good decisions. Remember, machines cannot interpret and extrapolate category labels or scope notes like humans can. The reason machine categorization fails is not that machines cannot do this work. It is because we have not provided them with the equivalent of the human categorizer's knowledge base. It is entirely unreasonable to expect a machine to take a description of the Dewey Decimal System, or the Library of Congress Classification Scheme, or even the AMS classification scheme, and categorize it as well as a human. It is not unreasonable to expect us to build these knowledge bases to achieve this result, though. They should be an essential component of our functional categorization architecture.

Much of what is described as the machine categorization research focuses on concept clustering and text analytics. These are different forms of

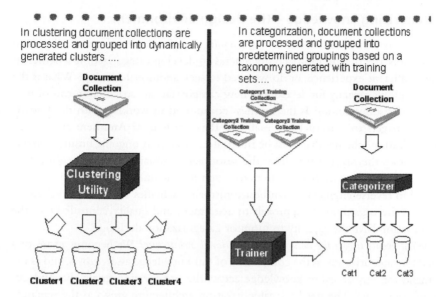

In clustering document collections are processed and grouped into dynamically generated clusters ....

In categorization, document collections are processed and grouped into predetermined groupings based on a taxonomy generated with training sets....

FIGURE 13.4 Comparison of Clustering and Rule–Based Categorization

categorization (Figure 13.4). They are more appropriately described as concept networks or semantic networks. These are covered in Chapter 15. This research leverages statistical methods to discover the proximity and occurrence of words – sometimes concepts – in a document or a corpus. These strategies are not technically categorization because (1) they do not begin with a categorization scheme comprised of defined categories, and (2) they assign entities to defined categories.

Instead, they discover clusters of concepts and, depending on the parameters of a cluster (usually defined by the distance from the central node or concept), define a category based on the concepts that fall within those parameters. This approach may help you to discover patterns within a defined corpus. However, experience suggests that the clusters, e.g., derived categories, change with the addition or deletion of items from the collection. The derived categories do not generally translate to other collections. One of the most significant challenges of working with this approach is that the larger the collection we analyze, the less meaningful are the derived clusters. It is the result of simple linguistic and statistical facts. While nouns are important, they become increasingly scarce in comparison to other grammatical forms in larger and larger collections. And, statistically, we will revert to the mean – the larger and less focused (e.g., curated) the population – the more the generic nouns and words will rise to the top. While it is important to explain these methods in the context of categorization functions, they are more appropriately treated as semantic networks. They are discussed in greater detail in Chapter 15.

Categorizing knowledge – the design environment

What factors do we need to consider in designing this functional architecture? We need to consider the organization's competencies to develop categorization schemes. Is there sufficient experience, or do we need to seek additional training? What is the organization's capacity for developing new categorization capacity in terms of new roles and responsibilities? Is the business committed to working with the knowledge managers to construct and maintain these structures? Are there entrenched categorization schemes that must be integrated to support ongoing business operations? Does the organization have the resources to sustain human categorization efforts, or do they have the resources to invest in machine categorization? Is there a need to reverse engineer or synthesize historical schemes with current schemes? What is the organization's approach to assessment and quality control? Does the organization have the capacity to monitor categorization decisions?

What events trigger the need for this functional architecture? We become aware of a need for categorization as the complexity of our knowledge assets grows, and as the demand for easy access to knowledge across the organization grows, beyond our immediate assets. The need for categorization architecture grows as the semantic complexity of our work grows, i.e., as the depth of treatment and specialization increases, and as the scope of our work expands. The more complex the language, the greater the need to provide a higher-level structure to make sense of the language. We also realize the need for a categorization architecture as we try to navigate our knowledge assets over time, space, and changing administrative structures. The greater the expanse of our knowledge asset landscape, the greater the need to provide high-level views to navigate the landscape.

What are the impacts of having a functional architecture for categorization? Having this well-developed functional architecture means the organization can effectively describe the scope of its assets in a simple navigable view, explain the focus of those categories by defining subcategories, or providing meaningful descriptions of those categories, design an enterprise search that can be parameterized to search within categories, sort results by categories, and enable the organization to operationalize machine-based categorization.

What sources do we leverage to search for knowledge? We can organize any collection of assets into sense-making categories. Our sources for categorization architectures could include existing subject categorization structures, personal expert categorization structures, professional categorization structures, historical topical categorization structures, domain-based categorization structures (e.g., library subject classes, legal classifications, financial classifications, etc.), personal categorization schemes, expert categorization schemes, machine-generated categories, and emerging topic lists or new business areas. These are critical sources for human categorization, but they are insufficient for machine categorization. Machine categorization requires additional components that represent the functionality of the human categorizer's knowledge base.

What outputs does this functional architecture produce? Categorization architectures can provide the capability to create and maintain any categorization scheme or process the organization needs. This architecture might produce enterprise-level administrative categorization schemes, enterprise topic or subject categorization schemes, enterprise resource-document categorization schemes, or business function categorization schemes.

Designing activities and tasks for knowledge categorization

There are five activities essential to the knowledge of functional categorization architecture, including:

- Activity 1. Define the access points
- Activity 2. Define categories and their scope
- Activity 3. Design the categorization scheme
- Activity 4. Desk test the categorization scheme
- Activity 5. Integrate categorization into business systems
- Activity 6. Assess categorization decisions and actions

Activity 1. Define the access points

How do we do this? This activity begins by defining the community of stakeholders who will use the categorization scheme to navigate the context. Next, we need to understand how these stakeholders think about the context – what are their mental models of the space? Remember that categorization is about translating and aligning personal and community models. From this understanding, we should be able to identify the most common access points for discovering knowledge assets. We can now determine which of these access points is best supported by a categorization scheme. It may be the case that multiple schemas are embedded in these different mental models. For example, do some include identifiers and descriptors? Do others include academic domains, and others include processes and methods? The knowledge architect should be able to see and distinguish these views into schemes.

What inputs does this activity need? For this activity, it is essential to have specifications and logs from any categorization schemes in use across the organization. There are likely many schemes in place around the organization – it is essential to consider all of them. This Activity has an element of discovery. It is also essential to have access to any categorization schemes that are used in the broader and external business community. Business stakeholders should be able to 'see' their business views in the schemas. In addition to having access to these schemas, the knowledge architect should be able to determine their behaviors, business rules, and guiding principles.

What outputs does this activity generate? This activity should produce guidance for the knowledge architect concerning the essential access points that require a governing categorization structure. This prepares us to develop a set of design principles for each schema. At this point, we can also synthesize the different mental models into a high-level structure. The final step is the design of a high-level architecture for an individual schema.

What other resources does it use? This activity also leverages any requirements and specifications that may have been developed for search systems in the past.

Activity 2. Define categories and their scope

How do we do this? This activity begins by defining the scope and coverage of each category in the high-level structure. After you have made the first pass at each top category, look across the scheme to determine whether an additional level of categories will be necessary. It is generally unwise to define more than two or three levels to any categorization scheme because users tend to lose sight of the larger structure and the tendency to violate the principle of exclusivity, uniqueness, and relevance. Additional levels increase the level of uncertainty as to which category is the best fit. Remember that a category label does not constitute a sufficient definition of any category. Develop the conceptual-level definitions, e.g., elaborated knowledge base, for each category. If an organization expects to deploy machine categorization, the categories will require extensive and in-depth conceptual definitions. The organization should plan for several weeks of human and machine investment for each category in the scheme.

Additionally, thresholds for good fit matches must be defined and integrated into the application's rule base. It is the equivalent of the human indexer's decision-making process. Realize that as you develop these definitions and elaborate the knowledge base, you will discover problems with how you've defined categories. It is entirely reasonable. Expect to iterate between definition and refinement. Once you have a good enough set of categories and definitions, step back and consider how other relevant schemes align with your structure. Are there gaps? Is there a good mapping? Are there redundancies? We can earn much about how to label or name a category through this exercise.

What inputs does this activity need? The essential inputs are the schemas we collected in Activity 1, and the determination of the essential access points for categorization.

What outputs does this activity generate? This activity generates a strawman categorization scheme for each essential access point identified in Activity 1. It means a preliminary structure for each of the access points that are supported by a categorization structure.

What other resources does it use? This activity leverages any feedback, explanations, and performance information available on the existing categorization schemas.

Activity 3. Design the categorization schemes

How do we do this? This activity involves defining the behaviors, business rules, and specifications for the schema. These rules explain how the scheme is aligned with attributes and fields and how it will be displayed in different contexts. Categorizers do not assign assets to categories in a vacuum – there is always a context in which they're categorizing. The rules should also explain what kinds of assets the schema is intended to organize. This activity explains whether we classify to all levels of the scheme, or to a single level of the scheme. This activity also explains how engineers and developers implement the schema. What does it mean to display the top-level category? Is it a display of second-level categories, or is it a whole listing of all the assets in that category? How you design this will depend on the size of the collection, and how the stakeholders expect to work with the schema.

What inputs does this activity need? This activity leverages the preliminary structure developed in Activity 2, the established principles for usability and navigation, as well as internal guiding principles for creating categorization structures. It should also leverage working business rules for those enterprise systems that support core business operations. These systems should be primary consumers of categorization structures.

What outputs does this activity generate? This activity produces a working design specification for each categorization scheme identified as essential to the knowledge architecture. Those schemas that support essential business may have enterprise or master data value. Where this is the case, the working designs would also require review at the organizational governance level.

What other resources does it use? This activity leverages good practice internal and external guidelines for navigation and behaviors for interfaces.

Activity 4. Desk test the categorization scheme

How do we do this? This activity focuses on verifying and validating the categorization scheme by conducting test categorization runs. Select a sample set of assets, ensuring they are representative of what you intend to organize. It is important to include both information professionals and business stakeholders to participate in your test – the results will help you learn how others understand the scheme. It will also highlight challenges that you can resolve before you operationalize the scheme. This activity includes developing a mockup of the schema to test how easy it is to navigate and discover within the scheme. This activity should produce results that you can feed back into the design process to improve the scheme before you release it. Machine categorizers will require additional development and testing, including the evaluation of machine categorization decisions by human categorizers

What inputs does this activity need? This activity leverages storyboards, usability testing methods in everyday use for testing other systems and interfaces.

What outputs does this activity generate? This activity produces feedback on the initial design and an adjusted design specification for each categorization structure. The output should be in a form that can be handed off to developers. This activity should also produce a final specification for business rules for each schema. These specifications should explain how each structure is expected to be used and where adjustments may or may not be made.

What other resources does it use? This activity makes extensive use of feedback from business stakeholders. The goal is to design a schema that works for and will be used by business stakeholders.

Activity 5. Integrate categorization into business systems

How do we do this? Once the scheme is designed and formalized, it can be operationalized. This activity is a collaboration between the knowledge architect and the application architect. It should also include human categorizers. Human categorizers can begin using the schema wherever it is deployed. Machine categorizers can start using the schema after signoff from human categorizers.

What inputs does this activity need? At this point in the design process, the blueprint is ready to hand to developers and system administrators. In Activity 4, we leveraged the knowledge and experience of human categorizers to test the usability and performance of our design. These same individuals should be involved in the work of integrating the design into business systems.

What outputs does this activity generate? This activity should result in the successful integration of the design into working systems. The knowledge architect's role in this activity is as an adviser, not as an active developer. What is learned here, though, should be fed back into the blueprint and design specifications.

What other resources does it use? The other primary resource for this activity is knowledge of how individual business systems function, and how they will leverage the categorization design.

Activity 6. Assess categorization decisions and actions

How do we do this? The research on evaluating categorization is noteworthy. It tends to focus on several contexts for evaluation, including a comparison of human and machine categorization practices; assessment of the variability of categorization decisions among human and machine classifiers; comparison of machine-generated categorization structures and well-established categorization schemes and thesauri; the quality of categorization in the context of information retrieval; and evaluations of the quality of statistically generated classes. One fundamental perspective that appears to receive less treatment is the simple question of how well the object fits a category in a categorization scheme. There are two explanations of why this perspective has not received more attention. First, to date, most categorization is done by people, and we have always assumed that humans make optimal decisions. Second, until recently, we could not evaluate choices in a direct and controlled way. Instead, we could only assess them from an information-retrieval and end-user perspective. What would a direct evaluation of the fit between an object and a chosen class look like?

What inputs does this activity need? The primary input for this activity is an understanding of how human and machine categorizers make categorization decisions. This Activity also calls for performance objectives for categorization actions.

What outputs does this activity generate? The primary output of this activity is an optimal categorization decision for each asset for each access point. In an expanding universe of information, categorization decisions are often made by people who have neither professional information science training nor subject expertise. Machine classifiers may also make categorization decisions. Regardless of who makes decisions, the goal is to ensure that those decisions are optimal. An optimal categorization decision reflects the best choice that can be made given the information available at the time. An optimal choice may be defined as a good fit between the object and possible classes. An optimal decision also reduces the risk of mis-categorization, which may take two forms. The first form occurs when we assign the object to a class for which it is not a good fit. In this case, the object will be presented to the user in error. The second form occurs when we fail to assign the object to a class for which it is a good fit. In this case, the object will be overlooked because it is not in the class. So our evaluation point for categorization decisions is determining how well the classified object aligns with the chosen class(es).

What other resources does it use? This activity may leverage existing research on challenges with categorization performance. However, the challenge is that little research exists. The organization may need to consider developing a set of internal targets.

Evolution of knowledge categorization designs

Categorization has been with us for millennia. It has evolved over the centuries. Experience and a review of the literature suggest there are five phases of evolution of categorization (Figure 13.5):

- Phase 1. Personal sense-making categorization
- Phase 2. Domain- and collection-focused categorization
- Phase 3. Universal or generic categorization
- Phase 4. Industry-specific categorization
- Phase 5. Machine-generated corpus categorization

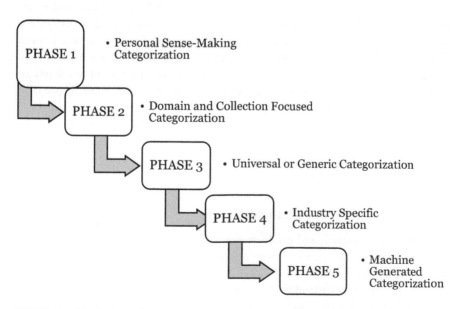

FIGURE 13.5 Evolution of Categorization

Phase 1. Personal sense-making categorization

In the earliest days, categorization consisted of our mental models and how we saw and organized our worlds to make sense. Our worlds were limited in those days – they consisted of our immediate social groups and the resources we could readily access or acquire. These structures were simple, but they were essential to managing growing levels of knowledge. Knowledge grew more slowly in those early times than it does today, but there has always been a body of knowledge that supported our survival.

Phase 2. Domain- and collection-focused categorization

The increased scale and scope of knowledge, products, and services lead to the development of categories that made sense to groups of individuals. In some cases, these groups of individuals represented subject domains or professions, areas of practice, or commonly available products or resources. Consider that the earliest categorization schemes focused on organizing things into categories. As knowledge advances, these community-based schemes expanded to include more abstract things.

Phase 3. Universal or generic categorization

In this stage, we see the development of universal categorization schemes – schemes for organizing things that are sufficiently general to make sense to everyone. This stage might describe the development of library categorization schemes used to organize physical resources on the shelves – into groups of like things – to support browsing, particularly in the 19th century with the growth of chemistry and information science. As librarians have rapidly observed, one undesirable consequence of such decimal schemes is the increasing fragmentation of subjects as taxonomists' work proceeds. For example, though the Dewey Classification is a useful public access scheme and was designed for extensibility, the variant pace of development of different categories has left the scheme unbalanced and difficult to navigate over the decades. The solution has been to 'phoenix' the schema – to reconstruct and redefine different categories – to reflect the public's current understanding of the context. Many categorization schemes were constructed around perceptions of knowledge at the time and of the relationships between academic disciplines that existed from 1890 to 1910.

Phase 4. Industry-specific categorization

As industries, businesses, and products expanded during the industrial revolution, they developed categorization schemes to manage operations and products. These included high-level schemes that helped us to understand what an organization does and to better understand what products they offer. Remember the mail-order retail catalogs we described in Chapter 12? These catalogs have indexes to support search, but the products and offerings are organized into a linear section that makes it easier for us to navigate. These catalogs were a reflection of how businesses managed their internal product inventories. While the industry is familiar with these schemes, the information science professionals have paid little attention to them. As more organizations realized the need to represent their business capabilities and functions, these schemes have gained greater focus.

As technology developed and as computing capacity grew, so did our ability to design categorization schemes and support categorization processes effectively. We were no longer constrained to single-dimension structures. Nor were we limited to a single schema because we had only one descriptive field with which to work. As our awareness of the need for multiple categorization schemes grew, our initial tendency was to combine them into a single structure. As a result, some of the earlier schemes will have designs confounded. It is a poor design to design business functions, formats, geographical concepts, and subjects into a single scheme. There can be no single set of design principles for such a scheme because each of these dimensions has different behavior. They change at different rates and are neither easily navigated nor maintained. This design creates confusion in the relationships among categories that are not strictly hierarchical. Categorization schemes may work in concert with semantic networks, but they should not be combined into a single structure. The unintended consequences of this confounded design are to define relationships among categories that are not hierarchical or based on characteristics. This confounded design tends to undermine the essential design principles of the categorization structure. The advance in technologies and increase in computing capacity allows us to avoid these artificial constraints and adopt a design that better represents how people make sense of the environment.

Phase 5. Machine-generated corpus categorization

Machine-based categorization represents a significant shift from the categorization of human domain experts or information professionals to machines. This stage generates significant confusion about what is meant by categorization and differentiates the two different processes. Current practices and methods will not work in the future, because the future will look a lot like the very distant past. Individuals will have the capability to develop their categorization schemes and do their own categorizing. They must understand how to do this well – and that the tools they have to work are consistent with good functional architecture design principles.

Knowledge categorization in the enterprise architecture

This functional architecture fits squarely in the knowledge architecture practice. If no knowledge architecture practice exists, this architecture should align with the information and data architecture practice. While there are some affinities with the application architecture, particularly in the integration of schemes into applications, this is a human-managed process. There are also affinities with the business architecture practice, but business stakeholders will play the role of consumers rather than managers of this architecture.

Chapter review

After reading this chapter, you should be able to:

- explain the role that categorization plays in knowledge architecture;
- define categories and categorization methods;
- describe the design principles of categorization;
- explain how we develop a categorization scheme;
- describe the different categorization methods;
- explain categories that have value to different kinds of knowledge assets.

References and recommended future readings

Baker, S. L., & Shepherd, G. W. (1987). Fiction classification schemes: The principles behind them and their success. *RQ*, 245–251.

Bedford, D. (2013). Evaluating classification schema and classification decisions. *Bulletin of the American Society for Information Science and Technology, 39*(2), 13–21.

Beghtol, C. (2008). From the universe of knowledge to the universe of concepts: The structural revolution in classification for information retrieval. *Axiomathes, 18*(2), 131–144.

Berlin, B. (2014). *Ethnobiological classification: Principles of categorization of plants and animals in traditional societies.* Princeton University Press.

Bliss, H. E. (1929). Standardization in classification for special libraries. *Special Libraries, 20*(3), 74–76.

Borko, H. (1962, May 1–3). The construction of an empirically based mathematically derived classification system. *Proceedings of the Joint Computer Conference, 21,* 279–289.

Borko, H. (1964). Measuring the reliability of subject classification by men and machines. *American Documentation, 15*(4), 268–273.

Borko, H., & Bernick, M. (1963). Automatic document classification. *Journal of the Association for Computing Machinery, 10*(2), 151–162.

Borko, H., & Bernick, M. (1964). Automatic document classification. Part II. Additional experiments. *Journal of the Association for Computing Machinery, 11*(2), 138–151.

Boros, E., Ibaraki, T., & Makino, K. (1998, November). Error-free and best-fit extensions of partially defined Boolean functions. *Information and Computation, 140*(2), 254–283.

Broughton, V., & Slavic, A. (2007). Building a faceted classification for the humanities: Principles and procedures. *Journal of Documentation, 63*(5), 727–754.

Chan, L. M. (1995). *Library of Congress subject headings: Principles and application.* Libraries Unlimited, Inc., PO Box 6633.

Chen, M.-H., Dey, D. K., & Ibrahim, J. G. (2004). Bayesian criterion based model assessment for categorical data. *Biometrika, 91*(1), 45–63.

Ciesiak, D., & Chowla, N. (2009). A framework for monitoring classifiers' performance: When and why failure occurs. *Knowledge and Information Systems, 18*(1), 83–108.

Dahlberg, I. (1976). Classification theory, yesterday and today. *Ko Knowledge Organization, 3*(2), 85–90.

Devlin, K. (1993). *The joy of sets.* Springer Verlag.

Dobrowolski, Z. (1964). Étude sur la construction des systèmes de classification. http://hdl.handle.net/123456789/124386.

Garland, K. (1983). An experiment in automatic hierarchical document classification. *Information Processing and Management, 19*(3), 113–120.

Hammer, P. L., Kogan, A., Simeone, B., & Szedmak, S. (2004). Pareto-optimal patterns in logical analysis of data. *Discrete Applied Mathematics, 114*(1–2), 79–102.

Hanson, B. A., & Brennan, R. I. (1990). An investigation of classification consistency indexes estimated under alternative strong true score models. *Journal of Educational Measurement, 27*(4), 345–359.

Hjørland, B. (2008). What is knowledge organization (KO)? *KO Knowledge Organization, 35*(2–3), 86–101.

International Standards Organization. (2006). *ISO 11179-2 Information technology – Metadata registries (MDR). Part 2. Classification.* Retrieved September 15, 2012, from http://metadata-standards.org/11179/.

Larson, R. R. (1992). Experiments in automatic library of congress classification. *Journal of the American Society for Information Science, 43*(2), 130–148.

Lee, W.-C., & Brennan, R. L. (2009). Classification consistency and accuracy for complex assessments under the compound multinomial model. *Applied Psychological Measurement, 33*(5), 374–390.

Lee, W.-C., Hanson, B. A., & Brennan, R. I. (2002). Estimating consistency and accuracy indices for multiple classifications. *Applied Psychological Measurement, 26*(4), 412–432.

Losee, R. M. (1993). Seven fundamental questions for the science of library classification. *KO Knowledge Organization, 20*(2), 65–70.

Ma, K. G. (1954). The basic principles of the new library classification at University College, London. *Journal of Documentation, 10*(4), 169–192.

Painter, A. F. (1974). Classification: Theory and Practice. *Drexel Library Quarterly, 10*(4), n4.

Rafferty, P. (2001). The representation of knowledge in library classification schemes. *KO Knowledge Organization, 28*(4), 180–191.

Ranganathan, S. R. (1937). *Prolegomena to library classification.* Madras Library Association.

Ranganathan, S. R. (1945). *Elements of library classification: Based on lectures delivered at the University of Bombay in December 1944.* NK Publishing House.

Ranganathan, S. R. (1957). *Prolegomena to library classification.* The Library Association.

Ranganathan, S. R. (1965). *Library classification on the march. Herald of Library Science, 4*(1), 84–91.

Ranganathan, S. R. (1989). *Philosophy of library classification.* Sarada Ranganathan Endowment for Library Science.

Satija, M. P. (2000). Library classification: An essay in terminology. *KO Knowledge Organization, 27*(4), 221–229.

Sayers, W. C. B. (1918). *An introduction to library classification: With readings, questions and examination papers.* HW Wilson Company.

Van der Walt, M. S. (1998). The structure of classification schemes used in Internet search engines. *Advances in Knowledge Organization, 6*, 379–387.

Wang, J. (2009). An extensive study on automated Dewey Decimal Classification. *Journal of the American Society for Information Science and Technology, 60*(11), 2269–2286.

Zins, C., & Santos, P. L. (2011). Mapping the knowledge covered by library classification systems. *Journal of the American Society for Information Science and Technology, 62*(5), 877–901.

14

FUNCTIONAL ARCHITECTURES FOR INDEXING AND KEYWORDING

Chapter summary

This chapter explains the role that concept indexing and keywording plays in supporting access to knowledge assets. The chapter lays out the five activities that support the design of an indexing and keywording architecture for knowledge assets. The chapter also considers why it is essential to understand the use of language to describe concepts and ideas, domain vocabularies, focal vocabularies, listening vocabularies, speaking vocabularies, and reading and writing vocabularies. The chapter also explains the difference between unmanaged and managed vocabularies and explains how structured vocabularies are different from controlled vocabularies. We consider the primary challenge in designing this functional architecture for designing effective conceptual indexing and keywording. It is the integration and harmonization of terms used to index from different sources and over time.

Why we care about indexing and keywording

There are two contexts in which we talk about indexing. The first was in Chapter 12, where we described an index as a component in a search system. The second context is a focus on what goes into an index – the keywords, concepts, and indexing terms. We can create an index for any parameter in a knowledge landscape. Keywords, indexing terms, and concepts are a kind of parameter that describes the ideas and concepts that are treated or represented in knowledge assets.

We care about indexing terms because they enable us to access ideas and concepts in and about knowledge assets. We care about indexing terms because they are often confused with the labels we use for categories. This confusion leads to poor access to knowledge assets because it creates an unbalance in our expectations for and the underlying behavior of indexing terms. Today we understand a keyword is a way to get to the author or creator's use of that term in the asset. We expect it to get us to the idea or the concept. We do not expect it to take us to assets that someone else thinks are about that keyword. The underlying design of keyword or concept level indexes is fundamentally different from the design for indexes that help us to navigate categories. A keyword or concept index is designed to rank results by the incidence rate of a term or phrase in an asset, or based on the position of that concept in the asset. It is not designed to be assigned by an intermediary or broker who thinks this asset is 'about' that concept.

This distinction is challenging for information professionals to grasp because the structural designs of card and online catalogs have conflated concept-level indexing with subject indexing, i.e., categorization. Just because a subject heading has the same 'label' as an indexing term does not mean they behave in the same way or are applied in the same way. Card and online catalogs have imposed artificial limitations on the number of indexing terms assigned to a knowledge asset. It constrained the natural tendency to index an asset like we index a book (e.g., the back-of-the-book index), but identifying those concepts that were substantively treated in a document. That is why it is challenging for application architects to design search indexes that combine both machine-generated concepts and subject terms assigned by information professionals. The underlying assumptions of behavior and design are different. How do we effectively combine subject headings that behave like category names with concept-level terms assigned by machines, authors, and stakeholders? Experience suggests that it is more effective to map subject headings and category names assigned by professional indexers to categorization schemes, rather than to add them to keyword level indexes. It is more effective because it aligns with users' expectations for results.

We care about indexing terms, keywords, and concepts because our access behaviors have changed in the age of full text and broader access to assets. When we know what we're looking for – on an idea or a concept level – we are no longer satisfied to navigate through extensive collections of results that reflect someone else's interpretation of that concept. While it is true that there are challenges with berrypicking and information grazing through this expansive knowledge landscape, some of these challenges are better met by synthesizing and harmonizing assets at the concept level rather than the category level. Categories serve an important access function, but they are no longer the only solution we have available.

We care about indexing terms, keywords, and concepts because this new level of access to assets has created new challenges that call for new solutions. The primary challenge is that access to the full asset is now available to the public. Some of this access is supported by full-text indexing (e.g., where every word in the text becomes an index entry), and some are supported by direct searching of any word or concept within the asset through direct access. It is the challenge of navigating language, one that professional indexers have masked for decades. In a nutshell, professional indexers have mentally interpreted the language of an asset and translated it to an 'indexing term' they think will have meaning for their stakeholders. For example, a chemist will write about a compound using chemical terminology, but a doctor needs to translate it into a medical context. A medical indexer will do that translation and assign a medical term. It is not just a terminology challenge, though; it is a fundamental language challenge. Consider how authors are taught to write well – they are encouraged to vary their language, to avoid repeating the same phrases within a document or a book. As a result, there might be ten different ways to express a concept – poverty mitigation, poverty alleviation, poverty reduction, poverty elimination. Full-text searching – out of the box – will not consider all of these variations as a single relevance factor. Each term is assigned its relevance ranking. Additionally, depending on the formality of the asset, there may be spelling errors in the asset. To test whether this is a challenge in your landscape, conduct a simple test. Do a full-text search of a commonly misspelled term in your enterprise search. How many actual matches are returned?

Another reason to care about indexing terms, concepts, and keywords are that greater access to publishing and a more literate population means we have more non-professional and casual indexers than professional indexers. The scatter and fragmentation of terms, concepts, and keywords have expanded rather than coalesced. Accessing knowledge assets through user-generated keywords is now a high-stakes probability game. Consider the challenge of even navigating a run of journal issues trying to guess or match author-generated keywords. While authors may know their articles and their research topics, they are remarkably poor at selecting terms that represent the concept they have addressed.

All of these reasons make a case for intentionally and deliberately designing a functional architecture that supports concept-level indexing and harmonizes these variant practices. The trend will not subside. Instead, we expect the fragmentation and scattering will increase with broader access to knowledge assets, and with the availability of increasingly sophisticated semantic analysis technologies to interpret and represent those assets in different formats. When concept-level indexing is well designed and supported at the architecture level, it complements and supplements categorization architectures. Working together, these two architectures provide an accessible environment that is both flexible and manageable for stakeholders. A deliberately and intentionally designed concept-level functional architecture will contribute to more effective and efficient access to increasingly complex and varied knowledge assets. It will enable organizations to better understand the language and terminology of their work and to better manage the increasingly complex access environment. It will also enable application developers and knowledge architects to design better and more effective index structures and to introduce machine-based semantic technologies effectively.

Indexing knowledge – design concepts

To develop this functional architecture, we must have a good understanding of the use of language to describe concepts and ideas, domain vocabularies, focal vocabularies, listening vocabularies, speaking vocabularies, reading vocabularies, writing vocabularies, subject indexing schemes, subject headings, controlled versus uncontrolled vocabularies, professional indexing practices, generalized keywording practices, indexing exhaustivity, pre- and post-coordinated index terms, and indexing for precision and recall. The primary challenge we face in designing this functional architecture is integrating and harmonizing terms used to index from different sources and over time.

This functional architecture focuses on the selection of index terms or keywords to describe the concepts that are substantively treated in or by a knowledge asset. We are not discussing the structure or nature of the index to which these concepts or terms are added. We are talking about how well they describe the substance of the asset. The primary question is, where do we get the keywords? What is their source? And how do we manage them? It is an important design factor for the functional architecture because it determines how difficult it will be for stakeholders to understand and interpret the meaning of a keyword. To design this functional architecture, we need to understand the definitions and meanings of concepts, keywords, and vocabularies. All three of these concepts are practical sources of indexing terms. The more we understand each source, its behaviors, and its structures, the better architecture we can design.

What is a concept?

A concept is a thought or idea – it refers to the process of taking an idea into the mind. It is an abstract idea or a notion that we hold in our thoughts, in speech, in our minds. A concept is the fundamental element of thoughts and beliefs. We have a centuries-old tradition of thinking and research about the relationship of concepts, ideas, and knowledge (Armstrong et al., 1999; Biocca et al., 2003; Brown, 1978; Carey, 1999, 2009; Eysenck, 2012; Fodor, 1998; Fodor et al., 1980; Fodor & Lepore, 1996; Gomez-Milan et al., 2013; Hume, 1739; Kant, 2012; Margolis & Laurence, 2007; Margolis and Lawrence, 2012; Mill, 1843; Murphy, 2004; Murphy & Medin, 1985; Nikolic, 2009; Paton, 1936; Prinz, 2002; Quine, 1999; Rey, 1999; Somov, 2010; Wittgenstein, 1999). In terms of our characterization of knowledge assets, concepts live in and are essential to every type of asset. Concepts are the fundamental elements of the discipline of cognitive science. When we talk about improving discovery, seeking, and searching, we're talking about leveraging our cognitive abilities and the cognitive agents we design for machine-level understanding. A concept is instantiated in actual or potential instances – as physical things, but most often as words. The words that appear in explicit knowledge or procedural knowledge are an individual or a group's representation of a concept in language form. Concepts are essential to knowledge acquisition, representation, sharing, and use. We must have a place for concepts in knowledge architecture.

What do we mean by concept-level indexing? There is no universal agreement on what this term means. How you define it depends on your perspective and your experiences. The Society of American Archivists equates concept-level indexing with the use of a controlled vocabulary. They represent the more generic form of concept indexing as extractive indexing. It is not accurate to limit our definition of concept-level indexing to either a controlled vocabulary or a machine-level extraction from text. In this definition, there is no room for author-assigned concepts, for reader-assigned terms, or for non-professional indexers to assign keywords. While this definition is not quite accurate, it is not difficult to understand. Archivists are accustomed to working with categories and collections. They understand word-level indexing in what is practical and reasonable for archival materials. Extended concept level indexing is challenging for one of a kind, print-based materials. It becomes prohibitively labor-intensive and costly.

On the other hand, systems developers and computer scientists understand concepts as closely related terms or term expansions – as in concept groups or grammatical clusters. They may also understand concepts in a linguistic structure perspective, i.e., in terms of discoverable noun phrases in a text. Text analysts and developers define concepts as a way to expand their analytical methods beyond simple word clusters. This approach is important because a concept is not necessarily the same as the words that comprise it. For example, 'girls education' is a concept that is different from 'girls' and 'education.' Searching the two words as distinct concepts will produce many results that are not about these concepts. It is another essential view of concepts, but it is not complete or sufficient for knowledge architecture.

Information scientists are perhaps the closest to defining concepts well for knowledge architecture purposes. They represent it indirectly, though. They suggest that the process of indexing is the representation of a concept in the form of either a term derived from natural language or a controlled source. In practice, though, given the constraints and traditional practices of subject indexing, the definition defaults to word-level indexing (Bedford & Gracy, 2012; Blouw et al., 2016; Fauconnier & Turner, 1998; Hausser & Hausser, 1999; Hjørland, 2009; Kapetanios & Sugumaran, 2008; Maron, 1961; McEnery, 2012; Mitkov, 2004; Mroczko-Wasowicz & Nikolic, 2014; Putnam, 1999).

We incorporate all of these definitions for this text because we will find all of them in our organizations today. It is essential to recognize them when we see them because our task will be to harmonize and synthesize them into an effective functional architecture.

What is a keyword?

Keywords are most often defined simply as words or concepts of great significance. It is a good definition because it accurately describes keywords as concept-level terms. And, it highlights their role – they are chosen because we believe they best represent the ideas expressed in the asset. It is common practice for keywords to be unmanaged and free form. We expect them to be free form expressions of our mental concepts. Keywords are a closer representation of concept-level indexing than indexing with a controlled vocabulary for the simple reason that they reflect an individual's implicit thoughts and their understanding of meaning. Consider the different sources of keywords. Authors assign keywords to their publications and presentations. Publishers and editors assign keywords to submitted manuscripts. Staff across organizations assign keywords to their documents. People assign keyword tags to their social posts, web publications, posted photographs, posted videos, audios, and words of art. Keywords are probably the primary access point for any kind of knowledge asset published to the Web today. The practice of informal and unmanaged keywording far outpaces either professionally managed term indexing or even machine-based semantic indexing.

Just as there are variant definitions for concepts, so are there different views of keywords (Agrawal et al., 2002; Bhattacharyya et al., 2011; Guo et al., 2003; Hristidis et al., 2006; Li et al., 2010; Liu et al., 2006; Myers, 1994; Pfitzner et al., 2008; Reynolds & Vahdat, 2003; Strader, 2009). Computer scientists and text analysts understand keywords as the words that found to occur most frequently (i.e., have a high incidence rate) in a document that is full-text indexed. Full-text indexing algorithms may select these terms and tend to weight them more heavily as 'keywords' in a text. Another definition from the computer science and systems view is simply a term or set of terms entered into the search box of a search engine. These 'keywords' are captured by search system engineers and used to optimize, i.e., to weight index entries, the search index. In other words, if someone thinks this keyword is important enough to search, it must be something important to flag and enhance in the index. Search engine engineers may further refine this definition to include only the nouns or adjectives in the keywords entered – because these grammatical forms represent ideas and concepts more than do verbs, adverbs, and prepositions.

It is essential to accept all of these definitions because they represent the broader organization's perceptions. Just as for concepts, we must incorporate and accommodate all of these views in our knowledge architecture.

What is a managed vocabulary?

A vocabulary is simply defined as the body of words used in a particular language. We tend to think of vocabulary in terms of dictionaries. There are, though, four types of vocabularies, including listening vocabulary, speaking vocabulary, reading vocabulary, and writing vocabulary. Vocabularies are essential for communicating and accessing knowledge. It is the basis for the development of all the other skills, such as reading comprehension, listening comprehension, speaking, writing, spelling, and pronunciation. Everyone has a vocabulary. Vocabularies can be managed or unmanaged (free form and reflecting common usage – no deliberate control or formal management of the vocabulary. When we refer to a managed vocabulary, we typically think of an *intentionally managed and curated vocabulary*. A managed vocabulary is a carefully selected list of words and phrases used to describe assets (document or work) so that a search may more easily retrieve them (ANSI, 2010; International Standards Organization, 2011). Managed vocabulary schemes mandate the use of predefined, authorized terms that have been preselected by the designers of the schemes, in contrast to natural language or unmanaged vocabularies, which have no such restrictions (Cimino et al., 1989; Dubois, 1987; Fidel, 1991, 1992; Gross & Taylor, 2005; Markey et al., 1980; Mili et al., 1997; Muddamalle, 1998; Noruzi, 2006, 2007; Patrick et al., 2001).

A managed vocabulary is most often referred to as a controlled vocabulary. Controlled vocabularies are often equated with subject headings, thesauri, and knowledge organization system (KOS) lists. While each of these examples is managed and controlled, they go beyond simple management to add structural relationships and meaning. For this text, we characterize a controlled vocabulary more as a managed vocabulary. What is typically described as a controlled vocabulary, we will characterize as a semantically enhanced structure. Well-designed knowledge architectures must support the simple management of a defined vocabulary and the relationships we may assign to those concepts. It is an essential design consideration because we need to support the harmonization of concepts first and address the harmonization and synthesis of relationships and their meanings. Assigned relationships do not necessarily translate well to different business concepts. We cannot merely adopt or inherit them as defined. The architecture must be able to identify, distinguish, discard, and redefine relationships.

A domain vocabulary is a specialized set of terms and distinctions of particular importance to one specific group. The group may be a subject domain, a business industry, a genre-focused community, or any other community with a shared experience or goal. The vocabulary is essentially the linguistic register of that community. It is a set of concepts and ideas that describe what they do and their common interests. It represents their particular perspective on these concepts. A domain vocabulary is a living list of concepts and ideas that reflects the evolution of learning and growth in that domain.

Contrary to popular opinion, though, a controlled vocabulary does not have to be a structured vocabulary with fully elaborated relationships to other terms. A list in a SharePoint object is a controlled vocabulary, though not necessarily structured. An approved set of publisher's keywords from which authors can choose is also a controlled vocabulary. A collection of essential terms for the field of mechanical engineering, regardless of whether or not they have relationships, is a controlled vocabulary.

A subject heading can also be described as a predefined set of authorized terms preselected by an authoritative group (Fischer, 2005). Subject headings are, in fact, headings or lead terms. They are a uniform set of words or phrases intended to be assigned to books, articles, or other documents to describe the subject or topic of the texts and to group them with texts having similar subjects. These headings are designed to help us understand what the asset is 'about,' but not what concepts or ideas are discussed 'in' the asset. The most common headings are preferred terms or phrases that professional indexers and catalogers are taught to use. These headings are often pre-coordinated, meaning that they combine several unique and different concepts in a string. It is a practice developed for card catalogs. It has been carried over to online catalogs and cataloging practices. Pre-coordination of headings is often supported by multiple lists of subheadings – e.g., geographic locations – that may be combined with preferred headings. Subject headings are often represented as simple alphabetical lists. Some lists are presented as thesaurus structures, but these structures are designed to help indexers and catalogers to discover other. more relevant headings. While information professionals often talk about indexing subject headings, the assignment of subject heading is aligned more with categorization than with a concept.

What are indexing parameters and processes?

There are as many variations of indexing processes as there are variant definitions of concepts (Armstrong, 1994; Basch, 1996; Cleveland & Cleveland, 2013; Hlava, 2002; Luhn, 1957; Riaz, 1989; Salton, 1987). The differentiating factors appear to be the purpose of the index, who is doing the indexing, the indexing training they have, the tools they have to work with, and the business rules of the system used for indexing. The design of the indexing process and the index begins with an understanding of the purpose of the index and how it will work. We begin the discussion which a brief explanation of how we determine the purpose of the index.

Experience and a review of the literature suggest we create indexes to navigate specific physical knowledge assets such as books that help us locate where the author has talked about a specific concept. Another purpose is to help us identify the place in a collection where a concept is treated, such as a run of journal issues or a collection of artifacts. Perhaps the most common purpose today is to create a tool that helps us to find concepts in a searchable source, e.g., a search system index. Each of these purposes has a consistent element – finding the location of a concept in an asset. An essential design question for each purpose is, how are we defining a concept? And, who makes this decision? For a back-of-the-book index, the definition and decision are made jointly by the indexer and the author. In the case of a collection, it is generally the curator of the collection that makes this decision based on their knowledge of the collection and how people will look for concepts. In the case of a search system, information engineers and systems developers make the definition and decision.

Part of the decision process is deciding whether there needs to be a managed vocabulary or whether free-form, unmanaged vocabulary can be effective. If there is a finite number of concepts, broad acceptance of the vocabulary, and little variation, an unmanaged vocabulary may be sufficient. If the vocabulary is extensive, varied, and dynamic, some degree of management and oversight is important. Regardless of whether the vocabulary is managed or unmanaged, it is essential to know the following: (1) What are the rules for adding a concept to the index – e.g., will we index every index of the word or just the substantive treatment of the idea? (2) What constitutes substantive treatment and who will judge that – e.g., is it important enough to call out a historical site on a roadmap, or is that not of interest to the user? And (3), whether the index is static or dynamic, e.g., will it be updated and refreshed, how often, and how do we rebuild it?

Another critical design consideration is who is doing the indexing. Is it a person, a website crawling program, or a rule-based application? How does design vary with each of these approaches? It is interesting to highlight common practices for those who create an index. For fictional or imaginative assets, the author or creator is generally responsible for creating the index. For non-fiction assets, it can be either the author or a professional indexer who creates the index. One of the important questions in a knowledge architecture is who is responsible for identifying concepts for an asset? Should it be the individual whose human capital is described who identifies these concepts, or should it be a professional indexer? Who should create concepts that describe our cultural profiles and cultural knowledge assets and artifacts? Or, our procedural knowledge?

Concept indexing can be done by individuals who are familiar with the asset, e.g., authors, artists, collectors, or individuals who are seeing the asset for the first time. When the indexer is familiar with the asset, they begin by brainstorming the critical concepts they know are treated and proceed to highlight where they are addressed and the degree of treatment. When the indexer is not familiar with the asset, they generally begin by scanning the asset, first focusing on the key elements that identify and define the asset. The indexer will then create a list of concepts they think are most substantively treated. If the vocabulary is managed, the preliminary list of concepts is compared to the managed vocabulary, and close terms are selected. It is not a straightforward task. The indexer has a sense of the treatment of that concept, but the permissible term in the controlled vocabulary may be too general or specific to capture the meaning. What if the term is new, and there is no equivalent in the managed vocabulary? If the vocabulary is not managed, the next step is to consider which of these should be given greater weight than others, and what form they should take. Another important task for the human indexer is to give voice to a term the stakeholder community might know but has not been used in the asset. The challenge with this approach is that it is labor-intensive and costly. Because of the simple labor ceilings, this approach does not scale well and will result in a limited number of conceptually indexed assets.

Machine-based concept indexing is a computerized process that should replicate the human indexing process when it is done well. In most cases, machine-level indexing simply focuses on identifying the most frequently occurring words or concepts. It is rarely the case that these approaches to machine indexing do not leverage a managed or controlled vocabulary. The advantages of this approach are the low cost and the ability to handle the scale of text-based knowledge assets.

More advanced semantic methods have been developed to compensate for the historical deficiencies of machine-based concept indexing, These approaches are expensive to acquire because they have more sophisticated components including dictionaries, morphological analysis, and rule-based threshold analysis. They require upfront investments to develop and elaborate the vocabularies to a point where they can approximate the human indexer decision process. Once that investment has been made, concept indexing methods can increase the scale of processing and reduce the processing costs of processing large volumes of text assets.

In addition to the issue of scale and cost, conceptual indexing methods vary in quality. It would seem intuitive to believe that human indexing produces the highest-quality results, and that machine-level indexing will produce lower-quality results. However, quality depends on the level of knowledge of the indexer about the asset. Counterintuitively, experience suggests that authors and creators do not create the highest-quality indexing concepts because their intimate knowledge of the asset prevents them from seeing the wealth of concepts that other stakeholders see. Indexers who are not familiar with the subject area have been shown to either overspecify or underspecify the indexing concepts. Machine-level indexing generally makes acceptable choices but leaves gaps wherever concepts are not explicitly called out in the text. Surprisingly, semantic methods for concept selection can produce higher-quality results than human indexing if they have a strong knowledge base from which to work. These methods are verifiable and are more objective than either an author indexer or a professional indexer. Additionally, semantic methods will identify more concepts that are important, providing a richer set of potential matching points for discovery. These methods have also been demonstrated to achieve a higher degree of exhaustivity – the level of detail with which the asset is indexed – because minor but important concepts are more likely to be identified.

Indexing human capital

The critical access points for human capital are the name of the person and any aspects of that individual's tacit knowledge, skills and competences, and attitudes and behaviors. We might search for topics and terms that describe their knowledge, methods they've learned or can perform, the level of expertise, the languages they write and speak, their experiences or jobs held, their certifications and licenses, and any skills they may possess.

Indexing explicit knowledge

The critical access points for explicit knowledge are the name of the asset and any descriptors we might use to look for it, including title, author, date, format, length, language, subject, concept, country, business function, and publisher or issuing entity.

Indexing procedural knowledge

The critical access points for procedural knowledge are the name of the process it pertains to, the name of the function it supports, process methods, products or results it generates, inputs it uses, job classes that support it, people who are assigned to it, life cycle or dates of the process, and the units using the process.

Indexing cultural knowledge

The critical access points for cultural knowledge are the community that creates it, values and behaviors, types, periods, locations, business functions, disciplines, and the kind of organization that it represents.

Indexing network knowledge

The critical access points for network knowledge are the topic, function, network or community members, dates the network is/was active, the community's language, whether it is sponsored or informal, and whether it is virtual or physical.

Knowledge indexing – the design environment

What factors do we need to consider in designing this architecture? There are several factors to consider when designing this functional architecture, including whether the organization has the functional competencies and technical capacity to support concept-level indexing, to create and manage concept-level vocabularies, and to manage updates to those vocabularies. We must also consider the age of the organization and the extent of its business operations, as terminologies over time and domains need to be represented. It is also important to consider stakeholders' expectations for concept-level access to knowledge assets, and the extent of the knowledge assets that must be indexed.

What events trigger the need to design a functional architecture for indexing? Several types of events trigger the need to design a functional architecture, including the need to improve the precision of search, to improve search recall, to bridge vocabularies of multiple domains, and to improve the efficiency of indexing processes (e.g., reduce unit processing times, to increase the number of objects indexed). The need is highlighted when we realize the breadth of concepts in our organizational lexicon, the need to harmonize the way we've talked about ideas over time, and the need to establish authoritative vocabularies in some cases (e.g., master data vocabularies).

What are the consequences of having this functional architecture in place? Ideally, this functional architecture results in improved search precision, improved search recall, increased indexing efficiency and effectiveness, expanded coverage of indexing, and improved currency of managed vocabularies.

What sources does this functional architecture use? Designing this functional architecture requires the use of multiple sources, including domain or focal vocabularies, business function vocabularies, personal vocabularies, subject headings, and the organization's master data vocabularies, machine-generated vocabularies, user-generated keyword lists, frequently misspelled terms, and organizational glossaries.

What products and services does this functional architecture produce? The functional architecture enables us to produce concept-level indexed knowledge assets, indexing tools for human indexers, knowledge bases for machine indexing applications, commercially available controlled vocabularies for use by others, and knowledge bases for machine translation dictionaries.

Design activities and tasks for knowledge indexing

The functional architecture for concept indexing support five essential activities, including:

- Activity 1. Define acceptable indexing concepts, including specifications and behaviors
- Activity 2. Harmonize and integrate existing structures and sources (including retrospective indexing of sources)
- Activity 3. Define indexing principles for humans and machine applications
- Activity 4. Define indexing methods and rules
- Activity 5. Define index quality monitoring and assessment methods and metrics

Activity 1. Define acceptable indexing concepts, including specifications and behaviors

How do we do this? This activity includes identifying the scope of the domain, the community of stakeholders, and descriptions of existing vocabularies the community uses to talk about the domain including applied, theoretical, and popular terms. An essential decision made at this time is whether the vocabulary should be managed or can be unmanaged. If the decision is to manage the vocabulary, it is crucial to determine whether there are existing vocabularies that can be used or adapted. The knowledge architect must design an application to manage and make it easily accessible if the vocabulary is controlled. If controlled, the knowledge architect must know whether indexing will leverage human, machine, or semantic-based methods. The knowledge architect must configure the application and integrate the vocabulary if semantic methods are to be used. This activity should determine how keywords will be identified and integrated into the source application if the vocabulary is not controlled. Keywords might be created by end users, extracted from keywords in existing assets, or simply generated by machine indexing methods.

What inputs does the activity need? The inputs include sample vocabularies from the community, existing controlled vocabularies, knowledge of how people in the community look for concepts, and how indexers or applications will use the vocabulary.

What outputs and outcomes does it produce? This activity generates either a managed vocabulary and the indexing routines that will use it, or a decision to not manage the vocabulary. It also produces a design for the specifications and the behavior of the keyword attribute regardless of whether the vocabulary is managed or unmanaged.

What other resources does it use? This activity uses the knowledge of application architects, the business community, and individuals with knowledge of semantic applications.

Activity 2. Harmonize and integrate existing structures and sources (including retrospective indexing of sources)

How do we do this? This activity focuses on ensuring that for managed vocabularies, there is a single integrated and harmonized source that can be used in source applications. Many different approaches have been adopted over the years, but the most widely accepted and sustained approach is one that integrates and synthesizes the existing vocabularies. Where stakeholders can see a familiar source in place, they are inclined to work with it. If they must learn to work with an entirely new source that is unfamiliar, adoption will be slower and more difficult. Harmonizing vocabularies is different from harmonizing categories. With concepts, it is most effective to begin at the concept level, to look for overlaps across sources, and to integrate variations.

What inputs does the activity need? This activity requires an inventory of all of the existing vocabularies and lists of keywords, in addition to any relevant external vocabularies.

What outputs and outcomes does it produce? This activity produces a comprehensive and inclusive managed vocabulary for a single field. Over time, it also produces vocabularies to represent all of the organization's business operations.

What other resources does it use? This activity also leverages the negotiation and facilitation skills of the knowledge architect in encouraging all of the custodians of existing vocabularies to collaborate.

Activity 3. Define indexing principles for humans and machine applications

How do we do this? This activity focuses on the development of guidelines for human indexers and rules for semantic applications. Human indexers should have a good explanation of exhaustivity, an understanding of the minimum and the maximum number of concepts the field will allow, guidelines on selecting terms from a controlled vocabulary, and the acceptability of terms from popular, applied, and theoretical vocabularies.

What inputs does the activity need? For this activity, we need to know the specifications of the field that will hold the indexing concepts and the nature of the data entry. If semantic applications are in place, this activity requires that we define the thresholds for selecting keywords that are matched by the system.

What outputs and outcomes does it produce? This activity produces the guidelines and rules that will be used to select and manage the concepts that will be indexed.

What other resources does it use? This activity leverages the knowledge of information professionals to create the controlled vocabulary, the knowledge of application architects to ensure the conceptual indexing applications can work with the vocabulary, and the knowledge architect's understanding of how concept indexing words with search and metadata applications.

Activity 4. Define indexing methods and rules

How do we do this? This activity focuses on methods and rules for constructing the keyword index for use in the search system. These methods and rules describe how each concept is entered into the index (e.g., as multiple words and index entries, or as a single whole phrase), how its reference to the asset will be noted (e.g., a simple link to the asset or a position in the asset), and whether it will be added to the index as it is recorded or whether it is modified (e.g., in its original form or grammatically stemmed). These rules have a significant effect on how well concepts in the index match with keywords searched. This activity also determines whether a single harmonized keyword is constructed or a concept-specific index that includes only indexing concepts, and a separate generic keyword index that combines entries from multiple fields.

What inputs does the activity need? The primary input is knowledge of index-building rules and the effects of those rules on query matching and index performance.

What outputs and outcomes does it produce? The primary output is a set of decisions governing the design and construction of concept and keyword indexes.

What other resources does it use? This activity also leverages application architects and search system engineers to understand common practices for designing and constructing indexes across the organization.

Activity 5. Define index quality monitoring and assessment methods and metrics

How do we do this? Concept indexes are among the indexes that grow most rapidly. It is essential to monitor and manage this index. It is also essential to ensure that the human and/or machine indexing methods are effective – that a level of quality and consistency is maintained. It means defining an architecture role – assigned either to the knowledge or the application architect – to monitor and report on the state of this index.

What inputs does the activity need? There are two primary inputs. The first is routine reports on the selection of indexing terms added to the index, and the concepts selected for searching. The second is periodic samplings of search results to determine terms that are searched but not included in the controlled vocabulary.

What outputs and outcomes does it produce? This activity produces suggestions for new terms to add to the managed vocabularies and an understanding of terms in the vocabulary that are not used in a search. The un- or underutilized concepts may be removed or archived from the vocabulary over time to manage the size of the vocabulary better.

What other resources does it use? This activity requires the collaboration and cooperation of search system administrators in setting up the concept logs and generating periodic reports.

Evolution of knowledge indexing and keywording designs

The evolution of concept indexing reflects the evolution and use of language. Experience and a review of the literature suggest there are six phases of evolution (Figure 14.1), including:

- Phase 1. The era of language development
- Phase 2. The era of specialized language
- Phase 3. The era of traditional stand-alone indexing
- Phase 4. The era of controlled vocabularies
- Phase 5. The era of keywords
- Phase 6. Semantic era

Phase 1. The era of language development

In the earliest phase, we see the simple development of language and language structures. Language evolves based on the need to communicate with others. As our knowledge grew, there was a need for more sophisticated languages, including word-level vocabularies that helped us understand simple meanings. Languages developed structures, and concepts became an essential element in representing both concrete and abstract objects.

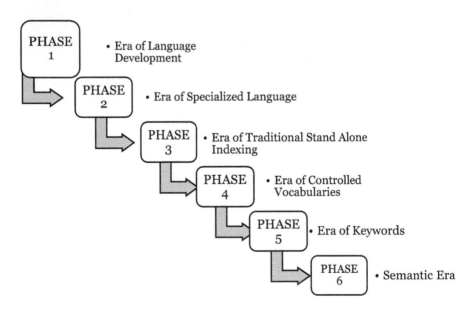

FIGURE 14.1 Evolution of Concept Indexing

Phase 2. The era of specialized language

As communities continued to develop knowledge, and knowledge grew around domains, areas of application and scientific inquiry, particularly in specialized languages, developed. These specialized languages were used to communicate within designated communities and stakeholders. They evolved specialized meanings for both abstract and concrete things. As these specialized languages evolved, they became part of the education and learning system of that domain. We have the first mental associations of concepts with ideas, and written references to these concepts.

Phase 3. The era of traditional stand-alone indexing

As print books proliferated, and as the size of those assets grew, the practice of indexing emerged. The indexes, typically positioned in the back of the book, served as location and navigation tools for primarily scientific works. Over time, these indexes became important descriptions and explanations of the coverage of ideas in books. As other physical formats developed, concept-level indexing became an important method of providing access. Concept-level indexing of audio assets, visual assets, images, and artifacts were important access points for assets that did not have full-text equivalents.

Phase 4. The era of controlled vocabularies

The rise of the concept index and the rapid expansion of collections of assets generated the need to control concepts as managed vocabularies. Controlled vocabularies first emerged as publishers generated access points to databases and collections. At this same time, the concept of headings, specifically subject headings, emerged in academia.

Phase 5. Era of keywords

The scale and scope of knowledge assets requiring concept-level indexing exploded with the development of the Web and the capability to self-publish. It became apparent that human indexing and controlled vocabularies would not scale to meet this rapidly growing demand. An alternative method of generating concepts emerged – keywording. Keywording solved one challenge – meeting the demand for associating concepts with assets – but it created new problems. The primary consequence of keywording was a proliferation of concepts, widely varied in their form and specificity, that became overwhelming to manage from the search angle.

Phase 6. Semantic era

The current and evolving phase might be described as the semantic era because it leverages semantic applications to both generate and select concepts for indexing. Semantic applications have their origins in machine-based indexing and human indexing methods. Machine-based methods were efficient at identifying 'key concepts' in text assets but were not as successful as humans in concept indexing. Quality was often not acceptable. The emergence of semantic engines, text analytics, and the automated management of controlled vocabularies created a foundation for designing a human-like machine approach. At present, only the best resources organizations have been able to afford semantic applications. However, as they become more widely available as open-source applications, and with the increased sharing of controlled vocabularies within domains, these technologies will become more practical and affordable.

Semantic technologies will become the norm in the future. Individuals will have the capability to access them and will be able to configure them to reflect the vocabularies that reflect their interests and specializations. They will have the capability to apply these semantic applications to source collections to generate user-focused indexes for any knowledge source or landscape.

Knowledge indexing in the enterprise architecture

Concept indexing is an area of specialization of information professionals. We would most logically place it in the information and data architecture practice. The expansion of this practice to cover all knowledge assets, though, moves it more closely to the knowledge architecture practice. It may best be placed within the knowledge architecture practice if one exists or on the border between business and information architecture practices where a knowledge architecture does not yet exist. While there are alignments with application architectures, it does not fit within that practice. It is vital to ensure that where machine indexing methods are in place, they are designed and managed by knowledge architects.

Chapter review

After reading this chapter, you should be able to:

* explain the difference between indexing and keywording;
* define concepts and explain how they relate to knowledge assets;
* define keywords and explain how they relate to knowledge assets;
* explain what we mean by a managed vocabulary;
* describe indexing and keywording processes.

References and recommended future readings

Agrawal, S., Chaudhuri, S., & Das, G. (2002). DBXplorer: Enabling keyword search over relational databases. In *Proceedings of the 2002 ACM SIGMOD international conference on Management of data* (pp. 627–627). ICDE.

American National Standards Institute. (2010). *ANSI/NISO Z39.19 (R2010) guidelines for the construction, format, and management of monolingual controlled vocabularies*. Retrieved September 15, 2012, from www.niso.org/apps/group_public/project/details.php?project_id=46.

Armstrong, S. L. (1994). *Using large corpora* (p. 291). MIT Press.

Armstrong, S. L., Gleitman, L. R., & Gleitman, H. (1999). What some concepts might not be. In E. Margolis & S. Lawrence (Eds.), *Concepts* (pp. 225–261). MIT Press.

Basch, R. (1996). *Secrets of the super net searchers: The reflections, revelations, and hard-won wisdom of 35 of the world's top internet researchers* (p. 271). Information Today, Inc.

Bedford, D. A. D., & Gracy, K. F. (2012). Leveraging semantic analysis technologies to increase effectiveness and efficiency of access to information. *Qualitative and Quantitative Methods in Libraries (QQML)*, *1*(1), 13–26.

Bhattacharyya, P., Garg, A., & Wu, S. F. (2011). Analysis of user keyword similarity in online social networks. *Social Network Analysis and Mining*, *1*(3), 143–158.

Biocca, F., Harms, C., & Burgoon, J. K. (2003). Toward a more robust theory and measure of social presence: Review and suggested criteria. *Presence: Teleoperators & Virtual Environments*, *12*(5), 456–480.

Blouw, P., Solodkin, E., Thagard, P., & Eliasmith, C. (2016). Concepts as semantic pointers: A framework and computational model. *Cognitive Science*, *40*(5), 1128–1162.

Brown, R. (1978). *A new paradigm of reference* (pp. 159–166). Academic Press Inc.

Carey, S. (1999). Knowledge acquisition: Enrichment or conceptual change? In E. Margolis & S. Lawrence (Eds.), *Concepts: Core readings* (pp. 459–489). MIT Press.

Carey, S. (2009). *The origin of concepts.* Oxford University Press.

Cimino, J. J., Hripcsak, G., Johnson, S. B., & Clayton, P. D. (1989). Designing an introspective, multipurpose, controlled medical vocabulary. In *Proceedings. Symposium on computer applications in medical care* (pp. 513–518). American Medical Informatics Association.

Cleveland, A., & Cleveland, D. (2013). Introduction to indexing and abstracting (4th ed., p. 289). ABC-CLIO.

Dubois, C. P. R. (1987). Free text vs. Controlled vocabulary: A reassessment. *Online Review*, *11*(4), 243–253.

Eysenck, M. W. (2012). *Fundamentals of cognition* (2nd ed.). Psychology Taylor & Francis.

Fauconnier, G., & Turner, M. (1998, April–June). Conceptual integration networks. *Cognitive Science*, *22*(2), 133–187.

Fidel, R. (1991). Searchers' selection of search keys: II. Controlled vocabulary or free-text searching. *Journal of the American Society for Information Science*, *42*(7), 501–514.

Fidel, R. (1992). Who needs controlled vocabulary. *Special Libraries*, *83*(1), 1–9.

Fischer, K. (2005). Critical views of LCSH, 1990–2001: The third bibliographic essay. *Cataloging & Classification Quarterly*, *41*(1), 63–109.

Fodor, J. A. (1998). *Concepts: Where cognitive science went wrong.* Oxford University Press.

Fodor, J. A., Garrett, M. F., Walker, E. C., & Parkes, C. H. (1980). Against definitions. *Cognition*, *8*(3), 263–267.

Fodor, J. A., & Lepore, E. (1996). The red herring and the pet fish: Why concepts still can't be prototypes. *Cognition*, *58*(2), 253–270.

Gómez Milán, E., Iborra, O., de Córdoba, M. J., Juárez-Ramos, V., Rodríguez Artacho, M. A., & Rubio, J. L. (2013). The Kiki-Bouba effect: A case of personification and ideaesthesia. *The Journal of Consciousness Studies*, *20*(1–2), 84–102.

Gross, T., & Taylor, A. G. (2005). What have we got to lose? The effect of controlled vocabulary on keyword searching results. *College & Research Libraries*, *66*(3), 212–230.

Guo, L., Shao, F., Botev, C., & Shanmugasundaram, J. (2003). XRANK: Ranked keyword search over XML documents. In *Proceedings of the 2003 ACM SIGMOD international conference on Management of data* (pp. 16–27). https://doi.org/10.1145/872757.872762.

Hausser, R., & Hausser, R. (1999). *Foundations of computational linguistics.* Springer.

Hjørland, B. (2009). Concept theory. *Journal of the American Society for Information Science and Technology*, *60*(8), 1519–1536.

Hlava, M. M. (2002). Automatic indexing: A matter of degree. *Bulletin of the American Society for Information Science and Technology, 29*(1), 12–12.

Hristidis, V., Koudas, N., Papakonstantinou, Y., & Srivastava, D. (2006). Keyword proximity search in XML trees. *IEEE Transactions on Knowledge and Data Engineering, 18*(4), 525–539.

Hume, D. (1739). Book one part one: Of the understanding of ideas, their origin, composition, connexion, abstraction etc. In D. Hume (Ed.), *A treatise of human nature.* Reprint. Penguin Publishing Group. Retrieved May 1, 2020, from https://www.gutenberg.org/files/4705/4705-h/4705-h.htm.

International Standards Organization. (2011). *ISO 25964 Thesaurus schemas.* Retrieved September 15, 2012, from www.niso.org/schemas/iso25964/.

Kant, I. (2012). *Fundamental principles of the metaphysics of morals.* Courier Corporation.

Kapetanios, E., & Sugumaran, V. (2008, June 24–27). *Natural language and information systems: 13th international conference on applications of natural language to information systems, NLDB 2008 Proceedings* (Vol. 5039). Springer Science & Business Media.

Li, J., Wang, Q., Wang, C., Cao, N., Ren, K., & Lou, W. (2010). Fuzzy keyword search over encrypted data in cloud computing. In *2010 Proceedings IEEE INFOCOM* (pp. 1–5). IEEE.

Liu, F., Yu, C., Meng, W., & Chowdhury, A. (2006). Effective keyword search in relational databases. In *Proceedings of the 2006 ACM SIGMOD international conference on Management of data* (pp. 563–574), June 27–29, 2006, Chicago, Illinois, USA.

Luhn, H. P. (1957). A statistical approach to mechanized encoding and searching of literary information. *IBM Journal of Research and Development, 1*(4), 309–317.

Margolis, E., & Laurence, S. (2007). The ontology of concepts – abstract objects or mental representations? *Noûs, 41*(4), 561–593.

Margolis, E., & Lawrence, S. (2012). *Concepts.* Stanford Encyclopedia of Philosophy. Metaphysics Research Lab at Stanford University. Retrieved 6 November 2012, from https://plato.stanford.edu/entries/concepts/

Markey, K., Atherton, P., & Newton, C. (1980). An analysis of controlled vocabulary and free text search statements in online searches. *Online Review, 4*, 225–236.

Maron, M. E. (1961). Automatic indexing: An experimental inquiry. *Journal of the Association for Computing Machinery, 8*(3), 407–417.

McEnery, T. (2012). *Corpus linguistics* (Vol. 978019). Oxford University Press Inc.

Mili, H., Ah-Ki, E., Godin, R., & Mcheick, H. (1997). Another nail to the coffin of faceted controlled-vocabulary component classification and retrieval. *ACM SIGSOFT Software Engineering Notes, 22*(3), 89–98.

Mill, J. S. (1843). *A system of logic.* Reprinted in 2002.

Mitkov, R. (Ed.). (2004). *The Oxford handbook of computational linguistics.* Oxford University Press.

Mroczko-Wąsowicz, A., & Nikolić, D. (2014). Semantic mechanisms may be responsible for developing synesthesia. *Frontiers in Human Neuroscience, 8*, 509.

Muddamalle, M. R. (1998). Natural language versus controlled vocabulary in information retrieval: A case study in soil mechanics. *Journal of the American Society for Information Science, 49*(10), 881–887.

Murphy, G. L. (2004). *The big book of concepts.* MIT Press.

Murphy, G. L., & Medin, D. L. (1985). The role of theories in conceptual coherence. *Psychological Review, 92*(3), 289.

Myers, E. W. (1994). A sublinear algorithm for approximate keyword searching. *Algorithmica, 12*(4–5), 345–374.

Nikolic, D. (2009). Is synaesthesia actually ideaesthesia? An inquiry into the nature of the phenomenon. In *Proceedings of the third international congress on Synaesthesia. Science & Art*, April 26–29.

Noruzi, A. (2006). Folksonomies: (un)controlled vocabulary? *KO Knowledge Organization, 33*(4), 199–203.

Noruzi, A. (2007). Folksonomies: Why do we need controlled vocabulary? *Webology, 4*(2).

Paton, H. J. (1936). *Kant's metaphysic of experience* (Vol. 1–2). G. Allen & Unwin.

Patrick, T. B., Monga, H. K., Sievert, M. C., Hall, J. H., & Longo, D. R. (2001). Evaluation of controlled vocabulary resources for development of a consumer entry vocabulary for diabetes. *Journal of Medical Internet Research, 3*(3), e24.

Pfitzner, D., Treharne, K., & Powers, D. (2008). User keyword preference: The Nwords and Rwords experiments. *International Journal of Internet Protocol Technology, 3*(3), 149.

Prinz, J. (2002). *Furnishing the mind: Concepts and their perceptual basis.* Cambridge University Press.

Putnam, H. (1999). Is semantics possible? In E. Margolis & S. Lawrence (Eds.), *Concepts: Core readings* (pp. 177–189). MIT Press.

Quine, W. (1999). Two dogmas of empiricism. In E. Margolis & S. Lawrence (Eds.), *Concepts: Core readings* (pp. 153–171). MIT Press.

Rey, G. (1999). Concepts and Stereotypes. In E. Margolis & S. Laurence (Eds.), *Concepts: Core readings* (pp. 279–301). MIT Press.

Reynolds, P., & Vahdat, A. (2003). Efficient peer-to-peer keyword searching. In *ACM/IFIP/USENIX international conference on distributed systems platforms and open distributed processing* (pp. 21–40). Springer.

Riaz, M. (1989). *Advanced indexing and abstracting practices.* Atlantic Publishers & Distributors.

Salton, G. (1987). The past thirty years in information retrieval. *Journal of the American Society for Information Science, 38*(5), 375–380.

Somov, G. Y. (2010). Concepts and senses in visual art: Through the example of analysis of some works by Bruegel the Elder. *Semiotica, 2010*(182), 475–506.

Strader, C. R. (2009). *Author-assigned keywords versus library of congress subject headings: Implications for the cataloging of electronic theses and dissertations.* Library Resources.

Wittgenstein, L. (1999). Philosophical investigations: Sections 65–78. In E. Margolis & S. Lawrence (Eds.), *Concepts: Core readings* (pp. 171–175). MIT Press.

15

FUNCTIONAL ARCHITECTURE FOR KNOWLEDGE SEMANTICS

Chapter summary

This chapter explains the role that semantic structures play in knowledge access. The chapter covers the seven essential activities that support designing a semantic architecture. The chapter also considers why it is crucial to have a good understanding of thesauri, semantic networks, concept and topic maps, semantic relationships, semantic relatedness, and meaning in different contexts. The chapter lays out the similarities and differences in human and machine approaches to defining meaning and relatedness. The primary challenge in designing this functional architecture is identifying a harmonized, common semantic approach to suit different communities.

Why we care about semantics

Semantic structures are essential tools to help us find and understand the meaning embedded in knowledge assets. These structures are often poorly formed and misunderstood. As a result, they are poorly integrated into the overall knowledge landscape and not an essential element of our knowledge architecture. We can change this situation by developing a more effective understanding of semantic structures' elements and comparing the practices that have emerged over the past half-century.

Semantics is about how we use language, the meaning we assign to language, and the structure of language (Collins & Loftus, 1975; Collins & Quillian, 1969; Helbig, 2006; Klein, 2002; Poon & Domingos, 2009; Quillian, 1968, 1969; Simmons et al., 1964; Van de Riet, 1992; Yngve, 1960). From a linguistic perspective, semantics is also about the structure of language – the essential elements and rules of language. Language is a rich and amorphous thing. Semantics is about the meaning and how we use language to convey meaning. Knowledge is a representation of meaning. By extension, semantics speak to how we use language to express, convey, share, hear, and understand knowledge. In this text, we're interested in understanding how we design semantic architectures to support access to knowledge. Language is essential to working with knowledge in any form. Knowledge creators and knowledge interpreters begin with language. Our focus in this chapter is understanding and representing how people use semantic models and structures to convey knowledge. We are not interested in the linguistic structure of language except where we might be focusing on a specific unit of language in our semantic models.

Semantics – design concepts

To develop this functional architecture, we must have a good understanding of thesauri; semantic networks, concept and topic maps, semantic relationships such as synonym rings, and hierarchical and associative relationships. The knowledge architect must understand semantic relatedness, distance, and centrality. We must consider those vocabularies designed for administrative and business functions, as well as semantic principles, policies, and governance processes. The primary challenge in designing this functional architecture is developing a harmonized, common design strategy for designing semantic structures that suit different communities (Bendeck, 2008; Cormack, 2010; Daoud et al., 2011; Davis, 2008, 2011; Dietze & Schroeder, 2008; Dong et al., 2004; Giunchiglia et al., 2004; Grimmes, 2010; Guha et al., 2003; Haveliwala et al., 2002; Imielinski & Signorini, 2009; Shvaiko & Euzenat, 2004; Sussna, 1993; Weber & Schek, 1998; Zezula et al., 2006).

It is essential to understand that semantics are not simple words. Semantic structures include five essential elements, including: (1) a definition or warrant that describes the domain – essentially the scope and coverage of the field the structure is defined to support or represent; (2) the concepts that define the field (which may be expressed with one or more words); (3) connections that define the relationships among the concepts; and (4) a way to define or convey the meaning of the concept.

Semantic structures

We must understand the purpose and design of semantic structures because they will be essential tools for accessing knowledge in the future (Allen & Frisch, 1982; Bedford & Gracy, 2011; Bordes et al., 2013; Hulpus et al., 2015; Radaa et al., 1989; Sowa, 1987, 2014; Speel et al., 1993; Steyvers & Tenenbaum, 2005; Sun & Zhuge, 2018; Van Atteveldt, 2008; Zhuge, 2004, 2009, 2011, 2012; Zhuge & Zheng, 2003; Zhuge et al., 2004). What are the dimensions of semantic structures? How do we represent and design these structures? And, how are these structures different from the other architectures we discussed in Chapters 13 and 14? There are five essential elements to a semantic structure, including:

- concepts or nodes;
- semantic relationships and nodes;
- semantic relatedness and similarity;
- semantic distance;
- semantic centrality.

What is the source of these elements? Where do we look for design guidance for these elements? We look to the fields of semantic engineering and network science to understand how semantic structures behave. The translation of these elements to knowledge contexts is relatively recent, and there is much yet to be discovered.

Concepts and nodes

A concept in a semantic structure is represented as a node. A node can take the form of a word, a phrase, a subject heading, a chemical element, a geographical feature, a name of something such as a person or an organization, a brand name or a generic product name, a disease, a business function, or any type of descriptor. Some examples of semantic structures predetermine what form a node can take, whereas others do not. It is essential to apply our definition consistently throughout the structure. When nodes are not consistently applied, relationships will require more interpretation to arrive at a semantic meaning, or only simple statistical meanings can be applied. It is necessary to describe more complex relationships than simple equivalence, hierarchy, or associative. The challenge with most semantic structures today is that they are not well-disciplined at the node or concept level. Structures with more varied concepts require more clearly defined and more granular relationships. Working with an existing semantic structure that does not follow these guidelines may tend to generate questionable or unreliable linkages or relationships that are challenging to interpret.

Let's assume we will define the nature of nodes consistently. We can take this approach regardless of which level of semantic meaning we assign to relationships. We can specify the types of nodes we want to discover as long as we can describe them to the machine or a human knowledge analyst. At the machine level, we are working with a tool or application that can leverage grammatical rules (e.g., recognize the parts of speech we want nodes to represent) or a defined set of rules for a human analyst to interpret. Let's assume we're writing the rules for a human analyst. What would these rules cover? Here are a few of the most common questions we find for which rules have been addressed in the most advanced of semantic structures:

- What types of terms are we looking for (i.e., nouns, noun phrases, pronouns, verbs, or verb phrases?

- Will we include only single word nouns, and treat phrases as multiple nodes?
- Will we allow both singular and plural forms of nouns, or restrict to only singular forms?
- Will we support all conjugations and tenses of verbs, or restrict to present tense infinitives?
- Will we include proper nouns and place names, i.e., identifiers, or exclude these and focus only on descriptive words and phrases?
- Will we include acronyms, abbreviations, and initialisms as nodes?
- Will we allow misspellings (i.e., 'reduction' and 'reducation') and variant spellings (i.e., 'labor' and 'labour,' 'organization' and 'organisation') to represent nodes, or is there only on preferred spelling?
- What level of specificity will we support (i.e., must the node represent the equivalent of a category rather than a concept)?
- Will we allow slang and jargon from different domains?
- How will we treat expert and novice concepts?
- Will we allow loanwords, i.e., words borrowed from other languages – force majeure – to represent nodes?
- Will we allow or strip the use of punctuation (e.g., hyphens, apostrophes, parentheses)?
- Must terms be represented in their natural language form, or will they be inverted (i.e., noun, adjective)?
- If there is an inherent number in a noun phrase, must it be spelled out as characters, represented as an Arabic or a Roman numeral?

On a practical level, if you are working with a concept cluster, concept map, a semantic network, or a topic map and you predefine the type of node, you will limit your rules to nouns and noun phrases, proper nouns and place names. If you are working with a subject or functional thesaurus where the nodes themselves are predetermined (e.g., specific words or phrases are allowed or disallowed), you will need to consider all of them.

Semantic relationships and meaning

Semantic relationships are the associations that exist between the nodes. Links have meaning. There is a spectrum of meanings we might assign to links (Figure 15.1). The meaning may be source-specific or source-agnostic. Source-specific relations derive their meaning from a specific context, in this case, a business context. As we move up the spectrum, the meaning we assign to links is 'source agnostic.' Meaning is predefined based on the types of relationships we expect to exist in any source. These points on the spectrum represent a shift from deriving the meaning from a predefined source to predefined meanings that can be applied to any source. Let's consider each point on the spectrum.

At the simplest end of the spectrum, we have those kinds of links that call out the existence of a relationship but do not interpret or assign semantic meaning to

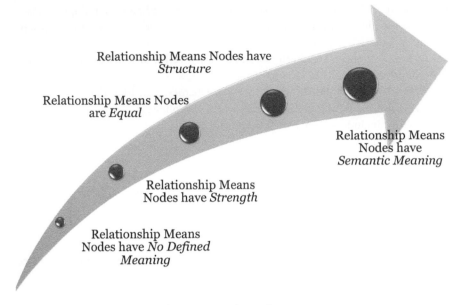

FIGURE 15.1 The Spectrum of Semantic Relationships

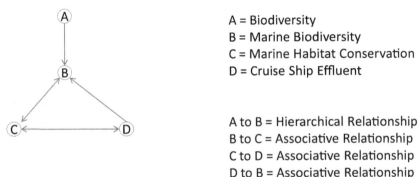

A = Biodiversity
B = Marine Biodiversity
C = Marine Habitat Conservation
D = Cruise Ship Effluent

A to B = Hierarchical Relationship
B to C = Associative Relationship
C to D = Associative Relationship
D to B = Associative Relationship

Directed Graph with 4 Nodes

FIGURE 15.2 Holistic View of Higher-Order Semantic Relationships

the relationship (Level 1). As we move up the spectrum, the next category of links convey meaning about the strength or frequency of the appearance of the relations between two nodes (Level 2). In some semantic structures such as semantic networks, concept clusters, or topic maps, these links might be defined simply as 'distance' or 'relatedness and similarity' relative to other concepts in the context. Distance and degrees of related are often determined based on position, location, or statistical occurrence (Budanitsky & Hirst, 1999; Cooper 2000; Kenett et al 2017; Simmons, 1963; Figure 15.2). In the most primitive semantic structures, distance and related-ness-similarity are expressed numerically and statistically, or in a matter of degrees.

As we will see later, though, these underlying assumptions can also be translated into relationships with deeper semantic meaning. Links and relationships for Levels 3, 4 and 5 are more complex, and require deeper discussion and understanding.

Level 3: when the relationship means nodes are equal

Of these three categories, the most basic is what we find in our historical dictionaries and thesaurus – synonyms. Given the word or concept as a source node, this relationship suggests that all of the other nodes mean the same thing. While it is the most basic of all relationships, there is still not one simple, single meaning. There are exact synonyms – these other concepts can be used interchangeably without any further impacts. There are partial synonyms – they have essentially the same meaning, but there are slight variations. For example, some would argue that the terms 'poverty alleviation' and 'poverty elimination' are equivalent in the broadest sense. But, in a practical sense, they have different meanings and impacts. Brand names and generic names are equivalent in some contexts but not in others. Correct and incorrect spellings are exact synonyms in some contexts but not in others. It is generally the case that what we call cross-language equivalents might be good enough in some settings but are only partial synonyms to experts in those fields. Synonym relationships have essential significance for knowledge discovery because they speak to the first challenge of language – that we may each use different words to express the same idea. Synonym relationships can provide an essential remedy for addressing knowledge scatter. A more extensive description of the types and degrees of synonyms can be found in established standards such as ANSI/NISO Z39.19 2005 or BS ISO 25964–1:2011.

We refer to these relationships as equivalents. These relationships link synonymous concepts. Synonyms are concepts whose meanings are the same or nearly the same in a wide range of contexts. It commonly includes true synonyms, lexical variants, quasi-synonyms or near-synonyms, initialisms, abbreviated forms, commonly misspelled forms, other language equivalents, popular terms and scientific names, generic nouns and trade names, variant names for emergent concepts, current or favored terms versus outdated or deprecated or superseded terms, common nouns and slang terms, and dialectical variants.

Equivalence relationships solve important discovery and seeking challenges, specifically those related to language variants and fragmentation. They reduce the ambiguity inherent in the ordinary human language, where the same concept has different names. Equivalence relationships also help us manage variations in meanings associated with the same word (i.e., swimming pools and gaming pools). Equivalence relationships also help us to handle preferred and variant concepts, whether they be current and outdated or acceptable, and unacceptable ways of talking about an idea.

Level 4: when the relationship means nodes have structure

From the simpler equivalence relationships, we move up the spectrum to relationships that mean the nodes have structure. These relationships are hierarchical.

Hierarchical relationships are defined by degrees or levels of superordination and subordination. The structure also conveys a degree and type of reciprocity. The link has an underlying meaning of the direction of the relationship. For example, if we move from one node to another, the direction of the movement signals a type of relationship. They link terms that have the following structural relationships:

- one term represents the class, and the other term represents a member of the category (i.e., one node represents the category and the other node represents the member of the category);
- one term represents a whole, and the other represents the part of the whole (e.g., one node is included in the other);
- one term represents a general category, and the other term represents an instance of the category (e.g., one node identifies the general category of things or events, and the other node represents an instance of that thing or event).

Level 5: when the relationship means nodes have extended semantic meanings

The final category of relationships is too frequently described as 'others.' These types of relationships describe a finer breakdown of what is meant by 'associated in some other way.' These kinds of links define relationships that are semantically or conceptually related though not in an equal or hierarchical-directional way. From a behavior perspective, the links signified by these relationships are symmetrical – meaning that it can go in either direction. The difference, though, is that the direction signifies a particular meaning or role. Thesaurus standards refer to these as associative relationships simply because it is easier to group them all as 'RTs – Related Terms' for thesaurus formatting and publishing. And, it is generally the case that while standards offer finer breakdowns, these breakdowns are rarely used in traditional library thesaurus constructions or indexing. For this text, we suggest the category might better be described as having 'extended semantic meanings.' Traditionally, associative relationships include but are not limited to the types detailed in Table 15.1. While symmetrical, the relationship is not necessarily equal.

Predefined semantic relationships have great value for knowledge discovery. For the most part, though, these relationships are implemented either as quantitative distance measures in managing search results or in the specific structured domain and focal vocabularies. In other words, they are either not explicitly interpreted in a particular context or are fully interpreted in a particular field or context. Research suggests that while the former is invisible to most of us, the application creates a lower risk than what we encounter when these relationships are explicitly interpreted in a domain or focal vocabulary. The risk is higher because these relationships are often poorly defined and not verified or validated before use. This risk has emerged when we have operationalized traditionally structured vocabularies in

TABLE 15.1 Types of Relationships With Extended Semantic Meanings

Relationship Type	Relationship Description
Sibling Links	Concepts that have sibling relationships, or are loosely associated and sometimes interchangeable.
Familiar or Derivational Links	Concepts that have familial or derivational relationships (i.e., one of the concepts is derived from the other).
Disciplines and Practitioners – Object Links	Concepts that represent disciplines or fields of study and the objects or phenomena studied, or the discipline's practitioners
Operations – Process and Agent Links	Concepts that represent operations, processes, and their agents and instruments.
Processes and Counteragent Links	Concepts that represent objects, processes, and counteragents.
Actions and Results Links	Concepts that represent actions and their results or concepts that describe processes and their products.
Actions and Target Links	Concepts that represent actions and their targets.
Objects – Substances and their Properties	Concepts that represent objects or substances and their properties.
Phenomenon and Causes	Concepts that represent some phenomenon and its causes.
Phenomenon and Units of Measure	Concepts that represent some phenomenon and its units of measurement.
Everything Else	There may be many other ways that concepts or nodes are semantically related. This category includes everything else that is not otherwise specified. This category is potentially rich for future semantic discovery. We expect these kinds of relationships to emerge in a semantic exploration of concept clusters, concept maps, semantic networks in specific contexts.

search engines and observed the results. Research suggests that the primary causes of risk are:

- equivalent relationships that are not synonymous or equal but are somehow related;
- hierarchical relationships that do not reflect the three conditions of meaning but have a range of other meanings;
- extensive and overuse of associative relationships as a quick remedy for relationships that have not been well thought through.

Consider the impacts to search when associative relationships are ranked at 90% to 99% relevance versus 35%. Consider the impact to search when hierarchical relationships are ranked at 65% rather than 35%. And, consider the effect to search if terms that do not have a well-articulated relationship are included in the results.

We have not thought of the effect these relationships might have on seeking, discovery, and search. Consider the impact of building these kinds of relationships into a navigation map of our knowledge landscape. Practical experience suggests that stakeholders react strongly to these effects when they encounter them in these contexts. The lesson we have learned over the years is: if you're going to use semantic relationships and semantic structures, do so carefully, deliberately, and intentionally. And, verify and validate any semantic relationships that you create to test your interpretation of meaning.

Measures of semantic relationships

It is also essential to consider the nature of semantic relationships, including (1) semantic relatedness and similarity, (2) semantic distance, and (3) semantic centrality.

Semantic relatedness and similarity

Semantic relatedness and similarity are often used interchangeably. It is a measure of the distance (or closeness) of the meaning of two things. For example, 'spoon' and 'fork' will have high semantic similarity because of the similar meaning of tableware, but terms such as 'alien' and 'chair' will not because they are not close or similar in meaning. The same two concepts will have different similarity relatedness in two different contexts. For example, there is a strong relationship between 'girls education' and 'village footpaths' in the economic development context. It is because in real life, if there are not well-established and protected footpaths, girls are not likely to attend school – traveling from home is simply too dangerous. In the transportation context or environmental sciences, there will be a very distant or non-existent relationship between these two concepts because a girl's education is simply not a concern. Semantic relatedness may be measured as the simple proximity of concepts in source materials. Semantic relatedness is an important quality control factor – it is an indication of how well the semantics represent the domain. Another type of relationship that is important to these more primitive structures is 'centrality.' Centrality focuses on the position of the node in the overall source relative to other nodes. It is not a relationship we normally track in predefined semantic structures because we cannot and do not intend to predetermine the semantic structure.

Having said that these measures are primarily applied in a 'source-specific' context, it is also possible to translate the three higher-level categories of relationships to a numerical or quantitative value. Relatedness and similarity are measures that are sometimes integrated into the query-matching algorithms of search systems. In the more sophisticated search architectures, results that are synonymous with the query terms can be given a higher weight than other results. Research has shown that synonymous terms are often ranked at a 90%–99% level. Research has shown that terms that have a hierarchical relationship are often ranked at between 55%–75%. Research has also shown that terms that have an associative relationship are often ranked at around 35% relevance. These quantitative settings reflect two decades of search system research on the part of historically effective search application engineers. It is important to note that these quantitative measures are not directly assigned to the terms. Rather, these measures are applied to the results set.

Semantic distance

Semantic distance is one way of measuring the closeness in the meaning of two concepts or things in a specific context. Specifically, semantic distance is a statistical measure of how close or distant two units of language are in terms of their meaning. This measure was developed in the natural language processing context to help resolve some common semantic challenges such as machine translation, word sense disambiguation, speech recognition, spelling corrections, and so on. In a given context, a fundamental assumption is that words that are found in proximity have some meaningful relationship. It does not indicate that they have 'similar meanings,' but that the relationship between these things is meaningful in this particular context. Semantic distance is vital to knowledge seeking, discovery, and search because we want to be able to detect and understand the meaningful relationships among concepts and across concepts. In the future, such semantic networks or semantic explanations may become a kind of 'relational knowledge' in and of themselves. They are sources of knowledge that help us to understand the meaning or to make sense of a domain.

The context for these first two points on the spectrum may be serendipitous, i.e., we want to discover relationships, but we are not ready or interested in assigning any greater degree of meaning to them. We are interested only in describing the distance or occurrence of relationships. The biggest challenge we find in using these kinds of semantic structures is the leap often taken from seeing a relationship to assuming it has a significant meaning and assigning meaning without further exploration of the context. An additional risk is created when these 'undefined' relationships are extended to other contexts whose semantic foundations we do not yet understand. For example, drawing political observations from the clusters without first understanding the nature of the relationships or testing the reliability beyond that one communication channel. Or, generating a concept cluster of a set of tweeted messages from a political uprising and presuming those concepts and relationships can be reliably applied to other types of communications in different political contexts.

The last three points on the spectrum begin with a predefined meaning. We have a sense of the kinds of meaning we are looking for before we start looking at the source. These meanings are all open to significant interpretation. These types of relationships can be applied to any source or context, but they require additional elaboration.

Semantic centrality

Semantic centrality speaks to the degree of relatedness of a concept or thing to other things in the network. For example, a person's tacit knowledge may have

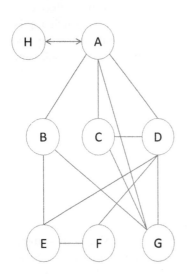

Network Connectivity = Total Number of Edges/Links

Degree Centrality = No. of Unique Edges for a single node

Edge Distance/Weight = Aggregate Value of Edges

FIGURE 15.3 Graphic Representation of Semantic Centrality

high semantic centrality in a knowledge network for a division of an organization if that person has the expertise that drives the work and innovation of that division. If people are going to that individual for advice and guidance, many other people will be linked to that individual through communications and knowledge flows. These semantic connections contribute to the centrality of that individual's tacit knowledge. The same can be said of a concept, which is one of the core ideas of a paper or text (Figure 15.3).

Common semantic structures

There are several common semantic structures, including (1) concept clusters, (2) semantic networks, (3) concept maps, (4) topic and mind maps, (5) common language thesauri, (6) structured vocabularies and thesauri, (7) ontologies, and (8) cross-language knowledge bases and dictionaries. We order and describe these structures consistent with the spectrum of meaning assigned to their relationships.

Concept clusters

The simplest form of a semantic structure is what we find in concept clusters. In its simplest form, a concept cluster tells us that there is 'some kind of' relationship between these two 'things' in this particular context (Figure 15.4). What the nature of that relationship is, though, is dependent upon the design of the clustering algorithm. A concept cluster is a grouping of related concepts generated by clustering algorithms. These groups derive from a predefined source, a collection of assets that represents a domain, a defined collection, or even a single document.

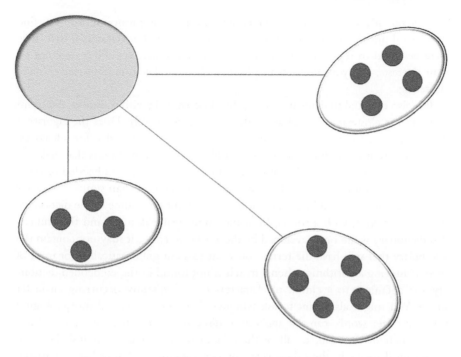

FIGURE 15.4 Graphic Representation of a Concept Cluster

Clustering algorithms are designed to identify the source's concepts and record how often those concepts occur in the source and where they appear in the source. The design factors for clustering algorithms are: (1) What do we mean by a concept? (2) What do we mean by 'where'? and (3) Are there thresholds or baselines for occurrence?

If you are working with a concept clustering application and have the opportunity to define a concept, you might want to consider whether you are interested in tracking 'things' or 'actions' or another kind of entity (Berkhin, 2006; Cai et al., 2010; Carullo et al., 2009; Collins & Quillian, 1970; Dhillon & Modha, 2001; Kominek & Kazman, 1997; Osinski & Weiss, 2005; Xy & Gong, 2004). For example, are you interested in any noun, any noun phrase, verbs, or pronouns? Are you interested in specific nouns, or do you have a profile of verbs and actions you're interested in tracking? Or, in tracking specific names of people, organizations, or places? It is not a factor you can manage in all clustering applications. Some are simple statistical clustering programs that look at words as character strings separated by spaces. If this is the case, the minimum engineering you should do before you apply it is to create a stopword list. A stopword list is a list of terms that you do not want to highlight or track in the source. It is important because a fundamental rule of statistics is that what is most common will rise to the top. If you don't have a stopword list, you will likely find that certain parts of speech occur more frequently, e.g., articles, conjunctions, and possibly pronouns. You can find some good practice stopword lists published to the Web, but remember that these were designed to represent the issuing organization's interests. They may not be your interests, and your interests may vary with the collection and sources you're clustering.

It is also essential to determine what the clustering algorithm does to the terms it selects for clustering. It will affect the results significantly. Does the algorithm stem each term? Consider what this means for nouns, for verbs, for adjectives. Does it create meaningful clusters? Or, is it likely to develop clusters that make no sense for your goals? Does the clustering application have an embedded diction-ary? If so, is stemming defined by grammatical roots rather than simple 'character chunks'? If there is an embedded dictionary, ask about the source of the dictionary. If you're working with a source from the engineering domain and the embed-ded dictionary is the one developed by the *Financial Times*, it may not contain the vocabulary that will have the terms you want to stem grammatically. For most of these clustering algorithms, when a match is not found in the embedded diction-ary, the default is to a chunk of characters or a frequently occurring character string. You might also want to ask whether there are embedded morphological rules. In other words, can the application discern whether the source is in Eng-lish, French or German, or all of these languages? Can it distinguish between grammatical forms in those languages, or is it looking only for character strings across languages? We can understand the level of non-sense that will be inherent to our clusters where there are no dictionary or morphological rules or are not well aligned with your interests.

The second design question is, what do you mean by 'where'? In the simplest clustering applications, you will not be able to specify where because they will have designed this into the clustering algorithm directly. In the more sophisticated applications, though, you should be able to define 'whereas': the adjacency of words in the text, e.g., 'girl's education,' or 'girl's' and 'education' within the same sentence, or 'girl's and education' within the same paragraph or three paragraphs. These questions will affect the semantic centrality of your clusters and the semantic distance of those clusters. It will also influence how you interpret the relatedness in the final cluster 'girl's education' may have a higher degree of relevance whereas 'girl's cooking' and the 'education of older adults' may have a low level of semantic relatedness.

The third consideration is the threshold level set for identifying relationships. A threshold is the minimum level of semantic relatedness you will tolerate in the clusters the algorithm generates. If you want to simply explore the whole source, you might want to set a low threshold. However, if you are looking for specific concepts or entities, it might be wise to begin with a high threshold. The thresh-old simply defines the level of noise or non-sense you are willing to tolerate in the clusters. In the simplest clustering applications, you may not be able to set a threshold. Instead, the full set of semantically related clusters will be generated, and you would simply decide when to stop exploring the clusters.

Semantic networks

We might describe semantic networks as having the next degree of semantic relatedness. A semantic network or frame network is a knowledge base representing semantic relations between concepts in a network (Figure 15.5). It is often used as a form of knowledge representation. It is a directed or undirected graph consisting of vertices, which represent concepts, and edges. Edges is a network term for *links* – what we in knowledge architecture refer to as the semantic relations between nodes. We place this at the next level of relatedness because semantic networks allow us to identify and represent concepts and links as semantic triples. Semantic networks leverage natural language processing methods such as semantic parsing and word-sense disambiguation to identify and select concepts. In a semantic network, we take another step toward deliberately defining what we mean by a concept and what we mean by a link. Natural language processing allows us to tell the application to 'look for nouns' and 'look for verbs and other grammatical forms that connect those nouns.' Look first for commonly occurring nouns, which then tell us about the verbs and other grammatical forms that link them.

It is an essential semantic method because it can reveal the most commonly occurring verb associations between concepts. These revelations may fall into the three predefined types of relationships we described earlier. But, it is more likely that these revelations will help us to understand better that last category of 'associative relationships,' i.e., the 'other' or 'everything else.' Semantic network graphs derived from intentionally developed collections can help us to understand semantics at a level we can use to teach machines. They can help us to expose our tacit knowledge of a context or domain. We leverage a semantic network when we understand it as a set of concepts that are related to one another. Most semantic networks are cognitively based. Semantic networks and graphs are essential tools for the field of computational linguistics. While semantic networks have been the

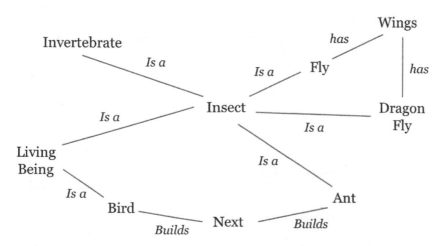

FIGURE 15.5 Graphic Representation of a Semantic Network

focus of research since the 1950s, the increased computing capacity of the past 20 years has led to an explosion of applications and new insights. One notable example of this research is WordNet, a lexical database of the English language. Wordnet organizes English into sets of synonyms called synsets, provides short, general definitions, and records the various semantic relations between these synonym sets and some degree of hierarchy. It provides a first primitive understanding of common relationships that mean nodes are equal or have some inherent structure.

Concept maps

A concept map takes a similar form to those we see in concept clusters, but they leverage a different method (Cañas & Novak, 2014; Heinze-Fry & Novak, 1990; Johnson & Henderson, 2011; Novak, 1990, 1995; Novak et al., 1983; Novak & Canas, 2006; Quillian, 1963, 1967; Ruiz-Primo & Shavelson, 1996). A concept map is a way of representing nodes and links, where the nodes may represent ideas, images, words, or topics, and links represent the type of semantic relationship the 'mapper' determines exists (Figure 15.6). In a concept map, each word or phrase connects to another and links back to the original idea, word, or phrase. Concept maps may be machine-generated, or they may be human developed. When they are machine-generated, we are leveraging a sophisticated clustering or semantic network graphic method. When they are human developed, the source is the human being's understanding of the context. Concept maps are essential learning

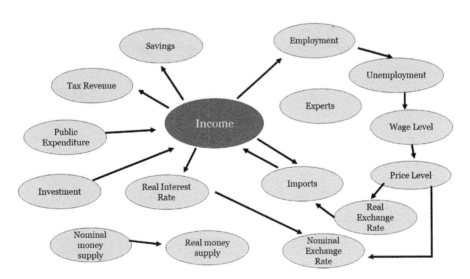

FIGURE 15.6 Graphic Representation of a Concept Map

and teaching tools. Concept maps can enhance meaningful learning in the sciences. A well-made concept map grows within a *context frame* defined by a specific focus question.

Concept maps are designed to describe what we call a declarative memory system – essentially a representation of our tacit knowledge of the context. Concept maps are valuable for representing how an individual makes sense of the context and how an individual might communicate or explain how they think about that context. Concept maps will be essential tools in the future – they will be a starting point for individual designing and representing their knowledge semantics.

Topic maps

Topic maps are maps of concepts that identify concepts and their relationships (Dicheva & Dichev, 2006; Garshol, 2002, 2004; Le Grand & Soto, 2002; Pepper, 1999, 2000; Vatant, 2004). The relationship between concepts can be articulated in *linking phrases* such as 'causes,' 'requires,' or 'contributes to.' The difference between a concept map and a topic map is that a topic map uses graphs to represent the links (Ficapal Vila, 2019; Ji et al., 2015; Lin et al., 2017; Nickel et al., 2016; Pujara et al., 2013; Wang et al., 2014). The linking phrases in topic maps are not unlike those we call out in the three semantic meaning forms. Topic maps represent ideas and information as boxes or circles, connecting with labeled arrows in a downward-branching hierarchical structure (Figure 15.7). The challenge – and the confounding factor – is that the graph takes the form of a hierarchy, whereas the linking phrases may not be hierarchical. While the visual representation (e.g., a concept map) is an essential tool for understanding and sense-making, it is essential to call out and further categorize the linking phrases identified in the concept map. Topic maps that are simply converted to hierarchical semantic relationships and integrated into discovery and search applications without further discernment increase the level of risk of confusion and non-sense making.

Topic maps are useful for transforming tacit knowledge into an organizational resource and mapping team and procedural knowledge, for preserving institutional knowledge through the elicitation and mapping of expert and employee knowledge before retirement. Topic maps are also essential tools for modeling collaborative knowledge, the transfer of expert knowledge, and facilitating the creation of shared vision and shared understanding within a team or organization. We also make use of topic maps for an instructional design where they can provide an initial conceptual framework for capturing future knowledge, and for training where they can help to align the training concepts with roles and responsibilities. Topic maps are also essential tools for communicating complex ideas and arguments, and for balancing complex ideas and shared vocabularies.

FIGURE 15.7 Graphic Representation of Topic Map

Mind maps

A mind map is a representation of how an individual or a group makes sense of a context. Mind maps are similar to concept and topic maps in their content, but they have a defined structure and visual presentation (Beel & Langer, 2011; Eppler, 2006; Wheeldon, 2011; Wheeldon & Faubert, 2009; Whiting & Sines, 2012; Wickramasinghe et al., 2011; Willis & Miertschin, 2006). Mind maps are also less systematic in elaborating on the meaning of links. Mind maps are expressed as radial hierarchies and tree structures (Figure 15.8). Mind maps create links among nodes or concepts, but they do not assign a specific meaning or a type of semantic relationship to the link. It is tempting to interpret the links in the essential hierarchical form of a mind map to mean inheritance structures, but this is not the intention. The link simply means – for this individual or this group – there is some kind of a semantic relatedness to this other thing.

Mind maps are generated quickly and spontaneously. In addition to representing how an individual makes sense of a context, they represent that sense-making at this point. They are often time-sensitive and designed to communicate that sense to others. A mind map typically has a central focus point – a core idea or concept. All other branches or concepts must derive from and be linked, whether directly or indirectly, to this central hub. Concept clusters, concept maps, and topic maps may have multiple focus points with different numbers and lengths of links. They tend to be more free form, with multiple hubs and clusters.

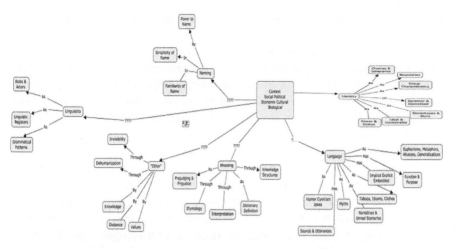

FIGURE 15.8 Graphic Representation of Hand Drawn Mind Map

Common language thesauri and dictionaries

Common language thesauri have value for their elaboration of synonymous words. *Roget's Thesaurus*, the Power Thesaurus, and the simple extraction of synonyms and antonyms from online dictionaries are the most common forms of within-language thesauri (Collinson, 1939; Hassler, 1999; Hullen, 2004a, 2004b, 2009; Tudhope et al., 2001; Warner, 2002). These sources provide synonyms, though they do not usually elaborate on the degree or type of similarity. Additionally, these synonym sources focus on common meanings – an important knowledge discovery and search consideration. They do not, though, include common language variants and spellings, including misspellings. If you choose to work with these sources, and you have a stakeholder population whose first language is not your most common language of business, you might find value in extending your synonym lists to include these other variants.

These sources are relevant, but remember that they are focused on words rather than concepts. In many cases, a word is a concept, but not in all cases. Where the concept is a noun phrase, the dictionary will not provide synonyms or trying to construct a synonym simply from other word combinations that introduce semantic risk. These are essential synonyms in any business context. – 'Poverty mitigation' and its 12 synonyms are essential for the World Bank. 'Sediment transport' is a critical concept in the Environmental Protection Agency – as are its 12 synonyms. These synonyms are discovered only through an analysis of the organization's knowledge stocks.

Synonyms may be time-sensitive. Consider that in the 1960s, it was acceptable to talk about 'underdeveloped countries.' Today, this is not an acceptable language because it is no longer an accurate representation of how we understand economic development. In the information science community, these types of synonyms are called predecessor and successor terms. By definition, a predecessor term is a synonym, but it is not 100% equivalent from a user perspective. We no longer support its use, though it would be unwise to ignore the earlier term. If we ignore the earlier term, we lose the connection to all of our earlier knowledge stocks. Synonyms, and predecessor terms, are essential to connecting knowledge stocks over space and over time.

Synonyms also reflect simple administrative and functional changes. For example, a company is known today by one name, but ten years ago, it had a different name. Consider how often your organization changes its organizational structure. How do you trace the evolution of units? Do you identify and track predecessor and successor names? If not, consider the loss of semantic meaning to your organization's ability to track and manage its functional knowledge – specifically its procedural and cultural knowledge assets. Without the tracing of these synonyms, you have lost the continuity of that meaning. Consider how you might use synonyms and relationships where the meaning is equal to track mergers of knowledge stocks when companies are acquired or where units are combined.

These kinds of synonymous tracings are often referred to in the information science community as Name Authority Control semantics. Consider all of the different ways we might represent the name of a CEO – full formal name, nickname and last name, initials, with a salutation, maiden name, changed the name, and so on. Name authority can help us synthesize the tacit knowledge of individuals by ensuring that we have a way to semantically relate all of the names they have used over their lifetime.

Name authority control is essential for managing geographic synonyms. While most countries do not change their names frequently, names and geographic identities do change. If we refer only to Myanmar, we will lose access to those knowledge stocks that referred to Burma. If we refer only to Saint Petersburg (Russia), we lose access to all of the knowledge created for Leningrad and Petrograd.

Synonyms are the first level of managing the semantics of a language. Even if you do not advance to representing relationships with structural or more advanced semantic meanings, managing synonymous relationships are essential to a knowledge architecture.

Cross-language knowledge bases and dictionaries

Multilingual dictionaries help us to find equivalent or synonymous concepts across languages (Richens, 1956). They are more than the simple synonym sets we find in common language dictionaries or glossaries because it is rarely the case that cross-language terms are exact synonyms. There are always inherent variations and shades of meaning. Establishing correspondence is not always easy. The challenges and risks increase when we try to map translated concepts in more complex structural vocabularies. There are examples of multilingual thesauri, but the majority are designed for explicit browsing rather than embedded semantic tools for discovery and search. While there are standards for multilingual thesauri, experience suggests that these have inherent risks and unintended consequences when integrated without further functional design.

Structured vocabularies and thesauri

Structured vocabularies and thesauri are semantic sources that include the three categories of relationships representing equivalence, hierarchical, and associative (Alani et al., 2000; ANSI/NISO, 2010; Collinson, 1939; Eden et al., 2005; Hassler, 1999; Hersh et al., 2000; Hullen, 2004a, 2004b, 2009; Noyes, 1951; Roddick et al., 2003; Stanley, 2004; Tsatsaronis et al., 2007; Tudhope et al., 2006). We will not repeat the extensive discussion of these relationships here. Instead, we simply note that thesauri may include all or some of these relationships, and that the original intention of these thesauri was to assist indexers in the choice of terms for keywording and indexing. Over time, they have also been integrated into search systems or published to aid searchers in selecting search terms. Many thesauri call out explicit equivalence and hierarchical relationships without referencing associative links. We recommend that the user critically assess these sources because they may not represent true interpretations. These types of thesauri and structured vocabularies may be available in print or digital form. Some thesauri are also represented in a visual rather than just a text display (Figure 15.9). We also note that national and international standards governing the production of these thesauri, including the British Standard, BS 8723 *Structured Vocabularies for Information Retrieval, the International Standard*, ISO 25964, and an American standard, ANSI/NISO Z39.19.

The primary challenge with using the earlier editions of the domain and focal thesauri is that they were designed for indexers and not for searching. The

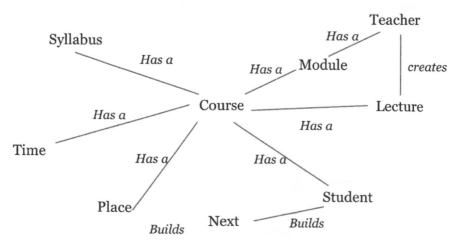

FIGURE 15.9 Sample ANXI/NISO Z39.19 Thesaurus Display

relationships should be critically tested before integrating them into an application. Additionally, research suggests that extensive structured vocabularies are rarely consulted by subject matter experts when a simple keyword search option is available. Research also indicates that intentionally selected thesaurus terms infrequently appear in search system logs. The most effective approach to leveraging these earlier domain vocabularies in today's discovery environment may be an embedded search tool. It is the semantic relationships and structures that have value, rather than the specific nodes and concepts that are represented in the vocabularies. An additional challenge is the expense of maintaining these structured vocabularies, and the slow rate at which they are traditionally updated. These traditional practices are not, though, inherent to the use of thesauri. It is possible to leverage some of the other semantic methods discussed in this chapter to develop and manage thesauri more effectively and efficiently.

Ontologies

Ontologies are a set of concepts and categories in a subject area or domain (Figure 15.10) that shows their properties and the relations between them (Euzenat et al., 2008; Leadbetter et al., 2010). We describe ontologies as the last example because they may be designed to include elements of all the other structures we've described to this point. What we have observed about the formulation of practical ontologies

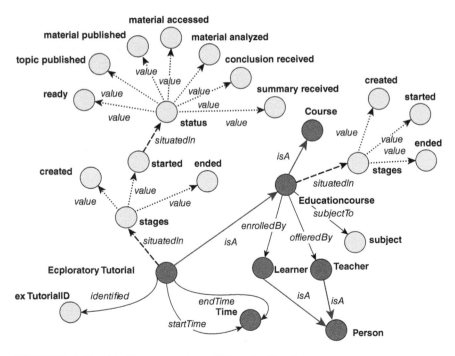

FIGURE 15.10 Graphic Representation of Domain Ontology

is: (1) they may consist of a variety of types of concepts and entities as nodes; (2) they may or may not assign meaning to the link; and (3) the links are often presumed to be hierarchically structured and designed to represent inheritance. In practice, ontologies vary in the degree of abstraction and the nature of the application.

The most common forms of ontologies are upper ontologies, domain ontologies, interface ontologies, and process ontologies. An upper ontology is not unlike an object model and an object class – it tells us about the nature of primary, secondary, and tertiary categories and their attributes. A domain ontology elaborates on the concepts relevant to a particular topic, context, or area of interest. An interface ontology elaborates and relates the concepts pertinent to the juncture of two disciplines. Finally, a process ontology elaborates on the inputs, outputs, constraints, and process concepts associated with an operation or function. In a nutshell, any of the semantic structures described earlier could be represented as and referred to as an ontology. From our experience, ontologies are described because of the encoding methods used to represent them – the RDF schema or languages used to represent them.

Semantic structures for human capital

Semantics for human capital are related to the access points and the concepts that define those access points. It means the values, the vocabularies, and the relationships among values for each of the critical access points. Semantics for human capital might include a topic thesaurus, a topic map, a concept map of subjects or themes, an authority control list of functions, a thesaurus of methods, a controlled list of levels of expertise, a controlled list of languages, and a controlled vocabulary of types of experiences and skills.

Semantic structures for explicit knowledge

Semantics related to explicit knowledge might include controlled lists of formats and languages, a subject or topic thesaurus, a function thesaurus, and an authority control of country names and publishers.

Semantic structures for procedural knowledge

Semantics related to procedural knowledge might include a functional thesaurus, a controlled list of process methods, a controlled list of products and results, a controlled list of ingredients and materials, an authoritative list of job classes, a predefined list of life cycle stages, and an authority control list of units and their tracings over time.

Semantic structures for cultural knowledge

Semantics for cultural knowledge might include an authoritative list of types of cultural values and behaviors, a defined list of types of cultures, a standardized list of life cycle stages of a culture, an authoritative list of business functions, an official list of unit names, and a topic or functional thesaurus.

Semantic structures for network knowledge

Semantics for network knowledge might include a topic map, a topic thesaurus, a concept map, an authoritative list of business functions, a controlled list of languages spoken in the community, a predefined list of values that tell us whether the community was sponsored or informal, and a list of values that tell us whether the community is virtual and physical.

Semantic structures – the design environment

What factors do we need to consider in designing this architecture? This functional architecture is complex in its essential elements. The environment in which it is applied is equally complex. We must take into account the semantic capacity of all existing search applications, and must design to suit different levels of capacity. We also need to consider the current human and machine-based indexing processes and consider how our semantic structures will align with them. We must also consider where other semantic structures are in use across the organizations and design an architecture that allows us to leverage them. Most importantly, though, we must consider how to design all of these approaches into a harmonized enterprise architecture.

What events cause us to design a functional architecture for semantics? We develop functional architecture to support semantics when we need to manage language to support knowledge discovery and search when our organizations have a long history, and that language has changed over time, and when we have nationalities and language variants in common usage. We need to have a strong semantics foundation when our language is complex. Our stakeholders may not always know how to express what they're looking for, when the language and the knowledge landscape are complex. We need to provide some implicit guidance, and when we need an intuitive way to explain the scope and coverage of what we do. We need a strong semantics architecture if we want to consider machine-assisted indexing or categorization. Perhaps most importantly, we need a robust semantic architecture when we work in a dynamic and rapidly changing knowledge economy.

What are the impacts and consequences of having this functional architecture? Having a semantic architecture in place improves the effectiveness and efficiency of knowledge seeking and discovery, of search, of cross-language and organizational searching, and of the cost-effectiveness of machine-based indexing of a broader range of knowledge assets. It also enables any organization to harmonize administrative, business, and domain language over time and space.

What inputs do we need to consider when designing this functional architecture? There are several essential inputs for the design of a semantics architecture, including exiting semantic structures such as concept clusters, glossaries, existing controlled vocabularies, indexing vocabularies, specialized language dictionaries, concept maps, topic maps, semantic networks, standardized thesaurus, and cross-language dictionaries. It also includes current and historical administrative and business vocabularies and semantic tools.

What are the outputs and outcomes this functional architecture generates? Having this functional architecture in place makes it possible for an organization to provide increasingly effective navigation and search capabilities, expose and share semantic structures, develop user-assisted search options, increase the precision of results ranking, and design our semantic structures into increasingly intelligent tools and technologies.

Design activities and tasks for semantic structures

This functional architecture is supported by and supports six activities, including:

- Activity 1. Develop a profile of the knowledge space or context
- Activity 2. Define the semantic and linguistic registers at play in the context
- Activity 3. Define the kinds of relationships important to the context
- Activity 4. Design the larger architecture of the structure
- Activity 5. Design a process for applying the structure to the context
- Activity 6. Harmonization and integration of semantic sources

Activity 1. Develop a profile of the knowledge space or context

How do we do this? It is an important starting point for defining the scope and coverage of the source we're using to develop the semantic structure or the domain we strive to profile with our controlled vocabulary. In the best-case scenario, we should be able to use the description of the knowledge landscape we described in Chapter 11. The inclusion of sources should reflect the language and vocabulary we intend to represent.

What inputs does this activity need? Sources may include both digital and print, but print sources will need to be converted to digital before we can apply any of the computer-based methods we described. The sample set of sources should represent all types of language you need to model. The selection of samples should reflect the stakeholders whose knowledge discovery will be supported by semantic structure.

What products and services does it generate? This activity produces the knowledge base that will be used to identify the concepts and semantic relationships.

What other resources does it need? Stakeholder knowledge of sources and the knowledge architect's knowledge of the landscape are the two essential inputs. In assembling these sources, additional resources would be some type of capacity or platform for a test collection.

Activity 2. Define the semantic and linguistic registers at play in the context

How do we do this? It is an essential activity. We need to understand the kinds of language – specifically the semantic and linguistic registers – of the stakeholders we aim to support. For example, we would be misadvised to develop a 'research-oriented register' when the stakeholder community is interested in policy development. The types of concepts we're interested in would be significantly different in these two contexts. We need to pay attention to how our stakeholders talk about their interests.

What inputs does this activity need? We must begin with samples of how the stakeholders write about, talk about, and represent important concepts. It means casting a broader rather than a narrower net to understand all dimensions of a domain rather than to restrict it early on. Scoping and refining can take place after we have a full set of concepts and semantic relationships. Eliminating any of these in this early stage introduces risks of oversight and gaps.

What products and services does it generate? Ideally, this activity generates a strong working list of concepts included in the semantic structure's scope.

What other resources does it need? The analytical and critical thinking required for this task should not be underestimated. Additionally, this activity requires strong communication skills and competencies.

Activity 3. Define the kinds of relationships important to the context

How do we do this? This activity is as important as identifying the concepts because it determines how these relationships will 'behave' or work when they are automated or embedded in other applications. Once you have a good grasp of the kinds of semantic relations possible, review the corpus you've assembled and begin to analyze the use of verbs and verb phrases. Focusing on verbs and verb phrases, walk through a series of questions:

- What kinds of relationships are essential to the domain? While there are some basic kinds of relationships, relationships can have many different interpretations. Be aware of, but be cautious of, very generic relationships because they are more prone to errors in assignments. More detailed relationships require more care, time, and effort to assign.
- Can the relationships be demonstrated or exposed to the results?
- Does your architecture expect that users will be able to query or explore relationships as a direct access tool rather than just as a meaningful pointer?
- We should be aware of the rigor of validation that was applied to creating relationships among concepts.
- Does this relationship hold outside of the domain? If not, we should be clear about the warrant that drives the field and the semantic structures.
- Do the experts in the field support this relationship? Or was the relationship established just because the two concepts had similar words?
- Are the two concepts that are related defined at the same level of granularity?
- What is the degree of subjective meaning or interpretation associated with the meaning of the relationships among concepts?

What inputs does this activity need? To complete this activity, you need to have a corpus to start with. Ideally, you've created that in the last two activities. Another approach you can take is to focus on verbs and noun phrases if you have the resources and the capacity to run a concept extraction. This strategy essentially mimics the creation of semantic networks and topic maps – discovering noun and verb phrases that are common to the corpus. The extracted verb phrases will give us a hint of the frequently occurring semantic relationships. Other good sources for discovering semantic relationships are existing structured vocabulary, thesauri, or glossaries. Be cautious, though, in accepting these interpretations without critical evaluation.

What products and services does it generate? This activity should produce a list of semantic relationships that are important to the domain. Combined with the list of concepts, it should also give you a good start on the overall vocabulary you will need to structure.

What other resources does it need? It is essential to validate all of your work with subject matter experts. Be sure to make it easy for them to review and provide feedback. Experience suggests that providing a digital copy of your proposed vocabulary (e.g., nouns and noun phrases) and inviting the experts to (1) note what is missing, and (2) cross out what is not essential, will make it easy for them to provide the feedback you need. Do not ask them to review linking phrases. You can work with your verb extraction to accomplish that.

Activity 4. Design the larger architecture of the structure

How do we do this? This activity focuses on the business rules and developing a design with which your systems developers and application architects can work. Is your semantic structure designed to integrate with search systems? Will it be integrated into data entry templates for indexing or categorization? Do you need a presentation design for general public access? Business rules guide developers – they explain how you expect the semantic structure to work. The more you can communicate with the developers, the better chance you will have to achieve a well-designed application. There are some business rules which cannot be adjusted, and there are some that are more flexible. For example, will you allow a developer to select only portions of your semantics, or must they use it in total? If they can choose, should they work with you? Or can you provide general guidance in the ruleset?

What inputs does this activity need? The knowledge architect should have a good understanding of the architecture and functions of any applications that will consume the application. You should be able to anticipate some of the challenges an application architect or developer will encounter in integrating your semantic structure.

What products and services does it generate? At a minimum, this activity should explain the architecture and functionality of your semantic structure. It should also have a specific set of design guidelines and business rules.

What other resources does it need? Ideally, this activity would also leverage any architecture design software or applications. The knowledge architect generates a formal architecture specification for the structure. Where these resources are not available, the knowledge architect can use other graphic forms to explain the underlying structure and working methods.

Activity 5. Design a process for applying the structure to the context

How do we do this? This activity focuses on operationalizing the process that you just walked through to manage in the future. Remember that no semantic structure is static. There are a few functions or disciplines that have stopped growing or evolving. As they evolve, new concepts are added to the vocabulary, and old concepts may be updated or superseded. What aspects of the activities you worked through to get to this point worked well? Which did not work well? What will be practical and effective going forward? Do you need to have additional support? Will you continue to involve domain experts in the review of vocabulary changes? Or will you rely on indirect feedback from the consuming applications? How do you plan to engage the information professionals? Semantic structures are essential elements of knowledge architecture. They need some form of business continuity and contingency plan, in case the knowledge architect's attention is redirected, or the function needs to be handed off to another group.

What inputs does this activity need? The primary input for this activity is an 'after-action review' of the prior four activities. The knowledge architect should consider how the activities can be streamlined and integrated into a new capability. And, this new capability should have a clear place and role in the knowledge architecture.

What products and services does it generate? This activity generates procedural knowledge that supports the architecture specifications developed in the previous activity. It ensures the function can be repeated in the future to keep the semantic structures current and relevant. This procedural knowledge should be documented in a way that allows other functions and groups to contribute. For example, there may be a master data group charged with maintaining the semantics of administrative vocabularies. The documentation should explain how to document any changes and should detail which applications consume these semantics and how to push the changes to those applications.

What other resources does it need? This activity leverages any conventions for documenting procedural knowledge as an essential knowledge asset.

Activity 6. Harmonization and integration of semantic sources

How do we do this? Few semantic structures will be entirely new. Having established a functional architecture for any semantic support across the organization, you now need to make sure that you've provided a way to integrate what exists. Your new semantic architectures have a better chance of being adopted and supported if you can demonstrate to stakeholders that their current sources and structures are 'in there.' In other words, they can continue to work with what they have, but it is now part of a larger resource. Be sure to demonstrate how the new resource provides additional value and how it relieves them of the burden of maintaining it. Be sure to develop training materials and examples that represent their interests.

What inputs does this activity need? These materials were considered back in Activities 1 and 2. At this stage, you can look back at how those sources were integrated into the overall vocabulary and extract examples. If you overlooked any sources, this last step provides an opportunity to map them in.

What products and services does it generate? This activity provides a final check and validation of your functional semantic architecture and the actual semantics. If you can demonstrate it to stakeholders, and if you can assure yourself and other architects that it will function as promised, you have accomplished your goals.

What other resources does it need? The most input resource is the knowledge architect's ability to review and analyze the semantic architecture design critically. It requires an ability to be objective, to walk through the overall design and functionality, and to conduct an internal assessment. This activity also requires the ability to communicate well with business stakeholders and other architects.

Evolution of the design of semantic structures

Experience and a review of the literature suggest that semantic structures have evolved over five phases (Figure 15.11). The primary factor contributing to this evolution is the expanding scale and scope of knowledge in society. These structures – other than simple language dictionaries and thesauri – are relatively recent.

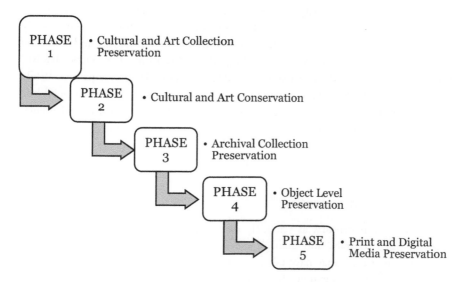

FIGURE 15.11 Evolution of Semantic Structures

Consider that it is only in the past 300 years that we have seen the rapid growth of scientific and theoretical knowledge bases.

The need for these structures arose when the scale of knowledge and information sources grew and when the complexity of those sources deepened (e.g., the more specialized the domain, the broader the concepts and meanings, and the greater the need for semantic tools). The five phases of semantic structures evolution include:

*   Phase 1. Simple language semantics
*   Phase 2. Domain semantics
*   Phase 3. Formalized structures
*   Phase 4. Source-specific semantics
*   Phase 5. Personalized semantics

Phase 1. Simple language semantics

The language was simple in the earliest centuries. In these early millennia, we had dictionaries, but not explicit thesauri. Dictionaries did list synonyms or antonyms, but the primary purpose of a dictionary was to provide definitions and explanations. Before the 19th century, a thesaurus was equated with any dictionary or encyclopedia, the *Dictionary of the Latin Language* (1532), and the *Dictionary of the Greek Language* (1572). As written language developed and as literacy increased in the general population, the variety and richness of language grew. The simple growth in written language gave rise to the need for general language thesauri. The earliest of these were referred to as synonym dictionaries. The more formal term, thesaurus, was first used in 1852 by Roget in the development of *Roget's Thesaurus*. Roget's thesaurus presents sets of words in a hierarchical structure. Other thesauri, though, provide simple alphabetical, dictionary-like orders. Today, formal language thesauri are differentiated from dictionaries in that they do not include definitions. These early thesauri were designed to assist writers and communicators in varying and enriching their language, and the avoidance of word repetition. Over time, this practice has had a significant impact on the effectiveness of our discovery and search semantics. While other semantic structures have emerged in the centuries since Roget first published his thesaurus, these general language thesauri have continued to serve a fundamental purpose. Their purpose has been supplemented but not overtaken by other semantic structures. These tools have continued to evolve, and many now provide more extensive distinctions between the degrees of meaning among synonyms.

Phase 2. Domain semantics

In the early 20th century, as scientific disciplines developed and expanded, the need emerged to track and manage specialized scientific terms and vocabularies. The earliest tools may have taken the form of glossaries. As scientific journals grew in popularity and extent, the need to provide consistent concept-level access emerged. The earliest domain semantics came out of the fields of engineering, chemistry, and biology. In the 1940s and 1950s, the earliest scientific vocabularies were collections of indexing terms. The first scientific thesauri were the chemistry thesaurus produced by E. I. Dupont de Nemours Company (1959), the *Thesaurus of ASTIA Descriptors* (1960), and the American Institute of Chemical Engineers' *Chemical Engineering Thesaurus* (1961). Subsequent scientific thesauri included the *Thesaurus of Engineering and Scientific Terms* (TEST) (1967). This last thesaurus provided the first guidance for the construction of thesauri. The relationship categories we associate with thesauri today emerged from these early vocabulary management communities. While academic and public libraries developed extensive subject headings listings, it was only later that the traditional 'See' (e.g., equivalence) and 'See also' (e.g., other relationships) were adapted with formal thesaurus labels.

In the second half of the 20th century, there was a dramatic expansion in the publication of scientific journal articles, conference proceedings, book chapters, and technical reports. Initially, thesauri were published in print form and intended to be used by indexers in providing concept- or topic-level access to these sources. As the sources moved from print to digital form, thesauri were engineered into the commercial database search systems.

Phase 3. Formalized semantics

The formalization of semantic structure in the late 20th century led to the creation of other domain thesauri in other scientific domains, the social sciences, and in the popular press and literature. These developments, though, coincided with the explosion of digital information and the emergence of the Web and self-publishing. The inherent limitations of these formalized semantic structures were evident – the labor-intensive nature of thesaurus development, their inherent limitations in comparison to full-text access, and the general expense of maintaining them in rapidly changing domains.

Phase 4. Source-specific semantics

Alternative methods of discovering underlying semantics emerged, particularly with the increase in computing capacity. It was in the early 2000s that topic maps, concept maps, concept clusters, and semantic networks emerged. These new approaches were collection-specific and, as noted earlier in this chapter, did not explicitly call out semantic relationships. Semantic relationships were defined statistically or through co-occurrence. While these semantic methods had value for discovering the scope and coverage of sources, they have limitations beyond those sources. In the early 2020s, we see a blending of the human-generated predefined semantics and the machine-supported discovery in the form of semantic analysis tools and technologies. These tools have several key components, including embedded language dictionaries, morphological and grammatical rules, embedded domain vocabularies, and extensive semantic characterizations of subdomains. As these semantic tools gain acceptance and greater use, the development of these embedded components will become more affordable and practical to a broader group of stakeholders.

Phase 5. Personalized semantics

We expect this current path to continue but to radically shift from general community or group use to personalized use. Consider the earlier discussions of our individual linguistic and social registers. How we talk about and see the world of knowledge is personal. Eventually, we expect these large and cumbersome semantic tools to behave like personal audio assistants. Just as we train our audio assistants, we will each be training our semantic assistants. We may have one or more domain vocabularies, a news vocabulary, and a shopping vocabulary. These will simply become applications in our everyday digital environment.

Semantic structures in the enterprise architecture blueprint

Historically, semantic structures have aligned with both information and application architecture practices. The semantic architecture draws upon and leverages sources from information architecture practices. Semantic architectures are implemented and leveraged in search and discovery applications.

Chapter review

After reading this chapter, you should be able to:

- define semantics and semantic structures;
- discuss the goal and purpose of semantic structures in knowledge accessibility;
- explain the most common forms of semantic relationships;
- explain historical and current semantic tools and processes;
- describe the spectrum of semantic structures in use today.

References and recommended future readings

Alani, H., Jones, C., & Tudhope, D. (2000, September). Associative and spatial relationships in thesaurus-based retrieval. In *International conference on theory and practice of digital libraries* (pp. 45–58). Springer.

Allen, J., & Frisch, A. (1982). *What's in a semantic network*. Proceedings of the 20th Annual meeting of ACL, Toronto, 19–27.

ANSI/NISO Z39.19–2005. (2010). *Standard. In Guidelines for the construction, format, and management of monolingual controlled vocabularies*. National Information Standards Organization.

Bedford, D. A. D., & Gracy, K. F. (2011). Leveraging semantic analysis technologies to increase effectiveness and efficiency of access to information. *Qualitative and Quantitative Methods in Libraries, 1*(1), 13–26.

Beel, J., & Langer, S. (2011). An exploratory analysis of mind maps. In *Proceedings of the 11th ACM symposium on document engineering* (pp. 81–84). Association for Computing Machinery.

Bendeck, F. (2008). *WSM-P workflow semantic matching platform*. Verlag Dr. Hut.

Berkhin, P. (2006). A survey of clustering data mining techniques. In *Grouping multidimensional data* (pp. 25–71). Springer.

Bordes, A., Usunier, N., Garcia-Duran, A., Weston, J., & Yakhnenko, O. (2013). Translating embeddings for modeling multi-relational data. In *Advances in neural information processing systems* (pp. 2787–2795). South Lake Tahoe: NIPS

Budanitsky, A., & Hirst, G. (1999). *Semantic distance in WordNet: An experimental application-oriented evaluation of five measures.* Workshop on WordNet and Other Lexical Resources.

Cai, D., He, X., & Han, J. (2010). Locally consistent concept factorization for document clustering. *IEEE Transactions on Knowledge and Data Engineering, 23*(6), 902–913.

Cañas, A. J., & Novak, J. D. (2014). Concept mapping using CmapTools to enhance meaningful learning. In *Knowledge cartography* (pp. 23–45). Springer.

Carullo, M., Binaghi, E., & Gallo, I. (2009). An online document clustering technique for short web contents. *Pattern Recognition Letters, 30*, 870–876.

Collins, A. M., & Loftus, E. F. (1975). A spreading-activation theory of semantic processing. *Psychological Review, 82*(6), 407.

Collins, A. M., & Quillian, M. R. (1969). Retrieval time from semantic memory. *Journal of Verbal Learning and Verbal Behavior, 8*(2), 240-247

Collins, A. M., & Quillian, M. R. (1970). Does category size affect categorization time? *Journal of Verbal Learning and Verbal Behavior, 9*(4), 432–438.

Collinson, W. E. (1939, November). Comparative synonymics: Some principles and illustrations. *Transactions of the Philological Society, 38*(1), 54–77.

Cooper, M. (2000). Semantic distance measures. *Computational Intelligence, 16*(1), 79–94.

Cormack, G. (2010, December 6). Keyword searches disappoint. *Computerworld.*

Daoud, M., Tamine, L., & Boughanem, M. (2011). A personalized search using a semantic distance measure in a graph-based ranking model. *Journal of Information Science, 37*(6), 614–636.

Davis, M. (2008, October). *Semantic wave 2008 report: Industry roadmap to web 3.0 & multibillion dollar market opportunities.* Retrieved February 2, 2020, from www.eurolibnet.eu/files/Repository/2009050/165103_SemanticWaveReport2008.pdf.

Davis, M. (2011). *Web 3.0 manifesto: How semantic technologies in products and services will drive breakthroughs in capability, user experience, performance, and life cycle value.* Retrieved November 11, 2011, from http://project10x.com/about2.php.

Dhillon, I. S., & Modha, D. S. (2001). Concept decompositions for large sparse text data using clustering. *Machine Learning, 42*(1–2), 143–175.

Dicheva, D., & Dichev, C. (2006). TM4L: Creating and browsing educational topic maps. *British Journal of Educational Technology, 37*(3), 391–404.

Dietze, H., & Schroeder, M. (2008). *Semantic search engine for the life science web.* Presentation delivered to e-Science Institute, Edinburgh, Scotland. November 28, 2008.

Dong, X., Halevy, A., Madhavan, J., Nemes, E., & Zhang, J. (2004). *Similarity search for web services.* Proceedings of the 30th VLDB Conference, Toronto, Canada, 2004.

Eden, B. L., Dalmau, M., Floyd, R., Jiao, D., & Riley, J. (2005). Integrating thesaurus relationships into search and browse in an online photograph collection. *Library Hi Tech.*

Eppler, M. J. (2006). A comparison between concept maps, mind maps, conceptual diagrams, and visual metaphors as complementary tools for knowledge construction and sharing. *Information Visualization, 5*(3), 202–210.

Euzenat, J., Mocan, A., & Scharffe, F. (2008). Ontology alignments. In *Ontology management* (pp. 177–206). Springer.

Ficapal Vila, J. (2019). *Anemone: A visual semantic graph.* School of Electrical Engineering and Computer Science, Kth Roya Institute of Technology.

Garshol, L. M. (2002). What are topic maps. In *XML.Com* (pp. 580–590). Retrieved May 1, 2020, from http://www.xml.com/pub/a/2002/09/11/topicmaps.html.

Garshol, L. M. (2004). Metadata? Thesauri? Taxonomies? Topic maps! Making sense of it all. *Journal of information science*, *30*(4), 378–391.

Giunchiglia, F., Shvaiko, P., & Yatskevich, M. (2004). *S-Match: An algorithm and an implementation of semantic matching*. Technical Report #DIT-04-015. University of Trento, Department of Information and Communication Technology.

Grimmes, S. (2010, January 21). Breakthrough analysis: Two + nine types of semantic search. *InformationWeek*.

Guha, R., McCool, B., & Miller, E. (2003). *Semantic search*. WWW2003, Budapest, Hungary, May 20–24.

Hassler, G. (1999). Lafaye's *Dictionnaire des synonymes* in the history of semantics. In S. Embleton, J. E. Joseph, & H.-J. Hiederehe (Eds.), *The emergence of the modern language sciences*. John Benjamins.

Haveliwala, T. H., Gionis, A., Klein, D., & Indyk, P. (2002). *Evaluating strategies for similarity search on the Web*, Honolulu, Hawaii, May 7–11, 2002.

Heinze-Fry, J. A., & Novak, J. D. (1990). Concept mapping brings long-term movement toward meaningful learning. *Science Education*, *74*(4), 461–472.

Helbig, H. (2006). *Knowledge representation and the semantics of natural language*. Springer.

Hersh, W., Price, S., & Donohoe, L. (2000). Assessing thesaurus-based query expansion using the UMLS Metathesaurus. In *Proceedings of the AMIA symposium* (p. 344). American Medical Informatics Association.

Hüllen, W. (2004a). *Roget's thesaurus, deconstructed in historical dictionaries and historical dictionary research*. International Conference on Historical Lexicography and Lexicology, University of Leicester, 2002, Max Niemeyer Verlag 2004.

Hüllen, W. (2004). *A history of Roget's thesaurus: Origins, development, and design*. Oxford University Press.

Hüllen, W. (2009, January). *Networks and knowledge in Roget's thesaurus*. Oxford University Press.

Hulpuş, I., Prangnawarat, N., & Hayes, C. (2015, October). Path-based semantic relatedness on linked data and its use to word and entity disambiguation. In *International semantic web conference* (pp. 442–457). Springer.

Imielinski, T., & Signorini, A. (2009). *If you ask nicely, I will answer: Semantic search and today's search engines*. 2009 IEEE International Conference on Semantic Computing.

Ji, G., He, S., Xu, L., Liu, K., & Zhao, J. (2015). Knowledge graph embedding via dynamic mapping matrix. In *Proceedings of the 53rd annual meeting of the association for computational linguistics and the 7th international joint conference on natural language processing (volume 1: Long papers)* (pp. 687–696). Association for Computational Linguistics.

Johnson, J., & Henderson, A. (2011). Conceptual models: Core to good design. *Synthesis Lectures on Human-Centered Informatics*, *4*(2), 1–110.

Kenett, Y. N., Levi, E., Anaki, D., & Faust, M. (2017). The semantic distance task: Quantifying semantic distance with semantic network path length. *Journal of Experimental Psychology: Learning, Memory, and Cognition*, *43*(9), 1470–1489.

Klein, S. (2002). The analogical foundations of creativity in language, culture & the arts: The Upper Paleolithic to 2100CE. *Advances in Consciousness Research*, *35*, 347–372.

Kominek, J., & Kazman, R. (1997). Accessing multimedia through concept clustering. In *Proceedings of the ACM SIGCHI conference on human factors in computing systems* (pp. 19–26). New York, NY: Association for Computing Machinery.

Le Grand, B., & Soto, M. (2002). Visualisation of the semantic web: Topic Maps Visualisation. In *Proceedings sixth international conference on information visualisation* (pp. 344–349). IEEE.

Leadbetter, A., Hamre, T., Lowry, R., Lassoued, Y., & Dunne, D. (2010). Ontologies and ontology extension for marine environmental information systems. In A. J. Berre, D. Roman, & P. Maue (Eds.), *Proceedings of the workshop environmental information systems and services-infrastructures and platforms, (envip'2010)*. CEUR Workshop Proceedings.

Lin, H., Liu, Y., Wang, W., Yue, Y., & Lin, Z. (2017). Learning entity and relation embeddings for knowledge resolution. *Procedia Computer Science, 108*, 345–354.

Nickel, M., Rosasco, L., & Poggio, T. (2016). Holographic embeddings of knowledge graphs. *arXiv preprint arXiv:1510.04935*.

Novak, J. D. (1990). Concept mapping: A useful tool for science education. *Journal of Research in Science Teaching, 27*(10), 937–949.

Novak, J. D. (1995). Concept mapping: A strategy for organizing knowledge. *Learning Science in the Schools: Research Reforming Practice*, 229–245.

Novak, J. D., & Cañas, A. J. (2006). The origins of the concept mapping tool and the continuing evolution of the tool. *Information Visualization, 5*(3), 175–184.

Novak, J. D., Bob Gowin, D., & Johansen, G. T. (1983). The use of concept mapping and knowledge vee mapping with junior high school science students. *Science Education, 67*(5), 625–645.

Noyes, G. E. (1951). The beginnings of the study of synonyms in England. *Publications of the Modern Language Association of America, 66*(6), 951–970.

Osinski, S., & Weiss, D. (2005). A concept-driven algorithm for clustering search results. *IEEE Intelligent Systems, 20*(3), 48–54.

Pepper, S. (1999). Euler, topic maps, and revolution. In *Proceedings of XML Europe* (Vol. 99). Retrieved May 1, 2020, from https://ontopia.net/topicmaps/materials/euler.pdf.

Pepper, S. (2000). The TAO of topic maps. In *Proceedings of XML Europe* (Vol. 3, p. 77). Retrieved from May 1, 2020, from https://badame.vse.cz/2005/tao/TheNewTAO.pdf.

Poon, H., & Domingos, P. (2009, August). Unsupervised semantic parsing. In *Proceedings of the 2009 conference on empirical methods in natural language processing: Volume 1-volume 1* (pp. 1–10). Association for Computational Linguistics.

Pujara, J., Miao, H., Getoor, L., & Cohen, W. (2013). Knowledge graph identification. In *International semantic web conference* (pp. 542–557). Springer.

Quillian, M. R. (1967). Word concepts: A theory and simulation of some basic semantic capabilities. *Behavioral Science, 12*(5), 410–430.

Quillian, M. R. (1968). *Semantic memory. Semantic information processing* (pp. 227–270). Bolt Beranek and Newman Inc.

Quillian, M. R. (1969). The teachable language comprehender: A simulation program and theory of language. *Communications of the ACM, 12*(8), 459–476.

Quillian, R. (1963). *A notation for representing conceptual information: An application to semantics and mechanical English para- phrasing. SP-1395*. System Development Corporation.

Rada, R., Mili, H., Bicknell, E., & Blettner, M. (1989). Development and application of a metric on semantic nets. *IEEE Transactions on Systems, Man and Cybernetics, 19*(1), 17–30.

Richens, R. H. (1956). General program for mechanical translation between any two languages via an algebraic interlingua. *Mechanical Translation, 3*(1), 20–25.

Roddick, J. F., Hornsby, K., & de Vries, D. (2003). *A unifying semantic distance model for determining the similarity of attribute values*. Twenty-Sixth Australasian Computer Science Conference (ACSC2003), Adelaide, Australia.

Ruiz-Primo, M. A., & Shavelson, R. J. (1996). Problems and issues in the use of concept maps in science assessment. *Journal of Research in Science Teaching: The Official Journal of the National Association for Research in Science Teaching, 33*(6), 569–600.

Shvaiko, P., & Euzenat, J. (2004). *A survey of schema-based matching approaches*. Technical Report#DIT – 04–087. Department of Information and Communication Technology, University of Trento.

Simmons, R. F. (1963). Synthetic language behavior. System development *Corporation. Data Processing Management, 5*(12), 11–18.

Simmons, R. F., Klein, S., & McConlogue, K. (1964). Indexing and dependency logic for answering English questions. *American Documentation, 15*(3), 196–204.

Sowa, J. F. (Ed.). (2014). *Principles of semantic networks: Explorations in the representation of knowledge*. Morgan Kaufmann.

Sowa, J. F. (1987). Semantic networks. In S. C. Shapiro (Ed.), *Encyclopedia of artificial intelligence*. John Wiley & Sons.

Speel, P. H., van der Vet, P. E., ter Stal, W., & Mars, N. (1993). Formalization of an ontology of ceramic science in classic. In *Proceedings of the seventh international symposium on methodologies for intelligent systems, poster session* (pp. 110–124). Springer Nature.

Stanley, E. (2004). *Polysemy and synonymy and how these concepts were understood from the eighteenth century onwards in treatises, and applied in dictionaries of English*. Historical Dictionaries and Historical Dictionary Research, papers from the International Conference on Historical Lexicography and Lexicology, University of Leicester, 2002, Max Niemeyer Verlag.

Steyvers, M., & Tenenbaum, J. B. (2005). The large-scale structure of semantic networks: Statistical analyses and a model of semantic growth. *Cognitive Science, 29*(1), 41–78.

Sun, X., & Zhuge, H. (2018). *Summarization of scientific paper through reinforcement ranking on semantic link network*, IEEE ACCESS.

Sussna, M. (1993). *Word sense disambiguation for free-text indexing using a massive semantic network*. Proceedings of the Second International Conference on Information and Knowledge Management, ACM Press.

Tsatsaronis, G., Vazirgiannis, M., & Androutsopoulos, I. (2007). Word sense disambiguation with spreading activation networks generated from thesauri. In *IJCAI* (Vol. 27, pp. 223–252). AAAI Press/International Joint Conferences on Artificial Intelligence.

Tudhope, D., Alani, H., & Jones, C. (2001). Augmenting thesaurus relationships: Possibilities for retrieval. *Journal of Digital Information, 1*(8), 254484.

Tudhope, D., Binding, C., Blocks, D., & Cunliffe, D. (2006). Query expansion via conceptual distance in thesaurus indexed collections. *Journal of Documentation, 62*(4), 509–533.

Van Atteveldt, W. (2008). *Semantic network analysis: Techniques for extracting, representing, and querying media content*. BookSurge Publishing.

Van de Riet, R. P. (1992). *Linguistic instruments in knowledge engineering*. Elsevier Science Publishers.

Vatant, B. (2004). Ontology-driven topic maps. In *XML Europe* (pp. 18–21). Retrieved May 1, 2020, from http://citeseerx.ist.psu.edu/viewdoc/download?doi=10.1.1.130.2846&rep=rep1&type=pdf.

Wang, Z., Zhang, J., Feng, J., & Chen, Z. (2014). Knowledge graph embedding by translating on hyperplanes. In *Twenty-Eighth AAAI conference on artificial intelligence*. Palo Alto, CA: AAAI.

Warner, A. J. (2002). A taxonomy primer. *Lexonomy*. www.lexonomy.com/publications/aTaxonomyPrimer.html.

Weber, R. & Schek, H.-J. (1998). A quantitative analysis and performance study for similarity-search methods in high-dimensional spaces. In *Proceedings of the 24th VLDB Conference on Very Large Data Bases*, August 24–27, New York City, New York.

Wheeldon, J. (2011). Is a picture worth a thousand words? Using mind maps to facilitate participant recall in qualitative research. *Qualitative Report, 16*(2), 509–522.

Wheeldon, J., & Faubert, J. (2009). Framing experience: Concept maps, mind maps, and data collection in qualitative research. *International Journal of Qualitative Methods, 8*(3), 68–83.

Whiting, M., & Sines, D. (2012). Mind maps: Establishing 'trustworthiness' in qualitative research. *Nurse Researcher, 20*(1), 21–27.

Wickramasinghe, A., Widanapathirana, N., Kuruppu, O., Liyanage, I., & Karunathilake, I. M. K. (2011). Effectiveness of mind maps as a learning tool for medical students. *South East Asian Journal of Medical Education, 5*(1), 2–9.

Willis, C. L., & Miertschin, S. L. (2006). Mind maps as active learning tools. *Journal of Computing Sciences in Colleges, 21*(4), 266–272.

Xu, W., & Gong, Y. (2004). Document clustering by concept factorization. In *Proceedings of the 27th annual international ACM SIGIR conference on Research and development in information retrieval* (pp. 202–209). Association for Computing Machinery.

Yngve, V. H. (1960). A model and an hypothesis for language structure. *Proceedings of the American Philosophical Society, 104*(5), 444–466.

Zezula, P., Amato, G., Dohnal, V., & Batko, M. (2006). *Similarity search – The metric space approach. Advances in database systems* (Vol. 32). Springer.

Zhuge, H. & Zheng, L. (2003). *Ranking semantic-linked network.* Retrieved May 1, 2020, from http://www2003.org/cdrom/papers/poster/p148/P148-Zhuge/P148-Zhuge.html.

Zhuge, H., (2004). *Knowledge grid.* World Scientific Publishing Co.

Zhuge, H., (2009). Communities and emerging semantics in semantic link network: Discovery and learning, *IEEE Transactions on Knowledge and Data Engineering, 21*(6), 785–799.

Zhuge, H., (2011). Semantic linking through spaces for cyber-physical-socio intelligence: A methodology. *Artificial Intelligence, 175*, 988–1019.

Zhuge, H., (2012). *The semantic link network, in the knowledge grid: Toward cyber-physical society.* World Scientific Publishing Co.

Zhuge, H., Zheng, L., Zhang, N. & Li, X. (2004). An automatic semantic relationships discovery approach. *WWW, 2004*, 278–279.

16

FUNCTIONAL ARCHITECTURE FOR KNOWLEDGE ABSTRACTION AND SURROGATION

Chapter summary

This chapter explains the role that abstracting and surrogation plays in making knowledge accessible. The chapter lays out the five activities essential to developing abstracts and surrogates of knowledge assets. The chapter also considers why it is essential to have a good understanding of forms abstracts can take, the different ways we structure abstracts, and the design of abstracts for different formats such as images, audio and visual formats, and text. This chapter also considers why we still develop abstracts. Abstracts enable us to access knowledge in other languages, to access assets we cannot experience directly, to market and promote products and services, and to overcome technical impediments to accessing the full asset. We consider the primary challenge in designing this functional architecture for abstracting. It is raising awareness of the growing importance of abstracts to access in the age of full text, and of learning to see abstracts and summaries in non-traditional information professions.

Why we care about abstracting and surrogation

We care about any surrogate of a knowledge asset because regardless of whether it is a gist or a snapshot or a full structured abstract, surrogates serve an essential access purpose. Surrogates help us to determine the relevance of an asset when we cannot access the asset. We take this purpose for granted today because surrogates are such an essential part of our everyday lives. Consider that surrogates provide a form of asset whenever the asset: (1) is classified and secured and we must request access; (2) is in another language and we need to determine if it is essential to translate it; (3) has no digital version available and proximity to the source is not possible; (4) is costly to acquire and we need to make a special borrowing request; (5) is in fragile condition and cannot be handled for conservation reasons; (6) is a large object and the seeker is in a low bandwidth location and cannot download it; (7) is encoded for an application or packaged for use with a tool the seeker does not have; (8) has a custodian who is not trusted and presents a risk to the seeker; (9) is one of many results and the opportunity costs of opening and reading every result are too high; (10) is being considered for acquisition or purchase and a brief description helps make that decision; or (11) suggests there may be a cultural, political or moral risk to access and a trailer or snippet is needed to assess. In an electronic environment, surrogates are more critical than they have ever been. Sometimes the surrogate is the only thing a seeker will see, and it is the one chance we have of persuading them to access the knowledge asset.

Additionally, consider that what we have traditionally considered 'information objects' or kinds of documents are, in fact, surrogates. A person's profile, their photos, their CVs are, in fact, surrogates or abstracts of that person. We cannot always 'access' the person, but we can use any of these surrogates to decide whether it would be worth our time to contact the person. A company's website or its stock exchange profile is a surrogate for investors. A trailer is a surrogate for a movie. A thumbnail or a painting or a cultural artifact is a surrogate. We cannot all experience a sculpture physically, but we can experience a photograph or a video representing it. We care about surrogates of knowledge assets because they are likely to be more prevalent and more valuable in the future than they have been in the past. Our awareness of their value has been overshadowed by the common presumption that all assets are now and will be digitally accessible. This presumption ignores language, tools and applications, physical conditions, costs, and places in access.

Knowledge abstraction and surrogation – design concepts

To develop this functional architecture, we must have a good understanding of the types of abstracts and the methods we use to produce them. We use surrogates rather than abstracts because abstracts have a strong traditional definition associated with print or text assets. The broader term surrogates allows us to think more broadly and to cover all types and forms of knowledge assets. Surrogates include extracted highlights, summaries, explanations, lists, descriptive abstracts, informative and indicative abstracts; structured and unstructured abstracts; summarization methods for different formats such as images, audio and visual formats, and text; embedded versus linked abstracts; author-generated abstracts; professional abstracting methods; and the full range of goals for abstracting and summarizing, including surrogate access for other language assets, marketing and promotion, and overcoming impediments to full asset access. The primary challenges we face in designing this functional architecture are recognizing the importance and growing need for abstracts in the age of full text, and of learning to see abstracts and summaries in non-traditional information professions.

A surrogate is designated or authorized to act on behalf of another and act as a substitute for something else. Surrogacy can have many purposes. We create a surrogate to provide a partial representation of another asset. A surrogate can be a partial representation of something else, a representation that provides some level of understanding but not a complete understanding. A surrogate can assume some of the other entity's roles – it can be a simulation of the original, such as an expert system that represents some small portion of an expert's knowledge in diagnosing a specific condition. A surrogate might represent an individual's experience of another asset, i.e., a summary of a recital or a performance. All of these are legitimate surrogates. When we think of surrogates in this broader sense, it expands the scope considerably – well beyond what we typically think of as an abstract for a published scientific paper. When we think of surrogates for all five categories of knowledge assets, an interesting knowledge architecture emerges. What is a surrogate for human capital? What is a surrogate for procedural knowledge or cultural knowledge? Is there a surrogate for relational capital assets? As we work through these questions, our traditional thinking around metadata shifts – from the generic definition of data about data to a descriptive surrogate. We see that surrogates are an essential rather than merely a convenience element of knowledge architecture.

The primary purpose of a surrogate is to give the consumer a condensed and objective account of an asset's ideas and features. There are conventions for different kinds of surrogates, but there are no standards. Their length, scope, and coverage are dependent upon the source asset. The best surrogates are valuable because they inform the consumer without demanding more time than necessary to determine whether they should access and consume the asset. Being able to convey the most elements and characteristics of the asset concisely and accurately, without wasting any time or causing misunderstandings, is a characteristic of a good-quality surrogate.

Surrogates can also serve another purpose – the control of access and consumption. Consider when a surrogate takes the form of a deliberate or intentional representation that masks the asset's true nature. In this case, the person or agent creating the surrogate intentionally wants to hide essential parts or elements of the knowledge object. From this perspective, we also understand a surrogate as taking away or removing characteristics of the asset to reduce it to a set of acceptable or non-risky components. Surrogation includes both encapsulation and data hiding.

Additionally, some surrogates may be created to mislead or falsely promote an asset. Consider movie trailers that extract scenes of a movie that are not representative of the quality of the film. Consider photos of an artifact that do not represent the artifact, whether intentional or deliberate. These examples are borderline surrogates and new derivative assets. There has not yet been sufficient discussion around these questions to draw that boundary in this text.

Surrogates are the kinds of knowledge assets that we often find difficult to categorize and manage. A surrogate can have some new elements, but by and large, it's purpose is to serve as a representation of another asset. The most critical characteristic of a surrogate, then, is that there is a source asset. The crucial attribute for any surrogate is a link to the source asset.

Spectrum of surrogates

There is a broad spectrum of surrogates of knowledge assets. We have defined five broad categories of surrogates based on a set of characteristics. They are: (1) summaries and explanations; (2) gists and extractions; (3) derivative surrogates; (4) informative surrogates; and (5) critical surrogates. Surrogates may be structured or unstructured, intended for personal and limited use or public consumption, human- or machine-generated, in the language of the source asset or another language; is created by a subject matter expert, the asset creator, or an information professional; may be embedded in or inherent to the source asset; and may have been created at the same time as the source asset or well after the creation of the source asset.

It is essential to define a framework that supports the full spectrum of surrogates to ensure our functional architecture can support all of them (Figure 16.1). At the low end of the spectrum, we have summaries and explanations. These more primitive forms of surrogates give us a 'sense' of the object's 'aboutness.' At the highest end of the spectrum, we find a well-structured, full representation of the core attributes or elements of the object. Professional abstractors define three types of abstracts at the high end of the scale, including descriptive, informative, and critical. In the middle of the spectrum, we find extracts or gists generated by search engines, programmatically defined machine-generated gists, current awareness blurbs and extraction of sentences, practitioner or professionally written abstracts, author-generated summaries and abstracts, and abstracts written by translators to increase awareness and access.

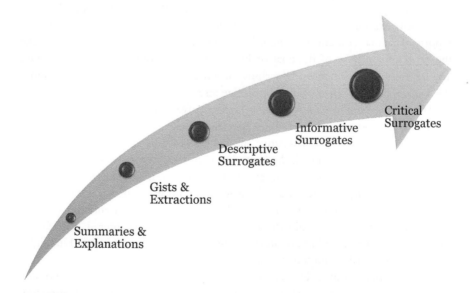

FIGURE 16.1 Types of Surrogates

Summaries, explanations, and highlights

This category of surrogates serves as a memory aid. They may be intended for informal or limited sharing, or as a low-effort, easy way to explain 'aboutness.' This category includes formal and informal summaries, explanations, outlines, synopses, executive summaries, event summaries, or highlights. In the past, we paid little attention to these surrogates because they were considered informal communications or aid that did not rise to the level of formal surrogates. However, in the larger scheme of access and use, these surrogates may be important preliminary ways to share and exchange knowledge.

Summaries are brief statements or accounts of the main points of something. Most summaries are written by non-professionals, in their own words, of another source such as an article, a book chapter, a play, or a whole book. We also develop summaries to represent something the writer heard or an event in which they participated, i.e., a speech, a movie, a play, or a music performance. Summaries provide a general account of the theme, the major points, or purpose (Chuang & Yang, 2000; Kling & McKim, 1999; Mani & Bloedorn, 1998; Nakayama et al., 2005; Neto et al., 2002; Neufeld et al., 1983; Salton et al., 1994; Torres-Moreno, 2014).

Summaries can also be described as informative or descriptive. Informative summaries include outlines and synopses. As informative summaries take on more formality and intention, they may resemble abstracts. Outlines present the plan or the structure of an asset and show the order and relationships of the parts. A *synopsis* is a brief overview of an article, story, book, film, or other works. A synopsis is a concise, chronological description of a historical event, news event, historical event, or other experiences as they develop in time. We expect an informative summary to be objective in presenting the ideas in the asset. We typically write informative summaries for scientific, non-fictional works or to present objective reports of factual content. On the other hand, descriptive summaries might take the form of a review of fictional or literary works: books, movies, video clips, articles, essays, performances. Descriptive summaries can include statements about the sense and significance of the knowledge asset.

An executive summary is a high-level informative summary. An executive summary is what most executives read or experience, representing what they take away from the knowledge asset. Executive summaries describe the project or event, a course of action, or a proposal. We write an executive summary because we expect the executive will not have time to experience and take in the full asset.

We design a highlight to attract the reader's attention to the study or the asset. A highlight is not intended to present either a complete or an entirely objective assessment of the source. Highlights may be written to attract interest. A highlight may serve as a surrogate but not an altogether honest or objective one. Highlights are generally informal and unverified.

Event summaries provide surrogate access to an event, or they may serve as a memory aid. One kind of event summary is a clinical summary – an after-visit summary that provides a patient with relevant and actionable information and instructions. These summaries reference the patient's name, provider's office contact information, date and location of the visit, an updated medication list, updated vitals, reason(s) for the visit, procedures, and other instructions based on clinical discussions that took place during the office visit. A clinical summary also includes updates to a problem list, immunizations, or medications administered during the visit, and a summary of topics covered during the visit. These summaries are often written for the physician's benefit but not always made available to the patient. They serve as a record or surrogate of the event and the conversations. Police notes of conversations with witnesses and accident parties are also a kind of event summary. They do not constitute a formal report or document but are important surrogates or records of the knowledge exchange with law enforcement.

Gists and extractions

A gist or extraction is a literal representation of an object. The word 'gisting' has been used in a variety of settings. Informally, it simply means 'getting the gist,' that is, given some information conveyed by natural language, understanding some characteristics or essential aspects of that information. Gisting is an activity in which the information taken into account is less than the full information content available. There is no subjective interpretation of the source asset. There are several ways we can create a gist, though. We differentiate gists by the level of intelligence we use to do the extraction (Maksymowicz, 1990; Marchionini et al., 2009; Resnik, 1997; Rohlicek, 1993; Rubino et al., 2013; Stokes et al., 2004).

The simplest form of gist or extraction is identifying a chunk of an asset to use as a surrogate. A surrogate might include a photograph of an individual, a shot from a moving image, a fragment of text from a paper, a snapshot of a process, or an artifact from a culture. We simply identify the type of chunk and take the chunk. We may define the fragment by the number of characters, the number of shots, the number of snapshots, or the number of artifacts. No further intelligence or meaning is associated with the 'chunk.'

A slightly smarter gist or extraction is produced based on a parameter, i.e., the text around a keyword or concept, a moving image shot of a kind of action, or an extract of a recording for the use of a verb or verb phrase.

An example of intelligent gisting today is where we select an asset's elements and combine or correlate them with elements from another asset. Today we refer to this kind of gisting as conversational and data gisting. Consider the emerging practice in air traffic control of automatic, real-time gisting of voice traffic for updating information in databases, in report production, and event notification. The intelligence identifies flights referenced and determines whether they are landings or takeoffs, departures, arrivals, etc. The goal of this form of gisting is to create a system where we can process the radio communication of air traffic controllers and pilots to generate a continuous stream of information. Intelligence combines a variety of speaker-identification techniques, speech recognition, natural-language processing, and artificial intelligence. Additionally, this type of gisting can be applied to large databases of air traffic and radio conversations where the controllers and operators need to decide whether to route information to electronic warfare analysts (Elsaesser, 1995). This type of continuous speech recognition and gisting has benefits for air traffic control, specifically for automated target tagging, aircraft compliance monitoring, controller training, automatic alarm disabling, and display.

Abstracted surrogates

An abstracted surrogate is different from the gist and is more like a summary because it has new value-added. It is not just an excerpted or extracted portion of the source asset (Bayley & Eldredge, 2003; Beck & Manuel, 2008; Booth & O'Rourke, 1997; Borko & Bernier, 1971; Brown & Faibisoff, 1977; Cleveland & Cleveland, 1983; Collison, 1971; Falagas & Vergidis, 2004; Fontelo et al., 2013; Hartley, 2004; Hartley & Sydes, 1997; Hartley et al., 1996; Haynes et al., 1990; Hernon & Schwartz, 2008; Kulkarni, 1996; Lancaster, 1991; Ripple et al., 2011, 2012, 2020; Rowley, 1988; Sharma & Harrison, 2006; Sollaci & Pereira, 2004; Stevenson & Harrison, 2009; Wong, 2005). While we do not have formal standards for abstracted surrogates, there are conventions and common practices. There are conventions for structure, including (1) the overall purpose of the asset and the intent, (2) the basic design of the asset, and (3) conclusions or outcomes. There are different kinds of gists and summaries; there are different types of abstracted surrogates – descriptive, indicator or informative, and critical. We differentiate these types based on the extent and nature of the value-added in the surrogate. We need an interpretation of these kinds of surrogates for all of our knowledge assets.

Descriptive surrogates

A descriptive surrogate 'describes' the type of information found in work. It is sometimes called an indicative surrogate because it merely indicates 'aboutness.' It makes no judgments about the work. It does incorporate key concepts expressed in the asset and may include the purpose, methods, and scope of the research. Mainly, the descriptive abstract describes only the work summarized. Some researchers consider it an outline of the work, rather than a summary. Descriptive abstracts are usually concise – 100 words or less. A descriptive abstract indicates the type of information found in work. As in a descriptive summary, a descriptive surrogate makes no judgments about the work and does not address the source's results or conclusions. A descriptive abstract references critical concepts from the source asset and may describe the purpose, methods, and scope of the work.

A descriptive surrogate summarizes the significant aspects of the source asset. What constitutes a description varies with the type of asset and the discipline or context. An abstract of social science or scientific work may contain the scope, purpose, results, and contents of the work. An abstract of a humanities work may contain the thesis, background, and conclusion of the larger work. A descriptive surrogate is not a review, nor does it evaluate the work being abstracted.

In some contexts, the abstract is a new knowledge asset as well as a surrogate. As we move up the spectrum, the form of the surrogate may differ from the form of the asset. We might have a text abstract of a scientific text paper, or a text abstract of a moving image, or an audio abstract of a scientific paper. As we expand our vision of descriptive surrogates, we see that creating a surrogate involves creating added value and, in some cases, a new creative effort. Consider the role that movie trailers, thumbnail images, photosculptures, and photo artifacts play as descriptive surrogates.

One of the most common forms of descriptive abstracts we encounter every day is a movie trailer. A trailer is a preview or commercial advertisement for a film that will be released in the future. Trailers describe the film in a way that incentivizes the viewer to attend the film or purchase a copy. As descriptive surrogates, trailers consist of a series of selected shots from the film. The excerpts often are drawn from the most exciting, funny, or otherwise noteworthy parts. The scenes are not necessarily in the order in which they appear in the film. Most of the time, the trailers include footage of the film, but they can also add footage that is not in the full version. We categorized trailers as descriptive surrogates rather than as extracts or excerpts because there is some degree of creative or artistic effort involved. Most trailers include only footage from the film, but others include additional footage and are more than simple excerpts. These trailers are designed to create a different impression from what we might gain if we saw the whole film.

There are some historical instances of trailers that were a misleading or false surrogate of the source. They may be false or 'not entirely true' surrogates in that they created the impression that a celebrity who had only a minor role as a main cast member or suggesting the film was more action-filled than it actually was.

Trailers may include elements of the source asset, but they are distinct assets released at a different time. A trailer has approximately two minutes to achieve this purpose. The two-minute guidelines were issued in 2014 by the National Association of Theatre Owners. The guideline is not mandatory and allows for limited exceptions. They are intended to be distributed before the release or publication of the source. Movie trailers are a popular form of a surrogate, highly viewed and consumed around the world. In addition to movies and films, they are descriptive surrogates for television shows, video games, books, and theatrical events and concerts.

Thumbnails are another kind of descriptive surrogate. We've chosen to categorize them as a descriptive surrogate rather than as a summary or a gist because new value was added to the source asset in creating the surrogate. Thumbnails are reduced-size versions of pictures or videos, designed to help us better understand, recognize, and organize them. They serve the same role as a descriptive abstract of a paper or book. Just like targeted text extracts might be used to boost a search index, so might thumbnails support visual search. These descriptive surrogates also serve one of those crucial goals of providing a sense without having to download the full asset. They are also essential surrogates when there is only one copy of the visual asset, and it is under protection or conservation status. Also, consider the informative images we create to describe art or image collections. To generate this surrogate, we select a representative set of images from a larger set of images. Another form of descriptive surrogates of physical objects is photosculptures, or photographs of physical artifacts. This type of descriptive abstracting often involves taking multiple photographs or representations from different points of view. These surrogates describe an asset that requires artistic and creative interpretation to produce.

Informative surrogates

Descriptive or indicative surrogates tell us just the basics – without interpretation. Informative surrogates explain more about the source asset and do more than describe it. A good informative surrogate can substitute for the source asset itself. An informative surrogate presents and explains the main arguments, important results, and supporting evidence of the source asset. An informative surrogate includes the information that can be found in a descriptive surrogate but goes further to describe the asset's results and impacts. An informative asset's length and extent vary according to the context, but an informative abstract is usually around 10% of the full asset.

Because of their extended nature, informative surrogates tend to have additional structure. Consider the extended informative surrogates written for health professionals who need sufficient information to choose between alternative therapies. They need to know more about the therapy than just mere descriptions. They have limited time and must manage risks. They need to know enough about the project or procedural knowledge to see whether it is a good fit for their clinical patients and what risks they might encounter if they adopted the therapy.

Informative abstracts written for scientific communications are commonly structured. The use of structured abstracts ensures that better information is supplied and that what is communicated is predictable and consistent across sources. A structured informative surrogate contains several elements, including purpose, design, data collection, methodology, analysis findings and conclusions, recommendations, value, and implications.

Critical surrogates

Our goal is to provide a representation of the source asset in the case of descriptive and informative surrogates. The representation may include some value-added structures and creative activity to design and create the surrogate. The intention, though, is not to evaluate or to critique the source asset. A critical surrogate, on the other hand, takes this next step. From an architecture perspective, this presents a challenge. An important surrogate has many of the same design requirements as summaries, gists, and descriptive and informative surrogates. The most compelling of these is the need to link to or reference the source asset. A critical surrogate cannot exist without the source asset. There is a critical process point where the critique may become more of a critical thinking exercise than a critique of a distinct asset. When we cross that line, we must think of the critical surrogate as a new asset that may build upon another asset, but not one whose purpose is to provide a critique of the source. In the latter case, we are designing a functional architecture to support the use and consumption of knowledge assets in general.

A critical surrogate has all of the elements of an informative surrogate but adds a critical opinion from the writer (Basuroy et al., 2003; Dixon-Woods et al., 2006; Grant & Booth, 2009; Kling et al., 2003; Langston, 1996; Odlyzko, 2002; Silberhorn et al., 1990; Sompel et al., 2004; Yeung, 1994). In most cases, the writer of this surrogate is an expert on the source asset's topic. Consider the reviews of mathematical research and publications published by the American Mathematical Society's *Mathematical Reviews* service. These reviews are designed to serve researchers and scholars in the mathematical sciences by providing timely information on articles, books, and other published material that contain new contributions to mathematical research. This service critically reviews articles and books in other disciplines that include new mathematical results or give a novel and interesting applications of known mathematics. These reviews are written by experts selected by the editors of *Mathematical Reviews*. Reviews leverage the author's written descriptive or informative abstracts wherever they are available. The reviews are critical evaluations of the published research and closely resemble a peer review, with full references and citations from the reviewer.

Surrogation processes

A surrogate is an accurate representation of a knowledge asset. Surrogates may be created by the individual or agent that created the asset, by another expert who is familiar with that kind of asset, or by an information or knowledge professional. There is a slight variation to the process, depending on who is creating the surrogate. Our knowledge architecture should support all three approaches. The process of creating the surrogate also means having access to the source asset. For physical assets or assets which are secured or protected for conservation reasons, this means being in proximity to the asset and having the

When the abstractor *knows the knowledge asset*, they follow a reverse engineering process. The challenge is that the creator knows the asset so well, it can be difficult for them to select the key elements. They may skim through the source asset and extract features to include in the surrogate. The creator may be creating a surrogate for a particular audience or consumer. It works well, but creators tend to overlook essential elements that may be of interest to other stakeholders. If the source asset is an audio, visual, or a physical artifact, additional expertise and skills are required to create the surrogate.

Subject matter experts who are familiar with the topic or subject but not the asset take a slightly different approach. They begin by reviewing the source asset, looking for key concepts, ideas, and events. We look to the asset structure to find those key elements – the opening or introduction, the purpose or central theme, the conclusion, or the outcome. It helps to extract or excerpt parts and then go back and recompose or rewrite the surrogate.

Information or knowledge professionals may or may not be familiar with the subject or context. They take a similar but more analytical approach. They consider why the asset was created, its purpose, and the challenge or problem it addresses. They consider the scope of the asset and the main point or argument the creator is trying to make, and they explain how it fits into the broader knowledge landscape. Depending on the nature of the asset, they may also describe the methods or techniques used to produce the asset. Depending on whether the goal is a descriptive or informative surrogate, they may also describe the implications and outcomes.

In addition to human surrogation processes, few semantic applications allow us to imitate the human abstractor's thought process to generate a descriptive surrogate. These surrogates are not as good as what a human creates, but they can be an affordable alternative when we need surrogates but do not have unlimited support for a human process. Consider that, on average, a human-produced surrogate will take a minimum of 45 minutes to create. Given simple labor constraints, in an eight-hour workday, a human could create nine abstracts. This approach is limited to only the most valuable knowledge assets. The semantic applications require time and effort to develop – they are not out-of-the-box, off-the-shelf applications. They come with morphological and dictionary components, but each organization must define the set of rules for identifying the extracts or excerpts the program will select. The rules include (1) identifying parts of the asset to target; (2) key phrases or terms to highlight; (3) number of excerpts to select; and (4) the order in which to place the excerpts. There are several challenges with these applications, the primary being the inability of the application to provide referential integrity. It means that the internal references that a human can interpret are missing from a machine-generated surrogate.

In general, the surrogation process is resource and labor-intensive. Publishers tend to ask authors to write abstracts that they then repurpose. Media companies have specialized marketing roles that create promotional materials (Baltes, 2015; Chaffey & Chadwick, 2019; Kannan, 2017; Parsons et al., 1998; Taiminen & Karjaluoto, 2015; Wind & Mahajan, 2002). Search engines develop algorithms that generate gists. And, individuals create summaries and outlines because they have personal value. In the future, we expect to see smarter and more efficient processes to create surrogates. We expect that efficiency gains will come as side effects and collateral effects from creative and innovative applications of open-source artificial intelligence tools.

Surrogates for human capital assets

Human capital is inherent to an individual, so any representation we create for their tacit knowledge, skills and competencies, attitudes, and personality is a surrogate. It is vital to ensure we have a rich stock of surrogates for every individual because it helps us better to understand the nature of their current and potential value. It is essential to guard and respect their privacy. Knowing an individual's competencies, interests, and ways of working can help us decide when to reach out to them, when to include them on a team, and how to invest in them further.

Surrogates for explicit knowledge assets

Explicit knowledge is any physical representation of knowledge. It can take the form of a book, journals, photos, audio, images, graphics, and video. It can be digital or physical. Surrogates for these kinds of assets are in everyday use today. Many of the examples we provided in this chapter focus on explicit knowledge. It is important to increase our awareness of and respect for the rich stock of surrogates for explicit knowledge assets. It is also important to improve our understanding of what we have learned about creating surrogates.

Surrogates for procedural knowledge assets

A surrogate of procedural knowledge is any summary or short representation of the knowledge of people who perform a process or do it in a line of work. It can take many forms. Perhaps the way to distinguish surrogates from other tangible representations is to understand why the representation was created. Was it created to discover who is currently using the process? Was it created to understand better the process to perform it, to join the team, to conduct a quality review, to award a patent, or to look for process improvements? All of these are important reasons for creating a surrogate because they contribute business value to the organization.

Surrogates for cultural knowledge assets

Surrogates for cultural knowledge are similar in purpose and challenges to procedural knowledge. Culture is practiced – it is inherent in our behaviors and values. Any explicit representation of an organization, unit, or team culture may be considered a surrogate. Why is it essential to have a surrogate of cultural knowledge? A surrogate can help us to 'see' our culture. We live our culture every day – it is often difficult for us to recognize our culture. Having a surrogate can increase our awareness and better understand our culture. It can also help others outside of that culture to better understand how to work with us effectively – to understand how we work, our work values and behaviors, and our assumptions and beliefs. While we may have a single espoused organizational culture, our unit, and team cultures are variations of that espoused culture (Bedford & Kucharska, 2020).

Surrogates for network knowledge assets

Surrogates of relational and network knowledge include any summary description that tells us what we need to know about a community or a network. It might include the group's members, the group's focus, the group's activities, its age and life cycle stage, whether it is still active, and whether it is open to others to join or a closed network. Discovery of networks is essential in the knowledge economy because it is within these spaces that we see the greatest density of knowledge exchange and use. Knowing what communities exist internal to an organization is essential to ensuring that knowledge is accessible to other areas of the business and is leveraged to the greatest extent.

Knowledge abstraction and surrogation – the design environment

What factors do we need to consider in designing this architecture? There are several factors to consider, including the organization's capacity for human abstracting, its capacity for machine abstracting, its need for multilingual access to information and knowledge, and its search and content management architectures.

What events cause us to design a functional architecture for semantics? The primary trigger for any organization is simple information and knowledge overload. In most organizations, individuals are trying to solve the overload problem themselves. They are creating their outlines and summaries, setting up their current awareness profiles, writing their executive summaries, and producing surrogates for their websites. It is a highly redundant, costly, and inefficient approach for an organization. The primary trigger events will be redundant technologies, redundant development work, and redundant staff time to generate surrogates. Additionally, these redundant efforts will tend to produce suboptimal outputs and results. In essence, the trigger event is an accumulation of poor business decisions and investments.

What are the impacts and consequences of having this functional architecture? The impacts include broader access to resources inside the organization, broader access to assets outside the organization, increased ease of access to selection information, and increased multilingual access.

What inputs do we need to consider when designing this functional architecture? There are several inputs for designing this functional architecture. These include the inventory of internal knowledge assets, all formats of knowledge assets, and knowledge assets made available to external stakeholders – in essence, any knowledge object that may need to have a surrogate to support access and use. Also essential is an understanding of both the internal and external demand for the organization's knowledge assets.

What are the outputs and outcomes this functional architecture generates? The simple answer is surrogates for any knowledge asset the organization produces. These surrogates may be in a language, format, or structure other than the source asset.

Design activities and tasks for knowledge abstracting and surrogation

Five activities are supported, including:

- Activity 1. Define the purpose of a goal of the surrogate
- Activity 2. Identify the environment that will host or manage the surrogate

- Activity 3. Define the type and structure of the abstract
- Activity 4. Define the abstracting process and rules
- Activity 5. Produce the abstract or summary

Activity 1. Define the purpose and goal of the surrogate

How do we do this? An essential first step is understanding the audience, why they need a surrogate, and how they will use them. Think both internal to the organization and outside the organization. Do you have one internal audience, or many different audiences? Do executives and managers need a different kind of surrogate than the frontline staff? Is the source asset sensitive or fragile? Is there a need for a partial view of the asset for external audiences? Is an extended metadata record a sufficient external surrogate, or is more information needed? Does the external audience need a visual as well as a textual surrogate? Or, an audio surrogate? Is there a need for other language surrogates?

What inputs does this activity need? The two primary inputs for this activity are the knowledge of the internal and external audiences and the surrogate nature.

What outputs does this activity generate? Historically, organizations have created surrogates to support internal knowledge and information management practices. We had created surrogates if and when the metadata practices called for an abstract, if the search system required an extended gist for indexing purposes, or if document or web content templates had a required field for summary or abstract. But, outside of publishing units, publishing industries, and marketing industries, we have not included it as a distinct process or a dedicated information management process. Organizations can be more deliberate in developing surrogates where a supportive, functional architecture is in place. The primary output for this activity is a description of current and future demands for surrogates, their formats, and their expected distribution channels.

What other resources does the activity require? This activity leverages the knowledge of information and knowledge professionals, but also communications and marketing professionals. Internal and external communications teams are likely to be the source of most surrogates in your organization. It is a core task to identify the audience, determine what they want and need to know or access, and how. Your marketing teams also have a good understanding of how to develop and support a marketing plan.

Activity 2. Identify the environment that will host or manage the surrogate

How do we do this? This activity is challenging because the practices are likely to be varied and fragmented. You may be targeting an enterprise functional architecture to support the creation of surrogates, but surrogates will live in different places and be consumed through multiple channels.

What inputs does this activity need? The plan from Activity 1 is a good starting point for this activity. For each target audience, we can identify the most likely environment for the surrogate. Will the surrogate be embedded in the asset? Or, is it intended to be a distinct asset? Where will the surrogate be housed or stored? Is the surrogate embedded in the source asset? How will the surrogate be distributed? When will the surrogate be distributed? What is the life span of the surrogate? Is it intended to be short-lived, or to have long-term value? The answers to these questions help us to understand the design environment. It may take time for the full environment to emerge. Perhaps the best vantage point for answering these questions is to focus on the source attribute and consider the demand for surrogates. Because surrogates are labor-intensive and costly to produce, it is essential to design 'smart' – to meet the demand but not to overproduce. It is also important to consider potential partnerships. Are there external stakeholders who want their surrogates of your knowledge assets? If they are willing to produce them, how can you access and leverage them? In the long term, these other surrogates become part of the semantic network for a knowledge asset. They become part of the knowledge derived and interpreted from the source asset.

What outputs does this activity generate? This activity generates additional detail for the plan prepared in Activity 1. At this point in the process, we have the beginning of a surrogate strategy – we know what types of assets are associated with what kinds of surrogates, their formats, how and where they will be stored, and how they will be distributed. We also have a sense of the estimated useful business life of a surrogate, which helps us to understand the long-term disposition and preservation strategies.

What other resources does the activity require? This activity relies primarily on the knowledge of information and knowledge management professionals, their understanding of the application architecture within the organization, and their knowledge of the broader information industry that produces surrogates in the same business sector.

Activity 3. Define the type and structure of the abstract

How do we do this? This activity focuses on designing the surrogate(s) for the range of knowledge assets. What kinds of surrogates are needed? Is there a convention in the business sector for surrogates? Do we need only informal summaries? Will gists suffice? Can we rely on machine-generated gists? Do we need descriptive and informative surrogates? Do we need to consider critical surrogates?

What inputs does this activity need? The knowledge of demand from Activity 1 and the knowledge of source and storage architectures are essential inputs. The primary input, though, is knowledge of the surrogation methods and practices – for different formats, structures, and fields.

What outputs does this activity generate? This activity should produce internal best practices or standards for different types and formats of surrogates. These should align with the types of knowledge assets the organization generates. Internal best practices should address both internal and external demands.

What other resources does the activity require? This activity draws upon well-established practices and structures for surrogates, but it also looks to the future and considers emerging trends for semantic and intelligent surrogates.

Activity 4. Define the abstracting process and rules

How do we do this? This activity focuses on developing the processes and the capacity to produce surrogates. This activity shifts our focus from filling in a field in a metadata record, a web content template, or a document template to providing distinct surrogates that may be embedded in or linked to the source attribute itself. We shift the process from creating a surrogate embedded in another surrogate to a new knowledge asset.

What inputs does this activity need? At this point, we have a sense of the demand, an understanding of the storage and application requirements, and a set of best practices for the types of surrogates we need. At this point, we are developing a new process, a new set of competencies, and a new resource budget. We may also be leveraging existing competencies but expanding their scope and scale. This activity involves continually surveilling the market for surrogation practices, particularly those that use innovative approaches, semantic methods, and artificial intelligence.

What outputs does this activity generate? This activity produces actual procedural knowledge for surrogation, new or expanded business operations, and budgets to ensure we can implement the guidelines and practices.

What other resources does the activity require? This activity involves the input of managers and decision-makers. We need to determine who or what will create the surrogates, what tools are necessary, any arrangements or accommodations to provide access to the source asset, investment decisions for developing or acquiring application software, and the commitment to develop and sustain the competences.

Activity 5. Produce the abstract or summary

How do we do this? This final activity involves the actual production and distribution of the surrogate. With this final action, we have established the capability to generate surrogates. This activity may also include making the surrogate available to consuming applications such as search engines or broadcasting organizations.

What inputs does this activity need? The primary challenge is finding the level of knowledge and competence within the organization to support these processes. The probability is high that these competencies do not exist, that they will have to be developed or procured externally. The primary input will likely be resources – financial and personnel – to support the process. A semantic application may also be essential, depending on whether the focus is on human or machine-generated surrogates.

What outputs does this activity generate? The answer to this question is simple – this activity produces the finished surrogates.

What other resources does the activity require? The primary resources supporting this activity are the competences and the efforts of the architects, designers, and information professionals who produce the surrogates.

Evolution of knowledge abstracting and surrogation

Experience and a review of the literature suggest there are five phases in the evolution of knowledge surrogation, including:

- Phase 1. Direct promotion and communication of knowledge
- Phase 2. Expansion of knowledge consumption and distribution
- Phase 3. Global growth of scholarly community and communications
- Phase 4. Knowledge time to markets
- Phase 5. Machine-generated surrogates and machine-generated new knowledge from recombinant assets

These five phases are influenced by the development of scholarly and scientific knowledge, an increasingly literate population, growing scientific and scholarly communities, a shift first to a global information economy and finally to a global competition for knowledge and reduced time to market of fundamental research (Figure 16.2).

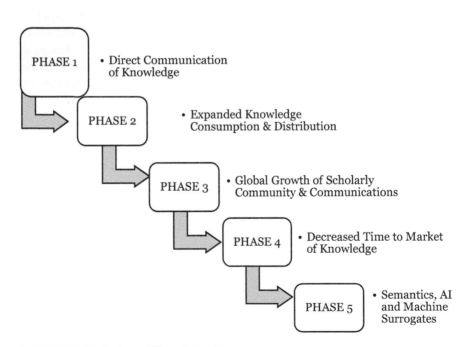

FIGURE 16.2 Evolution of Knowledge Surrogates

Phase 1. Direct promotion and communication of knowledge

In the earliest phase, there was a small demand for knowledge, and any demand could be satisfied directly. Little new knowledge was created beyond what was needed to survive, and there was low demand for creating explicit forms of knowledge to be shared broadly within or outside the community. Much of the early knowledge was shared through stories because literacy rates were low.

Phase 2. Expansion of knowledge consumption and distribution

With increased exploration came an expanded production of knowledge. Exploration expanded communication and contact, and the reach of knowledge sharing and exchange grew. The most primitive forms of scholarship emerged. Abstracts and surrogates emerged as a way to communicate the essentials of research and scholarship. These early abstracts may have taken the form of letters or scientific communications. The increasing rates of literacy and the increased interest in learning created a demand for scholarly works. In the early phases, a practice of compiling books of abstracts and summaries emerged. These surrogates provided access to knowledge where the source assets or the scholars were physically limited. Books of abstracts served the purpose of making the knowledge remotely accessible.

Phase 3. Global growth of scholarly community and communications

The global explosion of scholarship and scientific development created new demand for abstracts and surrogates. Disciplines developed, and specializations grew. A need arose to have more concise access to developments within broader fields. Access to new knowledge became time-sensitive. Scholars needed access to more precise descriptions of scholarship and developments, and they needed it more quickly. The tolerance for time delays in publication declined, particularly in fields like physics, chemistry, and engineering. At this same time, the scholarly community expanded globally, and communication was now in six or seven major languages. Access to knowledge in other languages was now essential.

Additionally, world conflicts increased the demand for information that may be classified for national security or foreign intelligence purposes. Surrogates served an essential role in providing enough access to make an acquisition request. These international conflicts also introduced shortages in print supplies. With the technological advances of later wars, the production and distribution of abstracts moved from print to electronic form. This phase saw the rapid expansion and distribution of scientific abstracts and the earliest conventions for the structure of abstracts. The rapid rise of scholarly journals and scholarly publications further incentivized the production and distribution of abstracts.

About this same time, the rise of consumerism and the entertainment industry created new demands for promotional materials. These promotional materials took the form of abstracts and descriptions. These promotional materials exploited new distribution channels.

Phase 4. Knowledge time to market

In the later decades of the 20th century, there was an explosion of knowledge and technologies. It became difficult for scholars to keep pace with developments in their field. As we shifted from an industrial to an information economy, the value of information increased dramatically. Increased costs of access to scholarly and scientific work made direct personal purchases improbable. This phase saw the emergence of publishers' abstracting and indexing services as initial points of access to their journals and publications. It was also the age of information brokers. There was increased funding for research and scholarship, and publishing requirements increased. Academic tenure became further dependent upon publishing. During this time, the emergency of the Web and full-text access appeared to diminish the need for human-generated abstracts. While full text alleviated one access challenge, it did not address the overload challenge. The ability to self-publish increased the overload challenge. During this phase, critical reviews gained popularity and became an essential element of the scientific communication system.

Phase 5. Machine-generated surrogates and machine-generated new knowledge from recombinant assets

In the early years of the 21st century, increased technology capacity, the advancement of semantic technologies, and artificial intelligence agents provided an environment conducive to machine-generated surrogates. New web search engines produced too many results for seekers to review – new forms of gists and extractions emerge. The entertainment industry and commercial promotion of new products generated the need to develop and repurpose surrogates for different markets. The number and type of marketing and distribution channels were exposed. New formats and multimedia production tools emerged. Surrogates are now multiformat and recombinant. Anyone with access to open-source artificial intelligence tools could now develop surrogates. Finally, the growing shift in research from theoretical to applied, and from academic to community-based problem-solving created a need for surrogates for general consumers and non-academic investors.

Knowledge abstraction and surrogation in the enterprise architecture blueprint

Abstracting and surrogation architecture most closely aligns with information architecture practices. There is some affiliation and synergy with business architecture because the surrogates are designed to support efficient access of business stakeholders to knowledge assets.

Chapter review

After reading this chapter, you should be able to:

- define abstracts and surrogates;
- explain abstracting and surrogation methods and processes;
- explain how abstracts and surrogates relate to knowledge assets;
- describe the spectrum of types of surrogates;
- describe the goal and purpose of surrogates in knowledge accessibility.

References and recommended future readings

Baltes, L. P. (2015). Content marketing – the fundamental tool of digital marketing. *Bulletin of the Transilvania University of Brasov. Economic Sciences. Series V, 8*(2), 111.

Basuroy, S., Chatterjee, S., & Ravid, S. A. (2003). How critical are critical reviews? The box office effects of film critics, star power, and budgets. *Journal of marketing, 67*(4), 103–117.

Bayley, L., & Eldredge, J. (2003). The structured abstract: An essential tool for researchers. *Hypothesis, 17*(1), 11–13.

Beck, S. E., & Manuel, K. (2008). *Practical research methods for librarians and information professionals.* Neal-Schuman.

Bedford, D. A., & Kucharska, W. (Eds.). (2020). *Relating information culture to information policies and management strategies.* IGI Global.

Booth, A., & O'Rourke, A. J. (1997). The value of structured abstracts in information retrieval from MEDLINE. *Health Libraries Review, 14*(3), 157–166.

Borko, H., & Bernier, C. L. (1971). *Abstracting concepts and methods.* Academic Press.

Brown, P. P., & Faibisoff, S. (1977). *Abstracts and abstracting services: A manual for students.* University of Arizona Graduate Library School.

Chaffey, D., & Ellis-Chadwick, F. (2019). *Digital marketing.* Pearson.

Chuang, W. T., & Yang, J. (2000). Extracting sentence segments for text summarization: A machine learning approach. In *Proceedings of the 23rd annual international ACM SIGIR conference on Research and development in information retrieval* (pp. 152–159). Retrieved from https://doi.org/10.1145/345508.345566

Cleveland, D. B., & Cleveland, A. D. (1983). *Introduction to indexing and abstracting.* Libraries Unlimited.

Collison, R. L. (1971). *Abstracts and abstracting services.* ABC-Clio.

Dixon-Woods, M., Bonas, S., Booth, A., Jones, D. R., Miller, T., Sutton, A. J., & Young, B. (2006). How can systematic reviews incorporate qualitative research? A critical perspective. *Qualitative Research, 6*(1), 27–44.

Elsaesser, D. S. (1995, December). *Data fusion and correlation techniques testbed (FACT): A command and control information system for land electronic warfare,* Defence Research Establishment Ottawa, Ottawa, Canada.

Falagas, M. E., & Vergidis, P. I. (2004). Addressing the limitations of structured abstracts. *Annals of Internal Medicine, 141*(7), 576–567.

Fontelo, P., Gavino, A., & Sarmiento, R. F. (2013). Comparing data accuracy between structured abstracts and full-text journal articles: Implications in their use for informing clinical decisions. *BMJ Evidence-Based Medicine, 18*(6), 207–211.

Grant, M. J., & Booth, A. (2009). A typology of reviews: An analysis of 14 review types and associated methodologies. *Health Information & Libraries Journal, 26*(2), 91–108.

Hartley, J. (2004). Current findings from research on structured abstracts. *Journal of the Medical Library Association, 92*(3), 368.

Hartley, J., & Sydes, M. (1997). Are structured abstracts easier to read than traditional ones? *Journal of Research in Reading, 20*(2), 122–136.

Hartley, J., Sydes, M., & Blurton, A. (1996). Obtaining information accurately and quickly: Are structured abstracts more efficient? *Journal of Information Science, 22*(5), 349–356.

Haynes, R. B., Mulrow, C. D., Huth, E. J., Altman, D. G., & Gardner, M. J. (1990). More informative abstracts revisited. *Annals of Internal Medicine, 113*(1), 69–76.

Hernon, P., & Schwartz, C. (2008). Leadership: Developing a research agenda for academic libraries. *Library & Information Science Research, 30*(4), 243–249.

Kannan, P. K. (2017). Digital marketing: A framework, review and research agenda. *International Journal of Research in Marketing, 34*(1), 22–45.

Kling, R., & McKim, G. (1999). Scholarly communication and the continuum of electronic publishing. *Journal of the American Society for Information Science, 50*(10), 890–906.

Kling, R., McKim, G., & King, A. (2003). A bit more to it: Scholarly communication forums as socio-technical interaction networks. *Journal of the American Society for Information Science and Technology, 54*(1), 47–67.

Kulkarni, H. (1996). Structured abstracts: Still more. *Annals of Internal Medicine, 124*(7), 695–696.

Lancaster, F. W. (1991). *Indexing and abstracting in theory and practice*. University of Illinois, Graduate School of Library and Information Science.

Langston, L. (1996). *Scholarly communication and electronic publication: Implications for research, advancement, and promotion*.

Maksymowicz, A. T. (1990). Automated gisting systems for voice communications. In *IEEE Conference on Aerospace Applications* (pp. 103–115). IEEE.

Mani, I., & Bloedorn, E. (1998). Machine learning of generic and user-focused summarization. In *AAAI/IAAI* (pp. 821–826). New York, NY: AAAI/IAAI.

Marchionini, G., Song, Y., & Farrell, R. (2009). Multimedia surrogates for video gisting: Toward combining spoken words and imagery. *Information Processing & Management, 45*(6), 615–630.

Nakayama, T., Hirai, N., Yamazaki, S., & Naito, M. (2005). Adoption of structured abstracts by general medical journals and format for a structured abstract. *Journal of the Medical Library Association, 93*(2), 237.

Neto, J. L., Freitas, A. A., & Kaestner, C. A. (2002). Automatic text summarization using a machine learning approach. In *Brazilian symposium on artificial intelligence* (pp. 205–215). Springer.

Neufeld, M. L., Cornog, M., & Sperr, I. L. (1983). *Abstracting and indexing services in perspective*. Information Resources Press.

Odlyzko, A. (2002). The rapid evolution of scholarly communication. *Learned Publishing, 15*(1), 7–19.

Parsons, A., Zeisser, M., & Waitman, R. (1998). Organizing today for the digital marketing of tomorrow. *Journal of Interactive Marketing, 12*(1), 31–46.

Resnik, P. (1997). *Evaluating multilingual gisting of web pages*. Laboratory for Language and Media Processing, Institute for Advanced Computer Studies, University of Maryland [at College Park].

Ripple, A. M., Mork, J. G., Knecht, L. S., & Humphreys, B. L. (2011). A retrospective cohort study of structured abstracts in MEDLINE, 1992–2006. *Journal of the Medical Library Association: JMLA, 99*(2), 160.

Ripple, A. M., Mork, J. G., Rozier, J. M., & Knecht, L. S. (2012). *Structured abstracts in MEDLINE: Twenty-five years later*. National Library of Medicine. Retrieved February 2,

2020 from https://structuredabstracts.nlm.nih.gov/Structured_Abstracts_in_MEDLINE_Twenty-Years_Later.pdf

Ripple, A. M., Mork, J. G., Thompson, H. J., Schmidt, S. C., & Knecht, L. S. (2020). *Performance comparison of MEDLINE structured abstracts to unstructured abstracts.* Poster session presented at National Institutes of Health Research Festival, 2014 September 22–24. Retrieved February 2, 2020 from https://researchfestival.nih.gov/festival14/poster-RSCHSUPP-19.html

Rohlicek, J. R. (1993). Gisting continuous speech. In *Proceedings of the workshop on human language technology* (pp. 384–384). Association for Computational Linguistics.

Rowley, J. E. (1988). *Abstracting and indexing.* C. Bingley.

Rubino, R., de Souza, J., Foster, J., & Specia, L. (2013). *Topic models for translation quality estimation for gisting purposes.*

Salton, G., Allan, J., Buckley, C., & Singhal, A. (1994). Automatic analysis, theme generation, and summarization of machine-readable texts. *Science, 264*(5164), 1421–1426.

Sharma, S., & Harrison, J. E. (2006). Structured abstracts: Do they improve the quality of information in abstracts? *American Journal of Orthodontics and Dentofacial Orthopedics, 130*(4), 523–530.

Silberhorn, E. M., Glauert, H. P., & Robertson, L. W. (1990). Critical reviews in: Carcinogenicity of polyhalogenated biphenyls: PCBs and PBBs. *Critical Reviews in Toxicology, 20*(6), 440–496.

Sollaci, L. B., & Pereira, M. G. (2004). The introduction, methods, results, and discussion (IMRAD) structure: A fifty-year survey. *Journal of the Medical Library Association, 92*(3), 364.

Sompel, H. V. D., Payette, S., Erickson, J., Lagoze, C., & Warner, S. (2004). Rethinking scholarly communication: Building the system that scholars deserve. *D-Lib Magazine; 2004 [10] 9.*

Stevenson, H. A., & Harrison, J. E. (2009). Structured abstracts: Do they improve citation retrieval from dental journals? *Journal of Orthodontics, 36*(1), 52–60.

Stokes, N., Newman, E., Carthy, J., & Smeaton, A. F. (2004). Broadcast news gisting using lexical cohesion analysis. In *European Conference on Information Retrieval* (pp. 209–222). Springer.

Taiminen, H. M., & Karjaluoto, H. (2015). The usage of digital marketing channels in SMEs. *Journal of Small Business and Enterprise Development, 22*(4), 633–651.

Torres-Moreno, J.-M. (2014). *Automatic text summarization* (p. xii). John Wiley & Sons.

Wind, J., & Mahajan, V. (2002). Digital marketing. *Symphonya. Emerging Issues in Management* (1), 43–54.

Wong, H. L. (2005). Quality of structured abstracts of original research articles in the British medical journal, the Canadian medical association journal and the journal of the American medical association: A 10-year follow-up study. *Current Medical Research and Opinion, 21*(4), 467–473.

Yeung, H. W. C. (1994). Critical reviews of geographical perspectives on business organizations and the organization of production: Towards a network approach. *Progress in Human Geography, 18*(4), 460–490.

SECTION 4

Functional architectures to support knowledge consumption

We often assume that there is an extensive stock of research on knowledge consumption, and the architecture that supports use. The recent rise of the enterprise architecture discipline has highlighted a significant gap in coverage. The knowledge management discipline focuses on the process and impacts of knowledge sharing, transfer, and exchange. Similarly, the communication science field focuses on the process of knowledge transmission. The information science literature focuses on information use and information systems interface design. The field of computer science focuses on human–computer interaction and usability engineering. And, the business literature focuses on the use of knowledge and information in decision-making. Except for knowledge management and communication science, all focus on information and explicit forms of knowledge. All are essential perspectives, but none addresses the design of an architecture that supports the consumption and use of knowledge.

This section addresses how we consume knowledge assets, how that use changes or effects knowledge assets, the benefits and the use of the risk introduces, and how a knowledge architecture can facilitate value creation while managing risk. The chapters in this section focus on designing four functional architectures essential to working with and consuming knowledge, including: (1) knowledge authenticity and provenance; (2) knowledge security; (3) knowledge privilege controls; and (4) translation, interpretation, and surrogate creation. Section 3 focused on access to support discovery. In this section, we look at access from a control and management perspective. Access control and management involve doing something with the asset that is just beyond reading or seeing. It means changing or effecting the asset in some way. In this section, the reader will also find a different treatment of 'surrogates,' including those activities that result in augmenting, deriving new value, or synthesizing assets.

17

FUNCTIONAL ARCHITECTURE FOR KNOWLEDGE AUGMENTATION, DERIVATION, AND SYNTHESIS

Chapter summary

This chapter considers a range of ways we can consume knowledge assets. We abstract these different practical actions into three general types – asset translations, asset interpretations, and asset augmentations. The chapter outlines the four essential activities we need to consider when designing an architecture to support this rich set of practices. It also discusses why it is essential to have a good understanding of the way the knowledge management field describes knowledge use, exchange, transfer, uptake, and sharing but with the realization of the limitations inherent to historical definitions of knowledge assets. The chapter explains the activities included in translating, interpreting, and augmenting knowledge assets. We consider the primary challenge in designing this functional architecture. It is learning to see and understand how we are consuming our knowledge assets and keeping pace with the rapid evolution of different patterns of consumption.

Why we care about knowledge augmentation, derivation, and synthesis

In Chapter 5, we argued that the value of knowledge is gained or lost, grown, or diminished through use. We explained that the practice of achieving growth and value through stockpiling physical and financial assets does not work for knowledge assets. Stockpiling knowledge assets diminishes its business value and prevents an organization from achieving a return on investment. The knowledge sciences literature discusses use variously as knowledge translation, knowledge transfer, knowledge exchange, knowledge uptake and utilization, knowledge implementation, knowledge dissemination, knowledge diffusion, and knowledge sharing. All of these terms describe some form of knowledge flow. Our challenge in designing a knowledge architecture is to find the common elements.

We find the most significant treatment of knowledge consumption and use in fields where research is actively and immediately translated into practice. These fields include medical sciences, scientific research, environmental sciences – domains where the research can have a positive or a negative effect on people, the environment, and general life and well-being concerns. The challenge is that most of these discussions are isolated within the domains and have not been significantly touched by knowledge scientists. There is little to begin working with for this functional architecture in terms of existing solutions or existing thinking. We need to start with the functional models that have been developed in these scattered domains and extract what we can about functional activities and architectures – just because there is not much to work from does not mean we can avoid this critical knowledge function.

In this text, our goal is to design a knowledge architecture that will support the consumption of knowledge assets in every business context. However, we do need to understand how the business and knowledge sciences define consumption. We need to understand what the process looks like to ensure that any architecture we design is suited to the purpose.

The challenge we face is finding a well-formed, inclusive, and comprehensive characterization of knowledge consumption. Experience and a review of the literature on knowledge use reinforce our earlier characterization of knowledge asset economic behaviors and properties. Knowledge augmentation, derivation, and synthesis are inherently dynamic, interdependent, unpredictable, and human. Throughout the framework, we can see aspects of Nonaka and Takeuchi's socialization, externalization, combination, and internalization processes. A key design element is ensuring that people and agents can move seamlessly from one form of consumption to another. It is not currently the case in our 'built' information and knowledge environments today. It must be possible for the individual and teams to move from one form of knowledge capital to another without having to think about it consciously or to travel from one application to another deliberately. The consumption architecture must be constructed as an intermediary level – a support level – embedded functionality that works behind any explicit business application.

Knowledge augmentation, derivation, and synthesis – design concepts

Developing this functional architecture requires a good understanding of the full spectrum of use, including knowledge translation, interpretation, and augmentation. To understand knowledge translation, we need to have a good grasp of knowledge exchange, transfer, uptake, and sharing. Translated knowledge takes the source knowledge that is actionable, including translations of research into practice, clinical procedures, explanations, testing procedures and results, representations of knowledge in other languages, or any other activity that transforms the knowledge asset to generate business value. Knowledge interpretation is the representation of knowledge in other forms such as performance or rendering in other channels, creating knockoffs and copies, plagiarism, adaptations, parodies or satires, critical reviews, peer reviews – in essence, any type of use that is best understood in the context of the original asset. Interpretive knowledge cannot be fully understood or meaningfully realized without knowledge of the source. Knowledge augmentation changes the original knowledge asset, including annotations in all media forms (e.g., text, film, image, audio, dramatic, story), errata and corrections, versions and revisions, renditions, redactions, or partially censored versions, annotations, mark-ups, comments, and note bene.

The primary challenge we face in designing this functional architecture is learning to see and understand how we are consuming our knowledge assets, and keeping pace with the rapid evolution of different patterns of consumption, changing roles in consumption, and the rapidly expanding and evolving knowledge use landscape. This functional architecture not only supports knowledge consumption but also increases our awareness of common forms of consumption.

There is a rich literature in knowledge sciences focused on human capital. There is a rich literature in information sciences dedicated to the use of explicit knowledge. There is a rich business process management, engineering, and workflow literature focused on procedural knowledge. Despite the rich literature on cultural assessment, there is little research to draw from to understand how we leverage the business value of culture. While there is a rich literature on networks and how they work, there is no widely supported characterization of how we use network knowledge. Across all of these disciplines, though, there is a generic treatment of knowledge use concepts. While the terminology varies, they provide a foundation from which to establish an architectural design framework.

- *Knowledge translation* is defined as the exchange, synthesis and ethically-sound application of knowledge – within translation a complex system of interactions among researchers and users – to accelerate the capture of the benefits of research . . . through improved health, more effective services and products, and a strengthened health care system. It involves collaborative and systematic review, assessment, identification, aggregation, and practical application of research by key stakeholders (i.e., consumers, researchers, practitioners, policymakers) (Tetroe, 2007).
- *Knowledge transfer* is defined as

> a systematic approach to capture, collect and share tacit knowledge for it to become explicit knowledge. This process allows individuals and organizations to access and utilize essential information, which was previously known intrinsically to only one or a small group of people. Knowledge transfer depends on access to people, information, and infrastructure. It is about transferring good ideas, research results, and skills between universities, other research organizations, business, and the wider community to enable innovative new products and services to be developed (Tetroe, 2007).

- *Knowledge exchange* is a collaborative problem-solving between researchers and decision-makers that happens through linkage and exchange. Effective knowledge exchange involves interaction between decision-makers and researchers. It results in mutual learning through the process of planning, producing, disseminating, and applying existing or new research in decision-making. In this context, knowledge transfer ensures that the knowledge generated is relevant and applicable to stakeholder decision-making and is useful to researchers.
- *Knowledge uptake or utilization* is defined as a process by which specific research-based knowledge (science) is implemented in practice.
- *Knowledge implementation* is the execution of the adoption decision, that is, the innovation of the research becomes practice.
- *Knowledge dissemination* is accomplished through the promotion and publication of results, for example as in scientific journals and at scientific conferences.
- *Knowledge diffusion* is the process by which an innovation is communicated through certain channels over time among members of a social system.

We leverage all of these concepts and their supporting research to present an architectural design framework for knowledge consumption. Experience and literature suggest that consumption represents a spectrum of activities. Every organization has a different business process and workflow. Every business process leverages a different set of knowledge use activities. A knowledge consumption architecture must be flexible and adaptable to support how an organization works. The framework does not supplant or supersede any of the literature on knowledge use, knowledge translation, knowledge exchange, or knowledge sharing. Instead, it draws and synthesizes elements from each of these characterizations.

The framework is comprised of three high-level categories (Figure 17.1). The first category of use is our augmentation of knowledge. We define augmentation as the business value created through knowledge review or critiques, or the annotation of knowledge based on what was learned through use. The second category is derived knowledge. Derived knowledge describes the new business value that is generated from the asset during its use. This new derived value may be achieved through knowledge translation of knowledge interpretation. The third category is integrated knowledge, which includes the transformation of knowledge assets through synthesis and collaboration. Our goal is to design an architecture that helps us to grow, manage, and leverage knowledge. Our focus throughout the text has been on knowledge assets. From an architecture perspective, we need a model of each form of use. The model should help us understand the actions involved, effects, or results in knowledge assets, and the value generated through business transformation.

Each use category can be presented as a system of actions, outputs, and business value generated. When taken as a whole, these six models give us a comprehensive and inclusive view of the different ways knowledge can be used, the effects they produce, and the business value that is generated. These models also help us

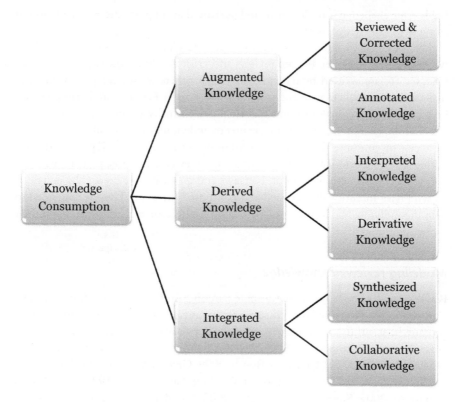

FIGURE 17.1 Knowledge Consumption and Its Effects

to understand what kinds of processes (e.g., actions) our functional architecture should support, the changed and new assets we need to manage, and the types of value we want to track and report on.

Augmented knowledge

Every use of knowledge assumes that we access and consume the source asset in some way. Augmented knowledge refers to how we add knowledge directly to the original knowledge object. Augmentation focuses on what happens to that asset after we have consumed it. We might augment the source knowledge by creating a review or critique of the asset. A review does not change the source asset directly but attempts to influence or qualify the asset by offering comments, corrections, errata, suggestions, criticisms, or questions. Reviews may be formal or informal. Formal reviews would be created for use by others, and informal reviews might be intended for personal or limited use. Another way we augment knowledge is by suggesting or making changes to the asset. This form of augmentation is defined as an annotation. An annotation may or may not change the source asset immediately, but it adds ideas or notes to the asset. Annotations are common practice in many fields. Our challenge is to design an architecture that supports the augmentation of all types of knowledge assets.

It is essential to differentiate between the development of surrogates, which we discussed in Chapter 16, and reviews and critiques. Surrogates, as described in Chapter 16, are written by individuals to assist others in discovery – to find and make a decision whether to access a knowledge asset. Reviews and critiques may be written by individuals or teams, informally or formally, to serve the purpose and needs of the creator. Surrogates are created by individuals who would not necessarily access or consume the asset if they were not charged to develop the surrogate. Surrogates create externalized knowledge assets – they take an explicit form – whether they are formally published or not. Reviews and surrogates are created by individuals who have intentionally accessed and consumed the asset. They are intended to help the individual build their understanding of the source asset and to build their knowledge stocks.

Modeling reviewed knowledge

Reviewing a knowledge asset means examining it for understanding, building a memory, internalizing, or evaluating it. To review an asset means to assess it, appraise it, scrutinize it, inspect it, or explore it (Bailar, 2011; Benos et al., 2007; Biagioli, 2002; Bornman, 2008; Boswell & Cannon, 2009; Devereaux et al., 2001; Godlee et al., 1998, 2012; Grant & Booth, 2009; Greenhalgh et al., 2007; Lee et al., 2013; Pawson et al., 2005; Sampson et al., 2009; Sandelowski, 1997; Sandelowski & Barroso, 2003; Shepperd, 2009; Spier, 2002; Stemler, 2000). Evaluative reviews may also rate or rank an asset in comparison to other assets. We might undertake a review simply to gain a better understanding of it, or we may intend to suggest or provoke a change. A critical review will highlight the strong and weak points. A critical review may approve or disapprove of the asset, accept it, or recommend it to others (Brown, 2006; Brunton et al., 2006; Caldwell et al., 2005; Callahan et al., 1998). The expected result of a review depends on whether it is undertaken for personal use and learning or for consumption by others. If it is intended for personal use, the end goal is internalization, which builds the consumer's knowledge base, adding to their tacit knowledge or skills. If it is intended for consumption by others, it might take the form of a new explicit knowledge asset – a formal review, a written report, or a prescribed set of actions. In the latter case, the intended result is a change to the original knowledge asset. Reviews may also vary from subjective to objective. Where the intended use is personal and informal, reviews tend to be more subjective – they are compared to and integrated into an individual's knowledge stocks. Where the intended use is public and formal, reviews will tend to be objective and part of a formal and more rigorous process.

We need to be able to conceptualize how we conduct these reviews and what they produce to design a functional architecture that supports the review of human capital, explicit knowledge, procedural knowledge, cultural knowledge, and network knowledge. Reviews and critiques are common today – consider book reviews, movie reviews, performance reviews, product reviews, project reviews, design reviews, restaurant reviews, service or company reviews, and performance reviews. Health care and medical practitioners are familiar with systematic reviews – reviews of everything we know about a condition, a disease, treatment, or therapy. We are also accustomed to participating in performance reviews of our work over some time. How do these kinds of reviews and review processes align with knowledge assets? Most of these reviews pertain to explicit knowledge. Some apply to procedural knowledge and cultural knowledge – particularly as they apply to project, design or process reviews, and performance or engagement.

Modeling knowledge critiques

A critique is an analysis tool that we use to evolve and improve something. We have created something and analyzed it to make it better by revising choices we might have made – we have an opportunity for critique. The primary purpose of a critique is to improve or iterate on an idea or process, in this case, a knowledge asset. Critiques may be stand-alone and one time, or continuous and iterative. Individuals or groups may conduct them. They may be formal or informal. They may be created during or after an asset is developed, or after it has assumed a tangible form.

The functional architecture for reviews and critiques should support actions, outputs, and business value (Figure 17.2). The annotation architecture must also provide access to the source asset, including the tools that allow stakeholders (e.g., experts, consumers, individuals, team members, etc.) to analyze the asset, ask questions about the asset, collect a broader range of perspectives, brainstorm, share

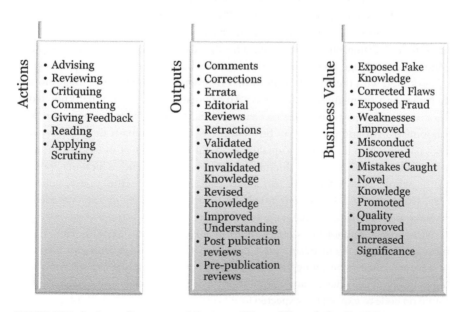

Actions
- Advising
- Reviewing
- Critiquing
- Commenting
- Giving Feedback
- Reading
- Applying Scrutiny

Outputs
- Comments
- Corrections
- Errata
- Editorial Reviews
- Retractions
- Validated Knowledge
- Invalidated Knowledge
- Revised Knowledge
- Improved Understanding
- Post pubication reviews
- Pre-publication reviews

Business Value
- Exposed Fake Knowledge
- Corrected Flaws
- Exposed Fraud
- Weaknesses Improved
- Misconduct Discovered
- Mistakes Caught
- Novel Knowledge Promoted
- Quality Improved
- Increased Significance

FIGURE 17.2 Actions, Outputs, and Business Value of Knowledge Reviews

their thoughts with others, collect additional information, share insights, generate new ideas, provide feedback, structure and write a formal review or critique, and to publish or share that review and critique. Critiques, in particular, can also be an integral element of every business process.

Reviews and critiques produce a rich set of outputs including anonymous and public comments, commentaries, corrections, and errata, validated knowledge, invalidated knowledge, revised knowledge, more in-depth and improved understanding, blogs, retractions, actionable feedback, revised methodologies, revised designs, improved quality, cautions and limitations, and assessments. The architecture should allow for a single user, for collaboration, for 'in-process' or 'post-process' capture and release.

Reviews and critiques generate considerable business value. They provide the opportunity to expose fake knowledge, flaws or fraud, weaknesses, misconduct, mistakes, and opportunities for improvement. Additionally, the process uncovers opportunities for growth and training, strengthens the organization's ability to critique, increases engagement among teams, improves facilitation and presentation skills, encourages collaboration among stakeholders, accustoms the organization to giving and receiving feedback, and can provide a boost to positive team culture.

Modeling knowledge annotations

Annotations are most commonly associated with explicit knowledge assets, specifically with documents, reports, articles, and books (Cadiz et al., 2000; Campbell, 2002; Farkas & Poltrock, 1995; Fischer et al., 1993; Einsohn, 2000; Kaufer et al., 2011; Marshall, 1997, 2009; Mendenhall et al., 2011; Shabajee & Reynolds, 2018; Virbel, 1993; Wolfe, 2000, 2002, 2008; Wolfe & Neuwirth, 2001). Annotations can be understood as explicit additions or changes, or as a simple change or supplement to an existing knowledge asset. The foundation for annotations, though, is a current knowledge asset. The annotation may be attached to the source asset or be associated with the asset in some way. The essence, though, is the suggestion of a change or a supplement of the asset. An annotation is an additional knowledge associated with a particular idea or characteristic. It can include an explanation or a comment. An annotation may be a simple point of emphasis or highlight that draws attention to an idea or a quality. It might be a series of individual or team notes and observations. It is different from a review or critique, which may pertain to the whole knowledge asset. An annotation targets a specific aspect, concept, idea, or quality of a knowledge asset. Annotations are targeted and intended to provoke an immediate change.

Many forms of annotations are in common use today. Document annotation is the most common. Mathematicians use annotations to translate symbols and formulae into natural language meaning, to handle disambiguation, and support recommendations. In computer science, annotation refers to documentation and comments that found on code to explain the expected functionality. In computational biology, annotations identify the locations of genes, defining what those genes do, and eventually making sense of a sequenced gene. Digital imaging uses annotations to superimpose descriptions onto an image without changing the underlying image – similar to a sticky note. Dramatic annotations identify the elements that characterize the drama, often leveraging a formal annotation scheme. Story annotation adds comments and notes to narratives (Schank, 1975). Legal annotations interpret legal statutes and are critical tools for legal research. Film annotations tend towards a critique of films and their presentations – these are in context commentaries. They support the scholarly use of films and take the form of writing in a film. They are different from a film review or critique because they are embedded in or closely attached to the film. They are often attached to the shot or frame level in a film.

The functional architecture for annotation should enable highlighting, interpreting, marking, reading, summarizing, tracking, underlining, making marginal notes, asking and answering questions, calling attention to critical points, editing, writing, sharing, explaining, creating links to other assets, referencing prior knowledge, reviewing others' comments, private reading of other comments, and social reading. The annotation may be both active or passive. Highlighting or emphasizing is a passive activity intended to draw attention. Active annotation presumes engagement and consumption of the asset. As an individual engages with a knowledge asset, they generate questions or ideas. Active annotation contributes directly to monitoring and improving comprehension and understanding. Active understanding and awareness will provoke ideas and concepts, which may provoke a need for an explanation or further information. The architecture must support both active and passive annotations (Figure 17.3).

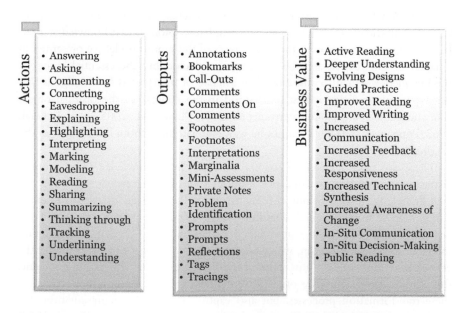

Actions
- Answering
- Asking
- Commenting
- Connecting
- Eavesdropping
- Explaining
- Highlighting
- Interpreting
- Marking
- Modeling
- Reading
- Sharing
- Summarizing
- Thinking through
- Tracking
- Underlining
- Understanding

Outputs
- Annotations
- Bookmarks
- Call-Outs
- Comments
- Comments On Comments
- Footnotes
- Footnotes
- Interpretations
- Marginalia
- Mini-Assessments
- Private Notes
- Problem Identification
- Prompts
- Prompts
- Reflections
- Tags
- Tracings

Business Value
- Active Reading
- Deeper Understanding
- Evolving Designs
- Guided Practice
- Improved Reading
- Improved Writing
- Increased Communication
- Increased Feedback
- Increased Responsiveness
- Increased Technical Synthesis
- Increased Awareness of Change
- In-Situ Communication
- In-Situ Decision-Making
- Public Reading

FIGURE 17.3 Actions, Outputs, Business Value of Knowledge Annotation

Reviews and critiques produce a rich set of outputs including annotations, bookmarks, callouts, comments, footnotes, interpretations, marginalia, mini-assessments, private notes, problem identification, prompts, reflections, tags, and tracings. Reviews and critiques generate considerable business value. They create an incentive for active reading and writing, promote a deeper understanding of all forms of knowledge assets, contribute to improved designs, generate guided practice, increase opportunities for communication, feedback, responsiveness, and decision-making. They also promote an in situ awareness of change.

Derivative knowledge

Derivative knowledge refers to knowledge generated while performing or expressing the knowledge object which has been appropriately accessed or arises from the use of or reference to the knowledge. Derivative knowledge is intended to be a secondary product – though it can be related to the source. Derivative knowledge is intended to be not simply a more concise representation of the item, but a new object with new substantive additive value. We divide derivative knowledge into two categories because the functional architecture to support them may vary. The first category we label as 'Interpretive knowledge.' The second category we label as 'Translated knowledge.' These labels are selected for convenience purposes – we expect that as the discussion advances in the field of knowledge sciences, better labels might be provided.

Modeling knowledge interpretation

The functional architecture of interpreted knowledge involves direct changes to the original knowledge asset – and the complete version of that knowledge asset. In essence, it is a variation of the outer layers of the onion model we presented in Chapter 6. The format and the package may change, but the essential kernel of the knowledge remains consistent. The essence of interpreted knowledge is that this type of knowledge is best understood in the context of the original object (Onwuegbuzie et al., 2003; Paterson et al., 2001; Pluye et al., 2005, 2009; Polanyi, 1962; Pope et al., 2000) – it cannot be well understood without the context of the original knowledge asset.

There are several characterizations of interpreted knowledge. The simplest characterization relates to concepts of implicit and tacit knowledge. We call out tacit knowledge as one of our important types of knowledge assets – an essential component of human capital. The knowledge sciences literature reminds us that tacit knowledge is implicit – it cannot be fully codified. Through engagement, interaction, and socialization, we transform tacit knowledge into a form that others can hear, see, or read. In its simplest and broadest way, interpretation represents this transformation. In terms of architecture, this means the design should support these transformation processes, but also capture the explicit representation that results. Explicit knowledge, though, is also interpreted to create tacit knowledge. It is closely linked to competence and skill acquisition and the growth of tacit knowledge. Nonaka and Takeuchi refer to this kind of use as internalization (Nonaka & Takeuchi, 1995). It involves the learner's active reflection and interpretation of knowledge that is new to them. In a nutshell, knowledge interpretation of the simplest characterization of knowledge interpretation is the cognitive activity of knowledge processing. (Camerer, 2009; Hartmann & Sure, 2004; Schneckenberg, 2008). By interpreting knowledge, every individual in the organization develops a self-learning competence, and thus creates the capacity to generate business value. Self-learning competence is a prerequisite for improving the individual's work-related performance.

Knowledge interpretation is also a team activity. Interpretation adds greater business value when it is practiced in a cooperative and participative business context. Knowledge interpretation is closely associated with learning cultures and learning environments of organizations (Krause et al., 2009). Organizational learning is grounded in the cooperative and participative interpretation of knowledge. The architecture should support active, self-directed constructive, situative, and social engagement around knowledge assets. This form of active learning is essential to the active construction of knowledge assets of business value to the organization. Knowledge interpretation is an ongoing cyclical activity (Winterton et al., 2005; Kim, 1999). Knowledge interpretation is essential to knowledge acquisition and retention. Interpretation contributes to acquisition when we assess new knowledge and use it for a specific action. We develop mental models when we interpret knowledge, and these mental models are the foundation of our knowledge retention, e.g., tacit knowledge. Knowledge interpretation is essential to the transformation of knowledge assets into business value (Samuelson & Nordhaus, 1985).

Perhaps the most advanced form of knowledge interpretation is those that generate new knowledge assets or new versions of the source asset. In this case, the individual must develop such a deep understanding of the source asset as to produce a new version or edition, a new format, or even a parody, satire, or spoof.

The functional architecture for annotation should support knowledge acquisition, an adaptation of assets, assessments, design, modeling, process and product development, interpretation, individual and group learning, informal and formal learning, observation, moving ideas to action, performance, presentation, copying, generating one-off assets such as knockoffs, parodies, satires, and knowledge retention. Knowledge interpretation is an essential function to support consumption (Figure 17.4).

As an essential knowledge management function, knowledge interpretation produces a rich set of outputs including assessments, instructions and recipes, new products, copies and knockoffs, new designs, new ideas, new processes and products, performances, and presentations. The architecture must be able to track and capture all of these outputs.

Knowledge interpretation generates considerable business value. These actions create enhanced insights, improved assessments, improved performance, improved

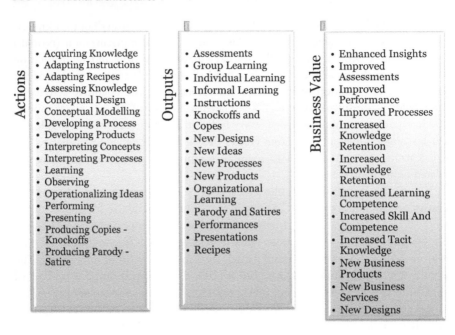

Actions
- Acquiring Knowledge
- Adapting Instructions
- Adapting Recipes
- Assessing Knowledge
- Conceptual Design
- Conceptual Modelling
- Developing a Process
- Developing Products
- Interpreting Concepts
- Interpreting Processes
- Learning
- Observing
- Operationalizing Ideas
- Performing
- Presenting
- Producing Copies - Knockoffs
- Producing Parody - Satire

Outputs
- Assessments
- Group Learning
- Individual Learning
- Informal Learning
- Instructions
- Knockoffs and Copes
- New Designs
- New Ideas
- New Processes
- New Products
- Organizational Learning
- Parody and Satires
- Performances
- Presentations
- Recipes

Business Value
- Enhanced Insights
- Improved Assessments
- Improved Performance
- Improved Processes
- Increased Knowledge Retention
- Increased Knowledge Retention
- Increased Learning Competence
- Increased Skill And Competence
- Increased Tacit Knowledge
- New Business Products
- New Business Services
- New Designs

FIGURE 17.4 Actions, Outputs, Business Value of Knowledge Interpretation

processes, increased knowledge retention, increased learning capacity, increased skills and competence, and increased tacit knowledge.

Modeling knowledge translation

Knowledge translation is a term that is used generically and interchangeably with knowledge exchange, knowledge distribution, knowledge transfer, knowledge sharing, and so on. Knowledge translation is a model and a process that has significant business value when it is complete (Brink & Wood, 2001; Davis et al., 2003; Estabrooks et al., 2006; Graham et al., 2006; Graham Tetroe and KT Theories Research Group, 2007; Grimshaw et al., 2012; Handy, 1973; Higgins et al., 2019; Jacobson et al., 2003; Kastner et al., 2011, 2012; Linn et al., 2003; Meyer et al., 2019; Novak et al., 2012; Ring et al., 2011; Straus et al., 1988, 2013; Strauss & Corbin, 1998; Sudsawad, 2007). The challenge, though, is that the process is not often complete, and the process does not accommodate all stakeholders. Knowledge translation focuses on the relevance, pertinence, quality, adoption, and uptake of knowledge. In most business contexts, knowledge translation is closely associated with evidence-based practice and accountability. Knowledge translation focuses on a core challenge of knowledge use – the Knowledge-to-Action (KTA) gap. Additionally, this type of use focuses on the use of knowledge by practitioners, decision-makers, consumers, and the public.

For this text, translated knowledge includes moving theoretical knowledge to applied knowledge, translating research into products, services, advice, guidance, clinical tests, experiments, and replicated research. It also includes representation of the knowledge in another language – because translations are never exact. Translated knowledge is what knowledge economists and engineers refer to as the business transformation of knowledge.

The functional architecture of translated knowledge takes as a starting point a knowledge asset or a body of knowledge. The bulk of the use process does not depend on direct and immediate access to the original knowledge asset. This type of derivative knowledge presumes some degree of use or translation to a different environment. It is essential to see the translated knowledge asset in the broader context of other uses, tests, feedback, criticisms, explanations, and errata (Figure 17.5). Translated knowledge provides the ultimate demonstration of the value of a knowledge asset.

The functional architecture for knowledge translation should enable individuals and groups to adopt a knowledge asset, apply feedback to the asset, diffuse and disseminate knowledge, distill knowledge, exchange knowledge, interact around knowledge assets, transfer ideas, implement the asset or test the asset, and discover and resolve challenges.

Knowledge translation produces a rich set of outputs including new applied knowledge, behavioral change, business intervention, experimental results, explanations, extended and enhanced tacit knowledge, feedback, good practices,

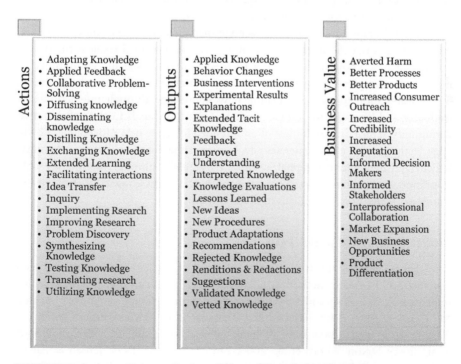

FIGURE 17.5 Actions, Outputs, Business Value of Knowledge Translation

evaluations, lessons learned, rejected knowledge, renditions, and redactions, validated and vetted knowledge.

Knowledge translation generates considerable business value. It helps to avert harm and manage risk, improves products and services, enables an organization to increase stakeholder outreach, and results in increased communication with network partners, enhanced reputation and credibility, informed decision-makers and stakeholders, new business opportunities, market expansion, and product differentiation.

Integrated knowledge

The category of knowledge integration includes two forms of use and consumption, including knowledge synthesis and collaboration, focused on knowledge. Knowledge synthesis focuses more heavily on integrating existing sources of knowledge to produce high-level understanding; it generates a high-level description and summary, often a recommendation or review – a 'state of the art.' Additionally, synthesis tends to focus on explicit knowledge assets – and spans time and space. In some ways, knowledge synthesis tells us about the state of knowledge on a topic – intended to provide a new foundation or plateau upon which new knowledge will build. In those disciplines where it is used, it often provides a new jumping-off point for change or a shift in focus and discovery. Knowledge synthesis tends to look at the past – what is known about a topic or question – without regard to who has created the knowledge or its intended purpose.

The collaboration focused on knowledge may include some of these elements, but synthesis is not the intended outcome. Here the intended result is the development of new knowledge around a focused topic by a specific community of individuals, at a given point in time, and concentrating on a particular problem. The collaboration focuses on creating new knowledge through interaction and exchange and leverages the human capital of the individuals in the collaborative community. Collaboration is most often intended to create new procedural knowledge. In the process, it also generates new human capital for those in the community. It generates new network capital – simply because a community defines the collaboration. Collaboration also often produces new explicit knowledge through the team's work and from individuals in the community.

Modeling knowledge synthesis

Knowledge synthesis involves a review of clearly formulated questions that uses systematic and explicit methods to identify, select, and critically appraise relevant research and to collect and analyze knowledge from a range of sources (Arksey & O'Malley, 2005; Atkins et al., 2007; Banning, 2012; Barnett-Page & Thomas, 2009; Barroso et al., 2003; Beise & Stahl, 1999; Cook et al., 1997; Dixon-Woods et al., 2005; Dixon-Woods et al., 2006; Droitcour et al., 1993; Jensen & Allen, 1996; Lucas et al., 2007; Moss et al., 2019; Noblit & Hare, 1988; Popay et al., 2006;

Roberts et al., 2002; Rycroft-Malone et al., 2012; Sutton & Abrams, 2001; Ten-kasi & Boland, 1996; Thomas & Harden, 2008; Tricco et al., 2016; Weed, 2005; Yin, 2003; Yin & Heald, 1975). Knowledge syntheses are intentionally broad and thorough. They vary from the other forms of use discussed earlier: they begin with the collection of 'everything that is known' about a topic or problem or question. The starting point is explicit knowledge and knowledge in any format or package. Once collected, a variety of analytical and intelligence methods might be applied. Methods include the full range of diagnostic analysis, forensic analysis, content analysis, and common qualitative and quantitative research methods. There is no prescribed sequence of methods – each knowledge synthesis is a design challenge.

From an architecture perspective, knowledge synthesis is cumulative, i.e., it must support and leverage the architecture for knowledge augmentation and derivation. Additionally, it should provide ready access to advanced synthesis tools and technologies, including Bayesian meta-analysis, content analyses, critical interpretive syntheses, cross-design syntheses, triangulations, framework syntheses, grounded theory, interpretive and integrative synthesis, meta-ethnographies, meta-interpretations, meta-narratives, meta-studies, meta-summaries, meta-syntheses, mixed studies reviews, narrative reviews and summaries, narrative syntheses, qualitative cross-case analyses, qualitative meta-syntheses, systematic qualitative reviews (Figure 17.6), quantitative case surveys, textual narrative syntheses, and thematic analysis. Additionally, knowledge synthesis may leverage any of those semantic

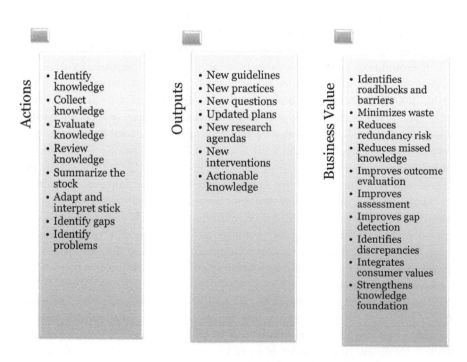

Actions
- Identify knowledge
- Collect knowledge
- Evaluate knowledge
- Review knowledge
- Summarize the stock
- Adapt and interpret stick
- Identify gaps
- Identify problems

Outputs
- New guidelines
- New practices
- New questions
- Updated plans
- New research agendas
- New interventions
- Actionable knowledge

Business Value
- Identifies roadblocks and barriers
- Minimizes waste
- Reduces redundancy risk
- Reduces missed knowledge
- Improves outcome evaluation
- Improves assessment
- Improves gap detection
- Identifies discrepancies
- Integrates consumer values
- Strengthens knowledge foundation

FIGURE 17.6 Actions, Outputs and Business Value of Knowledge Synthesis

structures, categorization, or indexing methods we discussed in the chapters of Section 3. We discussed these methods from the perspective of supporting access, but they also provide essential analytical and synthesis capabilities.

Knowledge synthesis is most effective when undertaken by a group or team. The functional architecture for knowledge translation should enable groups of designated individuals to identify and collect all the existing knowledge on a topic, evaluate, review and summarize the knowledge stock, adapt and interpret that knowledge to the problem at hand, and identify gaps and issues with the existing knowledge stock.

Knowledge synthesis produces a rich set of outputs, including new guidelines, new practices, new questions, updated plans, new research agendas, new interventions, and actionable knowledge.

Knowledge synthesis generates business value. It helps to identify and assess barriers to use of processes, products, and services, ensures that wastage is minimized, reduces the chance that existing knowledge will go undetected or unused, supports outcome evaluation and assessment, improves understanding of existing knowledge gaps, highlights discrepancies in existing knowledge stocks, integrates consumers values and preferences, and strengthens the foundation from which an organization developed guidelines, practices, and operations.

Modeling collaborative knowledge

Collaboration means working with others to produce or create something or a result. For this text, collaboration creates a business result or value (Arnott et al., 2020; Brown & Duguid, 1991; Brunton et al., 2006; Brush, 2002; Donath et al., 1999; Frommholz et al., 2003; Gennari et al., 2004; Gunawardena et al., 2010; Kaplan & Chisik, 2005; Lave & Wenger, 1991; Weng & Gennari, 2004; Weng et al., 2004). Collaboration generates what economists refer to as comparative advantages. When individuals pool their knowledge, engage around knowledge assets, focus their tacit knowledge on the creation of procedural knowledge, they create value that is greater than what a single individual can offer. The collaboration leverages knowledge reviews and critiques, knowledge interpretation, and knowledge translation. However, what is different is the inherent interaction, exchange, pooling of knowledge through conversations, and joint work. Collaboration is the one form of knowledge consumption heavily dependent on relational capital – the establishment of communities and networks. For collaboration to succeed, the community must also build a productive culture. Effective collaboration depends heavily upon the behaviors, attitudes, and personality traits of the community members.

The literature of collaboration is rich and spans several disciplines, including communications, sociology, psychology, industrial design, management science, learning, and knowledge management. This rich literature reminds us that our knowledge architecture must be designed to support formal and informal engagement, planned and serendipitous, to capture work in progress, to link to and integrate with other knowledge stocks and sources. The essential design principle is that a collaborative knowledge architecture must be seamlessly integrated into the everyday work environment. It cannot be a stand-alone space that requires community members to remember and access intentionally. The design should be real-time, not after action or end of process or project. It is a tall design effort. These designs have consistently failed over the past 25 years.

Knowledge synthesis is most effective when undertaken by a group or team. The functional architecture for knowledge translation should support several activities (Figure 17.7), including active reading, active and argumentative writing, collaborative learning, collaborative problem-solving, social understanding, critical reading and thinking, discussions, group decision-making, idea exchange, interpretations, iterative design and development, iterative reviews, knowledge sharing, persuasion, progress tracking, social learning, turn-taking, and group culture development.

Knowledge synthesis produces a rich set of outputs including articulations, brainstorming, clarifications, cultural artifact development, decision-making, document-centric discussions, formal knowledge representations, formalized knowledge, group revisions, mental gap filling, negotiated perspective, new understanding, personal understanding, scientific collaboration, scientific dissemination, suggestions, and the development of group language and terminology.

Knowledge synthesis generates business value. It exposes errors, increases personal capacity for understanding and communication, and develops shared

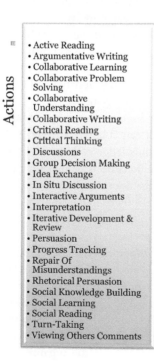

Actions

- Active Reading
- Argumentative Writing
- Collaborative Learning
- Collaborative Problem Solving
- Collaborative Understanding
- Collaborative Writing
- Critical Reading
- Critical Thinking
- Discussions
- Group Decision Making
- Idea Exchange
- In Situ Discussion
- Interactive Arguments
- Interpretation
- Iterative Development & Review
- Persuasion
- Progress Tracking
- Repair Of Misunderstandings
- Rhetorical Persuasion
- Social Knowledge Building
- Social Learning
- Social Reading
- Turn-Taking
- Viewing Others Comments

Outputs

- Articulations
- Brainstorming
- Clarifications
- Cultural Artefact Development
- Decision-Making
- Document Centric Discussions
- Formal Knowledge Representations
- Formalized Knowledge
- Group Revisions
- Mental Gap Filling
- Negotiated Perspective
- New Understanding
- Personal Understanding
- Scientific Collaboration
- Scientific Dissemination
- Suggestions
- Symbolic Language

Business Value

- Error Detection
- Increased Personal Understanding
- Shared Analysis
- Shared Culture
- Shared Meaning
- Shared Repertoire
- Shared Social Interactions
- Shared Social Structures
- Shared Understanding
- Socially Shared Annotations
- Thought Shaping

FIGURE 17.7 Actions, Outputs and Business Value of Knowledge Synthesis

analytical methods, shared group, and business culture, shared meanings and repertoires, builds trust and confidence through social interactions, creates long-term social relationships, and develops tacit knowledge sharing.

Knowledge augmentation, derivation, and synthesis – the design environment

What factors do we need to consider in designing this architecture? There are many factors to consider for this layer, but the most crucial factor is the business culture. We may identify good practice design principles. However, the consumption architecture must be designed into the business of the organization. It means designing the culture as well as the technology in place.

What events cause us to design a functional architecture for consumption? Every organization invests in knowledge assets, directly and intentionally and indirectly, and as a simple way of working. Every organization must realize the value of these assets, and the only way to realize that value is through the business transformation and use of those assets. The challenge in most organizations is that taking full advantage of knowledge assets is time-consuming, cumbersome, and costly. In many cases, it appears to business managers to be an ineffective use of time and personnel. Often organizations find it more convenient to recreate or reinvent knowledge when it is needed. It leads to suboptimal decisions and to use of flawed or inappropriate knowledge. In the end, the way that knowledge consumption is designed into the business environment determines whether and how those assets are used.

What are the impacts and consequences of having this functional architecture? Ideally, the result is that the full business value of the organization's knowledge assets is realized. Everyone across the organization leverages a seamlessly integrated architecture that supports knowledge use. And, that architecture is continuously updated and calibrated to maintain currency with each of the underlying components.

What inputs do we need to consider when designing this functional architecture? Many inputs are required to achieve an elegantly integrated design. The knowledge of all of the other architecture practices is essential, as is a knowledge of how the business works every day. The goal of this layer of the architecture is to make it easy for every business area to create and leverage knowledge assets in everything they do every day. The architecture should make it possible for them to develop and use these assets without thinking about it – the architecture should be integrated into how and where they work.

What are the outputs and outcomes this functional architecture generates? Keeping in mind that architecture is about design, not about build or construction, this architecture generates the blueprints, guiding principles, and resource requirements necessary to construct the integrated architecture layer. The blueprint, and all of the consultations that go into developing the blueprint, should also provide the organizational support for moving forward. This architecture also raises awareness of what we mean by knowledge use. It helps individuals across the organization 'see' how they use knowledge assets in their daily work.

Design activities for knowledge augmentation, derivation, and synthesis

The architecture that supports knowledge consumption is complex because it includes many different activities and links to many stocks and sources. We must design this into the business architecture of the organization. Earlier, we walked through all of the actions and outputs the architecture should support – across all forms of knowledge consumption. An elegantly designed architecture supporting use will be integrative. It means looking across all of the forms to find those common actions and outputs. It also means looking for existing functions, adapting, and integrating those functions to support the knowledge architecture. Of all of the functional architectures we've discussed in this text, this is the architecture that best illustrates the principles and practices of enterprise architecture. Therefore, our activities will resemble an enterprise architecture design methodology. The five activities that support this functional architecture include:

- Activity 1. Define business capabilities the architecture will support
- Activity 2. Define the existing business architecture working environment
- Activity 3. Define application architecture support requirements
- Activity 4. Define information architecture support requirements
- Activity 5. Design principles for knowledge consumption interface

Activity 1. Define business capabilities the architecture will support

How do we do this? Initially, it is simple. It becomes complex, though, as we progress. This activity begins with the gathering of all of the types of actions we take to consume knowledge. In this chapter, we have taken a first step in defining what those actions might include. It is a long list, and it is not a coherent list because it does not represent one type of action that can be supported by one application. And, the lack of coherence is true of all six of the types of knowledge use categories. No one of these knowledge architectures will rely on a single application. Across the categories of use, though, all of the same functions should be available. The architectures across all types are inherently intertwined. It is the knowledge consumer's role or the knowledge agent to determine which of the architecture components to access when. Each choice will be dependent upon the task at hand, then.

What inputs does it require? What do we know about the functions that must be supported in this architecture? We know there must be a foundation component that supports access to sources of knowledge assets, discovery, preservation and disposition, and essential management of knowledge assets. The knowledge architecture must support version control and tracking, annotations, reviews, critiques, presentations, performances, group discussions, community building, links to any form of communication applications including text and audio communications, interactive meetings, notifications, annotation tracking and a dedicated annotation repository, personal profiles, group profiles, community profiles, access to directories, access to external sources, a glossary function, support for cross-language translation and interpretation, and a dedicated community focused knowledge base.

What outputs does it generate? This activity generates the first design of a 'to be functional architecture' blueprint. It lays out the ideal design without any form of evaluation or reduction.

What other resources does it require? This activity leverages the knowledge and experience of the knowledge architect, the business architecture, and the application architecture practice.

Activity 2. Define the existing business architecture working environment

How do we do this? Activity 1 frames this activity. The goal is to identify applications that can be leveraged to support knowledge consumption across the organization. The first step in accomplishing this activity is identifying the applications that are currently in place. It means working with the application architects who will have the responsibility of maintaining an application inventory. In all probability, the challenge will be that multiple applications support the function, and preferences may be voiced. Choosing among multiple applications will have cultural implications. The most effective application may not be the one that is most widely used, or is preferred by stakeholders who have more influence than others. It will be essential to consider the preferences of those who perform the organization's most critical business capabilities. This step requires the knowledge architect to work closely with the business architecture practice.

What inputs does it require? The task is to assess these applications for interoperability. Can they pass knowledge assets to other applications? Is there an organization-level bridge that can connect all of the applications? If so, the knowledge architect should be prepared to work with the application architecture practice to ensure any development work is efficient. If not, it will be essential to identify some underlying connecting applications to support integration. This activity requires an organizational inventory of applications. It also requires a description of who is using which applications and their satisfaction with those applications. The integrated architecture must also be loosely integrated into the business architecture, specifically the workflow architecture. The cost and licensing issues for each application should be considered, along with their market sustainability.

What outputs does it generate? This activity produces a blueprint for an integrated design that leverages existing applications and identifies gaps and proposed development work. This activity should also produce an explanation of how this design aligns with the knowledge architecture design principles.

What other resources does it require? This activity requires the knowledge of the business architect, the application architect, and the knowledge architect. It also leverages any architecture development methods and tools the organization uses to analyze and prepare enterprise architecture proposals.

Activity 3. Define application architecture support requirements

How do we do this? The integrated knowledge architecture will require a dedicated team of application architects and developers. Keep in mind that integration is an additional architecture support service. It is sometimes the case that the integration architecture can be as resources-intensive as supporting a significant financial or communication technology. It is also not a one-time development activity – the integrated nature of this functional architecture means continuous calibration of all of the components – like the gears in a complex engine. Support may not take the form of a dedicated team, but at a minimum, there should be designated roles and responsibilities for the application team.

What inputs does it require? The primary inputs for this activity will come from the application architecture practice, as they will have the most accurate knowledge of the level of support needed, the development work involved, and the cost of any extended licenses if the use of these applications is extended. This activity should also consider any additional training requirements to ensure the business stakeholders have full knowledge of the functionality to be supported.

What outputs does it generate? This activity provides an estimated budget for the integrated architecture design. The estimated budget supplements the proposed blueprint and provides the information management needs to move the design forward to development.

What other resources does it require? Any additional information about roles, responsibilities, and staffing costs will draw upon the expertise of human resource management professionals.

Activity 4. Define information architecture support requirements

How do we do this? We need to know where the knowledge assets are currently managed. Identify which knowledge assets are not sufficiently managed – go back to the knowledge object models, and the knowledge preservation architecture. This architecture should build upon the designs that have been promoted by other functions, not begin from scratch or propose any design that competes with the other knowledge asset availability functions. Additionally, accessing knowledge assets from the consumption interface will make extensive use of the accessibility architecture designs – these should be a part of the 'intermediate' or supporting layer of the architecture. Those accessibility functions which may be explicit in other places in the organization may need to be invisible or embedded into this architecture.

What inputs does it require? Knowledge of the assets that are likely to be produced and consumed by each business capability. Ideally, this information is assembled when designing the knowledge availability architecture. The design must ensure that assets can be accessed from whatever source and made available quickly in the business workflow.

What outputs does it generate? This activity generates additional design specifications that must be designed into the blueprint. This activity may generate additional requirements – both from integration and from a support perspective.

What other resources does it require? This activity requires the input of the information architecture practice, as well as the information management professionals supporting the different business functions.

Activity 5. Design principles for knowledge consumption interface

How do we do this? This task also involves considerable design work to ensure the interface is seamless and non-obtrusive. Keep in mind that the knowledge architect's role is to develop design specifications, not to do the construction and development of a solution. In establishing the knowledge architecture practice, a set of design principles should be established. This functional architecture will require an explicit interpretation of those general guidelines. These guidelines are essential – given the complexity of this integration, governance will be crucial. The design guidelines should be the foundation for governance, and governance will involve all of the other architecture practices.

What inputs does it require? Generic principles developed to set up the knowledge architecture practice are the starting point. Knowledge architects should lead to the interpretation of the design guidelines. The guidelines should be acceptable and workable for all of the architecture practices. They should be sufficiently relevant to be practical and interpreted by the development team.

What outputs does it generate? A practical working set of design guidelines that focus on the integration of applications.

What other resources does it require? This piece of architecture requires continuous governance and engagement. As individual parts of the design evolve, there is a need for continuous calibration. And, the calibration must involve all other areas of architecture practice, as well as the business stakeholders. The fundamental knowledge architecture design guidelines are the governing principles for this layer of the architecture.

Evolution of knowledge augmentation, derivation, and synthesis

Experience and a review of the literature suggest there are five phases to the evolution of knowledge use and consumption (Figure 17.8), including:

- Phase 1. Development of literacy
- Phase 2. Development of learning capacities
- Phase 3. Increased value assigned to knowledge in the general public
- Phase 4. Exponential growth of technology
- Phase 5. Development of demand for knowledge and knowledge economy

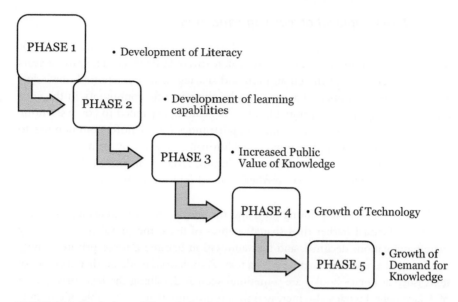

FIGURE 17.8 Evolution of Knowledge Use and Consumption

Phase 1. Development of literacy

Knowledge augmentation, derivation, and synthesis all presume we have the competences to recognize, access, and use some form of knowledge – initially, literacy meant reading and writing literacies. Our first forms of literacy related to the use of language – but it is not sufficient to limit our understanding of the evolution of knowledge consumption when we had access to the written word. Our history with knowledge synthesis – a collaboration among people regardless of whether they had reading and writing skills – is timeless. People have worked in teams – as communities, as guilds – for millennia. The traditional form of knowledge exchange, transfer, and retention have been from person to person, using conversational, verbal, and oral methods or through performance and presentation. Thus, knowledge interpretation and the translation is also historically older than is augmentation. So, if we're tracing the evolution of human knowledge consumption, we would begin with synthesis, consider derivative methods, and finally look at augmentation. It is because augmentation does presume some tangible form, whereas derivative and synthesis do not. We can trace text annotation back to 1000 AD, when it became a prominent activity in Talmudic commentaries and Arabic rhetorics treaties. In the medieval era, scribes made marginal annotations on manuscripts that were shared with the literate community. While text annotation is old, it was limited to those who had literacy competencies. Text annotation may be as old as writing on media, where it was possible to produce an additional copy with a reasonable effort.

Phase 2. Development of learning capacities

The first wave of literacy coincided with the emergence of the printing press. Print technologies supported broader access to all forms of knowledge. The earliest years of printing gave rise to the publication and sharing of new scientific knowledge. We see the first examples of annotations by the scientific community in the centuries following the early printed books. As printing expanded to cover scientific letters and catalogs, there were more opportunities for scientific communities to record their thoughts and responses. Additionally, as scholarly printing evolved, we also see the use of footnotes and endnotes, rather than marginal, handwritten comments. These practices further evolved into scholarly commentaries and formal letters.

With the rise of the printing press and the relative ease of circulating and purchasing individual (rather than shared) copies of texts, the prevalence of socially shared annotations declined, and text annotation became a more private activity consisting of a reader interacting with a text. Annotations made on shared copies of texts (such as library books) are sometimes seen as devaluing the text, or as an act of defacement. Literacy also increased the community that was capable of consuming all forms of knowledge assets – which in turn created new opportunities for derivation and translation. We have been less intentional in tracking the expansion of the use of human capital, procedural capital, and cultural capital; it may be the case that these grew at a more rapid rate than did explicit information derivation and translation. Procedural knowledge derivation and translation began to expand with the initial decades of the industrial revolution – there was a need to codify and continuously improve procedural knowledge. It was not seen as a 'knowledge use' activity until the last decades of the 20th century. It was the standard way of doing business.

Phase 3. Increased value assigned to knowledge in the general public

Increased production of knowledge, and an increasingly educated and literate public, increased the demand for and value of knowledge – of all types. A market for knowledge began to emerge. The increased value of knowledge means increased scrutiny and greater opportunities for new copies, versions, knockoffs, fraud, fakes, losses, theft, and misuse. New markets gave rise to an awareness of quality and trustworthiness. Quality and trustworthiness of knowledge became an issue, whereas, in past centuries, knowledge was taken on faith based on the source. As education became more widely available, the demand for knowledge increased. As more people engaged in organizations and businesses that leverage knowledge, human capital grew exponentially. The boost in human capital gave rise to more opportunities to interpret and create new knowledge assets. As knowledge stocks began to grow, the idea of knowledge synthesis emerged. The more concentrated human capital is concentrated in organizations and businesses, the greater incentive for people to collaborate.

One of the essential new processes to emerge over this phase is peer review. Peer review was introduced to scholarly publication in 1731 by the Royal Society of Edinburgh. Peer review was mainly the purview of editors until the mid-20th century, when a sufficiently large community of scientists and engineers – in essence, a scholarly community – began to support professional peer review. Peer review became an essential quality management and control mechanism in a world of increasing knowledge production and distribution.

Phase 4. Exponential growth of technology

Computer-based technologies have provided new opportunities for individual and socially shared text annotations that support multiple purposes, including readers' individual reading goals, learning, social reading, writing, and augmentation. The explosion of technology at the end of the 20th century accelerated awareness of knowledge use and management. The discipline had been evolving since the 1950s, but increased technical capacity and capability provided the opportunity to put our concepts and theories into practice. What had been mostly invisible and unacknowledged everyday knowledge consumption was now visible and acknowledged. Knowledge technologies became a new market segment. Every form of knowledge use became a dedicated development area for technology development. In turn, these new technologies opened the door to new ways of doing things. Over the past 30 years, we have made knowledge consumption commonplace. Knowledge technologies are now open source and plentiful. The challenge is that we have deferred our understanding of knowledge use patterns to the built environment. The new goal of knowledge architecture is to walk back from those engineered solutions to a more fundamental understanding of behaviors and design.

Phase 5. Development of demand for knowledge and knowledge economy

In the early 21st century, knowledge is a core asset in the economy. The focus has now shifted from knowledge as a by-product of doing business or an asset used by managers to make decisions to a common commodity in the new economy. More people are producing knowledge, and more are consuming knowledge; there are greater interpretation and derivation. Behaviors supporting synthesis and collaboration are still emerging, particularly in economic systems with advanced financial and industrial economies. The tension in this current phase is around competition for and protection of knowledge assets as a competitive business asset. This is in addition to the tension arising from three centuries of evolution of intellectual property protection, which tends towards stockpiling rather than circulating knowledge and intellectual capital. Competing forces, though, such as open access and vendor initiatives to make knowledge more widely available outside of academic or licensed environments, and the rise of social media, are shaping our expectations for access to and use of knowledge assets. We are not yet at the point, though, where we have a clear picture of how these tensions will be resolved, and how all of the different forms of use will be seamlessly integrated into our everyday environments. In the 2020s, it is the person who continues to integrate across all forms and sources of use.

Knowledge augmentation, derivation, and synthesis in the enterprise architecture

This functional architecture aligns with business capabilities and with the business architecture practice. It speaks to the crux of why and how the organization consumes and manages its knowledge assets. All other alignments to the architecture practice are secondary or indirect. For example, we might think to align annotation and review with information management, but in fact these represent activities of business stakeholders.

Chapter review

After reading this chapter, you should be able to:

- explain the positive effects that knowledge consumption can have for an organization;
- explain why we have a gap in coverage of knowledge architecture to support and manage knowledge use;
- describe what we mean by knowledge augmentation, and provide examples from your context;
- describe what we mean by knowledge derivation, and provide examples from your context;
- describe what we mean by knowledge synthesis, and provide examples from your context;
- discuss why it is essential to increase our awareness of how we use knowledge every day, and the need to manage the new value that results from that use.

References and recommended future readings

Arksey, H., & O'Malley, L. (2005). Scoping studies: Towards a methodological framework. *International Journal of Social Research Methodolog, 2005*(8), 19–31.

Arnott, J. C., Neuenfeldt, R. J., & Lemos, M. C. (2020). Co-producing science for sustainability: Can funding change knowledge use? *Global Environmental Change, 60*, 101979.

Atkins, D. E., Brown, J. S., & Hammond, A. L. (2007). *A review of the open educational resources (OER) movement: Achievements, challenges, and new opportunities* (Vol. 164). Creative Common.

Bailar, J. (2011). Reliability, fairness, objectivity and other inappropriate goals in peer review. *Behavioral and Brain Sciences, 14*(1), 137–138.

Banning, J. (2012). *Ecological triangulation: An approach for qualitative meta-synthesis*. Retrieved February 2, 2020 from http://mycahs.colostate.edu/james.h.banning/PDFs/Ecological%20Triangualtion.pdf

Barnett-Page, E., & Thomas, J. (2009). Methods for the synthesis of qualitative research: A critical review. *BMC Medical Research Methodology, 9*(1), 59.

Barroso, J., Gollop, C. J., Sandelowski, M., Meynell, J., Pearce, P. F., & Collins, L. J. (2003). The challenges of searching for and retrieving qualitative studies. *Western Journal of Nursing Research, 25*(2), 153–178.

Beise, M., & Stahl, H. (1999). Public research and industrial innovations in Germany. *Research Policy, 28*(4), 397–422.

Benos, D. J., Bashari, E., Chaves, J. M., Gaggar, A., Kapoor, N., LaFrance, M., & Qadri, Y. (2007). The ups and downs of peer review. *Advances in Physiology Education, 31*(2), 145–152.

Biagioli, M. (2002). From book censorship to academic peer review. *Emergences: Journal for the Study of Media and Composite Cultures, 12*(1), 11–45.

Bornman, L. (2008). Scientific peer review: An analysis of the peer review process from the perspective of sociology of science theories. *Human Architecture: Journal of the Sociology of Self-Knowledge, 6*(2). Retrieved from https://www.researchgate.net/publication/254693844_Scientific_Peer_Review_An_Analysis_of_the_Peer_Review_Process_from_the_Perspective_of_Sociology_of_Science_Theories.

Boswell, C., & Cannon, S. (2009). Critique process. In C. Boswell & S. Cannon (Eds.), *Introduction to nursing research: Incorporating evidence-based practice* (pp. 291–316). Retrieved February 2, 2020 from http://samples.jbpub.com/ 9780763794675/Critique_Process.pdf

Brink, P. J., & Wood, M. J. (2001). *Basic steps in planning nursing research from question to proposal* (5th ed.). Jones and Bartlett.

Brown, J. S., & Duguid, P. (1991). Organizational learning and communities-of-practice: Toward a unified view of working, learning, and innovation. *Organization Science, 2*(1), 40–57.

Brown, R. (2006). Double anonymity and the peer review process *The Scientific World Journal, 6*, 1274–1277.

Brunton, G., Oliver, S., Oliver, K., & Lorenc, T. (2006). *A synthesis of research addressing children's, young people's and parents views of walking and cycling for transport.* London: University of London.

Brush, A. J. (2002). *Annotating digital documents for asynchronous collaboration* (PhD), Dissertation Department of Computer Science and Engineering, University of Washington, Seattle, 119.

Cadiz, J. J., Gupta, A., & Grudin, J. (2000). *Using web annotations for asynchronous collaboration around documents.* Proceedings of CSCW 2000, Philadelphia, PA, 309–318.

Caldwell, K., Henshaw, L., & Taylor, G. (2005). Developing a framework for critiquing health research. *Journal of Health, Social and Environmental Issues, 6*(1), 45–54.

Callaham, M. L., Baxt, W. G., Waeckerle, J. F., & Wears, R. L. (1998). Reliability of editors' subjective quality ratings of peer reviews of manuscripts. *Jama, 280*(3), 229–231.

Camerer, R. (2009). Sprache, Kultur und Kompetenz. Überlegungen zur interkulturellen Kompetenz und ihrer Testbarkeit. *Kompetenzen für die globale Wirtschaft: Begriffe–Erwartungen–Entwicklungsansätze.* Bielefeld: W.Bertelsmann Verlag, pp. 41–64.

Campbell, D. G. (2002). The use of the Dublin core in web annotation programs. In *International conference on Dublin core and metadata for e-communities.* Firenze University Press.

Cook, D. J., Mulrow, C. D., & Haynes, R. B. (1997). Systematic reviews: Synthesis of best evidence for clinical decisions. *Annals of Internal Medicine, 126*(5), 376–380.

Davis, D., Davis, M. E., Jadad, A., Perrier, L., Rath, D., Ryan, D., & Zwarenstein, M. (2003). The case for knowledge translation: Shortening the journey from evidence to effect. *BMJ: British Medical Journal, 327*(7405), 33–35.

Devereaux, P. J., Manns, B. J., Ghali, W. A., Quan, H., & Guyatt, G. H. (2001). Reviewing the reviewers: The quality of reporting in three secondary journals. *CMAJ, 16411*, 1573–1576.

Dixon-Woods, M., Agarwal, S., Jones, D., Young, B., & Sutton, A. (2005). Synthesising qualitative and quantitative evidence: A review of possible methods. *Journal of Health Services Research and Policy*, *10*(1), 45–53.

Dixon-Woods, M., Cavers, D., Agarwal, S., Annandale, E., Arthur, A., Harvey, J., & Riley, R. (2006). Conducting a critical interpretive synthesis of the literature on access to healthcare by vulnerable groups. *BMC Medical Research Methodology*, *6*(1), 35.

Donath, J., Karahalios, K., & Viegas, F. (1999). Visualizing conversation. *Journal of Computer-Mediated Communication*, *4*(4), JCMC442. Stahl and Herrmann, 1999.

Droitcour, J., Silberman, G., & Chelimsky, E. (1993). Cross-design synthesis: A new form of meta-analysis for combining results from randomized clinical trials and medical-practice databases. *International Journal of Technology Assessment in Health Care*, *9*(3), 440–449.

Einsohn, E. (2000). *The copyeditor's handbook*. University of California Press.

Estabrooks, C. A., Thompson, D. S., Lovely, J. J. E., & Hofmeyer, A. (2006). A guide to knowledge translation theory. *Journal of Continuing Education in the Health Professions*, *261*, 25–36.

Farkas, D. K., & Poltrock, S. E. (1995). *Online editing, mark-up models, and the workplace lives of editors and writers* (Vol. 38, No. 2, pp. 110–117). Professional Communication, IEEE Transactions.

Fischer, G., Nakakoji, K., Ostwald, J., Stahl, G., & Sumner, T. (1993). Embedding critics in design environments. *The Knowledge Engineering Review*, *8*(4), 285–307.

Frommholz, I., Brocks, H., Thiel, U., Neuhold, E., Iannone, L., Semeraro, G., & Ceci, M. (2003, August). Document-centered collaboration for scholars in the humanities – The COLLATE system. In *International conference on theory and practice of digital libraries* (pp. 434–445). Springer.

Gennari, J. H., Weng, C., McDonald, D. W., Benedetti, J., & Green, S. (2004). An ethnographic study of collaborative clinical trial protocol writing. *Studies in Health Technology and Informatics*, *107*(Pt 2), 1461–1465.

Godlee, F., Gale, C. R., & Martyn, C. N. (1998). Effect on the quality of peer review of blinding reviewers and asking them to sign their reports: A randomized controlled trial. *JAMA*, *280*(3), 237–240.

Gough, D., Thomas, J., & Oliver, S. (2012). Clarifying differences between review designs and methods. *Systematic Reviews*, *1*(1), 28.

Graham, I. D., Logan, J., Harrison, M. B., Straus, S. E., Tetroe, J., Caswell, W., & Robinson, N. (2006). Lost in knowledge translation: Time for a map? *Journal of Continuing Education in the Health Professions*, *26*(1), 13–24.

Graham, I. D., Tetroe, J., & KT Theories Research Group. (2007). Some theoretical underpinnings of knowledge translation. *Academic Emergency Medicine*, *14*(11), 936–941.

Grant, M. J., & Booth, A. (2009). A typology of reviews: An analysis of 14 review types and associated methodologies. *Health Information and Libraries Journal*, *26*(2), 91–108.

Greenhalgh, T., Kristjansson, E., & Robinson, V. (2007). Realist review to understand the efficacy of school feeding programmes. *BMJ: British Medical Journal*, *335*(7625), 858–861.

Grimshaw, J. M., Eccles, M. P., Lavis, J. N., Hill, S. J., & Squires, J. E. (2012). Knowledge translation of research findings. *Implementation Science*, *7*(1), 50.

Gunawardena, A., Tan, A., & Kaufer, D. (2010). Encouraging reading and collaboration using classroom salon. In *Proceedings of the fifteenth annual conference on innovation and technology in computer science education* (pp. 254–258). ITiCSE '10: Bilkent Ankara Turkey. Association of Computing Machinery.

Handy, R. (1973). The Dewey-Bentley transactional procedures of inquiry. *The Psychological Record*, *23*(3), 305–317.

Hartmann, J., & Sure, Y. (2004, July). A knowledge discovery workbench for the Semantic Web. In *International Workshop on Mining for and from the Semantic Web* (p. 56). Retrieved May 1, 2020, from https://www.kde.cs.uni-kassel.de/wp-content/uploads/hotho/pub/2004/msw2004_proceedings.pdf#page=62.

Higgins, J. P., Thomas, J., Chandler, J., Cumpston, M., Li, T., Page, M. J., & Welch, V. A. (Eds.). (2019). *Cochrane handbook for systematic reviews of interventions.* John Wiley & Sons.

Jacobson, N., Butterill, D., & Goering, P. (2003). Development of a framework for knowledge translation: Understanding user context. *Journal of Health Services Research and Policy, 8*(2), 94–99.

Jensen, L. A., & Allen, M. N. (1996). Meta-synthesis of qualitative findings. *Qualitative Health Research, 6*(4), 553–560.

Kaplan, N., & Chisik, Y. (2005). In the company of readers: The digital library book as practiced place. In *Proceedings of the 5th ACM/IEEE-CS joint conference on digital libraries* (pp. 235–243). ACM Press.

Kastner, M., Estey, E., Perrier, L., Graham, I. D., Grimshaw, J., Straus, S. E., & Bhattacharyya, O. (2011). Understanding the relationship between the perceived characteristics of clinical practice guidelines and their uptake: Protocol for a realist review. *Implementation Science, 6*(1), 69.

Kastner, M., Tricco, A. C., Soobiah, C., Lillie, E., Perrier, L., Horsley, T., & Straus, S. E. (2012). What is the most appropriate knowledge synthesis method to conduct a review? Protocol for a scoping review. *BMC Medical Research Methodology, 12*(1), 114.

Kaufer, D., Gunawardena, A., Tan, A., & Cheek, A. (2011). Bringing social media to the writing classroom: Classroom salon. *Journal of Business and Technical Communication, 25*(3), 299–321.

Kim, S. (1999, August 20–28). The roles of knowledge professionals for knowledge management, in IFLA Council and General Conference. *65th Conference Programme and Proceedings,* Bangkok, Thailand. Retrieved May 1, 2020, from https://archive.ifla.org/IV/ifla65/papers/042-115e.htm.

Krause, U. M., Stark, R., & Mandl, H. (2009). The effects of cooperative learning and feedback on e-learning in statistics. *Learning and Instruction, 19*(2), 158–170.

Lave, J., & Wenger, E. (1991). *Situated learning: Legitimate peripheral participation.* Cambridge University Press.

Lee, C. J., Sugimoto, C. R., Zhang, G., & Cronin, B. (2013). Bias in peer review. *Journal of the American Society for Information Science and Technology, 64*(1), 2–17.

Linn, M. C., Clark, D., & Slotta, J. D. (2003). WISE design for knowledge integration. *Science Education, 87*(4), 517–538.

Lucas, P. J., Baird, J., Arai, L., Law, C., & Roberts, H. M. (2007). Worked examples of alternative methods for the synthesis of qualitative and quantitative research in systematic reviews. *BMC Medical Research Methodology, 7*(1), 4.

Marshall, C. C. (1997). Annotation: From paper books to the digital library. In *Proceedings of the second ACM international conference on Digital libraries* (pp. 131–140). Association for Computing Machinery.

Marshall, C. C. (2009). Reading and writing the electronic book. *Synthesis Lectures on Information Concepts, Retrieval, and Services, 1*(1), 1–185.

Mendenhall, A., Kim, C., & Johnson, T. E. (2011). Implementation of an online social annotation tool in a college English course. In *Multiple perspectives on problem solving and learning in the digital age* (pp. 313–323). Springer.

Meyer, R. M., Lemos, M. C., Mach, K. J., Meadow, A. M., Wyborn, C., Klenk, N., . . . Vaughan, C. (2019). Actionable knowledge and the art of engagement. *AGUFM, 2019,* PA51B-08.

Moss, R. H., Avery, S., Baja, K., Burkett, M., Chischilly, A. M., Dell, J., & Knowlton, K. (2019). Evaluating knowledge to support climate action: A framework for sustained assessment. Report of an independent advisory committee on applied climate assessment. *Weather, Climate, and Society*, *11*(3), 465–487.

Noblit, G. W., & Hare, R. D. (1988). *Meta-ethnography: Synthesizing qualitative studies* (Vol. 11). Sage.

Nonaka, I., & Takeuchi, H. (1995). *The knowledge-creating company: How Japanese companies create the dynamics of innovation*. Oxford University Press.

Novak, E., Razzouk, R., & Johnson, T. E. (2012). The educational use of social annotation tools in higher education: A literature review. *The Internet and Higher Education*, *15*(1), 39–49.

Onwuegbuzie, A. J., Teddlie, C., & Tashakkori, A. (2003). Handbook of mixed methods in social and behavioral research. In *Handbook of mixed methods in social and behavioral research*. Sage.

Paterson, B. L., Thorne, S. E., Canam, C., & Jillings, C. (2001). *Meta-study of qualitative health research: A practical guide to meta-analysis and meta-synthesis* (Vol. 3). Sage.

Pawson, R., Greenhalgh, T., Harvey, G., & Walshe, K. (2005). Realist review-a new method of systematic review designed for complex policy interventions. *Journal of Health Services Research and Policy*, *10*(S1), 21–34.

Pluye, P., Gagnon, M. P., Griffiths, F., & Johnson-Lafleur, J. (2009). A scoring system for appraising mixed methods research, and concomitantly appraising qualitative, quantitative and mixed methods primary studies in mixed studies reviews. *International Journal of Nursing Studies*, *46*(4), 529–546.

Pluye, P., Grad, R. M., Dunikowski, L. G., & Stephenson, R. (2005). Impact of clinical information-retrieval technology on physicians: A literature review of quantitative, qualitative and mixed methods studies. *International Journal of Medical Informatics*, *74*(9), 745–768.

Polanyi, M. (1962). Tacit knowing: Its bearing on some problems of philosophy. *Reviews of Modern Physics*, *34*(4), 601.

Popay, J., Roberts, H., Sowden, A., Petticrew, M., Arai, L., Rodgers, M., Britten, N., Roen, K., & Duffy, S. (2006). Guidance on the conduct of narrative synthesis in systematic reviews. *A Product from the ESRC Methods Programme Version*, *1*(2006), b92.

Pope, C., Ziebland, S., & Mays, N. (2000). Qualitative research in health care: Analysing qualitative data. *BMJ: British Medical Journal*, *320*(7227), 114.

Ring, N. A., Ritchie, K., Mandava, L., & Jepson, R. (2011). *A guide to synthesising qualitative research for researchers undertaking health technology assessments and systematic reviews*. Retrieved February 2, 2020, from www.healthcareimprovementscotland.org/programmes/clinical__cost_effectiveness/shtg/synth_qualitative_research.aspx

Roberts, K. A., Dixon-Woods, M., Fitzpatrick, R., Abrams, K. R., & Jones, D. R. (2002). Factors affecting uptake of childhood immunisation: A Bayesian synthesis of qualitative and quantitative evidence. *The Lancet*, *360*(9345), 1596–1599.

Rycroft-Malone, J., McCormack, B., Hutchinson, A. M., DeCorby, K., Bucknall, T. K., Kent, B., & Wallin, L. (2012). Realist synthesis: Illustrating the method for implementation research. *Implementation Science*, *7*(1), 33.

Sampson, M., McGowan, J., Cogo, E., Grimshaw, J., Moher, D., & Lefebvre, C. (2009). An evidence-based practice guideline for the peer review of electronic search strategies. *Journal of Clinical Epidemiology*, *62*(9), 944–952.

Samuelson, P., & Nordhaus, W. (1985). *Principles of economics*. McGraw-Hill.

Sandelowski, M. (1997). "To be of use": Enhancing the utility of qualitative research. *Nursing Outlook*, *45*(3), 125–132.

Sandelowski, M., & Barroso, J. (2003). Creating metasummaries of qualitative findings. *Nursing Research, 52*(4), 226–233.

Schank, R. C. (1975). Using knowledge to understand. In *Theoretical issues in natural language processing.* Association for Computing Machinery.

Schneckenberg, D. (2008). *Educating tomorrow's knowledge workers: The concept of eCompetence and its application in international higher education.* Eburon Uitgeverij BV.

Shabajee, P., & Reynolds, D. (2003). *What is annotation? A short review of annotation and annotation systems* (pp. 213–223). Tech. Rep. ILRT Research Report No. 1053, Institute for Learning & Research Technology.

Shepperd, S., Lewin, S., Straus, S., Clarke, M., Eccles, M. P., Fitzpatrick, R., . . . Sheikh, A. (2009). Can we systematically review studies that evaluate complex interventions? *PLoS Medicine, 6*(8), e1000086.

Spier, R. (2002). The history of the peer-review process. *TRENDS in Biotechnology, 20*(8), 357–358.

Stemler, S. (2000). An overview of content analysis. *Practical Assessment, Research, and Evaluation, 7*(1), 17.

Straus, S. E., Tetroe, J., & Graham, I. D. (1988). 1.1 Knowledge to action: What it is and what it isn't. *Knowledge translation in health care: Moving from evidence to practice* (Vol. 3). Wiley.

Straus, S. E., Tetroe, J., & Graham, I. D. (Eds.). (2013). *Knowledge translation in health care: Moving from evidence to practice.* John Wiley & Sons.

Strauss, A., & Corbin, J. (1998). *Basics of qualitative research techniques.* Sage.

Sudsawad, P. (2007). *Knowledge translation: Introduction to models, strategies and measures.* Southwest Educational Development Laboratory, National Center for the Dissemination of Disability Research.

Sutton, A. J., & Abrams, K. R. (2001). Bayesian methods in meta-analysis and evidence synthesis. *Statistical Methods in Medical Research, 10*, 277–303.

Tenkasi, R. V., & Boland, R. J. (1996). Exploring knowledge diversity in knowledge intensive firms: A new role for information systems. *Journal of Organizational Change Management.* Retrieved from http://www.tlainc.com/article4.htm

Tetroe, J. (2007). Knowledge translation at the Canadian Institutes of Health Research: A primer. *Focus Technical Brief, 18*, 1–8.

Thomas, J., & Harden, A. (2008). Methods for the thematic synthesis of qualitative research in systematic reviews. *BMC Medical Research Methodology, 8*(1), 45.

Tricco, A. C., Soobiah, C., Antony, J., Cogo, E., MacDonald, H., Lillie, E., & Welch, V. (2016). A scoping review identifies multiple emerging knowledge synthesis methods, but few studies operationalize the method. *Journal of Clinical Epidemiology, 73*, 19–28.

Virbel, J. (1993). Reading and managing texts on the Bibliotheque de France station. In *The digital word: Text-based computing in the humanities* (pp. 31–51).

Weed, M. (2005). Meta Interpretation: A Method for the Interpretive Synthesis of Qualitative Research. In *Forum qualitative sozialforschung/forum: Qualitative social research* (Vol. 6, No. 1). Institute for Qualitative Research and the Center for Digital Systems, Freie Universität Berlin.

Weng, C., & Gennari, J. H. (2004). Asynchronous collaborative writing through annotations. In *Proceedings of the 2004 ACM conference on computer supported cooperative work* (pp. 578–581). Association for Computing Machinery.

Weng, C., Gennari, J. H., & McDonald, D. W. (2004). A collaborative clinical trial protocol writing system. In *Medinfo* (pp. 1481–1485). IOS Press.

Winterton, J., Delamare-Le Deist, F., & Stringfellow, E. (2005, January 26). *Typology of knowledge, skills and competences: Clarification of the concept and prototype.* Centre for

European Research on Employment and Human Resources Groupe ESC Toulouse Research report elaborated on behalf of Cedefop/Thessaloniki. Final draft (CEDEFOP Project No RP/B/BS/Credit Transfer/005/04).

Wolfe, J. L. (2000). Effects of annotations on student readers and writers. In *Proceedings of the fifth ACM conference on Digital libraries* (pp. 19–26). Association for Computing Machinery.

Wolfe, J. L. (2002). Annotation technologies: A software and research review. *Computers and Composition, 19*(4), 471–497.

Wolfe, J. L. (2008). Annotations and the collaborative digital library: Effects of an aligned annotation interface on student argumentation and reading strategies. *International Journal of Computer-Supported Collaborative Learning, 3*(2), 141.

Wolfe, J. L., & Neuwirth, C. M. (2001). From the margins to the center: The future of annotation. *Journal of Business and Technical Communication, 15*(3), 333–371.

Yin, R. K. (2003). Applied social research methods series. *Case Study Research: Design and Methods, 5*(1).

Yin, R. K., & Heald, K. A. (1975). Using the case survey method to analyze policy studies. *Administrative Science Quarterly*, 371–381.

18

FUNCTIONAL ARCHITECTURE TO MANAGE RISK AND HARM

Chapter summary

This chapter considers the types of harm and risk an organization can incur from making available, accessible, and consumable knowledge assets. We consider the types of harm that might naturally result from the use of knowledge that has value to the organization. The chapter explains the importance of working with business managers to determine the degree of risk any business might encounter. It reminds us that every organization has a unique business context. This chapter walks through several design activities and tasks, including identifying risk factors, identifying the business custodians and stewards who can advise on the degree of risks, determining the cost-benefit model for safeguarding assets, and designing a risk management portfolio. This chapter also considers why it is essential to understand the spectrum of harm, including knowledge loss, knowledge theft, knowledge damage or misuse, asset tampering, and the creation of fake knowledge. The primary challenge in designing this functional architecture is exposing the harm that has occurred in the past and shaping systems and human behaviors to protect against harm.

Why we care about managing risk and harm

Knowledge use and consumption are what produce business value. With increased usage and consumption comes increased risk. As noted earlier, we have designed some methods for managing and mitigating risk, but our design is not complete. Every organization has its view of what constitutes risk based on the type of harm it might experience. Use creates the opportunity for harm. We manage potential business harm by managing risk. The range of risks associated with the use of knowledge assets expands significantly in the knowledge economy. Increased knowledge use creates opportunities and incentives for broader distribution, for changing and adding to, interpreting, and translating knowledge assets. These actions can also lead to damage, plagiarism, tampering, counterfeiting, misrepresentation, misappropriation, and theft. To support use and consumption while managing risk and harm, we need to understand the nature of the harm possible and the probability of the chance of that harm occurring. Once we know the nature of the harm to a type of knowledge asset and the probability of risk through use, we can design a strategy to mitigate those risks. First, let's understand the kinds of harm that can come to knowledge assets through use. Then let's focus on a strategy that minimizes the risk of the harm occurring.

Knowledge asset harm and risk – design concepts

To design a functional architecture to mitigate risk, we need to understand the types of harm possible, the degree of harm experienced, and the probability of risk to each type of knowledge asset. We should have a good understanding of the full spectrum of harm, including (1) asset loss, (2) asset theft, (3) physical harm, (4) tampering and misuse of assets, and (5) the creation of false and fake assets. We also need to understand business risk, risk mitigation, and risk portfolio development. The primary challenge we face in designing this functional architecture is recognizing the harm that can occur, raising awareness among staff, and providing the support structures for recording harm and alerting users to risk.

Types of harm to knowledge assets incurred through consumption

Recognizing and determining harm to actual knowledge assets is a human activity (Bate, 1964; Bogg & Stanton-Ife, 2003; Elvins, 2008; Eser, 1965; Riley & O'Hare, 2000; Riley et al., 1999; Steel, 2008). The knowledge architecture can support this human activity by providing the capability to tag assets that have been or are at potential risk of harm. To design those capabilities, we need a good understanding of the types of harm that can occur. Harm is defined as an injury that may include physical hurt, damage to reputation or dignity, the loss of a legal right, or a breach of contract. Harm may be inflicted willfully – intentionally causing harm – or negligently. Failing to understand harm can generate significant liabilities to the business. Harm may depend on the sensitivity of the object and the harm that it can cause if it is exposed to different kinds of risks. For this text, we identify five types of risks that may result from increased use of knowledge assets: (1) loss of the asset; (2) theft of the asset; (3) physical harm to the asset; (4) tampering with the asset; and (5) creation of a false asset (Figure 18.1). Each type of harm may occur to a greater or lesser degree.

Asset loss means the asset is no longer available for others to access or consume. The simple act of making an asset available creates an opportunity for loss. Loss may be intentional or unintentional; it may be caused by human negligence, a

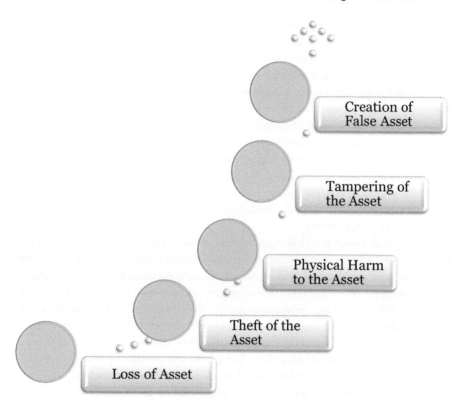

FIGURE 18.1 Degrees of Risk to Knowledge Assets Through Use

natural disaster or force majeure, or simple wear and tear. Loss of a critical business asset can be devastating to an organization. Microsoft can rebuild a facility within a matter of months. However, the loss of Microsoft's development engineers in a hurricane or an earthquake would take years to rebuild. Having a business continuity plan that backs up all their knowledge may shorten an otherwise impossible task. Organizations sustain 'planned' and intentional loss of human capital every day – in the form of retirements.

Only recently have we realized the impact this built-in loss has on our organizations. Several decades ago, academic research libraries realized the effect that normal wear and tear would have on explicit information, particularly books, journals, and special collections. A consortium of these libraries designed a plan to identify the most vulnerable and essential assets and to ensure that at least one copy was available for future use. Individual organizations may have archives management practices in place. In most cases, a natural disaster, limited incidents in key offices, and even simple power outages or server failure, can result in permanent loss of explicit assets. Loss can result from negligence. Consider the loss of years of critical project data due to the negligence of a project manager who fails to test a migration program in a development environment, but moves forward to a live migration and with no rollback strategy. It is not a deliberate loss, but it has a substantial business impact. We have only to recall the most famous loss of procedural knowledge – the failure of NASA managers to ensure that all of the working procedural knowledge that went into the Apollo missions was preserved. Consider what would happen if Heinz lost the recipe for its famous ketchup, or Kraft lost the recipe for the cheese used in so many products. The loss of cultural knowledge is continuous – in the form of change. Cultural change occurs when an individual leaves a group, and a new person joins. Cultural change is visible at the leadership level because the impact of leadership culture can be more significant. For cultural knowledge, the issue is, when does the degree of cultural change become a loss? Network knowledge is a vital mechanism for knowledge use and transmission. Loss of networks will most likely result from intentional administrative actions and organizational restructuring.

We can understand the challenges that use creates. The critical question is, how do we design a knowledge architecture that identifies and alerts us to potential losses, and how can that architecture help us to mitigate those losses? What kind of business strategy do we need to have to prevent or reduce the impact of loss? And, how does the knowledge architecture enable these strategies? We need to know which of our knowledge assets are vulnerable, and we should have security in place for vulnerable assets. The architecture should allow an organization to apportion the use of assets that are at risk of loss, and whose loss would impact the organization. It means we need an architecture that allows us to identify the risk, to secure the asset for its useful business life, and to permit access to ensure both values and to mitigate loss.

Asset theft means that providing access and permitting the use of the asset was stolen. The effect is similar to loss but different because the asset is still available for use. When a single instance asset is stolen, it is no longer available to the original custodian or owner, but it is now available to another party. From a legal perspective, theft implies intent and malicious action. And, the consequences of theft are judged by the value of the asset that has been stolen. Theft has been applied to property – physical property, financial property, and intellectual property. In a knowledge sciences context, property means assets. A challenge we face – and a significant challenge – is to expand our understanding from the simpler characterization of intellectual property to knowledge capital – all forms of knowledge assets. What does it mean to steal human knowledge? To steal explicit knowledge? To steal procedural knowledge? To steal cultural knowledge? And, to steal network capital?

A spectrum of actions come to mind when we ask these questions. Our first response to these questions is, 'Well, it depends on what you mean by theft.' And, this response is exactly correct. Theft represents a range of actions concerning knowledge capital – it is a spectrum of actions. And, the value of the theft varies with the action and the asset. The impact of the theft depends on who is responsible for the theft and who receives the benefit. Theft in the form of plagiarism gives benefit to the thief but does not necessarily confer an equivalent degree of harm to the owner. For example, theft of culture may more closely resemble deliberate sharing and may not have a negative value to the source. Plagiarism is a form of theft, but it does not diminish or steal value from the source – it merely confers unearned value on the recipient. And, how do we distinguish intentional plagiarism from deep and inherent learning from a source? Theft is easier to discover and easier to value for explicit knowledge than for human capital. When a competitor recruits an individual, this is a form of theft of human capital. When an individual is denied the opportunity to express or leverage their tacit knowledge or skills and competencies due to political or social discrimination, this is a form of theft. When procedural knowledge is leaked from an organization to a competitor or a national security source, this is a clear form of theft.

The challenges of use are clear here, as well. How do we design a knowledge architecture that supports use but reduces the opportunity for theft? And, different degrees of theft? At the low end of the stage, we want to make sure we know who is using which assets because this allows us to trace theft, appropriation, or reproduction in the future. The methods we use to track copies and to manage versions are an excellent place to begin. Contacts, custodianship, and provenance tracking provide a foundation for understanding where an asset has traveled and has been consumed. The methods we use to authenticate an asset are essential for detecting and deterring theft. Having a strong security infrastructure is also essential, as it can assign and manage access privileges.

Physical harm and damaged assets are those assets that are available but, for some reason, is no longer usable. Damage occurs in degrees. Some damage can be repaired, whereas other damage renders the asset unusable from a business perspective. It may have been altered or suffered damage in a way that makes it no longer accessible. For example, an original photograph of an early founder working in a laboratory may be poorly stored. The paper stock has deteriorated to such an extent that it cannot be repaired. Or, the damage may mean expiration or spoilage such that it is no longer consumable. For example, process knowledge that was dependent upon a natural ingredient is no longer relevant as it has been replaced with a new synthetic ingredient that has entirely different proportions. The process recipe has expired and must be replaced with a new recipe. The challenge is that knowledge assets don't come with an expiration date. We know their shelf life only by continuous review and comparison to new assets. In a business environment, we would refer to this as determining the useful business life of an asset, and by assigning a current value and a depreciated value over time. It may also have been damaged or tarnished in a way that makes it no longer trustworthy or desirable to use. For example, a subject matter expert has been found to have stolen or misrepresented his research. The organization can no longer trust his tacit knowledge as being real or effective.

We're accustomed to visible detection of damaged equipment for physical assets, and we can see when a financial asset has been damaged. But detecting errors and faults in knowledge assets is more challenging. What is enlightening is that it is only through use and consumption that we can discover faults and errors in tacit knowledge, skills, and procedural knowledge, in our business cultures, and our networks. The opportunity here is to have mechanisms built into the knowledge architectures that allow us to capture and isolate the faulty assets so they can be repaired or corrected. It was interesting to us to realize that this was the purpose of the earliest 'lessons learned' in the early years of knowledge management systems. Recently, there has been a resurgence of interest in building failure points into our projects or learning to value our mistakes and to learn from them. These strategies speak directly to how we trap and repair damaged assets.

The challenge is clear to a knowledge manager and a knowledge architect. It is also clear to an information professional and an archivist. It is not as clear, though, to business managers. The impact of damage becomes apparent once it has occurred. We tend to focus on loss, theft, unauthorized use, and tampering rather than on everyday or routine damage. It is perhaps the most common form of harm, though, and the most difficult to prevent or mitigate. How do we prevent harm from coming to an individual's tacit knowledge? How do we prevent or reduce the chance of procedural knowledge being damaged? Perhaps the critical design principle comes from how we manage explicit knowledge. The knowledge architecture can help to mitigate against damage by ensuring that the version of a knowledge asset that is used is accessible and consumable but not directly 'changeable.' It preserves the original asset and lessens the risk of damage. Or, when an asset is changed, the nature of the change is marked, and a new version or instance is created. It allows us to 'roll back' to the earlier version. A knowledge architecture that supports authentication and change tracking, and manages access is a good starting point.

Tampering with the asset results from well-intentioned and malicious actions. As with theft and damage, there are degrees of tampering. Physical assets that have been tampered with are more easily detected than are knowledge assets. We can detect a medication whose package seal has been broken and repaired. We can detect a tire that has been intentionally punctured, though it may still function for a while. A production line may be tampered with if something about the assembly line is deliberately changed, or if one of the workers fails to apply an important part. A manager may intentionally change a resource or method to save time or money without regard to the impact on the product.

One of the most common forms of tampering is censorship, which prevents us from seeing the true knowledge asset. What does it mean to tamper with an individual's tacit knowledge? It is challenging because it means ensuring that if an individual encounters bad or faulty knowledge, they can detect it and either not consume it or ensure that they can counteract the use. What does it mean to tamper with explicit knowledge? Tampering might take the form of a deliberate or dishonest change or attribution. It might involve removing an element from a document or a book. It might mean removing papers or presentations from a proceeding to ensure an unpopular idea is not promoted. An individual can misrepresent behaviors or intentionally sabotage a business unit's culture to prevent it from working together and achieving a business goal. Or, an individual's reputation might be questioned or their actions in a community misrepresented. All of these actions result from having access to and using the knowledge asset. While the method or nature of the change may vary, the impact will be consistent. The end use or product will have been altered, and the alteration means a lower-quality, less usable, or less trustworthy asset.

Tampering may also be extreme and take the form of deliberate destruction. Consider an out-going administrator who decides to erase servers so the incoming administration does not have access to vital business data. Consider the intentional destruction of management communication and records with legal discovery value by a corrupt manager. Perhaps the most extreme form of tampering is the intentional incapacitation or silencing of an individual whose tacit knowledge is a threat to a manager or a competitor organization. These are examples of tampering, though they are extreme and should be rare.

How can knowledge architecture help to reduce the chances of tampering? It is a design challenge. Three elements are crucial to managing or recovering from tampering, including: (1) detection of the change; (2) knowing what kinds of changes may cause harm; and (3) having a persistent version of the source asset to use for comparison. Knowledge architecture can prevent tampering by ensuring that the authentic source version is safeguarded from change or alteration and that any alteration is traceable. It is vital to have some way to authenticate the source asset to counter or roll back the changes that result from tampering. It is also essential to be able to acknowledge and record the tampering to ensure that the effects can be countered.

Additionally, the architecture should be able to link the source asset and the correction or errata. While security is essential, a security infrastructure does not prevent malicious action. Access control is a mitigating component, but it only reduces who has access. It does not prevent someone who has access from making a change that is intended to cause harm.

The creation of false assets is a form of harm that is relatively recent to knowledge management. Like the other forms of harm, false assets fall into a spectrum. At the low end of the spectrum, we have the kinds of false assets that create harm but may not be illegal or are created with the intention of false gain. These might include propaganda or disinformation. At the other end of the spectrum, we have complete forgeries – an asset created or developed to be something it is not. In the middle of the spectrum, we have reproductions, bootlegged copies, fake assets, and falsified assets.

A forged or a counterfeit asset is an illegal copy of an original that actually exists, or is an illegal representation of an asset that does not exist but is deliberately attributed to a source for illegal gain. A document may be produced with antique materials, using antique tools and methods, and made available with false credentials. Forged assets often mimic the style of a known creator. Forged assets may mimic the package or the encoding of the original asset. Forged assets often imitate the style of a famous author. If an original manuscript, typewritten text, or recording is available, the medium itself can be falsified.

Unauthorized reproduction or knockoff may be a legal or illegal copy intended to resemble an original asset but is consumed at a lower cost without fraud. Copying and making bootlegged copies of assets also falls along this spectrum. These are exact replications of the original intended for consumption without compensation or reciprocity. Organizations may inadvertently extend use to those who are not entitled to access (e.g., outside of a contract or a licensing agreement) and thus create 'bootlegged copies.'

Falsified or fake assets are those that cannot be authenticated or verified, do not have a known or credible source, and have a high probability of being untrue or false in some way. The intention may or may not be to achieve a monetary gain. Fake assets may be written to generate a profit and distributed through a variety of channels. Typically, they are targeted to consumers who are eager to trust the asset. Fake assets survive and have an impact when the consumer either does not have the means to verify the source or does not take the time to verify it. Fake assets have some semblance of legitimacy in that they mimic a processor that has sufficient characteristics to deceive the consumer.

A kind of false asset is disinformation – explicit information intended to mislead. Intentional falsifications are intentionally designed to deceive or create the desired effect. Consider falsified research results or falsified credentials. Falsified assets have something in common with tampered assets in that both have corrupted elements. A falsified asset is mostly or wholly false, though, whereas an asset that has been tampered with may only be partially changed. Satirical assets are a form of false assets but without the intention to defraud. Satirical assets have an aspect of the truth but are intentionally and openly presenting variations of the truth for entertainment purposes. Satirical assets can be misinterpreted and confused with source assets. Propaganda is a form of false explicit information that represents a bias and contains misleading or partial truth. Propaganda is designed to promote or publicize a particular point of view or cause. Propaganda most often takes an explicit form but may also be generated and spread as tacit knowledge, through cultural practices, or reflected in an individual or group's assumptions, beliefs, and behaviors.

How do we design a knowledge architecture to detect and prevent the use of false or bad knowledge assets? The knowledge architecture should enable us to determine the source, to verify the asset, to trace its provenance, and to discern any malicious intent. Attribution, identification, and provenance tracking are essential and effective authentication methods to mitigate the damage from false or forged assets. In the case of false or bootlegged copies, access controls are essential. The knowledge architecture must go one step further, though, in preventing access to forged assets, tagging them as false assets, and preserving the evidence of falsification or forgery.

Aligning types of risk with knowledge assets

Designing risk management into our knowledge architecture means understanding what functional architectures have the greatest value to which types of assets (Chapman, 2011; Gibb & Buchanan, 2006; Herbane et al., 2004; Hiles, 2010;

Hoyt & Liebenberg, 2011; Lam, 2014; Olsson, 2008; Petit, 2012; Sanchez et al., 2009). We present some generic and universal thoughts on common types of harm. However, every organization will have a different degree of risk. The probability of risk and the impact of harm is something that each organization must assess. If resources must be prioritized, understanding which functional architectures have the greatest value for the type of asset is a good starting point. We are all familiar with the examples of harm described in the following.

What tacit knowledge harm can include

An individual leaving an organization or being assigned to another unit is an example of lost tacit knowledge. An example of stolen tacit knowledge is appropriation of an idea by someone who is not its source, or an individual who takes credit for some tacit knowledge they have not developed. An example of damaged tacit knowledge is the knowledge that has expired, has errors, or has not been fully vetted. An altered asset is one that has been deliberately or intentionally changed to represent an illegitimate idea or partially accurate concept. An example of false tacit knowledge might be falsified ideas, a deliberate misrepresentation of facts, or the creation of counterfeit research results.

Harm to skills and competencies can include lost skills and competencies, including an individual who has changed roles and lost competencies due to lack of use in the new job. Over time, those skills and competencies may degrade through lack of practice. Consider a lawyer who fails to renew his license, or a carpenter who fails to keep up with the latest materials and building codes, or a dentist who fails to take the required continuing education courses to the main certification. An example of a stolen competence might include a sports team's intentional theft of a playbook or communication signals from another team, or theft of a political candidate's strategy and briefing book. Damaged skills or competence might refer to an individual who takes a training course that is not certified or apprentices with someone who does not have quality skills. An example of an altered skill or competence may be someone who knows how to do something but is told to do the work differently to reduce costs or speed up production. An example of a false or counterfeit skill is a false credential or a counterfeit diploma from a trade school.

Harm to explicit knowledge assets might include any of the examples we described earlier in the chapter, since our experience with the concept derives from established methods in physical and digital assets.

Harm to procedural knowledge assets might include lost procedural knowledge discovered after a team has retired without replacement. An example of a stolen procedural knowledge is intentional leakage of critical operational knowledge to a competitor. An example of damaged procedural knowledge is a changing process that is untested and corrupted but is transferred to another plant or location. Damage results when a business manager changes materials or tools and generates defective outputs. Or, where that manager deliberately ignores knowledge to reduce quality standards, creating faulty products. False procedural knowledge includes a patent application that describes a process an organization is not using, has not demonstrated or tested, or does not own.

Harm to cultural knowledge assets can include the loss of culture when a key leader leaves or a team is dispersed. Stolen cultural knowledge can include recruiting away a lead or team to a competitor, or taking another unit's assumptions and beliefs and associating them with a second unit. Damaged cultural knowledge includes negative or counterproductive behaviors and values. Altered cultural capital may include changes to espoused organizational values, or a negative critical incident such as a public feud between a CEO and a Board of Directors. False cultural capital may include espoused and publicized values and behaviors that do not truly represent the organization's culture.

Harm to relational knowledge assets can include lost network knowledge in the form of informal networks that lose members or are disbanded by the organization. Examples of stolen relational knowledge can include recruiting members from networks or creating a duplicate, closed network. Damaged relational knowledge may include actions that are sabotaging networks, planting false ideas, or creating discord among the members to render the network less effective. Altered relational knowledge may include censoring members' communications or exchanges within the network. False relational knowledge may include the creation of fake networks, fake community, fake social media groups, or fake messages within a network.

Managing risk to knowledge assets

Risk is essential to manage because any of these forms of harm can result in a negative business impact on business processes, products, and the bottom line. Risk is determined by the nature of potential harm and the probability that harm will occur. A knowledge architecture should have functionality that enables us to detect, mark, correct, disable, or destroy assets whose use may harm the business. The knowledge architecture must acknowledge and provide solutions for these new risks and threats. The knowledge architecture should help us determine whether the asset is authentic, whether the knowledge asset is secured from unauthorized access, and whether the knowledge has or will be appropriately consumed. Armed with a good understanding of the types of harm and the nature of the risks, we can consider how to design an architecture to support authentication and provenance tracking (Chapter 19), to support security control (Chapter 20), and to support access privileges (Chapter 21). Each of these functions requires its functional architecture, and each has warranted a full chapter in this text.

Some functionality exists today in our application architecture. But, this functionality may need to be extended or enhanced to ensure it applies to all kinds of knowledge assets. How do we decide what to expand, what to enhance? And how many resources can we devote to designing this layer of protection? How do we balance the value of the use of knowledge assets with the potential cost of harm? It is impractical to assume we can prevent all forms of harm. We need to understand the type of risk associated with any asset and the form of harm. What is the risk? And how do we build it into the design of a knowledge architecture?

Risk is measured by degrees of harm. We can never eliminate risk, but we can identify the levels of harm that are likely to occur and the degree of harm we can and cannot tolerate. The goal of effective risk management is to understand and manage uncertainty effectively. Executives must be the integrators of the different risk positions of the organization and its internal and external environments. Cultural and information risk models and methods need to be designed for integration into the organization's overall risk portfolio.

Risk assessment is a process that allows us to understand risks, define risk criteria, assess the probability and the consequences of that risk occurring, define a level of risk we can tolerate and afford, and define a cost-effective and efficient mitigation treatment. The authors provide a risk assessment and analysis method which you can use to (1) build cultural risk into your organizational risk management profile, and (2) adapt the organization's risk management profile to include cultural risks. The author has leveraged the ISO 31000/31010 risk management model, but has expanded and adapted it to account for the level of cultural risk an organization may carry. The author walks through and translate each of the seven steps to account for cultural risks.

Risk is inherent in everything that we do. Risk management helps us make better decisions in specific contexts. Risk management helps us to manage our organizations in real-world situations. Strategies are often formulated for ideal situations or the best of all possible worlds. In formulating strategies, it means that organizations fail to consider the everyday risks involved in conducting the organization's business. Risk assessment is a process that allows us to understand risks, define risk criteria, assess the probability and the consequences of that risk occurring, define a level of risk we can tolerate and afford, and define a cost-effective and efficient mitigation treatment. Chapter 10 provided a high-level description of the types of risks an organization might encounter – risks generated by suboptimal formulation and management of strategy, and risks generated by ignoring or failing to recognize the influence of culture. In this chapter, we describe how to translate those generic hazards and risks into actual risk calculations. I recommend aligning your strategic and cultural risks with the organization's risk management profile.

Knowledge asset harm and risk management – the design environment

What factors do we need to consider in designing this architecture? To design this functional architecture, we must consider how to affect the organization's casual approach to working with and selecting knowledge for business decisions without precautions to determine whether it is authentic, i.e., stolen, damaged, tampered with, or false. We must consider the lack of awareness of the harm that can result from business knowledge; the behavioral changes needed to ensure respect for the value of knowledge assets, the lack of mechanisms for staff to report knowledge at risk, and the lack of mechanisms for managers to track and manage this business risk systematically.

What events cause us to design a functional architecture for authentication? The most common triggers are critical incidents that alert the organization to business risks it had previously discounted. It might include the loss of a key founding document due to failure to preserve it and ensure proper handling, the theft of critical business process knowledge, the misrepresentation of an individual's reputation by a competitor, the release of an internal financial report with corrupted information, or the creation of a false news story about a corporate leader to damage the reputation of the organization.

What are the impacts and consequences of having this functional architecture? The effect of this functional architecture will include a reduced business risk from knowledge assets, an increased business value generated by knowledge assets available to business stakeholders, the enhanced reputation of the organization due to capability to manage risk to all sources of knowledge, and cultural changes in the form of behaviors that increase the understanding of the value and potential hazards in the knowledge economy.

What inputs do we need to consider when designing this functional architecture? Designing this functional architecture requires a broad knowledge of types of harm that can occur, an understanding of how to balance the business value of use and access with the potential risk, increased awareness of business risk and behavior change needed to avoid risks, a risk management strategy for each type of knowledge asset, training materials to increase awareness of harm, and methods to authenticate knowledge assets, to secure assets, and to control access.

What are the outputs and outcomes this functional architecture generates? This functional architecture makes it possible for an organization to track risks and report harm for individual knowledge assets, to tag assets that have some type of harm, to caution against their use, and to formulate, monitor, report, and manage a knowledge asset risk portfolio.

Design activities for knowledge asset harm and risk management

Designing an organization architecture to track and mitigate harm involves five activities, including;

- Activity 1. Identify risk factors
- Activity 2. Identify the business custodian and steward
- Activity 3. Determine the degree of risk
- Activity 4. Design a risk management portfolio for the unit
- Activity 5. Design an organization-level risk management portfolio

Activity 1. Identify risk factors

How do we do this? Risk begins with an understanding of the value of an asset and the kinds of harm that asset might sustain. The probability of harm is the likelihood of a specific threat occurring. Risk is entirely dependent on the business context. We can gauge the most common forms of harm for an asset. The probability of experiencing that harm and its significance to the organization varies from one business environment to the next. Calculating and planning for risk is a human activity, and not one that our architecture can perform for us. The architecture can record our calculations and assessments, though. Assessing risk is not a one-time event – it is continuous. Risk changes with the changes in the environment. The architecture must allow us to record but also change risk levels. When we talk about risk management, many organizations will understand business continuity planning. Our risk factors should be integrated into these strategies. Often, though, these strategies are separate from our working environments, and they rarely address business-critical knowledge assets other than systems. These strategies focus on technology backups and fallbacks and essential staff and remote working. They do not address critical knowledge assets unless they fall into the 'explicit knowledge' category. Working with your organization's business continuity team is a good place to start designing your knowledge risk management architecture. The knowledge architect should facilitate this task, but it should be 'owned' by business managers. We recommend that you take knowledge asset types as your starting point, then assess their types of harm and the probability of risk.

What inputs does it require? For this activity, we need to know our knowledge assets, and architects need to have a sense from business managers of the potential harm to those assets. We need a working framework to use to map out our risk portfolio.

What outputs does it generate? This activity should generate a working risk portfolio for knowledge assets. The portfolio should cover all assets across the organization, but the final output should be a risk management portfolio that each business manager has in hand. A risk portfolio is also a working tool for the business continuity team.

What other resources does it require? Perhaps the most important resource is the business managers' understanding of the business environment, the potential harm, and the practicality and cost of protecting and safeguarding.

Activity 2. Identify the business custodian and steward

How do we do this? We begin by identifying the custodians and stewards for business-critical knowledge assets. The place to begin is by focusing on business capabilities or functions, discovering units that perform common processes and whose knowledge assets have the greatest value to the organization. This activity involves consulting with those business managers and stakeholders to gain their guidance on what is business-critical. This outreach creates an essential connection for raising awareness and for tracking potential or historical risks.

What inputs does it require? This activity leverages the inventory of knowledge assets – the inventory you created to develop your knowledge object models. Business custodians and stewards will also benefit from a high-level description of kinds of harm to make it easier for them to gauge risk.

What outputs does it generate? This activity generates a working list of custodians and stewards in developing a risk management strategy and managing the risk management portfolio.

What other resources does it require? Knowledge of the business environment – internal and external – is essential to this activity. It is knowledge the business managers and stakeholders can provide.

Activity 3. Determine the degree of risk

How do we do this? This activity is communications-heavy. It involves consultation with business managers, particularly those responsible for business-critical operations and functions. The purpose of this activity is to gain sufficient knowledge about how these managers think about the risk to design prototype risk tracking and recording methods. This activity also involves understanding which systems and applications are most often used by the units to ensure that we can surface any risk attributes in those working environments.

What inputs does it require? This activity leverages a list of business managers as custodians and stewards of the knowledge assets at risk. It also leverages a list of business application administrators and stewards to ensure we understand how to best design an architecture for seamless integration.

What outputs does it generate? This activity generates descriptions of attributes for marking the risk factors for knowledge assets, preliminary design blueprints for risk management reports, and a risk management dashboard (Ballou et al., 2010; Bunting & Siegal, 2017).

What other resources does it require? This activity would benefit from business managers' experience with historical incidents involving harm and the business risks that resulted.

Activity 4. Design a risk management portfolio for the unit

How do we do this? Activity 3 should provide us with preliminary design blueprints for risk tacking, reporting, and portfolio management. In this activity, we review those blueprints with business managers to hear their feedback. Mainly, this activity involves integrating the feedback from individual business units to ensure that the architecture design is practical, efficient, and effective for business.

What inputs does it require? An essential input for this activity, if available, is the risk management portfolio framework, the organization uses to manage other types of assets. Managers are likely to consider a specification that looks like others they work with. This activity should leverage any best practice design guidelines used in other fields such as financial, banking, legal, or medical sciences.

What outputs does it generate? This activity generates feedback from business managers and stakeholders and a revised architecture blueprint. Ideally, this activity also produces a preliminary description of new capabilities and competencies needed to operationalize this new architecture.

What other resources does it require? This activity also leverages the knowledge of application architects and business continuity teams responsible for managing the organization's current technology and data risk portfolio.

Activity 5. Design an organization-level risk management portfolio

How do we do this? This activity involves synthesizing all of the feedback received in Activity 4 into an organization-level risk management portfolio. It means identifying common risk attributes to build back into the knowledge object models, designing standard and custom risk management reports, and designing an enterprise-level risk management dashboard for knowledge assets.

What inputs does it require? This activity leverages all of the knowledge we gathered through Activity 4, including APIs that may be used to collect information from business applications.

What outputs does it generate? This activity generates design blueprints for new attributes for knowledge object models, design specifications for existing or new risk attributes for business applications, blueprints for risk management reports, and design specifications for the enterprise dashboard.

What other resources does it require? The most crucial additional resource is knowledge of the design of existing business applications.

Evolution of knowledge asset harm and risk management

Experience and a review of the literature suggest there are five phases of evolution of knowledge misuse and risk management (Figure 18.2), including:

- Phase 1. Private access to precious objects
- Phase 2. Expanded markets for precious artifacts and theft
- Phase 3. The market for copies, fakes, and forgery grows
- Phase 4. Expanded demand for knowledge
- Phase 5. Incentives and methods for misuse

Phase 1. Private access to precious objects

This phase is characterized by primitive economies centered around localities and proximity to assets. Assets have value primarily grounded on personal use and survival. There is limited exposure to assets since they are owned and held by individuals. The risk of harm is caused by scarcity, loss, and damage through natural events rather than intentional harm. The value is inherent to the asset, compensation, or financial insurance is not yet considered. The threat of loss and damage means individuals hold these assets close and protect them through proximity and access.

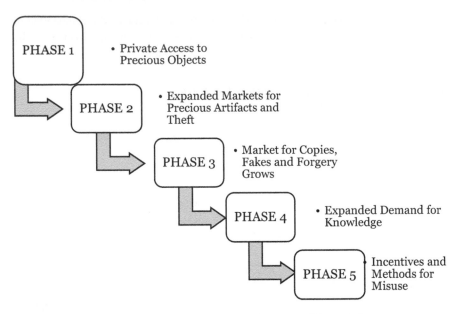

FIGURE 18.2 Evolution of Risk Management and Misuse of Knowledge

Phase 2. Expanded markets for precious artifacts and theft

In this phase, we see the growth of society and the expansion of travel and communication. With these developments come economic developments and the earliest forms of markets. The greater availability of resources produces more interest in objects of value and increased competition for objects. Markets grow across communities. There is a new incentive to steal due to the growth of value and its ability to convert to other sources. This phase also sees the growth of currencies, and greater access to currencies increase the financial value of other assets. The nature of value expands due to increased numbers of potential consumers. The incentive to steal increases due to increased market values. This phase also sees the emergence of the first 'protection societies' and 'insurance agencies' that arise to protect investments. The concept of loss of financial value gains acceptance, and insurance against loss emerges as a new form of investment.

Phase 3. The market for copies, fakes, and forgery grows

In this phase, we see an increase in wealth and increases in populations. Wealth is now available to a broader number of people. It creates a demand for valuable objects. Objects gain status value as well as an investment safeguard value. This growth in demand creates a new market for fakes, reproductions, and copies due to increases in learning and skills. A greater segment of the population now can produce valuable objects. With these new capabilities comes a need to identify the nature of harm from an investment and the probability of that harm to ensure insurance societies can survive as businesses.

Phase 4. Expanded demand for knowledge

With the growth of the industrial economy and society, there is an increased awareness of the business value of knowledge. As this recognition grows, particularly in business training and education, the value of information as a critical asset grows. The rapid advance of technology expands this awareness also to include knowledge. The models and methods for commodities and assets expand from art and precious materials to knowledge. The increased capability to create fakes and increased access to and availability of technology makes it easier to create fake knowledge or to generate knowledge. Just as the market for copies and imitations of precious objects increased, so now does the market for business information and knowledge.

Phase 5. Incentives and methods for misuse

As recognition of the value of knowledge assets expands, new incentives arise to damage or falsely promote organizations and individuals. The incentives for these actions expand from personal gain and status to social, political, and ethical gain. Technologies make it increasingly challenging to detect harm, and the nature of harm expands in this phase. To counter these practices, new capabilities to track and prevent harm emerge intentionally.

Designing knowledge asset risk management into the enterprise architecture

This chapter provided a risk assessment and analysis method which you can use to (1) build risk mitigation capabilities into your business architectures; (2) adapt the existing applications to cover all kinds of knowledge assets; (3) expand the functionality of existing applications to accommodate authentication, security, and access control of all assets; (4) ensure that all forms of use have appropriate levels of protection; and (5) ensure that the protective architecture is elegantly integrated into the business architecture.

Chapter summary

After reading this chapter, you should be able to:

- describe the types of harm that an organization's knowledge assets might incur;
- define business risk and explain how an organization might gauge the probability of risk to knowledge assets resulting from consumption;
- explain how to estimate degrees of risk for knowledge assets;
- describe examples of knowledge loss, theft, damage, tampering and forgeries;

- explain why it is essential for an organization to track and manage risk to knowledge assets.

References and recommendations for future reading

Ballou, B., Heitger, D. L., & Donnell, L. (2010). Creating effective dashboards. *Strategic Finance, 91*(9), 27.

Bate, F. L. (1964). The protection of company knowledge from theft – Legal remedies. *Research Management, 7*(4), 253–259.

Bogg, A. L., & Stanton-Ife, J. (2003). Protecting the vulnerable: Legality, harm and theft. *Legal Studies, 23*(3), 402–422.

Bunting, R. F. Jr., & Siegal, D. (2017). Developing risk management dashboards using risk and quality measures: A visual best practices approach. *Journal of Healthcare Risk Management, 37*(2), 8–28.

Chapman, R. J. (2011). *Simple tools and techniques for enterprise risk management* (Vol. 553). John Wiley & Sons.

Elvins, M. (2008). Identity theft? Re-framing the policing of organized drug crime in the UK as harm reduction. *Contemporary Drug Problems, 35*(2–3), 241–263.

Eser, A. (1965). Principle of harm in the concept of crime: A comparative analysis of the criminally protected legal interests, the. *Duquesne University Law Review, 4*, 345.

Gibb, F., & Buchanan, S. (2006). A framework for business continuity management. *International Journal of Information Management, 26*(2), 128–141.

Herbane, B., Elliott, D., & Swartz, E. M. (2004). Business continuity management: Time for a strategic role? *Long Range Planning, 37*(5), 435–457.

Hiles, A. (2010). *The definitive handbook of business continuity management.* John Wiley & Sons.

Hoyt, R. E., & Liebenberg, A. P. (2011). The value of enterprise risk management. *Journal of Risk and Insurance, 78*(4), 795–822.

Lam, J. (2014). *Enterprise risk management: From incentives to controls.* John Wiley & Sons.

Olsson, R. (2008). Risk management in a multi-project environment – An approach to manage portfolio risks. *International Journal of Quality & Reliability Management, 25*(1), 60–71.

Petit, Y. (2012). Project portfolios in dynamic environments: Organizing for uncertainty. *International Journal of Project Management, 30*(5), 539–553.

Riley, D., & O'Hare, P. (2000). Harm reduction: History, definition, and practice. *Harm Reduction: National and International Perspectives, 1000*, 1–26.

Riley, D., Sawka, E., Conley, P., Hewitt, D., Mitic, W., Poulin, C., . . . Topp, J. (1999). Harm reduction: Concepts and practice. A policy discussion paper. *Substance Use & Misuse, 34*(1), 9–24.

Sanchez, H., Robert, B., Bourgault, M., & Pellerin, R. (2009). Risk management applied to projects, programs, and portfolios. *International Journal of Managing Projects in Business, 2*(1), 14–35.

Steel, A. (2008). The harms and wrongs of stealing: The harm principle and dishonesty in theft. *UNSWLJ, 31*, 712.

19

FUNCTIONAL ARCHITECTURES FOR KNOWLEDGE AUTHENTICATION AND PROVENANCE

Chapter summary

This chapter explains the role that authentication plays in making knowledge assets consumable. The chapter lays out the six activities that support the design of functional architectures that enable authentication of knowledge assets. The chapter also considers why it is essential to have a good understanding of authenticity, authentication methods, package-based authentication, product-based authentication, and inferred authentication. The chapter also identifies and describes the range of authentication concepts, challenges, and methods. We consider the primary challenge in designing this functional architecture for authentication. It is raising awareness of the need to authenticate all types of knowledge assets and the importance of adapting technologies for different assets.

Why we care about authenticity

We care about the authenticity of knowledge assets because we need to know if we can trust them. We will use these assets to make business decisions or to support business actions. If the knowledge is not trustworthy or true, if we cannot verify the knowledge, we might be incurring a business risk by using it. To verify the authenticity of knowledge assets, we need new methods, and we need to adapt to existing methods. Current forms of authenticity may presume established identification methods – these may be grounded on formatting and packaging which may be modifiable in the knowledge economy.

We care about authenticity because the challenges increase when we expand the scope and definition of knowledge assets. We need to consider what these risks mean for the five categories of knowledge assets. As we expand the definition of knowledge assets, we also expand the community of actors, and the methods they have available to 'consume' knowledge objects expand. Additionally, we have a richer experience base to draw from in finding and adapting solutions. Given the expanded definition of knowledge objects, we need to draw principles and processes from several different environments; these need to be adapted and harmonized to apply to knowledge assets and to be usable in knowledge architectures.

Authenticity becomes simpler and more complex in the knowledge economy, as we have more advanced methods for authenticating and tracking assets. This is because the technologies make it easier to change, more people are knowledgeable about working with the tools, and there is broader access to knowledge. Authenticity becomes more complex with new forms of availability and new tools to support consumability. It introduces risks, particularly when we can consume and modify but do not track consumption and modification.

Knowledge authenticity – design concepts

The design of a functional architecture to support knowledge authentication depends on our understanding of a few essential concepts, including authenticity, authentication, inherent authenticity, demonstrated and inferred authenticity, and documented authenticity. Provenance and provenance tracking are also essential concepts (Creagh et al., 2007; Deelman et al., 2006; Feigenbaum et al., 2012; Ko & Will, 2014; Kühlenthal, 1974; Moreau et al., 2008; Munita et al., 2003; Niesse et al., 2017; Tan, 2004; Vijayakumar & Plale, 2006). We consider these concepts concerning documented authenticity. To develop this functional architecture, we must have a good understanding of authenticity; authentication methods; package-based authentication; product-based authentication; inferred authentication; plagiarism; digital signatures; watermarking; archival stamps; seals; plagiarism; provenance; custodial history; provenance tracking and recording; the chain of custody; proof markup language; and scientific workflow systems. The primary challenge we face in designing this functional architecture is to raise awareness and to keep up with the technologies and practices that make it easier to create copies and new versions, to falsify and misrepresent, or to appropriate or engage in knowledge theft.

What is authenticity?

Something authentic is genuine, bona fide, what it claims to be, reliable, of undisputed origin, evidence-based, trustworthy, original, a faithful representation of the original, legitimate, real, and transparent. We want to make sure the knowledge assets we use are authentic and authoritative because it could have business consequences. We want to avoid using knowledge assets that are false, suspect, of dubious origin, untrustworthy, or counterfeit.

What is authentication?

Authentication is the process or technique we use to verify the authenticity of an asset (Brocardo et al., 2017; Brodie, 2000; Burrows et al., 1989; Carroll, 2005;

Clancy et al., 2003; Committee on National Security Systems, 2020; Eliasson & Matousek, 2007; Federal Financial Institutions Examination Council, 2008; Giova, 2011; Kastenhofer, 2015; Lowe, 1997; McTigue et al., 2013; National Institute of Standards and Technology, 2013; Needham & Schroeder, 1987; Otway & Rees, 1987; Ratha et al., 2001; Turner, 2014; Vigil et al., 2015; Watson, 2013; Wu & Liu, 1998). Authentication is related to a concept we discussed in Chapter 8 – identification. Authentication is the process of verifying that identity – of proving, demonstrating, or documenting that what we have in hand is what it purports to be. It presumes that identity has been established. Authentication is the process of proving that what we have in hand is what we identified back in Chapter 8. We cannot and should not expect to establish an asset's identity in the process of authentication. Identity should already exist. Therefore, the knowledge object model and its identifying attributes is a foundational element for authentication.

Before making an asset available or accessible, we should be able to speak to its authenticity. Organizations should have defined authentication processes to ensure that any knowledge asset used to make business decisions is authentic. Some organizations, such as law firms, have internal review and authentication processes. Most organizations, though, do not and should be conscious of the fact that a lack of review and authentication may generate both internal and external risks. The functional architecture should also ensure that any of the results of any authentication process can be associated with the asset. We should be cautious not to conflate authentication with security classification or access control. Authentication tells us what something is, isn't, or might be. Authentication does not protect the asset.

Authentication methods

The literature on authentication is rich but scattered across several different disciplines. We find authentication methods, practices, and standards in several disciplines, including art and antique history, archeology, law enforcement and judicial systems, real estate, fashion design, financial services, computer science, archives management, broadcasting, intellectual property, and digital media rights management. Each of these disciplines interprets authentication to suit assets, methods of production, and common business methods. While there are a rich history and a wealth of practice and knowledge to draw from, the current approach does not provide a good foundation for working in knowledge architecture.

Knowledge assets represent a broad spectrum of assets – from physical to digital, from traditional to modern, from implicit to explicit, created by one or many, static and dynamic. Knowledge assets may span decades and centuries or have been created yesterday. There is something we can learn about authentication from each of these disciplines. It is unlikely that one method from any one discipline will work for all types of assets.

The natural affinities across disciplines may be challenging to see. The essence of our design challenge is to develop this holistic view. We need to bridge the practices and standards of each discipline. Additionally, technologies – particularly for establishing inherent or demonstrated authenticity – are advancing rapidly and at different rates across these disciplines. These developments create a more challenging environment that we have faced in the past. They speak to the importance of creative design for authentication architectures. In addition to authenticating assets, we may also need to 'unauthenticate' some assets – we need to be able to authenticate the knowledge kernel and those other layers of the asset.

Our experience and a review of the literature suggests that this holistic view does not exist either within or across any of the disciplines. As a first attempt to harmonize these methods, can we find a synthesized or generalized view of the different approaches to authentication? This text defines three conventional authentication methods (Figure 19.1), including authentication that is: (1) discoverable from the inherent characteristics of the asset itself without further investigation or documentation; (2) demonstrated through an established and accepted scientific method – a verifiable method for proving authenticity; and (3) documented or ascertained through external sources and documentation. The first method, *inherent authenticity*, is the most desirable because it is the most objective and rigorously verified, and is less susceptible to manipulation. The second method, *demonstrated authenticity*, is the second most desirable because it can also be objectively verified. It is less desirable than the first, though, because it can account only for tampering, change, or misrepresentation through comparison to other assets. Finally, the third method, *documented authenticity*, is trusted but may not always be objectively verified. It, too, does not entirely prevent tampering or change or misrepresentation. While one of these methods may be preferred in a discipline, every discipline leverages all three.

Experience suggests that authenticity is additive. By additive, we mean that authentication of a knowledge asset may require more than one of these assets – they may complement or supplement each other. Additionally, experience suggests that some of these authentication methods may not be feasible for some types of knowledge assets.

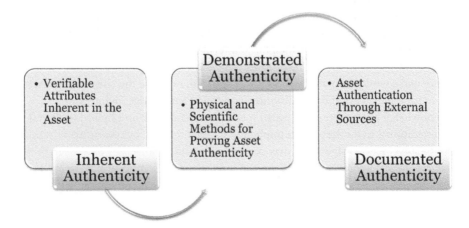

FIGURE 19.1 Three Common Authentication Methods

Inherent authenticity (Type 1)

Inherent authenticity means that we can determine whether an asset is authentic based on direct observation or experience with the asset – the authenticity is embedded in or inherent to the qualities of the asset. These qualities are part of their identity. For example, we can determine whether an individual is who they purport to be by checking their DNA. However, we cannot always rely on the inherent qualities of all types of knowledge assets. We are not interested in whether an individual is who they say they are. Rather, we are interested in whether the individual's human capital is authentic. Can we determine the authenticity of their tacit knowledge, skills and competencies, and personalities by examining them, or do we need the individual to demonstrate those assets, or to document them? What type of authentication do we need to have before we decide whether we will trust the knowledge?

What is inherently authentic about an individual's tacit knowledge, skills and competencies, and personality and behavior? The challenge is that while human capital is by definition embedded in and inherent to an individual, we cannot tell by looking at an individual whether they have the human capital they indicate unless we can experience it directly. If we include experiencing the human capital as inherent authentication, then we can determine that an individual knows what they say they know and has the personality and behavioral characteristics they describe by interacting with them. This type of authentication is limited, though. It has value to the immediate consumer but does not have an authenticity to anyone beyond that individual. To leverage this authentication, the consuming individual would have to document their experience – to offer a testimonial, reference, or rating. The inherent authenticity of human capital is not sufficient for others to trust without further demonstration – such as through testing, use, practice, expression, or actions that others can observe. The knowledge management literature describes this as turning tacit knowledge into actionable knowledge.

What is inherently authentic about explicit knowledge? We can establish the first level of authenticity by looking at explicit knowledge. The challenge is that with the advanced technologies and their widespread availability today, it is possible to create 'fakes' and copies that have flaws or have been changed. If the level of harm is significant, it is essential to supplement the observed inherent authenticity with either demonstrated or documentary evidence. For example, a book may look like a first edition, or a manuscript may look like an official copy from a well-known scientist. Still, unless we can test the paper's chemical composition or validate it against another instance, inherent authenticity may not be sufficient. Some types of explicit knowledge may have embedded watermarks, track and trace codes, water indicators which become visible upon contact with water, color-shifting ink or film, or embedded chips. Some of these characteristics can be exposed easily, whereas others require additional technologies or actions to detect them. It is further evidence of the addictive nature of authentication.

What is inherently authentic about procedural knowledge? We incline to think of procedures manuals rather than the actual performance of the process. Procedural knowledge is what we practice, what we implement, as validated in action. We authenticate procedural knowledge in the products and services it generates – when we produce a quality product with all the features of the 'brand,' it is authenticated. When an expert explains how they do a task or step, or how they make a decision or discloses the ingredients, this is inferred authenticity, because it is not the actual practice. Procedural knowledge is experienced by those who participate in it – so it is authenticated for them but not for others. In this case, procedural knowledge can be authenticated when we observe it directly or experience it directly, but as in other types of assets, the authenticity does not carry beyond the observer. For this authenticity to be trusted, it must be further supported by demonstrated or documented authenticity.

What is inherently authentic about cultural knowledge? While cultural profiles provide an essential representation of cultural knowledge, culture is what we practice and live each day. We can observe the culture in action and through the functioning of the organization. As expressed every day, it is authenticated for those who are part of the culture and who participate in it, but it is not authenticated for others beyond the organization. The challenge is that this authentication is not transferrable to others who are neither experiencing nor observing it.

What is inherently authentic about relational knowledge? For relational knowledge, we can establish inherent authenticity observed by those who are part of the network but not to others who do not experience it. The challenge is that the network's knowledge has multiple components and levels, so inherent authenticity may be complex – the explicit knowledge that is exchanged, the human capital of the network participants, and the developed relationships. Those who participate in the connections can authenticate the relationships, but those not engaged in the network require either demonstrated or documented authentication

Demonstrated or inferred authenticity (Type 2)

By definition, this type of authentication is separate from the asset. Demonstrated or inferred authenticity is indirectly achieved through a deliberate effort to text, examine, or explain the asset. In each case, there is an authoritative external source of evidence that we use to validate the asset. This form of authentication looks for aspects of the asset that are similar to aspects of assets we know to be authentic. For example, an art expert might look at the style of painting, consider the location and form of a signature, or compare the object to an old photograph. An archaeologist might use carbon dating to verify the age of an artifact, conduct a chemical analysis of the materials used, or compare the style of construction or decoration to other objects. We might use the physics of sound and light to evaluate the authenticity of recordings, photographs, or moving images, or test the ink and paper readily available at the time of the item's implied creation.

Demonstrated authenticity means identifying these characteristics through action, explanation, practice, interrogation, testing, or production. We can demonstrate that procedural knowledge is authentic because it produces the expected result. We can demonstrate that an individual has a level of skill or competence because we can watch them act. We can demonstrate essential characteristics through the use of trusted scientific and technical methods. For example, we can demonstrate the authenticity of a document's content using semantic technologies, if we have a copy of the original document.

We can also infer authenticity. The inference may take the form of packaging, labeling, tagging, a seal, microprinting, serialized barcodes, or ultraviolet embossing. We can design the package and label to reduce the risk of counterfeiting or theft. We can reduce tampering, material substitution, and tampering with authentication seals, security printing, electronic tags, or holograms. We can add a trademark or a watermark to an asset to infer that it is an authentic asset with legal protection from a source. All of these methods can infer authenticity to a consumer. The challenge, though, is that even these methods can be reproduced and counterfeited.

As with other types of authentication, though, demonstrated and inferred authenticity might not be sufficient. Skill and expertise, access to expertise, and technologies make it possible to create forgeries and copies. In many cases, supplementary documented authentication is required to establish credibility and trust. A forgery may be indistinguishable from a genuine artifact. It requires expert knowledge, and mistakes are easily made. Certificates of authenticity may be provided by experts as an indication of demonstrated authenticity. However, certificates can also be forged, and authenticating these poses a problem. Currency and other financial instruments commonly use this second type of authentication method.

What is demonstrated and inferred from the authenticity of human capital? Demonstrated authenticity is what knowledge management professionals refer to as turning tacit knowledge into action. We demonstrate our tacit knowledge, skills, competencies, and behaviors through practice, action, testing, sharing, and interrogation. The challenge we must address is how to represent this type of authenticity so it can be consumed by more than the individuals who participate in the activity.

What is demonstrated and inferred authenticity of explicit knowledge? Explicit knowledge assets may have features that have been embedded by their creators that, upon examination, can be determined to be authentic. For example, a book may have the publisher's imprint or copyright. A corporate document may be on the corporate letterhead or have an electronic signature. Any print asset may have a watermark that can be discovered and compared to a source mark. Digital assets may have embedded digital watermarks. Digital watermarks may be embedded in most formats, including text, audio, video, and image assets. Watermarks can be used to identify copyright owners and may also be used to validate the authenticity or source of origin of information assets. Watermarking can be essential to ensure that information assets that are released or disclosed in an unauthorized way can be traced. Digital assets can carry digital rights notices. Digital files can also be encrypted. Encryption uses cryptographic methods that leverage keys help by the source and the intended receiver. They are not entirely foolproof, though. Another form of demonstrated and inferred authenticity for physical assets can be their packaging, though packaging can be replicated, disassembled, and reassembled.

What is demonstrated and inferred authenticity of procedural knowledge? Procedures manuals, instructions, videotaped processes, mentoring sessions, process observations, quality control reviews, expert knowledge books, and expert systems are only a few examples of authenticating procedural knowledge. These forms of authentication can be shared with others not directly engaged in the activity, though they may require additional documentary evidence to confirm. Procedural knowledge can also be authenticated by the quality and nature of the outputs – the products generated.

What is demonstrated and inferred authenticity of cultural knowledge? Demonstrated or inferred authentication is what we can experience or observe. Concerning cultural knowledge, this form of authentication may include artifacts produced by or chosen to represent the culture, cultural expression in the form of social events or cultural behaviors. We would also include the organization's, unit's, team's, and individual's norms and ethics. Perhaps the most trusted forms of authentication, though, are the actual rewards and punishments, the management decisions and choices, that are exercised each day. These can be observed directly, but they can also be known through association and social exchange.

What is demonstrated and inferred authenticity of relational knowledge? We experience or observe network or relational knowledge through our community memberships, our network affiliations, our professional association memberships, social club participation, and our interactions in these communities and networks.

Documented authenticity (Type 3)

The third type of authenticity is documented authenticity. This form of authentication relies on documentation or other external affirmations. Common forms of documentation can include: (1) chain of custody and custodial history; (2) archival stamps and certificates of integrity; (3) watermarks and watermarking processes; (4) electronic signatures; (5) encryption methods; (6) scientific workflow systems and data lineage; and (7) embedded proof markup language.

Chain of custody is defined as the chronological documentation or paper trail that records the sequence of custody, control, transfer, analysis, and disposition of physical or electronic evidence (Constable, 1983; Cosic et al., 2012; Evans & Stagner, 2003; Garfinkel, 2009; Giannelli, 1982; Giova, 2011; Paradise, 1999; Prayvudi & Sn, 2015; Pravudi et al., 2014; Tomlinson et al., 2006; Vijayakumar & Plale, 2006). Chain of custody can have archival and legal significance. Chain of custody is the detailed account of who created an asset, who has owned the asset, who has made changes to the asset, and who has had custody of the asset. Chain of custody is applied to the full life of an asset. The most trustworthy chain of custody tells us about location and handling from its earliest state to its present state. The chain of custody is demonstrated.

From a legal context and in supply chain management, a chain of custody attests to the handling and traceability of evidence, assets, and products. Maintaining a chain of custody is time-consuming and spans the full life cycle of the asset. The change is how to document the different owners and custodians over time, and whether we can trust the documentation, we find. While historically, this level of effort was reserved for assets with high financial value, it has been translated and adapted for use with knowledge assets with significant business value. Chain of custody is pertinent today because of the increased and unpredictable movement of knowledge assets.

Chain of custody is often referred to as provenance outside the legal and business environments. Provenance is defined as the chronology of ownership, custody, or location of an object, document, or group of documents over its full history. The primary purpose of tracing the provenance of an object or entity is to provide contextual and circumstantial evidence for its original production or discovery, by establishing, as far as practicable, its later history, especially the sequences of its formal ownership, custody, and places of storage. Having detailed evidence of provenance can establish that an asset is what it purports to be, that it has not been altered or stolen and is not a forgery. Moral and legal validity of a chain of custody is important where forgeries, fakes, and reproductions are common in cases of theft, misappropriation, or 'looted' assets (Bubandt, 2009; Carter, 2007; Craddock, 2009; Graham, 2007; Hamilton, 1996; Karlen, 1986; Lee & Yoo, 2009; Lenain, 2014; Li, 2013; Marston & Watts, 2003; Mathews, 2015; Mills & Mansfield, 1979; Olson et al., 2007; Parker, 2018; Pennycook, 1996; Rusanov et al., 1993; Sanchirico, 2003; Savage, 1963; Shao et al., 2017; Shu et al., 2017; Spilsbury, 2009; Spink & Levente Feies, 2012; Stalnaker, 2005; Tandoc et al., 2018).

How do we document provenance? Trusted provenance documentation consists of two components. The first component is the semi-structured text that contains a list of transfers ordered from the first owner until the present day. It resembles a chronology with each entry having detailed information about locations, named events, transfer location, the period of ownership, purchase information, and citation markets. The second component is a collection of unstructured note text that provides explanatory information about custodianship and any asset changes.

What does the documented authenticity of human capital include? Documentary evidence of tacit knowledge is explicit. A person's curriculum vitae and resume are evidence of their credentials, as are their diplomas, certificates, and licenses. Performance evaluations are evidence of the quality of their competence and skills, their publications and reports are evidence of their tacit knowledge, as are presentations and lectures, interviews and recorded conversations, photographic documentation, the artifacts, and products they have created. References and recommendations are written for and about them, and rankings and ratings are the equivalents of testimonials. Documentation of critical life events such as vital documents would also be considered as documentary authentication. Individuals are complex, and their human capital is dynamic. Like any other documentary evidence, all the examples we listed are time-sensitive. And, like any other form of documentary evidence – and explicit knowledge – they are subject to forgery.

The cornerstone of documentary evidence is the chain of custody and provenance. An individual creates and maintains a chain of custody. In this case, documentary evidence must be supplemented with inherent and demonstrated authentication.

What does the documented authenticity of explicit knowledge include? Because explicit knowledge has a tangible form, creating a chain of custody is more straightforward. However, it is not without its challenges and opportunities for falsification and misrepresentation. Emails can be time-stamped, and the time-stamp can be verified through system logs. Applications can track and record transactions, data, and internally generated assets. Once a digital asset leaves a context, though, it is difficult to track its use unless the tracking is designed into the package or the encoding level.

While it is more straightforward to create a chain of custody for physical assets, it is time-consuming and requires coordination over time. Chain of custody of a publication, a document, or print conference proceedings means creating a separate tracking record. It means ensuring that anyone who has custody or ownership of that asset adds their information to the chain of custody record. In the case of rare items, art, or antiques, there is one instance of the asset. When the asset changes hands, the provenance record also changes hands. In the case of a digital asset or a physical asset that is not rare, there may not be one copy. The chain of custody must be specific to that asset. The provenance of a single copy may include sales or acquisitions records, inscriptions, marginalia, bookplates, physical descriptions, references to auction catalogs, or advertisements.

In the case of organizational records and documents, provenance should include an archival stamp and a full administrative record of changes and versions. In archival practice, proof of provenance is provided by the operation of control systems that document the history of records kept in archives, including details of amendments made to them.

Digital resources may also leverage embedded proof markup language intended to represent the provenance of web assets. An example is the Open Provenance Model. This language is designed to support interoperability and exchange of provenance information across applications.

What does the documented authenticity of procedural knowledge include? It might consist of oral histories of individuals involved in the process or their accounts of critical incidents. It can include patents and trademarks, or imprints and digital signatures or brands on products generated by the process. It might also include visual instructions, workflow documentation, process identifiers, and documented certified business rules. All of these are documentary evidence of process knowledge, but they do not constitute provenance of the process. The provenance of a process would be an authorized documented history of the process over time. Private sector organizations may be more conscientious about maintaining records of processes to ensure their intellectual property is protected.

Scientific workflow tracking is another form of documented evidence of procedural knowledge. Scientific research provenance is generally considered trustworthy when it supports the reproducibility of the research. Scientific workflow systems allow scientists and researchers to track their work and their data through all transformations, analyses, and interpretations.

What does the documented authenticity of cultural knowledge include? The challenges are similar to those of procedural knowledge. There are some clear forms through which we can document our cultural profiles, actions, and artifacts. While these may be authorized forms, they are only single instances of cultural knowledge at a given point in time. Documentary evidence of an organization's, a unit's, or individual's cultural knowledge would be an account that is created over time. Establishing the authenticity of cultural knowledge means leveraging more than one type of authentication.

What does the documented authenticity of relational knowledge include? A network that has a digital presence is more effectively documented than a network that is physical and in person. Digital networks have directories and membership lists; they have member profiles, community and member discussion forums, and network activity statistics and reports. To create this same type of evidence for a business unit, a cross-functional team, a leadership group means intentionally and deliberately documenting, tracking, and chronicling the activities, exchanges, and knowledge flows of the members. Establishing the authenticity of relational knowledge means leveraging all three authentication methods.

Designing authentication methods to suit assets

This functional architecture is dependent on the organization's having in place a means of tracking and managing the authenticity of its knowledge assets. Monitoring and managing authenticity mean being able to authenticate knowledge assets. The knowledge architect might leverage a framework for identifying authentication methods (Table 19.1) working in collaboration with business managers.

TABLE 19.1 Authentication Approaches for Knowledge Capital Assets

Knowledge Asset	Inherent Authenticity	Demonstrated Inferred Authenticity	Documented Authenticity
Human Capital			
Tacit Knowledge			
Skills and Competencies			
Personality and Behavior			
Explicit Knowledge			
Procedural Knowledge			
Cultural Knowledge			
Relational Knowledge			

Legend Precedence	Color Code
1	
2	
3	

This framework might be used to determine the most appropriate authentication method for each type of asset. We have suggested an order of precedence that might apply to different types of assets. The precedence does not suggest that any one of the methods can stand alone.

Knowledge authenticity – the design environment

What factors do we need to consider in designing this architecture? There are several factors to consider in designing an authentication architecture. We need to consider the sensitivity and vulnerability of our knowledge assets, the capacity of the organization to identify risks and support authentication, to review assets and to gauge levels of harm, and to mark and manage authentication records.

What events cause us to design a functional architecture for authentication? Authentication is something we have undertaken to protect high-profile assets or valuable artifacts and works of art. We had undertaken authentication as a legal activity when we had to produce evidence or a chronology of events. Given the changing nature of knowledge assets and their increasing value to the knowledge economy, we need an authentication architecture to ensure we can trust any kind of asset we might use to make a business decision. The motivation for authentication is the potential risk and harm that might result from lost or stolen assets or from using damaged, tampered, or falsified assets.

What are the impacts and consequences of having this functional architecture? The primary impact of having an authentication architecture is the ability to determine and manage business risks from knowledge assets. Another impact is an increased awareness of the harm that can come to and from knowledge assets.

What inputs do we need to consider when designing this functional architecture? Each of the three authentication methods should take as a starting point a kind of knowledge asset. As has been noted in walking through all three methods, there are many different elements, tools, and interpretations for each type of asset. To achieve authenticity means we must design a combination of all three methods. Perhaps an important input in deciding how much of a risk is tolerable, and how many resources we can devote to authentication. We must balance what it takes to authenticate with the potential harm and risk if we don't authenticate.

What are the outputs and outcomes this functional architecture generates? One output is a decision to authenticate or not authenticate, and what degree of authentication is needed. Another output is determining the potential harm of not authenticating. And, of course, the primary output is an authenticated knowledge asset, with a record of authenticity.

Design activities and tasks for knowledge authentication

This functional architecture supports five activities, including:

- Activity 1. Identify authentication risk factors
- Activity 2. Determine the appropriate type of authentication

- Activity 3. Determine the type of authentication that is possible
- Activity 4. Expand and enhance business solutions to support authentication
- Activity 5. Record the authenticity

Activity 1. Identify authentication risk factors

How do we do this? Risk begins with an understanding of the value of an asset and the kinds of harm that might result from using or maintaining knowledge assets that have expired, been tampered with, have questionable value, have poor quality content, or are not legitimate. The challenge for this activity is raising awareness of authentication issues and gaining an understanding of harm from poor quality or tainted assets. It is essential to work with the business stakeholders because detecting and preventing harm from bad or tainted knowledge assets is a judgment call, made each day, and often without formal acknowledgment. An important starting point is to identify the most likely kinds of risks and to ensure all stakeholders understand what is acceptable handling.

What inputs does it require? The starting point is understanding the business's most critical knowledge assets. Another essential input is the business stakeholders' knowledge of kinds of potential harm and degrees of risk. This input determines the reliability of your risk management portfolio. A set of key questions may be useful in working with stakeholders. Key questions might include:

- What kinds of risks might we encounter with this kind of asset?
- How much are we willing to devote to authentication? Is it worth the risk?
- What are the key attributes that would trigger concern about its authenticity?
- Do we know where it came from? Who created it?
- Can we establish its identity?
- Can we identify the knowledge asset, or are we focused on the package?
- Of the three authentication methods, which is the one we need? What level of rigor is needed for the business decision or use?
- Of the three authentication methods, which do we have the capability to perform?

What outputs does it generate? This activity provides essential input for your risk management portfolio. It also provides the basis for current awareness and response training for dealing with risk situations.

What other resources does it require? Another important resource might be a working knowledge of past incidents the organization has experienced, the response, and any current guidance. It may also be useful to ensure that any existing authentication methods are leveraged for the knowledge architecture and adapted or extended wherever possible.

Activity 2. Determine the appropriate type of authentication

How do we do this? This activity focuses on choosing a management strategy for authentication risks. It involves identifying an appropriate authentication solution for each type of asset and asking business managers to explain which authentication methods are preferred for the nature of the business.

What inputs does it require? In this chapter, we identified five general authentication methods. We also offered a first pass at the kinds of authentication challenges different types of assets might experience. Given an understanding of the risks, an organization can choose as to the preferred mitigation method.

What outputs does it generate? This activity produces a business unit-level assessment of the best choice authentication methods given a business risk.

What other resources does it require? This activity requires an understanding of what business units are currently doing in managing bad or tainted knowledge assets, and what is in place in the business architecture for these units.

Activity 3. Determine the type of authentication that is possible

How do we do this? This task focuses on determining what is possible based on what we can afford in terms of the level of effort, what we can afford in terms of a practical business application, what we have the competency to do, and what our infrastructure can support.

What inputs does it require? Business stakeholders should decide on what authentication method is possible. The knowledge architect's role is to design an architecture to support the business manager's preferred solution.

What outputs does it generate? This activity produces a practical set of affordable, supportable, sustainable choices that a knowledge architecture can use to design practical solutions.

What other resources does it require? The knowledge architect should have a good understanding of the existing authentication solutions. Knowing what is available is an important starting point. It also informs us of practical costs and types of investment needed to support those solutions.

Activity 4. Expand and enhance the business solutions to support authentication

How do we do this? Business stakeholders will have the responsibility of assessing the authenticity of a knowledge asset. The role of knowledge architecture is to provide the means of recording any concerns about authenticity. The most elegant design solution is defining a default that presumes authenticity but allows for other options where there is uncertainty, doubt, or knowledge of problems. This activity focuses on defining what those options might be and designing a solution for recording them. The most elegant solution will be to enable business stakeholders to record the status in the knowledge object model. It is critical, though, that business applications have access to these attributes. Having a metadata attribute that the business rarely sees and is not required to check will be a missed opportunity and a wasted level of effort.

What inputs does it require? This activity requires a set of status options that indicate the level of severity of risk associated with an asset. The status values should be supported by options to record: description of the authentication method and source used; who was involved in authenticating; the nature of the challenges or risks discovered; and the type of authentication 'stamp' applied to the asset.

What outputs does it generate? This activity should produce updated knowledge object model attributes, and also a way of 'marking' the asset itself for caution. An asset that does not have any associated risks might simply carry an authorizing mark. In this case, the absence of a mark would signal caution.

What other resources does it require? This activity may also trigger some development expansion or enhancement for other business applications to ensure that business stakeholders can see any cautionary information about the asset. It will be a sensitive design issue where human capital or cultural capital is concerned. In this case, the knowledge architect needs to work with human resources and legal experts.

Activity 5. Record the authenticity

How do we do this? This activity focuses on leveraging the architecture to record the authenticity of an asset. Ideally, this information is recorded in the knowledge object model and surfaced through business applications. It should also be easily accessed in the knowledge landscape through discovery and search solutions.

What inputs does it require? This activity requires the use of knowledge architecture by business stakeholders and knowledge analysts. It may also be a responsibility of information management professionals throughout the organization.

What outputs does it generate? This activity produces the actual authentication information and the authentication certificate or stamp that is associated with an asset.

What other resources does it require? This activity involves awareness of business stakeholders, training, and periodic audits of knowledge assets to determine whether access to assets with risks should be removed or their access restricted.

Evolution of knowledge authenticity designs

Experience and a review of the literature suggest there are five phases to the evolution of knowledge authentication (Figure 19.2), including:

- Phase 1. Collection of precious objects
- Phase 2. Increased market for precious objects
- Phase 3. The market for fakes, forgeries, and copies grows
- Phase 4. Demand for knowledge grows
- Phase 5. Authentication methods emerge

Phase 1. Collection of precious objects

This phase is fairly consistent across all types of harm and as a starting point for understanding risk. In this earliest phase, precious objects were the possessions of a few wealthy individuals and sources of power. In this earliest phase, precious objects

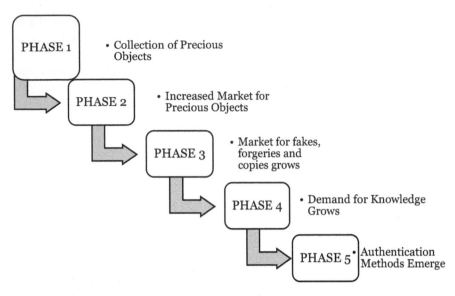

FIGURE 19.2 Evolution of Knowledge Misuse and Authentication Methods

included art, antiques, antiquities, currencies, and other objects with economic value. We can trace this phase back to Roman times with the creation of copies of Greek sculptures. These 'reproductions' were not intended to deceive and were known to not be authentic. The new art was created in classical times for historical reference, religious inspiration, or simple enjoyment – not intended to have intrinsic financial value beyond the original purpose. This phase is characterized by limited literacy and the availability of written knowledge. Few individuals were educated, though many were knowledgeable about essential social and survival functions.

Phase 2. Increased market for precious objects

As economies and communities stabilized and expanded, material wealth grew. With wealth came a greater interest in precious objects. During this phase, there was a greater appreciation for art. During the Renaissance, schools of art evolved, masters emerged, and a formal system of apprenticeship developed. In these workshops, works of art were intentionally copied by apprentices in the Renaissance to emulate a master's style. These copies were a form of compensation to the master, who then sold them for monetary gain. As the middle classes grew in some societies, the new increased prosperity of an emerging middle class created an increased demand for art. It is during this phase that we begin to see a financial value associated with works of art. Works of art were marked for source and authenticity. Signatures or graphics were an early brand for an artist. At the end of this phase, works of art were now commercial commodities.

Phase 3. The market for forgeries, fakes, and copies grows

With increased wealth and new forms of economic turbulence, tangible property that can hold its value becomes a popular investment. However, given the nature of art and the skill, competency, and knowledge required to create art, there are supply-side constraints. Simply put, there is an inherent limit to the number of works a single artist can produce. As the value for works of art from a particular master increases, so does the demand. As demand increases and cannot be met, a new market for forgeries and fakes emerges. Because investors look for marks of authenticity, both the work of art and the mark of authenticity may be forged. The growing wealth of a middle class and the growing levels of education and literacy increase the demand for works of art in general. The market expanded in this phase to include not only forgeries but also fakes, reproductions, copies, replicas, and reproductions. The new versions were copies of convenience intended for simple appreciation and adornment rather than as financial investments.

Phase 4. Demand for knowledge grows

In this phase, the value of and market for information grows. Information is seen as a critical capability in business, in economic and social advancement. The incentive to acquire information and knowledge is not for investment purposes, but as a way to increase competencies. In an economy that increasingly valued information and knowledge, access to information and knowledge creates a competitive advantage. It represents a shift from seeing sources of information as art in earlier centuries (e.g., rare books and manuscripts) to the indirect value of the information content of the object. The information value is authenticated through emerging practices of archival science and records management. The art value is authenticated through art and rare books and manuscript sciences. Authenticating the art value remains in the domain of art and antique experts and continues to focus on the authentication methods used in those fields. Archives and records management develop a new set of practices that continues to leverage provenance and chain of custody but also begins to focus on language and stylistic patterns for authentication. The principles of archival provenance were developed in the 19th century by both French and Prussian archivists. They gained widespread acceptance based on their formulation of archival practice and methods by Dutch archivists. Today's digital curation practices are an adaptation of these early methods. Archival science professional associations developed in the 20th century and continue as essential operations in many public sector organizations and large private sector organizations.

Phase 5. Authentication methods emerge

This phase began in the mid-20th century with the increased precision of production and manufacturing. Specifically, authentication received greater attention with the quality control and management movement of the 1950s and 1960s. It coincided with the growing population of trained engineers, engineering, and computer science. Quality control shed new light on the quality of the inputs used in production. As project management methods developed, we began to question the quality of information used in business decisions. The increased value and scrutiny of information created new quality standards for the generation and publishing of information. While peer review had existed for decades, it had been largely in the control of journal editors. In this phase, we see increased participation in peer review by academicians and practitioners. Ethical and scholarly norms developed to ensure some consistency in review. These included common practices for attribution of source ideas and knowledge to become commonplace. With the growth of education and a new middle class built around knowledge and information, there were increased opportunities and incentives for plagiarism (Angélil-Carter, 2014; Blum, 2011; Lazer et al., 2018; Park, 2003; Zu-Eissen & Stein, 2006). Increased collaboration and ready access to information provide opportunities to internalize knowledge – and to use without attribution inadvertently. Due to the increased value assigned to knowledge in the 21st century, and the increased opportunity to create fakes and misrepresent and misuse knowledge, new methods for authentication have emerged. These methods are still developing – we're still learning how to detect these forgeries, fakes, and appropriations.

Knowledge authenticity and provenance in the enterprise architecture

The functional architecture for managing authenticity most closely aligns with the information architecture practice. It is also closely aligned with business architecture because the business stakeholders have to operationalize the risk management strategy and manage the risk portfolio. There is also a connection to the application architecture practice, though, because the capability to track and tag assets are accomplished through business applications. It requires an integrated application design. Additionally, the risk management roles and responsibilities are assigned to business stakeholders who are best positioned to detect harm and manage risk.

Chapter review

After reading this chapter, you should be able to:

- explain to others the concept of authenticity and authentication;
- describe inherent authenticity and apply it to the organization's critical business knowledge;
- describe demonstrated or inherent authenticity and apply it to the organization's critical business knowledge;
- describe documented authenticity and apply it to the organization's critical business knowledge;
- work with business managers to identify methods for tagging and tracking knowledge assets with authenticity challenges.

References and recommended future readings

Angélil-Carter, S. (2014). *Stolen language? Plagiarism in writing*. Routledge.

Blum, S. D. (2011). *My word! Plagiarism and college culture*. Cornell University Press.

Brocardo, M. L., Traore, I., Woungang, I., & Obaidat, M. S. (2017). Authorship verification using deep belief network systems archived Wayback Machine. *International Journal of Communication Systems*. doi:10.1002/dac.3259

Brodie, N. (2000). Authenticity, preservation and access in digital collections. *New Review of Academic Librarianship*, *6*(1), 225–238.

Bubandt, N. (2009). From the enemy's point of view: Violence, empathy, and the ethnography of fakes. *Cultural Anthropology*, *24*(3), 553–588.

Burrows, M., Abadi, M., & Needham, R. M. (1989). A logic of authentication. *Proceedings of the Royal Society of London. A. Mathematical and Physical Sciences*, *426*(1871), 233–271.

Carroll, N. (2005). Unwrapping archives: DVD restoration demonstrations and the marketing of authenticity. *The Velvet Light Trap*, *56*(1), 18–31.

Carter, R. G. (2007). Tainted archives: Art, archives, and authenticity. *Archivaria*, *63*, 75–86.

Clancy, T. C., Kiyavash, N., & Lin, D. J. (2003). Secure smartcardbased fingerprint authentication. In *Proceedings of the 2003 ACM SIGMM workshop on biometrics methods and applications* (pp. 45–52). Association for Computing Machinery, Inc.

Committee on National Security Systems. *National information assurance (IA) glossary*. National Counterintelligence and Security Center. Retrieved February 2, 2020, from https://en.wikipedia.org/wiki/National_Information_Assurance_Glossary#:~:text= Committee%20on%20National%20Security%20Systems,for%20discussing%20 Information%20Assurance%20concepts

Constable, G. (1983). Forgery and plagiarism in the middle ages. *Archiv für Diplomatik*, *29*(JG), 1–41.

Cosic, J., Cosic, G., Ćosić, J., & Ćosić, Z. (2012). Chain of custody and life cycle of digital evidence. *Computer Technology and Application*, *3*, 126–129.

Craddock, P. (Ed.). (2009). *Scientific investigation of copies, fakes and forgeries*. Routledge.

Creagh, D. C., Kubik, M. E., & Sterns, M. (2007). On the feasibility of establishing the provenance of Australian Aboriginal artefacts using synchrotron radiation X-ray diffraction and proton-induced X-ray emission. *Nuclear Instruments and Methods in Physics Research Section A: Accelerators, Spectrometers, Detectors and Associated Equipment*, *580*(1), 721–724.

Deelman, E., Callaghan, S., Field, E., Francoeur, H., Graves, R., Gupta, N., & Mehringer, J. (2006). Managing large-scale workflow execution from resource provisioning to provenance tracking: The cybershake example. In *2006 Second IEEE international conference on e-science and grid computing (e-science'06)* (pp. 14–14). IEEE.

Eliasson, C., & Matousek, P. (2007). Noninvasive authentication of pharmaceutical products through packaging using spatially offset Raman spectroscopy. *Analytical Chemistry*, *79*(4), 1696–1701.

Evans, M. M., & Stagner, P. A. (2003). Maintaining the chain of custody evidence handling in forensic cases. *AORN Journal*, *78*(4), 563–569.

Federal Financial Institutions Examination Council. (2008). *Authentication in an internet banking environment*. Retrieved February 2, 2020, from www.ffiec.gov/pdf/authentication_ guidance.pdf

Feigenbaum, G., Reist, I., & Reist, I. J. (Eds.). (2012). *Provenance: An alternate history of art*. Getty Publications.

Garfinkel, S. L. (2009). Providing cryptographic security and evidentiary chain-of-custody with the advanced forensic format, library, and tools. *International Journal of Digital Crime and Forensics (IJDCF)*, *1*(1), 1–28.

Giannelli, P. C. (1982). Chain of custody and the handling of real evidence. *American Criminal Law Review*, *20*, 527.

Giova, G. (2011). Improving chain of custody in forensic investigation of electronic digital systems. *International Journal of Computer Science and Network Security*, *11*(1), 1–9.

Graham, M. (2007). Fake holograms a 3-D crime wave. *Wired*.

Hamilton, C. (1996). *Great forgers and famous fakes: The manuscript forgers of America and how they duped the experts*. Glenbridge Publisher.

Karlen, P. H. (1986). Fakes, forgeries, and expert opinions. *Journal of Arts Management and Law*, *16*(3), 5–32.

Kastenhofer, J. (2015). The logic of archival authenticity: ISO 15489 and the varieties of forgeries in archives. *Archives and Manuscripts*, *43*(3), 166–180.

Ko, R. K., & Will, M. A. (2014). Progger: An efficient, tamper-evident kernel-space logger for cloud data provenance tracking. In *2014 IEEE 7th international conference on cloud computing* (pp. 881–889). IEEE.

Kühlenthal, M. (1974). The Alberini sarcophagus: Renaissance copy or antique? *The Art Bulletin*, *56*(3), 414–421.

Lazer, D. M., Baum, M. A., Benkler, Y., Berinsky, A. J., Greenhill, K. M., Menczer, F., . . . Schudson, M. (2018). The science of fake news. *Science*, *359*(6380), 1094–1096.

Lee, S. H., & Yoo, B. (2009). A review of the determinants of counterfeiting and piracy and the proposition for future research. *Korean Journal of Policy Studies*, *24*(1), 1–38.

Lenain, T. (2014). 3 The narrative structure of forgery tales. In *Cultural property crime* (pp. 37–60). Brill.

Li, L. (2013). Technology designed to combat fakes in the global supply chain. *Business Horizons*, *56*(2), 167–177.

Lowe, G. (1997). A hierarchy of authentication specifications. In *Proceedings 10th computer security foundations workshop* (pp. 31–43). IEEE.

Marston, G., & Watts, R. (2003). Tampering with the evidence: A critical appraisal of evidence-based policy-making. *The Drawing Board: An Australian Review of Public Affairs*, *3*(3), 143–163.

Mathews, G. (2015). Taking copies from China past customs: Routines, risks, and the possibility of catastrophe. *Journal of Borderlands Studies*, *30*(3), 423–435.

McTigue, E., Thornton, E., & Wiese, P. (2013). Authentication projects for historical fiction: Do you believe it? *The Reading Teacher*, *66*(6), 495–505.

Mills, J. F., & Mansfield, J. M. (1979). *The genuine article: The making and unmasking of fakes and forgeries*. British Broadcasting Corporation.

Moreau, L., Groth, P., Miles, S., Vazquez-Salceda, J., Ibbotson, J., Jiang, S., & Varga, L. (2008). The provenance of electronic data. *Communications of the ACM*, *51*(4), 52–58.

Munita, C. S., Paiva, R. P., Alves, M. A., De Oliveira, P. M. S., & Momose, E. F. (2003). Provenance study of archaeological ceramic. *Journal of Trace and Microprobe Techniques*, *21*(4), 697–706.

National Institute of Standards and Technology, U.S. Department of Commerce. (2013). *Electronic authentication guideline*. NIST Special Publication 800–63–62. National Institute of Standards and Technology.

Needham, R. M., & Schroeder, M. D. (1987). Authentication revisited. *ACM SIGOPS Operating Systems Review*, *21*(1), 7–7.

Neisse, R., Steri, G., & Nai-Fovino, I. (2017). A blockchain-based approach for data accountability and provenance tracking. In *Proceedings of the 12th international conference on availability, reliability and security* (pp. 1–10). ACM Press.

Olson, B. J., Graham, M. R., Maltbie, J., & Epperson, R. (2007). The 10 things every practitioner should know about anti-counterfeiting and anti-piracy protection. *Journal of High Technology Law*, *7*, 106.

Otway, D., & Rees, O. (1987). Efficient and timely mutual authentication. *ACM SIGOPS Operating Systems Review, 21*(1), 8–10.

Paradise, P. R. (1999). *Trademark counterfeiting, product piracy, and the billion dollar threat to the US economy*. Greenwood Publishing Group.

Park, C. (2003). In other (people's) words: Plagiarism by university students – Literature and lessons. *Assessment & Evaluation in Higher Education, 28*(5), 471–488.

Parker, A. J. (2018). Fakes and forgeries in the brain scanner. *Frontiers for Young Minds, 6*(39).

Pennycook, A. (1996). Borrowing others' words: Text, ownership, memory, and plagiarism. *TESOL Quarterly, 30*(2), 201–230.

Prayudi, Y., Ashari, A., & Priyambodo, T. K. (2014). Digital evidence cabinets: A proposed framework for handling digital chain of custody. *International Journal of Computer Applications, 107*(9), 975–8887.

Prayudi, Y., & Sn, A. (2015). Digital chain of custody: State of the art. *International Journal of Computer Applications, 114*(5), 1–9.

Ratha, N. K., Connell, J. H., & Bolle, R. M. (2001). Enhancing security and privacy in biometrics-based authentication systems. *IBM Systems Journal, 40*(3), 614–634.

Rusanov, V., Angelov, V., Tsacheva, T., & Ormandjiev, S. (1993). On the possibility of the use of the Mössbauer test for bank-note forgeries and printer ink control. *Nuclear Instruments and Methods in Physics Research Section B: Beam Interactions with Materials and Atoms, 73*(3), 417–424.

Sanchirico, C. W. (2003). Evidence tampering. *Duke Law Journal, 53*, 1215.

Savage, G. (1963). *Forgeries, fakes and reproductions: A handbook for the collector*. Barrie and Rockliff.

Shao, C., Ciampaglia, G. L., Varol, O., Flammini, A., & Menczer, F. (2017). The spread of fake news by social bots. *arXiv preprint arXiv:1707.07592, 96*, 104.

Shu, K., Sliva, A., Wang, S., Tang, J., & Liu, H. (2017). Fake news detection on social media: A data mining perspective. *ACM SIGKDD Explorations Newsletter, 19*(1), 22–36.

Spilsbury, R. (2009). *Counterfeit! Stopping fakes and forgeries*. Enslow Publishing, LLC.

Spink, J., & Levente Fejes, Z. (2012). A review of the economic impact of counterfeiting and piracy methodologies and assessment of currently utilized estimates. *International Journal of Comparative and Applied Criminal Justice, 36*(4), 249–271.

Stalnaker, N. (2005). Fakes and forgeries. In *The Routledge companion to aesthetics* (pp. 533–546). Routledge.

Tan, W. C. (2004). Research problems in data provenance. *IEEE Data Engineering Bulletin, 27*(4), 45–52.

Tandoc, E. C. Jr., Lim, Z. W., & Ling, R. (2018). Defining "fake news" a typology of scholarly definitions. *Digital Journalism, 6*(2), 137–153.

Tomlinson, J. J., Elliott-Smith, W., & Radosta, T. (2006). Laboratory information management system chain of custody: Reliability and security. *Journal of Analytical Methods in Chemistry, 2006*.

Turner, D. M. (2014). *Digital authentication: The basics*. Cryptomathic. Retrieved February 2, 2020, from www.cryptomathic.com/news-events/blog/digital-authentication-the-basics

Vigil, M., Buchmann, J., Cabarcas, D., Weinert, C., & Wiesmaier, A. (2015). Integrity, authenticity, non-repudiation, and proof of existence for long-term archiving: A survey. *Computers & Security, 50*, 16–32.

Vijayakumar, N. N., & Plale, B. (2006). Towards low overhead provenance tracking in near real-time stream filtering. In *International provenance and annotation workshop* (pp. 46–54). Springer.

Watson, O. (2013). Authentic forgeries? *Creating Authenticity: Authentication Processes in Ethnographic Museums, 42*, 59.

Wu, M., & Liu, B. (1998). Watermarking for image authentication. In *Proceedings 1998 international conference on image processing*. ICIP98 (Cat. No. 98CB36269) (Vol. 2, pp. 437–441). IEEE.

Zu Eissen, S. M., & Stein, B. (2006). Intrinsic plagiarism detection. In *European conference on information retrieval* (pp. 565–569). Springer.

20

FUNCTIONAL ARCHITECTURES FOR SECURING KNOWLEDGE ASSETS

Chapter summary

This chapter explains the role that knowledge asset security plays in making knowledge assets consumable. It covers the five activities that support designing appropriate security methods for knowledge assets. The chapter also considers why it is essential to have a good understanding of harm and all of the different kinds and degrees of harm, of risks, the different kinds of risk, how we reduce the probability of harm and risk, and how different approaches to security may or may not reduce harm and risk. The primary challenge we face in designing this functional architecture is developing security measures and methods that are suited to types and levels of harm, and avoiding the temptation to adopt security classifications structures and methods from other organizations without full consideration.

Why we care about securing assets

In Chapter 18, we walked through five types of harm that might occur to put our knowledge assets at risk. Perhaps the most common business strategy to safeguard against harm is to secure these assets against access. While this is an effective strategy for many resources, it can be counterproductive for knowledge assets. Traditional security approaches are designed to lock down, protect, discourage use, and prevent access. These actions can impede our use of knowledge assets and may lower the expected business value from these assets. Additionally, security presumes we can restrict access by building it into the holding application (Burkett, 2012; Kim & Leem, 2005; Kissel et al., 2006; Murphy et al., 2000; Rodriguez et al., 2007; Sherwood, 2005; Wahe & Petersen, 2011). There is no application and no encryption method that has not been breached.

These traditional approaches to security design simply do not work in a knowledge economy, or for knowledge assets. The basic design principles of security architecture should be revisited for knowledge architectures. Redesigning security architecture begins with a basic understanding of how we support beneficial use, and how we discourage destructive use. It is a significant shift in thinking from historical security designs, which take as their core models bank safes, vaults, and jails, to a more 'beneficial balance' model. The traditional model presumes physical access based on limited proximity (Babar et al., 2010; Jain et al., 2006; Katic et al., 1998). In the 21st century, assets are now digitally balanced between physical and digital. Proximity is no longer a barrier but is instead a matter of degree. It is no longer a 'zero-sum' situation. The traditional approach presents a simple challenge to increasingly sophisticated hackers – any barrier is an invitation to break and trespass. Barriers are broken, good use is discouraged.

The traditional model leads to other adverse effects and unintended consequences, including overclassification and uneven coverage. Classification errors often result in an overly cautious interpretation of rules and guidelines. Overclassifying or underclassifying knowledge assets due to misunderstanding or mischaracterization of harm presents a risk in itself. Overclassification often results from an overabundance of caution and an attempt to prevent intended or unintended future bad behavior. Security should not be used to hide bad behaviors or to impede learning or business operation. Once overclassified, an asset's classification is rarely changed except through open disclosure projects.

Additionally, the 'vault and lock' design works well for some kinds of assets but leaves others vulnerable. The same object may be 'secured' in different ways in different organizations, in different parts of the organization, or at different times.

Additionally, organizations often tend to adopt a standard set of security parameters without considering the business implications. Organizations should not adopt other security methods and schemes. Security classification is not a one-and-done activity – it is ongoing. It should be revisited periodically.

In contrast, a 'beneficial balance' model supports and enables beneficial use and to discourage malicious use. The security design begins with an understanding of what we want to happen. We know from Chapter 18 what kinds of use we want to support. An organization can consider the types of harm that should be countered in every kind of asset. This exercise produces a more tailored and considered approach than the current 'vault and lock' approach.

Securing knowledge assets – design concepts

We must have a good understanding of harm, including legal harm, economic harm, willful harm, negligent harm, reputational damage, physical hurt or damage, levels and degrees of harm, risk reduction, risk of faults, risk from errors, uncertainty, unauthorized use, insurance against harm, security classes, security classification, overclassification, and underclassification. The primary challenge we face in designing this functional architecture is developing security measures and methods that are suited to types and levels of harm, and avoiding the temptation to adopt security classifications structures and methods from other organizations without full consideration.

Security is defined as the state of being free of danger, of being protected, and is free from care. No organization can ever by 100% free of risk or care. Every organization must decide what level of harm they will tolerate and how they want to achieve it. Traditional security is the practice of preventing unauthorized access, use, disclosure, disruption, modification, inspection, recording, or destruction of assets. Do we secure assets by asking what is the harm if this knowledge is accessed?

In the traditional approach, we rarely ask, what benefit is created if this asset is accessible? Going forward, we need a set of questions for a walkthrough for each type of asset in each business context (Allen, 2008; Anderson & Moore, 2006; Canadian Standards Association, 1994; Carlson, 2008; CNSS, 2010; Eloff & Eloff, 2003; Furnell, 2005; Gasmi et al., 2008; Lesnykh, 2011; Maconachy et al., 2001; McCumber, 1991; Peltier, 2005; Pereira & Dinis Santos, 2010; Sallos et al., 2019; Siponen, 2000; Swanson et al., 2006; Von Solms & Von Solms, 2005; Vroom & Von Solms, 2004; Whitman & Mattord, 2011; Whitman & Mattord, 2007). Traditional security is also 'one and done.' It is unrealistic from a business context and can lead to large stocks of unused stocks of assets, which are costly to manage.

Securing an asset means making a thoughtful choice as to (1) the level of internal protection needed, (2) the degree of external security required, and (3) a reasonable and practical security method (Figure 20.1). In contrast, consider how we do security today. Today, security is physical. Security is assigned to an object as metadata or assigned to the context and inherited by the asset. The object is secured against unwarranted access. In most situations, access is permitted or denied at an application or a folder level. It means that the security class is activated when someone tries to access the asset within an application or a folder. Once the object leaves

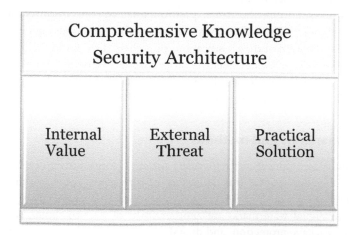

FIGURE 20.1 Factors to Consider in Designing a Knowledge Asset Security Solution

that space, though, security no longer applies if it is not encrypted. The essential protective components of a traditional approach include:

There is a rich world of security designs, markets, and built solutions. How do we put all of these into perspective? Security architectures for any kind of asset are like systems: there are inputs, there is a process, and there are results. Security inputs include security classes, security marks, security properties, metadata, and security rules. Security processes may be designed to secure applications, whole systems, folders, parts of assets, whole assets, and even metadata for assets. Security processes may be default based on the context, machine assigned, human assigned, encryption, and human declassification and disclosure. Security outputs may include secured assets, marked assets, and security metadata for individual assets.

To design a functional architecture to secure knowledge assets, we need to understand security classes and levels, security properties or metadata, security markups, security processes, and the business impacts of security decisions.

Security classes and levels

The two broadest categories of a classification typically used by organizations are (1) public, and (2) restricted. Restricted is often broken down further to reflect access and levels of harm. Examples of restricted classes might include Official Use Only, Confidential, Strictly Confidential, and For Eyes Only. Many business applications have built-in security controls that can be adjusted to align with the organization's security classes and level. Security classes and levels are most often registered as metadata in applications and enterprise registries.

Security properties and guidelines

Security properties include the levels and their definitions. They may also define the date of classification, the name, position title, and the organization of the authorized classifier. The reference is a guide to the conditions supporting classification, the duration of the classification, the office of origin of the information asset, and any special markings. Security properties may take the form of embedded properties or of externally represented and managed metadata. Ideally, properties are embedded in the asset so they can travel with the asset.

Security markings and methods

In addition to recording security metadata for assets, organizations typically mark or package the asset in a way that defines its security status. Some markings simply note the level which must be interpreted by learning the parameters of that level. Physical and digital watermarks are another form of asset marking. Encryption, public keys, package protection, and digital seals are other forms of applying security to assets.

Security processes

Security classification processes involve the interpretation and application of security classes. Human classification is the most common form of classification – performed by people using subjective judgment. Successful and effective processes are grounded in reliable guidance and consistent interpretation of security classes. Liabilities can result from both under- and overclassification of information assets. Manual classification is performed by individuals who review the source asset and interpret the classification guidelines to select and apply the most appropriate classification level. Two outcomes of human classification based on subjective judgment are overclassification and underclassification. Overclassification of knowledge assets results in reduced business value because access is constrained. Under the classification of knowledge, assets result in increased business risks because assets that may be harmed or cause business harm are more widely accessible.

Automated classification can be used where the classification rules are sufficiently well defined to allow a machine to understand them well enough to apply to assets. Machine-based classification can be used only where the asset is in digital form, or where there is sufficient digital information about the asset for the machine to apply the rules.

Classification processes are triggered by events such as filing when an asset might inherit the security classification of the folder to which it was assigned. Security may also be inherited or inferred from the context. A document filed into a content management system may inherit the security of the folder. An individual may inherit the classification associated with their job classification and work unit. Procedural knowledge may inherit the security classification assigned to the business-critical classification of the work unit or the system that supports it.

Security is commonly assigned to applications, to systems, to folders, to people, and to individual assets. We apply security classification to folders in an application or on a network drive to ensure that only those with the proper security clearance may access any information in the folder. The documents in a folder may have higher-level security clearance than the folder. Assuming that security properties are embedded in the object itself, Folder security is traditionally inherited by any documents added to the folder.

Classification of systems and applications

An entire system, such as an ERP system or an HR system, might have a default security classification assigned to any information managed in that system. An application is defined functionally – a specific application may have security assigned to it and inherited by any content created or maintained in that application.

Assets can also be declassified. When classified information of material no longer requires the level of protection previously assigned to it, it may be downgraded or declassified to preserve the effectiveness and integrity of the classification system. There should be clear guidance on the review process followed in approving or denying declassification requests. Additionally, organizations may choose to programmatically declassify information assets based on their types, creation dates, and ownership of business units. Ideally, declassification decisions are made based on a general declassification schedule. Declassification decisions should also apply to any copy of the source document.

Additionally, information may be declassified for limited periods, to pre-specified individuals, or in specific contexts. We may opt to classify the whole asset or just portions of an asset. There may be assets of an individual's tacit knowledge that are more highly classified than others. We may classify the metadata for an asset as well as the asset itself.

Security architectures for knowledge assets

Securing an asset assumes that we have ownership or custodianship rights for the asset, have determined that some form of physical or virtual security will add protection to the business value of the asset, and will not constrain use by those who have the rights to use it for business purposes, and that we can reverse the security protection as needed. Chapter 17 provided examples of the types of harm an asset might experience. Harm can take many forms. Securing an asset is not the only way, and not always the appropriate way, to protect the asset's business value. When is security appropriate, and what type of protection is practical?

Designing security for human capital assets

Security is appropriate for human capital when tacit knowledge has been learned on the job and is an investment of the organization in the individual. The investment needs to be protected and not shared with others in a way that gives others competitive knowledge. It is appropriate when skills and competencies are specific to what the organization does, and they have been taught by or developed on the job. It is important to remember that we can only affect or secure behavior or personalities in the organizational context and environment – through norms and ethics.

Who should secure the asset? Securing human capital is a joint effort of the organization, providing guidance, and the individual following the guidance. What type of security is practical? The most practical and effective strategy for securing human capital is establishing norms, standards of behavior, and reinforcement, such as rewards and recognitions. Nondisclosure agreements are common, but they are only a legal warning – they are not a real, physical security strategy. Similarly, intellectual property protections are a way of defining ownership, but they are only a legal mechanism that can be invoked when – and after – there is a security breach.

Designing security for explicit knowledge assets

When is security appropriate for explicit knowledge? It is appropriate when the explicit knowledge was created by an organization, was paid for, or was work for hire. It is appropriate when the knowledge has business value that should not be shared with others – it would create harm or an unintended competitive disadvantage if shared. It is appropriate when it is protected by copyright, trademark, and patents. It is appropriate when the organization formally procures it for some time or a specific type of use.

Who should secure the asset? Securing explicit knowledge assets is the responsibility of the organization because they are the owner and custodian. What type of security is practical? The most practical and effective strategy for securing explicit knowledge includes copyright protections, patent protections, trademarks, watermarks, encryption, disclosure policies and statements, and digital rights management where the explicit knowledge is available for a fee or some form of compensation. Licenses, contracts, and legal agreements to provide access or support use are another form of security.

Designing security for procedural knowledge assets

When is security appropriate for procedural knowledge? It is appropriate when the procedural knowledge has business value that can be safeguarded through control and protection against access. For private sector organizations, this includes any knowledge that has competitive value. For public sector organizations, it depends on the sensitivity or security risks associated with the process. General public service processes will not be appropriate for security, but national intelligence processes will be appropriate. In any organization, though, there should be security or safeguarding to prevent knowledge from leaking out of or intentionally leaving the organization.

Who should secure the asset? Security procedural knowledge is the responsibility of the organization, but the team and individuals who perform the process must secure it. What type of security is practical? There are several practical and effective strategies for securing procedural knowledge. The best choice depends on the nature of the process. The location where the process is performed might be secured or limited only to those who do the work. The procedural documentation or formula may be secured physically or legally. There may be patents, trademarks, or nondisclosure agreements in place. The most critical security solution, though, is training for those who have the procedural knowledge. The organization should map and preserve that knowledge to ensure it can be replicated if there is a loss of human capital.

Designing security for cultural knowledge assets

When is security appropriate for cultural knowledge? It is a more challenging question since culture is how we behave and how we interact. In this case, security takes the form of preventing access to the organization – having a secure location where only those permitted in can experience the culture, i.e., CIA, NSA, or a laboratory where classified research is conducted. Who should secure the asset?

The organization must set security guidelines and policies, but individuals enact those guidelines. What type of security is practical? It is not clear that there is an effective security strategy for cultural knowledge. Cultures are difficult to 'secure' – we can secure them only indirectly by preventing access or restricting participation.

Designing security for relational knowledge assets

When is security appropriate for relational knowledge? It is appropriate when the focus of the community is internal business or business-critical methods. It is appropriate when the community is a closed group of members representing secure collaborations. It is appropriate when the subject or focus of the network is itself secure or highly sensitive. Who should secure the asset? As with procedural and cultural capital, the organization sets the standards and guidelines, but it is the individual who practices the security. What type of security is practical? The most useful and effective strategy for securing relational capital is to secure access to the community if it is virtual. If the community is on-site or in-person, meetings and interactions can be located in a physically secure or undisclosed location. It is also possible to secure the identity of those individuals who participate in the network. The most effective security strategy is in the behavioral norms the network establishes for exchanging and developing knowledge.

From this exercise, we realize that given the properties and behaviors of knowledge assets, security is unlikely to be an effective method for managing harm and risks. Technology solutions are effective for explicit knowledge where they are embedded in the asset. Human behavior in the form of awareness, training, and certification is a more effective approach to maintaining the security of an organization's knowledge assets.

Securing knowledge assets – the design environment

What factors do we need to consider in designing this architecture? We need to consider the capacity of staff to understand and interpret security guidelines, the resources required for secure storage, the organization's ability to review and apply security to new knowledge assets, to classify documents early in their business life, to security tag parts of assets rather than just the whole asset, to security tag metadata differently from the asset, and to assign different security values to different metadata attributes.

What events cause us to design a functional architecture for security? Triggers include the need to manage potential risk and potential harm that might result from unauthorized access. Triggers might include different and conflicting security practices across the organization, the need to protect the business value of knowledge assets, the need to secure parts of assets or versions, or the need to apply security to metadata.

What are the impacts and consequences of having this functional architecture? The consequences of having this architecture in place are significant. They include a lowered risk of unauthorized disclosure, security breaches, and of accidental access to knowledge in a breach. The consequences also include an increased awareness of security risks and an increased awareness of potential harm due to security breaches.

What inputs do we need to consider when designing this functional architecture? There are several factors to consider, including whether the assets represent the current or historical business, existing human resource policies and practices, existing security classification policies and schemes, and technology solutions in place across the organization (Bulgurcu et al., 2010; Li et al., 2012). Perhaps the most important factor, though, is the general awareness of and behavior of the organization's people towards security.

What are the outputs and outcomes this functional architecture generates? Having a knowledge security architecture in place allows an organization to balance the opportunity to derive business value from knowledge while being confident that such use will not generate harm. A knowledge security architecture designed to suit different kinds of assets will reduce the potential under classification and overclassification.

Design activities for knowledge security

Designing a functional architecture for knowledge asset security involves five activities and tasks, including:

- Activity 1. Define types of harm and probability of risks for assets
- Activity 2. Design a security and safety strategy and infrastructure
- Activity 3. Determine what is possible for different types of assets
- Activity 4. Design a practical security strategy
- Activity 5. Establish updated security capabilities

Activity 1. Define types of harm and probability of risks for assets

How do we do this? This activity involves identifying a security strategy for each type of business–critical knowledge asset. The strategy should have both a physical-technology component and a human behavior component. Starting at the unit level, we work with the inventory of assets we generated earlier. With the advice of business managers, we create a preliminary strategy for their business-critical assets. Expanding the effort to other units provides the big picture we need to begin our architectural design. It is more likely that our design will address the physical-technical architecture component simply because the human behavioral aspect is not an architecture design task. However, the security risks that we find in our existing systems as part of this design effort can provide security experts with the information to develop further behavioral guidelines.

What inputs does it require? There are several inputs, including the inventory of knowledge assets, the business managers' guidance of which are business critical and which have the greatest security risks, and the knowledge architect's understanding of physical and behavioral challenges.

What outputs does it generate? This activity provides a rich stock of business advice on which knowledge assets can be safeguarded with traditional security methods, and which require new strategies. It is the foundation we need to develop the whole enterprise strategy.

What other resources are essential? The knowledge architect and the business managers should have a good understanding of harm and risk as it pertains to knowledge assets.

Activity 2. Design a security and safety strategy and infrastructure

How do we do this? This activity focuses on developing complete enterprise security and safety design blueprint for knowledge assets. The design blueprint should have two components: a blueprint for physical-technical security solutions, and a blueprint for human behavioral solutions. The human behavioral design may focus on building cautions, alerts, and traps into existing applications to remind users of security issues.

What inputs does it require? This activity is a synthesis of what we learned at the unit level. The unit-level feedback from business managers is the primary input. The knowledge architect's analytical competencies are essential to harmonizing needs across the organization.

What outputs does it generate? This activity creates a design blueprint for future security architecture. It represents a pre-evaluation vision.

What other resources are important? It is helpful to present the design in a format and framework that is consistent with the organization's security strategies for other types of assets. Knowledge of those other strategies is important to this activity.

Activity 3. Determine what is possible for different types of assets

How do we do this? This activity translates the vision into a practical solution for each type of knowledge asset. Every organization has a built security environment – any strategy proposed for knowledge assets must integrate with and supplement this environment.

What inputs does it require? The most important input is the knowledge architect's understanding of the existing security applications and strategies in place across the organization. Security policies and guidelines are another important input to this activity.

What outputs does it generate? This activity produces a security strategy at the knowledge asset level that will work across the organization.

What other resources are important? The results of this activity are fed back to the knowledge object models. The knowledge architect's understanding of the security attributes in that model is a vital resource.

Activity 4. Design a practical security strategy

How do we do this? This activity focuses on both the physical-technical solution and the human behavior solution. It is essential to present both in the design blueprint to emphasize the balance. It is the case for most organizations that both technical and behavioral solutions are in place. However, for knowledge assets, security behaviors are likely to be more impactful than security technologies.

What inputs does it require? This activity leverages all of the outputs from Activities 1, 2, and 3.

What outputs does it generate? This activity produces the whole organization's architecture design for knowledge assets. The design should speak to existing solutions and explain how those solutions are expanded or enhanced.

What other resources are essential? The knowledge architect should have a good understanding of the most effective way to present and explain the strategy.

Activity 5. Establish updated security capabilities

How do we do this? Most organizations have security training in place for all employees. This activity will update that training and possibly expand the coverage of the certification. This activity focuses on identifying competency updates that may be important for the security team, the training team, and business units.

What inputs does it require? This activity requires a knowledge of the existing security training materials and the training process. Any new capabilities or competencies will be integrated into what currently exists.

What outputs does it generate? This activity produces suggestions for expanding and enhancing existing security training and certifications.

What other resources are important? Since the new training will mean additional certification for every employee, it is essential to work closely with human resources experts to ensure they are professionally developed and approved.

The evolution of knowledge security

To understand the full history of security, we need to take a broad perspective – including focusing on and understanding how we have handled safety over millennia. From early security systems of moats and drawbridges and armed guards to today's systems, which can all be monitored, managed, and captured through the phone in your pocket, security has evolved with technological advances and demand for enhancements. There are many iterations and layers of security. The first layer we encounter is the security of physical spaces, structural safety, and perimeter control. Security has been applied to systems, to products, to commodities, to individuals, and now to knowledge. Over the millennia, these layers have been expanded and enhanced to apply to different environments. Today's sophisticated security solutions are a natural evolution of the earliest rope locks for doors

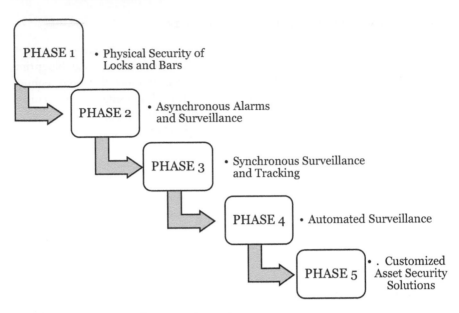

FIGURE 20.2 Evolution of Security Strategies

and spaces. Experience and a review of the literature suggest that there are five phases of evolution of security design (Figure 20.2), including:

- Phase 1. Physical security of locks and bars
- Phase 2. Asynchronous alarms and surveillance
- Phase 3. Synchronous surveillance and tracking
- Phase 4. Automated surveillance
- Phase 5. Customized asset security solutions

Phase 1. Physical security of locks and bars

In this phase, security solutions were physical, primitive, and one of a kind. In Chapter 17, we described the very early approaches to managing harm – rope locks, padlocks, and lock and key mechanisms. Over the millennia, security grew in complexity, but it was not until the early 1700s that we have anything more sophisticated than a lock and key. In the early 1700s, we see intrusion alerts built into security solutions. With the growth of the economy and the increased availability and distributions of goods and products, security was part of the packaging design. The packaging was designed to deter or prevent tampering and spoilage.

Phase 2. Asynchronous alarms and surveillance

This phase corresponds with the rise of the industrial revolution and economy. There are several significant advances during this phase. The increased rate of inventions created a demand for protection and security information about new methods, products, and formulae. The increased rate of development of technology led to new security systems and alarms. It was a shift from more primitive mechanical mechanisms or security guards for protection. The widespread installation of electricity in buildings made electric monitoring and security systems possible. This phase shifts from visible security strategies to invisible and anonymous security systems.

Phase 3. Synchronous surveillance and tracking

In this phase, security systems expanded beyond surveillance to prevent theft or intrusion to surveillance and monitoring to prevent a broader spectrum of harm. Fire and smoke alarms became commonplace, and the first site-based video surveillance systems emerged. Standards for security solutions emerged during this phase. Our awareness of the intrusive nature of security systems also increases, giving rise to privacy and legal concerns.

Phase 4. Automated surveillance

In this phase, video surveillance, first developed for the home, expanded to other buildings. New types of controls and new communications technologies emerged, and opportunities to customize security grew. Security solutions also became affordable and more commonplace. Security solutions are now designed to individual needs and individual devices because expectations, awareness, and competences grow within the larger population. With an increase in sophisticated attacks and global terrorism, security solutions are now designed into every aspect of our environments. In this phase, there is an expansion to secure information and knowledge rather than just physical assets or spaces. The expansion of security to information and knowledge created a demand for pre-access security classification, security classification schemes, and security markings.

Phase 5. Customized asset security solutions

In this phase, security solutions continue to expand in sophistication and complexity. We see the integration of artificial intelligence, sensor-based monitoring, and motion detection systems. The significant shift in this phase, though, is the focus on tracking and identifying individuals. Advances in identification technologies increased computing capacity to store large stocks of data, and tracings now make it possible for us to secure spaces, devices, and assets for and against specific individuals.

Knowledge security in the enterprise architecture

Security is not generally called out as a specific layer in the enterprise architecture practice. It is aligned with the application architecture and implemented or operationalized through the technology practice. There is a close affinity of knowledge security architectures and business architecture because it is the business managers who realize security behaviors every day in doing the organization's work. It is the business stakeholders who must make a case for how assets should be classified and disclosed. These stakeholders are responsible for monitoring any changes to classification. It is business managers who will suffer if a knowledge asset is wrongly classified. They will bear the costs of overclassification and suboptimized business value. They also bear the risks of exposed critical business information. There is also a strong affinity with the people's layer of the practice because good security is inherent to individuals' decisions and actions. People are the breaking point for any security strategy – regardless of how robust it is technically.

Chapter review

After reading this chapter, you should be able to:

- explain the business purpose of security;
- describe traditional approaches to security control and management;
- explain the challenges and opportunities of applying security to knowledge assets;
- describe the two components of a knowledge asset security architecture, i.e., technical and behavioral;
- explain why it is essential to develop new awareness training and behavioral competencies to safeguard knowledge assets.

References and recommended future readings

Allen, J. H. (2008). *Plan, do, check, act.* Build Security Retrieved August 14, 2008, from https://buildsecurityin.us-cert.gov/bsi/articles/best-practices/deployment/574-BSI.html

Anderson, R., & Moore, T. (2006). The economics of information security. *Science, 314*(5799), 610–613.

Babar, S., Mahalle, P., Stango, A., Prasad, N., & Prasad, R. (2010). Proposed security model and threat taxonomy for the Internet of Things (IoT). In *International conference on network security and applications* (pp. 420–429). Springer.

Bulgurcu, B., Cavusoglu, H., & Benbasat, I. (2010). Information security policy compliance: An empirical study of rationality-based beliefs and information security awareness. *Management Information Systems Quarterly, 34*(3), 523–548.

Burkett, J. S. (2012). Business security architecture: Weaving information security into your organization's enterprise architecture through SABSA®. *Information Security Journal: A Global Perspective, 21*(1), 47–54.

Carlson, T. (2008). Understanding information security management systems. In H. F. Tipton & M. Krause (Eds.), *Information security management handbook* (6th ed., Vol. 2, pp. 15–28). Auerbach Publications.

CNSS (Committee on National Security Systems). (2010). *National information assurance (IA) Glossary,* CNSSI 4009, 35. CNSS.

CSA (Canadian Standards Association). (1994). *ISO 8402:1994, Quality management and quality assurance – Vocabulary.* Canadian Standards Association.

Eloff, J., & Eloff. M. (2003, September 17–19). Information security management: A new paradigm. In *Proceedings of the 2003 annual research conference of the South African institute of computer scientists and information technologists on enablement through technology* (pp. 130–136). SAICSIT Press.

Furnell, S. (2005). *Computer insecurity: Risking the system*. Springer-Verlag.

Gasmi, Y., Sadeghi, A. R., Stewin, P., Unger, M., Winandy, M., Husseiki, R., & Stüble, C. (2008, October 27–31). Flexible and secure enterprise rights management based on trusted virtual domains. In *Proceedings of the 3rd ACM workshop on scalable trusted computing* (pp. 71–80). ACM Press.

Jain, A. K., Ross, A., & Pankanti, S. (2006). Biometrics: A tool for information security. *IEEE Transactions on Information Forensics and Security*, *1*(2), 125–143.

Katic, N., Quirchmay, G., Schiefer, J., Stolba, M. A. S. M., & Tjoa, A. M. (1998). A prototype model for data warehouse security based on metadata. In *Proceedings ninth international workshop on database and expert systems applications* (Cat. No. 98EX130) (pp. 300–308). IEEE.

Kim, S., & Leem, C. S. (2005). Enterprise security architecture in business convergence environments. *Industrial Management & Data Systems*, *105*(7), 919–936.

Kissel, R., Scholl, M., Skolochenko, S., & Li, X. (2006). *Guidelines for media sanitization: Recommendations of the national institute of standards and technology*. NIST Special Publication 800–88. Automated Information System Security.

Lesnykh, A. (2011). Data loss prevention: A matter of discipline. *Network Security*, *2011*(3), 18–19. [Crossref], [Web of Science ®].

Li, S., Xu, L., Wang, X., & Wang, J. (2012). Integration of hybrid wireless networks in cloud services oriented enterprise information systems. *Enterprise Information System*, *6*(2), 165–187. [Taylor & Francis Online], [Web of Science ®].

Maconachy, W. V., Schou, C. D., Ragsdale, D., & Welch, D. (2001, June 5–6). A model for information assurance: An integrated approach. In *Proceedings of the 2001 IEEE workshop on information assurance and security* (pp. 306–310). US Military Academy.

McCumber, J. (1991, October 11–14). Information systems security: A comprehensive model. In *Proceedings of the 14th NIST-NCSC national computer security conference* (pp. 328–337). NIST.

Murphy, B., Schlarman, S., & Boren, R. (2000). Enterprise security architecture. *Information Systems Security*, *9*(2), 1–14.

Peltier, T. R. (2005). *Information security risk analysis*. CRC Press.

Pereira, T., & Dinis Santos, H. (2010). An audit framework to support information system security management. *International Journal of Electronic Security and Digital Forensics*, *3*(3), 265–277. [Crossref], [Web of Science ®].

Rodríguez, A., Fernández-Medina, E., & Piattini, M. (2007). A BPMN extension for the modeling of security requirements in business processes. *IEICE Transactions on Information and Systems*, *90*(4), 745–752.

Sallos, M. P., Garcia-Perez, A., Bedford, D., & Orlando, B. (2019). Strategy and organisational cybersecurity: A knowledge-problem perspective. *Journal of Intellectual Capital*, *20*(4), 581–597.

Sherwood, N. (2005). *Enterprise security architecture: A business-driven approach*. CRC Press.

Siponen, M. T. (2000). A conceptual foundation for organizational information security awareness. *Information Management & Computer Security*, *8*(1), 31–41.

Swanson, M., Hash, J., & Bowen, P. (2006). Guide for developing security plans for federal information systems. NIST Special Publication 800–18, Revision 1. Author.

Von Solms, B., & Von Solms, R. (2005). From information security to . . . business security? *Computers & Security*, *24*(4), 271–273.

Vroom, C., & Von Solms, R. (2004). Towards information security behavioural compliance. *Computers & Security, 23*(3), 191–198.

Wahe, S., & Petersen, G. (2011). *Open Enterprise Security Architecture (O-ESA): A framework and template for policy-driven security.* Van Haren Publishing.

Whitman, M. E., & Mattord, H. J. (2007). *Principles of information security* (3rd ed.). Thomson Course Technology.

Whitman, M. E., & Mattord, H. J. (2011). *Principles of information security.* Cengage Learning.

21

FUNCTIONAL ARCHITECTURES FOR AUTHORIZATION AND ASSET MANAGEMENT

Chapter summary

This chapter explains how authorizing knowledge assets and designing privileges enables us to consume these assets. The chapter lays out the five activities that support authorization and access privileges. The chapter also considers why it is essential to have a good understanding of access, access controls, access rights, access control mechanisms, user identity management, and a range of approaches to privilege access management. The primary challenges we face in designing this functional architecture are understanding who is requesting access, why and what harm or risk they present, and overcoming the tendency to revert to the principle of least privilege – which results in lower knowledge flows and constraints the business value of knowledge assets.

Why we care about authorizing and privileging knowledge assets

The traditional approaches to security are not suitable or effective for knowledge assets. We need a new framework to balance risk and value, a framework that is tied to the new types of use and consumption we see in the 21st century. Most organizations have a good understanding of authorization but still struggle with authentication, access, and privileges. Lack of a full understanding of the authorization architecture and its relation to authentication and access control principles and processes can create security gaps that put the organization at risk. This requires enforcement, a compliance mechanism, and continuous monitoring. Authorization and access control require continuous monitoring of who gets access to which data/knowledge, how they should be able to access them, and under which conditions access is granted. Access to much information and knowledge assets is still managed within applications, at the folder level, and statically. These assumptions no longer hold because today, the expectation is that digital copies have mobility.

It is critical to embed authorization and access controls in each knowledge object to ensure that its security will be maintained wherever that asset travels. Perhaps the best analogy we have to understand this is the shift in air traffic authorization and privileging. In past decades aircraft used ground-based radar tracking – there was a location-based system that tracked which aircraft was where, where they were going, and what they could do when they reached their destination. Recently, aircraft authentication and credentialing have been designed into and embedded in the individual aircraft. We can determine what it is and what it can do based on the credentials we can access directly from its embedded properties. We need to adopt a similar design for our authorizing and privileging architecture for knowledge assets. We need to be able to authenticate users based on their credentials and to authorize users based on the credentials and sensitivities of the knowledge asset. It is a significant shift in thinking and design.

Authorizing and privileging knowledge assets – design concepts

To develop this functional architecture, we must have a good understanding of access – access control, access rights, access control mechanisms, user identify management, privilege access management, discretionary access control, mandatory access control, attribute-based access control, personally identifiable information, user accounts, privileged risk accounts, the principle of least privilege, authorization, and authorization methods. The primary challenge we face in designing this functional architecture is understanding who is requesting access, why, and what harm or risk they present. Another challenge is the tendency to revert to the principle of least privilege – which results in lower knowledge flows and constraints the business value of knowledge assets.

Designing an authorizing and privileging architecture resembles designing a system with inputs, processes, and outputs (Figure 21.1). We have inputs in the form of authenticated people, agents, and organizations – those entities we decide are trusted and can be identified and *authenticated*. We have processes in the form of authorized uses. *Authorization* focuses on who can do what with which assets. It is the central design question each organization must ask and answer. Authorized

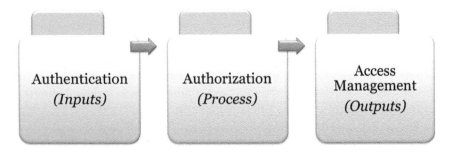

FIGURE 21.1 Core Design Concepts for Knowledge Authorizing and Privileging Architecture

use pertains to both internal and external use and consumption. Finally, we have outputs in the form of managed access based on access privileges. It is a challenging architecture to design because the application architecture practice 'owns' and is in control of authentication and access control. The essence of the design challenge is defining the authorization and privileging component in a way that leverages the authentication solutions in place and translates them so the access management solutions can implement them as intended.

The chapters in Section 2 addressed architecture designs that facilitate access to knowledge assets generally. These architecture designs are essential to discovering and finding knowledge assets. We use the term access differently in this chapter – assuming that knowledge assets can be discovered and found because of the internal functional architecture – we now ask who can access them, to do what, and how. We design for ease of access to ensure that we can transform knowledge assets into business value through use. We know that access can lead to unintended harm and consequences if it is not managed. We design authorization and privileging architecture to manage the balance between use and misuse. Chapter 17 outlined the harm and risk issues. Chapter 18 focused on the authentication of assets – the input to authorization and privileging. Chapter 19 focused on designing an architecture to secure assets. In this chapter, we consider how the architecture can help us to authenticate users and requests for access, how we authorize different uses, and how we design this into a manageable, functional architecture. We design each of the three components of the authorization and privileging architecture around key decision points (Figure 21.2).

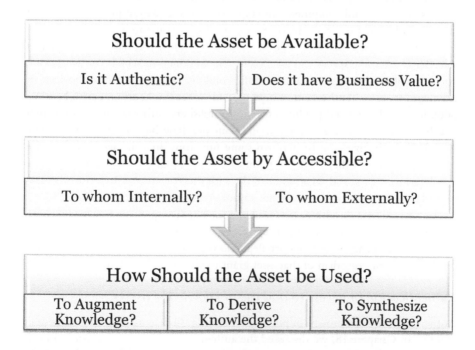

FIGURE 21.2 Critical Decision Points in Designing an Authorizing Architecture

Authorization of access to and use of knowledge assets

Authorization is a fundamental concept of access management. To authorize use is to assert ownership, custodianship, or privilege for an asset. Authorization is the act of giving permission, to endorse, to empower, to justify or to permit (Burt et al., 2003; Rabitti et al., 1991; Thomas & Sandhu, 1998). The owner or recognized authority confers authorization. Who is the owner or author for an asset is an essential question for knowledge architects to answer. We cannot assume the organization is the 'owner' of any knowledge asset. In some cases, the organization may have 'leasing' or 'renting' privileges to an asset (e.g., a salary means we can leverage an employee's tacit knowledge during work hours, but not beyond). In other cases, the organization is a temporary custodian of assets (e.g., leased commercial databases).

Authorization is the process the asset owner or custodians works through to grant managed access. Pre- or prior authorization may be granted to internal business stakeholders. On-demand authorization is often the process we follow for external business stakeholders and competitors. The authorization process revolves around three essential questions, including: (1) what authorization requested is, (2) when authorization is automatically granted based on credentials, (3) to what are we authorizing access? and (4) what kind of use is being authorized.

Authorization is the function of specifying access rights and privileges to assets. Authorization provides the set of business rules we follow to design access control – it defines our access policies. Authorization determines access to spaces and places, processes, devices and equipment, and types of access. For example, consider what you are authorized to access in your organization – you can access your human resource documents, but not those of a colleague unless you have a management role. There are some spaces you can access – the buildings in which you work. But, you may not be able to access another office building unless you are 'authorized' or privileged to enter. Authorization is granted for some books and journals by some publishers to the general public. Still, most publishers authorize access only after you have made a purchase, and you and your purchase have been authenticated. Your bank authorizes you to perform some functions on your accounts, but not on the accounts of others. They authenticate who you are, what accounts you are privileged to access, and what you can do with those accounts. In your organization, there are certain systems you are authorized to access, but not others.

Authorization is a multitiered consideration. The first question is, can you access the asset, i.e., a facility, a system, a repository, or an asset? The second question is, assuming you can access it, what privileges do you have? What rights and privileges do the owner or custodian of that asset grant to you while you have access?

Authentication of access to and use of knowledge assets

Authentication is the process of proving something, such as an asset or a requester's identity. In Chapter 18, we discussed the authenticity of knowledge assets. In this chapter, we consider the authenticity of a person or agent who is requesting access to those assets. Authentication is essential because it enables organizations to keep their assets secure by permitting only authenticated users to access those assets. Authentication focuses on identifying and proving the identity of the requester (Braz & Robert, 2006; Das, 2009; Das et al., 2004; Indovina et al., 2003; Li & Hwang, 2010; O'Gorman, 2003; Shen et al., 2010; Wahl et al., 2000). Just as we want to make sure any knowledge asset we're leveraging is authentic, we want to know that a requester is authentic.

Their credentials determine the authentication of users or requesters. By credentials, we mean those identifying attributes they can present to us, and which we can validate against a trusted source. Internal business stakeholders are often trusted because they are pre-authenticated when on-boarding to the organization. It may vary with their affiliation to the organization – if they are temporary affiliates or contracted affiliates, their pre-authentication may be indirect – and through another organization. Authentication is just the first gate a requester needs to open. Authorization then considers what we will let them access, and why.

Authentication begins when a user tries to access information. First, the user must prove his access rights and identity. If the requester or consumer has no known identity or does not provide authenticated information, they are assigned to a group of users commonly labeled 'Guest' or 'Anonymous.' Anonymous consumers or guests have no requirement to authenticate. We confer limited authorization privileges on these consumers. Most authentication, though, is multifaceted and can require several levels or forms of identification. Most authentication strategies are multifaceted, meaning that they rely on more than one form of identification. And, most authentication systems begin with a baseline of 'no identification' or 'anonymous requester.' Multi-factor authentication (MFA) is a method of logon verification where at least two different factors of proof are required. MFA is also referred to as 2FA, which stands for two-factor authentication. MFA helps protect your data (email, financial accounts, health records, etc.) or assets by adding an extra layer of security. There are generally three recognized types of authentication factors, depending on (1) something you know; (2) something you have; or (3) something you are. It is the easiest way to think about the architectures your organization likely has in the 'built' environment.

The first type of authentication is based on *something you know*. Something you know might include includes user names, passwords, personal identification numbers (PINs), code words, or secret handshakes. In short, anything you can remember and then type, say, perform, or otherwise recall when needed falls into this category. The challenge with this type of authentication is that it can be guessed or gamed. Depending on the potential harm and risk associated with a knowledge asset, this level may or may not be sufficient. This type of authentication aligns with our demonstrated or inferred authenticity, as discussed in Chapter 18.

The second type of authentication is based on *something you have*. Something you have includes physical objects, such as keys, smartphones, smart or key cards, USB drives, and token devices that generate a time-based PIN or can compute a response from a challenge number issued by the server, and digital certificates such as are used in a Public Key Infrastructure (PKI) method. This type of authentication aligns with our documented authenticity, as discussed in Chapter 18.

The third type of authentication is based on *something you are*. Something you are includes something inherent to you. It includes any part of the human body that can be used for verification, such as fingerprints, palm scanning, facial recognition, retina scans, iris scans, and voice verification. This form of authentication depends on the user's presence and proximity. This technology makes it more difficult for hackers to break into computer systems. It also requires a more complex application and technology architecture.

Multi-factor authentication means combining two or three factors from these three categories. Multi-factor authentication is preferred, as it is much more difficult for an intruder to overcome. With just a password, an attacker only has to have a single attack skill and wage a single successful attack to impersonate the victim. With multi-factor authentication, the attack must have multiple attack skills and must attempt multiple methods to impersonate the victim. It is extremely difficult and, thus, a more resilient authentication strategy.

Access management

The third component of our knowledge authorization architecture is access control (Bertino et al., 2001; Claycomb et al., 2007; Deng & Hong, 2003; Ferraiolo et al., 1999; Howes et al., 2003; Hu et al., 2015; Jin et al., 2012; Joshi et al., 2005; Oh & Park, 2003; Park et al., 2012; Shen & Hong, 2006; Sheresh & Sheresh, 2002; Yang et al., 2007). Access control is a method of guaranteeing that users are who they say they are and that they have the authorization they need to support the organization's business goals and work. The fundamental concept of access control and management is access rights. We assume that to be considered for access privileges, a stakeholder or consumer has been assigned to an authentication category and can be authenticated. We also assume that we know what they want to access and what they want to do with those assets.

Designing access control architectures means designing the matrix or decision points and applying them to spaces, places, systems, and assets. The challenge is that access control methods are usually built into applications and are inherited by the assets that reside in those applications. Our challenge from a knowledge architecture perspective is normalizing all of these different 'built' solutions into an architecture that allows us to protect and leverage assets. The risk often results from gaps and variations in access management designs. Knowledge assets are dynamic and fluid, but access control solutions are often static and isolated. Ultimately, our authorization and privileging design will be implemented by the enterprise or business-specific technologies, so the design principles must take into account calibration, translation, and continuous monitoring. Organizations must determine the appropriate *access control model* to adopt based on the type and sensitivity of their assets and their use.

There are three basic types of access control systems, including (1) discretionary access control (DAC), (2) mandatory access control (MAC), and (3) role-based access control (RBAC) or attributed base access control (ABAC). In discretionary access control systems, the asset owner or custodian decides on access and assigns access rights based on rules. It is the oldest access management design. It is the least sophisticated approach, but it is the most labor- and management-intensive in that we need to assign privileges to individuals for each asset. It is the model most organizations follow for access to facilities and spaces.

In mandatory access control systems, people or agents are granted access based on credentials and levels of authorization (e.g., clearance or privilege categories). Mandatory access controls typically operate from a common security classification scheme, as described in Chapter 20. It is the most common access control model in place today. This design leverages predefined access categories, including open access, access to pre-authenticated and pre-authorized users, restricted access granted only upon specific request, and embargo, which may allow access to metadata and metainformation but not the asset.

Finally, role-based access control systems grant access based on the requester or stakeholder's role. It is the most recent design. The principle is to authorize access to knowledge based on what is relevant to their work. In an attribute-based access control system, each resource and user is assigned a series of attributes. This dynamic method leverages a comparative assessment of the user's attributes, the time of day, position, and location to make an access determination.

The most common type of access control application is a directory structure (Sheresh & Sheresh, 2002). The term directory architecture refers to either the internal or the external design of a directory application. Directories provide information about the user. It can essentially deliver any information required to identify a user. Directories also provide information about the data that the users are allowed to see and what they can do with the data that they can access. Almost every directory keeps track of when an entry is created and when it is last modified. The most challenging aspect of a directory service implementation is the design stage. Like other functional architecture design challenges, our knowledge architecture needs to fit into the enterprise architecture. The three most essential directories in an organization are email, Network Operating System (NOS), and mainframe security. Secondary directories include human resources, secondary NOSs, applications that store lists of authorized users, router and firewall tables, and organization charts.

We can see how the ultimate authorization and privileging architecture leverages both authentications to verify the identity of requesters and authorization to determine what we will allow them to do (Zhang et al., 2006). When a consumer tries to access an asset, the access control process checks to verify the requester's credentials (or lack thereof) and that the requester has been authorized to use it. Authorization is the responsibility of a business manager, but it is often delegated to a custodian, such as a system administrator.

Authorization and privileging of knowledge assets

A few keys will help us to design an authorizing and privileging architecture for knowledge assets, including: (1) Who owns the asset? (2) Who has the authority to make it available? (3) Who monitors access and authorizations? (4) What is the best design for authorizing this type of asset? And (5) what are the built solutions that need to be leveraged and integrated?

Authentication, authorization, and access to human capital

Who owns this type of asset? The individual owns their tacit knowledge, their skills and behaviors, and their behaviors and personalities. By agreeing to work for an organization, you 'lease' or 'rent' your human capital to the organization for the time you're engaged in. Who has the authority to make human capital available? The organization may have the authority to make human capital available to others – internal and external – during the workday. However, what is made available is controlled by the individual.

Conversely, as we have seen in recent years, organizations can exercise a limit on what human capital may not be authorized for access. For example, individuals with expertise who are prohibited from sharing their tacit knowledge due to social or political preferences, or due to the competitive or comparative advantage of skill, may have business value. Who monitors access to human capital? It is a sensitive issue because it raises concerns about surveillance and intrusion. At present, authorization likely takes non-disclosure agreements, patents, intellectual property agreements and clauses, and copyrights. How might knowledge architecture facilitate privileging access to an individual's human capital? Perhaps one of the most effective solutions might be people portals with those full profiles with conditions for under what circumstances the individual will engage with others. What are the 'built systems' that are likely in place for these assets today? The primary built system is the organization's enterprise directory systems, communications systems, and the human resource management applications.

Authentication, authorization, and access to explicit knowledge

Who owns explicit knowledge? The answer here is clear – the organization owns whatever explicit information is produced by anyone working for hire or as an employee unless there is an explicit agreement in place to the contrary. The challenge is to ensure that these assets are identified and authenticated. Who grants access is generally determined by the owning unit or the business custodian. The organization may define a set of authorization rules and guidelines they are assigned and applied by individuals making decisions in the course of doing business. Because this is generally the richest stock of knowledge assets, monitoring authorization, and access is the challenge. It is particularly true when applications use 'inherited authorization' and inherited security practices. The more complex the authorization rules, the more challenging and labor-intensive the monitoring task. What is the best design for this type of knowledge asset? Perhaps the best design for this type of asset is to ensure that the authorization parameters are built into each asset. It takes us back to the knowledge asset object model. What are the 'built systems' that are likely in place for these assets today? The built solutions are document management systems, content management systems, web management systems, and any other general asset management systems. The challenge is that they will each have a different authorization protocol.

Authentication, authorization, and access to procedural knowledge

Who owns it? The answer to this question has two components. The clear answer is that the organization owns and is the authorizing agency for access to procedural knowledge. The second part, though, is challenging because procedural knowledge is manifested in the human capital of team members and business stakeholders. The organization can control access to formal procedural knowledge. Still, it is not possible to prevent an individual from learning or expanding upon what they have learned in doing the work. Who grants access? The organization is the authority for privileging access to procedural knowledge, but the individual and the team member is the final authority for what is 'released' or accessed. What is the best design for this type of knowledge asset? The design imperative for this type of asset is that the organization should know its procedural knowledge, design methods to protect it, and create a foundation for authorization or non-authorization. What are the 'built systems' that are likely in place for these assets today? The most common solution today is to document, patent, and protect procedural knowledge, and to classify it in a way that prevents external access to that documentation. A challenge is that procedural knowledge may be overprotected to prevent external access and, as a result, further restrict internal access.

Authentication, authorization, and access to cultural knowledge

Who owns it? Culture is a shared asset, and it is an action and practice. The default control here is open and accessible simply because it is difficult to hide or suppress a culture. Who grants access? Who is the authorizing agency? The authorizing agency here is the group that owns and shapes the culture – if you are allowed or privileged into the group, you have access to it. And, the answer to the question of who monitors is the same – the group monitors access. The design for culture is the nature of the space. To some extent, authentication for access to spaces and places is the built solution. It includes both virtual and physical spaces and places. The best design of an authorization architecture is likely defined by the leader of the group or unit.

Authentication, authorization, and access to network knowledge

Who owns it? Networks at work are owned and supported by the organization, but they are activated and realized by the individuals who comprise the networks. The organization manages the first level of authorization, but the members control authorization to access the actual activities and knowledge of the network. Typically, a network has a facilitator or moderator who, we would assume, is responsible for assigning privileges and manages access. What is the best design for this type of knowledge asset? The best design is a two-tiered authorization architecture, with the organization managing networks and privileging 'the door' to the network. Still, individual members setting the guidelines and rules for who is authorized to do what within the network. What are the 'built systems' that are likely in place for these assets today? The challenge here is that there is a proliferation of building solutions that support networks, social groups, and communities – and each of these solutions has a different approach to access management.

Knowledge asset authorization and privileging – the design environment

What factors do we need to consider in designing this architecture? While there are three components to this functional architecture, our focus is on factors that determine authorization rules and guidelines. It means understanding the level of business risk and business value and understanding how to balance them. It means understanding the range of business roles and responsibilities that are required and that would also benefit from access in a knowledge discovery perspective. It also means understanding and synchronizing levels of access to common types of knowledge assets across and within applications. Finally, it means understanding how we apply the authorization rules and methods to assets, not just applications.

What events cause us to design a functional architecture for semantics? Several events would trigger the need to authorize access to a knowledge asset. The most obvious is on-boarding new staff, establishing credentials, and authorizing access to any knowledge assets they need to do their job. Staff changing jobs within the organization is another trigger. Whenever we create new knowledge assets, they should be assigned an authorizing agent and assigned access privileges.

Authorizing agencies need to identify and access privileges established and synchronized with other applications whenever a new application or system is acquired. Another essential trigger is any critical incident that exposes vulnerabilities. Routine access audits are also important triggers.

What are the impacts and consequences of having this functional architecture? Having this functional architecture in place means that access is afforded to those who are entitled and denied to those who are not access is managed programmatically and that knowledge assets are assigned to asset categories appropriately.

What inputs do we need to consider when designing this functional architecture? This architecture is a design challenge because it involves leveraging authentication and access management solutions in place while designing authorization rules that are suited to knowledge assets. A challenge may be that some of these assets are already under permission by functions that do not recognize them as capital assets but treats them as resources. Enterprise directory structures are core elements of the built environment.

What are the outputs and outcomes this functional architecture generates? This architecture generates authorization guidelines and rules for all five categories of knowledge assets.

Design activities for knowledge authorization and privileging

Five activities are integral to the design of a knowledge asset authorization architecture, including:

- Activity 1. Design a practical authorization solution for all five categories of knowledge assets
- Activity 2. Review and align authorization solutions with existing authentication solutions
- Activity 3. Review and align authorization strategies with built access control solutions
- Activity 4. Revise authentication and access control rules to support knowledge assets
- Activity 5. Establish a knowledge management capability to monitor authorization and access to knowledge assets

Activity 1. Design a practical authorization solution for all five categories of knowledge assets

How do we do this? This activity begins with a focus on the business unit level. This activity focuses on identifying who can or should do what with the unit's assets. We look at what they can or need to do from a consumption or use perspective, not just the standard 'read, write, edit, delete' controls we find in most access control applications. We should consider what options are available in the business applications supporting the unit's work. We should consider who has access to these applications now and what they can do with the assets. This activity asks and answers how we track and capture what they have done with the asset; whether it is limited to simple system-level logging of their access; whether any changes to the asset were recorded in the system?; and whether the earlier version of the asset was preserved in some way. We should also consider how those who need the information but do not have access obtain the asset – are there any risks involved in these kinds of transactions? We work backward from what people are doing with assets to who is not doing anything with the asset. This activity also explains what those without access might do with it if they had access. Essentially, this activity provides us with the information we need to design the optimal authorization framework.

What inputs does it require? We need to know who the internal business stakeholders are, what they are doing now – how they are using the assets, the most critical business assets, current disclosure policies, current classification levels and processes for these assets, and the existing business applications used within and across units.

What outputs does it produce? This activity generates a positive and proactive description of an authorization framework for knowledge assets at the unit level.

What other resources are important? Also crucial to this activity is the knowledge of business stakeholders, the experience of application architects who support and design current access control, the knowledge and advice of the disclosure policy team, and the security team.

Activity 2. Review and align authorization solutions with existing authentication solutions

How do we do this? This activity focuses on comparing the proactive framework with the current approach. It involves gathering information on current access control methods and determining possible ways of adapting authentication credentials and access privileges. This activity also consists of looking across all internal and external access points to establish safe and secure methods for providing extended access in a controlled way.

What inputs does it require? This activity requires access to current authentication, authorization, and access control policies and practices at the unit level.

What outputs does it produce? This activity creates a practical authorization framework that can be presented to business managers for review and comment. It also generates an architectural design for adapting and expanding existing authorization practices to cover knowledge assets.

What other resources are important? This activity also leverages an understanding of security architectures, authentication methods, and business unit-level behaviors.

Activity 3. Review and align authorization strategies with built access control solutions

How do we do this? This activity translates the 'use' level categories – what are referred to in most business systems as 'privilege categories' to task level access controls. It is a survey and synthesizing activity that maps all of the most critical business applications. Some of these will be enterprise-level applications, but others will be local to the unit and others specific to individuals.

What inputs does it require? This activity leverages knowledge of and access control documentation for all business-critical applications and systems, and the architecture framework we designed in Activity 2.

What outputs does it produce? This activity creates a task-level authorization framework for all knowledge assets across all business systems.

What other resources are important? This activity also benefits from access to business application reference documentation and configuration settings.

Activity 4. Revise authentication and access control rules to support knowledge assets

How do we do this? This activity maps all of the access control methods across all units to a single enterprise framework.

What inputs does it require? This activity requires access to documentation about the enterprise directory. We need to know how the organization authenticates individual staff and how they allocate privileges across applications. The framework we designed in Activity 4 is a critical input as it provides a map of all existing access privileges.

What outputs does it produce? This activity creates a design for full access to control coverage of knowledge assets. The heart of this output is a new authorization framework that pertains to knowledge assets. It will likely include new privilege groups.

What other resources are important? This activity also leverages the enterprise directory team's knowledge of profiles and parameters.

Activity 5. Establish a knowledge management capability to monitor authorization and access to knowledge assets

How do we do this? This activity augments existing access control capabilities and functions and expands current roles and responsibilities from simple information and document management to knowledge access management. It is an integrated capability that will add to rather than redefine any existing roles and responsibilities. This activity creates a new community of experts from across several different business areas. It shifts the focus of these experts from seeing their assets as isolated or business-specific to enterprise level.

What inputs does it require? This activity leverages information about who plays these roles now, an understanding of what they do, and how their roles are described.

What outputs does it produce? This activity generates design specifications for permissioning people to applications. It generates recommendations for additional training for these roles.

What other resources are important? The human resource management approach to managing these responsibilities and competencies.

Evolution of knowledge asset authorization and privileging designs

Authorization and privileging are about determining the mechanisms that allow you to control who gets in, who does not, and what they can do with whatever assets are 'in the space.' It's about keeping the unwanted, unqualified, and

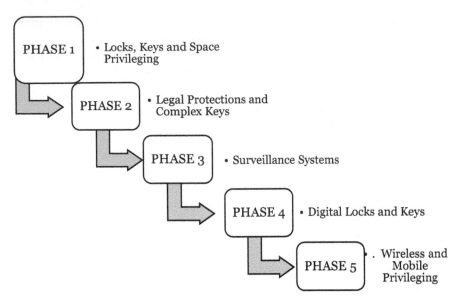

FIGURE 21.3 Evolution of Security Design

unverified out, and the wanted, qualified and verified in. Authorizing and privileging is ancient. Experience and a review of the literature suggest that these architectures have evolved over five phases (Figure 21.3), including:

- Phase 1. Locks, keys, and privileging of space and place
- Phase 2. Legal protections and complex keys
- Phase 3. Surveillance systems and protections
- Phase 4. Digital locks and keys
- Phase 5. Wireless and mobile privileging

Phase 1. Locks, keys and privileging of space and place

The earliest methods for authorizing access involved ropes and knots. These were the norm for the general population until around 4000 BC when we find the first mechanical locks. Locks were used by the wealthy and royalty to protect valuable places. These mechanical locks were designed to prevent access by human threats – unauthenticated and unauthorized intrusion and to safeguard gardens, works of art, mines, stocks of jewelry, bridges, irrigation and sewage systems, libraries, and any asset of value needing safeguarding. Solutions advanced from simple locks to locking systems that had multiple components. These kinds of authorization and privilege tools were intended to guard against physical force attacks. Over the centuries, the design of locks advanced from wooden to metal, to locks with uniquely fitted and customized keys. This advance was a significant design shift – it built-in permissioned or pre-authorized access (e.g., the keyholder) – from the simple barricade. This design advance built obstruction and challenges into access. These challenges were easy to overcome, though. For several centuries the strategy was to increase the complexity of the locking systems, including intricate key designs, obscuring keyholes, and even fake keyholes.

Phase 2. Legal protections and keys

Phase 2 of the evolution focused on other forms of protection, and protections targeted to inventions and assets. Specifically, during this phase, we note the rise of intellectual property, patent, and trademarking solutions. This phase corresponds to the early years of the industrial revolution. While there was a precedent for conferring monopoly and property rights to inventors starting in the Middle Ages, the first patent law appeared in the late 1700s. We continued to engineer better physical locking mechanisms simultaneous with the evolution of these legal protections. It is at this time that homes were equipped with mass-produced pin tumbler locks.

Phase 3. Surveillance systems and protections

It was during this broad phase that we see the first rudimentary surveillance systems emerge. Surveillance first took the form of trained and financed policing services. In the mid-20th century, we see the first video surveillance systems. Specifically, early home security systems utilized television surveillance. These systems worked in conjunction with physical locks and policing methods. They 'authenticated' the requester through video display and provided the homeowner with the controls to provide or deny access. These systems required human monitoring and intervention.

Phase 4. Digital locks and keys

The third phase is characterized by sophisticated threats, computer technology, data credentials, intellectual assets, remote control, and fast-paced convenience. The shift was incentivized by the advent of personal computers with data storage, digital keypads and remote access control systems for automobiles, and credential authentication through passwords for computer software. Security now shifts to individuals and is customizable by users. Authentication is grounded in a 'key or credential holder.' It introduces new risks because we have decentralized and fragmented access controls and privileges. During this phase, we also see new access control systems designed around user-defined keys and access codes. During this phase, we also see the earliest forms of intelligent systems designed into the access mechanisms – into the locking mechanism. We see the first use of security identification and passcards and devices. Today, these are the most common form of user authentication. During this phase, access control systems are primarily 'wired.' The user or requester must be in physical proximity to the system to activate the access control system.

Phase 5. Wireless and mobile privileging

Phase 5 is today and the future. This phase is characterized by a move from wired authorization and privileged access to wireless. In this phase, we see a significant expansion of the scale of coverage that goes beyond simple access. In this phase, we see a more aggressive and intentional use of artificial intelligence in authentication and detection. The guiding principle of access control in this phase is proactive and predictive. We see a shift from prevention of a requested or launched access action to a more comprehensive monitoring and surveillance approach. This phase considers integrating existing access control mechanisms and the ability to monitor well beyond physical proximity. Advances in technology also make access control more affordable. Access controls become commonplace in most organizations.

Authorization and privileging in enterprise architecture

This functional architecture aligns primarily with the application architecture because we are dealing with a heavily built and well-established application and technology environment. There is a strong affinity with the business architecture practices because these practices must be adapted to accommodate the new frame-work. Business managers are also essential because they will be responsible for monitoring who is authorized to access business-critical knowledge assets. This architecture is less dependent upon information architecture because the access control privileges of knowledge assets under information management control are unlikely to change in the new framework.

Chapter review

After reading this chapter, you should be able to:

- explain why it is crucial to authenticate stakeholders to use your knowledge assets;
- explain why it is essential to authorize access to knowledge assets;
- describe the role of authentication and authorization in defining access controls;
- describe the levels of access controls and management we might find in any organization;
- explain the importance of synthesizing and harmonizing access control to support knowledge assets.

References and recommended future readings

Bertino, E., Bonatti, P. A., & Ferrari, E. (2001). TRBAC: A temporal role-based access control model. *ACM Transactions on Information and System Security (TISSEC)*, 4(3), 191–233.

Braz, C., & Robert, J. M. (2006). Security and usability: The case of the user authentication methods. In *Proceedings of the 18th conference on l'interaction homme-machine* (pp. 199–203).

Burt, C. C., Bryant, B. R., Raje, R. R., Olson, A., & Auguston, M. (2003). Model driven security: Unification of authorization models for fine-grain access control. In *Seventh IEEE international enterprise distributed object computing conference, 2003. Proceedings.* (pp. 159–171). IEEE.

Claycomb, W., Shin, D., & Hareland, D. (2007). Towards privacy in enterprise directory services: A user-centric approach to attribute management. In *2007 41st Annual IEEE international Carnahan conference on security technology* (pp. 212–220). IEEE.

Das, M. L. (2009). Two-factor user authentication in wireless sensor networks. *IEEE Transactions on Wireless Communications, 8*(3), 1086–1090.

Das, M. L., Saxena, A., & Gulati, V. P. (2004). A dynamic ID-based remote user authentication scheme. *IEEE Transactions on Consumer Electronics, 50*(2), 629–631.

Deng, J. B., & Hong, F. (2003). Task-based access control model. *Journal of Software, 14*(1), 76–82.

Ferraiolo, D. F., Barkley, J. F., & Kuhn, D. R. (1999). A role-based access control model and reference implementation within a corporate intranet. *ACM Transactions on Information and System Security (TISSEC), 2*(1), 34–64.

Howes, T. A., Smith, M. C., & Good, G. S. (2003). *Understanding and deploying LDAP directory services.* Addison-Wesley Longman Publishing Co., Inc.

Hu, V. C., Kuhn, D. R., Ferraiolo, D. F., & Voas, J. (2015). Attribute-based access control. *Computer, 48*(2), 85–88.

Indovina, M., Uludag, U., Snelick, R., Mink, A., & Jain, A. (2003). Multimodal biometric authentication methods: A COTS approach. In *Proceedings of workshop on multimodal user authentication* (pp. 99–106). http://www.nist.gov/customcf/ge-t_pdf.cfm?pub_id=151579

Jin, X., Krishnan, R., & Sandhu, R. (2012). A unified attribute-based access control model covering DAC, MAC and RBAC. In *IFIP annual conference on data and applications security and privacy* (pp. 41–55). Springer.

Joshi, J. B., Bertino, E., Latif, U., & Ghafoor, A. (2005). A generalized temporal role-based access control model. *IEEE Transactions on Knowledge and Data Engineering, 17*(1), 4–23.

Li, C. T., & Hwang, M. S. (2010). An efficient biometrics-based remote user authentication scheme using smart cards. *Journal of Network and Computer Applications, 33*(1), 1–5.

O'Gorman, L. (2003). Comparing passwords, tokens, and biometrics for user authentication. *Proceedings of the IEEE, 91*(12), 2021–2040.

Oh, S., & Park, S. (2003). Task – Role-based access control model. *Information Systems, 28*(6), 533–562.

Park, J., Nguyen, D., & Sandhu, R. (2012). A provenance-based access control model. In *2012 tenth annual international conference on privacy, security and trust* (pp. 137–144). IEEE.

Rabitti, F., Bertino, E., Kim, W., & Woelk, D. (1991). A model of authorization for next-generation database systems. *ACM Transactions on Database Systems (TODS), 16*(1), 88–131.

Shen, H. B., & Hong, F. (2006). An attribute-based access control model for web services. In *2006 seventh international conference on parallel and distributed computing, applications and technologies (PDCAT'06)* (pp. 74–79). IEEE.

Shen, J. J., Lin, C. W., & Hwang, M. S. (2003). A modified remote user authentication scheme using smart cards. *IEEE Transactions on Consumer Electronics, 49*(2), 414–416.

Sheresh, B., & Sheresh, D. (2002). *Understanding directory services.* Sams Publishing.

Thomas, R. K., & Sandhu, R. S. (1998). Task-based authorization controls (TBAC): A family of models for active and enterprise-oriented authorization management. In *Database security XI* (pp. 166–181). Springer.

Wahl, M., Alvestrand, H., Hodges, J., & Morgan, R. (2000). Authentication methods for LDAP. *IETF Request for Comments, 2829.*

Yang, N., Barringer, H., & Zhang, N. (2007). A purpose-based access control model. In *Third international symposium on information assurance and security* (pp. 143–148). IEEE.

Zhang, X., Sandhu, R., & Parisi-Presicce, F. (2006, March). Safety analysis of usage control authorization models. In *Conference on computer and communications security: Proceedings of the 2006 ACM symposium on information, computer and communications security* (Vol. 21, No. 24, pp. 243–254). ACM Press.

SECTION 5

Pulling it all together – the big picture knowledge architecture

The two chapters in this section focus on pulling together all of the components and functional architectures into a coherent, manageable, sustainable, and elegant design. Metadata is an essential element across all the functional architectures – it supports availability, accessibility, and consumption. It is an essential architecture design concept in a dynamic asset management environment. We have saved this chapter for the 'big picture' section because it is no longer an isolated and one-off operation.

The final chapter pulls together all of the design issues from Chapters 6 through 22 into a holistic knowledge architecture blueprint. This chapter also highlights future research and engagement agenda to help us realize the architecture.

22

FUNCTIONAL ARCHITECTURE FOR KNOWLEDGE METADATA AND METAINFORMATION

Chapter summary

This chapter explains the role that metadata and metainformation play in making knowledge assets accessible. The chapter lays out the six activities that support designing metadata and metainformation architecture to support knowledge assets. The chapter also considers why it is essential to understand the designing to essential access points, why we need to understand metadata specifications and business rules, the semantics of each attribute, and how we instantiate or manage metadata structures. The chapter makes a case for designing metadata to suit your organization rather than merely adopting a standard framework.

Why we care about knowledge metadata and metainformation

Metadata structures are the mechanism for managing all of the attributes we identified in our object classes back in Chapter 6. Traditionally, metadata has been the primary tool for managing explicit information assets. Properties, whether in applications or embedded into documents and Web resources, have been essential tools for managing digital resources. We have tended to think about metadata as a composite record, comprised of multiple identifiers, descriptors, and access points. We've become accustomed to seeing these properties as a single object – with one set of guidelines or rules for filling out fields. This traditional view was sufficient when metadata lived in repositories and catalogs, and when information assets were created in and expected to spend their business live in a specific application. It may have been sufficient when the focus was on documents, publications, or textual information. But, it is not enough when knowledge assets can take many different forms and travel through many different distribution channels. It is also not sufficient when knowledge assets require tools and metainformation (e.g., instructions and explanations) for us to derive, interpret, and use them.

We need a new approach to designing a metadata and metainformation architecture because attributes, rather than the composite record, are not the essential element. Each organization must decide which attributes are essential to them, for which kinds of assets. Identifying and adopting an external standard will continue to be essential for sharing and exchanging information externally. Still, it is not a good starting point for designing a functional metadata architecture. Think back to the Chapter 6 discussion of object classes and attributes. Few existing external standards align with most of these classes. Designing new metadata and metainformation architecture begins with an understanding of the behaviors, specifications, and business rules for each attribute.

We care about designing a functional architecture for metadata and metainformation because the current approach can be resource-intensive, costly, and fragmented. The metadata we create and manage today is often dictated by the applications we use. Consider the metadata, property, and data element dictionaries defined by SAP, PeopleSoft, Web content management systems, document management systems, security systems, and workflow systems. The metadata and data dictionaries are all tied to the functions of those systems. We may have pieces of the knowledge asset scattered across all of these applications, each having different attributes, some with contradictory values, and some redundant attributes. There is no metadata or attribute life cycle across these applications. And, the quality of metadata will be uneven. In most cases, these metadata are not accessible for knowledge asset management purposes. Ideally, rather than having this fragmented and scattered approach, we manage knowledge assets as objects with an aggregated set of attributes and values.

The primary challenge we face in designing a functional architecture for metadata and metainformation is learning to see beyond our historical practices. We must see the role that metadata and metainformation will play in the future – and to view metadata and metainformation as a kind of abstract or surrogate for the object. Metadata has evolved as an intermediary tool for managing information and knowledge assets. Still, we have seen it primarily as a rigid data structure or set of properties rather than a surrogate. A primary challenge is learning to see the new role that object models play vis-à-vis metadata, and understanding how 'old metadata' becomes a new kind of asset.

Knowledge asset metadata – design concepts

To develop this functional architecture, we must have a good understanding of the principle of access points; metadata attributes, specifications, and business rules; metadata semantics; metadata profiles and records; metadata architectures; catalog and inventory applications; and metadata practices, policies, and standards. The primary challenges we face in designing this functional architecture are learning to see metadata as a kind of abstract description of the asset, integrating and harmonizing well-established and well-entrenched metadata practices and policies across domains, and making a case for redesigning metadata structures and referencing practices for knowledge asset mobility and extensibility.

Designing metadata and metainformation architecture for the future means designing to two goals. The first design goal is managing the knowledge object models, object classes, and attributes we discussed in Chapter 6. The second design goal is to create an architecture that enables us to treat and leverage metadata and metainformation like a knowledge asset surrogate. Metadata and metainformation has always been a kind of structured surrogate, though we have not managed it like a surrogate. The potential value of metadata and metainformation as a structured surrogate is far greater than merely a repository or registry management tool.

To design these two goals, we need to understand some basic concepts. We need to understand metadata. We need to understand the purpose of metadata, metadata attributes, metadata semantics, metadata profiles and attribute sets, metadata profiles and attributes sets, and metadata architectures. We also need to understand the types of metadata organizations are currently creating and managing today.

What is metadata?

Let's begin by describing what we have traditionally understood as metadata, and then let's consider how this description changes as we go forward. Historically, we've described metadata as 'data about data' – those elements or attributes that are essential to managing our information (Caplan, 2003, 2009; Duval et al., 2002; Foulonneau & Riley, 2014; Gilliland, 2008; Hayness, 2004; Hillmann & Westbrooks, 2004; Kroeger, 2013; Miller, 2011; Nilsson, 2010; Park, 2009; Pomerantz, 2015; Sowa, 2000). Traditionally, metadata has been developed and applied to explicit types of information – digital and physical assets. Metadata attributes are what we leverage to build out search architectures. They are what we use to describe topical and functional categories, what we use to store keywords and index terms, and to assign and track security classification, to preserve or destroy, or to authenticate. The challenge with traditional metadata is that it has been designed differently by different areas of practice and professions. It makes designing a knowledge architecture very challenging.

There is much to build on to support knowledge architecture. What we can build on is what sustains – and what sustains from our work on knowledge object classes and attributes. In many cases, the attributes we need for the knowledge architecture exist somewhere in our organization's applications. There are some gaps, though, and we should focus on those gaps in order to support a whole enterprise knowledge architecture.

If it is true that much of what we need for a metadata architecture exists, what is the design challenge? There are two design challenges. The first is designing the enterprise's approach to managing knowledge object models, classes, and attributes. In Chapter 6, we walked through what these classes will look like for knowledge assets, but we did not consider where and how these knowledge object models would be managed, governed, and used across the organization. The second design challenge is to expand the purpose of metadata to include metainformation, i.e., those attributes that explain how the asset was created, how to work with it, what quality standards it might or might not adhere to,

What is metainformation?

What is the difference between metadata and metainformation? It is a reasonable question to ask since we often interchange the two words – data, and information. If metadata is the essential fields and attributes that describe another object, then what is metainformation? The vital attributes for an object class might be sufficient if we're focusing only on availability and access. The challenge arises when we need to know more about that object before we decide whether we can use it. We have compared metadata to a label. Consider the label on a can of tomatoes or a bottle of glue or a medicinal drug. The label tells us much about the container – its brand name, its common or generic name, its size, how much of the product it contains, what the product is, and its basic ingredients. Sometimes, though, the package has other information beyond the label, including how the product was made, instructions for its use, what not to do with the product, or risks associated with it. The label and its metadata are often standardized by the business sector that produces the product, or through regulations and standards.

Metainformation, on the other hand, is unpredictable and may not always be available in a way we can all understand or in predictable places on the package. Consider how many times you have to go to the Web to find additional information about the product. Looking for instructions on how to assemble or use something is looking for metainformation. Consider how this translates to all kinds of knowledge assets, and we understand why metainformation becomes as essential as metadata. The more we access different kinds and sources of knowledge, the more we need to know its origins, the processes followed, the conditions under which it was created or developed, and what has happened to it since it was first created. If the knowledge asset was curated, we needed to know who curated it and how it was curated. Recall our onion graphic from Chapter 6. We are referring to the onion's outermost layers when we talk about metadata and metainformation (Figure 22.1). It is also the boundary between the knowledge asset, its surrogates, and other related assets.

Metainformation is also essential because it may form the first circle or level of extensions around metadata or a knowledge object's surrogates. We can see a larger architecture begin to emerge when we move from the knowledge object as a central node, to its metadata surrogates, to other types of surrogates, and extended metainformation. To this structure, we also connect other kinds of knowledge assets that evaluate, derive from, interpret, or extend the original knowledge asset.

The challenge with metainformation is that outside of the world of data curation; we do not have a good handle on metainformation practices and standards. For each type of knowledge asset, we need a new research effort – to identify the most essential and comment elements of metainformation. What we do suspect, though, is that these extended elements should form a second–degree surrogate

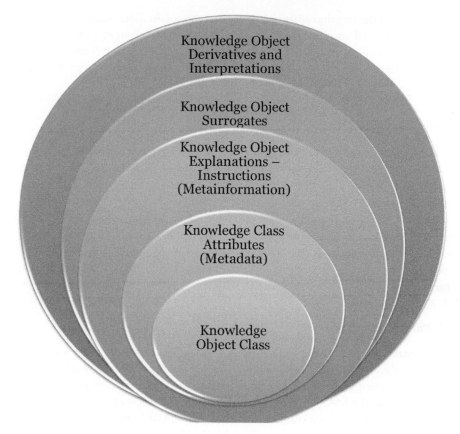

FIGURE 22.1 Conceptual Relationships of Knowledge Objects, Metadata, Metainformation, and Surrogates

for any knowledge object. Metainformation is an essential design element of our knowledge architecture, but it does not currently exist in a formal form.

The purpose of metadata – past, and future

Traditionally, metadata has served the purpose of a label or a surrogate. A metadata 'label' tells us what the content or document is, what it is about, which format it is presented in, where it is located, when it was created, why it was created, who can use it, what can be done with it, and how it should be managed. Metainformation goes beyond metadata in providing extended information that speaks to the authenticity, structure, composition, and risks associated with the knowledge asset. Metainformation is perhaps easiest understood in the context of statistical data or survey response data. The metainformation would explain where the data came from, its sampling methods, its years of coverage, and any changes made to the original data. If the data were reformatted or 'curated,' that information would be included in the metainformation. We can see how vital metainformation might be to the extended set of knowledge assets. For example, we need to know more about a team's cultural profile than simple metadata profiles can tell us. We need to know more about a network knowledge asset that simple metadata profiles can tell us.

Metadata attributes

Traditionally, metadata attributes have been defined by applications, by standards groups, or by business industries. Metadata attributes have been described in sets rather than individual attributes that could be extended and adapted to different contexts and assets. Additionally, we have 'taught' metadata as a set of rules to be learned and memorized for data entry purposes. This approach needs to be redesigned and rethought. Metadata needs to be taught as knowledge object attributes, assigned to and reusable across knowledge object classes. This new mental model allows us to understand the semantics, business rules, and behaviors of each attribute.

Metadata semantics

Traditionally, we have understood metadata semantics as the data entry rules and practices which govern and manage the specifications for fields in a specific application. For example, an integrated library system cataloging module has attributes defined around the MARC record (Avram, 1975; Baldonado et al., 1997; Greenberg, 2005). Library school students are taught the MARC record and the 'syntax' of values that can be entered into each field. Rarely, though, do we explain how these values are used outside of the cataloging module. Similarly, we might have a property template in a SharePoint application. We understand these properties as fields, but in fact, they are traditional metadata. The same fields may be defined in the MARC record and the SharePoint template, but with entirely different semantics. For example, consider the syntax (e.g., semantics) of an author field in the MARC record and compare that to the syntax of a SharePoint template, or even of a PeopleProfile or an operations portal report template. Do all of those fields have the same 'repeatable' behavior? Do they all have the same simple field lengths? The design challenge for metadata going forward is to design that functional architecture that allows us to manage knowledge object classes, their attributes, and their semantics efficiently and effectively across the organization.

The design challenge means looking across the organization at the metadata practices and designing the architecture to support a new management and governance framework. It means starting the review at the attribute level, not the record or profile level. It means looking at institutional metadata, at master data, and unique metadata across the organization.

Perhaps the most important design factor, though, is considering how to design a functional architecture that is extensible, expandable, and adaptable.

Metadata profiles and attribute sets

Metadata records or structures are the aggregations of all of the metadata attributes required to manage information assets. These structures or records take the form of a faceted taxonomy – where each node represents a distinct attribute and access point with its specifications and controlled reference sources. The focus of the metadata record is the information asset it describes. There are many different metadata standards pertinent to information assets, including MARC, COSATI, Access to Biological Collection Data, AgMes for agricultural information, Astronomy Visualization Metadata, CERIF – Common European Research Information Format, CF (Climate and Forecast) Metadata, CIF – Crystallographic Information Framework, CIM – Common Information Model, CSMD-CCLRC, Darwin Core, Data Package, DataCite Metadata, DCAT – Data Catalog, Data Documentation Initiative, DIF, Dublin Core, Ecological Metadata Language, FGDC/CSDGM, FITS – Flexible Image Transport System, Genome Metadata, PREMIS, Protocol Data Element Definitions, RDF Data Cube Vocabulary, QuDEx – Qualitative Data Exchange Format, and SDAC – Standard for Documentation of Astronomical Catalogues, among others (Corti & Gregory, 2011; Eaton et al., 2003; Fisher et al., 2016; Goh et al., 2008; Hall & McMahon, 2016; Hoshovsky, 1969; Hurt et al., 2007; Jeffery et al., 2002; Jorg, 2010; Neumann & Brase, 2014; Reddy et al., 2015; Stuempel et al., 2009; Uslar et al., 2012; Vardigan et al., 2008; Weibel et al., 1998; Wells & Greisen, 1979; Wieczorek et al., 2012; World Wide Web Consortium, 2014; Yee et al., 2003). There are internal functional practices for metadata, such as those designed into document management systems, content management systems, web publishing systems, learning management systems, financial management systems, human resource management systems, and so on.

Metadata and metainformation for knowledge assets

Traditional metadata structures were developed around the early card catalog designs. Most of the metadata schemes we have in our built environment today are variations on this early design. In designing metadata and metainformation architecture for knowledge assets, we need to start from a new foundation. Four questions can guide our designs, including:

- How do we look for and discover each type of knowledge asset? This question exposes the access points we need for each type of asset and leads us to the metadata attributes.
- What do we need to know about how the knowledge asset was developed to decide whether we can use it?
- What metadata do we need to manage access to the asset?
- What metadata do we need to manage and preserve the business value of the asset? It helps us to design the metainformation we need for each type of asset.

Metadata and metainformation for human capital

Question 1: How do we look for and discover human capital? To look for human capital, we need metadata that defines:

- topic and concept;
- methods;
- level of expertise;
- language;
- currency or date;
- experience;
- certifications;
- licenses;
- skills according to an inventory.

Question 2: What do we need to know about how the capital was developed to decide whether we can use it? Metainformation that helps us to assess human capital might include:

- where they learned it;
- who they worked with;
- how others have rated it;
- who taught them;
- where they've applied it;
- how others rate their integrity and honesty;
- how easy they are to work with.

Question 3: What metadata do we need to manage access to the asset? Metadata that helps us to manage human capital might include:

- continuous updates of information about the individual whose human capital we are representing;
- authoritative information from the individual or authoritative sources such as human resources, security, educational institutions, and authoritative external sources;
- information that tells us how to access the individual, since it is up to the individual to share or make that knowledge available and accessible.

Question 4: What metadata do we need to manage and preserve the business value of the asset? This information provides a chronicle of how the organization has managed and developed the individual's human capital for their association with the organization – these might include when the individual was hired, when they were promoted, any internal transfers, the date they left the organization.

Metadata and metainformation for explicit knowledge

Question 1: How do we look for and discover explicit knowledge? To look for explicit knowledge, we need metadata that defines:

- title;
- author;
- date;
- format;
- length;
- language;
- subject;
- concept;
- country;
- business function;
- publisher or authorization.

Question 2: What do we need to know about how the capital was developed to decide whether we can use it? Metainformation that helps us to assess human capital might include:

- credentials of the author;
- the reputation of the publisher;
- reviews by other users;
- citations;
- methods used to generate it;
- variables;
- quality control methods used;
- currency or rate of update;
- scope and coverage.

Question 3: What metadata do we need to manage access to the asset? Metadata that help us to manage human capital might include:

- sensitivity business information;
- version or edition;
- the authenticity of the knowledge;
- the business value of the asset.

Question 4: What metadata do we need to manage and preserve the business value of the asset? Metadata that help us to manage and preserve the business value of human capital might include:

- official or unofficial status;
- whether it is a copy;

- changes that have been made;
- conversions of encoding, formatting, or packaging;
- disposition actions or decisions;
- destruction actions.

Metadata and metainformation for procedural knowledge

Question 1: How do we look for and discover procedural knowledge? To look for procedural knowledge, we need metadata that defines:

- the function it supports;
- process methods;
- products or results it generates;
- inputs it uses;
- job classes that support it;
- people who are assigned to it;
- life cycle or dates of the process;
- units using the process.

Question 2: What do we need to know about how the capital was developed to decide whether we can use it? Metainformation that helps us to assess procedural capital might include:

- patents associated with the process;
- process reviews;
- quality control standards or ratings.

Question 3: What metadata do we need to manage access to the asset? Metadata that help us to manage procedural knowledge might include:

- the currency of the process;
- business-critical status of the process;
- locations or facilities using the process.

Question 4: What metadata do we need to manage and preserve the business value of the asset? Metadata that help us to manage and preserve the business value of procedural knowledge might include:

- changes to the process;
- information about the current status of the process;
- when the process was archived;
- when jobs or agents performing the process change.

Metadata and metainformation for cultural knowledge

Question 1: How do we look for and discover cultural knowledge? To look for cultural knowledge, we need metadata that defines:

- the community that creates it;
- values and behaviors;
- types;
- periods;
- locations;
- business functions;
- disciplines;
- type of organization.

Question 2: What do we need to know about how the capital was developed to decide whether we can use it? Metadata that help us to manage cultural knowledge might include:

- ratings by those in the community;
- ratings by those outside the community;
- the methods used to develop the characterization.

Question 3: What metadata do we need to manage access to the asset? Meta-information that helps us to assess cultural capital might include:

- whether it is an open or a closed culture;
- whether it is a private or public sector organization.

Question 4: What metadata do we need to manage and preserve the business value of the asset? Metadata that help us to manage and preserve the business value of cultural knowledge is challenging since culture is dynamic and is part of our behaviors. The only way we can do this is to determine who the members of the community were that created the culture.

Metadata and metainformation for relational capital

Question 1: How do we look for and discover relational capital? To look for relational knowledge, we need metadata that defines:

- topic;
- function;
- network or community members;
- dates the network is/was active;
- language of the community;

- whether it is sponsored or informal;
- whether it is virtual or physical.

Question 2: What do we need to know about how the capital was developed to decide whether we can use it? Metadata that help us to manage relational knowledge might include who the members are, and the internal protocols for engagement.

Question 3: What metadata do we need to manage access to the asset? Metainformation that helps us to assess cultural capital might include:

- who the network leader is;
- where they meet;
- whether it is open or closed.

Question 4: What metadata do we need to manage and preserve the business value of the asset? Metadata that help us to manage and preserve the business value of relational knowledge might include whether the network is active or inactive and whether there are any records or transcripts of discussion.

Future metadata architecture design concept

Our traditional metadata architecture consists of (1) record structures or profiles (e.g., predefined sets of field); (2) a metadata registry (e.g., a database structure that houses the records); (3) a repository in some cases of the metadata records and links to the referenced object; (4) in many cases, the larger application that leverages the registry; and (5) references to the controlled reference sources that provide the permissible values for the attributes. In some cases, traditional architecture also includes a mechanism for embedding metadata into assets like properties. In some cases, the metadata architecture is an intentional, stand-alone application that services other applications. It will be an essential transition architecture, but it will not be a complete or sufficient metadata architecture for the future. Consider the size and inelegant nature of a huge metadata repository with a wide range of metadata profiles for different kinds of knowledge assets. Now add in the extended metainformation we need for those knowledge assets, and the additional links to derivative and interpretations. We suddenly have a very complex and difficult way to manipulate a database. Simply turning everything into links is not a practical solution. We need to think about a new design, beginning with objects and attributes. Perhaps the knowledge architecture of the future is grounded in an elegantly designed, more flexible and less rigid architecture.

There is a clear distinction between a registry and a repository. Organizations need to have at least a registry of their knowledge object models, object classes, and attributes. The essential design challenge is, what does the repository of these models, classes, and attributes look like? Perhaps we have registries of models and classes, but what about repositories of actual attributes – the values of actual assets? Do we have logical sets of attributes that may be designed to provide easy access for different applications and functions? Does a logical set of attributes have a link back to the object model's primary key? We know how to ground the new metadata and metainformation architecture; we just don't know how to build it. It would make sense for managing the different behaviors of sets of attributes. It would also make managing extensible non-core and unique attributes more efficient. Core attributes are those that must be there for every knowledge object model. Extensible attributes are those that are common to some models, but not essential to all. Unique attributes are those that pertain to one model but are neither common nor essential to others. And, it would allow us to manage access to these attributes better. It is a design challenge we need to work on with systems developers and design professionals.

Metadata and metainformation – the design environment

What factors do we need to consider in designing this architecture? There are several factors to consider in designing this functional architecture. These include the organization's current practices and capacity for working with metadata, the organization's need for metainformation, and its general engineering and development capacity. Perhaps the most critical factor is the organization's capacity to move beyond its traditional metadata models and embrace a new and different design in the future. It means realigning capabilities and competencies across the organization, which can be a significant cultural shift.

What events cause us to design a functional architecture for semantics? Perhaps the most significant trigger is the simple weight and cost of maintaining the current cumbersome metadata architectures, and the inability to adapt to changing demands and circumstances without additional new investments in applications. The organization realizes the number of resources that are being wasted in continuing to feed the fragmented and suboptimal metadata architecture designed to support the industrial economy.

What are the impacts and consequences of having this functional architecture? This functional architecture gives an organization the capability to manage all types of knowledge assets, ensure their long-term availability, manage access and discoverability better, and consume and track consumption.

What inputs do we need to consider when designing this functional architecture? We need to focus on the future and the future requirements, a practical view of the current architecture, and a transition plan for getting from where the organization is today to where it needs to be. The challenge is the lack of existing solutions and the uncertainty of what a future design will look like or what it will include. In addition to the functional architecture specifications, we need to develop new procedures, capabilities, and competencies to support the new functional architecture. It will also involve retooling the metadata functions of many of the enterprise applications. It may also involve the development of new machine methods for generating metadata and metainformation.

What are the outputs and outcomes this functional architecture generates? Having this architecture in place gives us a foundation for managing our knowledge assets in the future. It provides us with the flexibility and the agility to adapt to new formats, channels, and an extended set of knowledge assets and connections among assets. It also allows us to manage these new developments at a level of investment an organization can afford and can sustain.

Design activities supporting metadata and metainformation architectures

These should mirror the activities are defined for developing object models – starting with identifying the attributes:

- Activity 1. Review knowledge object model classes and attributes
- Activity 2. Compare classes and attributes to current metadata practices
- Activity 3. Map to existing sources
- Activity 4. Identify attribute gaps
- Activity 5. Develop methods for filling the gaps
- Activity 6. Design an application that makes the object models and attributes actionable as surrogates

Activity 1. Review knowledge object model classes and attributes

How do we do this? This activity assumes that you've already worked through the design of knowledge object models for your assets, as laid out in Chapter 6. Those activities are the foundation for designing the enterprise architecture that will help you operationalize, manage, and maintain the attributes. This activity involves gathering all those object models and working through an inventory of the attributes. In this activity, you're looking across object classes for attributes that serve a similar purpose. You might want to use the framework we've laid out in the chapters as a way to inventory and record the attributes in your organization. The models we described in Chapter 6 were intended as a starting point – your classes and attributes will be more targeted and specific to your organization's business and work.

What inputs do we need for this activity? The essential input is the object models, classes, and attributes. Specifically, you must have the attributes as a starting point. Another important input is the framework the knowledge architect develops to organize and synthesize the assets.

What outputs does this activity produce? This activity produces the first pass at a synthesis of attributes by purpose – across all of your knowledge object classes. It is a working framework for the 'to be' metadata architecture.

What other resources does this activity use? This activity does not require complex applications or tools. A simple spreadsheet or word processing table is more than sufficient for creating the framework.

Activity 2. Compare classes and attributes to current metadata practices

How do we do this? This activity is another inventory and mapping task. You may have completed some of this activity earlier in your design process. If you worked with existing data dictionaries, property models, metadata profiles, or standards to identify your knowledge object attributes, refer back to that work. For this activity, you're taking a slightly different perspective, though. You're looking at and for existing attributes that are intended to serve a purpose, whereas your intent may have been to synthesize and generalize current practice to find common ground. In this activity, you want to go back and make sure all of those existing attributes that are serving similar purposes are called out and mapped to the generic attributes.

What inputs do we need for this activity? You could use those notes and worksheets for this activity if you worked from existing dictionaries and sources. If not, you'll want to identify any application – whether it directly or indirectly creates metadata and metainformation – and walk through those applications to call out attributes. This activity, though, requires a further expansion of your framework. Recall the attribute specifications we called out in Chapter 6? For each attribute in your inventory, you'll need to know something about their specifications, behaviors, and business rules. The reason this is important is twofold. First, you will not be able to change the behavior of these attributes in the source application – you need to respect that. Second, you'll need to develop a process to ensure that they are normalized before they are pulled into the enterprise metadata architecture. What do we mean by normalization? In this case, we simply suggest adjusting them to whatever specifications, behaviors, and business rules we've defined for the enterprise metadata attributes.

What outputs does this activity produce? This activity produces an extensive mapping of existing attributes across all source applications. This activity sets you up to develop an extraction or 'reporting' method for each existing application.

What other resources does this activity use? For this activity, the knowledge architect needs to have an understanding of application designs. He or she will need to work with application administrators to retrieve copies of the embedded dictionaries or specifications. It is also important that the knowledge architect has good communication skills to work with the developers to understand how these dictionaries and specifications are managed.

Activity 3. Map to existing sources

How do we do this? This activity involves walking back from the completed mapping and inventory to individual source applications. The goal of this activity is to make the first pass at defining the extraction or reporting specifications for pulling attribute information from the source applications. Another important consideration is how often the attribute values change in the source systems, and how often the reports or extracts should be run.

What inputs do we need for this activity? The output from this activity is a set of design specifications for an attribute in a source application that we can use to extract or report out those values. Depending on the metadata architecture defined by the organization, it may be easier for us simply to run a report periodically or to do any actual extraction.

What outputs does this activity produce? Ideally, this activity provides reporting and extract specifications for all of the important attributes for any given application in the organization. We should remember that this is a learning exercise. The first round of extracts and reports will provide many opportunities to rethink and revise each strategy. Over time, the most effective and efficient approach will become clear.

What other resources does this activity use? One of the essential inputs for this activity is the knowledge architect's ability to discover when a single knowledge asset is a resident in more than one application, and to design a method for determining the most authoritative source of attributes, when there is duplication. Often this takes the form of determining which is the application that feeds other applications.

Activity 4. Identify attribute gaps

How do we do this? Activities 1, 2, and 3 will provide good coverage for our existing metadata practices. However, this does not address any or all of those other attributes we know we need for knowledge object models but are either not systematically managed or are not managed at all. This activity involves going back to those object-level attributes to identify the gaps. We need to look at attributes for metadata and particularly for metainformation. It means looking closely at those kinds of knowledge assets that we are not systematically managing now, simply because we don't have a good foundation for understanding how we manage their availability, accessibility, and consumability. We do not want to focus on their full life cycle because this will involve actions that are not in the organization's business interests.

What inputs do we need for this activity? The primary input for this activity is an extended set of attributes for metainformation. We described metainformation as those explanations, instructions, and guidance needed to access and consume the knowledge asset. If the asset requires tools to access or if explanations are needed to decide whether the procedural knowledge is suitable for your interests, this should be accessible through the extended architecture. It should not require an extra effort for the knowledge consumer to find and discover this metainformation. The challenge is to determine what these types of metainformation are likely to be for different kinds of knowledge assets. What metainformation do we need to decide whether we want to leverage an individual's skills and competencies? What metainformation do we need to decide whether the procedural knowledge is trustworthy? Or, whether the network is a high-risk engagement for us?

What outputs does this activity produce? This activity produces a list of additional metadata and metainformation attributes for knowledge assets. Working with these lists, the knowledge architect would backfill and augment the knowledge class models. Additionally, this activity produces a working framework for extended metainformation architecture.

What other resources does this activity use? To complete this activity, we need to walk through the metainformation issues for each knowledge asset. Walking through individual use case scenarios is essential to teasing out additional requirements and specifications. The knowledge architect should have a use case template in their toolkit to support this activity.

Activity 5. Develop methods for filling the gaps

How do we do this? In Activity 4, we identified the gaps and made the first pass at defining the new metainformation attributes we need to support our knowledge architecture. In this activity, we take that one step further and socialize our initial lists and specifications with business units that are likely stakeholders. Anything we design must be workable and practical. The additional meta-information will require an additional intentional effort to create and maintain. We cannot be adding an effort that does not produce additional business value.

What inputs do we need for this activity? The starting point for this activity is the initial specifications and requirements for the extended metadata and metainformation from Activity 4. For each new metainformation or metadata attribute, we need to conduct a desk check of the requirements, specifications, and methods we intend to design to fill the gap.

What outputs does this activity produce? This activity generates a desk-checked set of specifications and requirements for filling the metadata and metainformation gaps. The knowledge architect should have a design spec that can be shared with developers and with system administrators.

What other resources does this activity use? The other important resource for this activity is the knowledge architect's interview guidelines and notes from each conversation. These are important sources of correction and caution to be shared with developers and application managers.

Activity 6. Design an application that makes the object models and attributes actionable as surrogates

How do we do this? It is the most challenging of all the activities because it involves working with developers and application architects to design a new and sustainable architecture for managing metadata and metainformation. We don't know what this architecture will look like. We have some design principles we can draw upon. It is one that will involve trial and error, learning from experiments, and iterating over time.

What inputs do we need for this activity? The desk-checked set of specifications and requirements for existing and new attributes is the primary input for this activity. It is not just a document that is handed off to the development team but is the starting point for a design exercise.

What outputs does this activity produce? The output is not the development of a fully built metadata and metainformation application, but a design specification developed by the knowledge architect, the system developers, and the application administrators.

What other resources does this activity use? Perhaps the other important resource is the system developer's knowledge of what is required for a systems design specification. It is the starting point for actual development. Additional resources are notes or communications that track what is learned as the teams move forward to turn the design specs into a functioning application.

Evolution of metadata and metainformation

The evolution of this architecture is not too different from the evolution of the search presented in Chapter 12. The search has always been heavily dependent on the existence of catalogs and catalog entries. The search was impacted by the application of technologies to these catalogs as well. Metadata records have been the equivalent of the entries in these catalogs. The difference, though, is that these designs have been heavily influenced by other consumer applications, such as all of the processes and functional applications. Experience and a review of the literature suggest there are five phases of evolution of today's metadata and metainformation architectures (Figure 22.2), including:

- Phase 1. Collection inventories
- Phase 2. Catalog inventories
- Phase 3. Distributed and transported catalogs
- Phase 4. Metadata for functional applications
- Phase 5. Dedicated metadata architectures

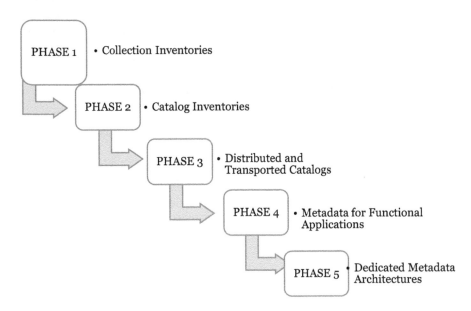

FIGURE 22.2 Evolution of Metadata and Metainformation

Phase 1. Collection inventories

The earliest phase of metadata coincided with the development of collections. When we had one of something, when we only had what we needed and what we would consume immediately, there was little need to manage many items in a collection. We did not have the luxury of keeping things for long periods when subsistence living was the norm. As knowledge grew, as economic systems developed, and there was some resource security, we began to 'collect' or 'store' things. As collections grew, we developed primitive methods of tagging and inventorying what we had in our collections. These early tags and the metadata they recorded were designed to meet the needs of those who owned or managed the collections. There was not a need to consider the needs of a wider community of stakeholders. For the most part, these metadata tags focused on simple identification. As collections grew and there was a need to organize within collections or to describe different perspectives, we moved on to other access points.

Phase 2. Catalog inventories

As collections grew, though, and as the level of knowledge and literacy of the population increased, there was an increased demand for access to the assets in these collections. Collections could be art, artifacts, books, letters, or manuscripts. We created catalogs to describe the items in these collections. As the size of the collections grew, we needed more than just identifying metadata – we needed metadata that described the asset and metadata that defined different categories and access points.

Phase 3. Distributed and transported catalogs

This phase spans several centuries. This phase represents a logical and gradual transition from the handwritten catalogs of Phase 2 to print catalogs. Over time, with the advances in transportation and distribution systems, these print catalogs became mass-produced and distributed widely. Over time, the catalog becomes an essential retail and marketing tool. Over time, these retail catalogs take on the definition and structure of the business's functional applications. It is where we see the early signs of what became Phase 4. Catalogs become an everyday resource for acquiring and requesting items from sources and services. With the emergence of technology and increased technology capacity, catalogs and thus metadata practices were simply ported to electronic format. Unfortunately, in most cases, there was little rethinking or redesign work. Perhaps the classic example was the translation of the physical library card catalog record to the MARC format. As formats of information and knowledge assets have expanded over the past centuries, and as the web developed, the existing structures were simply adjusted to fit. The challenge of rethinking and looking at designs needed in the future was not taken.

Phase 4. Metadata for functional applications

This phase evolves from Phase 2 and overlaps from Phase 3. It becomes a primary focus of development and design, though it represents a rethinking and redesign effort. Functional applications create and manage information and knowledge assets. Each functional area has its practices and standards for how those assets are managed. In some ways, these applications have been more responsive to business needs than have the generic metadata standards of the information science applications. From these applications, we derive many of our extended attributes for managing information and knowledge assets in distinct and dedicated metadata architectures. The challenge is that each of the functional architectures is grounded in different metadata standards, and practices emerge. At an enterprise level, we have redundant and sometimes conflicting requirements. It was this complex and resource-intensive environment that gave rise to the practice of enterprise architecture. As a result, we have a competing set of practices, specifications, and standards – some de facto, some de jure, most functional, and few aligned or synthesized. This phase continues through to today in the form of metadata in financial systems, security systems, project management systems, human resource management systems, and any other functional application.

Phase 5. Dedicated metadata architectures

Phase 5 is a natural and logical outcome of Phase 4. The proliferation of applications and different technologies created a need for an enterprise architecture perspective and practice. Because information and knowledge assets are scattered across all of these functional applications, it made sense for organizations to develop a centralized and dedicated architecture to manage metadata. The earliest source of these structures can be traced back to the catalog modules of the early integrated library systems of the 1980s. These early applications were designed to support the life cycle management of library collections. Standards evolved to ensure that data created in these systems could be exchanged, and migrated from one system to another. As other business function applications took over some of the modules of these early systems (e.g., procurement for acquisition, asset management and directory structures for circulation, search systems for online catalogs), the core metadata module became the prototype for today's metadata registries and repositories. These now form the essential structures for the information and data architecture layers in the enterprise architecture layer cake.

The design of this information architectures has been suboptimized and overwhelmed by the 'built environment' and 'built solutions' offered by content and document management system vendors in particular. The challenge of this phase is that the application and technology environment is so overwhelming that we must focus just on making the existing environment function. The challenge and the opportunity are to get beyond the 'feeding the beast' mode and refocus on design. The challenge of the future is to reverse engineer what exists to see what is essential and is needed that is not yet supported.

Chapter review

After reading this chapter, you should be able to:

- define metadata and explain its role and purpose in the knowledge architecture;
- define and distinguish metainformation and explain its role and purpose in the knowledge architecture;
- describe the traditional approach to and evolution of metadata in information science;
- explain the relationship of metadata attributes and semantics and knowledge object models and attributes;
- explain how we adapt and expand the concepts of metadata and metainformation to apply to knowledge assets.

References and recommended readings for the future

Avram, H. D. (1975). *MARC, its history and implications.* Library of Congress.

Baldonado, M., Chang, C. C. K., Gravano, L., & Paepcke, A. (1997). The Stanford digital library metadata architecture. *International Journal on Digital Libraries, 1*(2), 108–121.

Caplan, P. (2003). *Metadata fundamentals for all librarians.* American Library Association.

Caplan, P. (2009). *Understanding premis.* Library of Congress.

Corti, L., & Gregory, A. (2011). CAQDAS comparability. What about CAQDAS data exchange? In *Forum: Qualitative social research* (Vol. 12, No. 1). FQS.

Duval, E., Hodgins, W., Sutton, S., & Weibel, S. L. (2002). Metadata principles and practicalities. *D-lib Magazine, 8*(4), 1082–9873.

Eaton, B., Gregory, J., Drach, B., Taylor, K., Hankin, S., Caron, J., & Pamment, A. (2003). *NetCDF Climate and Forecast (CF) metadata conventions.* http://cfconventions.org/

Fisher, S. M., Barnsley, F., Chung, W., Da, S., Ramos, G., De Maria, A., & Matthews, B. (2016). The growth of the ICAT family. NoBugs 2016, Copenhagen, Denmark, 17–19 October.

Foulonneau, M., & Riley, J. (2014). *Metadata for digital resources: Implementation, systems design and interoperability.* Elsevier.

Gilliland, A. J. (2008). Setting the stage. *Introduction to Metadata, 2*, 1–19.

Goh, K. N., Weber, K., & GISP, D. P. A. (2008). *Developing a geo-spatial search tool using a relational database implementation of the FGDC CSDGM model* (Doctoral dissertation), Idaho State University, Idaho.

Greenberg, J. (2005). Understanding metadata and metadata schemes. *Cataloging & Classification Quarterly, 40*(3–4), 17–36.

Hall, S. R., & McMahon, B. (2016). The implementation and evolution of STAR/CIF ontologies: Interoperability and preservation of structured data. *Data Science Journal, 15*, 1–15.

Haynes, D. (2004). *Metadata for information management and retrieval* (Vol. 1). Facet Publishing.

Hillmann, D. I., & Westbrooks, E. L. (2004). *Metadata in practice.* American Library Association.

Hoshovsky, A. G. (1969). *COSATI information studies-what results* (No. OAR-69–0021). Office of Aerospace Research, Arlington, VA.

Hurt, R. L., Gauthier, A. J., Christensen, L. L., & Wyatt, R. (2007). Sharing images intelligently: The astronomy visualization metadata standard. In *CAP'07: Proceedings of the conference on communicating astronomy with the public* (pp. 450–453). Eugenides Foundation.

Jeffery, K. G., Lopatenko, A., & Asserson, A. (2002). *Comparative study of metadata for scientific information: The place of CERIF in CRISs and scientific repositories.* Kassel University Press.

Jörg, B. (2010). CERIF: The common European research information format model. *Data Science Journal.* doi:10.2481/1006280236-1006280236

Kroeger, A. (2013). The road to BIBFRAME: The evolution of the idea of bibliographic transition into a post-MARC future. *Cataloging & Classification Quarterly, 51*(8), 873–890.

Miller, S. J. (2011). *Metadata for digital collections: A how-to-do-it manual.* Neal-Schuman Publishers.

Neumann, J., & Brase, J. (2014). DataCite and DOI names for research data. *Journal of Computer-Aided Molecular Design, 28*(10), 1035–1041.

Nilsson, M. (2010). *From interoperability to harmonization in metadata standardization: Designing an evolvable framework for metadata harmonization* (Doctoral dissertation), KTH, Stockholm.

Park, J. R. (2009). Metadata quality in digital repositories: A survey of the current state of the art. *Cataloging & Classification Quarterly, 47*(3–4), 213–228.

Pomerantz, J. (2015). *Metadata.* MIT Press.

Reddy, T. B., Thomas, A. D., Stamatis, D., Bertsch, J., Isbandi, M., Jansson, J., & Kyrpides, N. C. (2015). The Genomes OnLine Database (GOLD) v. 5: A metadata management system based on a four level (meta) genome project classification. *Nucleic Acids Research, 43*(D1), D1099–D1106.

Sowa, J. F. (2000). Ontology, metadata, and semiotics. In *International conference on conceptual structures* (pp. 55–81). Springer.

Stuempel, H., Salokhe, G., Aubert, A., Keizer, J., Nadeau, A., Katz, S., & Rudgard, S. (2009). Metadata application profile for agricultural learning resources. In *Metadata and semantics* (pp. 499–507). Springer.

Uslar, M., Specht, M., Rohjans, S., Trefke, J., & González, J. M. (2012). *The common information model CIM: IEC 61968/61970 and 62325-A practical introduction to the CIM.* Springer Science & Business Media.

Vardigan, M., Heus, P., & Thomas, W. (2008). Data documentation initiative: Toward a standard for the social sciences. *International Journal of Digital Curation, 3*(1), 107–113.

Weibel, S., Kunze, J., Lagoze, C., & Wolf, M. (1998). Dublin core metadata for resource discovery. *Internet Engineering Task Force RFC, 2413*(222), 132.

Wells, D. C., & Greisen, E. W. (1979). FITS-a flexible image transport system. In *Image processing in astronomy* (p. 445).

Wieczorek, J., Bloom, D., Guralnick, R., Blum, S., Döring, M., Giovanni, R., & Vieglais, D. (2012). Darwin core: An evolving community-developed biodiversity data standard. *PLoS One, 7*(1), e29715.

World Wide Web Consortium. (2014). *Data catalog vocabulary (DCAT).* World Wide Web Consortium.

Yee, K. P., Swearingen, K., Li, K., & Hearst, M. (2003). Faceted metadata for image search and browsing. In *Proceedings of the SIGCHI conference on human factors in computing systems* (pp. 401–408). ACM Press.

23

THE WHOLE KNOWLEDGE ARCHITECTURE – PULLING IT ALL TOGETHER

Chapter summary

This chapter assesses the current state of knowledge architecture, working across architecture segments and types of knowledge assets. We consider what we need to do to bring the current state up to an acceptable level – that is, an equilibrium state across all assets. Drawing from the factors identified in the evolution of the 17 functional architectures, we observe that knowledge architecture has followed the path of economic systems. We align the knowledge architecture segments with the essential elements of an economic system. We explore what economists, media, and broadcasting experts tell us about the economic trends that will shape the future. And, we translate these trends to help us envision the future knowledge architecture.

The big picture – current state

Our big picture of the current state of knowledge architecture begins with the view from knowledge segments. What is the current state of knowledge availability, knowledge accessibility, and knowledge consumability? Next, we consider the coverage of the five categories of knowledge assets. Both states require attention for us to attain equilibrium with other architecture practices across the organization.

Current state of functional architectures

Knowledge availability has some good practice examples we can leverage, but in most cases, they must be expanded and enhanced to (1) support knowledge architecture; and (2) meet the needs and expectations of the knowledge economy (Table 23.1). Knowledge consumption is perhaps the most uneven in its development of all of the architecture segments.

TABLE 23.1 High-Level Assessment of Knowledge Availability Segment

Architecture Function	Current State
Knowledge object models	Good practices for object modeling exist and are in widespread use in other areas of enterprise architecture. It is essential to use them to establish good practices for knowledge object modeling.
Knowledge encoding formatting packaging	The built environment for this architecture is extensive. It is essential to leverage existing good practices. The challenge is working backward from the built environment to design principles.
Knowledge identification and distinction	There are good practices in place for some types of assets, but there is a need to expand and enhance them. They also need to be reverse engineered from the built environment to design principles.
Knowledge disposition and destruction	There are good practices to place for some assets, but these are not sufficient for the current environment.
Knowledge preservation and conservation	There is an extension built environment for conservation related to media, but the practice of preservation is largely underdeveloped for any but explicit assets. Preservation of explicit assets is primarily limited to fragile, unique historical materials and business-critical paper documents.

The functional architectures in the knowledge accessibility segment are uneven in their grounding, principles, and practices (Table 23.2).

Search is more extensively developed in terms of the built environment but is often less effectively applied to assets or grounded in designed principles. Perhaps the greatest challenge in this segment is the gap in understanding between professional practices and business needs. Those architectures that have well-established design principles are mainly reserved for professionals. In contrast, we address everyday business needs in a fragmented and more haphazard way, leaving the task to business stakeholders. Another intervening factor is the extent of the built environment, particularly components that are built into other applications commonly used by the business. Rarely do we ground these components in sound design principles.

The functional architectures in the knowledge consumability segment are perhaps the least well-developed of all. They require extensive investment, adaptation, enhancement, and expansion before they can be applied to knowledge assets (Table 23.3). Knowledge augmentation, derivation, and synthesis require the most work – starting with a new understanding of the six categories of use. The knowledge sciences field should address this work. It is essential to create a more practical applied and theoretical understanding of how knowledge assets are used, and the effects of that use on assets.

Similarly, harm and risk management architecture require extensive foundational design work. We have little foundation upon which to build today – this work should be taken up by the knowledge sciences community. Authentication requires significant work, but there is a growing awareness upon which to build.

TABLE 23.2 High–Level Assessment of Knowledge Accessibility Segment

Architecture Function	*Current State*
Looking for and discovering knowledge	This architecture is significantly underdeveloped both in terms of the audit and inventory of sources and in terms of its presentation and navigation. There are good practices to draw from, including collection development, usability engineering, and interface design. These are practices not generally associated with discovery, though. There is a need to adjust our view away from search and refocus it on landscape and the full range of sources.
Searching for knowledge	This architecture is significantly advanced in terms of capabilities and the built environment. However, it is little understood and poorly applied to different kinds of assets. The predominant view today is on embedded applications and improving the performance of a search. It is essential to refocus it on index design and access points before adding further intelligence to the process.
Knowledge categorization	It is an architecture with a significant built environment, but it often lacks fundamental design principles. The challenge is to re-establish a foundation at the enterprise level, develop principles, and to expand the practice to include the business view. Most of the built environment today concentrates on a topic or subject.
Knowledge indexing and keywording	This architecture is well developed in terms of practices but has a confused design history. There is a need to distinguish indexing from categorization, and to extend indexing to address business access and needs. It is also important to bridge the different understandings of formal professional indexing and keywording.
Knowledge semantics	This architecture has a very uneven design and development history. And, it is often applied indiscriminately to knowledge assets. There is a need to understand the basic design principles and essential functionality. There is significant confusion about functionality across semantic solutions today. It may be the case that more than one kind of semantic solution will be applied to the same knowledge asset in the same context. There are significant design challenges for this architecture.
Knowledge abstraction and surrogation	The full scope of this functional architecture is not well-understood. Some elements have well-established design principles and practices, but others remain informal and unanchored in sound practices. This architecture ranges from informal personal to professional public practice. There is also a need to re-establish the value of this functional architecture in the light of technological advances.

TABLE 23.3 High-Level Assessment of Knowledge Consumability Segment

Architecture Function	Current State
Knowledge Augmentation Derivation and Synthesis	It is perhaps one of the most underdeveloped of all the segments. It is a concern because it is the primary architecture to support business use and the transformation of business value. While there is some recognition of the impacts and effects of the use of knowledge assets in the knowledge management literature, the treatment is at a generalized level. Of all the six sub-architectures here, only annotation and synthesis have any treatment. And, to be precise, the treatment we find is from technology rather than from a design view. Annotation is considered in terms of how we engineer it. Synthesis is considered from the viewpoint of the techniques that we use to analyze it. This architecture needs extensive work – not only its effects on the source but also the new and varied assets it generates.
Knowledge Harm and Risk Management	While our awareness of harm and risk has increased, the focus has been on physical assets. We have developed risk management strategies to protect our facilities, technology, and business-critical data in business continuity plans. The challenge is that this simply allows us to provide access to these assets – it does not address the full range of harm. It is vital to expand our understanding of harm and to ensure we have strategies for managing the risk of all kinds of knowledge assets.
Knowledge Authentication	Of all the potential arm types, we have devoted little attention to authenticating the assets we use to create leverage in business operations. Our awareness of harm has increased through the proliferation of false information through social media, but we do not yet have standard good practices for any of the types of harm. This architecture requires substantial new investment and development. Organizations must then select and adapt designs to suit their levels of risk with greater access to solutions.
Knowledge Security	Security architecture is generally one of the most robust built environments in an organization. However, it is designed on an outdated premise of perimeter breach and need-to-know principles. We need to design and apply a new kind of security architecture that will address all of the types of security risks we face.
Knowledge Authorization and Privileging	Access control is also one of the most extensively built-out architectures. However, it is designed to support security as traditionally defined. Access control architectures should be reconsidered in terms of levels of business value and business risk. Overclassification and impediments restrict our ability to transform and leverage our knowledge assets.

This work should include the knowledge sciences community, but it should also draw from the financial, legal and judicial, and broadcasting sectors. Security and access control have extensive built environments today, but these environments are not suitable for knowledge assets. We need extensive work on design principles and expansion.

Current state of coverage of knowledge capital assets

What is the current state of coverage of knowledge asses in the knowledge availability segment? Table 23.4 offers a view of where we have made progress, where we have something to build upon, and where we have significant work. What do we see in terms of support for those functional knowledge architectures associated with making knowledge capital available? We see no dark green. It suggests we have a lot of work to do – no single type of knowledge capital is in good shape in terms of availability. There is an excellent foundation to work for explicit knowledge, but that is because there is a long history – about 500 years – of working with explicit knowledge. There are fragmented practices – suggesting an emerging practice – for human capital and one hopeful sign for procedural capital. The most significant challenges for availability pertain to procedural knowledge, cultural knowledge, and relational knowledge

What do we see for individual functional architectures? There are some hopeful signs for knowledge object modeling. Perhaps the most extensively developed architecture in this segment is encoding, formatting, and packaging. The knowledge disposition and destruction architecture and the preservation and conservation architecture require the most work. We characterize the current state as: (1) we have a well-developed design environment; (2) a foundation exists upon which to build; (3) there are fragmented good practices; (4) there are significant gaps; and (5) there is no current practice, and we need to start from scratch. We offer a color-coded legend to interpret the architectures in each segment.

What is the current state of knowledge accessibility? Table 23.5 offers a view of the level of progress in this area. We see no dark green anywhere in the representation of this segment. For the most part, 'No current practice' is the norm. We do

TABLE 23.4 Current State of Knowledge Availability Segment

Architecture Function	Human Capital	Explicit Knowledge	Procedural Knowledge	Cultural Knowledge	Relational Knowledge
Object Models					
Encoding Formatting Packaging					
Identification Distinction					
Disposition – Destruction					
Preservation – Conservation					

Legend Precedence	Color Code
Well Developed	
Foundation Exists to Build Upon	
Fragmented Good Practices	
Significant Gaps Exists	
No Current Practice – Start from Scratch	

TABLE 23.5 Current State of Knowledge Accessibility Segment

Architecture Function	Human Capital	Explicit Knowledge	Procedural Knowledge	Cultural Knowledge	Relational Knowledge
Looking For – Discovery					
Searching					
Categorization					
Indexing – Keywording					
Semantics					
Abstraction – Surrogation					

Legend Precedence	Color Code
Well Developed	
Foundation Exists to Build Upon	
Fragmented Good Practices	
Significant Gaps Exists	
No Current Practice – Start from Scratch	

still have some good practices related to explicit knowledge, but there is still some work to be done here. Human capital appears to be the area that is developing after explicit knowledge. Yet a significant amount of work remains to be done for procedural knowledge, cultural knowledge, and relational knowledge. What do we see for individual functional architectures? Three functional architectures – looking/ discovery, searching, and categorization offer some existing or fragmented good practices. Most, though have significant work to do

What is the current state of knowledge consumability? Table 23.6 offers a view the level of progress we have made in this area as well. Perhaps more concerning than all other segments, this segment seems to place greater emphasis on security and access than use, risk management, and authentication. We need a significant shift in focus here – this is a sign that we've been placing the attention on the 'wrong' part of the knowledge architecture. A change is required – specifically, a shift is needed to consumability first, and then to availability followed by accessibility. There is still a significant amount of work to be done

This review suggests a need to establish and build out knowledge architectures if organizations are to remain competitive in the knowledge economy.

Getting to equilibrium state in knowledge architecture

Equilibrium is defined as achieving parity with other architecture practices in place throughout the organization. Essentially, equilibrium means integrating knowledge architecture segments into the enterprise architecture layer cake (Figure 23.1). We reach equilibrium by the building out of the 17 functional architectures. The purpose of the big picture is to provide a comprehensive and inclusive framework from which to design a knowledge architecture for our organizations. A big picture is also a working tool that

TABLE 23.6 Current State of Knowledge Consumability Segment

Architecture Function	Human Capital	Explicit Knowledge	Procedural Knowledge	Cultural Knowledge	Relational Knowledge
Knowledge Augmentation Derivation and Synthesis					
Harm Risk Management					
Authentication					
Security					
Authorization – Privileging					

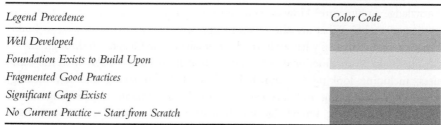

Legend Precedence	Color Code
Well Developed	
Foundation Exists to Build Upon	
Fragmented Good Practices	
Significant Gaps Exists	
No Current Practice – Start from Scratch	

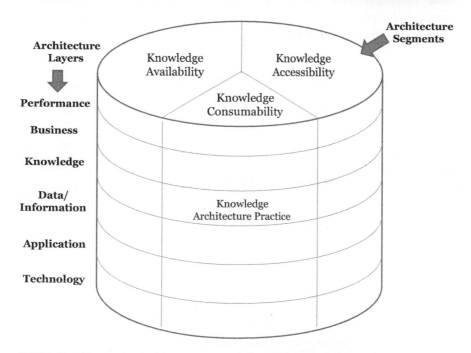

FIGURE 23.1 Enterprise Architecture Layer Cake With Knowledge Architecture

allows us to calibrate, adjust, and adapt that architecture blueprint as the individual parts evolve and change. Initially, we may not have a dedicated knowledge architecture practice. Over time, though, as we design and develop each component, as we work with other architecture practices, that knowledge architecture practice and layer will emerge.

Designing knowledge architecture into enterprise architecture

To achieve our goal of a big picture, knowledge architecture means systematically and intentionally walking through the architecture design process described in Chapter 3. Organizations that have an existing enterprise architecture practice have an advantage – they may use that practice as a foundation for expanding the practice to cover the three knowledge architecture segments, and to expand coverage to all forms of knowledge assets.

In Chapters 6 through 22, we laid out activities that would guide an organization through the build-out of these functional architectures. Integration and equilibrium begin with seeing affinities and building relationships with existing practices. Where do these affinities exist? What relationships should you cultivate to advance the knowledge architecture? How do you best position what you have to get to where you need to be? What are the relationships and alignments you need to build? Figure 23.2 summarizes what we learned about alliances in Chapters 6 through 22.

There are seven functional architectures that most closely align with the business, including looking for knowledge, knowledge indexing and keywording, knowledge abstracting and surrogation, knowledge semantics, knowledge harm and risk management, knowledge authentication, and knowledge use. Some have strong traditional ties to information architecture but need to be reoriented to support and align with business architecture. These architectures derive from the accessibility and consumability segments.

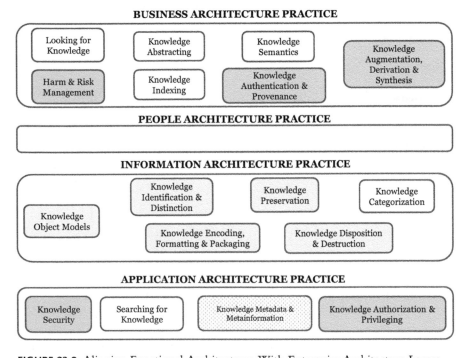

FIGURE 23.2 Aligning Functional Architectures With Enterprise Architecture Layers

Five of the functional architectures closely align with information architecture practices, including knowledge object models, knowledge identification and distinction, knowledge encoding formatting and packaging, knowledge preservation, knowledge disposition and destruction, and knowledge categorization. These architectures derive from the availability and accessibility segments. Four of the functional architectures have an affinity to the application architecture, including searching, knowledge security, knowledge authorization and privileging, and metadata. Metadata is traditionally an information management responsibility, but the increased value in a knowledge architecture argues for its alignment with the application layer. Reviewing the alliances across chapters made it clear that the people's architecture layer has no claim or close alignment with any of these functional practices. Instead, the people architecture practice's affinity lies with a type of knowledge asset – human capital.

Designing knowledge assets into the knowledge architecture

We must also ensure that the current and future functional architectures are expanded and enhanced to support the full spectrum of knowledge assets. Our current architectures are designed to help explicit knowledge assets, but this is only one element of the organization's knowledge capital. In Chapters 6 through 22, we also explored expanding and enhancing those architectures to support each category of knowledge assets. Just as it is essential to understand our functional alignments, so it is essential to know where the essential support for and investment in knowledge assets lies.

As Figure 23.3 suggests, four of the five types of knowledge assets are essential areas of investment and growth for business architecture practices. Explicit

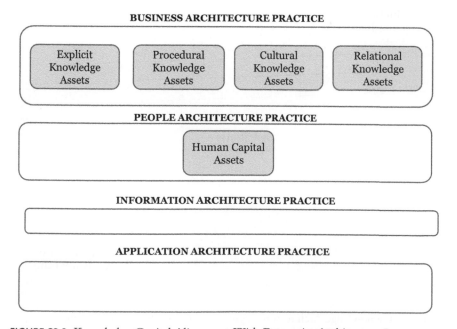

FIGURE 23.3 Knowledge Capital Alignment With Enterprise Architecture Layers

knowledge assets are created by and for the business. Procedural knowledge is the essence of what the organization does and how it does it. Cultural knowledge is the underlying assumptions, beliefs, values, and behaviors that determine the organization's way of working. Relational knowledge assets represent the knowledge fiber of our organizations. All are essential to achieving our business goal and realizing business value. While human capital represents the core of our business knowledge, its greatest current affinity is people's architecture. It is because we currently treat people as stock resources rather than as capital assets. It is essential to start with this alignment and to calibrate it to achieve a new perspective.

What the future holds for knowledge architecture

Today's knowledge architectures strive to support the organization's business and economic needs in a knowledge economy. In Chapters 6 through 22, we considered the evolution of our 17 functional architectures, specifically the factors that affected the economy and shaped those architectures over millennia. Looking at those factors across the architectures reminds us that knowledge architecture segments resemble an economic system (Figure 23.4). Knowledge availability is influenced by factors that shaped the production and nature of commodities – the supply side. Knowledge access factors shaped availability, proximity, and geographical aspects of the market – the economic system's distribution element. Knowledge

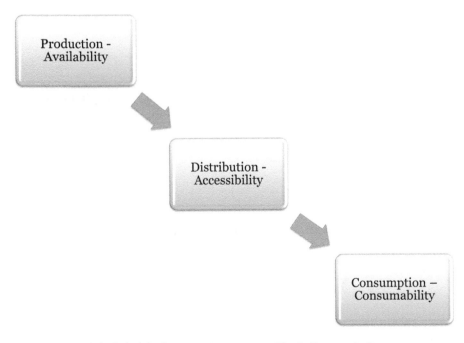

FIGURE 23.4 Knowledge Architecture Segments as Classic Economic System

consumability is influenced by factors that shape the demand and consumption element of the system. As resources became more abundant, as producers gained the skills and competencies to produce more goods, architectures expanded to support supplies. As economic markets grew and evolved beyond individual households to villages, cities, regions, and countries, architectures evolved to meet new exchange and distribution needs. As commodities and markets expanded, consumption grew. As the competencies and skills of consumers increased, the demand for and creation of new products expand. Just as these factors have influenced the economy of today, so will they affect the future economy.

The knowledge architecture of the future will be influenced by the same factors that have shaped the evolution of our historical economies. Yes, the current state is not yet equilibrium – we strive to achieve the equilibrium of our architecture with the needs of the knowledge economy. But, we cannot focus on the past or the present without regard to the future. It is ineffective and inefficient to strive only for equilibrium. It is essential to look to the future. What will that knowledge economy look like 25 or 50 years from now? How will it be different from today? And, what does this mean for our knowledge architecture?

We cannot know the shape and look of the knowledge economy 25 or 50 years from now. We can, though, understand the factors that will influence that will shape that future economy. To understand what economists and industry experts foresee for that future knowledge economy, we look to two sources – the World Economic Forum and the media and broadcasting industry (World Economic Forum, 2018). How do these sources characterize the future economic systems, markets, and assets changing in the future? We apply their advice to the five types of knowledge assets to understand how the design of knowledge architecture may change. From these sources, we derive 15 future trends projected to influence the future of knowledge capital, including:

- Trend 1. Widespread adoption of technology, including automation, across the value chain
- Trend 2. Global climate change and resource scarcity
- Trend 3. Human migration on a mass scale
- Trend 4. Shifting consumer demands and changing market demographics
- Trend 5. Mixed signals on trade and transparency in the years ahead
- Trend 6. Plan for the supply chain impacts of automation and migration
- Trend 7. Build responsible regional sourcing hubs
- Trend 8. Digitalize supplier assessment and engagement
- Trend 9. Strengthening supply chain transparency and disclosure
- Trend 10. The labor supply is shifting
- Trend 11. Machines are intelligent
- Trend 12. Everything is connected
- Trend 13. Circular is the mainstream economy
- Trend 14. Frictionless economy and free movement of knowledge
- Trend 15. Increased levels of and expanded types of harm

We explore each of these trends in terms of how they influence the economic system and translate that to the future of knowledge architecture segments and functional designs and the future of knowledge assets.

Trend 1. Widespread adoption of technology, including automation, across the value chain

In the future, economists suggest that supply chains will be hyper-transparent as suppliers, workers, and communities access increasingly sophisticated technologies and use them to create and share knowledge about environmental and social performance. Economists predict increased digitalization and virtualization of supply chain management. This trend will change how products and services are made and delivered. It will also enable the creation and sharing of supply chain information in new ways by a more diverse set of actors (Globescan, 2015, 2018; Norman Broadbent, 2019). Companies will digitally transform the management of their supply chains by piloting and applying technologies such as machine learning, blockchain, and augmented reality to traditional supply chain management activities. This trend affects the future of distribution. It speaks directly to knowledge accessibility. It will impact all of the functional architectures in this segment because individually, they contribute to the more efficient discovery and distribution. There will be an increased demand for these architectures. In the future, smarter supply chain management means being able to discover, find, describe, and characterize knowledge assets from multiple dimensions, and for numerous and varied markets. Rather than decrease the need for these architectures, expanded digital markets mean increased demand.

We expect this trend to affect all types of knowledge assets but in different ways. We expect the effect will be smarter discovery and distribution of human capital and explicit knowledge. We expect the impact will be more intense use of procedural knowledge to enable supply chain management and delivery. We expect the effect will be to elevate the importance of relational capital as supply chains expand and focus on new types and sources of supply and new distribution channels.

Trend 2. Global climate change and resource scarcity

While the exact effects of climate change in supply chains cannot be precisely predicted, supply chains are particularly vulnerable to the impacts of climate change due to their reliance on raw materials and concentration in countries likely to be impacted by climate change. Organizations have shifted their focus to adapt to the risks of climate change – availability of raw materials, commodity price volatility, severe supply disruptions due to natural disasters, and worker health impacts due to rising temperatures.

These impacts are likely to increase in frequency and intensity and to have a significant effect on the supply side of the economic system. We expect this trend to influence the production and supply of knowledge assets, focusing mainly on the functional architectures that support knowledge availability. How do we see these trends playing out? We expect this trend will influence the demand for explicit knowledge assets in digital form, and the conversion of historical physical assets into digital format. It will have a significant effect on encoding, formatting, and packaging. It will also directly affect the development of preservation and conservation strategies.

We expect this trend will also increase the demand for direct access to human capital – reduced use of physical assets may result in an increased demand for access to the source itself – the human author or the team as the source. We can see how the demand for direct access to sources may increase the value and importance of managing relational capital.

Trend 3. Human migration on a mass scale

In the past few decades, there has been an increase in mass migration, with more than 240 million people living outside their countries of birth. This mass movement of people and their migrations' circumstances have shifted economic potential within countries and introduced new challenges and opportunities for companies seeking to respect and support human rights across their global supply chains. This trend speaks to two components of the economic system – the production of economic goods, or the supply side, and the consumption of economic goods, or the demand side. Who can produce knowledge assets now expands significantly, as does the scope and nature of those goods. Who consumes and expects to leverage those assets also changes.

This trend affects all three knowledge architecture segments because it represents a full market disruption. In the knowledge availability segment, we see impacts on knowledge encoding, formatting, and packaging because who creates now crosses cultures and who consumes crosses cultures. It impacts the language of every type of asset, and it has a direct effect on cultural knowledge. It may also affect how we identify and distinguish knowledge assets because different cultures have different views of ownership and use. In the knowledge accessibility segment, this trend affects two functional architectures more significantly than the others – looking for – discovery and search. With expanded and relocated populations, markets will no longer be language predictable. It indirectly affects all of the other functional architectures, including abstracting and surrogation and the need for summaries in other languages. In terms of consumption, we can expect knowledge augmentation, derivation, and synthesis to change in different cultural and economic contexts. We may also expect some aspects of harm and risk management to increase simply because different cultures have different perceptions of legitimate use and reuse.

Trend 4. Shifting consumer demands and changing market demographics

Advances in digital technology will enable high levels of personalization in marketing and product design and fuel the growing on-demand economy (Bowman & Willis, 2003; World Economic Forum, 2018, 2020a, 2020b). In the United

States alone, consumers are spending nearly US$60 billion in on-demand services such as online marketplaces and transportation. As companies look to meet the demand for custom goods and faster delivery times in some parts of the world, they are also looking for growth opportunities in new markets and among new customer groups. This trend will have a significant direct impact on the knowledge consumption segment as consumers' expectations for custom assets. While the immediate effect is on consumability, the ultimate result is on knowledge availability. Consumers' expectations for custom goods will affect what we produce. The direct impact will be on procedural knowledge and the adaptation of existing processes to customize products. We can also expect customization to influence how we design and market explicit knowledge.

Trend 5. Mixed signals on trade and transparency in the years ahead

This trend addresses fundamental changes to supply chains, including reshoring, vertical integration, and increased sourcing from new geographies. Economists see this trend resulting from confusion and disruption in the global trade system and mixed signals in existing trade relationships (Schwab & Davis, 2018). It speaks directly to a shift from global to more regional or local sourcing and distribution. This trend will tend to affect both the production and distribution components of the economic system. The impacts will affect knowledge availability and knowledge accessibility segments. Where we produce knowledge, assets may become more focused. Rather than defining human capital sources as global labor markets, we may focus on restoring and reshoring human and procedural capital. Shifting supply chains from global to local sources translates to an increased value of local networks, particularly sources and distribution channels. With more local control comes increased opportunity to identify and distinguish assets for local consumption and reinvent encoding formatting and packaging to suit local norms and cultures. This trend also speaks directly to human capital and procedural capital as sources of knowledge assets.

Trend 6. Plan for the supply chain impacts of automation and migration

Economists project that mass migration on a scale previously unimaginable, combined with projections that significant numbers of workers will be displaced by automation, will increase volatility in supply chain labor dynamics. Organizations will evolve their approaches as a result. Organizations will mitigate this volatility by fostering responsible and inclusive labor practices. Businesses sourcing from regions impacted by mass migration can redirect resources to engage with industry peers and cross-border actors, including government, labor unions, and employers. It will reinforce legal frameworks and insist on better enforcement of labor laws. Organizations with supply chains that expect significant uptake of automation through 2025 can insist that key suppliers will develop plans to support a sustainable workforce transition.

Organizations will also shift to a higher degree of empowerment of individual workers within their supply chains by enabling them to participate in and lead trade unions and other forms of worker representation, by using technology like mobile apps to help workers understand their legal rights, and through evolving technologies that directly gather workers' views. This trend will have a significant effect on production – and our knowledge availability. While global supply chains and distribution may shrink, we do not expect to narrow the producers and consumers. Migrations and population relocations mean that different languages, traditions, and cultures are now concentrated in single geographic areas. It affects what we produce locally and what we consume locally. It affects how we encode, format, and package assets, and it affects the use practices we observe in local communities.

Trend 7. Build responsible regional sourcing hubs

Economists project that growth in new markets and demographics and meeting customer demands for customized, on-demand goods and services will require understanding and satisfying new consumption patterns and preferences and providing goods and services in new locations and formats. Supply chain leaders will have an opportunity to develop agile, regional supplier networks that can meet both commercial expectations and sustainability aspirations. Organizations can build on the lessons learned in well-worn sourcing locations from developing and emerging economies.

On the supply side of the economic system, organizations now have the opportunity to embed social and environmental responsibility into the design of these regional sourcing hubs and to leapfrog supplier monitoring activities that have not delivered improvements in labor conditions or ecological resilience. This trend will have a significant effect on the production component of the economic system. It translates to the knowledge availability segment. Perhaps the most direct impact of this trend will be the identification and distinction architecture. Understanding what something is and where it comes from, who produced it, and sourcing will be critical to whether an asset is consumed. It pertains to all types of knowledge assets, but mainly to human capital and procedural capital because they speak to sourcing.

Trend 8. Digitalize supplier assessment and engagement

This trend speaks to an opportunity to rethink producing and distributing organizations to collect and interpret supply chain information. Practitioners will need to hone in on the supply chain information that is decision-useful in a sea of available data and dashboards. It will also need to reconsider which data they need to commission and how it is collected. Supply chain leaders looking to the future should firmly weigh the value of investing resources in a battery of one-time, on-site supplies. This trend speaks directly to distribution, but indirectly to production.

It will influence the knowledge accessibility segment of our architecture. Perhaps the most significant effect of this trend is procedural knowledge – the increased scrutiny of the quality of decisions made. Increased scrutiny of the supply chain will expose issues with knowledge consumption in the form of authentication, particularly of authentication of human capital and the tacit knowledge used to make those decisions. There may also be an effect on relational capital if increased scrutiny also means scrutinizing who we rely on for tacit knowledge.

Trend 9. Strengthening supply chain transparency and disclosure

Economists' projects' enhanced visibility and disclosures will reshape how supply chain leaders will manage those supply chains. Increased transparency means that global trade may shift with political events moving toward economic nationalism. Improving the quality and scope of supply chain disclosure enables practitioners to respond more quickly and effectively respond to both regulatory requirements and stakeholder scrutiny. This trend will have a significant effect on the distribution elements of the economic system. It translates to the knowledge accessibility segment of our architecture. Greater transparency means greater visibility of assets. It brings to light more access points and to access points that reflect how people in different places and spaces look for and discover knowledge. It also means greater visibility of relational capital, particularly distribution and sourcing networks. Transparency also affects explicit knowledge in the form of more encoded information and data. It also means having increased human skills and competencies to analyze and better manage the source.

Trend 10. The labor supply is shifting

In the future economy, economic and business roles will blur. Anyone can produce, consume, and distribute assets. The primary impact is on the production element of the system. While there may be some constraints for commodities produced from material resources, the only limitations for knowledge assets are the producers' human capital. The labor supply will look very different in the future. Scientists expect rapid growth in emerging economies and more moderate growth in developed economies. This trend has a significant effect on talent management and planning, and on how organizations think of labor. It will shift from seeing labor as a resource to be stockpiled or disposed of to a valuable capital asset essential to economic growth and investment. Organizations will compete for human capital in the future. While every segment of the knowledge architecture is impacted, the most significant impact is on the knowledge availability segment. We expect the most significant impact will be on human capital assets. These assets become increasingly valuable. And, this applies to all forms of human capital. Tacit knowledge becomes critical, but so are learning and collaborative skills and competencies. Digital and skills dexterity are vital sources of capital for organizations. It is more important to engage individuals who can learn than to employ individuals who 'know' everything.

Trend 11. Machines are intelligent

Along with the increased use of technology, the future will also be characterized by increasing intelligence. Artificial intelligence can have many applications that will affect all economic system elements, but most directly the distribution element. The most significant effect will be on analytics and insights gained from the increased capability to analyze information and data. It will shift how distribution is done, how quickly decisions are made, and the factors that influence those decisions. We expect the primary impact to be on the knowledge accessibility segment – how we make assets accessible. Increased intelligence in business rules and business repositories means increased use of and familiarity with business language. The business language will receive greater attention as functional categories, managed vocabularies, and business semantics. We expect these three architectures to grow simultaneously. Increased access to vast sources of business data and business rules repositories will provide a foundation for advanced business semantics.

We also envision this trend will affect procedural knowledge – AI will be increasingly embedded into procedural knowledge. It means we need to extend our definition of structural capital to include business rules repositories, expert systems, and decision support systems. Currently, the embedding of rules has a high error rate. As rules are encoded, they become more vulnerable to theft. New forms of protection are needed. And, the competencies of workers to create, maintain, or work with these rules increases.

Trend 12. Everything is connected

Economists suggest that digital sharing will be the norm rather than the exception in the future economy. It will have a dramatic effect on collaboration, simulation, and decision-making. Economists and technologists suggest that we will see an increase in what they call – digital twins. Digital twins are copies of the same asset. In the future, economists suggest that digital twins represent not only physical or virtual commodities but also process characteristics. This trend may pose impediments to production, or it may create new opportunities and markets for experimentation, modeling, and simulation. We may be able to simulate processes to identify faults and errors before we invest in them. While this trend creates new opportunities for the creation of new assets, it also increases levels and degrees of harm. Digital twins might mean new capabilities to run scenarios and to understand the implications of our decisions. Digital twins also introduce and accelerate harm and risk and highlight the need for more significant authentication. This trend will affect all types of knowledge assets, but it will heighten our awareness and valuation of relational knowledge. Networks, communities, and relationships will be increasingly important in the knowledge economy

Trend 13. Circular is the mainstream economy

This trend considers the effects of many of the preceding trends on the economy as a whole. Economists refer to the shape of the future economy as a circular economy. What is a circular economy? The circular economy is one where all three components are connected. The industrial and agricultural economies were linear. These earlier economies followed a life cycle model – we produce, we consume, and we dispose. This linear economy is sometimes referred to as 'take, make, waste' production and consumption. This approach is not consistent with other trends emerging today and increasing in the future. Climate change, population growth, and unsustainable lifestyles mean we will ground the future economy's design on circular economic principles. These principles reflect the economic properties and behaviors of knowledge highlighted in Chapter 1. We expect reuse, repurposing, smarter resourcing, and recycling. A circular economy is much easier to achieve for knowledge assets than for other types of capital assets.

Organizations that invest in knowledge assets will achieve a circular economy more efficiently and more quickly than organizations that do not. While this trend affects all types of knowledge assets, it heightens our awareness of relational and reputational knowledge. Reputation and responsibility increase in value. Relational knowledge gains greater visibility and recognition within and outside an organization. The organization takes on more of a 'network' model and is seen in its broader community.

Trend 14. Frictionless economy and free movement of knowledge

The internet has made our lives easier in many ways. We can purchase items online and have them delivered almost immediately. We can find people who like that same rare dog breed as we do and share an endless number of photos with them on Instagram. We can react to content – be it funny memes or breaking news – in real-time. The frictionless economy is more closely aligned with knowledge assets than other capital assets. Knowledge now moves freely and abundantly online. Every minute, 500 hours of video are posted to YouTube, and 243,000 photos are uploaded on Facebook.

This trend speaks directly to consumers in the economic system. It translates to our knowledge consumability segment. A frictionless economy means increased consumption, including augmentation, derivation, and synthesis. It means we can build communities and establish relationships more efficiently and effectively. It is easier to leverage relationships to develop our human capital and to showcase and display our human capital. While the frictionless economy facilitates the free movement of knowledge, the most significant impact may be on relational and network capital. Assets will flow unpredictably through these networks.

Trend 15. Increased levels of and expanded types of harm

The frictionless economy we described in Trend 14 also increases the challenge of tracing use and accountability. A frictionless economy also introduces harm and risk. We find all forms of harm rising in the future economy, and increased demand for authentication, security, and access control. The circular economy's increased volatility means that we can create copies and fakes and do harm much more quickly than in the past. A new form of harm in the future economy will be waste. The supply chain may be increasingly murky in terms of authenticity and fraud. Waste and fraud are now a possible economic impact on individuals, groups, and organizations. With this trend comes the need for increased discernment and caution in engaging in knowledge markets. It means that consumers must become much more sophisticated in terms of where they shop, what they shop for, and who they trust. This particular trend speaks directly to the consumption element of the system. It translates to the knowledge consumability segment of the architecture. Specifically, this trend addresses the need to increase our awareness of harm and risk management, and to pay greater attention to authentication. It means rethinking security and access management to suit the unpredictable and serendipitous flows of all kinds of knowledge assets.

Future research agenda for knowledge architecture

Earlier in this chapter, we suggested strategies for aligning the knowledge architecture segments with other architecture practices. In this section, we consider building coalitions and communities to move forward at the functional architecture level. Our review of the design environment for each functional architecture identified factors and challenges that might create impediments. Perhaps the most significant challenge and the potential obstacle is the built and well-established environment. It is difficult to redesign or rethink design principles where we have a heavily invested and built environment. To overcome these impediments, we must develop partnerships and establish new design communities. What are these new partnerships and communities?

A critical new partnership is with academic and professional education. It means greater collaboration with the academic fields of business, information science, economics, computer science, and design. These are the fields with the most significant investment in the pertinent built environments today. It means greater engagement and collaboration at the department and school levels. Within business schools, we must find opportunities to work with personnel and human resources. Within information science schools, we must find opportunities to establish a new and expanded framework for information architecture. We must also critically assess the treatment of knowledge management in either business administration or information science curricula. As we hope we have demonstrated throughout this text, all of these must have an economic foundation of some sort. It also means working with professional associations and certification organizations. It is as essential to reach practitioners as it is to reach students. The continuing and lifelong learning events offered by these organizations are essential partnerships.

The most critical collaboration is the partnership with the knowledge management community of academics and practitioners. Knowledge scientists must expand their view of knowledge architecture from the now-arcane life cycle model to the evolving knowledge economy. While knowledge exchange, sharing, and transfer are all essential concepts, they are insufficient for understanding the true nature of knowledge economy systems.

Chapter review

After reading this chapter, you should be able to:

- explain the current state of the three segments of knowledge architecture;
- describe the current state of functional architectures vis a vis each type of knowledge asset;
- explain how to use the activities of earlier chapters to achieve parity with other architecture practices;
- explain how the three knowledge architecture segments resemble an economic system;
- describe the economic trends that will shape the 21st-century knowledge economy;
- describe the effects these economic trends will have on knowledge assets.

References and recommended readings for the future

Bowman, S., & Willis, C. (2003). *We media: How audiences are shaping the future of news and information* (p. 66). The Media Center at the American Press Institute.

Globescan. (2015). *The state of sustainable business 2015*. Annual Results September 2015. Retrieved February 2, 2020, from www.bsr.org/reports/BSR_GlobeScan_State_of_Sustainable_Business_2015.pdf

Globescan. (2018). *Future of supply Chais 2025*. Retrieved February 2, 2020, from www.bsr.org/files/work/BSR_Future_of_Supply_Chains_Primer.pdf

Norman Broadbent. (2019). *Automation & digital transformation: Getting your supply*. Retrieved February 2, 2020, from www.normanbroadbent.com/2019/02/27/the-supply-chain-getting-match-fit-for-2020-and-beyond/

Schwab, K., & Davis, N. (2018). *Shaping the future of the fourth industrial revolution*. Currency.

World Economic Forum. (2018). *Creative disruption: The impact of emerging technologies on the creative economy*. World Economic Forum White Paper. Retrieved February 2, 2020, from www.weforum.org/whitepapers/creative-disruption-the-impact-of-emerging-technologies-on-the-creative-economy

World Economic Forum. (2020a). *Shaping the future of media, entertainment and culture*. Retrieved February 2, 2020, from www.weforum.org/platforms/shaping-the-future-of-media-entertainment-and-culture

World Economic Forum. (2020b). *How to help slow the spread of harmful content online*. Retrieved February 2, 2020, from www.weforum.org/agenda/2020/01/harmful-content-proliferated-online/

INDEX

Note: Page numbers in italics indicate a figure and page numbers in bold indicate a table on the corresponding page.

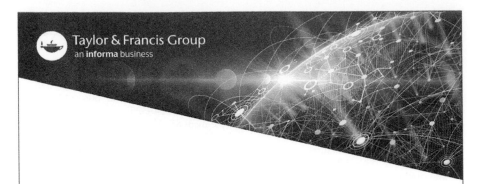

Printed and bound by CPI Group (UK) Ltd, Croydon, CR0 4YY

23/10/2024

01778262-0006